W9-CAX-340

FOURTH EDITION

An Introduction to Group Work Practice

Ronald W. Toseland
State University of New York at Albany

Robert F. Rivas
Siena College

Allyn and Bacon
Boston • London • Toronto • Sydney • Tokyo • Singapore

To our parents
Stella and Ed
Marg and Al

Series Editor, Social Work and Family Therapy: Judy Fifer
Editorial Assistant: Alyssa Pratt
Executive Marketing Manager: Jackie Aaron
Production Editor: Christopher H. Rawlings
Editorial-Production Service: Omegatype Typography, Inc.
Composition and Prepress Buyer: Linda Cox
Manufacturing Buyer: Julie McNeill
Cover Administrator: Linda Knowles
Electronic Composition: Omegatype Typography, Inc.

Copyright © 2001, 1998, 1995, and 1984 by Allyn & Bacon
A Pearson Education Company
160 Gould Street
Needham Heights, MA 02494

Internet: www.abacon.com

Library of Congress Cataloging-in-Publication Data

Toseland, Ronald W.
  An introduction to group work practice / Ronald W. Toseland, Robert F. Rivas.—4th ed.
    p. cm.
  Includes bibliographical references and index.
  ISBN 0-205-30763-9
  1. Social group work. I. Title: Group work practice. II. Rivas, Robert F. III. Title.
HV45.T68 2001
361.4—dc21

                                                          99-087491

Printed in the United States of America

10 9 8 7 6 5 4 3   05   04   03   02

this text, specialized knowledge and skills are often needed when practicing with special populations such as children, adolescents, and older adults. Therefore, this text also presents specialized knowledge and skills useful for practice with these populations.

Most experienced practitioners continue to learn by exposure to different approaches to group work. Although some approaches, such as behavioral and humanistic, are not easily integrated with one another, aspects of divergent approaches can often be integrated in a particular practice situation. A major tenet of the generalist approach is that practice should be based on a comprehensive assessment of the needs of a particular group in a particular situation. An integration of practice approaches is often preferable to using a single approach. Exclusive adherence to one approach may work well for a group with a particular set of needs, but it may not work well when leading a group with other needs. Rigid adherence to one approach tends to make a worker oblivious to other potentially useful methods and to distort a worker's assessment of a situation. A worker might mistakenly attempt to fit data from a situation to a particular practice approach rather than choosing the practice approach to fit the situation. For these reasons, group workers can be most effective when they are familiar with several approaches to group work and when they apply specialized knowledge and skills differentially depending on the particular group work endeavor.

This approach also recognizes the interactional nature of the helping process. A static, prescriptive approach to group work practice often appeals to novice practitioners because of its simplicity but does not match the complexity and diversity of the real world of group work practice. The interactional model of group leadership presented in Chapter 4 presents some of the factors that workers should consider when deciding how to proceed with a group.

VALUES AND ETHICS IN GROUP WORK PRACTICE

Practice Values

In social work, the focus of group work practice is influenced by a system of personal and professional values. These values affect workers' styles of intervention and the skills they use in working with clients. They also affect clients' reactions to the worker's efforts. Despite the emphasis on ethics and values in the new *Curriculum Standards* published by the Council on Social Work Education, Strozier (1997) found that few social group work course syllabi gave any emphasis to the topic of values or ethics in group work practice.

Values are beliefs that delineate preferences about how one ought to behave. They refer to a goal that is worth attaining (Rokeach, 1968). There is no such thing as value-free group work practice. All group workers operate on the basis

Most group work texts are focused on the use of groups for clinical practice, and many focus only on therapy or support groups, with little attention to social, recreational, or educational purposes. Also, scant mention is made of committees, teams, and other administrative groups that social workers are expected to participate in as members and leaders. Despite the distinctive emphasis of the social work profession on the interface between individuals and their social environment, in most group work texts, even less attention is paid to social action groups, coalitions, and other community groups. This text examines work with a broad range of groups in generalist practice with individuals, organizations, and communities.

Some prominent group workers (Hartford, 1971; Klein, 1972) focus on the group as a whole as the unit of intervention and place less emphasis on work with individuals in the group. Others place their emphasis on changing individual group members within the group context (Rose, 1998; Sundel, Glasser, Sarri, & Vinter, 1985). Both perspectives are useful. When leading any group, workers should direct their attention to individuals, the group as a whole, and the community in which the group functions. The worker focuses on individual members to help them accomplish their goals. The worker intervenes with the group as a whole to achieve an optimal level of group functioning and to ensure that the group accomplishes its purposes. The worker also assesses the group's environment and decides whether to help the group adapt to it or change it.

The purpose of the group helps determine the emphasis that each focal area should receive. For example, in a support group for recently separated people, the worker might focus on the development of mutual aid among members of the group as a whole. In an assertion training group, the worker might focus on assessing members' specific skills and deficits and developing individualized treatment plans.

In both cases, however, other focal areas should not be neglected. For example, in the support group it is necessary to help individual members develop plans for dealing with specific problems they are facing. In the assertion training group, it is important to enhance group cohesion, mutual sharing, and mutual aid in the group as a whole.

In both groups, attention must also be given to the community in which the groups function. For example, a close examination of the community in which members of the assertion training group function might suggest a need to make community services more responsive to members of the group. This may, in turn, lead to the development of a social action group to address this problem. Later, this text examines in detail these three focal areas.

Another aspect of group work practice is that workers draw on a broad base of knowledge and skills from generalist practice, which they apply to their work with a broad range of groups. The generalist approach emphasizes that social workers are called on to perform many roles in their professional lives. It suggests that there is foundation knowledge and skills that transcend specific roles. For example, in-depth knowledge about human development and skill in empathic responding are essential for effective work with individuals, families, groups, and communities. Although foundation knowledge and skills are described throughout

We have found that it is helpful to understand the practice of group work as consisting of six developmental stages:

1. Planning
2. Beginning
3. Assessment
4. Middle
5. Evaluation
6. Ending

Groups exhibit certain properties and processes during each stage of their development. The group worker's task is to engage in activities that facilitate the growth and development of the group during each stage of its development. With the exception of Part I, which focuses on the knowledge base needed to practice with groups, this text is organized around each of these six stages of group work. Practice examples illustrating each developmental stage can be found at the end of Chapters 6 through 14.

THE FOCUS OF GROUP WORK PRACTICE

Social work practitioners use group work skills to help meet the needs of individual group members, the group as a whole, and the community. In this text, group work is conceptualized from a generalist practice perspective. Group work involves the following:

1. Practice with a broad range of treatment and task groups
2. A focus on individual group members, the group as a whole, and the group's environment
3. Application of foundation knowledge and skills from generalist social work practice to a broad range of leadership and membership situations
4. Integration and use of specialized knowledge and skills based on a comprehensive assessment of the needs of a particular group
5. A recognition of the interactional and situational nature of leadership

This text is firmly grounded in a generalist approach to practice. To accomplish the broad mission and goals of the social work profession, generalist practitioners are expected to possess basic competencies that enable them to intervene effectively with individuals, families, groups, organizations, and communities. This text is designed to help generalist practitioners understand how group work can be used to help individuals, families, groups, organizations, and communities function as effectively as possible.

Introduction

This text focuses on the practice of group work by professional social workers. Group work entails the deliberate use of intervention strategies and group processes to accomplish individual, group, and community goals using the value base and ethical practice principles of the social work profession. As one prepares to become an effective social work practitioner, it is important to realize the effect that groups have on people's lives. It is not possible to be a member of society without becoming a member of numerous groups and being influenced by others (Falck, 1988). Although it is possible to live in an isolated manner on the fringes of groups, our social nature makes this neither desirable nor healthy.

Groups provide the structure on which communities and the larger society are built. They provide formal and informal structure in the workplace. But more important, they provide a means through which relationships with significant others are carried out. Participation in family groups, peer groups, and classroom groups helps members learn acceptable norms of social behavior, engage in satisfying social relationships, identify personal goals, and derive a variety of other benefits that result from participating in closely knit social systems. Experiences in social, church, recreation, and other work groups are essential in the development and maintenance of people and society.

ORGANIZATION OF THE TEXT

Group work can be understood as a series of activities carried out by the worker during the life of a group. Whereas certain foundation activities, such as empathic responding, are essential throughout the life of the group, other activities such as confrontation are more appropriate during particular stages of a group's development (Rivas & Toseland, 1981). Group workers' interventions, therefore, should be guided by the developmental needs of individual members and the group as a whole.

The Knowledge Base of Group Work Practice

on dealing with conflict and working with reluctant and involuntary group members. We have added features that we hope will appeal to educators. For example, Appendix B on group work films and videotapes has been expanded, and Appendix G on program activities for groups of children and adolescents has been expanded and updated.

The ideas expressed in this book have evolved during many years of study and practice. Some of the earliest and most powerful influences that have shaped this effort have come about through our contact with Bernard Hill, Alan Klein, Sheldon Rose, and Max Siporin. Their contribution to the development of our thinking is evident throughout this book. Perhaps even more important, however, were their support and encouragement in the early years of our professional development and their belief in our ability to make a contribution to knowledge about group work practice.

The ideas in this book were also greatly influenced by Albert Alissi, Martin Birnbaum, Leonard Brown, Burton Gummer, Margaret Hartford, Motier Haskins, Grafton Hull, Jr., Norma Lang, Catherine Papell, William Reid, Beulah Rothman, Jarrold Shapiro, and Peter Vaughan. We would also like to thank the reviewers of previous editions: Mel L. Goldstein, State University of New York at Stony Brook; Beverly Hagen, University of Nebraska at Omaha; Jerome Kolbo, West Virginia University; and Anthony Mazzaro, Northern Kentucky University. The reviewers of this edition were Marcia B. Cohen, University of New England; Kendra Garrett, University of St. Thomas; Patricia Guillory, Southern University at New Orleans; and Deborah Padgett, University of Wisconsin–Milwaukee. Their comments, suggestions, and reactions were invaluable in improving the quality of the book. We are also indebted to the many practitioners and students with whom we have worked over the years. Sharing practice experiences, discussing successes and failures, and giving and receiving constructive feedback helped us clarify and improve the ideas presented in this text.

We would also like to acknowledge the material support and encouragement given to us by our respective educational institutions. The administrative staff of the School of Social Welfare and the Rockefeller College of the University at Albany, State University of New York, and Siena College have played important roles in helping us to accomplish this project. In particular, we would like to acknowledge the support of Dean Lynn Videka-Sherman and the secretarial assistance of B. J. Kelly.

But most important of all, we are especially grateful to our spouses, Sheryl Holland and Donna Allingham Rivas. Their personal and professional insights have done much to enrich this book. Without their continuous support and encouragement, we would not have been able to complete this work. A special note of thanks also goes to Heather, Rebecca, and Stacey for sacrificing some of their dads' time.

R. W. T.
R. F. R.

p r e f a c e

We are gratified by the wide use of this text by professionals, as well as by educators and students in undergraduate and graduate courses in schools of social work throughout the United States and the world. We decided to prepare a fourth edition after receiving a great deal of feedback from readers of the third edition. Based on the suggestions received from fellow practitioners, educators, scholars, and students, we have revised each chapter, thoroughly updated reference material, and added new content.

Because we remain committed to presenting a coherent and organized overview of the field, the fourth edition includes a sharper focus on generalist practice and comprehensive typologies for both treatment groups and task groups. The typologies illustrate group work practice at the micro-, meso-, and macropractice level. Over the years, we have been especially pleased that our text has been used by educators who are dedicated to improving task group practice within social work. Although group work is a neglected area of social work practice, most social workers spend much time in meetings of various sorts, and many social workers have leadership responsibilities in task groups. We also believe in the importance of macropractice and, therefore, in this edition, we have expanded the emphasis on practice with community groups.

In the fourth edition, we have continued to emphasize three focal areas for practice: (1) the individual group member, (2) the group as a whole, and (3) the environment in which the group functions. We continue to emphasize the importance of the latter two focal areas because our experiences in supervising students and conducting workshops for professionals have revealed that the dynamics of a group as a whole and the environment in which groups function are often neglected aspects of group work practice.

Because we remain keenly aware that students and practitioners want practical suggestions about how to proceed when facilitating treatment and task groups during each stage of their development, we have expanded the emphasis on practice principles and leadership skills in each chapter dealing with the stages of group work practice. We have added case examples at the end of Chapters 6 through 14 to illustrate some of the practice principles used in each stage of social group work. There is also new material on confidentiality in group work practice, and expanded sections on telephone and computer groups, as well as

c h a p t e r **14**

Ending the Group's Work 430

c h a p t e r **15**

Case Examples 453

a p p e n d i x **A**

a p p e n d i x **B**

a p p e n d i x **C**

a p p e n d i x **D**

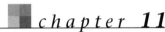
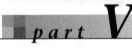

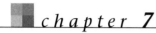

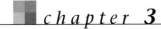
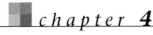

contents

of certain specific assumptions and values regarding the nature of human beings, the role of members, and the role of the group leader. Values influence the methods used to accomplish group and individual goals. Even a leader who is completely permissive and nondirective reveals the values embodied in such a stance.

A worker's actions in the group are affected by contextual values, client value systems, and the worker's personal value system. The context in which the group functions affects the values exhibited in the group. Contextual sources of values include the values of society, values of the agency sponsoring the group, and values of the social work profession. Brill (1998) has identified four values that are dominant in American society:

1. Judeo-Christian doctrine with its emphasis on the dignity and worth of people and people's responsibility for their neighbor
2. Democratic values that emphasize equality and participation, including men's and women's rights to life, liberty, and the pursuit of happiness
3. The Puritan ethic, which emphasizes men's and women's responsibility for themselves, and the central role of work in a moral life
4. Social Darwinism, which emphasizes the survival of the strongest and the fittest in a long-term evolutionary process

The organization and the community that are sponsoring the group are also part of the contextual value system that can influence a worker's stance toward the group. The health and social service organizations sponsoring the group have a history and a tradition with regard to the services they provide.

Before proposing to begin a group, the worker should become familiar with the agency's formal and informal values, which are embodied in its mission, goals, policies, procedures, and practices. Are treatment groups a preferred method of delivering therapeutic services? Are decisions often made in task groups consisting of staff members, or are decisions imposed on staff by the agency's administrators? Becoming aware of the policies, procedures, and practices regarding the use of groups in a particular agency can help the worker prepare for possible resistance and evaluate and use sources of support within the agency.

The community where the group conducts its business can also influence the functioning of the group. For example, community standards and traditions, as well as racial, ethnic, and socioeconomic composition, differ widely among communities. When planning a group, the worker needs to consider how these aspects of communities are likely to influence the group and its members.

The worker and the group are also affected by professional values. Important social work values summarized by Siporin (1975) include respecting the worth and dignity of the individual, respecting a person's autonomy and self-direction, facilitating a person's participation in the helping process, maintaining a nonjudgmental attitude, ensuring equal access to services and social provisions, and affirming the interdependence of the individual and society.

Beyond the values held by all professional social work practitioners, group workers share a special concern and interest in values that are basic to group work practice. Some of the key values of group work have been stated by Gisela Konopka (1983). She suggests that all group workers should agree on the importance of

1. Participation of and positive relations among people of different color, creed, age, national origin, and social class in the group
2. The value of cooperation and mutual decision making embodied in the principles of a participatory democracy
3. The importance of individual initiative within the group
4. The importance of freedom to participate, including expressing thoughts and feelings about matters of concern to individual members or the group as a whole, and having the right to be involved in the decision-making process of the group
5. The value of high individualization in the group so that each member's unique concerns are addressed

These values are not absent in other aspects of social work practice, but in group work they are of central importance. The group is uniquely suited for the exercise of these values, and all group workers should give them their careful attention. Leading treatment and task groups over the years have indicated three particularly important values.

First is the members' ability to help one another. The power and the promise of relationships to help members grow and develop, to help them heal, to satisfy their needs for human contact and connectedness, and to promote a sense of unity and community are vital. Thus, promoting member-to-member helping relationships and de-emphasizing the role of the leader as expert are important.

Second is the groups' ability to empower people. Groups help members feel good about themselves and their abilities to make a difference in their own lives and in their community.

Third is the power of groups to promote understanding among people from diverse backgrounds. Members' respect and appreciation for one another grow as their relationships deepen. Thus, the power of social group work strongly helps bridge the gaps between people from diverse backgrounds.

In addition to values derived from the context of practice, the worker and the members bring their own values to the group. Part of the worker's task is to help members clarify their values and to identify and resolve value conflicts between the leader and members, among members, and among members and the larger society. More information about resolving conflicts is discussed in Chapters 4 and 11.

The worker should be especially sensitive to the effects that cultural diversity have on values. For example, Lewis and Ho (1975) point out that in Native American culture, although cooperation is an important value, it is considered impolite to offer advice, help, or opinion to someone unless it is solicited. Giordano

(1973) suggests that group members with Irish ethnic backgrounds often prefer not to express their feelings openly, whereas Italian Americans are more likely to express their feelings freely.

Workers' personal value systems also affect how they practice. If workers are uncomfortable discussing certain value-laden topics, or if they impose their own values on the group, their work will be seriously impaired. Similarly, if they are not aware of the implications of their values, they are likely to get into conflicts with members who have different values.

Workers who are not aware of their own values will also have difficulty when faced with ambiguous and value-laden situations. Sometimes the goals of the worker, the agency, the community, and the group members differ. This often occurs with involuntary clients who are receiving the service of a worker at the request of law-enforcement officials or others in the community who find the client's behavior unacceptable. The clearer workers are about their own values and their own purposes and stances in relation to working with the group, the easier it will be for them to sort through conflicting goals and make their own purposes known to group members.

One of the best ways for workers to become aware of their own values and their own stance in working with a group is to obtain supervision. Although workers will never become value-free, supervision can help them become aware of the values they bring to the group. Supervision can help workers modify or change values that are not consistent with those of the social work profession or helpful in their practice with groups of people. Value-clarification exercises can also help workers identify personal and professional values that might influence their work with a group (Gibbs & Gambrill, 1998; Loewenberg & Dolgoff, 1996; Smith, 1977).

Practice Ethics

The National Association of Social Workers (NASW) has developed a code of ethics to guide the practice of its members. The code of ethics is an operational statement of the central values of the social work profession. Social workers who lead groups should be thoroughly familiar with it. It is available directly from NASW and is reproduced in many social work practice textbooks.

Corey and Corey (1997) point out that a code of ethics specifically for group workers is a helpful adjunct to the more general codes of ethics developed by professional associations. Unfortunately, a code of ethics specifically for social work practice with groups has not been developed (Dolgoff & Skolnik, 1992; Strozier, 1997). Two organizations, the Association for Specialists in Group Work (ASGW) and the American Group Psychotherapy Association (AGPA), have taken the lead in developing specific codes of ethics for interdisciplinary group work practice. The codes of ethics of these associations appear in Appendixes A1 and A2. Both codes focus on three main areas: (1) informed consent, (2) leader competence and training, and (3) the appropriate conduct of group meetings.

The first area includes telling members about the purpose and goals of the group and giving them information such as the potential risks of participation; the cost, timing, and duration of sessions; whether participation is voluntary; what is expected of group members during meetings; procedures to ensure confidentiality; and screening and termination procedures. In a survey of 300 group psychotherapists, Roback, Ochoa, Bloch, and Purdon (1992) found that the limits of confidentiality are rarely discussed with potential group members even though breaches of confidentiality by members are fairly common. Group leaders may also be required to report certain information, such as child abuse, even without the permission of a group member. To avoid ethical and legal problems associated with a group leader's failure to provide sufficient information about the limits of confidentiality, Roback, Moore, Bloch, and Shelton (1996) suggest having members and the leader sign an informed consent form (Table 1.1).

The second area covered in codes of ethics for group practitioners includes ensuring that workers have the proper education, training, and experience to lead a particular group. Practitioners should not offer a group, or use a procedure or technique within a group, without sufficient education, experience, and supervision to ensure that it is implemented properly. Practitioners should seek out additional supervision when they anticipate or encounter difficulties with a particular group.

As they continue to practice, group workers have the additional responsibility to engage in ongoing professional development activities including workshops, seminars, and other professional educational opportunities. They should also keep up with current clinical and empirical findings that relate to their ongoing work with group members.

The third broad area in both codes of ethics focuses on ethical principles for the conduct of group meetings. These include ensuring that

- Screening procedures lead to the selection of members whose needs and goals can be met by the group
- Workers help members develop and pursue therapeutic goals
- Members are protected from physical threats, intimidation, the imposition of worker and member values, and other forms of coercion and peer pressure that are not therapeutic
- Members are treated fairly and equitably
- Workers avoid exploiting members for their own gain
- Appropriate referrals are made when the needs of a particular member cannot be met in the group
- The worker engages in ongoing assessment, evaluation, and follow-up of members to ensure that the group meets their needs

Galinsky and Schopler (1977) point out that violation of these ethical principles can be damaging to group members. They suggest, for example, that the harm

TABLE 1.1 ■ *Informed Consent Form*

INFORMED CONSENT FORM

1. The law may require the therapist to notify the authorities if you reveal that you are abusing children or if you express an intent to harm yourself or to harm other people.
2. If you reveal secrets in the group, the secrets may be told outside the group by other members of the group. If your secrets are told outside the group, people you know may learn your secrets. You could be hurt emotionally and economically if your secrets are told outside the group.
3. Other group members may tell their secrets to you. If you tell the secrets outside the group, the member whose secrets you tell might have legal grounds to sue you for money for telling the secrets.
4. If you violate the confidentiality rules of the group, the group leader may expel you from the group.

I have read and fully understand the information provided above about the risks of group psychotherapy. I have discussed the risks with the group leader, and I have had the chance to ask all the questions that I wished to ask about the matters listed above and about all other matters. The group leader has answered all my questions in a way that satisfies me. I understand that I can leave the group at any time. By signing this document, I agree to accept the risks listed in this form and the risks explained to me by the group leader.

SIGNATURE OF THE GROUP MEMBER	DATE
SIGNATURE OF GROUP LEADER	DATE
SIGNATURE OF WITNESS	DATE

Reprinted by permission from the American Group Psychotherapy Association, Inc.

encounter groups do to some members can be traced to inappropriate screening procedures and the failure of group workers to describe the risks and requirements of group membership. Similarly, Harold Lewis (1982) points out that although the NASW code of ethics indicates the primacy of clients' interests, workers sometimes choose to give primacy to their own definitions of clients' needs or to give some group members' needs primacy over the needs of other members.

Lakin (1991) suggests that even well-intentioned, enthusiastic group workers can subtly violate ethical principles and that these violations can be harmful to members. He presents evidence, for example, that pressures to conform in some feminist-oriented therapy groups can lead members to suppress particular opinions, thoughts, or points of view simply because they clash with the dominant ideology expressed in the group. Further, he points out that group dynamics are abused when they are developed for the purpose of ideological recruitment or persuasion rather than to address therapeutic needs. To guard against these potential ethical violations, he suggests that all group workers should consider the extent to which (1) workers' values are consonant with the needs and problems of group members, (2) workers are pushing their own agendas without regard to the needs and wishes of group members, and (3) each member's needs are individualized rather than treated as identical to needs of other members.

In October 1998, the Association for the Advancement of Social Work with Groups adopted a set of standards for social work groups. The standards include (1) the essential knowledge and values that underlie social work practice with groups, (2) the tasks that should be accomplished in each phase of group work, and (3) the knowledge that is needed to carry out the tasks in each phase. The standards provide social workers with needed guidance for the effective and ethical practice of social group work, and they help group workers to avoid unintended ethical violations. The standards have been reprinted in Appendix A3.

DEFINITION OF GROUP WORK

Although there are divergent approaches to group work within the social work profession and allied disciplines, a generalist approach suggests that each approach has its merits and particular practice applications. The broad definition offered in this chapter allows beginning practitioners to understand the boundaries of group work, specialized approaches, and many practice applications. *Group work* can be defined as

> *Goal-directed activity with small treatment and task groups aimed at meeting socioemotional needs and accomplishing tasks. This activity is directed to individual members of a group and to the group as a whole within a system of service delivery.*

The definition describes group work as goal-directed activity, which refers to planned, orderly worker activities carried out in the context of professional practice with people. Goal-directed activity has many purposes. For example, group workers may aim to support or educate members, help them socialize and achieve personal growth, or provide treatment for their problems and concerns.

Workers may also help members of a group develop leadership skills so that members can take increasing responsibility for the group's development. Workers should also enable their groups to change the social environment. This includes helping members gain greater control over the organizations and communities that affect their lives. Some writers advocate a person-in-situation view of practice (Anderson, 1997; Glassman & Kates, 1990; Shulman, 1999). Others focus on techniques of individual change within small groups (MacKenzie, 1990, 1996; Rose, 1989, 1998; Rose & LeCroy, 1991). Both approaches are valuable, and attention should be given to both when groups set their goals.

The next component of the definition of group work refers to working with small groups of people. In this text, the term *small group* implies the ability of members to identify themselves as members, to engage in interaction, and to exchange thoughts and feelings among themselves through verbal and nonverbal communication processes.

The definition of group work also indicates that workers practice with both treatment and task groups. Most workers are called on to help clients meet their personal needs and to help their agency or organization accomplish its tasks. For example, most direct service workers have many opportunities to work with both treatment and task groups. Within treatment and task groups, attention should be paid to meeting members' socioemotional needs as well as to accomplishing tasks.

Our definition of group work also emphasizes that the worker should have a dual focus within any group: goal-directed activities with individual members and with the group as a whole. Although some writers favor working with the goals of individual members (Rose, 1989, 1998; Rose & LeCroy, 1991), and others emphasize working with the group as a whole as the primary focus of attention (Klein, 1972), few hold views that are mutually exclusive. Writers who emphasize individual members as the primary client system usually note the importance of the group as a whole. Those who focus on the group as the primary client system frequently note the importance of individualizing the members' needs, concerns, and goals. Both individuals and groups have life histories, developmental patterns, needs, goals, and characteristic behavior patterns that should be of concern to the worker. Therefore, both individual members and the group as a whole should receive the attention of the worker.

The final portion of the definition of group work emphasizes that groups do not exist in a vacuum. They exist in relation to a community that sponsors, legitimizes, and influences their purposes and in relation to an existing service delivery system. Even self-help groups and groups conducted in private practice are influenced by organizational and community support, sponsorship, and sanction.

There is an exchange of influence between a group and its sponsoring agency. A group is often influenced by its sponsoring organization's resources, mission, goals, and policies. At the same time, a group may be the catalyst for a needed change in agency policies or procedures. For example, an agency policy may limit membership in a support group for young parents to a specific geographical area served by the agency. Because of the large number of single parents interested in attending the meetings and the need for child care during meetings, the group may highlight the need for child care services. In this example, the group is influenced by—and influences—the agency that sponsors it.

CLASSIFYING GROUPS

To understand the breadth of group work practice, it is helpful to become familiar with the variety of groups in practice settings. Because there are so many kinds of groups that workers may be called on to lead, it is helpful to distinguish among them. In the following two sections, distinctions are made among groups on the basis of whether they are formed or occur naturally and whether they are treatment or task oriented.

Formed and Natural Groups

Formed groups are those that come together through some outside influence or intervention. They usually have some sponsorship or affiliation and are convened for a particular purpose. Some examples of formed groups are therapy groups, educational groups, committees, social action groups, and teams. *Natural groups* come together spontaneously on the basis of naturally occurring events, interpersonal attraction, or the mutually perceived needs of members. They often lack formal sponsorship. Natural groups include family groups, peer groups, friendship networks, street gangs, and cliques.

This text is primarily concerned with formed groups. Natural groups such as families are neither planned nor constructed by a group worker. Generally, natural groups have a longer developmental history, which has unique implications for the relationships among members and the interventions used by workers. For these reasons, a separate body of knowledge has been developed for work with natural groups such as families.

Despite the differences between formed and natural groups, many of the skills and techniques presented in this text are readily applicable to work with natural groups, and we encourage group work practitioners to use them. Some efforts have already been made in this regard, such as attempts to use group work skills in working with the family unit (Bell, 1981), working with gangs (Klein, 1997), and enhancing the social networks of persons who are socially isolated (Maguire, 1991).

Purpose and Group Work

Formed groups can be classified according to the purposes for which they are organized. The term *purpose* can be defined as the general aims of a group. The importance of purpose in group work cannot be overemphasized. According to Wilson (1976), "the nature of the framework for the practice of group work depends on the purpose of the group [that is] served" (p. 41). A group's purpose identifies the reasons for bringing members together. As Klein (1972) notes, "purpose guides group composition" (pp. 31–32). It also helps guide the group's selection of goal-directed activities and define the broad parameters of the services to be delivered.

In this text, the term *treatment group* is used to signify a group whose major purpose is to meet members' socioemotional needs. The purposes for forming treatment groups might include meeting members' needs for support, education, therapy, growth, and socialization. In contrast, the term *task group* is used to signify any group in which the overriding purpose is to accomplish a goal that is neither intrinsically nor immediately linked to the needs of the members of the group. Although the work of a task group may ultimately affect the members of the group, the primary purpose of task groups is to accomplish a goal that will affect a broader constituency, not just the members of the group.

Treatment and Task Groups

In classifying groups as either treatment or task oriented, it is important to consider how the two types differ. Table 1.2 points out some of the major differences between treatment and task groups in terms of selected characteristics. These include the following:

- The bond present in a group is based on the purpose for which it is convened. Members of treatment groups are bonded by their common needs and common situations. Task group members create a common bond by working together to accomplish a task, carry out a mandate, or produce a product. In both types of groups, common cultural, gender, racial, or ethnic characteristics can also help to form bonds among members.

- In treatment groups, roles are not set before the group forms, but develop through interaction among members. In task groups, members take on roles through a process of interaction and also are frequently assigned roles by the group. Roles that may be assigned include chair or team leader, secretary, and fact finder.

- Communication patterns in treatment groups are open. Members are usually encouraged to interact with one another. Task group members are more likely to address their communications to the leader and to keep their communication focused on a particular group task. In some task groups, the amount that members communicate on a particular agenda item may be limited by the worker. In other task groups, members may limit their own communication because they believe they will not be well received by the group.

- Treatment groups often have flexible procedures for meetings, including a warm-up period, a period for working on members' concerns, and a period for summarizing the group's work. Task groups are more likely to have formalized rules such as parliamentary procedure that govern how members conduct group business and reach decisions.

TABLE 1.2 ■ *A Comparison of Task and Treatment Groups*

Selected Characteristics	Type of Group	
	Treatment	**Task**
Bond	Members' personal needs	Task to be completed
Roles	Develop through interaction	Develop through interaction or are assigned
Communication patterns	Open	Focused on the discussion of a particular task
Procedures	Flexible or formal, depending on the group	Formal agenda and rules
Composition	Based on common concerns, problems, or characteristics	Based on needed talents, expertise, or division of labor
Self-disclosure	Expected to be high	Expected to be low
Confidentiality	Proceedings usually private and kept within the group	Proceedings may be private but are sometimes open to the public
Evaluation	Success based on members' meeting treatment goals	Success based on members' accomplishing task or mandate, or producing a product

- Treatment groups are often composed of members with similar concerns, problems, and abilities. Task groups are often composed of members with the necessary resources and expertise to accomplish the group's mission.

- In treatment groups, members are expected to disclose their own concerns and problems. Therefore, self-disclosures may contain emotionally charged, personal concerns. In task groups, member self-disclosure is relatively infrequent. It is generally expected that members will confine themselves to discussions about accomplishing the group's task and will not share intimate, personal concerns.

- Treatment group meetings are often confidential. Some task group meetings, such as the meetings of treatment conferences and cabinets, may be confidential, but the meetings of other task groups, such as committees and delegate councils, are often described in minutes that are circulated to interested persons and organizations.

- The criteria for evaluating success differ between treatment and task groups. Treatment groups are successful to the extent that they help members meet their individual treatment goals. Task groups are successful when they accomplish group goals, such as generating solutions to problems and making decisions, or when they develop group products, such as a report, a set of regulations, or a series of recommendations concerning a particular community issue.

An example in which a worker is responsible for leading both types of groups may help illustrate the differences between treatment and task groups. In the first group, the worker meets with adults who have recently become parents for the first time. The purpose of the group is to provide a forum for discussion about their adjustment to parenthood. In the second group, the worker brings together several community representatives to study day-care resources and make recommendations to a government agency regarding changes in government support for day care.

The parents' group is classified as a treatment group because it is convened to meet the personal needs of its members. The group is bonded by its common purpose and the common needs and concerns of its members. It is expected that friendships may develop among group members and that members will help each other in their adjustment to parenthood. It is also expected that the feeling level and the level of self-disclosure will be high because of the similar characteristics of the members and the problems they face. Because members may self-disclose about personal issues, the proceedings of the group are confidential. Roles develop on the basis of how members assist in accomplishing the purpose of the group and how members meet each other's needs.

Because parenting is a developmental phenomenon involving constant discovery and change, the procedures of the group are flexible to allow members to share their immediate weekly concerns. The parents' group is composed with the similarity of members' needs in mind. Patterns of communication focus on members' needs, such as adjusting to parenthood and becoming effective parents. To evaluate the success of the group, the worker focuses on members' satisfaction with the group experience and whether the group has met their needs.

In the group discussing day-care services, the focus is task oriented, and the purpose is external to the personal needs of the members. Members are bonded by the common cause of improving day-care services. They are expected to reveal their personal viewpoints only to the extent that they contribute to the group's task. Personal feelings are occasionally shared, but factual data are given greater weight. The group is publicized and seeks outside, expert testimony to contribute to its deliberations. Confidentiality is impractical because it would hinder the accomplishment of the group's task. Roles are assigned by the worker on the basis of members' preferences. For example, members are appointed to subcommittees to collect needed data. Roles develop on the basis of how each member contributes to the task of the group.

To facilitate an organized approach to the task, the group works from an agenda, which is published in advance to give participants time to prepare for the proceedings. To facilitate a division of labor and encourage different perspectives, the group is composed by selecting members who have some knowledge of day-care programs and needed areas of expertise. Patterns of communication focus on the task rather than on members' personal concerns. In evaluating the effectiveness of the group, the worker examines the group's decisions, actions, written reports, and recommendations for clarity, thoroughness, and feasibility.

GROUP VERSUS INDIVIDUAL EFFORTS

There are several advantages and disadvantages to using a group rather than an individual effort to meet individual, organizational, and community needs. In describing these advantages and disadvantages, it is important to distinguish between the effectiveness and efficiency of treatment and task groups.

Advantages and Disadvantages of Treatment Groups

In relation to meeting client needs, Levine (1979) suggests that "group therapy can help with most anything that individual therapy can, providing an appropriate group is available and the individual will accept the group as the mode of treatment" (p. 11). Several writers have suggested that group treatment has advantages over individual treatment (Lieberman & Borman, 1979; Northen, 1995; Piper & Joyce, 1996; Shulman, 1999; Toseland & Siporin, 1986; Yalom, 1995). Groups help members realize that they are not alone with their problems. They allow members to hear that others have similar concerns (Shulman, 1999; Yalom, 1995). They also give members the opportunity to help each other by being supportive, giving feedback, making suggestions, and providing useful information. Lieberman and Borman (1979) have noted the therapeutic benefit of the "helper-therapy principle" for members of groups that develop on a mutual-aid basis. As members give and receive help, they observe others achieving their goals. This process provides what Yalom (1995) refers to as an "installation of hope" that is absent in individual treatment.

Treatment groups provide vicarious learning opportunities and peer feedback that cannot be replicated in individual treatment. According to Northen (1995), group treatment is the preferred modality when a client's main problem concerns relationships with others. The presence of others gives members a chance to learn from hearing about the experiences of others and to receive feedback that can help them in their efforts to change. Peer feedback can be particularly beneficial for adolescents and involuntary adult clients who may resist the suggestions of the worker because he or she is viewed as an authority figure (Northen, 1995). It can also be beneficial for those who are socially isolated, such as older people who have lost peers and social roles, people who have been removed from their families, and people in hospitals and other institutions. Opportunities for vicarious learning are limited in individual treatment.

Groups can be valuable because they enable members to engage in reality testing (Klein, 1972; Rose, 1998). Groups can develop into "social microcosms" (Yalom, 1995) in which members recreate problems they have experienced in the outside world. This can enable members to work through previously unsatisfying relationships with family members, peers, or friends.

Groups can provide members with multiple opportunities to engage in role playing, test new skills, and rehearse new behaviors in the safe environment of the group (Rose, 1989). Opportunities to practice new behaviors with peers do not exist in individual treatment.

Although these advantages provide justification for using group work in treatment, several potential disadvantages of group treatment should be considered. Groups can encourage member conformity (Corey & Corey, 1997) and member dependency (Klein, 1972). When members open themselves to other members through self-disclosure, they are vulnerable to breaches of confidentiality and other harmful responses (Corey & Corey, 1997). Groups can scapegoat individual members (Konopka, 1983). Groups sometimes focus on a few particularly assertive or talkative members, which creates a danger that these members' problems will receive attention and other, less assertive or less talkative members will receive little help (Yalom, 1995).

In general, members can benefit from treatment groups when they have some ability to communicate with others and when their concerns or problems lend themselves to group discussion. To the extent that certain group members, such as autistic children and schizophrenic adults, cannot communicate effectively, group work must be modified to include nonverbal program activities and, where appropriate, simple, brief verbal activities that are consistent with those members' skill levels. People who have an extreme need for privacy or confidentiality may also be unable to take part in group treatment without considerable support or reassurance. Groups are contraindicated for people whose behavior is so alien to others' that it results in negative rather than positive interactions or when it leads to the failure of others to continue with the group.

Empirical studies tend to support clinical reports of the effectiveness of treatment groups. In a comprehensive review of well-designed studies comparing group and individual treatment, Toseland and Siporin (1986) found that group treatment was more effective than individual treatment in 25 percent of the studies that were reviewed, but individual treatment was not found to be more effective than group treatment in any of the studies. Group work was also found to be more efficient than individual treatment and to produce fewer dropouts from treatment.

Unfortunately, the empirical literature that was reviewed by Toseland and Siporin (1986) did not yield a clear pattern of the types of problems most effectively treated in groups. Subsequent work, however, has revealed that group treatment may be more effective than individual treatment for enhancing social supports and less effective for dealing with intense, highly personal, psychological problems (Toseland, Rossiter, Peak, & Smith, 1990).

Most other reviews of the literature have focused on group therapy. For the most part, these reviews confirm that group therapy is as effective as individual therapy (Fuhriman & Burlingame, 1994; Piper & Joyce, 1996).

Overall, findings from both the clinical and the empirical literature suggest that social workers should consider recommending group treatment for individuals who suffer from isolation or who have other difficulties with interpersonal relationships, and individual treatment for those with highly personal psychological problems. Combinations of individual and group treatment appear to be effective for clients with both needs. It is always important to remember, however, that before recommending group or individual treatment, the practitioner should carefully consider individuals' needs and preferences.

Advantages and Disadvantages of Task Groups

A group approach, as compared with an individual effort, has advantages in helping individuals, organizations, and communities accomplish tasks. In working with groups of people in organizations and communities, democratic participation is highly desirable (Gummer, 1991, 1995). Participation through group interaction helps members feel they have a stake in their organization or community. Also, resistance to change is minimized when those who are to be affected are given the opportunity to participate in the change through group discussion and shared decision making.

Group discussion, deliberation, and decision making can have other benefits. The increased quantity of information available in groups can be beneficial for generating alternative action plans, for problem solving, and for making decisions. Certain tasks are complex, requiring a pool of talents, expertise, or opinions for them to be completed in a satisfactory manner (Hare, Blumberg, Davies, & Kent, 1995). The division of labor that occurs in well-run groups can help members complete tasks quickly and efficiently (Tropman, 1995).

Some disadvantages should be kept in mind when considering selecting a group approach for accomplishing tasks. For example, group problem solving may take more time than individual problem solving, and the presence of others may interfere with the effectiveness of best members' problem-solving abilities (Hare et al., 1995). Napier and Gershenfeld (1993) note that poorly run groups can make members feel frustrated, bored, or unappreciated. In addition, such groups often accomplish little (Edson, 1977). Groups are also sometimes used to make simple decisions or solve simple problems that could be dealt with more easily by individuals. Under these conditions, group meetings can be costly to an organization and frustrating and unnecessary for group members.

Findings about the effectiveness of group versus individual problem solving and decision making suggest that groups are more effective than the average individual, but rarely more effective than the best individual (Hare et al., 1995). Also, groups are more effective than individuals only in certain situations (Davis & Toseland, 1987; Hare et al., 1995; McGrath, 1984). Groups tend to be more effective than individuals on difficult and complex tasks requiring high levels of creativity (Hare et al., 1995).

Overall, the advantages and disadvantages of using a task group for problem solving and decision making should be evaluated within the context of a particular situation and in reference to the types of goals to be achieved. For example, shared decision making may be more important than the time it takes to make a decision or even the quality of the decision.

Although this text suggests that group work methods have a fairly wide applicability for many different types of individual, organizational, and community problems, these problems are sometimes best approached by using several practice methods. Thus, although group work is a valuable method by itself, within a generalist practice framework, it is also valuable as part of a larger, planned change effort that may use additional methods such as social casework or community organization to achieve particular goals.

A TYPOLOGY OF TREATMENT AND TASK GROUPS

The broad distinctions between formed and natural groups and between treatment and task groups can be further refined and developed into a classification system of the many types of groups workers may encounter in practice settings. One way to develop a classification system is to categorize treatment and task groups according to their primary purpose. Many writers have attempted to identify the primary purposes of the groups that workers may lead in practice settings. Hartford (1964) suggests groups may focus on "the social functioning, growth or change or rehabilitation of the group members" (p. 14). Schwartz (1974) suggests that groups are "an enterprise in mutual aid" (p. 218), and Murphy (1959) suggests that groups enhance members' "social functioning through a purposeful group experience" (pp. 34–35).

Other writers have attempted more ambitious classifications. For example, Douglas (1979) suggests that group purposes may include (1) individual growth and adjustment; (2) group development toward specific needs; and (3) social action, social change, and changing society through the group experience. Klein's (1972) "objectives for group workers" define a wide range of purposes for treatment and task groups. According to Klein, group purposes can include the following:

- Rehabilitation—restoring members to their former level of functioning
- Habilitation—helping members grow and develop
- Correction—helping members who are having problems with social laws or mores
- Socialization—helping members learn how to get along with others and do what is socially acceptable
- Prevention—helping members develop and function at an optimal level and helping them prepare for events that are likely to occur
- Social action—helping members change their environment
- Problem solving—helping members resolve complex issues and concerns
- Developing social values—helping members develop a humanistic approach to living

The rest of this chapter presents typologies of treatment groups and task groups that social workers encounter in practice. The typologies are based on the primary purposes of each type of treatment and task group. Although groups with only one purpose rarely exist in practice, developing pure categories—that is, groups with a single purpose—is useful in illustrating differences between groups and in demonstrating the many ways that groups can be used in practice settings.

TREATMENT GROUPS

Five primary purposes for treatment groups are (1) support, (2) education, (3) growth, (4) therapy, and (5) socialization. In practice settings, there are innumerable variations of treatment groups that combine these five primary purposes. For example, a group for parents of children with Down syndrome might be oriented toward both education and growth. A group for alcoholics might have all five primary purposes. Table 1.3 is designed to show clearly the similarities and differences among groups with different purposes. Table 1.3 can be used as a guide by workers who are planning to lead groups with only one purpose or to lead groups that combine several purposes.

Support Groups

The description of the treatment typology begins with support groups because support is a common ingredient of many successful treatment groups (Galinsky & Schopler, 1995). Support groups can be distinguished from other groups using supportive intervention strategies by their primary goals: to foster mutual aid, to help members cope with stressful life events, and to revitalize and enhance members' coping abilities so they can effectively adapt to and cope with future stressful life events. Examples of support groups include the following:

- A group of children meeting at school to discuss the effects of divorce on their lives
- A group of people diagnosed with cancer, and their families, discussing the effects of the disease and how to cope with it
- A group of recently discharged psychiatric patients discussing their adjustment to community living
- A group of single parents sharing the difficulties of raising children alone

Leadership of support groups is characterized by a facilitative approach that emphasizes helping members share their collective experiences in coping with a

TABLE 1.3 ■ *A Typology of Treatment Groups*

Selected Characteristics		Purpose of the Group			
	Support	Education	Growth	Therapy	Socialization
Purpose	To help members cope with stressful life events and revitalize existing coping abilities	To educate through presentations, discussion, and experience	To develop members' potential, awareness, insight	To change behavior Correction, rehabilitation, coping, and problem solving through behavior change interventions	To increase communication and social skills Improved interpersonal relationships through program activities, structured exercises, role plays, etc.
Leadership	A facilitator of empathic understanding and mutual aid	Leader as teacher and provider of structure for group discussion	Leader as facilitator and role model	Leader as expert, authority figure, or facilitator, depending on approach	Leader as director of the group's actions or programs
Focus	The ability of the individual to cope with a stressful life experience Communication and mutual aid	Individual learning Structuring of the group for learning	Either member or group focus, depending on the approach Individual growth through the group experience	Individual members' problems, concerns, or goals	The group as a medium for activity, participation, and involvement
Bond	Shared stressful experience, often stigmatizing	Common interest in learning, skills development	Common goals among members Contract to use group to grow	Common purpose with separate member goals Relationship of member with worker, group, or other members	A common activity, enterprise, or situation
Composition	Based on a shared life experience Often diverse	Similarity of education or skill level	Can be diverse Based on members' ability to work toward growth and development	Can be diverse or can be composed of people with similar problems or concerns	Depending on location of group and purpose, can be diverse or homogeneous
Communication	Much sharing of information, experiences, and coping strategies Frequent self-disclosure of emotionally charged material	Frequently leader-to-member, didactic Sometimes member-to-member during discussions Self-disclosure low	Highly interactive Members often take responsibility for communication in the group Self-disclosure moderate to high	Leader-to-member or member-to-member, depending on approach Self-disclosure moderate to high	Often represented in activity or nonverbal behavior Self-disclosure low to moderate and often nonverbal

stressful event. The group worker helps members share their experiences and empathically respond to each other. Simply recounting events, ventilating feelings, and reflecting on efforts to cope can promote self-understanding and help overcome loneliness, isolation, and despair. The group worker also helps members overcome feelings of alienation, stigmatization, and isolation by validating, affirming, and normalizing their experiences.

A major role of the worker is to facilitate hope in the future and motivate members to improve coping skills through self-help and mutual aid (Steinberg, 1997). The worker fosters group norms that encourage members to share information and suggestions for more effective coping and to try out new coping strategies. Because support is basic to many types of groups, these strategies for assisting members are also used, to varying degrees, in other treatment and task groups.

Strong emotional bonds often develop quickly in support groups because of members' shared experiences. Emotional bonding may also occur because members are stigmatized by the larger community and find comfort and power in their association with each other. Frequently, there is a high level of self-disclosure of emotionally charged material in support groups.

In addition to directly facilitating support groups, workers are often called on to provide indirect assistance to support groups led by lay leaders. A worker might be asked to consult with the lay leader, serve as a referral source, or provide material assistance. Consultation may take the form of speaking at a meeting, helping the group resolve a problem in its functioning, or assisting members with specific problems or issues. The worker may be asked to refer appropriate individuals to a support group, provide a meeting place, or offer other support, such as help with printing a newsletter or distributing publicity.

Some writers have pointed out that professionals might interfere with the effective functioning of lay-led, self-help support groups (Katz et al., 1992; Katz & Bender, 1987). The potential does exist for professionals to dominate, interfere with, or take over the functioning of such groups. Members of self-help groups are sometimes wary of professional involvement because they fear it will compromise the autonomy and confidentiality of the group. This is particularly true of self-help groups such as Parents Anonymous, in which members share concerns about child abuse or neglect—situations often considered socially stigmatizing.

Most evidence, however, suggests that there are strong connections between self-help support groups and professionals and that both professionals and lay leaders benefit by cooperating with each other (Kurtz, 1997; Powell, 1987; Toseland & Hacker, 1982, 1985). Professionals gain an additional treatment resource that is often more flexible and responsive than the formal service system. Lay leaders have someone to turn to when they need particular types of expertise, resources, or assistance. Both can join forces when lobbying for additional community resources and services.

Educational Groups

The primary purpose of educational groups is to help members learn new information and skills. Educational groups are used in a variety of settings, including treatment agencies, schools, nursing homes, correctional institutions, and hospitals. Examples of educational groups include the following:

- An adolescent sexuality group sponsored by a family planning agency
- A wellness-in-the-workplace group designed by a social worker directing an employee assistance program
- A group for prospective foster parents sponsored by a child welfare agency
- A group sponsored by a community planning agency to help board members become more effective

All educational groups are aimed at increasing members' information or skills. Most groups routinely involve presentations of information and knowledge by experts. They also often include opportunities for group discussion to foster learning. When leading educational groups, workers concentrate on both the individual learner and the group as a whole as vehicles for learning, reinforcement, and discussion.

Members of educational groups are bonded by a common interest in the material to be learned and by common characteristics, such as being an adolescent, a prospective foster parent, a union worker, or a board member. In composing educational groups, workers consider each member's knowledge of the subject matter and level of skills and experience so that all members can derive the most benefit from the learning process.

Some educational groups seek members with different levels of exposure to the subject matter so that beginners can learn from advanced members. When the group is small, there are usually opportunities for member-to-member communication and group discussion. Depending on the norms of the group and the subject matter, member self-disclosure varies from low to moderate. In general, a relatively low level of self-disclosure is expected in an educational group because the group is often structured around a presentation of material by the worker, a guest speaker, or a member. Usually, the material to be learned is seen as more important than the needs of members to self-disclose. However, workers often use a personalized approach to learning that emphasizes the developmental learning needs of individual members. This is especially true in residential and institutional settings in which members' emotional or social functioning is impaired.

Other approaches to leading educational groups emphasize learning as a social experience. Workers who use this approach focus on group discussion and group activities rather than on didactic methods. Community center workers often use this approach to attract and hold the interest of members who participate in educational groups for personal enjoyment and enrichment.

Growth Groups

Growth-oriented groups offer opportunities for members to become aware of, expand, and change their thoughts, feelings, and behaviors regarding themselves and others. The group is used as a vehicle to develop members' capabilities to the fullest. Growth groups focus on promoting socioemotional health rather than remediating socioemotional illness. Examples of growth groups include the following:

- An encounter group for married couples
- A values-clarification group for adolescents
- A consciousness-raising group sponsored by a women's community center
- A gay-pride group sponsored by a community health clinic serving the gay community in a large urban area

Growth groups generally stress self-improvement and the potential of human beings to live a full and rewarding life, especially through improved relationships with others. They provide a supportive atmosphere in which individuals can gain insights, experiment with new behaviors, get feedback, and grow as human beings. The bond in growth groups stems from members' commitment to help one another develop and maximize their potential.

When composing growth groups, workers often select members who have diverse backgrounds and the potential to enrich and broaden each other's experiences. However, some growth groups are composed of members with similar characteristics to enhance empathy and support within the group. In most growth-oriented groups, self-disclosure is moderate to high.

Communication in growth groups is member centered and highly interactive. In-depth self-disclosure is expected, with members encouraged to reveal more about themselves as they become comfortable with their participation in the group.

Therapy Groups

Therapy groups help members change their behavior, cope with and ameliorate personal problems, or rehabilitate themselves after physical, psychological, or social trauma. Although there is often an emphasis on support, therapy groups are distinguished from support groups by their focus on remediation and rehabilitation.

In group work practice, particular importance is often accorded to leading therapy groups, even to the exclusion of other types of group work, possibly because of the traditional importance attributed to the medical model, which stresses therapy and treatment to bring sick or dysfunctional people back to health. Konopka (1983) noted that the high status of psychiatry on the North American continent helped to make the term *therapy* more precious and more important than the terms *casework* and *group work* (terms used by the social work profession). Thus, therapy groups are often associated with the professionalism of group work as a method of practice. Examples of therapy groups include the following:

- A psychotherapy group for outpatients at a community mental health center
- A group, sponsored by a voluntary health association, for people who want to stop smoking
- A first-offenders group in a juvenile diversion program sponsored by a probation department
- A hospital-sponsored group for people addicted to drugs

In therapy groups, members come together to solve their problems. The group leader is often viewed as an expert, an authority figure, and a change agent. Members' problems are assessed and treatment goals are developed with the help of the worker. Although the group has a common purpose, each member may have a different problem with different symptoms. In addition, the etiology and development of each member's problem is unique. Therefore, to achieve individual goals, the worker often focuses on one member at a time. Depending on the approach or stance of the worker, the members of a therapy group may be expected to help each other work on problems. The level of member self-disclosure is usually quite high but can depend somewhat on the types of problems experienced by group members.

Members of therapy groups have much to gain: relief from symptoms, loss of emotional pain, or resolution of a problem. Still, to ensure that members' needs are met, much planning usually takes place before the beginning of a therapy group. Therapeutic interventions are selected after a careful assessment of individual members, and the group is composed in relation to the members' problems. Often, members participate in an intake procedure so the worker can assess their interest in participating in the group, determine suitability for group treatment, and explain the purpose of the group. Although these procedures are also used with other types of groups, they are often given greater emphasis in therapy groups.

Socialization Groups

Socialization groups help members learn social skills and socially accepted behavior patterns so they can function effectively in the community. Socialization groups frequently use program activities such as games, role plays, or outings to help members accomplish individual goals (Middleman, 1978, 1980, 1982; Whittaker, 1985).

The personal needs of members and the goals of the group are often met through program activities rather than exclusively through group discussion. Thus, socialization groups feature a learning-through-doing approach in which members improve their interpersonal skills by participating in program activities. Examples of socialization groups include the following:

- A Catholic Youth Organization (CYO) activity group
- A social club for outpatients of a psychiatric center
- A monthly Vietnam Veterans evening social at a rural Veterans of Foreign Wars (VFW) post
- A Parents Without Partners group, which includes picnics, dances, and other social activities

Leadership of socialization groups can be directive or nondirective, depending on the complexity of program activities and the competencies of group members. Member participation is the key to successful individual and group outcomes. The group is a medium for activity, participation, and involvement, and members are bonded to each other through these activities. The composition of socialization groups can be based on the similar interests and needs of members or on the common experiences offered by a particular program activity.

There are at least three common forms of socialization groups: (1) social skills groups, (2) governance groups, and (3) recreation groups. Some social skills groups, such as assertiveness training groups, are formed for adults who wish to improve their existing skills. Unlike the other types of groups in our typology, social skills groups can be particularly useful for individuals who are unable or unwilling to communicate effectively and for those who have difficulty engaging in satisfying social relationships. Young children, shy adolescents, and mildly retarded adults are examples of client populations that can benefit from social skills groups. Program activities can help draw out these types of group members by helping them form meaningful relationships and learn social skills. Activities provide the basis for interaction and communication without the need for direct, verbal communication. Thus, by using program activities, group work can take place through nonverbal means.

In other cases, role plays, psychodrama, and other activities requiring both verbal and nonverbal communication can be used to increase members' skills and promote socialization. The behavior displayed during these activities can help a worker assess members' problems and plan effective interventions.

Governance groups are often found in residential settings such as nursing homes, psychiatric hospitals, correctional facilities, and residential treatment centers. The purpose of these groups is to involve residents (of the unit, ward, floor, or house) in the daily governance of the institution. Although governance groups are closely related to task groups because they solve problems and make decisions, they have been classified as treatment groups because their primary focus is on the needs of their members.

Through their participation in the governance process, members learn advocacy, communication, conflict resolution, and empowerment skills. They also learn to share with others, take responsibility for their actions, and participate in decision-making processes. The concept of a governance group is borrowed, in part, from the idea of the therapeutic community in which members have input into the rules that govern their behavior. Examples of governance groups include house meetings, ward meetings, resident councils, family meetings, and patient-rights meetings.

Participation in governance groups provides a method for members to identify with and become committed to the goals of the therapeutic community. It helps clarify members' roles, responsibilities, and rights within the community. All members of therapeutic communities are encouraged to attend meetings so that they have a voice in the way the community functions. In some settings, such as residential treatment centers, attendance may be required.

A third type of socialization group focuses on recreational activities. Much of the recent group work literature has understated the importance of recreational groups in meeting members' personal needs. The roots of group work can be traced to recreational groups like scouting, camping, sports, and club groups (Boyd, 1935; Slavson, 1945, 1946; Smith, 1935; Wilson, 1976). Recreation can be both an end and a means to an end. As an end, recreation can be a desirable leisure time activity. As a means, recreation can help a particular population become involved in an activity that has therapeutic benefits, such as increasing social skills.

Recreational groups are particularly important for working with children, adolescents, and older adults in neighborhood centers. Because the groups are enjoyable, they are often helpful in engaging resistant clients such as gang members and predelinquent, latency-age children. They can help members learn community values and accepted norms of behavior, develop interpersonal skills, and feel a sense of belonging. In addition, recreational groups help members develop confidence in their ability to function as a part of a group and to function in other social situations. To carry out these important purposes, recreation groups require leaders who are skilled in both group work and the featured recreational mode or program activity.

TASK GROUPS

Task groups are common in most agencies and organizations. They are used to find solutions to organizational problems, to generate new ideas, and to make decisions. Task groups can have three primary purposes: (1) meeting client needs, (2) meeting organizational needs, and (3) meeting community needs.

Task groups with the primary purpose of serving client needs include teams, treatment conferences, and staff-development groups. Task groups with the primary purpose of serving organizational needs include committees, cabinets, and boards of directors. Task groups with a primary purpose of serving community needs include social action groups, coalitions, and delegate councils.

Selected characteristics of each type of group are presented in Table 1.4. As with the typology for treatment groups, there is often some overlap between different types of task groups in actual practice situations. Thus, instead of a rigid classification system, the typology is intended as a guide for workers who may be called on to lead different types of task groups.

Groups to Meet Client Needs

Teams

Although empirical evidence for the effectiveness of interdisciplinary teams is limited (Gummer, 1995; Halstead, 1976; Keith, 1991; Schmitt, Farrell, & Heinemann, 1988), team work is often considered the most effective method of delivering comprehensive social and health services to those in need (Abramson, 1989; Brill, 1976; Fatout & Rose, 1995; Gummer, 1995; Kane, 1975a, 1975b). A *team* can be defined as

> *A number of individual staff members, each of whom possesses particular knowledge and skills, who come together to share their expertise with one another for a particular purpose. (Toseland, Palmer-Ganeles, & Chapman, 1986, p. 46)*

Team members coordinate their efforts and work together on behalf of a particular client group. Examples of teams include the following:

- A group of professionals working with stroke victims and their family members in a rehabilitation hospital
- A group of professionals who deliver home-based hospice care
- Professional and paraprofessional helpers trained in crisis intervention sponsored by a county mental health agency
- A group of professionals and aides who work with patients in a psychiatric hospital

The functioning of the team is the responsibility of the team leader. Team leaders are often appointed by an administrator from the team's sponsoring agency, but in some settings they are elected or nominated by team members. The team leader is a facilitator and coordinator for the group and is accountable to the agency for the actions of the team. The team leader is responsible for conducting meetings, motivating team members, coordinating individual efforts, and ensuring effective team functioning.

In most, if not all, cases an agency sanctions the mutual involvement of team members on behalf of a particular client population. Often, the team is composed of members with different professional orientations, such as social work, nursing, physical and occupational therapy, and medicine. The team might also be composed of paraprofessionals, such as mental health therapy aides.

TABLE 1.4 ■ *A Typology of Task Groups*

Selected Characteristics	Client Needs		
	Teams	**Treatment Conferences**	**Staff Development**
Purpose	To engage in collaborative work on behalf of a client system	To develop, coordinate, and monitor treatment plans	To educate members for better practice with clients
Leadership	Appointed by sponsoring agency	Neutral chair or chaired by member with most responsibility	Leader, supervisor, consultant, or educator
Focus	Build team to function smoothly High member focus	Decision-oriented Low member focus High client focus	Focus on staff members' needs and their performance with clients
Bond	Team spirit Needs of organization and client	Client system Treatment plan Inter- or intra-agency agreement	Continuing education needs Interest in client welfare Professional development
Composition	Often heterogeneous	Diversity by function, specialty, and expertise	Individuals with similar educational needs
Communication	Theoretically close, sometimes artificial or inspirational Low to moderate self-disclosure	Consideration of all points of view about the client system High disclosure	Leader-to-member Didactic and experiential instruction Member-to-member

(continued)

TABLE 1.4 ■ *Continued*

Selected Characteristics	Organizational Needs		
	Committees	**Cabinets**	**Board of Directors**
Purpose	To discuss issues and accomplish tasks	To advise an executive officer about future directions or current policies and procedures	To govern an organization
Leadership	Appointed or elected	Appointed by chief executive officer of an organization	Officers designated by bylaws are nominated by subcommittee and approved by vote of the membership
Focus	A specific task or charge	The development of procedures and policies for organizational management	Policy making Governance Monitoring Fiscal control Fundraising
Bond	Interest in a task	Loyalty to the organization and the chief executive officer	Commitment to the mission of the organization Service orientation
Composition	Diversity to aid decision making and division of labor	Appointment based on administrative responsibilities and expertise	Diverse members often selected for their status, power, influence in the community, expertise, representation of particular interest groups and constituencies
Communication	Relative to task Low member self-disclosure	Members present points of view based on their position in an organization To build a power base	Formal communication Parliamentary procedures Less formal in subcommittees Low member self-disclosure

TABLE 1.4 ■ *Continued*

Selected Characteristics	Community Needs		
	Social Action Groups	Coalitions	Delegate Councils
Purpose	To devise and implement social change tactics and strategies	To exert greater influence by sharing resources, expertise, and power bases of social action groups with common goals	To represent different organizations, chapters, or other units
Leadership	Indigenous leadership emerging from the groups Practitioner often is staffer or adviser	Often a charismatic or dedicated individual leading by consensus or elected by vote of the membership	Representatives appointed by the sponsoring organization
Focus	Consumer, community, social justice	Building consensus and a partnership for maximum influence	Collective input and action Equality of representation Focus on larger issues, concerns, and positions
Bond	Perception of injustice, inequity, or need for change	Interest in an issue Commitment to an ideological position	Larger purpose or community concern, rather than individual or agency concern
Composition	Based on common interest, shared purpose, and investment in community	Loose, temporary confederation of groups or organizations working in partnership to achieve a common goal	Diverse by definition Represents interest of sponsoring organization
Communication	Informal member-to-member discussion Formulation and implementation of tactics and strategies for change High member self-disclosure in relation to social problems	Formal or informal, depending on type of coalition Less formal in caucuses and subgroups Moderate member self-disclosure representing group interests	Provides a forum for communication among organizations Delegates are communication links between council and the sponsoring organization Low member self-disclosure

Usually, particular attention is paid to how team members work together as a group, frequently referred to as *team building*. Thus, meetings should avoid focusing solely on service delivery—some time should be devoted to how members function as a group (Toseland, Palmer-Ganeles, & Chapman, 1986). Neglecting team functioning can lead to a variety of problems such as interpersonal conflict and rivalry, duplication of effort, and uncoordinated or incomplete service.

Members are bonded by a team spirit that assists them in their work as a group rather than being a collection of individuals representing disparate concerns and professional agendas. When building and maintaining an effective team, the worker must foster the organization's support of teamwork, encourage members' personal and professional orientations toward collaboration, and help members to develop skills to clarify roles and negotiate conflicts (Steckler & Fondas, 1995).

Ideally, team members should meet regularly to discuss their service delivery efforts and their functioning as a team (Abramson, 1989). Communication among team members varies according to the working situation of the team (Fatout & Rose, 1995). Sometimes team members work independently of each other. For example, within a residential program for children, child-care workers might be considered important team members although they work different shifts. To promote adequate communication and a coordinated team effort in such situations, it is a good practice to schedule meeting times when shifts overlap.

Treatment Conferences

Treatment conferences meet for the purpose of developing, monitoring, and coordinating treatment plans for a particular client or client system. Members consider the client's situation and decide on a plan for working with the client. Examples of treatment conferences include the following:

- An interdisciplinary group of professionals planning the discharge of a patient in a mental health facility
- A group of child-care workers, social workers, nurses, and a psychiatrist determining a treatment plan for a child in residential treatment
- A parole board considering testimony regarding the release of a prisoner in a correctional facility
- A group of community mental health professionals considering treatment methods for a young man experiencing severe depression

Although treatment conferences may at first appear similar to team meetings, they differ in five respects:

1. Members of a treatment conference might not all work together as do members of teams. They may be employees of different organizations who come to a treatment conference to discuss ways to coordinate their efforts on behalf of a particular client.

2. Participants may not have the same close working relationships and shared sense of purpose that are essential in teamwork. Members may not work together from day to day. In fact, they may never have met before the treatment conference.

3. Treatment conference groups often meet less frequently than teams; they gather as the need arises in particular situations.

4. The composition of teams is relatively stable, but the composition of treatment conference groups varies depending on the clients being discussed.

5. The plan of action might be carried out by only one member who is entirely responsible for the client's care. For example, during a treatment conference in a family service agency, a worker gets advice from colleagues about how to help a group member with a particularly difficult issue. The other members of the treatment conference have no direct contact with the client. In contrast, all members of a team usually have some contact with clients served by the team.

In treatment conferences, participants generally focus on one client at a time. Members who are familiar with the client contribute information that may be helpful in developing or improving a treatment plan. Other members, who might not be familiar with the client, can also contribute their expertise about how to most effectively treat the type of problem the client is experiencing. On the basis of this information, the group discusses the client's overall circumstances and considers alternative treatment plans. The group decides on one plan that all members agree will be the most helpful for the client.

Treatment conferences are oriented toward decision making, problem solving, and coordinating the actions of members. The group focuses its attention on the needs of the client rather than on the needs of the group members. The bond that group members feel is based on their concern for a client and their commitment to an agreed-on treatment plan.

Treatment conferences usually include all helping professionals who are working with a client. The group can also include consultants or experts who do not work directly with the client but who can contribute to the treatment plan by offering insight, resources, or advice. Treatment conference membership is diverse by design. Participants are invited because they have new insights and treatment opportunities based on their area of expertise and their unique experiences with a client.

It is the policy of some agencies to have clients and their spouses, parents, guardians, or significant others participate in treatment conferences. However, the staff of some agencies believe that inviting clients to treatment conferences may inhibit open discussion. Also, some staff believe that the conflicting facts, multiple options in treatment planning, or emotionally charged issues that are sometimes discussed during treatment conferences can confuse or upset clients. These agencies sometimes invite the client and significant others to the portion of the treatment conference that occurs *after* treatment staff have had a private, freewheeling discussion about the client's situation. However, these agencies are in a minority. Most agencies simply opt not to have the client present at treatment conferences (Toseland, Ivanoff, & Rose, 1987).

No data are available to address when, or even if, it is best to invite clients and their significant others to treatment conferences. Still, because a client's right to self-determination is an important part of the value base of social work practice, careful consideration should be given to soliciting clients' input into the treatment-planning decisions that will affect their lives.

Treatment conference leadership can be determined in a variety of ways. In some agencies, the conferences are always led by the same person. This person might be the program director or a member of the staff, such as the social worker whose job includes responsibility for treatment coordination. Commonly, the designated leader is the worker with the most responsibility for, or involvement with, the client's care. In some agencies, leadership is rotated or a supervisor leads the meeting. In these situations, the leader can lend objectivity to the proceedings because he or she does not work directly with the client. For a detailed description of the functioning of a treatment conference see Jacobsen and Jacobsen (1996).

Staff Development Groups

The purpose of staff development groups is to improve services to clients by developing, updating, and refreshing workers' skills. Staff development groups provide workers with an opportunity to learn about new treatment approaches, resources, and community services; to practice new skills; and to review and learn from their previous work with clients. Examples of staff development groups include the following:

- A group of professionals who attend a series of seminars about pharmacology offered by a regional psychiatric center
- An in-service development seminar on codependency for the staff of an alcoholism treatment agency
- Group supervision offered by an experienced social worker for social workers who work in school districts in which there are no supervisors
- A program director who conducts a weekly supervisory group for paraprofessionals who work in a community outreach program for isolated elderly people

Ideally, leaders of staff development groups are experts in a particular field. Often they also possess extensive experience and knowledge gathered through specialized training, study, and reflection on difficult practice issues.

The focus of staff development groups is on improving workers' skills so they can perform more effectively on behalf of their clients. The trainer or leader can use many methods to aid learning, such as lectures, discussions, audio- and videotape presentations, simulations, and live demonstrations. Members may be given the opportunity to practice new skills in the group and to receive feedback from the trainer and the other members.

Members are bonded by their desire to improve their skills. Often they share an interest in a similar client population or treatment method. They may also share in the camaraderie that comes from being at similar stages in their professional development.

In some staff development groups, the leader takes primary responsibility for the content of each session. The leader may make presentations, arrange for guest speakers, or prepare and conduct simulations and other staff development exercises. In other groups, members are responsible for structuring the group by taking turns presenting their work with particular clients.

Members are expected to risk opening their work to the scrutiny and critique of the rest of the group and to participate in staff development exercises and discussions. They are also expected to learn from their own mistakes and the mistakes of others in the group. Honest, frank, constructive communication and feedback among members is valued, as is a high level of self-disclosure.

Groups to Meet Organizational Needs

Committees

The most common type of task group is the committee. It is almost impossible to be associated with an agency or organization without having some contact with committees. Although they are most often used to meet organizational needs, in human service fields, organizational needs often overlap client needs. For example, a committee may meet to respond to a request by the United Way to improve service. The results of the committee's work are beneficial to both the agency and its clients.

A committee is made up of people who are appointed or elected to the group. Their task is to "accomplish a charge" (Pincus & Minahan, 1973, p. 61) that is delegated to the committee from a higher authority such as organizational by-laws or an agency executive. Committees may be temporary creations (ad hoc committees) or more permanent parts of the structure of an organization (standing committees). Examples of committees include the following:

- A group of young people responsible for recommending activities for the local community center
- A group of employees assigned the task of studying and recommending changes in the agency's personnel policy
- A group of social workers considering ways to improve service delivery to pregnant teenagers
- A group of staff members developing recommendations for an employee assistance program

In these examples, members are concerned with producing reports, accomplishing tasks, issuing recommendations, or making decisions. In each example, the committee's work requires the collective wisdom of a number of people with varied viewpoints, expertise, and abilities.

Although members are expected to share their personal views during deliberations, the level of self-disclosure in committees is frequently low. In some cases, however, there are variations in the level of self-disclosure, depending on the norms that have developed in the committee and on the nature of the issues being discussed. For example, when the subject matter is of a sensitive nature, discussing personal viewpoints may require a high level of members' self-disclosure.

Most committees tend to follow a standard set of procedures. Sometimes committees rely on parliamentary procedure to conduct their meetings. In other cases, committees develop their own rules and regulations that control how members introduce and discuss issues and how decisions are reached.

It is useful for each meeting to have an agenda so committee members can follow the activity of the group and know what to expect during the rest of the meeting. The agenda provides structure, focus, and direction for the group. The chairperson is responsible for seeing that the agenda and the formalized procedures are carried out. The chairperson may be appointed by the authority that has given the committee its mandate or may be elected by committee or organization members.

Committees frequently deal with complex issues, requiring the group to divide large tasks into a series of smaller subtasks. To deal with these subtasks, a committee often authorizes the formation of one or more subcommittees from its membership. Subcommittees report back to the larger committee, which coordinates subcommittee reports and activities and deliberates about any recommendations made by the subcommittees.

The composition of subcommittees is sometimes the responsibility of the chairperson, who considers the qualifications and abilities of each committee member and selects subcommittee members on the basis of their ability to complete a particular task. The chairperson may also ask for volunteers rather than appoint members. This is particularly true when the subcommittee deals with a particularly onerous task and highly motivated members are needed. In other cases, subcommittee members are elected by members of the full committee.

Committees are generally accountable to an administrator or other individual or group who gave the committee its charge. The power vested in a committee depends on the group's mandate and the extent to which its actions are binding. It is common, however, for committees to be given the power to make recommendations rather than issue binding decisions.

The importance of the committee as a type of task group cannot be overemphasized. Most other types of task groups mentioned in our typology use elements of committee structure to complete their tasks. It can be argued that other forms of task groups, such as cabinets and treatment conferences, are special forms of committees.

Cabinets

Cabinets are designed to provide advice and expertise about policy issues to chief executive officers or other high-level administrators. Policies, procedures, and practices that affect the entire organization are discussed, developed, or modified in cabinets before being announced by a senior administrative officer. Cabinets enable formal communications among senior administrators in an organization and help garner support for particular policies and procedures among senior and midlevel administrators. Examples of cabinet groups include the following:

- A meeting of section heads in a large state health department to discuss long-term care reimbursement policies
- A weekly meeting of supervisory social work staff and the director of social services in a large municipal hospital
- A series of meetings of senior United Way staff to discuss potential changes in methods of allocating money among member agencies
- A meeting of department heads in a county social services department

Cabinets focus their efforts on administrative and policy issues that may have important implications for the entire organization or subdivisions within it. Although committees often make recommendations to a high-level administrator who is not part of the group, cabinet members often give advice about developing and changing policies and procedures directly to the chief executive officer or other administrator who leads the meeting. In some organizations, cabinets are delegated the authority to make decisions by the chief executive officer.

Unlike committee members, who may be elected or appointed, cabinet members are often appointed by the chief executive officer. Cabinet members are typically supervisors, department heads, or senior managers with powerful positions within the organization. Occasionally, the executive might ask an outside consultant to join the group because of that person's background and knowledge.

Authority and power are particularly important in cabinets. Members often vie for the chief executive's attention and for the chance to influence policy decisions. Members sometimes take stances on policy issues that will benefit the program or section they lead within the larger organization.

The proceedings of cabinet meetings are often kept confidential. Self-disclosure is typically low, with members thinking strategically about how their statements on issues will affect their own standing within the group and the likelihood that they will be able to influence current and future policy decisions.

Boards of Directors

There are two primary types of boards: the governing board and the advisory board (Conrad & Glenn, 1976). Under the articles of incorporation and the bylaws of not-for-profit organizations, governing boards—sometimes referred to as boards of trustees—are legally and financially responsible for the conduct of the organization.

The members of governing boards are stewards of the public trust and are accountable to the state government that granted the organization its charter; to the federal government, which granted tax-exempt status; and, ultimately, to the public, whom the organization serves (Wolf, 1990). Members of advisory boards provide counsel and guidance to the management of an organization. However, they have no official power to make policy or fiscal decisions. Examples of board groups include the following:

- Trustees of a large public hospital
- Members of the governing board of a family service agency
- Individuals on the citizens' advisory board to a county department of social services
- Members of the board of a corporation that includes several affiliated social service and health agencies

The primary functions of boards of directors are policy making, oversight of agency operations, ensuring the financial integrity and stability of the organization, and public relations (Tropman, 1995). Boards of directors determine the mission and short- and long-range goals of the organization. They set personnel and operating policies. They offer counsel and advice to the chief executive officer and monitor the organization's operations. They establish fiscal policy, set budgets, and install monitoring and auditing mechanisms. They also engage in fundraising, hire the chief executive officer, and manage public relations (Howe, 1998). Boards, however, are not supposed to engage in the day-to-day operations of the organization, the hiring of staff (other than the executive director), or the details of programmatic decisions (Wolf, 1990).

The position and duties of the president, vice-president, secretary, treasurer, and any other officers of a board of directors are generally specified in the articles of incorporation and bylaws of the organization. The terms of these officers and how they are selected are specified in the board's operating procedures. Usually, officers are nominated by a subcommittee of the board and are elected to specified terms by the entire membership.

It has been estimated that 11.5 million people sit on the boards of not-for-profit agencies in the United States (Waldo, 1986). Board members are bonded by their commitment to the mission and goals of the organization and by their commitment to community service.

They are often a diverse group of individuals who are selected on the basis of their power, status, and influence in the community; their expertise; and their representation of particular interest groups and constituencies. For example, a board might contain lawyers who can provide advice on legal matters, accountants or bankers who can provide advice on fiscal matters, business people who can assist with fundraising and advertising, other media experts who can help with public relations, and policy experts and consumers who can provide guidance on programmatic and service issues.

Written agendas are usually circulated before board meetings. Communication is often formal, following the rules of parliamentary procedure. Much of the actual work, however, is often conducted in less formal subcommittee meetings. Boards often have several standing and ad hoc committees that report at board meetings and recommend actions in the form of motions. For example, the finance committee might recommend that the board approve the annual budget of the agency, the personnel committee might recommend a change in health benefits for employees of the organization, or the nominating committee might present a slate of new officers for board approval.

Groups to Meet Community Needs

Social Action Groups

Social action groups empower members to engage in collective action and planned change efforts to alter some aspect of their social or physical environment. They are often referred to as "grass roots" organizations because they arise from the concerns of individuals in the community who may have little individual power or status. Although the goals of social action groups are frequently linked to the needs of the individual members of the group, goal achievement generally also benefits people outside the group. Thus, social action groups serve the common good of both members and nonmembers. Examples of social action groups include the following:

- A citizens' group advocating increased police protection on behalf of the elderly population in a neighborhood
- A group of social workers lobbying for increased funding for social services
- A tenants' group seeking support for a playground area in their housing complex
- A group of community leaders working to increase the access of African Americans to a mental health agency

A worker involved in a social action group can assume one of many leadership roles, depending on the nature of the change effort and the needs of the group. A worker assumes an enabler role to help the group acquire information or resources, determine priorities and procedures, and plan a strategy for action. For example, in working with tenants concerned about their rights, the worker might help organize a tenant-rights group to help the individuals pursue their common goals.

Alternatively, workers might take a directive role because of their expertise regarding the change effort. In a lobbying effort, for example, a worker might be particularly knowledgeable about techniques for influencing legislators. In this instance, the worker might be asked to speak for the social action group or might encourage the group to examine particular issues or use particular strategies, such as collaboration, bargaining, or conflict.

Although directive approaches to leading social action groups are sometimes useful and appropriate, the worker should be guided by the purpose of the group and the preferences of group members. The worker should make sure that a directive approach does not inhibit indigenous leadership from developing among members. Abels (1980) suggests that the worker should assume the role of an "instructed" advocate for the group. Using this approach, the worker's role is defined and limited by the social action group and includes four major goals: "(1) to help the group achieve its purpose, (2) to help the group remain together as a unit long enough to achieve these purposes, (3) to enable members to function in an autonomous manner, and (4) to help the group to come to terms with its community" (Abels, 1980, p. 327).

The bond that holds members of action groups together is a shared perception of injustice, inequity, and a need for a change in the current social structure. Yet, Mondros and Wilson (1994) point out that less than 2 percent of a potential constituency ever becomes involved in a social action group and that large numbers of individuals drop out after their initial enthusiasm fades. Five factors that help people stay involved in social action groups are (1) the importance of the work of the group, (2) the group's effectiveness, (3) a sense of community and peer support, (4) interest in the task, and (5) the feeling of making a contribution (Mondros & Wilson, 1994). Methods to enhance and sustain membership based on these and other factors are described in Chapters 3 and 12.

The composition of social action groups can vary depending on the nature and circumstances of the change effort. Sometimes workers take a leadership role in composing social action groups; in other cases, groups may form as a result of the interests of one or more concerned citizens. In the latter case, the worker is often asked to be a facilitator, enabler, or consultant to lend expertise to the change effort without necessarily influencing the composition of the group.

When the worker does have a role in composing the group, consideration should be given to the level of support for the change effort among key community leaders. In some instances, the worker may seek members who can exert influence in the environment or who have the diverse skills and resources needed to empower the group.

Communication patterns in social action groups vary with the circumstances of the group. The worker helps the group develop open communication patterns so that all members have a chance to become involved. The worker also helps the group establish communication links with its environment. Good communication helps avoid misunderstandings and promotes a cooperative effort among all those who may have some stake in the change effort (Mondros & Wilson, 1994).

Coalitions

Coalitions—or alliances, as they are sometimes called—are groups of organizations, social action groups, or individuals that come together to exert influence by sharing resources and expertise. Coalition members agree to pursue common goals, which they believe cannot be achieved by any of the members acting alone.
    Examples of coalitions include the following:

- A group of family planning and community health-care clinics who have formed a pro-choice coalition to influence state and federal legislation on abortion
- Not-for-profit home-care agencies who gather to lobby for greater access to community care for the chronically ill elderly
- Community agencies that want to bring public attention to the need for a community teen center
- Business, community, and civic leaders who team up to explore ways to reduce racial tensions in a large urban area

Despite scant attention to coalitions in the social work literature, the formation of coalitions as political and social forces to improve the responsiveness of the social environment to human beings has a long tradition in social group work (Mizrahi & Rosenthal, 1998). For example, Newstetter (1948) described principles for interagency collaboration that have formed the basis for more recent writings on the formation and development of coalitions (Bailey & Koney, 1996; Dluhy, 1990; Gentry, 1987; Hula, 1999; Mayer, Soweid, Dabney, & Brownson, 1998; Merenda, 1997; Mondros & Wilson, 1994; Prigmore, 1974; Schopler, 1994; Weisner, 1983; Winer & Ray, 1996).
    Coalitions are often formed by a charismatic or dedicated individual who has high visibility and respect within the community. This individual helps organizations, groups, and individuals understand that they have common goals and purposes that could be better served by working together.
    Because members of coalitions are often concerned about preserving their autonomy while joining with others in the group, coalitions sometimes experience conflict in establishing mutual goals, working agreements, plans of action, and equitable ways of sharing resources and accomplishments. Therefore, a primary task throughout coalition formation and development is building and maintaining consensus and a smooth partnership in which efforts can be focused on the goals to be achieved rather than on intragroup rivalry. Charismatic leaders are helped in their efforts by the coalition members, who are bonded by their ideals, common ideology, and interest in a particular issue or set of issues.
    Coalitions take many forms (Dluhy, 1990). Frequently, they are loose, temporary confederations of organizations or social action groups that coalesce to share resources and gain strength in numbers. In such informal coalitions, the autonomy of the individual members is strictly protected. Over time, however,

some coalitions become stable, long-term organizations with centralized staff and resources.

Meetings may be characterized by ideologically fervent speechmaking and position taking. Much emphasis is placed on developing strategies to accomplish specific goals and coordinating activities involved in the action plan. Sometimes, coalition meetings are characterized by formal interactions following the rules of parliamentary procedure. Although parliamentary procedures are often not as strictly adhered to as they are in board meetings or delegate councils, they are used in coalitions to promote a sense of inclusion and belonging so that members feel they have the opportunity to fully participate in the collective deliberations and decision making of the coalition. Still, Dluhy (1990) notes that coalitions often have one or more elite decision makers who may have considerable influence on the decision making and operation of the group.

Although parliamentary procedure is frequently used during formal meetings of the members, freewheeling interaction often occurs during caucuses, and in subgroup and one-to-one discussions between coalition meetings. Less formal procedures are also frequently used in ad hoc, single-issue coalitions that do not have a long history of operation.

Delegate Councils

Delegate councils are composed for the purposes of facilitating interagency communication and cooperation, studying communitywide social issues or social problems, engaging in collective social action, and governing large organizations. Members of delegate councils are appointed or elected by a sponsoring unit. The members' primary function is to represent the interests of their sponsoring unit during council meetings. A variation of the delegate council is the delegate assembly, which is usually larger. Examples of delegate councils include the following:

- A number of agency representatives who meet monthly to improve interagency communication
- A group of elected representatives from local chapters of a professional organization who meet to approve the organization's budget
- A state task force to study family violence composed of members appointed from each county
- A yearly meeting of representatives from family service agencies throughout the county

Representation is an important issue in delegate councils. A member represents a group of people, an agency, or another system. The member is often given authority to speak for the represented unit. Because the unit has agreed to participate by sending a representative, the represented unit generally agrees to abide by decisions made by the delegate council.

There are differing ways to achieve representation. The number of representatives for each sponsoring unit can vary with the size or importance of the unit. For example, legislative bodies frequently determine the number of representatives by considering the population of each voting district, county, or state, and apportioning an appropriate number of representatives for each district.

Other councils' representation may be dictated by a sanctioning authority to ensure control over policy decisions. For example, a consumer council for a large department of social services may have more employees than clients to ensure departmental control over the decisions made by the group.

Delegate councils are usually concerned with broad issues that affect several agencies, a large segment of a population, or a group of people in a wide geographic area. Delegate councils provide an effective communications link among groups of people who otherwise might not be able to communicate in a formal way. For example, delegate councils frequently serve as a forum for communication among diverse human service agencies within a city, state, or nation. Such agencies might not otherwise communicate effectively with each other. They may also form part of the governance structure of unions or professional organizations that represent a diverse and geographically dispersed membership.

Delegate councils can be either discussion oriented or action oriented, or they may have components of both orientations. White House Conferences on Aging, for example, involve a series of delegate councils that discuss issues of concern to older U.S. citizens and make recommendations for government action.

Delegate councils are formed in a number of ways. Some councils are the product of ad hoc task forces or coalitions that have been meeting informally for some time. Other councils begin with the support and sponsorship of a particular agency and gradually establish their own identities, rules and procedures, and sources of funding. Representatives to delegate councils are either elected or appointed, and leadership is usually determined through an election.

Because council members are responsible for representing the views, interests, and positions of their sponsors to the delegate council, members often act formally on behalf of their constituencies. Delegates communicate with their sponsors regarding the proceedings of the council. The effectiveness of the delegate council depends on the ability of each delegate to achieve two-way communication between the council and the represented unit. The individual delegates are not expected to engage in a high level of personal self-disclosure because they are bound by a mandate to represent the collective views of a group of people.

SUMMARY

This introductory chapter provides a framework for studying and working with groups. Group work is a broad field of practice conducted by professional social workers with, and on behalf of, many different client groups in many different settings. A definition of group work is offered that encompasses the breadth of group work practice and is sufficiently flexible to allow specialized approaches and objectives. To understand the types of groups that exist in practice, a distinction is made between treatment and task groups. Although some functions and objectives of task and treatment groups overlap, they are distinguished by a variety of characteristics.

This chapter also helps clarify the kinds of task and treatment groups often encountered in practice and illustrates the commonalities and differences among these groups. The typology of treatment groups distinguishes among those with five primary purposes: (1) support, (2) education, (3) growth, (4) therapy, and (5) socialization.

The typology of task groups distinguishes among nine types of task groups that are organized to serve three primary purposes: (1) meeting client needs, (2) meeting organizational needs, and (3) meeting community needs. Types of task groups that serve client needs include teams, treatment conferences, and staff development groups. Types of task groups that serve organizational needs include committees, cabinets, and boards of directors. Types of task groups that serve community needs include social action groups, coalitions, and delegate councils.

LEARNING ASSIGNMENTS

1. After reading Appendix A, interview an experienced group leader. Ask this person to identify three problems encountered while trying to implement social work values when practicing group work. For example, ask the person whether the encounters involved (a) violations of confidentiality, (b) conflicts between the rights of an individual member and the rights of the group, (c) problems in member-to-member and member-to-leader relationships within the group, and (d) problems in member-to-member and member-to-leader relationships outside the group. Ask how the person attempted to resolve the problems.

2. Attend several meetings of a treatment group or view one of the films listed in Appendix B. Following the list of selected characteristics in Table 1.3, record your observations about the group. After you have observed the group, answer the following questions:

   a. What was the primary purpose of the group? Was there more than one purpose?

   b. Comment on the role played by the leader in the group. Was the leader directive or nondirective?

   c. Was the focus of the group on the individual member or the group as a whole? To what extent was the focus on members' emotional needs versus the tasks the group was convened to accomplish?

   d. What was the basis on which members bonded? Was the bond strong or weak?

    e. Describe the composition of the group. How were group members similar? How were they different?

    f. Describe the communication patterns you observed. Were all members involved in the interaction? What was the level of self-disclosure?

3. Interview two middle or upper managers in one or two social service agencies. Ask the managers to list the task groups in which they are (a) leaders and (b) members. Ask them to estimate the amount of time task group participation takes each week and the importance of this component of their jobs. Also, ask how well their education prepared them to be leaders and members of the task groups in which they are involved.

Historical Developments

To develop a broad perspective concerning the potential uses of groups in practice settings, it is helpful to understand the developments that have occurred in the study of groups and in the practice of group work over the years. This historical perspective also gives the group worker a firm foundation on which to build a knowledge base for effective group work practice.

Two general types of inquiries have enhanced the understanding of groups. One type has come from social scientists who have experimented with groups in laboratories. This inquiry has led to social science findings about basic properties and processes of groups. The other type has come from group work practitioners who have examined how groups function in practice settings. The results of both inquiries have led to improved methods for working with groups.

KNOWLEDGE FROM GROUP WORK PRACTICE: TREATMENT GROUPS

Although casework began in England and the United States in charity organizations in the late nineteenth century, group work grew up mainly in English and American settlement houses. The use of group work in settlement houses and casework in charity organizations was not by accident. Group work—and the settlement houses in which it was practiced—offered citizens the opportunity for education, recreation, socialization, and community involvement. Unlike the charity organizations, which focused on the diagnosis and treatment of the problems of the poor, settlement houses offered groups as an opportunity for citizens to gather to share their views, gain mutual support, and exercise the power derived from their association for social change.

There were some exceptions to this trend. For example, as early as 1895, some people in the charity organization movement realized there was a need to organize the poor for social change as well as to work with them one-to-one (Brackett, 1895). Group work was also used for therapeutic purposes in state mental institutions (Boyd, 1935), but much of the interest in group work stemmed from those who had led socialization groups, adult education groups, and recreation groups in settlement houses and youth service agencies (McCaskill, 1930). In fact, during these early years, the term *club work* was often used interchangeably with the term *group work* (Slavson, 1939, p. 126).

It is often believed that group work is considerably younger than casework, but group work agencies actually started only a few years after casework agencies. There were courses for group workers in schools of social work in the early 1900s (Maloney, 1963), and both casework and group work were used by social workers in the early twentieth century.

Casework soon became identified with the social work profession, but group work did not become formally linked with social work until the National Conference of Social Work in 1935. The identification of group work with the social work profession increased during the 1940s (American Association of Group Workers, 1947), although group workers continued to maintain loose ties with recreation, adult education, and mental hygiene until 1955, when group workers joined with six other professional groups to form the National Association of Social Workers.

Differences between Casework and Group Work

Compared with caseworkers, who relied on insight developed from psychodynamic approaches and on the provision of concrete resources, group workers relied on program activities to spur members to action. Program activities of all types were the media through which groups attained their goals (Addams, 1909, 1926; Boyd, 1935, 1938; Smith, 1935). Activities such as camping, singing, group discussion, games, and arts and crafts were used for recreation, socialization, education, support, and rehabilitation. Unlike casework, which was mainly focused on problem solving and rehabilitation, group work activities were used for enjoyment as well as to solve problems. Thus, the group work methods that developed from settlement house work had a different focus and a different goal than did casework methods.

Differences between casework and group work can also be clearly seen in the helping relationship. Caseworkers sought out the most underprivileged victims of industrialization and diagnosed and treated worthy clients by providing them with resources and acting as examples of virtuous, hardworking citizens.

Although group workers also worked with the poor and impaired, they did not focus solely on the poorest people nor on those with the most problems. They preferred the word *members* rather than *clients* (Bowman, 1935). They emphasized members' strengths rather than their weaknesses. Helping was seen as a shared relationship in which the group worker and the group members worked together for mutual understanding and action regarding their common concerns for their community. As concerns were identified, group members supported and helped one another, and the worker mediated between the demands of society and the needs of group members (Schwartz, 1981).

Shared interaction, shared power, and shared decision making placed demands on group workers that were not experienced by caseworkers. The number of group members, the fact that they could turn to one another for help, and the democratic decision-making processes that were encouraged meant that group workers had to develop skills different from those of caseworkers. Group workers used their skills to intervene in complex and often fast-paced group interactions but remained aware of the welfare of all group members. Schwartz (1966) summed up the feelings engendered by the new group work method very well in the statement "there are so many of them and only one of me" (p. 572).

Unlike the early writings of caseworkers, which emphasized improving practice outcomes by careful study, diagnosis, and treatment (Richmond, 1917), the early writings of group workers (Coyle, 1930, 1935) emphasized the processes that occurred during group meetings. For example, Grace Coyle, one of the first social workers to publish a text on groups, titled her 1930 work *Social Process in Organized Groups,* whereas the first text on casework, published in 1917 by Mary Richmond, was called *Social Diagnosis.*

The emphasis on group processes has remained throughout the history of group work. Group workers have always been concerned with how best to use the unique possibilities offered by the interaction of different people in a group. Thus, workers focus on the group as a whole as well as on individual members.

Intervention Targets

During the 1940s and 1950s, group workers began to use groups more frequently to provide therapy and remediation in mental health settings. Therapy groups were insight oriented, relying less on program activities and more on diagnosis and treatment of members' problems (Konopka, 1949, 1954; Redl, 1944; Trecker, 1956).

The emphasis on the use of groups for therapy and remediation was the result, in part, of the influence of Freudian psychoanalysis and ego psychology and, in part, of World War II, which created a severe shortage of trained workers to deal with mentally disabled war veterans. It was also spurred on by Fritz Redl and Gisela Konopka, who helped make group services an integral part of child guidance clinics. Interest in the use of groups in psychiatric settings continued into the 1950s, as can be seen in the proceedings of a national institute on this topic in 1955 (Trecker, 1956).

Although there was an increased emphasis in the 1940s and 1950s on using groups to improve the functioning of individual members, interest remained in using groups for recreational and educational purposes, especially in Jewish community centers and in youth organizations such as the Girl Scouts and the YWCA. During the 1950s and 1960s, groups were also used for community development and social action in neighborhood centers and community agencies. At the same time, there was an increase in the study of small groups as a social phenomenon. According to Hare (1976), the 1950s were the golden age of the study of groups.

The Weakening of Group Work

During the 1960s the popularity of group services declined. This can be seen in accounts of well-known projects such as the Mobilization for Youth experiment (Weissman, 1969). Weissman stated, "the planners of Mobilization for Youth did not accord group work services a major role in the fight against delinquency" (p. 180). Work training programs and educational opportunities were viewed as more significant than group work services—except in the area of community organization, in which the skill of group workers played an important role in organizing youths and adults around important social concerns.

Also, during the 1960s, the push toward a generic view of practice in schools of social work and the movement away from specializations in casework, group work, and community organization tended to weaken group work specializations in professional schools and reduce the number of professionals trained in group work as their primary mode of practice. Taken together, these factors contributed to the decline of group work in the 1960s.

During the 1970s interest in group work continued to wane. Fewer professional schools offered advanced courses in group work, and fewer practitioners used it as a practice method. To increase awareness among practitioners about the potential benefits of groups, group workers throughout the United States and Canada came together in 1979 for the First Annual Symposium for the Advancement of Group Work. Each year since then, an annual group work symposium has been convened. The symposia bring together social group workers from the United States and other countries, who present clinical findings, research results, and workshops based on the work they have done with groups in their own communities.

During the 1980s and 1990s, attempts to revitalize group work within social work have continued and increased. The Association for the Advancement of Social Work with Groups (AASWG) has expanded into an international association with many affiliated local chapters. In addition to the annual symposia it sponsors, the AASWG has a person who is a liaison to the Council on Social Work Education to promote group work curriculum in schools of social work. The AASWG has also developed standards on group work education and submitted testimony to the Commission on Educational Policy of the Council on Social Work Education.

Also, each year since 1985, a group of social work practitioners and educators has convened a seminar on group work research, sometimes in conjunction with the annual AASWG symposium. The seminar is designed to promote research by encouraging participants to share findings and innovative methodological approaches and to collaborate on social group work research endeavors.

Current Practice Trends

Treatment Groups

In an article that has had a profound effect on social work practice with groups, Papell and Rothman (1962) outlined three historically important models of group work practice, shown in Table 2.1, that are still widely used today. These three models are (1) the social goals model, (2) the remedial model, and (3) the reciprocal model.

Social Goals Model

The social goals model focuses on socializing members to democratic societal values. It values cultural diversity and the power of group action. It was used, and continues to be used, in settlement houses and in group work with youth organizations such as the Girl Scouts, the YWCA, and Jewish community centers. It also has been used by community development agencies to change societal norms and structures and improve the social welfare of all citizens.

The worker acts as an enabler who uses program activities, such as camping, discussions, and instructions about democratic processes, to socialize members. The worker also acts to empower members by helping them make collective decisions and use their collective strength to make society more responsive to their needs.

The writings of Klein (1953, 1970, 1972) and Tropp (1968, 1976) helped to refine the social goals model. Tropp focused on how group development can be used to empower members to achieve the goals they have set for themselves. He was strongly opposed to the worker's establishing goals for members, believing instead that groups could promote growth only when the worker encouraged group self-direction toward common goals. Klein's writings emphasized the importance of matching members' needs to environmental opportunities for growth. Like Tropp, Klein emphasized the autonomy of group members and their freedom to pursue their own self-defined goals. Middleman (1980, 1982) has also made important contributions to the model by emphasizing the importance of program activities. Breton (1994, 1995), Cohen and Mullender (1999), Cox (1988), Cox and Parsons (1994), Lee (1990), Mondros and Wilson (1994), Mullender and Ward (1991), Parsons (1991), and Pernell (1986) have also made significant contributions by focusing on empowerment strategies in social group work.

Remedial Model

The remedial model focuses on restoring or rehabilitating individuals by helping them change their behavior. The worker acts as a change agent and intervenes in the group to achieve specific purposes determined by group members, the group worker, and society. The remedial model uses a leader-centered approach to group work, with the worker actively intervening in the group's process, often using step-by-step problem solving and task-centered or behavioral methods.

TABLE 2.1 ■ *Three Models of Social Group Work*

Selected Characteristics	Social Goals Model	Remedial Model	Reciprocal Model
Purpose and goals	Social consciousness, social responsibility, informed citizenship, and informed political and social action	To restore and rehabilitate group members who are behaving dysfunctionally	To form a mutual aid system among group members to achieve optimum adaptation and socialization
Agency	Settlement houses and neighborhood center settings	Formal agency setting, clinical outpatient or inpatient settings	Compatible with clinical inpatient and outpatient settings and neighborhood and community centers
Focus of work	Larger society, individuals within the context of the neighborhood and the social environment	Alleviating problems or concerns Improving coping skills	Creating a self-help, mutual aid system among all group members
Role of the group worker	Role model and enabler for responsible citizenship	Change agent who engages in study, diagnosis, and treatment to help group members attain individual treatment goals	Mediator between needs of members and needs of the group and the larger society Enabler contributing data not available to the members
Type of group	Citizens, neighborhood, and community residents	Clients who are not functioning adequately and need help coping with life's tasks	Partners who work together sharing common concerns
Methods used in the group	Discussion, participation, consensus, developing and carrying out a group task, community organizing, and other program and action skills to help group members acquire instrumental skills about social action and communal living and change	Structured exercises, direct and indirect influence—within and outside of the group—to help members change behavior patterns	Shared authority where members discuss concerns, support one another, and form a cohesive social system to benefit one another

Adapted from Papell and Rothman, 1980a.

Garvin (1997), Rose (1998), and Vinter (1967) are often associated with this approach to group work. With the increased attention to time-limited, goal-directed practice and measurable treatment outcomes, this model has received increasing attention in the group work literature in recent years (Edleson & Syers, 1990; Ellis, 1992; MacKenzie, 1990, 1996; Piper & Joyce, 1996; Rose & LeCroy, 1991; Shapiro, Peltz, & Bernadett-Shapiro, 1998). It is used widely in inpatient and community-based settings with individuals who have severe behavioral problems and social skills deficits.

Time-limited, highly structured remedial groups are also being used with increasing frequency in managed care settings as cost effective alternatives to long-term individual and group psychotherapy (MacKenzie, 1995). A recent survey of directors and providers in managed care companies suggests that this trend is likely to accelerate in future years (Taylor & Burlingame, in press). Although the survey indicated that social workers were more familiar than psychologists and psychiatrists with short-term structured group work approaches, it also indicated that practitioners from all disciplines tended to be more familiar and more comfortable with the traditional process-oriented, long-term group models, suggesting that more graduate and undergraduate education and more in-service training are needed about how to conduct short-term, structured, remedial model groups (Taylor & Burlingame, in press).

Reciprocal Model

The third model presented by Papell and Rothman (1962), the reciprocal model, is sometimes referred to as the *interactional model* (Reid, 1997). The model derives its name from the emphasis on the reciprocal relationship that exists between group members and society. Members both influence and are influenced by the environment. The worker acts as a mediator, helping group members find the common ground between their needs and societal demands. The worker also acts as a resource person who facilitates the functioning of the group and helps members form a mutual-aid system and explore new ways of coping with and adapting to environmental demands.

As contrasted with the remedial model, in which the work of the group is often focused on helping individual members with specific problems, the reciprocal model encourages workers to use group processes to foster a therapeutic environment in the group as a whole. The reciprocal model also encourages the worker to help the agency and the wider community better understand and meet individual members' needs. Gitterman and Shulman (1994), Schwartz (1976), and Shulman (1999) are best known for the group-centered, process-oriented approach to group work practice, but other authors such as Brown (1991), Falck (1988), Glassman and Kates (1990), and Wasserman and Danforth (1988) have made important contributions to this model of group work practice.

The reciprocal model is closely aligned with ecological systems theory, which has received criticism for being too vague to guide practice (Wakefield, 1996). Despite this criticism, the reciprocal model has wide appeal because of its humanistic orientation, which emphasizes the potential for growth and development of group members, the activation of members' adaptive capacities through mutual-aid efforts, and the attempt at making the social environment more responsive to members' needs.

Divergent and Unified Practice Models

The different foci of current practice models are equally valid, depending on the purposes, practice situations, and tasks facing the group. Group work practice has an eclectic base, which developed as a response to diverse needs for educational, recreational, mental health, and social services (Alissi, 1980; Lang, 1972, 1979a, 1979b; Papell & Rothman 1980; Roberts & Northen, 1976). A remedial purpose, for example, may be particularly appropriate for some populations and in some settings, such as alcohol and drug treatment centers and residential centers for delinquent youth. In contrast, the reciprocal model is ideally suited for support groups designed to help members cope with distressing life events. It is also ideally suited to the facilitation of self-help groups in which reciprocal sharing of mutual concerns and the giving and receiving of support are central. For example, in Make Today Count, a medical self-help group for cancer patients, members are encouraged to share their concerns, experiences, and the reactions of their family members to help each other cope with their illness.

The usefulness and appropriateness of different practice models suggest that group workers should make differential use of group work methods, depending on the purposes, objectives, and goals of the groups they are leading. In a comprehensive review of the history of group work, Reid (1981) concludes that there has always been more than one model of group work operating in the United States and that there will continue to be several models in use to meet the many purposes and goals of group work.

In recent years, there has also been a greater attempt to integrate different models of group work practice (Papell, 1997). For example, Papell and Rothman (1980) proposed a "mainstream model" of group work practice that incorporates elements of many different practice models. They suggested that this model was characterized by "common goals, mutual aid, and nonsynthetic experiences" (p. 7). They pointed out that the fostering of a mutual-aid system among members is a common ingredient of many seemingly polarized approaches to group work practice. They suggested that group development and the creation of group structures for increasing the autonomy of members as the group develops are also common elements of most current conceptualizations of group work practice.

Similarly, in considering the past, present, and future of group work in social work, Middleman and Wood (1990) also conclude that, in practice, there is a blending of models of group work. They suggested that a mainstream model of social work with groups should include the worker (1) helping members develop a system of mutual aid; (2) understanding, valuing, and respecting group processes as powerful dynamics for change; (3) helping members become empowered for autonomous functioning within and outside the group; and (4) helping members "re-experience their groupness at the point of termination" (p. 11). Thus, they concluded that some clinical work with groups, especially when it focuses exclusively on one-to-one work with individual members within a group context, would be excluded from a mainstream model of social work with groups.

In the first edition of this book, Toseland and Rivas (1984) also had as a primary goal bridging the chasm between the reciprocal, remedial, and social goals approaches to group work. The intent of the first edition, and this edition, is to elucidate a core body of knowledge, values, skills, and procedures that are essential for professional, competent group work practice, regardless of ideological orientation.

KNOWLEDGE FROM GROUP WORK PRACTICE: TASK GROUPS

Task groups have operated in social agencies since settlement houses and charity organizations began more than one hundred years ago. The distinction between task groups and treatment groups made today was not made in the earlier history of group work. Groups were used simultaneously for both task and treatment purposes. Earlier in the history of group work, the journals *The Group,* published from 1939 to 1955, and *Adult Leadership,* published from 1952 to 1977, devoted much space to articles about leading task groups.

With a few notable exceptions (Brill, 1976; Trecker, 1980) during the 1960s and 1970s, interest in task groups waned. However, interest has been rekindled during the 1980s and 1990s with the renewed emphasis on the value of participatory management practices (Gummer, 1991, 1995). For example, Dluhy (1990), Ephross and Vassil (1988), Fatout and Rose (1995), Toseland and Ephross (1987), and Tropman (1996) have all made outstanding contributions to the task group literature. Still, the current need for expertise in task group practices is becoming critical as more and more agencies are using participatory management practices and team approaches to service delivery. This text is designed, in part, to address this gap in the literature.

KNOWLEDGE FROM SOCIAL SCIENCE RESEARCH

Practitioners sometimes criticize the findings of social scientists as not being generalizable to real-world practice settings. Some social scientists conducting their research in laboratory settings use analogue designs, which may include short-term groups, artificial problems, and students who are not always motivated. Despite these limitations, the precision of laboratory studies enables social scientists to examine how different group dynamics operate. Findings from these studies increase practitioners' understanding of how helpful and harmful group dynamics develop.

Social scientists also use naturalistic observations to study the functioning of community groups. Some classic observational studies are those conducted by Bales (1955), Lewin (1947, 1948), Roethlisberger and Dickson (1939), Thrasher (1927), and Whyte (1943). Although not as precise as laboratory studies, naturalistic studies overcome some of the limitations of laboratory studies and provide many insights into the way groups develop.

According to Hare (1976), the scientific study of groups began at the turn of the century. A basic research question, which was asked at that time and continues to receive much attention today, concerns the extent to which being a part of a group influences the individual group member. Triplett (1898), for example, examined the effect that cyclists had on each other during races and found that a racer's competitiveness appeared to depend on the activities of others on the track. Taylor (1903) found that productivity increased among workers who were freed from the pressure to conform to the standards of other workers. Those early findings suggest that the presence of others has a significant influence on an individual group member. The presence of others tends to generate pressure to conform to the standards of behavior that are expected of those who belong to the group.

Other early social scientists also recognized the influence of groups on individual behavior. LeBon (1910) referred to the forces that were generated by group interaction as "group contagion" and "group mind," recognizing that people in groups react differently than do individuals. McDougall (1920) extended the concept of the group mind. He noted the existence of groups as entities and pointed out a number of group-as-a-whole properties that could be studied as phenomena separate and distinct from properties affecting individuals working outside of a group.

The concept of a primary group was also an important contribution to the study of groups. Cooley (1909) defined a *primary group* as a small, informal group—such as a family or a friendship group—that has a tremendous influence on members' values, moral standards, and normative behaviors. The primary group was therefore viewed as essential in understanding socialization and development.

Few studies of small-group processes were published between 1905 and 1920, but activity in this area increased after World War I (Hare, 1976). Several experiments conducted during that time illustrated the powerful effects of group forces on the judgments and behavior of group members. Allport (1924), for example, found that the presence of others improved task performance, and Sherif (1936) and Asch (1957) found that members were highly influenced by the opinions of others in the group.

After World War I, social scientists began to study groups operating in the community. One of the earliest social scientists to study groups in their natural environments was Frederick Thrasher (1927). He studied gangs of delinquents in the Chicago area by becoming friendly with gang members and observing the internal operations of gangs. He noted that every member of a gang had a status within the group that was attached to a functional role in the gang. Thrasher also drew attention to the culture that developed within a gang, suggesting there was a common code that all members followed. The code was enforced by group opinion, coercion, and physical punishment. Thrasher's work and the works of Shaw (1930) and Whyte (1943) have influenced how group work is practiced with youths in settlement houses, neighborhood centers, and youth organizations.

Later, Sherif and colleagues (Sherif, 1956; Sherif & Sherif, 1953; Sherif, White, & Harvey, 1955) relied on naturalistic observations of boys in a summer camp program to demonstrate how cohesion and intergroup hostility develop in groups. Groups of boys who spent time together and had common goals, such as winning a tug-of-war, became more cooperative, developed a liking for one another, and felt solidarity with their teammates. At the same time, antagonism between groups increased. Bringing boys from different groups together only increased the tension until tasks were assigned that required the joint efforts of boys from different groups.

Social scientists also learned more about people's behavior in groups from studies done in industry and in the U.S. Army. Perhaps the most famous of all industrial studies is the classic series of studies at Western Electric's Hawthorne Plant in Chicago (Roethlisberger, 1941; Roethlisberger & Dickson, 1939, 1975). These studies were designed to test whether piece-rate wage incentives increased the output of workers who assembled telephone equipment. The incentives were designed in such a way that wage increases gained by one team member would also benefit other team members. Management believed such a system would encourage individual productivity and increase group spirit and morale because all team members would benefit from the increase in productivity.

It was found that an informal group had developed among team members. Despite the opportunity to improve individual and group wages, workers did not produce more under the new incentive system. Results of the studies suggest that informal norms of what constituted a fair day's work governed the workers' behavior. Members of a work group that produced too much were ridiculed as "rate busters" and those who produced too little were called "chiselers." Occasionally, more severe sanctions called "binging" were applied by team members when a worker did not conform to the team's notion of a fair day's work. Binging consisted of striking a fellow worker as hard as possible on the upper arm while verbally asking the worker to comply with the group's norms.

Studies conducted on combat units during World War II also helped identify the powerful effects that small groups can have on the behavior of their members. For example, in describing the fighting ability of combat soldiers, Shils (1950) and Stouffer (1949) found that the courage of the average soldier was only partially sustained by hatred of the enemy and the patriotic ideas of a democratic society. Their studies revealed that soldiers' loyalty to their particular unit strengthened their morale and supported them during periods of intense combat stress.

During the 1950s, an explosion of knowledge about small groups took place. Earlier experiments by Bales (1950), Jennings (1947, 1950), Lewin, Lippitt, and White (1939), and Moreno (1934) spurred interest in the study of both task and treatment groups. Some of the most important findings from this period are summarized in the work of Cartwright and Zander (1968), Hare (1976), Kiesler (1978), McGrath (1984), Nixon (1979), and Shaw (1976). Because these viewpoints are reflected in a discussion of group dynamics and leadership in Chapters 3 and 4, they are not presented here. It is interesting to note, however, that the major themes of small-group research that were initially developed in the first half of the twentieth century—that is, cohesion, conformity, communication and interaction patterns, group development, leadership, and social cognition and perception—continue to dominate the research efforts of social scientists investigating the dynamics of small groups today (Garvin, 1998). But Garvin (1998) also notes that new themes have emerged. These include an increased emphasis on the effects of gender and diversity on group development. Horne and Rosenthal (1997) note that in recent years there has been a greater emphasis on research on teamwork and also on short-term structured groups for persons with specific problems such as depression, eating disorders, and adjustment to divorce.

INFLUENTIAL THEORIES

From knowledge about small groups accumulated over the years in laboratory and natural settings, investigators of group phenomena began to develop comprehensive theories to explain group functioning. An enormous variety of these theories exist (Douglas, 1979). This chapter considers five of the most important theories: (1) systems theory, (2) psychodynamic theory, (3) learning theory, (4) field theory, and (5) social exchange theory. Although a thorough knowledge of systems theory is basic to all group work practice, the text also summarizes four additional theories that have had an important influence on group work practice. As they become more experienced, group workers should consider learning more about these theories.

Systems Theory

Systems theory attempts to understand the group as a system of interacting elements. It is probably the most widely used and broadly applied theory of group functioning (Anderson, 1979; Olsen, 1968). Several influential theorists have developed conceptualizations of groups as social systems.

To Parsons (1951), groups are social systems with several interdependent members attempting to maintain order and a stable equilibrium while they function as a unified whole. Groups are constantly facing changing demands in their quest to attain goals and to maintain a stable equilibrium. Groups must mobilize their resources and act to meet changing demands if they are to survive. According to Parsons, Bales, and Shils (1953), there are four major functional tasks for systems such as a group: (1) integration—ensuring that members of groups fit together; (2) adaptation—ensuring that groups change to cope with the demands of their environment; (3) pattern maintenance—ensuring that groups define and sustain their basic purposes, identities, and procedures; and (4) goal attainment—ensuring that groups pursue and accomplish their tasks.

Groups must accomplish these four functional tasks to remain in equilibrium. The work of carrying out these tasks is left to the group's leader and its members. The leader and members act to help their group survive so they can be gratified as the group reaches its goal (Mills, 1967). To do this, group members observe and assess the group's progress toward its goals and take action to avoid problems. The likelihood that a group will survive depends on the demands of the environment, the extent to which members identify with group goals, and the degree to which members believe goals are attainable. By overcoming obstacles and successfully handling the functional tasks confronting them, groups strive to remain in a state of equilibrium.

Robert Bales, another important systems theorist, has a somewhat different conception of groups as social systems. Whereas Parsons was interested in developing a generalizable systems model to explain societal as well as group functioning, Bales concentrated his efforts on observing and theorizing about small task groups in laboratory settings. According to Bales (1950), groups must solve two general types of problems to maintain themselves. These include (1) instrumental problems, such as the group's reaching its goals, and (2) socioemotional problems, which include interpersonal difficulties, problems of coordination, and member satisfaction. Instrumental problems are caused by demands placed on the group by the outside environment; socioemotional problems arise from within the group.

The implications of Bales' work is that the worker should be concerned about group processes and outcomes, that is, members' social and emotional needs and the task accomplishments expected of the group. Exclusive attention to tasks leads to dissatisfaction and conflict within the group. Exclusive attention to members' socioemotional needs leads to the group's failure to accomplish its objectives and goals.

Because instrumental and socioemotional needs often conflict, it is usually impossible to attend to both sets of problems simultaneously. Therefore, the worker is placed in the precarious position of attending alternately to task and socioemotional needs to maintain the group's optimal functioning.

In contrast with Parsons, who emphasized harmony and equilibrium, Bales' systems model emphasizes tension and antagonism. Groups tend to vacillate between adaptation to the outside environment and attention to internal integration. Bales (1950) calls this the group's "dynamic equilibrium." Swings in attention are the result of the functional needs of the group in its struggle to maintain itself.

To study this "dynamic equilibrium," Bales observed interactions in several different kinds of task groups such as juries and teams (Bales, 1950, 1954, 1955). Bales found that, to deal with instrumental problems, group members asked for or gave opinions, asked for or gave information, and asked for or made suggestions. To handle socioemotional problems, group members expressed agreement or disagreement, showed tension or released tension, and showed solidarity or antagonism. Through these interactions, group members dealt with problems of communication, evaluation, control, decision making, tension reduction, and integration.

Bales (1954, 1955) also suggests that groups go through a natural process of evolution and development. Analysis of the distribution of interactions in each category in problem-solving groups suggests that typical task groups emphasize giving and receiving information early in group meetings, giving and asking for opinions in the middle stage, and giving and asking for suggestions in later stages (Shepard, 1964).

Bales (1950) developed a scheme for analyzing group interaction on the basis of his theory about how group members deal with instrumental and expressive tasks. This scheme is called Interaction Process Analysis. It puts members' interactions into 12 categories. Bales, Cohen, and Williamson (1979) have continued to develop and refine this system of analyzing group interactions. The new system, Systematic Multiple Level Observation of Groups (SYMLOG), is explained in Chapter 8.

The final conception of systems theory relevant to our understanding of group dynamics has been presented in Homans' (1950) early work, *The Human Group*. It is also evident in the writings of Germain and Gitterman (1996) and Siporin (1980) on ecological systems theory. According to these writers, groups are in constant interaction with their environments. They occupy an ecological niche. Homans suggests that groups have an external system and an internal system. The external system represents a group's way of handling the adaptive problems that result from its relationship with its social and physical environment. The internal system consists of the patterns of activities, interactions, and norms occurring within the group as it attempts to function.

Like Bales, Homans notes that the relative dominance of the internal system or the external system depends on the demands of the external and the internal environment of the group. Homans, however, denies the homeostatic idea of equilibrium proposed by Parsons and Bales, preferring to conceive of groups as ever changing entities. Change and the constant struggle for equilibrium are ever present.

Within the social work profession, Germain and Gitterman (1996), Meyer (1983, 1988), Siporin (1980), and other ecological systems theorists emphasize the constant exchange that all social systems have with their environment. They also emphasize the possibilities for growth and change, called *morphogenic properties,* that are a part of all social systems.

The different conceptualizations of systems theory may at first appear confusing. However, when one considers the vast array of groups in modern society and people's different experiences in them, it becomes easier to understand how different conceptualizations of systems theory have developed. It is important to recognize that each conceptualization represents a unique attempt to understand the processes that occur in all social systems.

Concepts derived from these differing views of systems theory that are particularly relevant for group workers include the following:

- The existence of properties of the group as a whole that arise from the interactions of individual group members
- The powerful effects of group forces on members' behavior
- The struggle of groups to maintain themselves as entities when confronted with conflicts
- The awareness that groups must relate to an external environment as well as attend to their internal functioning
- The idea that groups are in a constant state of becoming, developing, and changing, which influences their equilibrium and continued existence
- The notion that groups have a developmental life cycle

Workers can use these concepts to facilitate the development of group processes that help treatment and task groups achieve their goals and help members satisfy their socioemotional needs.

Psychodynamic Theory

Psychodynamic theory has had an important influence on group work practice. In his work *Group Psychology and the Analysis of the Ego,* Freud (1922) set forth his theoretical formulations about groups and their influence on human behavior. Many of Freud's other works have also influenced group work practice. For example, commonly used terms such as *insight, ego strength,* and *defense mechanisms* originated in Freud's work. Although psychodynamic theory focuses primarily on the individual, and Freud did not practice group psychotherapy, many of his followers, including Bion (1991), Redl (1942, 1944), Rutan (1992, 1993), and Yalom (1995), have adapted psychodynamic theory for working with groups. Psychodynamic theory has also influenced the founders of other practice theories used in groups, such as Eric Berne's transactional analysis, Fritz Perl's gestalt therapy, and Frank Moreno's psychodrama.

According to psychodynamic theory, group members act out in the group unresolved conflicts from early life experiences. In many ways, the group becomes a re-enactment of the family situation. Freud (1922), for example, describes the group leader as the all-powerful father figure who reigns supreme over group members. Group members identify with the group leader as the "ego ideal" (Wyss, 1973). Members form transference reactions to the group leader and to each other on the basis of their early life experiences. Thus, the interactions that occur in the group reflect personality structures and defense mechanisms that members began to develop early in life.

The group leader uses transference and countertransference reactions to help members work through unresolved conflicts by exploring past behavior patterns and linking these patterns to current behaviors. The group leader might, for example, interpret the behavior of two group members who are struggling for the leader's attention as unresolved sibling rivalry. When interpretations made by the group worker are timed appropriately, members gain insight into their own behavior. According to psychodynamic theory, insight is the essential ingredient in modifying and changing behavior patterns inside and outside the group.

More recent conceptions of psychodynamic group treatment (Yalom, 1995) have adapted and modified classical psychodynamic theory to include a greater emphasis on the here-and-now experiences of group interaction. Because of this emphasis this application is often referred to in the literature as *interpersonal group therapy* (Leszcz, 1992). Emphasizing the here-and-now experiences of group members is useful in ensuring that members deal with issues of immediate concern to them. From an analysis of here-and-now behavior patterns in the microcosm of the group, the leader can help members reconstruct unresolved childhood conflicts and have "corrective emotional experiences" (Leszcz, 1992, p. 48). Through direct, mutual interpersonal communications, members build interpersonal skills, adaptive capacities, and ego strength, as well as gain insight into their behavior. The cohesiveness of the group encourages members to reveal intimate details about their personal lives and to describe and act out their conflicts in a safe, supportive environment.

Psychodynamic theory has also been influential in furthering our understanding of how individuals behave in groups. Wilford Bion, who was psychodynamically trained, developed the Tavastock approach to help people understand the primitive emotional processes that occur in groups. He suggested that group members often avoid the work of the group by reacting to the leader's authority with flight-fight responses and dependency (Bion, 1991).

A thorough discussion of psychodynamic theory of group functioning is beyond the scope of this book. For further explanation of modern adaptations of psychodynamic theory to group work practice, see Konig (1994), Janssen (1994), Rice (1987), Rutan (1992, 1993), and Yalom (1995).

Learning Theory

Perhaps no theory has stirred more controversy within social group work than learning theory. As with psychodynamic theory, the primary focus of learning theory is on the behavior of individuals rather than on the behavior of groups. Thus, learning theory has generally ignored the importance of group dynamics. Also, like the early emphasis on primitive drives in psychodynamic theory, the early emphasis on environmental contingencies and the de-emphasis of free will has led some group workers to conclude that learning theory is deterministic. For these reasons, some view learning theory as antithetical to the values and traditions of growth, autonomy, and self-determination that are so much a part of the heritage of group work practice.

Despite the controversy, learning theory has had an important influence on current methods of group work practice. The emphasis on clear and specific goal setting, contracting, the influence of the environment on the group and its members, step-by-step treatment planning, measurable treatment outcomes, and evaluation can be traced, at least in part, to the influence of learning theory. The growing importance of short-term, structured psychoeducational groups attests to the important influence that learning theory principles have had on group work practice (Budman, Simeone, Reilly, & Demby, 1994; Grayson, 1993; MacKenzie, 1990; Piper, 1992; Piper & Joyce, 1996; Rose, 1998; Wells, 1994).

According to social learning theory (Bandura, 1977), the behavior of group members can be explained by one of three methods of learning. In the classical approach to learning theory, behavior becomes associated with a stimulus. For example, a worker responds by making a negative verbal comment each time a member turns and speaks to another member while the worker or other group members are speaking. After several times, the mere stimulus of the member's turning, without speaking, will be enough to cue the worker to respond with a negative verbal comment.

A second and more common method of learning is called operant conditioning. In this paradigm, the behaviors of the group members and the worker are governed by the consequences of their actions. Thus, if member A acts in a certain way and member B reacts positively, member A is likely to continue the behavior. Similarly, if a group worker receives negative feedback from group members about a particular behavior, the worker will be less likely to behave that way in the future.

In the group, the worker might use praise to increase member-to-member communications and negative verbal comments to decrease member-to-leader communications. To help a member with a problem he or she has experienced in the outside environment, such as being overweight, the group leader might ask the member to develop a plan that specifies self-imposed rewards for behavior that decreases caloric intake and self-imposed sanctions for behavior that increases caloric intake.

Several writers (Feldman, Caplinger, & Wodarski, 1983; Feldman & Wodarski, 1975; Rose, 1989, 1998; Rose & Edleson, 1987) use operant learning theory principles in their approach to group work. For example, Rose (1989) suggests that tokens, praise, or other reinforcers can be used to increase desired behavior and decrease undesired behavior in the group or in the external environment. Groups that focus on themes such as social skills training, assertiveness, relaxation, and parenting skills also frequently rely heavily on learning theory principles.

Bandura (1977) has developed a third learning paradigm called social learning theory. If group members or the group worker were to wait for classical or operant conditioning to occur, behavior in groups would be learned very slowly. Bandura proposed that most learning takes place through observation and vicarious reinforcement or punishment. For example, when a group member is praised for a certain behavior, that group member and other group members reproduce the behavior later, hoping to receive similar praise. When a group member who performs a certain behavior is ignored or punished by social sanctions, other group members learn not to behave in that manner because such behavior results in a negative outcome.

In response to concerns that learning theory has not taken into consideration motivations, expectations, and other cognitive aspects of behavior, Ellis (1992) and others have described cognitive-behavioral approaches to treatment (Beck, 1995; Leahy, 1996; Sheldon, 1995). Although learning theorists have not attempted to explain the functioning of groups as a whole, learning theory principles have been shown to be useful in helping members make desired changes. All group workers should be familiar with the basic principles of learning theory and cognitive behavior modification. Because of their particular relevance to treatment groups, some principles of classical, operant, social learning theory, and cognitive-behavioral approaches are used in the discussion of specialized methods for leading treatment groups in Chapter 10.

Field Theory

Kurt Lewin, more than any other social scientist, has come to be associated with the study of group dynamics. He conducted numerous experiments on the forces that account for behavior in small groups. For example, in an early study investigating leadership, Lewin, Lippitt, and White (1939) created three types of groups with authoritarian, democratic, and laissez-faire leadership. The results of this study are reported in Chapter 4. Lewin and his colleagues were the first to apply the scientific method in developing a theory of groups. In 1944, he and his colleagues set up laboratories and formed the Research Center for Group Dynamics at the Massachusetts Institute of Technology.

According to Lewin's field theory, "a group has a life space, it occupies a position relative to other objects in this space, it is oriented toward goals, it locomotes in pursuit of these goals, and it may encounter barriers in the process of locomotion" (Shepard, 1964, p. 25). The unique contribution of field theory is that it views the group as a gestalt, that is, an evolving entity of opposing forces that act to hold members in the group and to move the group along in its quest for goal achievement. According to Lewin (1947), groups are constantly changing to cope with their social situation, although there are times in which a "quasi-stationary equilibrium" exists for all groups. In all cases, however, the behavior of individual group members and the group itself must be seen as a function of the total situation (Lewin, 1946).

In developing field theory, Lewin introduced several concepts to aid in understanding the forces at work in a group. Among these are (1) roles, which refer to the status, rights, and duties of group members; (2) norms, which are rules governing the behavior of group members; (3) power, which is the ability of members to influence one another; (4) cohesion, which is the amount of attraction the members of the group feel for one another and for the group; (5) consensus, which is the degree of agreement regarding goals and other group phenomena; and (6) valence, which is the potency of goals and objects in the life space of the group.

Lewin sought to understand the forces occurring in the group as a whole from the perspective of individual group members. He did this mathematically and topographically, using vectors to describe group forces. Emphasizing the importance of properties of the group that act on the individual member, most field theorists have focused their research efforts on *cohesion,* which they define as the totality of forces acting on individual members to keep them in the group. Studies by field theorists have shown that cohesion is related to agreement on goals and norms, shared understanding, and similar demographic backgrounds of members, as well as to productivity, satisfaction, and cooperative interaction patterns (Cartwright, 1951; Cartwright & Zander, 1968; Lippitt, 1957).

Along with his interest in formulating a theoretical model of group dynamics, Lewin was interested in the effect of groups on individuals' psychological makeup. Before his death in 1947, Lewin developed the t-group as a way to observe the effects of group processes on group members and as a means to help individual group members change their own behavior. Although he was not directly involved, he helped found the first National Training Laboratory in Group Development in 1947. Since then, t-groups have been used extensively at the National Training Laboratories as an experiential means to train group facilitators, to teach individuals about the effects of group dynamics, and to help individuals examine and change their own behavior.

Relying on a principle in Lewin's field theory that suggests individuals will not change their own behavior unless they see their behavior and their attitudes as others see them, the t-group experience attempts to provide participants with extensive feedback about their own behavior. Members are confronted with the effects of their behavior on other group members and on the group's facilitator. Role plays, simulations, and other experiential program activities are often used to illustrate how group processes develop and how they affect members.

Social Exchange Theory

Although field theory emphasizes the group as a whole, social exchange theory focuses on the behavior of individual group members. Blau (1964), Homans (1961), and Thibaut and Kelley (1959) are the principal developers of this approach to groups. Deriving their theory from animal psychology, economic analysis, and game theory, social exchange theorists suggest that when people interact in groups, each attempts to behave in a way that will maximize rewards and minimize punishments. Group members initiate interactions because the social exchanges provide them with something of value, such as approval. According to social exchange theorists, because ordinarily nothing is gained unless something is given in return, there is an exchange implied in all human relationships.

In social exchange theory, group behavior is analyzed by observing how individual members seek rewards while dealing with the sustained social interaction occurring in a group. For an individual in a group, the decision to express a given behavior is based on a comparison of the rewards and punishments that are expected to be derived from the behavior. Group members act to increase positive consequences and decrease negative consequences. Social exchange theory also focuses on the way members influence one another during social interactions. The result of any social exchange is based on the amount of social power and the amount of social dependence in a particular interaction.

Guided Group Interaction (Empey & Erikson, 1972; McCorkle, Elias, & Bixby, 1958) and Positive Peer Culture (Vorrath & Brendtro, 1985) are two specialized group work methods that rely heavily on principles from social exchange theory. They are frequently used with delinquent adolescents in residential and institutional settings. In both approaches, structured groups are used to confront, challenge, and eliminate antisocial peer group norms and to replace them with prosocial norms through guided peer-group interaction.

Social exchange theory has been criticized as being mechanistic because it assumes people are always rational beings who act according to their analysis of rewards and punishments (Shepard, 1964). For the most part, these criticisms are unfounded. Social exchange theorists are aware that cognitive processes affect how people behave in groups (Keller & Dansereau, 1995; Knottnerus, 1994). Group members' perceptions of rewards and punishments are influenced by cognitive processes such as intentions and expectations. Thus, the work of social exchange theorists in psychology and of symbolic interaction theorists in sociology has helped to account for the role of cognitive processes in the behavior of individuals in groups and other social interactions. The influence of symbolic interaction theory and social exchange theory on social work practice with groups can be seen in the work of Balgopal and Vassil (1983) and Early (1992).

SUMMARY

This chapter describes historical developments in the practice of group work and in the social sciences. A historical perspective is presented to help workers develop a broad understanding of the uses of groups in practice settings and develop a knowledge base they can use to practice effectively with different types of groups.

The historical overview of group work practice presented in this chapter suggests that throughout the twentieth century, groups have been used for a variety of purposes, such as education, recreation, socialization, support, and therapy. The early emphasis on the use of groups for education, recreation, and socialization has waned in recent years in favor of an increased interest in the use of groups for support, mutual aid, and therapy. This trend parallels the gradual transition during the 1930s and 1940s away from group work's amorphous roots in adult education, recreation, and social work to its formal incorporation into the social work profession during the 1950s.

Currently, social group work is being revitalized in schools of social work and in practice settings. As current trends indicate, in recent years there has also been an increased recognition of the roots of social group work and the multiple purposes group work can serve.

This chapter also briefly explores historical developments in social science research that have relevance for understanding group processes. Findings from these studies emphasize the powerful influence that the group as a whole has on individual group members. The chapter closes with a review of five theories: (1) systems theory, (2) psychodynamic theory, (3) learning theory, (4) field theory, and (5) social exchange theory, all of which have had an important influence on group work practice.

LEARNING ASSIGNMENTS

1. Read about the lives of two famous group workers in the early history of group work practice. Possible sources are NASW's *Encyclopedia of Social Work*, K. Reid's *From Character Building to Social Treatment: The History of the Use of Groups in Social Work Practice*, and A. Alissi's *Perspectives on Social Group Work Practice*. Compare and contrast how they practiced with groups. How did their practice differ from your understanding of modern practice?

2. Interview a group worker and ask the individual to describe the theoretical foundation(s) of his or her work style. Does the worker draw on theories of group work practice in an eclectic manner or rely primarily on one theory of practice? Ask the individual to comment on the extent to which theory guides his or her day-to-day practice. Which seems to be more important to the individual: theory or practice wisdom generated from previous experience?

3. Observe a treatment group, or, if this is not possible, interview a treatment group leader. Using the characteristics described in Table 2.1, determine the extent to which the group leader is practicing within the traditions of the social goals, remedial, and reciprocal models of group work practice. To what extent does the worker blend traditions? What particular tradition is most appealing to you? Why?

chapter *3*

Understanding Group Dynamics

A thorough understanding of group dynamics is useful for practicing effectively with any type of group. Although many theories describe group functioning, fundamental to all these theories is an understanding of groups as social systems (Anderson, 1979). A system is made up of elements and their interactions. As social systems, therefore, task and treatment groups can be conceptualized as individuals in interaction with each other.

The forces that result from the interactions of group members are often referred to as *group dynamics*. Because group dynamics influence the behavior of both individual group members and the group as a whole, they have been of considerable interest to group workers for many years (Coyle, 1930, 1937; Elliott, 1928).

THE DEVELOPMENT OF HELPFUL GROUP DYNAMICS

One of the worker's most important tasks is to help groups develop dynamics that promote the satisfaction of members' socioemotional needs while facilitating the accomplishment of group tasks. Some years ago, Northen (1969) reminded group workers that this is not an automatic process.

Inattention to group dynamics can have a negative effect on the meeting of members' socioemotional needs and on goal attainment. Groups can unleash both harmful and helpful forces. The Hitler youth movement of the 1920s and 1930s, the Ku Klux Klan, the religious groups in Jonestown and at the Branch Davidians' ranch in Waco, Texas, and other harmful cults are familiar examples of group dynamics gone awry. In an in-depth examination of a variety of encounter groups, Lieberman, Yalom, and Miles (1973) found that many groups produced casualties, some of which were severe mental disorders among group participants. Similar findings reported by Galinsky and Schopler (1977) suggest the forces exerted in groups can have a powerful influence on group members and on the functioning of the entire group. In contrast, appropriate development of group dynamics can lead to positive outcomes for the group and its members (Bednar & Kaul, 1994).

This chapter seeks to help group workers recognize and understand the dynamics generated through the group process. People who are familiar with group dynamics are less likely to be victimized by harmful leaders and groups. The chapter is also designed to help workers establish and promote group dynamics that satisfy members' socioemotional needs and that help groups achieve goals consistent with the humanistic value base of the social work profession.

GROUP DYNAMICS

In this text, four dimensions of group dynamics are of particular importance to group workers in understanding and working effectively with all types of task and treatment groups:

1. Communication and interaction patterns
2. Cohesion
3. Social control mechanisms, that is, norms, roles, and status
4. Group culture

In-depth knowledge of group dynamics is essential for understanding the social structure of groups and for developing beginning-level skills in group work practice.

Communication and Interaction Patterns

According to Northen (1969), "Social interaction is a term for the dynamic interplay of forces in which contact between persons results in a modification of the behavior and attitudes of the participants" (p. 17). Verbal and nonverbal communications are the components of social interaction. Communication is the process by which people convey meanings to each other by using symbols. Communication entails (1) the encoding of a person's perceptions, thoughts, and feelings into language and other symbols, (2) the transmission of these symbols or language, and (3) the decoding of the transmission by another person. This process is shown in Figure 3.1. As members of a group communicate to one another, a reciprocal pattern of interaction emerges. The interaction patterns that

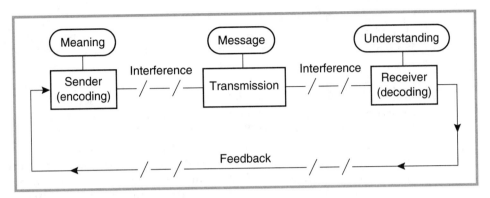

FIGURE 3.1 ■ *A Model of the Process of Communication*

develop can be beneficial or harmful to the group. A group worker who is knowledgeable about helpful communications and interactions can intervene in the
patterns that are established to help the group achieve desired goals and to ensure the socioemotional satisfaction of members.

Communication as a Process

The first step in understanding and intervening in interaction patterns is for the
worker to be aware that, whenever people are together in a group, they are communicating. As shown in Figure 3.1, all communications are intended to convey
a message. Silence, for example, can communicate sorrow, thoughtfulness, anger,
or lack of interest. In addition, every group member communicates not only to
transmit information but also for many other reasons. Kiesler (1978) has suggested that people communicate with such interpersonal concerns as (1) understanding other people, (2) finding out where they stand in relation to other
people, (3) persuading others, (4) gaining or maintaining power, (5) defending
themselves, (6) provoking a reaction from others, (7) making an impression on
others, (8) gaining or maintaining relationships, and (9) presenting a unified image to the group. Many other important reasons for communication could be
added to this list.

Workers who are aware that group members communicate for many reasons
can observe, assess, and understand communication and interaction patterns. Because patterns of communication are often consistent across different situations,
group workers can use this information to work with individual members and
the group as a whole. For example, a worker observes that one member is consistently unassertive in the group. The worker might help the member practice
responding assertively to situations in the group. Because the pattern of a lack
of assertiveness is likely to occur in situations outside the group, the worker suggests that the member consider practicing the skills in situations encountered
between meetings.

In addition to meanings transmitted in every communication, the worker should also be aware that messages are often received selectively. *Selective perception* refers to the screening of messages so they are congruent with one's belief system. As shown in Figure 3.1, messages are decoded and their meanings are received. Individual group members have a unique understanding of communications on the basis of their selective perception. Selected screening sometimes results in blocking of messages so that they are not decoded and received. Napier and Gershenfeld (1993) suggest that the perception of a communication can be influenced by (1) life positions that result from experiences in early childhood, (2) stereotypes, (3) the status and position of the communicator, (4) previous experiences, and (5) assumptions and values. Thus, what might appear to a naive observer as a simple, straightforward, and objective social interaction might have considerable hidden meaning for both the sender and the receiver.

It is not possible, or even desirable, for workers to analyze each interpersonal communication that occurs in a group. However, with a little practice, workers can develop a "third ear," that is, become aware of the meanings behind messages and their effect on a particular group member and on the group as a whole. Group workers are in a much better position to intervene in the group when they have a full understanding of the meanings of the messages being communicated and received by each member.

Communications can also be distorted in transmission. In Figure 3.1, distortion is represented as interference. Among the most common transmission problems are language barriers. In the United States, workers frequently conduct groups with members from different cultural backgrounds and for whom English is a second language. In addition to problems of understanding accents and dialects, the meanings of many words are culturally defined and may not be interpreted as the communicator intended. Special care must be taken in these situations to avoid distorting the meanings intended by the communicator (Kadushin & Kadushin, 1997).

Noise and other distortions inside or outside the meeting room can interfere with effective communication. Similarly, hearing or eyesight problems can create difficulties in receiving messages. For example, almost one third of older people suffer from hearing impairments (Jette, 1996), and 25 percent suffer from visual impairments (Lighthouse, 1995). Thus, when working with groups, the practitioner should be alert to physical problems that may impair communication. Some strategies for working with visually impaired and hearing-impaired members of groups are presented in Tables 3.1 and 3.2.

To prevent distortions in communications from causing misunderstandings and conflict, it is important that members receive feedback about their communications. Feedback is a way of checking that the meanings of the communicated messages are understood correctly. For feedback to be used appropriately it should (1) describe the content of the communication or the behavior as it is perceived by the group member, (2) be given to the member who sent the message as soon as the message is received, and (3) be expressed in a tentative manner so that

TABLE 3.1 ■ *Techniques for Communicating with Hearing-Impaired Group Members*

1. Position yourself so you are in full view of the person and your face is illuminated.
2. Speak in a normal voice.
3. Speak slowly and clearly. Stress key words. Pause between sentences.
4. Make sure no one else is talking when a group member is speaking to a hearing-impaired person or when a hearing-impaired person is speaking to a group member.
5. Make sure the room is free of background noises and has good acoustics.
6. Look for cues, such as facial expressions or inappropriate responses, that indicate the individual has misunderstood.
7. If you suspect that the individual has misunderstood, restate what has been said.
8. Speak *to* the individual, not *about* the person.

Adapted from Blazer, 1978.

TABLE 3.2 ■ *Techniques for Communicating with Visually Impaired Group Members*

1. Ask the individual whether assistance is needed to get to the meeting room. If the reply is yes, offer your elbow. Walk a half step ahead so your body indicates a change in direction, when to stop, and so forth.
2. Introduce yourself and all group members when the meeting begins. Go around the group clockwise or counterclockwise. This will help the group member learn where each member is located.
3. When you accompany a visually impaired person into a new meeting room, describe the layout of the room, the furniture placement, and any obstacles. This will help orient the individual.
4. Try not to disturb the placement of objects in the meeting room. If this is unavoidable, be sure to inform the person about the changes. Similarly, let the individual know if someone leaves or enters the room.
5. When guiding visually impaired individuals to their seat, place their hand on the back of the chair and allow them to seat themselves.
6. Speak directly to the visually impaired person, not through an intermediary.
7. Look at the individual when you speak.
8. Don't be afraid to use words such as *look* and *see*.
9. Speak in a normal voice. Do not shout.
10. Visually impaired people value independence just as sighted people do. Do not be overprotective.
11. Give explicit instructions about the location of coffee or snacks, and during program activities. For example, state, "The coffee pot is 10 feet to the left of your chair," rather than "The coffee pot is right over there on your left."

Adapted from a handout prepared by The Lighthouse, 111 E. 59th St., New York, NY 10222.

those who send messages understand that the feedback is designed to check for distortions rather than to confront or attack them.

Examples of feedback are "John, I understood you to say . . . " or "Mary, if I understand you correctly, you are saying. . . ." Feedback and clarification can help to prevent communications from being interpreted in unintended ways. For an in-depth discussion about the effects of feedback on task group behavior, see Nadler (1979); for the effect of feedback on members of treatment groups see Rhode and Stockton (1992).

Interaction Patterns

In addition to becoming aware of communication processes, the worker must also consider patterns of interaction that develop in a group. A variety of interaction patterns have been identified in social work literature (Middleman, 1978), such as (1) maypole, in which the leader is the central figure and communication occurs from leader to member or from member to leader; (2) round robin, in which members take turns talking; (3) hot seat, in which there is an extended back and forth exchange between the leader and a member as the other members watch; and (4) free floating, in which all members take responsibility for communicating according to what is being said and not said in the group. The first three patterns are leader centered because the leader structures them. The fourth pattern is group centered because it emerges from the initiative of group members.

In most situations, workers should strive to facilitate the development of group-centered rather than leader-centered interaction patterns. In group-centered patterns, members freely interact with each other. Communication channels between members of the group are open. In leader-centered patterns, communications are directed from members to the worker or from the worker to group members, thereby reducing members' opportunities to communicate freely with each other.

Group-centered communication patterns tend to increase social interaction, group morale, members' commitment to group goals, and innovative decision making (Carletta, Garrod, & Fraser-Krauss, 1998). However, such patterns can be less efficient than leader-centered patterns because communication may be superfluous or extraneous to group tasks (Shaw, 1964). Sorting out useful communications can take a tremendous amount of group time. Therefore, in task groups that are making routine decisions, when time constraints are important and when there is little need for creative problem solving, the worker may deliberately choose to encourage leader-centered rather than group-centered interaction patterns.

To establish and maintain appropriate interaction patterns, the worker should be familiar with the factors that influence them. Patterns of interaction are affected by (1) the cues and the reinforcements that members receive for specific interactional exchanges, (2) the emotional bonds that develop between group members, (3) the subgroups that develop in the group, (4) the size and physical arrangement of the group, and (5) the power and status relationships in the group. Workers can change interaction patterns by modifying these important factors.

CUES AND REINFORCERS.   After discussing changes in interaction patterns that may enhance the group's functioning, workers and members can decide to use verbal and nonverbal behaviors to facilitate modifications in established patterns. Cues such as words or gestures can act as signals to group members to talk more or less frequently to one another or to the worker. Workers and members can also use selective attention and other reinforcers to encourage beneficial interactions. As more appropriate interaction patterns are established, cues and reinforcers can be used intermittently and then be allowed to fade gradually to maintain newly developed patterns (Toseland, Krebs, & Vahsen, 1978).

EMOTIONAL BONDS.   Positive emotional bonds such as interpersonal liking and attraction increase interpersonal interaction, and negative emotional bonds reduce solidarity between members and result in decreased interpersonal interaction. Attraction and interpersonal liking between two members may occur because they share common interests, similar values and ideologies, complementary personality characteristics, or similar demographic characteristics (Hare, Blumberg, Davies, & Kent, 1995).

Hartford (1971) calls alignments based on emotional bonds *interest alliances*. For example, two members of a planning council might vote the same way on certain issues and they may communicate similar thoughts and feelings to other members of the council on the basis of their common interests in the needs of the business community. Similarly, members of a minority group might form an interest alliance based on similar concerns about the lack of community services for minority groups.

SUBGROUPS.   Subgroups also affect the interaction patterns in a group. Subgroups form from the emotional bonds and interest alliances among subsets of group members. They occur naturally in all groups. They help make the group attractive to its members because individuals look forward to interacting with those to whom they are particularly close. The practitioner should not view subgroups as a threat to the integrity of the group unless the attraction of members within a subgroup becomes greater than their attraction to the group as a whole.

There are a variety of subgroup types, including the dyad, triad, and clique. Also, there are isolates, who do not interact with the group, and scapegoats, who receive negative attention and criticism from the group.

In some situations the worker may actively encourage members to form subgroups, particularly in groups that are too large and cumbersome for detailed work to be accomplished. For example, subgroup formation is often useful in large task groups such as committees, delegate councils, and some teams. Members are assigned to a particular subgroup to work on a specific task or subtask. The results of the subgroup's work are then brought back to the larger group for consideration and action.

Regardless of whether the worker actively encourages members to form subgroups, they occur naturally because not everyone in a group interacts with equal valence. The formation of intense subgroup attraction, however, can be a problem. Subgroup members may challenge the worker's authority. They may substitute their own goals and methods of attaining them for the goals of the larger group. They can disrupt the group by communicating among themselves while others are speaking. Subgroup members may fail to listen to members who are not a part of the subgroup. Ultimately, intense and consistent subgroup formation can negatively affect the performance of the group as a whole (Gebhardt & Meyers, 1995).

When intense subgroup attraction appears to be interfering with the group as a whole, it can be helpful to

- Examine whether the group as a whole is sufficiently attractive to members
- Promote the development of norms that emphasize the importance of members' listening to and respecting each other
- Promote the development of norms restricting communication to one member at a time
- Change seating arrangements
- Ask for certain members to interact more frequently with other members
- Use program materials and exercises that separate subgroup members
- Assign tasks for members to do outside of the group in subgroups composed of different members

If intense subgroup loyalties persist, it can be helpful to facilitate a discussion of the reasons for them and their effect on the group as a whole. A frank discussion of the reasons for subgroup formation can often benefit the entire group because it can reveal problems in the group's communication patterns and in its goal-setting and decision-making processes. After the discussion, the worker should try to increase the attraction of the group for its members and help them reach out to one another to reopen channels of communication.

In some cases, the worker may wish to use subgroups for therapeutic purposes. For example, Yalom (1995) suggests that the worker can use relationships between members to recapitulate the family group experience. Transference and countertransference reactions among members may be interpreted to help members gain insight into the impact of their early development on their current way of relating to others in the group and their broader social environment.

SIZE AND PHYSICAL ARRANGEMENTS.   Other factors that influence interaction patterns are the size and physical arrangement of the group. As the size of the group increases, the possibilities for potential relationships increase dramatically. For example, with three people there are six potential combinations of relationships, but in a group with seven people there are 966 possible relationships (Kephart, 1951). Thus, as groups grow larger, each member has more social relationships to be aware of and to maintain, but less opportunity to maintain them.

With increased group size there are also fewer opportunities and less time for members to communicate. In some groups, the lack of opportunity to participate might not be much of a problem. It should not be assumed that members who are not actively participating are uninvolved in the group, although this may be true. Some group members welcome a chance for active involvement but speak only when they have an important contribution that might otherwise be overlooked. Often, however, a reduced chance to participate leads to dissatisfaction and a lack of commitment to decisions made by the group. Increased group size also tends to lead to subgroup formation as members strive to get to know those seated near them.

The physical arrangement of group members also influences interaction patterns. For example, members who sit in circles have an easier time communicating with each other than do members who sit in rows. Even members' positions within a circular pattern influence interaction patterns. Members who sit across from each other, for example, have an easier time communicating than do members on the same side of a circle who are separated by one or two members.

Because circular seating arrangements promote face-to-face interaction, they are often preferred to other arrangements. There may be times, however, when the group leader prefers a different arrangement. For example, the leader of a task group may wish to sit at the head of a rectangular table to convey his or her status or power. The leader may also wish to seat a particularly important member in close proximity. In an educational group, a leader may choose to stand before a group seated in rows, an arrangement that facilitates members' communications with the leader and tends to minimize interactions among members of the group.

Physical arrangements can also be used to help assess relationships among members and potential problems in group interaction. For example, members who are fond of each other often sit next to each other and as far away as possible from members they do not like. Similarly, members who pull chairs out from a circle, or sit behind other members, may be expressing their lack of investment in the group.

An interesting physical arrangement that often occurs in groups results from members' tendency to sit in the same seat from meeting to meeting. This physical arrangement persists because members feel secure in "their own" seat near familiar members. When seating arrangements are modified by the leader, or by circumstance, communication patterns are often affected.

POWER AND STATUS.   Two other factors affecting communication and interaction patterns are the relative power and status of the group members. Initially, members are accorded power and status on the basis of their position and prestige in the community, their physical attributes, and their position in the agency sponsoring the group. As a group develops, members' status and power change, depending on how important a member is in helping the group accomplish its tasks or in helping other members meet their socioemotional needs. When members carry out roles that are important to the group, their power and status increase. When a member enjoys high status and power, other members are likely to direct their communications to that member (Napier & Gershenfeld, 1993).

Principles for Practice

With basic information about the nature of communication and interaction patterns in groups, workers can intervene in any group to modify or change the patterns that develop. Workers may find the following principles about communication and interaction patterns helpful:

1. Members of the group are always communicating. Workers should assess communication processes continually and help members communicate effectively throughout the life of a group.

2. Communication patterns can be changed. Strategies for doing this start with identifying patterns during the group or at the end of group meetings during a brief time set aside to discuss group process. Workers then can reinforce desired interaction patterns; increase or decrease emotional bonds between members; change subgroups, group size, or group structure; or alter the power or status relationships in a group.

3. Members communicate for a purpose. Workers should help members understand each other's intentions by clarifying them through group discussion.

4. There is meaning in all communication. Workers should help members understand and appreciate the meaning of different communications.

5. Messages are often perceived selectively. Workers should help members listen to what others are communicating.

6. Messages may be distorted in transmission. Workers should help members clarify verbal and nonverbal communications that are unclear or ambiguous.

7. Feedback and clarification enhances accurate understanding of communications. The worker should educate members about how to give and receive effective feedback and model these methods in the group.

8. Open, group-centered communications are often, but not always, the preferred pattern of interaction. The worker should encourage communication patterns that are appropriate to the purpose of the group.

Workers who follow these principles can intervene to help groups develop patterns of communication and interaction that meet members' socioemotional needs while accomplishing group purposes.

Group Cohesion

Group cohesion is the result of all forces acting on members to remain in a group (Festinger, 1950). People are attracted to groups for a variety of reasons. According to Cartwright (1968), four interacting sets of variables determine a member's attraction to a group:

- The need for affiliation, recognition, and security
- The resources and prestige available through group participation
- Expectations of the beneficial and detrimental consequences of the group
- The comparison of the group with other group experiences

Cohesive groups satisfy members' need for affiliation. Some members have a need to socialize because their relationships outside the group are unsatisfactory or nonexistent. For example, Toseland, Decker, and Bliesner (1979) have shown that group work can be effective in meeting the needs of socially isolated older persons. Cohesive groups recognize members' accomplishments, and promote members' sense of competence. Members are attracted to the group when they feel that their participation is valued and when they feel they are well-liked. Groups are also more cohesive when they provide members with a sense of security. Schachter (1959), for example, has shown that fear and anxiety increase people's needs for affiliation.

The cohesion of a group can also be accounted for by incentives that are sometimes provided for group membership. Many people join groups because of the people they expect to meet and get to know. Opportunities for making new contacts and associating with high-status members are also incentives. In some groups, the tasks to be performed are enjoyable. Other groups might enable a member to accomplish tasks that require the help of others. Prestige may also be an incentive. For example, being nominated to a delegate council or other task group may enhance a member's prestige and status in an organization or the community. Another inducement to group membership may be access to services or resources not otherwise available.

Expectations of gratification and favorable comparisons with previous group experiences are two other factors that help make groups cohesive. For example, members with high expectations for a group experience and little hope of attaining similar satisfactions elsewhere will be attracted to a group. Thibaut and Kelley (1959) have found that members' continued attraction to a group depends on the "comparison level for alternatives"—that is, the satisfaction derived from the current group experience compared with that derived from other possible experiences.

Members' reasons for being attracted to a group affect how they perform in the group. For example, Back (1951) found that members who were attracted to a group primarily because they perceived other members as similar or as potential friends related on a personal level in the group and more frequently engaged in conversations not focused on the group's task. Members attracted by the group's task wanted to complete it quickly and efficiently and maintained task-relevant conversations. Members attracted by the prestige of group membership were cautious not to risk their status in the group. They initiated few controversial topics and focused on their own actions rather than on those of other group members.

Cohesion can affect the functioning of individual members and the group as a whole in many ways. Research and clinical observations have documented that cohesion tends to increase

- Expression of positive and negative feelings (Pepitone & Reichling, 1955; Yalom, 1995)
- Willingness to listen (Yalom, 1995)
- Effective use of other members' feedback and evaluations (Yalom, 1995)
- Members' influence over each other (Cartwright, 1968)
- Feelings of self-confidence and self-esteem, and personal adjustment (Seashore, 1954; Yalom, 1995)
- Satisfaction with the group experience (Widmeyer & Williams, 1991)
- Perseverance toward goals (Cartwright, 1968; Spink & Carron, 1994)
- Willingness to take responsibility for group functioning (Dion, Miller, & Magnan, 1970)
- Goal attainment, individual and group performance, and organizational commitment (Evans & Dion, 1991; Gully, Devine, & Whitney, 1995; Mullen & Cooper, 1994; Wech, Mossholder, Steel, & Bennett, 1998)
- Attendance, membership maintenance, and length of participation (Prapavessis & Carron, 1997)

Although cohesion can have many beneficial effects, workers should be aware that cohesion operates in complex interaction with other group properties. For example, although cohesive groups tend to perform better than less cohesive groups, the quality of decisions made by cohesive groups is moderated by the nature of the task (Gully et al., 1995) and by the size of the group (Mullen & Cooper, 1994). Cohesion has more influence on outcomes, for example, when task interdependence is high rather than when it is low (Gully et al.). Cohesion also varies over the course of a group's development. For example, Budman, Soldz, Demby, Davis, and Merry (1993) have shown that what is viewed as cohesive behavior early in the life of a group may not be viewed that way later in the group's development.

It also should be pointed out that cohesion can have some negative effects on the functioning of a group. Cohesion is a necessary, albeit not sufficient, ingredient in the development of "group think." According to Janis (1972) *group think* is "a mode of thinking that people engage in when they are deeply involved in a cohesive ingroup, when the members' strivings for unanimity override their motivation to realistically appraise alternative courses of action" (p. 9). In analyzing how group think develops, Janis (1972, 1982) emphasized cohesion more than authoritarian leadership, methodical search and appraisal procedures, or other qualities of a group.

In addition to encouraging pathological conformity, cohesion can lead to dependence on the group. This can be a particularly vexing problem in intensive therapy groups with members who started the group experience with severe problems and poor self-images. Thus, while promoting the development of cohesion in groups, the worker should ensure that members' individuality is not sacrificed. Members should be encouraged to express divergent opinions and to respect divergent opinions expressed by other group members. It is also important to adequately prepare members for group termination and independent functioning. Methods for this preparation are discussed in Chapter 14.

Principles for Practice

Because cohesion has many benefits, workers should strive to make groups attractive to members. Workers may find the following principles helpful when trying to enhance a group's cohesiveness:

1. A high level of open interaction promotes cohesiveness. The worker should use group discussions and program activities to encourage interaction among members.

2. When members' needs are met, they want to continue participating. Therefore, the worker should help members identify their needs and how they can be met in the group.

3. Achieving group goals makes the group more attractive to its members. The worker should help members focus on and achieve goals.

4. Noncompetitive intragroup relationships that affirm members' perceptions and points of view increase group cohesion. The worker should help group members to cooperate rather than compete with each other.

5. Competitive intergroup relationships help to define a group's identity and purpose, thereby heightening members' cohesion. The worker can use naturally occurring intergroup competition to build intragroup bonds.

6. A group that is too large can decrease members' attraction to the group by obstructing their full participation. The worker should compose a group that gives all members the opportunity to be fully involved.

7. When members' expectations are understood and addressed, members feel as if they are part of the group. The worker should help members clarify their expectations, and should strive for congruence between members' expectations and the purposes of the group.

8. Groups that offer rewards, resources, status, or prestige that members would not obtain by themselves tend to be attractive. Therefore, workers should help groups to be rewarding experiences for members.

9. Pride in being a member of a group can increase cohesion. The worker should help the group develop pride in its identity and purpose.

If the costs of participation in a group exceed the benefits, members may stop attending (Thibaut & Kelley, 1954). Although workers cannot ensure that all factors are present in every group, they should strive to make sure that the group is as attractive as possible to each member who participates.

Social Control Dynamics

Social control is the term used to describe the processes by which the group as a whole gains sufficient compliance and conformity from its members to enable it to function in an orderly manner. Social control results from forces generated by several interrelated factors, including the norms that develop in the group and the roles and status of individual group members.

Without a certain amount of conformity and compliance, group interaction becomes chaotic and unpredictable, and the group is unable to function effectively. Social order and stability are prerequisites for the formation and maintenance of a cohesive group. Social controls can be used by workers and members to gain compliance from deviant group members. Yet social controls that are too stringent can reduce group attraction and lead to intragroup conflict and dissatisfaction.

The extent of social controls varies from group to group. In groups with strong social controls, members must give up a great deal of their freedom and individuality. In some groups this is necessary for effective functioning. For example, in a delegate council in which members are representing the views of their organization, there may be little room for individual preference and viewpoints. In other groups, however, members may have a great deal of freedom within a broad range of acceptable behavior. The following sections describe how norms, roles, status, and other social control mechanisms can satisfy members socioemotional needs while simultaneously promoting effective and efficient group functioning.

Norms

Norms are shared expectations and beliefs about appropriate ways to act in a social situation such as a group. They refer to specific member behaviors and to the overall pattern of behavior that is acceptable in a group. Norms stabilize and regulate behavior in groups. By providing guidelines for acceptable and appropriate behavior, norms increase predictability, stability, and security for members and help to encourage organized and coordinated action to reach goals.

Norms result from what is valued, preferred, and accepted behavior in the group. The preferences of certain high-status members might be given greater consideration in the development of group norms than the preferences of low-status members, but all members share to some extent in the development of group norms.

Norms develop as the group develops. Norms develop directly as members observe one another's behavior in the group and vicariously as members express their views and opinions during the course of group interaction. As members express preferences, share views, and behave in certain ways, norms become clarified. Soon it becomes clear that sanctions and social disapproval result from some behaviors and that praise and social approval result from other behaviors. Structure in early group meetings is associated with increased cohesion, reduced conflict, and higher member satisfaction (Stockton, Rohde, & Haughey, 1992). The emergence of norms as the group progresses, however, reduces the need for structure and control by the worker.

Because norms are developed through the interactions of group members, they discourage the capricious use of power by the leader or by any one group member. They also reduce the need for excessive controls to be imposed on the group from external forces.

Norms vary in important ways. Norms may be overt or covert. Overt norms are those that can be clearly articulated by the leader and the members. In contrast, covert norms exert important influences on the way members behave and interact without ever being talked about or discussed.

Norms vary according to the extent that people consider them binding. Some norms are strictly enforced whereas others are rarely enforced. Some norms are more elastic than others; that is, some permit a great deal of leeway in behavior, but others prescribe narrow and specific behaviors.

Norms also have various degrees of saliency for group members. For some members, a particular norm may exert great influence, but for others it may exert little influence.

Deviations from group norms are not necessarily harmful to a group. Deviations can often help groups move in new directions or challenge old ways of accomplishing tasks that are no longer functional. Norms may be dysfunctional or unethical, and it may be beneficial for members to deviate from them. For example, in a treatment group, norms develop that make it difficult for members to express intense emotions. Members who deviate from this norm help the group re-examine its norms and enable members to deepen their level of communication. The worker should try to understand the meaning of deviations from group norms and the implications for group functioning. It can also be helpful to point out covert norms and to help groups examine whether these contribute to the effective functioning of the group.

Because they are so pervasive and powerful, norms are somewhat more difficult to change than role expectations or status hierarchies. Therefore, a worker should strive to ensure that the developing norms are beneficial for the group. Recognizing the difficulty of changing norms, Lewin (1947) suggested that three stages are necessary for changing the equilibrium and the status quo that hold norms constant. There must first be disequilibrium or unfreezing caused by a crisis or other tension-producing situation. During this period, group members re-examine the current group norms. Sometimes a crisis may be induced by the worker through a discussion or demonstration of how current norms will affect the group in the future. In other cases, dysfunctional norms lead to a crisis.

In the second stage, members return to equilibrium with new norms replacing previous ones. According to Lewin, the second stage is called *freezing*. In the third stage, called *refreezing*, the new equilibrium is stabilized. New norms become the recognized and accepted rules by which the group functions. Napier and Gershenfeld (1993) have suggested ways that norms can be changed, including the following:

1. Discussing, diagnosing, and making explicit decisions about group norms
2. Directly intervening in the group to change a norm
3. Deviating from a norm and helping a group to adapt a new response
4. Helping the group become aware of external influences and their effect on the group's norms
5. Hiring a consultant to work with the group to change its norms

Roles

Like norms, roles can also be an important influence on group members. Roles are closely related to norms. Whereas norms are shared expectations held, to some extent, by everyone in the group, *roles* are shared expectations about the functions of individuals in the group. Unlike norms, which define behavior in a wide range of situations, roles define behavior in relation to a specific function or task that the group member is expected to perform. Roles continue to emerge and evolve as the work of the group changes over time (Salazar, 1996).

Roles are important for groups because they allow for division of labor and appropriate use of power. They ensure that someone will be designated to take care of vital group functions. Roles provide social control in groups by prescribing how members should behave in certain situations. Performing in a certain role not only prescribes certain behavior but also limits members' freedom to deviate from the expected behavior of someone who performs that role. For example, it would be viewed as inappropriate for an educational group leader to express feelings and emotional reactions about a personal issue that was not relevant to the topic.

Changes or modifications of roles are best undertaken by discussing members' roles, clarifying the responsibilities and the privileges of existing roles, asking members to assume new roles, or adding new roles according to preferences expressed during the group's discussion.

Status

Along with norms and role expectations, social controls are also exerted through members' status in a group. *Status* refers to an evaluation and ranking of each member's position in the group relative to all other members. A person's status within a group is partially determined by his or her prestige, position, and recognized expertise outside the group. To some extent, however, status is also dependent on the situation. In one group, status may be determined by a member's position in the agency sponsoring the group. In another group, status may be determined by how well a member is liked by other group members, how much the group relies on the member's expertise or how much responsibility the member has in the group. It is also determined by how a person acts once he or she becomes a member of a group. Because status is defined relative to other group members, a person's status in a group is also affected by the other members who compose the group.

Status serves a social control function in a rather complex manner. Low-status members are the least likely to conform to group norms because they have little to lose by deviating. This behavior is less likely if they have hopes of gaining a higher status. Medium-status group members tend to conform to group norms so that they can retain their status and perhaps gain a higher status. High-status members perform many valued services for the group and generally conform to valued group norms when they are establishing their position. However, because of their position, high-status members have more freedom to deviate from accepted norms. They are often expected to do something special and creative when the group is in a crisis situation (Nixon, 1979). If medium- or low-status members consistently deviate from group norms, they are threatened with severe sanctions or forced to leave the group. If high-status members consistently deviate from group norms, their status in the group is diminished, but they are rarely threatened with severe sanctions or forced to leave the group.

Status hierarchies are most easily changed by the addition or removal of group members. If this is not possible, group discussion may help members express their opinions and feelings about the effects of the current status hierarchy and how to modify it. Changing members' roles in the group and helping them to achieve a more visible or responsible position within the group can also increase members' status.

Principles for Practice

Norms, roles, and status are interrelated concepts that affect the social controls exerted on individuals in the group. Social controls limit individuality, freedom, and independence. At the same time, social controls stabilize and regulate the operation of groups by helping them to function efficiently and effectively. Therefore, in working with task and treatment groups, workers should balance the needs of individuals and of the group as a whole, managing conformity and deviation, while ensuring that social controls are working to benefit rather than hinder or limit individual members and the whole group. Workers may find the following principles about social control dynamics helpful when facilitating a group.

1. Social control dynamics help regulate and stabilize group functioning so that members can accomplish individual and group goals. The worker should help group members assess the extent to which norms, roles, and status hierarchies are helping the group accomplish its goals.

2. Group structure helps ensure the development of social control dynamics. The worker should provide sufficient structure so that a group's functioning does not become chaotic, disorganized, unsafe, or unduly anxiety provoking.

3. Too much structure can produce social control dynamics that restrict members' ability to exercise their own judgment and free will, and to accomplish agreed-on goals. The worker should ensure that there is freedom and independence within the range of acceptable behaviors agreed to by the group.

4. Members choose to adhere to social control dynamics in groups that are attractive and cohesive. Workers should help make the group a satisfying experience for members.

5. Members choose to adhere to social control dynamics when they consider the group's goals important and meaningful. Therefore, workers should emphasize the importance of the group's work and the meaningfulness of each member's contributions.

6. Members choose to adhere to social control dynamics when they desire continued membership because of their own needs or because of pressure from sources within or outside the group. Therefore, workers should consider the incentives for members to participate in a group.

7. Rewards and sanctions can help members comply with norms, status, and role expectations. The worker should assess whether rewards and sanctions are being used to help members comply with fair and equitable social control dynamics agreed on by the group.

By following these principles, workers can ensure that the norms, role expectations, and status hierarchy that develop in a group satisfy members' needs while helping to accomplish individual and group goals.

Group Culture

Although it has often been overlooked in discussions of group dynamics, group culture is an important force in the group as a whole. *Group culture* refers to values, beliefs, customs, and traditions held in common by group members (Olmsted, 1959).

When the membership of a group is diverse, group culture emerges slowly. Members contribute unique sets of values that originate from their past experiences as well as from their ethnic, cultural, and racial heritages. These values are blended through group communications and interactions. In early meetings, members explore each other's unique value systems and attempt to find a common ground on which they can relate to each other. By later meetings, members have had a chance to share and understand each other's value systems. As a result, a common set of values develops, which becomes the group's culture. The group's culture continues to evolve throughout the life of the group.

Group culture emerges more quickly in groups with a homogeneous membership. When members share common life experiences and similar sets of values, their unique perspectives blend more quickly into a group culture. For example, members of groups sponsored by culturally based organizations, such as the Urban League or Centro Civico, and groups that represent a particular point of view, such as the National Organization for Women (NOW), are more likely to share similar life experiences and similar values than are groups with more diverse memberships. One of the attractions of these homogeneous groups is that they provide an affirming and supportive atmosphere.

Culture is also influenced by the environment in which a group functions. As part of the organizational structure of an agency, a community, and a society, groups share the values, traditions, and heritage of these larger social systems. The extent to which these systems influence the group depends on the degree of interaction the group has with them. For example, on one end of the continuum, an administrative team's operational procedures are often greatly influenced by agency policies and practices. On the other end, gangs tend to isolate themselves from the dominant values of society, the community, and local youth organizations. Group workers can learn a great deal about groups by examining how they interact with their environment.

Groups that address community needs often have much interaction with their environment. When analyzing a change opportunity, building a constituency, or deciding how to implement an action plan, groups that set out to address community needs must carefully consider dominant community values and traditions. The receptivity of powerful individuals within a community will be determined to some extent by how consistent a group's actions are with the values and traditions they hold in high regard. Whenever possible, groups attempting to address community needs should frame their efforts within the context of dominant community values. The practitioner can help by attempting to find the common ground in the values of the community and the group. When a group's actions are perceived to be in conflict with dominant community values, it is unlikely to receive the support of influential community leaders. In these situations, the group may rely on conflict strategies (described in Chapters 9 and 11) to achieve its objectives.

Principles for Practice

The culture that a group develops has a powerful influence on its ability to achieve its goals while satisfying members' socioemotional needs. A culture that emphasizes values of self-determination, openness, fairness, and diversity of opinion can do much to facilitate the achievement of group and individual goals. Sometimes members bring ethnic, cultural, or social stereotypes to the group and thus inhibit the group's development and effective functioning. Through interaction and discussion, workers can help members confront stereotypes and learn to understand and appreciate persons who bring different values and cultural and ethnic heritages to the group.

In helping the group build a positive culture, the worker should consider the following principles:

1. Group culture emerges from the mix of values that members bring to the group. The worker should help members examine, compare, and respect each other's value systems.

2. Group culture is also affected by the values of the agency, the community, and the society that sponsor and sanction the group. The worker should help members identify and understand these values.

3. Group members and workers can hold stereotypes that interfere with their ability to interact with each other. Workers should help members eliminate stereotypical ways of relating to each other and develop an awareness of their own stereotypes.

4. Value conflicts can reduce group cohesion and, in extreme cases, lead to the demise of the group. The worker should mediate value conflicts among members and between members and the larger society.

5. Group culture can exert a powerful influence on members' values. The worker should model values such as openness, self-determination, fairness, and acceptance of difference, which are fundamental to social group work and the social work profession.

6. Groups are most satisfying when they meet members' socioemotional and instrumental needs. Therefore, the worker should balance members' needs for emotional expressiveness with their needs to accomplish specific goals.

STAGES OF GROUP DEVELOPMENT

According to Northen (1969), "a stage is a differentiable period or a discernible degree in the process of growth and development" (p. 49). The rest of this text is organized around the skills that workers can use during each stage of a group's development. A group's entire social structure, its communication and interaction patterns, cohesion, social controls, and culture evolve as it develops. Therefore, an in-depth understanding of group development is essential for the effective practice of group work. This section reviews some of the ways that group development has been conceptualized by other group work theoreticians.

Many attempts have been made to classify stages of group development. Table 3.3 lists some of the models of group development that have appeared in the literature. Most are based on descriptions of groups that the authors of each model have worked with or observed. Most models propose that all groups pass through similar stages of development. As can be seen in Table 3.3, however, different writers have different ideas about the number and types of stages through which all groups pass. For example, Bales' (1950) model of group development has only three stages, but the model presented by Sarri and Galinsky (1985) has seven stages.

Relatively few empirical studies have been conducted of particular models, and little empirical evidence exists to support the notion that any one model accurately describes the stages through which all groups pass. Most empirical studies have relied on direct observation or tape recordings of a small number of closed-membership groups. Recently, however, an attempt has been made to develop a reliable and valid measure of group development that may lead to promising findings in the future (Wheelan & Hochberger, 1996).

Overall, the studies that have been conducted suggest that groups move through stages, but that the stages are not constant across different groups (Shaw, 1976; Smith, 1978). MacKenzie (1994), Wheelan (1994), and Worchell (1994) point out that both progressive and cyclical processes exist in groups; that is, although groups often move through stages of development from beginning to end, they also often come back to re-address certain basic process issues in a cyclical or oscillating fashion. For example, there is often a cyclical movement of group members from feeling (1) invested in the task to emotionally displaced from the task, (2) part of the group to autonomous, (3) defended to open, and (4) isolated to enmeshed.

There is some evidence that stages of group development may be affected by the needs of group members, the type of group, the goals of the group, the setting in which the group meets, and the orientation of the leader (Shaw, 1976; Smith, 1978). For example, a study of open-membership groups (Schopler & Galinsky, 1990) revealed that few moved beyond a beginning stage of development. *Open-membership* groups that are able to move beyond a beginning level of development are those that have a membership change less frequently than every other meeting and those with less than a 50 percent change in membership (Galinsky & Schopler, 1989).

Groups with frequent and extensive membership changes almost always remain at a formative stage. Such groups cope with problems in continuity and development by following highly ritualistic and structured procedures for group meetings. For example, a group in a stroke rehabilitation unit in a large teaching hospital in which a patient's typical stay is three to four weeks might be structured to begin with a half-hour educational presentation, followed by a half-hour discussion. The group would meet three times a week. Eight different topics could be presented before they are repeated. Therefore, patients with typical hospital stay of three to four weeks could learn about all eight topics, yet begin

TABLE 3.3 ■ *Stages of Group Development*

Development Stage	Bales (1950)	Tuckman (1963)	Northen (1969)	Hartford (1971)	Klein (1972)
Beginning	Orientation	Forming	Planning and orientation	Pregroup planning Convening Group formation	Orientation Resistance
Middle	Evaluation	Storming Norming Performing	Exploring and testing Problem solving	Disintegration and conflict Group function and maintenance	Negotiation Intimacy
End	Decision making		Termination	Pretermination Termination	Termination

and end their participation at any time. However, the intimacy that can be achieved during the middle stage of groups with closed memberships is rarely achieved in groups in which members are continually entering and leaving the group.

Despite the variable nature of the stages of group development described by different writers, many of the models contain similar stages. As can be seen in Table 3.3, the various phases of group development can be divided into three stages: beginning, middle, and end. Each model of group development is placed in relationship to these three broad stages.

Most writers suggest that the beginning stages of groups are concerned with planning, organizing, and convening. The beginnings of groups are characterized by an emergence of group feeling. Group feeling, however, often does not emerge without a struggle. For example, Klein (1972) emphasizes the resistance of members to group pressure; Garland, Jones, and Kolodny (1976) emphasize the desire of group members to become a part of the group while maintaining their autonomy. Thus, along with the tendency to approach one another, there is also a tendency for members to maintain their distance. Garland, Jones, and Kolodny (1976) identified this tendency as an approach-avoidance conflict. As the beginning stage progresses and norms and roles are differentiated, members explore and test the roles they are beginning to assume in the group. Conflict may emerge. The leader can help by encouraging members to discuss and resolve conflicts as they emerge during the group process. It is also helpful to point out that encountering conflict and dealing with it are normal steps in the development of smooth-working relationships in preparation for the intense work to come in

TABLE 3.3 ■ *Continued*

Trecker (1972)	Sarri & Galinsky (1985)	Garland, Jones, & Kolodny (1976)	Henry (1992)	Wheelan (1994)
Beginning Emergence of some group feeling	Origin phase Formative phase	Preaffiliation Power and control	Initiating Convening	Dependency and delusion
Development of bond, purpose, and cohesion Strong group feeling Decline in group feeling	Intermediate phase I Revision phase Intermediate phase II Maturation phase	Intimacy Differentiation	Conflict Maintenance	Counterdependency and flight Trust and structure Work
Ending	Termination	Separation	Termination	Termination

the middle stage. More information about conflict among members and how to resolve it is provided in Chapters 4, 7, and 11.

Although some work is accomplished in all stages of a group's development, most occurs in the middle stage. At the beginning of this stage, the conflicts over norms, roles, and other group dynamics found in the later part of the beginning stage give way to established patterns of interaction. A deepening of interpersonal relationships and greater group cohesion begin to appear. After this occurs, groups concern themselves with the work necessary to accomplish the specific tasks and goals that have been agreed on. The terms used to describe this stage include *problem solving, performing, maintenance, intimacy, work,* and *maturity.* Task accomplishment is preceded by a differentiation of roles and accompanied by the development of feedback and evaluation mechanisms.

The ending stage of a group is characterized by the completion and evaluation of the group's efforts. Bales' (1950) model of group development suggests that during this stage, task groups make decisions, finish their business, and produce the results of their efforts. Treatment groups, which have emphasized socioemotional functioning as well as task accomplishment, begin a process of separation, during which group feeling and cohesion decline. Often members mark termination by summarizing the accomplishments of the group and celebrating together.

Models of group development provide a framework to describe worker roles and appropriate interventions during each stage of a group. They also help workers organize and systematize strategies of intervention. For example, in the beginning stage, a worker's interventions are directed at helping the group define its purpose and helping members feel comfortable with one another. Models of group development can also prepare the leader for what to expect from a group during each stage of development.

The usefulness of theories of group development for group work practice, however, is limited by the uniqueness of each group experience. The developmental stages of groups vary significantly across the broad range of task and treatment groups that a worker might lead. It should not be assumed that all groups follow the same pattern of development or that an intervention that is effective in one group will automatically be effective in another group that is in the same developmental stage. Nevertheless, organizing content into specific developmental stages is a useful heuristic device when teaching students and practitioners how to lead and be effective members of treatment and task groups.

The model of group development presented in this text includes four broad stages: (1) planning, (2) beginning, (3) middle, and (4) ending. The beginning stage includes separate chapters on beginning groups and assessment. The middle stage includes five chapters focused on generic and specialized skills for leading task and treatment groups. The ending stage includes chapters on evaluating the work of the group and on terminating with individual members and the group as a whole. The rest of this text is organized around the skills, procedures, and techniques that help groups function effectively during each stage.

Principles for Practice

The worker should be knowledgeable about the theoretical constructs that have been proposed about the stages of group development. Knowing what is normative behavior for members at each stage can help the worker to assess whether the group is making progress toward achieving its goals. It can also help workers to identify dysfunctional behavior in an individual group member and problems that are the responsibility of the group as a whole. The following practice principles are derived from an understanding of group development.

1. Closed-membership groups develop in discernible and predictable stages. The worker should use systematic methods of observing and assessing the development of the group and should teach group members about the predictable stages of group development.

2. The development of open-membership groups depends on member turnover. The worker should help open-membership groups develop a simple structure and a clear culture to help new members integrate rapidly into the group.

3. Groups generally begin with members exploring the purpose of the group and the roles of the worker and each member. The worker should provide a safe and positive group environment so that members can fully explore the group's purpose and the resources available to accomplish the group's goals.

4. After the initial stage of development, groups often experience a period of norm development, role testing, and status awareness that results in expressions of difference among members and the leader. The worker should help members understand that these expressions of difference are a normal part of group development.

5. Structure has been demonstrated to increase member satisfaction, increase feelings of safety, and reduce conflict in early group meetings. A lack of structure can lead to feelings of anxiety, insecurity, and can lead to acting out and projection. Therefore, the worker should provide sufficient structure for group interaction, particularly in early group meetings.

6. Tension or conflict sometimes develops from differences among members. The worker should help the group resolve the conflict by helping the group develop norms emphasizing the importance of respect and tolerance and by mediating the differences and finding a common ground for productive work together.

7. Groups enter a middle stage characterized by increased group cohesion and a focus on task accomplishment. To encourage movement toward this stage, the worker should help members stay focused on the purpose of the group, challenge members to develop an appropriate culture for work, and help the group overcome obstacles to goal achievement.

8. In the ending stage, the group finishes its work. The worker should help members review and evaluate their work together by highlighting accomplishments and pointing out areas that need further work.

9. Groups sometimes experience strong feelings about endings. The worker should help members recognize these feelings, review what they accomplished in the group, and help members plan for termination.

SUMMARY

Groups are social systems made up of people in interaction. This chapter describes some of the most important forces that result from the interaction of group members. In working with task and treatment groups, it is essential to understand group dynamics and be able to use them to accomplish group goals. Without a thorough understanding of group dynamics, workers will not be able to help members satisfy their needs or help the group accomplish its tasks.

Group workers should be familiar with four dimensions of group dynamics: (1) communication and interaction patterns; (2) the cohesion of the group and its attraction for its members; (3) social controls such as norms, roles, and status; and (4) the group's culture. Communication and interaction patterns are basic to the formation of all groups. Through communication and interaction, properties of the group as a whole develop, and the work of the group is accomplished. This chapter presents a model of the communication process.

Groups are maintained because of the attraction they hold for their members. Members join groups for many reasons. The extent to which the group meets members' needs and expectations determines the attraction of the group for its members and the extent to which a group becomes a cohesive unit. As cohesion develops, group structures are elaborated and norms, roles, and status hierarchies form. Norms, roles, and status hierarchies are social controls that help to form and shape shared expectations about appropriate behavior in the group. Conformity to expected behavior patterns results in rewards, and deviation results in sanctions. Social controls help to maintain a group's equilibrium as it confronts internal and external pressure to change during its development. However, social controls can be harmful if they are too rigid, too stringent, or if they foster behavior that is contrary to the value base of the social work profession.

As the group evolves, it develops a culture derived from the environment in which it functions as well as from the beliefs, customs, and values of its members. The culture of a group has a pervasive effect on its functioning. For example, a group's culture affects the objectives of the group, which task the group decides to work on, how members interact, and which methods the group uses to conduct its business.

Although properties of groups are often discussed as if they were static, they change constantly throughout the life of a group. Many writers have attempted to describe typical stages through which all groups pass. Although no single model of group development is universally accepted, some of the major characteristics that distinguish group process during each stage of group development are discussed in this chapter. These characteristics can be a useful guide for group practitioners in the beginning, middle, and ending stages of group work, which are described in later portions of this text.

This chapter points out the power of group dynamics in influencing group members and in contributing to or detracting from the success of a group. As workers become familiar with properties of groups as a whole, their appreciation of the effects that natural and formed groups have on the lives of their clients is enhanced. In addition, workers can use their understanding of group dynamics to enhance their ability to work effectively with both task and treatment groups.

LEARNING ASSIGNMENTS

1. During a meeting of a group you currently participate in, take notes about the group's communication and interaction patterns. What pattern dominates? Who sends and receives the most communications? Who sends and receives the fewest communications? After the meeting, discuss your observations with another member of the group.

2. Audiotape or videotape a group session, or use one of the case examples in Chapter 15. Review the tape or the case example for the level of cohesion in the group. What circumstances led to the highest and lowest levels of cohesion? What did the leader do to foster cohesion in the group?

3. Choose a film or novel that features a group in its plot, such as *The Breakfast Club, Dead Poets Society, Lord of the Flies,* or *Animal Farm*. Analyze the development of the group over time using one of the models described in Table 3.3. Focus specifically on the development of social control mechanisms. How did norms, roles, status hierarchies, and power develop and evolve in the group? How did this affect the overall culture of the group?

chapter 4

Leadership

Leadership is the process of guiding the development of the group and its members. The goal of effective leadership is to meet the socioemotional needs of members and to help the group as a whole, and each of its members, achieve goals that are consistent with the value base of social work practice.

Although the leadership role is most often associated with the designated leader—that is, the worker—it is important to distinguish between the worker as the designated leader and the indigenous leadership that emerges among members as the group develops. Leadership is rarely exercised solely by the worker. As the group unfolds, members take on leadership roles.

Workers should do as much as possible to stimulate and support indigenous leadership. Encouraging indigenous leadership helps to empower members. Members begin to feel that they have some influence, control, and stake in the group situation. Exercising leadership skills in the group increases members' self-esteem and increases the likelihood that they will advocate for themselves and for others outside of the group context. Encouraging indigenous leadership also helps members to exercise their own skills and abilities. This, in turn, promotes autonomous functioning and ensures that members' existing skills do not atrophy. Thus, this chapter emphasizes both the importance of the worker as group leader and the importance of members' sharing in leadership functions as the group develops.

There is an increasing amount of evidence that gender roles play an important role in emerging leadership. In studies of emerging leaders, males are generally viewed more positively than females (Kolb, 1997). Also, the same leadership behaviors are often viewed more positively when attributed to males than to females (Shimanoff & Jenkins, 1991). Group leaders who are aware of this evidence will be better prepared to provide females with opportunities to assert their leadership abilities, and to guard against male dominance of leadership roles within task and treatment groups.

LEADERSHIP AND POWER

Workers who are new to the leadership role are sometimes uncomfortable with their power and influence and react by denying their power or by trying to take too much control. These strategies are rarely effective. Especially in early group meetings, members look to the leader for guidance about how to proceed. Experienced leaders are comfortable with their power and influence. They use it to empower members, which gradually enables members to take increasing responsibility for the group as it develops.

Workers use their influence as leaders within and outside the group to facilitate group and individual efforts to achieve desired goals. Within the group, the worker intervenes to change the dynamics of the group as a whole or to help individual members change. In exercising leadership outside the group, the worker intervenes to influence the environment in which the group and its members function. For example, the worker might try to change organizational policies that influence the group or obtain additional resources from a sponsor so the group can complete its work. In exerting leadership inside or outside the group, the worker is responsible for the group's processes, actions, and task accomplishments.

In considering a worker's power, it is helpful to distinguish between attributed power and actual power. *Attributed power* comes from the perception among group members or others outside the group of the worker's ability to lead. Workers who take on the responsibilities inherent in leading a group are rewarded by having attributed to them the power to influence and the ability to lead. Such power is attributed by group members, peers, superiors, the sponsoring agency, and the larger social system.

The attributed power of the worker comes from a variety of sources. Among these sources are professional status, education, organizational position, experience, defined boundaries between worker and group members' roles, fees for service, and the commonly held view that a group's success or failure is the result of its leadership. Workers should recognize that attributed leadership ability is as important as actual power in facilitating the development of the group and its members.

Workers can increase the power attributed to them by group members. Studies have shown that members' expectations about the group and its leader influence the group's performance (Bednar & Kaul, 1994; Piper, 1994). Preparing members with films, brochures, or personal interviews that offer information about the group, its leader, and the success of previous groups has been shown to be effective in increasing the change-oriented expectations of members and in helping individuals and groups accomplish their goals (Bednar & Kaul, 1994; Kaul & Bednar, 1994). When formal preparation is impossible, informal preparation by word of mouth or reputation can be used.

When attempting to increase their attributed power, workers should keep in mind that their motive is to increase their ability to help group members function independently and at an optimal level. As their attributed power increases, workers are more likely to be regarded with esteem by group members and to be looked to as models of effective coping skills whose behaviors are emulated and whose guidance is followed. Workers should not, however, attempt to gain power for its own sake or unilaterally impose their own values, standards, and rules concerning conduct inside or outside the group.

Actual power refers to the worker's resources for changing conditions inside and outside the group. Actual power depends on the sources of a worker's influence. Following are seven power bases (French & Raven, 1959) that the worker may possess:

1. Connection power—being able to call on and use influential people or resources

2. Expert power—having the knowledge or skill to facilitate the work of the group

3. Information power—possessing information that is valuable to and needed by others

4. Legitimate power—holding a position of authority and the rights that accrue to that position in the organization or larger social system

5. Reference power—being liked and admired; the group members want to be identified with the worker

6. Reward power—being able to offer social or tangible rewards

7. Coercive power—being able to sanction, punish, or deny access to resources and privileges

Use of power can have both negative and positive consequences. For example, coercive power is sometimes used to compel clients to receive treatment. However, coercion can have negative effects such as hostility, anger, rebellion, and absence from group meetings. Therefore, the worker should exercise power judiciously, in a manner consistent with personal, professional, and societal values.

At the same time, the worker's power as leader cannot, and should not, be denied, which sometimes occurs when suggestions are made that members should take total responsibility for leading the group. Groups need leaders to avoid disorganization and chaos; leadership and power are inseparable (Etzioni, 1961).

Anyone who has attended the first meeting of a new group recognizes the power the worker has as the designated leader. This power can be illustrated most vividly by examining members' behaviors and feelings during the initial portion of the first group meeting. Members direct most of their communications to the worker or communicate through the worker to other group members. Members are often anxious and inquisitive, wondering what they can expect from the group and its leader. They comply readily with requests made by the worker. Although members may wonder about the worker's ability to help them and the group as a whole, they usually give the worker latitude in choosing methods and procedures to help the group achieve its objectives.

Beginning with the first group meeting, it is essential that workers move as rapidly as possible to share their power with members and the group as a whole. The worker can do this in a variety of ways: (1) encouraging member-to-member rather than member-to-leader communications; (2) asking for members' input into the agenda for the meeting and the direction the group should take in future meetings; (3) supporting indigenous leadership when members make their first, tentative attempts at exerting their own influence in the group; and (4) encouraging attempts at mutual sharing and mutual aid among group members.

Theories of Group Leadership

Early theories about the best method to use in leading a group focused primarily on leadership style. Leadership was considered a trait rather than a cluster of behaviors that could be learned (Halpin, 1961). Three positions on a continuum of leadership behavior—laissez-faire, democratic, and autocratic—were the subject of early investigations (Lewin & Lippitt, 1938; Lewin, Lippitt, & White, 1939). The continuum can be seen in Figure 4.1. Findings from these studies

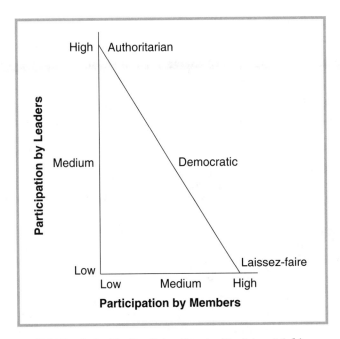

FIGURE 4.1 ■ *Participation in Decision Making by Leaders and Members in Groups Using Three Leadership Styles*

indicated that there were more aggression, hostility, and scapegoating in autocratic groups than in democratic groups. There were no differences in the tasks completed by the groups, although there was some indication that the products of democratic groups were qualitatively superior to those of groups that used autocratic or laissez-faire styles of leadership. Group members also preferred the democratic group's process—that is, they liked the leader better and felt freer and more willing to make suggestions. These early findings seemed to suggest that allowing members to participate in the group's decision-making process was the preferred leadership style. More recent findings have also suggested that a friendly, helpful, inclusive leadership style that is open to new ideas results in more effective groups than an autocratic style (Gummer, 1995).

Factors Influencing Group Leadership

Situational factors help determine what skills and leadership style are most appropriate and effective for a particular group. For example, Nixon (1979) has suggested that at least seven factors must be assessed before predicting what leadership styles or behaviors are most effective. These include the following:

1. The leadership expectations held by group members
2. The way leadership has been attained
3. Whether there is competition between designated leaders and the leaders that emerge as groups develop
4. The needs, tasks, and goals of the group as a whole
5. The task and socioemotional skills of members
6. The nature of authority within and outside of the group
7. The environmental demands placed on the group and its leadership

The growing recognition that group leadership is affected by a variety of interacting factors has resulted from empirical findings in social psychology, sociology, and business administration (Fiedler, 1967; Gibb, 1969; Hersey & Blanchard, 1977; Luft, 1984; McClane, 1991; McGrath, 1984, 1992; Nixon, 1979; Vroom & Yetton, 1973). These investigators found that to understand the dynamics of leadership in diverse treatment and task groups, several factors in addition to the personality and leadership style of the worker must be considered.

For example, in analyzing leadership in task groups, a number of investigators have shown that leaders develop different relationships with different members of a group (Dienesch & Liden, 1986; Graen & Schiemann, 1978; McClane, 1991). Others have demonstrated that the social environment, properties of the group as a whole, the type of problem the group is working on, and the purposes and functions of the group influence the nature of leadership (Fiedler, 1967; Gibb, 1969; McGrath, 1984, 1992; Nixon, 1979; Vroom & Yetton, 1973).

Several group work practitioners have also suggested that leadership must be seen as a process within the context of the group and its environment. For example, Garvin (1997) emphasizes the role of the agency in influencing the work of treatment groups.

In examining group leadership, Heap (1979) suggests that the degree of activity of a worker is directly related to the social health of the group's members. Thus, a worker should be more active in groups in which members are "out of touch with reality" or "withdrawn or very aggressive" (p. 50). For example, a worker might need to be directive and structured in a remedial group for severely mentally ill inpatients of a state hospital. The worker, as "expert," may work with each member in turn for 5 or 10 minutes. Other members may be asked to offer opinions or provide feedback, but the primary focus is on helping an individual achieve particular treatment goals.

Similarly, Toseland (1995) notes that group workers have to be active when working with the frail elderly in groups. The energy level of these group members is often low, and they are often preoccupied with their own physical functioning. Also, frail, older group members tend to relate to the group leader rather than to each other. Being energetic and working hard to establish connections among members can counteract these tendencies.

In contrast, when working with interested, eager, competent members, the worker should take on a less active, enabler role. For example, a group-centered leadership approach is usually more effective in support, growth, and socialization groups in which members are eager, competent, and not severely impaired. In using a group-centered method, the worker facilitates communication, interaction, understanding, and mutual aid and encourages members to help one another rather than to look to the worker as an expert who can solve their concerns or problems.

Overall, one conclusion that can be drawn from social science findings and from data accumulated from group work practice is that one method of leadership is not effective in all situations. Approaches that suggest one method for all circumstances are oversimplified. In her development of a broad-range model of group leadership, Lang (1972) underscored this point. She demonstrated how workers should vary their leadership depending on the characteristics of the group. The worker's leadership skills and intervention strategies should vary depending on the degree to which the group as a whole and its individual members can function autonomously. The less autonomous the group, the more the worker must play a central role in leading the group. Conversely, the more autonomous the group, the more the worker can facilitate the members' own self-direction and indigenous leadership abilities.

Effectiveness of Leaders

Most people assume leaders exert considerable influence on the outcome of task and treatment groups, but what is the empirical evidence to justify this faith in the leader? As Lieberman (1975) notes, "It is quite possible that the leader's behavior, personality, and skill level have taken on mythic proportions as basic causal forces explaining successful . . . change" (p. 357). Most theories emphasize the role of the leader in helping the group achieve its objectives and helping group members feel satisfied with the group's process. Many of these theories, however, are backed by little or no evidence.

Empirical evidence does not fully support the notion that group leadership is central in helping the group attain its objectives. Some evidence supports claims that leaders' behaviors are important to the success of the group (Bednar & Kaul, 1994; Dies, 1994; Feldman & Caplinger, 1977), but other evidence suggests that this may not be so. Lieberman, Yalom, and Miles (1973), for example, found that tape-led (virtually leaderless) groups were more effective than three fourths of the leader-led groups they studied. McLaughlin, White, and Byfield (1974) found that a programmed tape format with the leader present as a member was a better method for achieving group objectives than were five other leadership structures, including the traditional leader-led group format. Similarly, in a study of a leaderless women's group that had been meeting for 17 years, Counselman (1991) found that the group performed effectively because functions typically performed by the leader were assumed by members of the group. Therefore, when acting as the designated leader, workers should do everything possible to enable members to exercise their own leadership capacities. Workers should also recognize that other factors in addition to their skills may affect group outcomes. Taken together, these factors may be just as important as the worker's skill in helping a group to achieve its objectives.

AN INTERACTIONAL MODEL OF LEADERSHIP

Figure 4.2 presents factors that affect group leadership. The interactional model incorporates the empirical findings of others who have developed comprehensive models of group leadership (Likert, 1967; Tannenbaum & Schmidt, 1972; Vroom & Yetton, 1973). Because this model views leadership as being derived from the interactions of the group, its members, the leader, and the environment, the model is closely related to the ecological systems perspective of social casework proposed by Germain and Gitterman (1996) and Siporin (1980) as well as the interactional perspective presented by Gitterman and Shulman (1994) and Maluccio (1979). The interactional model represents leadership as a shared function that is not lodged solely in the designated group leader. In addition to the worker's role as designated leader, the model in Figure 4.2 clearly shows that leadership emerges from a variety of interacting factors as the group develops.

As a heuristic device, the model can be useful in planning effective leadership methods for different types of groups. The model shows six separate but interrelated factors that should be considered when leading a task or treatment group. These factors are (1) the purposes of the group, (2) the type of problem the group is working on, (3) the environment in which the group works, (4) the group as a whole, (5) the members of the group, and (6) the leader of the group.

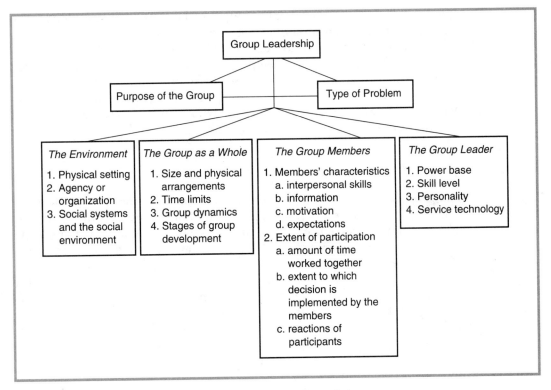

FIGURE 4.2 ■ *An Interactional Model of Group Leadership*

Purposes of the Group

When one considers how leadership emerges in a group, it is essential to consider the purposes of the group. According to Browning (1977), a group may be formed (1) to perform tasks that require more than one or two people, (2) to meet individual needs, (3) to bring people together who are involved in the same or similar problems, (4) to represent a larger collection of people, (5) to form the largest collection of people that can be managed together, (6) to help maintain an organization more economically than individuals, (7) to increase motivation, or (8) as a result of physical factors such as working together in the same office. To this list can be added the purpose of using the group to change conditions or situations outside the group in an organization, a service delivery system, or an entire social system.

A group may have a single purpose or several purposes. The worker should consider how a group's purposes are interpreted by all systems that interact with the group. The worker should ensure that the purpose of the group and the type of problem to be worked on are consistent. For example, if the purpose of a group is to meet the needs of socially isolated individuals, the types of problems on which the group works should be related to group members' needs for increased social interaction; that is, the group should not be working on problems of housing or finances unless they are linked to the primary purpose of decreasing isolation.

The purpose of a group helps determine how workers guide group processes. For example, in a group whose purpose is solely to complete a task or solve a problem, a worker might choose to encourage members to structure and focus the interactions more than one would in a group whose purpose is to have members share common concerns and ideas about an issue.

Type of Problem

The type of problem or task a group works on also has important implications for the leadership of a group. It has been found that groups do better than individuals on certain types of tasks, but individuals working alone do better on others (Hare, Blumberg, Davies, & Kent, 1995). Generally, groups do better when the task is additive, such as collecting information. Thus, it would be better to form a treatment conference group to collect information about a client from all the professionals working with the client rather than visit each professional separately. Groups also appear to improve on the decisions of individuals working alone in choosing between clearly delineated alternatives. For example, Toseland, Rivas, and Chapman (1984) found that groups improved on the decision-making ability of individuals working alone in deciding on funding priorities for medically underserved counties.

Groups also do better on tasks requiring a wide range of responses (Thorndike, 1938). For example, it is preferable to have group members and the leader generate alternative solutions with a woman who is having trouble expressing her anger rather than to have the woman generate the alternatives with one worker. For these kinds of tasks, the worker should promote interaction, input, and feedback from all group members so that a wide range of responses is generated and evaluated.

Individuals working alone solve some problems or accomplish some tasks faster and better than they would working in a group. Individuals working alone more readily solve complex problems requiring many variables to be synthesized into a whole. In these cases, the group's product was no better than the best performance of a member of the group (Thorndike, 1938).

Workers can effectively use the knowledge that individuals may solve some problems better by working alone. For example, in preparing a countywide plan for disseminating emergency energy allocation funds to low-income families, a worker might decide to use a nominal group procedure (see Chapter 11), which encourages members to work alone before sharing their ideas with the group. The worker might also help members form subgroups to work on specific ideas generated by the individuals before they are deliberated in the larger group.

Several other aspects of problems should be considered when leading a group. One is whether the problem is of concern to the group as a whole, to a subgroup, or to an individual. All members of the group might not be affected to the same extent by a particular problem or task being considered by a group. For example, when leading a group to teach parenting skills to foster parents, the worker should try to get all members involved in discussing parenting problems that are of interest to everyone in the group. When a member raises a problem unique to his or her particular situation, the worker should try to develop from this information generalized principles of child rearing of interest to all group members. This technique is often called *universalizing*.

When considering the type of problem confronting a group, workers should also be aware of where their legitimate influence ends. It may not be appropriate for the worker to encourage discussion of certain topics. For example, a worker leading a task group planning for an emergency housing shelter should not encourage a group member to talk about personal family life. In other situations, however, workers may want to encourage discussion of taboo areas. For example, when the problem being discussed is child abuse, it might be helpful for the worker to encourage all members to talk about how they were disciplined during their early childhood.

The Environment

The environment in which the group conducts its work has a profound effect on how leadership emerges in the group. Environmental influences come primarily from three interrelated factors: (1) the immediate physical setting, (2) the agency or organization in which the group functions, and (3) other social systems and the social environment. Each factor helps create the group's culture, which, in turn, affects how the worker's actions are perceived by the group.

The Setting

The worker should ensure that the setting facilitates the group's work. The decor and comfort of the waiting room and meeting area and the availability of equipment and supplies such as tables, blackboard, or newsprint all influence the group's leadership. It is important for the worker to match group members' needs and preferences to a setting that facilitates the group's work. For example, sitting around a table may facilitate the work of a task group because members can spread out papers and write more easily. In contrast, a table may interfere with the observation of nonverbal communication in a therapy group, and it may also hamper role playing and engagement in other program activities.

The Agency Context

In addition to the physical environment, the agency influences the group and its leader in several ways. The worker, for example, must be aware of agency policies, rules, and regulations that govern the group's behavior, its process, and its product. The worker is given legitimate authority by the agency or organization to help the group perform its tasks. The agency's delegation of this authority to the worker often assumes the worker will use the method of service delivery that currently exists in the agency. For example, two group workers trying to help pregnant women stop abusing alcohol may use quite different means, depending on the type of program sponsored by each agency. One group leader may use a reality-therapy group approach; the other may use a group format based on cognitive-behavioral self-control procedures.

A worker's position within an agency or organization can also affect the form leadership takes in a group. For example, a worker with a high-level administrative position may elicit different reactions from group members than would a worker with a lower-level position. Similarly, the leaders position in an organization often signifies the importance placed on the work of the group.

Other Social Systems

The third way the environment influences group leadership is through large social systems, such as the community in which the group operates. The worker's behavior is influenced by norms established by society. For example, in a group for abusive parents, the worker intervenes to help members comply with societal norms and values concerning appropriate parenting behaviors. Smaller social systems can also affect a group's work. For example, an agency committee might hesitate to become involved in a search for additional emergency housing if a delegate council formed by a community planning agency is already looking at ways to develop additional emergency housing resources.

The Group as a Whole

At least four properties of the group as a whole influence how leadership emerges in the group. These are (1) the size of the group, (2) the time limit in which the group is expected to accomplish its goals, (3) group dynamics, and (4) the stage of a group's development.

Group Size

As the size of a group increases, the opportunity for member participation decreases. The number of rules may increase as workers use them to maintain order and control in the group. Subgroups are more likely to form. The leader is more likely to be in the front of a large group, and leader-to-member and member-to-leader interactions are more likely to occur than are member-to-member interactions.

Time Limits

Time limits may be voluntary or mandatory. A treatment group, for example, might decide to use a time-limited method such as a behavioral group approach or a task-centered group approach. A task group, such as a delegate council, might feel responsible for making a speedy decision on an issue for an upcoming statewide meeting. In either case, time limits affect leadership behavior. Generally, time limits are associated with greater structuring of interactions, an increase in task-focused behavior, and fewer opportunities for indigenous leadership to emerge.

Group Dynamics

The third property that can influence leadership is the dynamics that operate in a group. As discussed in Chapter 3, these include communication and interaction patterns, cohesion, social control, and group culture. Workers should use their skills to foster the development of group dynamics that help the group accomplish its tasks and contribute to members' satisfaction. Interventions to change the dynamics of the group as a whole are discussed in Chapter 8.

Stage of Development

The stage of a group's development is the fourth group-as-a-whole factor that can affect leadership behavior. If the group is to develop successfully, the worker must be aware of the developmental tasks that face the group during each stage. A large portion of this text focuses on the specific skills and methods that workers can use during each stage of a group's development.

The Group Members

Group members influence how leadership emerges in three important ways: (1) through the unique characteristics and life experiences they bring to the group, (2) by the extent to which they participate in the group, and (3) by the extent to which they share in leading the group.

Member Characteristics

Several characteristics of members affect members' ability to influence the group. These include members' interpersonal skills, access to information, perceived responsibility for the work of the group, motivations, and expectations about the process and outcome of the group. The importance of these characteristics should not be overlooked when considering how leadership develops in a group. It has been shown, for example, that members' expectations influence outcomes in both treatment (Piper, 1994) and task groups (Gibb, 1969) and that interpersonal skill level and knowledge about a particular problem also help determine how well a group functions (Browning, 1977; Hersey, Blanchard, & Natemeyer, 1979).

Because members' attributes differ, one member who is knowledgeable about a particular topic may become the task leader while that topic is being discussed.

Another member may serve as the group's socioemotional leader by expressing feelings and responding to other members' feelings. This suggests that the worker should remain aware of each member's leadership potential as the group progresses and help members to take on appropriate leadership roles that match their interests and skills.

Extent of Participation

The extent of members' participation also influences how a worker leads a group. Some members' lack of interpersonal skills or motivation may prevent them from participating fully. In other cases, the worker may purposefully prevent a group member from making verbal communications, which limits to nonverbal means a member's ability to influence the group. For example, a worker leading a delegate council may decide to limit discussion and thereby effectively stop some members from speaking about an issue.

The worker should anticipate members' reactions when they are encouraged or discouraged from active participation in a group. Generally, discouraging or limiting a member's participation in a group leads to the member's dissatisfaction with the group. In some situations, however, members may be more interested in hearing what the worker or a guest speaker has to say than in what other members have to say, and they may readily accept limits on their participation. This response is particularly true in educational groups in which members' participation may be limited to a discussion period after a presentation by the worker. In task groups, some members may not have an interest in or a knowledge of certain issues, and the worker may want to encourage more knowledgeable or interested members to express their views. In other cases, the worker may want to limit discussion so the group can come to a speedy decision.

Sharing Leadership

Members' willingness to share leadership responsibilities is determined by their feelings of competency, their previous leadership experiences, and their perceptions of the openness of the designated leader to sharing leadership functions. It is also affected, in part, by the amount of time the member has been a part of the group. A new group member often has difficulty exerting leadership in a group in which the relationship among members has been established. Similarly, a member of a street gang that has been together for several years has more influence with the gang than a worker who is just beginning to work with the gang.

The Group Leader

When one examines how leadership emerges in a group, the power base, skill level, personality, and choice of service technology of the designated leader all play an important role. As indicated earlier, seven types of power bases can be used to influence a group: connection, expert, information, legitimate, referent, reward, and coercive. Most workers draw on a variety of power bases; workers should realize the power bases at their disposal when they are considering leading a group. For example, a worker planning to lead a group of alcoholics who have been referred because of a driving while intoxicated offense may influence members by refusing to certify that they are fit to have their licenses returned until they have successfully completed a group treatment program.

The level of skill that workers possess also influences their ability to lead. Experience and training of workers have been correlated with effectiveness in working with individuals and groups (Dies, 1994). Even when workers have a number of strong power bases they can use to influence group members, unskillful application of their power often results in members' becoming angry and uncooperative or submissive and passive. Through the appropriate use of leadership skills, the worker can more readily achieve objectives and satisfy group members. Leadership skills are described in greater depth in the next section of this chapter.

A worker's personality, interpersonal style, and preferences for how to lead all influence how leadership emerges in a group. For example, a worker who is shy and sensitive about others' feelings is less likely to use confrontation as a technique when leading a group. Workers should be aware of how their interpersonal style affects their attempts to objectively analyze what the group needs and their attempts to intervene in the group's processes. Some methods for becoming more aware of one's leadership style and how to modify it are described later in this chapter.

The service technology that workers use also affects how they conduct their groups. *Service technology* refers to particular theories or methods of intervention used by a worker. Three leaders of groups for alcoholics, for example, may intervene in quite different ways—by using transactional analysis or behavior therapy or, perhaps, reality therapy. Workers' choice of service technologies may be influenced by their personal preferences, their training, or the ideology of the agency in which they work.

A worker's technological and ideological stance often helps in organizing interventions. Workers may wish to receive specialized instruction in a particular service technology, such as transactional analysis or behavior modification; however, it is essential that they become familiar with basic practice principles of leading groups before they receive specialized training.

GROUP LEADERSHIP SKILLS

Group leadership skills are behaviors or activities that help the group achieve its purpose and accomplish its tasks and help members achieve their personal goals. Both workers and members use leadership skills, although the worker ordinarily uses them more than any other member of the group. Leadership skills are combined when conducting group meetings. For example, in using a problem-solving method, a worker calls on numerous leadership skills to help a committee arrive at a decision concerning personnel practices in a family service agency. Similarly, in an aftercare treatment group for recovering drug addicts, a worker relies on many different skills to help members remain drug free.

There has been long-standing interest in the "skillful use of self" in social work practice (Goldstein, 1983). Most evidence concerning the effect of skill level on desired outcomes has been gathered from the evaluation of work with individuals rather than from work with groups (Dies, 1994). Reviews of the literature suggest that skills can be learned and that skill level makes a difference in performance (Dies, 1994). There is some evidence that specific skills such as attending intently and responding empathically are directly connected to positive outcomes (Shulman, 1978; Toseland, Rossiter, Peak, & Hill, 1990). Results are tentative, however, because it is difficult to design studies to assess the independent effect of one particular skill.

Group leadership skills are somewhat different from skills used in working with an individual. Both members and the worker have greater choice regarding the level and focus of their interaction. For example, they may choose to be active or passive, and they may decide to interact with some members more than others. There is also a greater possibility of shared leadership and the delegation of various leadership responsibilities. There have been a few attempts to focus on the specific skills necessary to lead groups (Bertcher, 1994; Middleman, 1978; Middleman & Wood, 1990; Shulman, 1999). Some programs have also been designed to train group workers in specific skills. Evaluations of these programs suggest they can be effective in increasing a worker's skill level (Oxley, Wilson, Anderson, & Wong, 1979; Rivas & Toseland, 1981).

Some of the basic skills necessary for group leadership are categorized in Table 4.1. Skills are listed in three categories: (1) facilitating group processes, (2) data gathering and assessment, and (3) action. Skills are classified on the basis of their most likely functions in the group. However, skills listed under one category may, on occasion, be used in another category, particularly if they are combined with other skills. For example, responding is classified as a skill in facilitating group processes. Although responding to another group member's actions or words facilitates communication, responding may also lead to additional data gathering, assessment, or action.

Facilitating Group Processes

Table 4.1 lists several different skills in the category of facilitating group processes. All these skills can be used by workers differentially, depending on their intentions when attempting to influence various group processes. In general, however, skills in facilitating group processes contribute to positive group outcome when they improve understanding among group members, build open communication channels, and encourage the development of trust so that all members are willing to contribute as much as they can to the problem on which the group is working (Cabral, Best, & Paton, 1975).

TABLE 4.1 ■ *A Functional Classification of Group Leadership Skills*

Facilitating Group Processes	Data Gathering and Assessment	Action
1. Involving group members	1. Identifying and describing thoughts, feelings, and behaviors	1. Supporting
2. Attending to others	2. Requesting information, questioning, and probing	2. Reframing and redefining
3. Expressing self	3. Summarizing and partializing information	3. Linking members' communications
4. Responding to others	4. Synthesizing thoughts, feelings, and actions	4. Directing
5. Focusing group communication	5. Analyzing information	5. Giving advice, suggestions, or instructions
6. Making group processes explicit		6. Providing resources
7. Clarifying content		7. Modeling, role playing, rehearsing, and coaching
8. Guiding group interactions		8. Confronting
		9. Resolving conflicts

Involving Group Members

Ideally, all members should be involved and interested in what is being discussed in the group. Yalom (1995) has called this universalizing a group member's experience. Involving members who have been silent helps identify commonalities and differences in their life experiences. As members become involved they realize how particular problems affect them and how a solution to one member's problem can directly or indirectly help them. Involving others is also essential for building group cohesiveness, developing a sense of mutual aid, and encouraging shared decision making.

Involving group members also means helping them take on leadership roles within the group. The worker should be cautious about doing too much for members and thereby stifling individual initiative. Instead of jealously guarding the leadership role, workers should encourage members to contribute to the content of group meetings and help shape group dynamic processes. This can be done by providing members with opportunities for leadership roles during program activities, by praising members for their leadership efforts, and by inviting and encouraging members' participation and initiative during group interaction.

Attending Skills

Attending skills are nonverbal behaviors, such as eye contact and body position, and verbal behavior that convey empathy, respect, warmth, trust, genuineness, and honesty. Attending skills are useful in establishing rapport as well as a climate of acceptance and cohesiveness among group members. Egan (1998) suggests that, in addition to body position and eye contact, skills that indicate that a worker has heard and understood a member are part of effective attending. Research has shown that effective attending skills are an important characteristic of successful leaders (Johnson & Bechler, 1998). Effective attending skills include repeating or paraphrasing what a member says and responding empathically and enthusiastically to the meaning behind members' communications. They also include what Middleman (1978) has referred to as "scanning" skills. When scanning the group, the worker makes eye contact with all group members, which lets them know that the worker is concerned about them as individuals. Scanning also helps reduce the tendency of workers to focus on one or two group members.

Expressive Skills

Expressive skills are also important for facilitating group processes. Workers should be able to help participants express thoughts and feelings about important problems, tasks, or issues facing the group and to reiterate and summarize them when necessary. Members should also be helped to express their thoughts and feelings as freely as possible in an appropriate and goal-oriented manner. Members of task and treatment groups can often benefit from an open discussion of formerly taboo areas that affect the group or its members. Self-disclosure is an expressive skill that can be used effectively for this purpose. Although self-disclosures should be made judiciously, according to their appropriateness for particular situations, they can often be useful in helping the worker promote open communication about difficult subjects.

Responding Skills

Skillful responses help the group as a whole and individual members accomplish tasks. The worker might, for example, amplify subtle messages or soften overpowering messages (Middleman & Wood, 1990). The worker can also redirect messages that may be more appropriate for a particular member or the group as a whole.

Workers can use responding skills selectively to elicit specific reactions that will affect future group processes. For example, if a worker's response supports a group member's efforts, the member is more likely to continue to work on a task or a concern. If the worker disagrees with a member's statement or action, the member is likely to react either by responding to the worker's statement or by remaining silent. The member is not likely to continue to pursue the original statement. Thus, by responding selectively to particular communications, the worker can exert influence over subsequent communication patterns.

Focusing Skills

The worker can facilitate group processes by focusing them in a particular direction. This can be done by clarifying, asking a member to elaborate, repeating a particular communication or sequence of communications, or suggesting that group members limit their discussion to a particular topic. Helping the group maintain its focus can promote efficient work by reducing irrelevant communications and by encouraging a full exploration of issues and problems.

Making Group Processes Explicit

The skill of making group processes explicit helps members to become aware of how they are interacting. For example, a worker may point out implicit group norms, particular member roles, or specific interaction patterns. The worker may ask members whether they observed a particular pattern or type of interaction, whether they are comfortable with the interaction, and whether they would like to see changes in the ways members interact. Middleman and Wood (1990) point out that it is important for the worker to verbalize therapeutic group norms and to encourage the development of traditions and rituals. For example, pointing out that at the beginning of each group meeting members seem to take turns "telling their story" and receiving feedback about how they handled a particular situation encourages members to consider whether they want to continue this pattern of interaction.

Pointing out the here-and-now of group interaction is an underused skill. Sometimes, workers get so caught up in the content of interaction that they forget to pay attention to group processes. Other workers are reluctant to make their observations public. Workers who have difficulty directing the group's attention to group processes should consider practicing this skill by setting aside a few minutes at the beginning or end of each meeting for a discussion of group processes or by making a conscious effort to point out group processes in brief summary statements at intervals during meetings. Clinical and supervisory experience suggests that the process of pointing out here-and-now group interaction becomes easier with practice.

Clarifying Content

Just as it can be beneficial to make group processes explicit, it can also be beneficial to point out the content of members' interactions. The worker's purpose in clarifying content is to help members communicate effectively. The skill of clarifying content includes checking that a particular message was understood by members of the group and helping members express themselves more clearly. It also includes pointing out when group interaction has become unfocused or has been sidetracked by an irrelevant issue.

The skill of clarifying content can also be used to point out the possible avoidance of taboo subjects. For example, when working with a group of couples, the leader might point out that no mention has been made of the couples' satisfaction with their sex lives. Similarly, in a support group for caregivers of the frail elderly, the worker may point out that the subject of nursing home placement has not arisen.

Guiding Group Interactions

The last skill noted in Table 4.1 for facilitating group processes is that of guiding the interactions of group members. To help a group accomplish the goals it has set for itself, the worker will often find it helpful to guide the group's interaction in a particular direction. By limiting or blocking a group member's communications, by encouraging another member to speak, or by linking one group member's communication to those of other group members, the worker can guide the group's interaction patterns. This method has been referred to as selecting communications patterns purposely (Middleman & Wood, 1990).

The skill of guiding group interactions has many uses. For example, the worker may want to correct a dysfunctional aspect of the group's process, such as the development of a subgroup that disrupts other members. A worker who can skillfully guide group interaction patterns can limit the communication between subgroup members and increase their communication with other group members. The worker may also want to use guiding skills to explore a particular problem or help members sustain their efforts in solving a problem or completing a task. At other times, the worker may want to encourage open communication. For example, by redirecting a communication, the worker can help members speak to one another. The worker might say, "John, your message is really intended for Jill. Why don't you share your message directly with her rather than through me?"

Data Gathering and Assessment

Data-gathering and assessment skills are useful in developing a plan for influencing communication patterns as well as in deciding on the action skills to use to accomplish the group's purposes. These skills provide a bridge between the process-oriented approach of facilitating group processes and the task-oriented approach of using action skills to achieve goals and satisfy members' needs. Without effective data-gathering and assessment skills, workers' interventions are not grounded in a complete understanding of the situation. This can result in the use of premature, oversimplified, or previously attempted solutions that have not been carefully analyzed and weighed.

Identifying and Describing Skills

Perhaps the most basic data-gathering skill is helping members identify and describe a particular situation. This skill allows elaboration of pertinent factors influencing a problem or task facing the group. In using this skill, workers should attempt to elicit descriptions that specify the problem attributes as clearly and concretely as possible. To understand the problem, it is often useful for the worker to identify or describe historical as well as current aspects of the problem. It may also be helpful to share alternative ways of viewing the situation to obtain diverse frames of reference, alternative interpretations of events, and potential solutions to a problem.

Requesting Information, Questioning, and Probing

The skills of identifying and describing a situation are essential to workers' attempts to gather data by requesting information, questioning, and probing. Using these skills, workers can clarify the problem or concern and broaden the scope of the group's work by obtaining additional information that may be useful to all members. The worker should be careful to ask questions that are clear and answerable. Double questions or value-laden questions may be met with resistance, passivity, anger, or misunderstanding. For some issues and for some group members, questioning or probing may be seen as a confrontation or a challenge to what has already been stated, particularly in areas in which the member is reluctant to give additional information, because the information is perceived as emotionally charged or potentially damaging to the member's status in the group. The worker should be particularly sensitive to these concerns when seeking additional information from a member. Helping the member explore fears or concerns about the potentially damaging effect of a disclosure can be a helpful intervention. Another is having the member ask for feedback from other members about the realistic basis of personal fears.

Summarizing and Partializing

When information has been discussed about the problems or concerns facing the group, a worker can use summarizing or partializing skills. Summarizing skills enable a worker to present the core of what has been said in the group and provide members an opportunity to reflect on the problem. Summarizing skills give members and the worker an opportunity to consider the next steps in solving the problem and allow members to compare with the worker's summary their perceptions about what has gone on in the group. Partializing skills are useful for breaking down a complex problem or issue into manageable bits. Partializing is also helpful in determining group members' motivation to work on various aspects of the problem.

Synthesizing

Another useful data-gathering and assessment skill is synthesizing verbal and nonverbal communications. Examples of synthesizing skills include making connections among the meanings behind a member's actions or words, expressing hidden agendas, making implicit feelings or thoughts explicit, and making connections between communications to point out themes and trends in members' actions or words.

Synthesizing skills can be useful in providing feedback to members about how they are perceived by others. Because these skills often involve a considerable amount of judgment and conjecture about the facts available to the worker, they should be used cautiously, and all members should have the opportunity for input into the synthesis. Ideally, when the worker synthesizes a number of interactions or points out similarities in group problem solving or in group communication patterns, all members should be able to give feedback about their perceptions of the situation. For example, during a weekly staff meeting of an adolescent unit in a state mental hospital, a worker might mention the patterns of interactions that have developed among team members. In describing these patterns, the worker would ask members for feedback on how they perceived the group's interaction.

Analyzing Skills

Once the data have been gathered and organized, the worker can use analyzing skills to synthesize the information and assess how to proceed. Analyzing skills include pointing out patterns in the data, identifying gaps in the data, and establishing mechanisms or plans for obtaining data to complete an assessment. For example, in a treatment conference at a group home for adolescents, the worker can use analyzing skills to point out patterns used by staff members in previous work with a particular youngster. The group can then explore new methods and techniques for future efforts to work with the youngster. In an educational treatment group for potentially abusive parents, the worker can use analyzing skills to link parents' behavior patterns to the onset of physical abuse of their children.

Action Skills

Supporting Group Members

Action skills are most often used by the worker to help the group accomplish its tasks. Perhaps the most basic skill in this area is supporting group members in their efforts to help themselves and each other. Skills to support group members will not be effective unless members perceive the group to be a safe place in which their thoughts and feelings will be accepted. Thus, it is essential to begin by helping the group develop a culture in which all members' experiences and opinions are valued. The worker supports members by encouraging them to express their thoughts and feelings on topics relevant to the group, by providing them the opportunity to ventilate their concerns, by soliciting their opinions, and by responding to their requests and comments.

Support also means helping members respond empathically to each other and validate and affirm shared experiences. Skills in supporting members often involve pointing out their strengths and indicating how their participation in the group can help to resolve their problems. It also means providing hope for continued progress or success.

Ventilation and support are the primary goals of some groups. For example, support groups are often formed for the staff of neonatal intensive care units and burn units of regional hospitals. Such groups give staff a chance to talk about and reflect on the emotionally draining situations they frequently face. Medical social workers who form and facilitate these groups encourage staff to ventilate pent-up emotions and provide peer support for one another. Similarly, the therapeutic elements of a treatment group for recently widowed people include the ventilation of feelings about the loss of a loved one, the affirmation of similar feelings and experiences, and the encouragement to cope effectively with the transition despite feelings of grief.

Reframing and Redefining

Often, one of the greatest obstacles to the work of a group or an individual is failure to view a problem from different perspectives to find a creative solution (Clark, 1998). Redefining and reframing the problem can help members examine the problem from a new perspective. Thus, a worker may want to reframe or redefine an issue or concern facing the group. For example, in a group in which one member is being made a scapegoat, the worker might help members redefine their relationship to that member. Redefining can be done by having members talk about how they relate to the person who is being scapegoated and how they might improve their relationship with that person. In this case, reframing the problem from one that focuses on the scapegoated member to one that is shared by all members is a useful way to change members' interactions with this particular member. As the problem is redefined and group members change their relationship with the member being scapegoated, the problem often diminishes or disappears. Reframing is described in greater detail in Chapter 9.

Linking Members' Communications

The skill of linking members' communications involves asking members to share their reactions to the messages communicated by others in the group. Middleman and Wood (1990) refer to this skill as reaching for a feeling link or an information link. Members have a tendency to communicate with the worker rather than with other members, especially in early group meetings. The worker can prevent this from becoming a pattern by asking members about their reactions to a particular communication. For example, in a group in a psychiatric inpatient setting designed to prepare the members for independent living, the worker might say, "Mary, how do you feel about what Joe just said? I recall that during our last meeting, you expressed feeling anxious about living on your own." Alternatively, the worker might say, "Have any of you had the same feeling?" When members of the group validate and affirm each other's experiences and feelings, they develop a sense of belonging. Members no longer feel isolated or alone with their concerns. They stop questioning and doubting their own interpretations of a situation and their own reactions to it.

The skill of linking members' communications also involves asking members to respond to requests for help by other members. Helping members respond to each other fosters information sharing, mutual aid, and the building of a consensus about how to approach a particular problem. For example, in response to a query from a group member about whether the worker knows of a resource for helping her take care of her frail father while she is at work, the worker might ask whether any other members have used adult day care or respite care. Workers find that members are often more receptive to using a service or a resource when they hear positive reports about it from other members of the group.

Particularly when working with mandated and reluctant clients, workers who suggest use of a particular resource may be viewed with skepticism. Members sometimes believe that the worker has a vested interest in getting them to use a particular service. In contrast, the testimonials of one or more group members about the benefits of a particular service are often viewed with less skepticism. Workers should also be aware that once they provide a response, other members are less likely to provide their own perspective. Thus, although a direct response to a member's communication is often warranted, it is often a good practice for workers to turn to other members of the group for their input before jumping in with their own responses.

Directing

Whether the worker is clarifying the group's goal, helping members participate in a particular program activity, leading a discussion, sharing new information, or making an assessment of a particular problem, the worker is directing the group's action. Directing skills are most effective when coupled with efforts to increase members' participation and input (Stogdill, 1974). The worker should not use directing skills without obtaining members' approval or without involving them in decisions about the direction the group should take to accomplish its goals. The worker should be aware of how each member reacts to being directed in a new component of the group's work. For example, in directing role play in a remedial group designed to help teenagers learn how to handle angry feelings more effectively, the worker should be aware of how the action will affect each member. Depending on the way they express their anger, some group members may benefit from playing certain roles more than other members. Others may benefit most from observing the action.

Advice, Suggestions, and Instructions

Another cluster of action skills that both workers and members can use is giving advice, suggestions, and instructions. Workers use these skills to help group members acquire new behaviors, understand problems, or change problematic situations. Advice, suggestions, and instructions, however, are infrequently provided by professionals in practice. Studies have revealed, for example, that advice, suggestions, and instructions constitute 1 percent to 5 percent of all communications made by practitioners (Boatman, 1975; Mullen, 1969; Pinkus, 1968; Smith, Tobin, & Toseland, 1992).

Nonetheless, advice is expected and wanted by many clients, especially those of lower socioeconomic status (Aronson & Overall, 1966; Davis, 1975; Mayer & Timms, 1970). Further, these skills appear to have some beneficial effect in helping clients formulate new ideas and approaches to resolving problems (Davis, 1975; Ewalt & Kutz, 1976; Fortune, 1979; Reid & Shapiro, 1969; Smith et al., 1992). For example, in a review of studies of various therapeutic mechanisms of change, Emrick, Lassen, and Edwards (1977) reported that advice giving was strongly associated with positive changes in clients.

Advice, suggestions, and instructions should be timed appropriately so that group members are ready to accept them. They must be clear and geared to the comprehension level of the members for whom they are intended. For example, in an educational group for training Department of Social Service workers to lead parenting groups, each group worker should be sure the material is at a level that will be readily understood by the worker's clients. Similarly, a group of teenage parents who have not completed high school requires a presentation of ideas, advice, suggestions, and instructions quite different from a presentation to a group of highly educated women who have delayed child rearing until their early thirties.

Workers should also be sensitive to the language and culture of the members of their groups. Certain words in English might not translate appropriately or with the same meaning in another language. Further, the cultural heritage of a population may influence how such individuals receive and decode messages sent from the worker.

The worker should not act alone in giving advice, suggestions, and instructions. This sets the worker off as an expert who may be seen as too directive. The worker should encourage members to share information, advice, and instructions with each other. Middleman (1978) and Shulman (1999) refer to this as the worker's reaching for feelings and information that members may be hesitant to disclose.

To encourage members to share information and advice with each other, the worker should facilitate the development of helping networks in which members share their life experiences, information, and resources, as well as their opinions and views. One of the distinct advantages of group work over individual work is the ability of group members to rely on one another for help in solving problems and accomplishing goals. Experience suggests that well-established helping networks often continue outside the group long after the group experience has ended. For example, a worker who formed a support and parenting skills education group for single parents in an inner city area later helped the group members form a child-care cooperative that flourished for years after the 12-week parenting skills group ended. Similarly, the members of a support group for family members of patients recently discharged from inpatient settings in the inner city were helped by the worker to form a local chapter of a national welfare rights organization.

Providing Resources

Organizations that sponsor groups have access to a wide variety of resources such as medical treatment, home health care, financial assistance, job and rehabilitation counseling, family planning, and financial management consultation, which the worker can make available to members. Making skillful use of these resources through accurate assessment and referral can be helpful to group members. The worker can also help members to explore resources used by other members of the group. In this way, the cumulative knowledge of all group members can be used to help a member become familiar with and connect to a needed resource.

In task groups, workers can also provide a variety of resources for members. They can influence the environment in which a group works, either directly or indirectly, to make it easier for the group to accomplish its tasks. Workers may have access to important people or action groups that can give the group's work proper consideration. In addition, because task groups are often composed of members with a variety of skills and resources, members can also help one another achieve the group's goals.

Modeling, Role Playing, Rehearsing, and Coaching

The action skills of modeling, role playing, and rehearsing situations in the group can be helpful in both task and treatment groups. *Modeling* refers to the worker or a member demonstrating behaviors in a particular situation so that others in the group can observe what to do and how to do it. For example, the worker in an assertion training group might demonstrate how to respond to a spouse who has become quite angry. In another group, the worker might model caring and concern by going over to a group member who has begun to cry and placing an arm around the member's shoulder.

Role playing refers to having group members act out a situation with each other's help. The two primary purposes of role playing are to assess members' skill in responding to an interpersonal situation and to help members improve particular responses. Responses can be improved through feedback, rehearsal of a new response, and coaching from the worker or other group members during rehearsals (Etcheverry, Siporin, & Toseland, 1987).

Although role plays are commonly used so that members gain experience in the protected environment of the group before attempting a new response outside the group, role playing can also be used to improve responses in future situations. For example, in a group for couples trying to improve their relationships, the worker might ask each couple to role play an argument they had during the past week. During the role play, the worker asks each couple to switch roles so that each partner could experience how the other felt, thought, and acted in the situation. Role play can help members understand their partner's behavior and how their own behavior influenced their partner. The couples can use the feedback they received to experiment with new and better ways to communicate during an argument. In this way, the couples learn new communication skills and begin to use improved ways of responding to each other during disagreements.

Rehearsing refers to practicing a new behavior or response based on the feedback received after a role play. Because it is difficult to learn new behaviors or to diminish less adaptive but habituated behavior patterns, a member may have to practice a new response several times.

Coaching is the use of verbal and physical instructions to help members reproduce a particular response. For example, members of a group for the mentally retarded might practice expressing their feelings during interpersonal interactions. As members practice, the worker coaches them by giving instructions and demonstrating how to improve their responses. Additional information about different role-playing techniques is presented in Chapter 9.

Confrontation Skills

Confrontation is a useful action skill for overcoming resistance and motivating members. Confrontation is the ability to clarify, examine, and challenge behaviors to help members overcome distortions and discrepancies among behaviors, thoughts, and feelings (Egan, 1998; Toseland & Spielberg, 1982). Confrontation skills should be used only when the worker has carefully assessed the situation and decided that the confrontation will not be rejected by a member. If a member is not ready to examine thoughts, behaviors, or feelings, the member may react negatively to a confrontation by becoming passive, angry, or hostile.

Because confrontations are potent and emotionally charged, workers should be prepared for strong reactions. In certain circumstances, workers may want to make gentle or tentative confrontations to explore a member's reactions before making direct, full-scale confrontation. Although confrontations are often associated with pointing out a member's flaws or weaknesses, they can be used to help members recognize strengths and assets. For example, in a remedial group for psychiatric inpatients, a depressed group member who is self-deprecating might be confronted and challenged to begin to recognize his strengths and assets. Similarly, a member of a growth group might be confronted by pointing out how her words differ from her actions.

Resolving Conflicts

One of the most important action skills is helping resolve conflicts among the members of the group and with individuals and social systems outside the group. Group members may conflict with one another for a variety of reasons. For example, in a delegate council, members may represent constituencies that have quite different concerns, interests, and goals. In a treatment team, group members' responsibilities for different work functions and tasks may cause conflict or competition, particularly if resources for accomplishing a task are limited.

Many of the models of group development described in the previous chapter indicate that conflict may arise among members as the group develops. The worker should help the group view conflict as a healthy process that can clarify the purposes and goals of the group and the way members can work together.

Although conflicts inevitably arise, skillful group facilitation can help avoid unnecessary conflicts and resolve disagreements before they turn into hostile disputes. To help avoid unnecessary conflicts, workers can suggest that the group develop and maintain rules for participation. These rules are frequently expressed in early contractual discussions with members. Sometimes these rules, which should be developed with the participation of all group members, are stated in a written agreement that all members sign at the beginning of a new group. An example of such a written agreement is shown in Figure 4.3. Having agreed-on rules clearly written and displayed on a blackboard or flip chart is particularly helpful in children's groups. Children enjoy setting rules for their group, and, with the guidance of a leader, they can help each other follow rules they have made.

When conflicts arise among members, the worker may also use moderating, negotiating, mediating, or arbitrating skills to resolve disagreements before they turn into hostile disputes. Moderating skills help workers keep meetings within specified bounds so that conflict is avoided. Negotiating skills are used to help members come to an agreement or an understanding when initial opinions differ. Mediating skills are used when two or more members are in conflict and action is necessary to help them reach an agreement and resolve the dispute. Arbitration skills involve having an authoritative third person meet with the group. This person listens to the dispute and binds the members to a settlement. Arbitration is sometimes used in task groups that have reached an impasse when working on a labor contract. Specific methods that workers can use to help resolve conflicts in groups are described more fully in Chapters 8 and 10.

Members may also come into conflict with forces outside the group. The members of therapy groups, for example, often expect workers to provide guid-

FIGURE 4.3 ■ *Rules for Group Participation*

I, the undersigned, agree to:

1. Attend each group session or call one day before the group meeting to explain my absence.

2. Not talk about anything that occurs in the group to anyone outside the group, unless it applies only to myself and no other group member.

3. Carry out all assignments agreed to in the group between group sessions.

4. Speak in turn so that everyone gets a chance to talk.

5. Give the group two weeks' notice before terminating my participation.

_____   _____
          Name   Date

ance about how to resolve conflicts with spouses, other family members, friends, fellow workers, and acquaintances. In attempting to be more assertive, a member of a therapy group might receive hostile, angry, or aggressive responses from family members or friends. In such a case, the worker might attempt to reduce the conflict by intervening directly in the situation or by helping the member develop the skills necessary to overcome the conflict alone. When the conflict is an inevitable by-product of a change the member wishes to make outside the group, the worker can help the member feel comfortable with the conflict until a new state of equilibrium is achieved.

Sometimes it is helpful for the worker to meet with people outside the group to resolve a member's conflict. For example, a worker might meet with the parents of an adolescent group member to discuss how the parents set limits and rules for their child. In other cases, workers can prepare members for the reactions they may encounter outside the group. For example, a worker can help members learn how to respond to potential rejection or hostility when they are more assertive than usual with a particular person. Preparing members for what to expect in a wide range of situations and settings also helps ensure their success when they are using newly learned behaviors in unfamiliar settings or situations.

Workers may also need to resolve conflicts between the group as a whole and the larger society. For example, workers may help resolve conflicts between tenants' associations and housing authorities, welfare rights groups and county departments of social services, or support groups for individuals with chronic illnesses and health-care providers. Moderating, negotiating, mediating, and arbitrating skills can often be used successfully in these situations. However, in some situations, mobilization and social action skills (described in Chapter 11) may have to be used to resolve a conflict.

Learning Group Leadership Skills

Persons who are training to become group workers should begin by becoming thoroughly familiar with the theoretical knowledge about groups as a whole and the way members and leaders function in groups. However, to integrate theoretical knowledge about group dynamics with practical experience, trainees should (1) participate in exercises and role plays illustrating how group dynamics operate, (2) observe others leading and being members of groups, (3) examine their participation as members of natural or formed groups, and (4) lead or colead a group in a supervised field practicum.

In the classroom, trainees can learn to lead groups under a variety of conditions and circumstances by combining didactic and experiential methods of learning. Didactic material should expose trainees to the array of groups they may be called on to lead. Therefore, lectures, discussions, and examples should include groups in several settings with different purposes and clientele. Lecture material can be supplemented with films and videotapes of different social work groups in action. A list of available films is presented in Appendix B.

Cognitive knowledge is, by itself, insufficient for effective social work. Training should include exercises and role plays to illustrate and demonstrate the material presented during lectures. Often laboratory groups can be formed to help trainees practice the material that has been presented. Lab groups give trainees a sense of what it is like to be a member of a group. Also, leadership can be rotated in a lab group so that all members are responsible for leading a group at least once.

Laboratory group experiences can be enhanced by the use of video and audio equipment. These devices give trainees feedback about their verbal and nonverbal behavior as they participate in or lead a meeting. Tapes made during labs can be reviewed by trainees and the lab leader during supervisory sessions to help members develop their leadership skills.

Trainees can also learn how to lead a group by observing a group or by becoming a member of an existing group in the community. The trainee learns vicariously by observing the leader's behavior. The leader acts as a model of leadership skills for the member.

Learning also occurs through critiques of the group's process. Critiquing the group helps ensure that trainees do not accept all the activities of the group's leader without question. It gives trainees an opportunity to examine the development of a group over time and to observe the effects of leadership skills in action. It is relatively easy to structure lab groups so that part of the group's time is spent analyzing the group process, but trainees may not have this opportunity in community groups. Therefore, to achieve maximum benefit from participation in a community group, trainees should have an opportunity to discuss their experiences as members of a group in supervisory sessions or in the classroom.

When trainees become familiar with basic skills in leading a group through these experiences, they are ready for a field practicum. The field practicum may include leading several sessions of a group, coleading a group, or leading an entire group while receiving supervision. For purposes of learning about group leadership skills, group supervision is preferable to individual supervision because the supervisor models group leadership skills while reviewing a trainee's work with a group. Rivas and Toseland (1981) have found that a training group is an effective way to provide supervision. Methods for conducting group supervision are discussed by Rose (1989). If not enough practicum sites are available, trainees can form their own task or treatment groups by providing group services to students or community residents (Rivas & Toseland, 1981).

Before leading a group, it is helpful for trainees to discuss their concerns about the first meeting. Lonergan (1989) reports that these concerns can include (1) unmanageable resistance exhibited by members, such as not talking; (2) losing control of the group because of members' excessive hostility or acting out; (3) inability to deal with specific behaviors such as a member dropping out of the group capriciously, members dating each other, or individuals making sexual advances within the group or between group meetings; (4) overwhelming dependency demands by members; and (5) lack of attendance and the disintegration of the group. Because trainees react differently to their first group experience, supervisors should explore each individual's concerns and help them deal with their anxiety by discussing likely group reactions and reviewing what could be done in the unlikely event that a trainee's worst concern is realized. For additional information about effective methods for learning group leadership skills, see Berger (1996).

Leadership Style

It is important to recognize that, although leadership skills can be learned, they are not applied in a mechanical, objective fashion. Group work is a subjective encounter among the members of the group, all of whom have distinct personalities, viewpoints, and methods of relating to objective reality. Workers and members bring expectations, preferences, and styles of relating to the group. Although these may be modified during the course of interaction, they continuously color and shape the evolving interaction and the skills that workers use to facilitate the group. As Goldstein (1988) states, "As people enter into a group and take part in shaping its purpose and goals, the underlying premises that they bring to the encounter and their ways of perceiving, thinking and interpreting will inexorably determine how the process unfolds" (p. 25).

The degree to which styles of relating influence what occurs in the group depends on the nature of the group. The more a group is structured and the more it is focused on impersonal issues that the members have little stake in, the less likely group processes are to be affected by the personalities of the individuals. For example, in a delegate council using parliamentary procedure, the individual personalities of agency representatives are likely to have relatively little influence on group decisions. In contrast, Reid (1997) aptly points out that in therapy groups, "each [person] brings to the [group] experience a history of relating to others, sometimes with success and at other times without. In this therapeutic alliance group members may react to the therapist as if he or she were a significant figure out of their own original family. Similarly, the leader may react in exactly the same way, projecting onto others his or her own unresolved feelings and conflicts" (pp. 105–106).

In the psychoanalytic tradition, projection of feelings by members onto the leader is called *transference*. Projection of feelings onto members by the leader is called *countertransference*.

To become an effective group leader it is not sufficient, therefore, to learn group leadership skills without paying attention to how they are applied. It is essential for leaders to become self-reflective practitioners who consider carefully the meaning of their interactions with all members of the group. One of the hallmarks of an effective leader is the ability and willingness to examine the effect of personal beliefs, expectations, preferences, personality, style of relating, and subjective experience of reality on a particular group. Effective leaders are not afraid to explore with members, supervisors, or colleagues the possible ramifications of their behavior in a group. They observe carefully and think deeply about the meaning of members' reactions to particular interactions.

The first step in helping leaders become more aware of the effect of their style of interaction is for them to do a self-assessment of their strengths and weaknesses as a leader. Workshops around the country often begin by asking participants to complete the Leadership Comfort Scale (LCS) shown in Figure 4.4. The LCS allows participants to rate their degree of comfort with 10 situations that group leaders frequently experience. Participants are also asked to write down their responses to a series of open-ended questions, such as:

1. Describe what you perceive to be your major strengths and weaknesses as a leader.
2. What types of group members make you feel uncomfortable?
3. What situations or events during group meetings do you find particularly difficult to deal with?
4. What feedback have you received from others about your leadership skills?
5. What steps have you taken to improve your leadership skills? What steps have you considered but not yet taken?

Participants' anonymous answers to the LCS are tabulated and the aggregate answers are presented on a flip chart or blackboard. Volunteers who are willing are asked to share their answers to the open-ended questions, which inevitably leads

FIGURE 4.4 ■ *Leadership Comfort Scale*

Indicate your feelings when the following situations arise in the group. Circle the appropriate feeling.

1. Dealing with silence	Comfortable	Uncomfortable
2. Dealing with negative feelings from members	Comfortable	Uncomfortable
3. Having little structure in a group	Comfortable	Uncomfortable
4. Dealing with ambiguity of purpose	Comfortable	Uncomfortable
5. Having to self-disclose your feelings to the group	Comfortable	Uncomfortable
6. Experiencing high self-disclosure among members	Comfortable	Uncomfortable
7. Dealing with conflict in the group	Comfortable	Uncomfortable
8. Having your leadership authority questioned	Comfortable	Uncomfortable
9. Being evaluated by group members	Comfortable	Uncomfortable
10. Allowing members to take responsibility for the group	Comfortable	Uncomfortable

to a lively discussion of difficult leadership situations and participants' strengths and weaknesses in dealing with them. The discussion also helps point out the diversity of responses to challenging leadership situations.

Completing the Beliefs About Structure Scale (BASS), shown in Figure 4.5, can further the process of self-assessment. When completing the BASS, workshop participants sometimes state that their answers depend on the purpose of the group, the types of group members, and so forth. Leadership is interactive, but individuals have preferences about the degree of structure they are most comfortable with. Participants should be asked to respond to the inventory in a way that best describes their natural tendencies and preferences.

After completing the BASS, participants can be asked to total the number of items they circled in column A and column B and to form two groups—one for those who had higher column A scores favoring a higher level of structure, and one for those who had higher column B scores favoring a lower level of structure. Participants in each group are asked to discuss why they preferred a higher or lower level of structure. They may also be asked to prepare for a debate with members of the other group about the benefits of their approach to structuring the work of the group.

FIGURE 4.5 ■ *Beliefs About Structure Scale (BASS)*

Circle the statement in Column A or B that best describes your preference when running a group.

Column A	Column B
Time-limited group	Open-ended group
High structure/rules	Low structure/rules
Formal contract	Informal contract
Leader sets group purpose	Members decide purpose
Focus on member goals	Focus on group process
Leader-centered authority	Shared authority
Closed membership	Open membership
Homogeneous membership	Heterogeneous membership
Use of program activities	Use of open discussion
Focus on member behavior	Focus on meaning of communication
Directive leadership	Nondirective leadership

Summarize what you have learned about your style from the above choices. What are the major themes that emerge about your preferences for a particular level of structure within a group?

Workshop participants are also asked to complete the How Members Achieve Change Scale, which is presented in Figure 4.6. Once this scale is completed, different approaches to helping members change are discussed. For example, the importance of insight in psychoanalytic group psychotherapy is contrasted with the

FIGURE 4.6 ■ *How Members Achieve Change Scale*

Group leadership style is partly a function of how one believes members achieve change in their lives and how one believes the group should take responsibility for helping members change. Answer the following questions about these dynamics. Avoid using the term *it all depends*. Instead, choose the answer that best expresses your natural preference or inclination.

1. Do people achieve change best through insight or action?
2. Do people achieve change best by focusing on their affect (feelings) or their cognition (thoughts)?
3. When helping a member to achieve change, would you concentrate on changing the member's behavior or the member's thoughts?
4. When evaluating whether a member was making progress in the change efforts, would you assess whether the member did what the member wanted, what you wanted, or what society wanted?
5. Is it more important to give your attention to group content or group process?
6. Do you think the responsibility for the functioning of the group rests with the leader or the members?

Choose the statement that best characterizes your opinion. (circle one)

7. The purpose for group work is:
   a. Raising social consciousness, social responsibility, informed citizenship, and social and political action.
   b. Restoring and rehabilitating group members who are behaving dysfunctionally.
   c. Forming a mutual aid system among members to achieve maximum adaptation and socialization.
8. The role of the worker is to be a:
   a. Role model and enabler for responsible citizenship.
   b. Change agent, problem solving with members to meet their goals.
   c. Mediator between the needs of the members and the needs of the group and larger society.
9. Which methods would you tend to use in the group?
   a. Discussion, participation, consensus, group task
   b. Structured exercises, direct influence in and out of group
   c. Shared authority, support, building a positive group culture

Based on your responses to the previous nine questions, summarize your preferences for how to help members change.

importance of identifying here-and-now feelings in gestalt therapy. Similarly, the importance of cognition in cognitive therapy is contrasted with the importance of action in behavior therapy. Participants can also be asked to provide examples of the methods they use to help members change. For example, participants who prefer to help group members change through action strategies might describe role-playing or psychodrama procedures that they have found to be particularly effective.

Workshops also discuss preferences for process-oriented or outcome-oriented leadership styles and preferences for member-centered or leader-centered styles of leadership. Discussion is not intended to promote a particular style of leadership or even to help leaders identify what style of leadership they are most comfortable with. Rather, the aim is to encourage leaders to become more self-reflective, to consider their natural tendencies and preferences, and to gain greater insight into how their natural tendencies and preferences affect their interaction with group members.

COLEADERSHIP

Coleadership presents a dilemma for the practicing group worker (Kolodny, 1980). Do the benefits of coleadership exceed its potential disadvantages? An entire issue of the journal *Social Work with Groups* has been devoted to this topic.[1] Although there is little empirical evidence to suggest that two leaders are better than one (Yalom, 1995), there are many clinical reports of the benefits of having two leaders (Cooper, 1976; Davis & Lohr, 1971; Levine, 1980; MacLennon, 1965; McGee & Schuman, 1970; Roller & Nelson, 1991; Schlenoff & Busa, 1981; Starak, 1981). Among the most frequently cited benefits of coleadership are the following:

- Leaders have a source of support.
- Leaders have a source of feedback and an opportunity for professional development.
- A leader's objectivity is increased through alternative frames of references.
- Inexperienced leaders can receive training.
- Group members are provided with models for appropriate communication, interaction, and resolution of disputes.
- Leaders have assistance during therapeutic interventions, particularly during role plays, simulations, and program activities.
- Leaders have help setting limits and structuring the group experience.

This list suggests several ways in which coleadership can be helpful. For the novice worker, probably the greatest benefit of coleadership is having a supportive partner who understands how difficult it is to be an effective leader. As Galinsky and Schopler (1980) point out, "The support of a compatible co-leader lessens the strains of dealing with difficult and often complicated group interactions" (p. 54).

[1]*Social Work with Groups* (1980), 3 (4).

During group meetings, coleaders help each other facilitate the work of the group. Between group meetings, they share their feelings about the group and their roles in it. In addition to supporting each other's efforts at group leadership, coleaders can share feedback with each other about their mutual strengths and weaknesses and thereby foster each other's professional growth and development.

Coleadership can also be helpful because it allows workers to share alternative frames of reference regarding the interaction that has taken place in the group, which helps fill in gaps in each worker's memory of events and helps each view the interaction from a different perspective. This process, in turn, may lead to a more complete and accurate assessment as well as to more adequate planning when the coleaders prepare for future group meetings.

Another area in which coleadership has potential benefits is in intervening in a group. Coleadership provides a group with the benefit of having two experts who can help with problem solving. It provides two models of behavior for members to identify with and helps in role plays, simulation, and program activities engaged in by the group. Coleadership can increase workers' abilities to establish and enforce limits as long as they share common goals (Davis & Lohr, 1971). Coleaders also have the opportunity to structure their roles to meet the needs of members. For example, one worker can focus on members' socioemotional needs and the other worker can focus on members' task needs. In its most refined form, coleadership can be used strategically to promote therapeutic goals in a powerful and effective fashion. For example, in a thoughtful article about the benefits of male and female coleadership of spouse abuse groups, Nosko and Wallace (1997) point out that male and female coleaders who are perceived as different but equal can be effective at structuring their leadership and interaction to promote the resolution of faulty gender socialization among members. Effective coleaders use their relationship with each other to model effective interpersonal interactions that members can emulate both within and outside of the group.

Despite the benefits, coleadership has some potential disadvantages. Because it requires the time of two leaders, coleadership is expensive. Leaders must coordinate their actions in planning for the group. Between group sessions, communication can be a problem if workers do not make a concerted effort to find the time to discuss their work together (Herzog, 1980). If leaders do not function well together, they may not serve as therapeutic role models for members (Davis & Lohr, 1971). Yalom (1995) recommends that coleaders have equal status and experience. He suggests that the apprenticeship format—that is, training new group leaders by placing them in groups with experienced leaders—may create conflict and tension.

Conflict between coleaders can have detrimental effects on the outcome of a group (Cooper, 1976; Edelwich & Brodsky, 1992; Yalom, 1995). Members may be able to play one leader against the other or avoid working on difficult issues. When coleaders experience conflict with one another, it can be helpful to resolve the conflict in the group. This lets members know that the leaders are aware of the conflict and are able to work together to resolve it. It also enables the coleaders to act as models by demonstrating appropriate conflict-resolution strategies.

Galinsky and Schopler (1980) caution that, in some situations, it may not be helpful to resolve a conflict between coleaders in the group. For example, when conflicts are deep-seated and when there is little hope of a successful resolution, conflicts may be better handled in supervisory sessions. There is also a danger that conflict resolution can go awry, such as when members are pulled into the conflict and asked to take sides. It is also not a good idea to express conflict in early group meetings because this may add to the tensions that members are already experiencing (Yalom, 1995).

The decision about whether to resolve a conflict in a group should depend on its potential effect on members. Because members are usually aware of conflicts between coleaders, it is generally preferable to resolve them within the group, especially if the resolution process is amicable and not too distressing for members. When conflict is resolved outside the group, some members may not be aware that resolution has occurred. Also, resolving a conflict outside the group does not enhance members' conflict-resolution skills. Additional information about conflict-resolution skills is provided in Chapters 8 and 10.

Because of the lack of empirical evidence about its effectiveness, the benefits and drawbacks of coleadership should be carefully considered before two leaders are used in a group. In situations in which it is especially important to have models who represent different points of view, it may be important to have coleaders. For example, in a group of couples, it can be useful to have both male and female leaders. In other situations, however, the expense of coleadership or the incompatibility of potential coleaders may negate any potential benefits.

When the decision is reached to colead a group, it is essential that coleaders meet together regularly to plan for the group and to discuss group process issues that arise as the group develops (Davis & Lohr, 1971). To avoid coleaders' becoming too busy to meet together, it is helpful if they schedule a specific time to meet after each group meeting. During these meetings, coleaders should review what they did well in working together, what difficulties they experienced, how they plan to work together during the next meeting, and how members and the group as a whole are progressing. Coleaders should be particularly aware of any attempts to divide their effort that could result in working toward different purposes or on behalf of different group factions. Coleaders should schedule their review meeting soon after a group meeting because they are more likely to remember what has occurred, and they have more time to prepare for the next meeting.

To avoid the difficulties that may be associated with coleadership, it is recommended that coleaders feel at ease with one another's leadership style (Yalom, 1995). According to Davis and Lohr (1971), coleaders should be selected for their complementary characteristics rather than for their similarity. This will help broaden the perspective used to assess the group and its members, provide an additional model of ways to handle problematic behaviors, and widen the scope of intervention strategies that may be used in the group.

Experience has shown that it is worse to have a coleader with whom one does not agree than to lead a group alone. Therefore, group workers should be cautious in choosing a coleader. Difficulties may arise when workers agree to colead

FIGURE 4.7 ■ *Issues to Talk Over with a Potential Coleader*

1. Describe your leadership style. Discuss whether your style is characteristically nurturing or confrontational, whether you tend to be a high-profile or a low-profile leader, and to what extent you are comfortable with spontaneity as contrasted with sticking with a planned agenda.

2. Describe your strengths and weaknesses as a leader. What makes you feel uncomfortable when leading a group?

3. Describe your beliefs about how people change and grow, and how you will intervene in the group. For example, discuss your favorite interventions, and whether you typically intervene quickly or slowly, waiting for members of the group to engage in mutual aid.

4. Share your expectations for group accomplishments.

5. Discuss your respective roles in the group. Discuss specifically (1) where you will sit, (2) starting and ending group meetings, (3) how you will divide responsibility for any content you will be presenting, (4) what you will do about talkative and silent members, (5) scapegoating and gatekeeping, and (6) what you will do about lateness and absenteeism.

6. Discuss where, when, and how you will deal with conflict between you, and between either of you and the members of the group.

7. Discuss how you will deal with strong expressions of emotion such as crying and anger.

8. Is there anything that is nonnegotiable regarding your coleadership of a group?

a group without carefully considering whether they can work together effectively. Potential coleaders may want to examine each other's styles while leading a group or during team meetings before agreeing to colead a group. Figure 4.7 presents some issues to discuss before deciding to colead a group.

SUMMARY

This chapter focuses on leading task and treatment groups effectively. Although leadership is sometimes viewed as a function executed exclusively by the worker, leadership functions should be shared with group members. In this regard, the text distinguishes between the worker's role as the designated leader of the group and the leadership roles of group members that emerge as the group develops.

Leadership has been defined as the process of guiding the development of the group and its members to achieve goals that are consistent with the value base of social work practice. A worker's ability to guide group members depends on the power attributed to the worker by group members, by the supporting agency or organization, and by the larger society that sanctions the work of the group.

The power bases that can be used to guide the development of the group and its members include (1) connection power, (2) expert power, (3) information power, (4) legitimate power, (5) referent power, (6) reward power, and (7) coercive power. Leaders vary in the degree to which they have access to each power base and the extent to which they use the power bases to guide the group.

Leadership is affected by a variety of situational factors that act in combination. Thus, there is no one correct way to lead all groups. Rather, leadership methods should vary according to the particular group a worker is leading. This chapter reviews the remedial, social goals, and reciprocal models of group leadership and examines several variables that affect group leadership. To help workers examine situational variables, the text describes an interactional model of group leadership. The model includes (1) the purpose of the group, (2) the type of problem the group is working on, (3) the environment in which the group is working, (4) the group as a whole, (5) the members of the group, and (6) the leader of the group.

It is essential that workers be familiar with a range of leadership skills that can be applied in many different types of groups and in many different settings. Skills include (1) facilitating group processes, (2) data gathering and assessment, and (3) action. Together, these skills constitute the core skills needed for effective leadership of task and treatment groups.

It is also essential that workers be aware of their leadership styles. A number of exercises are presented to help workers identify their preference for a particular leadership style and understand how their preferences influence their practice with treatment and task groups.

The chapter ends with an examination of coleadership. The benefits, drawbacks, and pitfalls of coleadership are described.

LEARNING ASSIGNMENTS

1. Observe two leaders. Using Table 4.1, describe the leaders' use of facilitating, data gathering, and action skills. Compare and contrast the skillfulness of each leader.
2. Complete the inventories shown in Figures 4.4, 4.5, and 4.6. Prepare a written description of what you learn about your leadership style.
3. Compare your leadership style with that of a classmate by using both your responses to Figures 4.4, 4.5, 4.6, and 4.7. How would the similarities and differences in your leadership styles affect your ability to colead a group? How would you work together to overcome differences in leadership styles before coleading a group?

chapter 5

Leadership and Diversity

Group leaders often work with people from a wide range of backgrounds. Diversity within the group can be based on a variety of characteristics such as race, ethnicity, culture, national origin, religion, social class, gender, sexual orientation, and disability. When differences exist among members or between the leader and members, leadership can be particularly challenging.

APPROACHES TO MULTICULTURAL GROUP WORK

It is helpful for leaders to develop a perspective on how to work with people whose backgrounds are different from their own. Such a perspective has been referred to as ethnic-sensitive practice (Devore & Schlesinger, 1999), minority practice (Lum, 1996), a cross-cultural approach (Green, 1999; Pinderhughes, 1979; Sue & Sue, 1990), and cultural/multicultural competence (Diller, 1999; Vasquez & Han, 1995). According to Pinderhughes (1995), cultural competence includes (1) the ability to perceive others through their own cultural lens, (2) knowledge of specific beliefs and values in the client's community, (3) personal comfort with differences, (4) a willingness to change previous ideas and stereotypes, (5) the ability to be flexible and adapt one's thinking and behavior in novel settings, and (6) the skill to sort through diverse information about a community to understand how it might apply to particular individuals. Green (1999) points out that cultural competence can be learned. An empirically based approach for learning about issues of race, gender, and class in groups is presented by Davis and Proctor (1989). More recently, Davis, Galinsky, and Schopler (1995) developed a comprehensive framework for leadership of multiracial groups that highlights areas of potential difficulty for group workers and suggests practice guidelines for selecting appropriate intervention techniques. Important aspects of their framework, recognize, anticipate, problem-solve (RAP), suggest the group leader should

1. Engage in ongoing self-assessment and assessment of the group, its members, and their environment
2. Anticipate potential sources of tension in composing the group, in formulating the purpose, and in structuring the group's work together
3. Intervene at the individual, group, and environmental levels to promote harmony and understanding; to resolve racial, ethnic, and cultural issues; and to involve members in confronting and resolving problems within and outside the group

Understanding the dynamics of race, ethnicity, and culture is essential for effective group work practice, but people also differ from each other in gender, social class, geographic background, educational and disability level, language, level of acculturation and assimilation, and age. Thus, in addition to learning practice principles for use with particular groups such as Native Americans (Marsiglia, Cross, & Mitchell-Enos, 1998; Weaver 1999) and African Americans (Aponte, Rivers, & Wohl, 1995), leaders can benefit from using a broader conceptual framework about diversity within groups, which includes

-   Developing cultural sensitivity
-   Assessing cultural influences on group behavior
-   Intervening with sensitivity to diversity

Developing Cultural Sensitivity

The terms *identity* and *culture* are often used to refer to the many ways people can differ. To develop a perspective on effective work with people of diverse cultural backgrounds, the group leader should engage in a process of self-exploration. Green (1999) describes this process as developing "cultural competence" (pp. 88–108) and suggests that workers who are culturally competent have an awareness of their own cultural limitations, are open to cultural differences, and acknowledge the integrity of other cultures. It is difficult to develop cultural competence in multiple cultures, and some argue that this is impossible. However, recognizing one's limitations is a positive step.

Workers can become more culturally sensitive by exploring their feelings about their own identity. Sometimes leaders fail to take into account how they experience their identity and how this might affect their interactions with members from other backgrounds. Among both leaders and members, there may be little acknowledgment of identity issues and how these issues affect values, beliefs, and skills, perhaps because of discomfort with the subject of identity or because leaders fear that raising identity issues may reduce cohesion within the group. However, to ignore differences within the group denies the background and self-identity of each member. Davis, Galinsky, and Schopler (1995) note, for example, that "whenever people of different races come together in groups, leaders can assume that race is an issue, but not necessarily a problem" (p. 155).

Leaders can also benefit from knowledge about how members define and identify themselves. Because the manifestation of racial, cultural, ethnic, and other identity variables is the prerogative of the member rather than of the leader, the leader should provide opportunities for members to discuss their identities. For example, the leader can ask, "How do our cultural backgrounds affect how assertive we are in our daily lives?" or "How can we use our differing ethnic backgrounds to brainstorm some innovative solutions to the problem we are discussing here?"

It is often helpful for the worker to frame the discussion of differences so that members can see the strengths of their backgrounds and how diversity is an asset to the group. After reviewing the empirical evidence about the performance of homogeneous versus heterogeneous groups, Forsyth (1999) points out that "the value of diversity has been verified in a wide range of performance settings" (p. 279). McLeod and colleagues (McLeod, Lobel, & Cox, 1996), for example, found that groups that included Asian Americans, African Americans, Latinos, and Whites outperformed groups that included only Whites. Similarly, Watson, Johnson, and Merritt (1998) found that diverse teams performed better than non-diverse teams. A heterogeneity of member characteristics is associated with a variety of perspectives, and a variety of perspectives is associated with high-quality idea production. It is important to keep in mind, however, that "diverse teams that actually utilized the variety of perspectives . . . outperformed the homogeneous teams, whereas diverse teams that did not utilize their diversity performed worse than the homogeneous teams" (McLeod, Lobel, & Cox, 1996, p. 261). This finding clearly suggests that group leaders not only promote diversity in group composition but also should develop skills in helping members to understand and work with the different perspectives and experiences brought to the group by members with diverse backgrounds (Garvin, 1998).

Members may have a variety of self-identity issues that affect their participation in the group (Vasquez & Han, 1995). Some members may have clear self-identification with one race, ethnicity, or background or may identify with more than one. Others may have little knowledge about their racial, ethnic, or cultural heritage. It can be helpful if the leader provides members with opportunities to describe how they experience their cultural background and whether they experience any identity conflicts. For example, one Latino member was asked by other members why she was continually tired during group meetings. The leader asked the member whether her family duties posed difficult time constraints on her schedule and was told that her cultural background directed that she was expected to complete her family duties before doing other activities outside the home.

Self-identity issues are also important in group work with gay, lesbian, bisexual, and transgendered group members. Groups can provide an important support network and can be helpful in problem solving regarding issues of isolation, prejudice, stereotyping, and coming out. Groups can also be helpful in addressing interpersonal issues that arise with initiation and integration into gay organizations and communities. Getzel (1998) and Peters (1997) present useful information for working with gay, lesbian, bisexual, and transgendered individuals in groups.

Although it is not possible for a group leader to know all the complexities of diverse cultures and backgrounds, it is helpful for leaders to become familiar with the backgrounds of client groups with whom they frequently work. Green (1999) suggests that knowledge can be gained through several methods. For example, the leader can research literature and other information to develop a personal knowledge base about people from different cultures. When working with a group composed of members from a particular culture, the leader can visit that cultural community, interview key respondents in the community, and become a participant observer.

The leader can also gain knowledge about a particular cultural community through the process of *social mapping,* in which formal and informal relationships among members of a community are systematically observed and analyzed. For example, a leader assigned to conduct an afterschool group that included several Hispanic members visited the local parish priest serving the Hispanic community and interviewed several members of the parish to gain a better understanding of the needs of young people in the community. In addition, the leader attended several social functions sponsored by the church and met with parents and other community members who provided the worker with new insights into the needs of Hispanic youth.

When the leader has little knowledge about a particular culture or background, it is helpful to become immersed in that culture. Living or spending a concentrated period of time in a cultural community can help the leader better understand the common values, norms of behavior, and worldviews held by members of that culture. Immersion also assists the leader in establishing credibility among members of the community, in developing relationships important for connecting members to resources outside the group, and in understanding the importance of natural helping networks.

Leaders should be open to the differences exhibited by diverse cultures. It is particularly important for leaders to be accepting and nonjudgmental about the values, lifestyles, beliefs, and behaviors of others and to recognize the value of difference and diversity (Diller, 1999). Because our society tends to value being assertive and decisive, suspending judgment, being nonjudgmental, and taking time to systematically evaluate persons are sometimes seen as signs of weakness. The leader can learn much about other cultures, however, by asking members for information and assistance in understanding their diverse backgrounds because members are in the best position to describe how they experience their self-identity.

It is also important to acknowledge the effect of societal attitudes on members of diverse groups. Leaders should keep in mind that members of minority groups continually experience prejudice, stereotyping, and overt and institutional discrimination. The reality of ethnic and racial superiority themes in our society, as well as classism, sexism, and the history of depriving certain groups of rights and resources, should all be considered when attempting to develop a perspective on diversity. For example, the leader of an educational group for parents of children with developmental disabilities might discuss the effect of societal attitudes toward the disabled and the effects of discrimination on the parents and their children. As members discuss this issue, the leader might encourage all members to share their experiences with other forms of discrimination because of race, ethnicity, or sexual orientation. These experiences can help the whole group acknowledge and confront prejudice and stereotypes and more fully understand the dynamics of discrimination.

It can be helpful for leaders to honestly explore their prejudices, biases, and stereotypical assumptions in working with people from diverse backgrounds. Williams (1992) suggests leaders themselves may go through stages of ethnocultural development in which they experience cultural resistance and "color blindness" before acknowledging the importance of cultural influences and achieving cultural sensitivity. Leaders should acknowledge such thoughts and feelings and work on correcting them. Attending workshops on cultural sensitivity, doing self-inventories, researching one's own cultural heritage, attending specific cultural activities in the community, and joining cultural associations and organizations can help the leader achieve a fuller sense of cultural self-awareness. These activities can also help leaders gain a sense of their strengths and weaknesses in dealing with diversity. McGrath and Axelson (1999) and Hogan-Garcia (1999), for example, describe many exercises that can be used to increase leaders' awareness, knowledge, and sensitivity when working with multicultural groups.

Assessing Cultural Influences on Group Behavior

It is important for the group leader to recognize that the cultural backgrounds of members can have a profound effect on how they participate in the group. Assessing the cultural influences on group behavior requires constant vigilance throughout the life of a group. Diversity among members from differing cultural backgrounds as well as among members from the same cultural background requires careful consideration. Stereotyping members on the basis of preconceived notions of cultural behavior is an ineffective approach. Members must be individualized and differentially assessed. As Chau (1992) suggests, cultural sensitivity in assessing members is a prerequisite for becoming an effective group leader.

Early in the planning stage of a group, the benefits of matching member and leader backgrounds should be considered. There is some evidence that minority clients express a preference for ethnically similar workers (Atkinson & Lowe, 1995). However, there is little firm evidence that matching client and worker backgrounds leads to more effective treatment (Atkinson & Lowe, 1995; Proctor

& Davis, 1994; Sexton & Whiston, 1994; Sue, Zane, & Young, 1994). Also, there are benefits to having persons with different backgrounds interact, and practical difficulties often limit supervisors' choices in matching leaders and members.

Regardless of whether matching is attempted, some differences in the backgrounds of members and between members and the leader are likely. Therefore, when one plans a group, it is important for the leader to consider how members' backgrounds are likely to affect their participation in the group. For example, it is helpful to assess how potential members from differing cultural backgrounds will understand the purpose of the group. Members with different backgrounds bring differing expectations and experiences and that can affect how they view the group's purposes and the way work is conducted in the group. Confusion about the purpose of the group can lead to members' frustration and anxiety in the group's early stages.

The leader should also consider how members' backgrounds are likely to interact with the sponsorship of the group. The worker should consider, for example, how the sponsoring agency is viewed by members from different backgrounds. It is also important to consider how accessible the agency is, both physically and psychologically, to potential members. As Davis, Galinsky, and Schopler (1995) note, ethnic and socioeconomic boundaries of neighborhoods may be difficult for members to cross. When the sponsoring agency is perceived as being in a neighborhood that does not welcome persons from differing cultures, the leader may need to reach out to members or deal with members' perceptions of institutional or neighborhood prejudice and discrimination before continuing with further planning efforts.

When recruiting members, the leader should consider how to optimize outreach efforts. For example, in certain ethnic neighborhoods, key community members such as clergy, political leaders, and neighborhood elders may play an important part in helping the worker to gain support for the group and to reach potential members.

When composing a diverse group, the worker should consider how members from differing cultural groups are likely to relate to each other and to the leader. The literature on group composition gives suggestions for composing a diverse group (Brown & Mistry, 1994; Davis, Galinsky, & Schopler, 1995; Davis, Strube, & Cheng, 1995; McLeod, Lobel, & Cox, 1996). Davis, Galinsky, and Schopler (1995) suggest that workers need to be sensitive to racial composition to overcome tension. In addition, they warn that marked imbalance among members with one type of characteristic can cause problems of subgrouping or domination by members of one particular background. When reviewing the strengths of same-sex or same-race groups, Brown and Mistry (1994) noted that same-sex groups have advantages when the group task is associated with issues of personal identity, social oppression, and empowerment or issues of personal and political change.

A complete assessment of group members should consider the larger environmental context in which members live and how that context can influence behavior within the group (Chau, 1992). Davis, Galinsky, and Schopler (1995) list several environmental factors that can be considered sources of tension among members from diverse backgrounds—the climate of society, events in the members' neighborhoods, and the sponsoring organization's reputation for responsiveness to racial concerns. In addition, the direct experience of racism, sexism, and other forms of oppression can have profound effects on members' behavior. For example, in a group for resettled refugees, one member had difficulty trusting and self-disclosing in the group. The leader helped the member verbalize the torture, civil disorder, and fear she experienced in her country of origin. Through the discussion, the leader developed a fuller understanding of how the member's behavior in the group was influenced by the context of her cultural background.

It is also wise to keep in mind that members bring preferred patterns of behavior, values, and language to the group (Axelson, 1999). They also bring with them experiences with oppression and particular feelings about themselves, their group identity, and the larger society. When problems such as member dissatisfaction or conflict among members occur, the leader should keep in mind that the problems may be caused by cultural differences, not by an individual member's characteristics or flaws in group processes. For example, some members of a group became upset when an African American member became animated when discussing an issue of perceived racism. The members talked about their reaction to what they perceived as the member's loud, angry demeanor. The African American member explained, however, that this was a culturally acceptable way of expressing herself in the Caribbean community in which she grew up.

Several factors can interfere with the process of learning about how cultural background affects members' behavior in the group. The leader may fail to recognize that cultural differences exist or may diminish their importance. Facing difference is a difficult process, and leaders may think recognizing and expressing difference among members will cause conflict within the group. The leader may also fail to recognize differences among members of the same cultural group by assuming that all members of that culture have common behavioral characteristics and thereby overgeneralize and stereotype members with a common cultural heritage. Among Hispanic Americans, for example, there are wide differences in life experiences for people from a Mexican American background and people from Puerto Rico. Similarly, there are differences between African Americans with ancestry from different regions of Africa and African Americans with ancestry from Jamaica, Puerto Rico, and South America. It should not be assumed that all members of a common heritage share all perceptions, abilities, and characteristics. It should also be noted that even if members share a common cultural background, major differences in economic status may influence how the members experience the group. Different patterns and degrees of acculturation and assimilation also have a profound impact on the way cultural heritages are expressed in a group.

The leader should assess how members' backgrounds are likely to affect the way they experience communication and interaction patterns, cohesion, social controls, and the overall group culture. To assess communication and interaction patterns, it is important for the leader to understand the language, symbols, and nonverbal communication patterns of people from different cultural backgrounds. For example, in leading her first group with Chinese American members, a worker learned that group members from this cultural background felt uncomfortable with some of the attending behaviors she had learned in her social work education. Through some gentle probing and consultation with persons from that community, she learned that her direct eye contact, forward body position, and open body position were intimidating and communicated a level of disrespect to some members.

Johnson (1997) suggests that assessing communication and interaction patterns requires language sensitivity, knowledge of words and expressions that are appropriate and inappropriate in communicating with diverse groups. The leader should also have an awareness of the stylistic elements of communication, including how members of diverse cultural backgrounds communicate. For example, because of their respect for the authority of the leader's status and position in the group, some Asian Americans rely heavily on the group leader, especially in the first few sessions. Some groups of Native Americans may consider it impolite to give opinions in the group, and such attitudes may be mislabeled as resistance by the leader or by non-Native American members.

The group leader should strive to become aware of the nuances of messages sent by members, including how nonverbal messages differ across various cultures. People from different backgrounds use body language, gestures, and expressions to accompany and define the meaning of the verbal messages they send. In addition, the leader should consider how cultural groups differ in their use of space, that is, whether distance or closeness is the norm, and what other nonverbal communication norms govern interaction in the culture. It is also helpful for leaders to learn the language of members from diverse cultures. Earnest attempts to learn even rudimentary language skills are often respected by group members, an important factor in developing a trusting, professional helping relationship with members.

The leader should be aware of differing interaction patterns used by members of diverse cultural groups. Members from some cultural backgrounds may favor a member-to-leader pattern of interaction; others may favor a member-to-member pattern that supports mutual aid among members in the group. In task groups, members from diverse groups may have differing views of status hierarchies, which can affect interaction patterns between members and the leader. For example, in a committee planning a charity fundraising event, Chinese American members hesitated to criticize the behavior of a member who was monopolizing the group. The leader learned that the Chinese American members were hesitant to bring up their feelings because the monopolizing member was a person of advanced age and status in the community. According to Chinese American cultural heritage, interactions with older, high-status persons require respect. Criticism was not an acceptable behavior.

When the group has a membership drawn from many cultural groups, the leader should assess how subgrouping patterns may affect the group processes. Sociometric patterns can be influenced by cultural background, and this information is useful in assessing the behavior of members in the group and the behavior of the group as a whole. In a training group for college peer counselors, some members expressed their concerns about why most African American members sat together and communicated among themselves. The leader pointed out that cultural, racial, and ethnic groups often form informal subgroups on the basis of mutual interests and on common characteristics and experiences. The leader helped members to understand that members from minority groups on campus may also have needs for grouping as a protective, security-giving behavior. Through program activities and discussions, the leader helped all members of the group interact and become better acquainted.

The worker should consider the expectations and motivations that members from different cultural backgrounds bring to the group. For example, cohesion can be influenced by member expectations, which, in turn, can be influenced by the cultural background of members. In a support group for caregivers, some members with Hispanic backgrounds did not expect to divulge private family matters or publicly complain about their role as caregivers, and this affected how they bonded with other group members. If the cultural characteristics of members differ widely and are not explicitly taken into consideration, a climate of togetherness and a common sense of group goals can be difficult to achieve and the overall cohesion of the group is affected.

The leader should explore how members' cultural characteristics can affect their views of norms, roles, status, and power within the group. Group norms are often the result of the expectations that members bring to the group from previous experiences. The leader should assess how members' cultural backgrounds influence the norms that are developed in the group. For example, in many African American communities there is a strong belief in the power of spirituality and the "good" Christian life as antidotes to problems such as substance abuse, marital disharmony, difficulties in child rearing, depression, and alienation (Diller, 1999). Members' role expectations, developed within their particular cultural context, also often guide their behavior within the group. Gender-specific role expectations, for example, are prominent among certain ethnic groups. Thus, the leader should consider how members' culture influences their role expectations.

The leader should be sensitive to how members from diverse backgrounds experience power and control within the group. Many members from minority groups have had direct experience with oppression, discrimination, and prejudice, which can affect how members feel about the use of power within the group. The leader should understand that these experiences are likely to influence how some members may deal with power and control. It is also imperative for the leader to ensure that patterns of discrimination are not repeated within the group.

The leader should assess how the cultural backgrounds of members contribute to the overall group culture. Shared ideas, beliefs, and values held by group members are, in part, a reflection of what experiences individual members bring to the group. The group culture can include, for example, a heightened sense of spirituality when the group is composed of Native Americans or Hispanic Americans. The strengths of some cultural backgrounds can reinforce other important aspects of group culture. For example, in a caregivers group composed of African Americans, the cultural strength of the extended family as a natural helping network can help create a group culture of networking and mutual aid among members.

The level of group feeling and group morale may also be a function of the cultural context of the group's members. In a group composed of Hispanic Americans, one might expect the expression of a higher level of group feelings and emotions than that in a group composed of Asian Americans because in the latter group, members may believe strong expressions of emotion are not appropriate.

In addition to having an impact on group dynamics such as the culture of the group, it is important for workers to be aware that members' backgrounds can have a profound impact on group development and how leadership emerges in the group. Consider, for example, the impact of gender. Regarding group development, Schiller (1997) points out that affiliation and intimacy often appear earlier in women's groups and that conflict occurs later. Using Garland, Jones, and Kolodney's model of group development, Schiller (1995, 1997) proposes that the first and last stages of group development—preaffiliation and termination—remain the same, but that the three middle stages of group development—power and control, intimacy, and differentiation—would be conceptualized better as establishing a relational base, mutuality and interpersonal empathy, and challenge and change. Schiller (1997) goes on to describe the implications for practice of this alternative conceptualization of group development, which she refers to as the *relational model.*

Regarding leadership, Forsyth (1999) points out that women's leadership skills are often undervalued because they are viewed as socioemotional experts rather than as instrumental experts. Even though it is known that successful leadership depends on both expressive and instrumental skills, group members often overemphasize the instrumental side of leadership (Dodge, Gilroy, & Fenzel, 1995; Nye & Forsyth, 1991). Because of gender stereotypes and leadership prototypes, therefore, men are often viewed by both men and women as having more leadership potential, and men more often emerge as leaders of groups, even in groups that are composed largely of women (Forsyth, 1999). There is evidence, however, that by pointing out these dynamics in both task and treatment groups, workers can provide greater opportunities for women to take on leadership roles (Forsyth, 1999).

Intervening with Sensitivity to Diversity

There are many ways for a group leader to intervene with sensitivity to issues of diversity in the group. These include (1) using social work values and skills, (2) using a strengths perspective, (3) exploring common and different experiences among members, (4) exploring meanings and language, (5) challenging prejudice and discrimination, (6) advocating for members, (7) empowering members, and (8) using culturally appropriate techniques and program activities.

Using Social Work Values and Skills

Developing a culturally sensitive approach to group leadership means using social work values to guide interventions. The values of being nonjudgmental, genuine, and accepting can often compensate for wide differences in cultural backgrounds between the leader and members. Effective communication skills can also make a big difference. For example, good questioning skills, which stress open, nonjudgmental questions, can encourage members to respond in their own cultural styles. Similarly, the leader should be aware that for listening skills to be effective, the skills should be tailored to the cultural background of members. For example, a leader in a group for substance abusers used active listening skills with a Native American member, often paraphrasing and summarizing the content of the member's statements. When the member's participation became less frequent, the leader realized that the frequent paraphrasing was interpreted as being impolite. Recognizing this, the leader used passive listening skills, which conveyed to the member that he was being heard and that his participation was being carefully considered. Depending on the cultural style of the member, the leader may use active listening skills for some members and passive listening skills for others.

Using a Strengths Perspective

The leader should explore and use the strengths inherent in the cultural backgrounds of members. All cultures have strengths, which can be tapped to empower members. For example, in a group for adults who care for relatives with Alzheimer's disease, the leader discussed the strong natural helping networks of several African American members and how these networks supported the efforts of the caregivers. The African American members were able to recognize the networks as resources and make use of them for respite care for their relatives. Other members realized that they could also explore this arrangement, which contributed to the overall success of the group.

In the same group, a Hispanic member was criticized by one member for passively accepting the sole responsibility for caregiving in the family. The leader intervened, stressing that the role of caregiver was a culturally assigned one, usually given to a female in the household. The leader pointed out that commitment to the care of family members was viewed as a strength in the Hispanic culture. Other group members agreed with the leader's perspective. The Hispanic member became more active in the group as a result of this intervention because she believed that her cultural heritage had been acknowledged in a positive fashion.

In both task and treatment groups, it is important to point out how the group is strengthened by having members with diverse experiences and perspectives.

Unfortunately, although ratings by external evaluations found no differences based on team composition, there is evidence that members of teams that are heterogeneous with regard to gender, racial, and other characteristics perceive themselves to be less effective than teams with homogeneous membership (Baugh & Graen, 1997). It can be helpful, therefore, for workers to emphasize to members the accumulating evidence supporting the notion that diverse perspectives lead to more effective problem solving in groups (Forsyth, 1999). The worker can then go on to encourage members to express diverse perspectives, and to help the group to consider fully and grapple with the implications of each perspective. The worker's ultimate aim is to frame alternative perspectives as benefitting all members by enhancing the information exchange in the group. This will, in turn, enhance the group's ability to accomplish individual member and group goals.

Exploring Common and Different Experiences among Members

In working with members from diverse backgrounds it is often useful to acknowledge the differences that exist in the group and to explore the experiences that members may have in common. This process can begin by acknowledging diversity in the group and exploring how the cultural backgrounds of members may contribute to that diversity. For example, in a support group for parents who have experienced the death of a child, the leader began by self-disclosing that she was of Irish American background. She explained that, in her family, death was characteristically dealt with by planning large family gatherings, which sometimes took on a festive atmosphere. She also acknowledged that it may be particularly difficult for Irish American men to verbally express their grief. The members used this opportunity to explore their own cultural reactions to death and grieving by noting how different cultures express their feelings about death. The worker's initial disclosure and modeling helped the group explore their differing views of death and grieving and deal with difficult issues held in common by the members.

Exploring common and different experiences can also help overcome barriers to members' self-disclosure. Members are sometimes reluctant to disclose when they believe others may be judgmental about their cultural values, behavior, and lifestyle. Exploring cultural differences and fostering cultural appreciation can help members feel more secure in disclosing their thoughts and feelings. For example, in a support group for parents, it may be particularly difficult for members from certain backgrounds to share intimate details of their family life. Such matters may be considered private, to be discussed only among close family members. The worker can acknowledge this view and help members show sensitivity toward someone who may not self-disclose as readily as others.

The leader can also model the skill of empathy for members, which, in turn, can increase their responsiveness to differences. Helping members develop empathy allows them to comprehend more fully the experiences that result from diverse lifestyles.

Exploring Meanings and Language

Meaning is expressed through language. Many cultures do not attach common meanings to certain phenomena such as social problems or medical diseases (Dinges & Cherry, 1995). There may be no clear equivalent in the Spanish language, for example, for some psychiatric diagnoses. Likewise, an illness such as Alzheimer's disease may be defined in Spanish using nonmedical terms. The leader should help group members explore the differences in meaning reflected in different languages. Although some rudimentary knowledge of other languages is an asset, the leader should realize that language helps to shape reality. There are instances in which common terms and idiomatic expressions in English have no clear equivalent in another language. The leader should realize that members who speak English as a second language can define social situations, problems, and other conditions in culturally bound ways. It can be very helpful and interesting for all group members to discuss and explore culturally bound definitions.

The leader can help members interpret the significance of certain aspects of their culture to members of the group. In some instances, members may not understand the reasoning behind a cultural practice or phenomenon, which can lead to criticism or insensitivity among members. For example, in a rehabilitation group for spine-injured people, a member from Central America noted that he had visited the local *currandero,* who prescribed native herbs and other remedies. The initial reaction of several members was to discount this practice and accuse the member of going outside the traditional medical establishment. However, the leader and other members explained the importance of folk medicine and traditional healing in the member's culture and how the local healer contributed to the member's mental and physical well-being. Members learned the importance of this cultural practice and the significance of different sources of folk healing for some members (Koss-Chioino, 1995).

Similarly, spirituality may contribute significantly to the well-being of members of a group. It is important to acknowledge the importance of spirituality for particular members of a group and to explain the significance of different religious orientations. Group workers sometimes ignore spirituality because of the belief that it is linked to a specific religious denomination. It is important to take an ecumenical view and emphasize how spirituality transcends organized religion. The worker should avoid proselytizing about a particular religion but should acknowledge the importance of spirituality in the lives of some, if not all, the group members.

Challenging Prejudice and Discrimination

For members of diverse cultures, the realities of prejudice and discrimination can be heightened in a group. Challenging stereotypes and biases is an important leader skill. Some members may deny their individual biases, prejudices, or stereotypes, and it is important for the leader to challenge them to more realistically understand how they feel about people who are different from themselves. There is some evidence, for example, that suggests that psychoeducational group experiences can help members overcome stereotypes and biases (Rittner & Nakanishi, 1993).

Experience also suggests that task groups can help to overcome prejudice. For example, in a coalition planning a homeless shelter, several younger members discounted or ignored the suggestions made by older members. The leader asked all members to discuss how differences in the group might inhibit the group's work. After discussing what she had observed in the group, the leader helped the younger members confront their prejudices about the older members, and the group became more cohesive and goal oriented.

It is important for the leader to help members understand the discrimination that members have experienced in the past. Almost all minority groups have experienced discrimination and attempts to undermine their power and sense of positive self-identity. Burwell (1995) notes that extermination, expulsion, exclusion, and assimilation have all been used against minority group members. On a more subtle level, society often ignores the views of minorities and marginalizes their contributions. Schriver (1998) suggests, for example, that minorities do not partake of the privileges often accorded to members of the majority group. Access to a privileged status results in unearned advantages accruing to a particular group because of race, gender, socioeconomic status, or some other characteristic. In the United States, for example, white males have a more privileged status than do African American males, which has profound consequences for both groups.

The leader can help members to understand the effects of privilege and discrimination by asking members to identify a situation in which they felt discriminated against and to discuss the experience with other group members. After this exercise, members are better able to appreciate each other's experiences in dealing with discrimination and the effect it has had on their views of themselves, others, and their life position.

Advocating for Members

Members from minority groups may need special assistance in negotiating difficult service systems. Also, they may need help obtaining benefits and services. In working with people from different backgrounds, the group leader may need to advocate for members in situations outside the group. In a parenting skills group, for example, the leader became concerned about the absence of several Native American members. In investigating the reasons for their absence, she noted that these group members felt guilty about leaving their child-care duties to attend group sessions. The leader secured the support of her agency in providing child care at the agency during group meetings. Because of her efforts, members attended more regularly and their commitment and bond to the parenting group was greatly enhanced. Similarly, Brown (1995) points out that group process considerations are necessary for creating groups that are accessible for members with disabilities.

Leaders may wish to consider engaging in other advocacy activities on behalf of group members, such as, especially, working with family members and community support systems. For example, in a socialization group for the frail elderly, the leader experienced a good deal of absenteeism from members who nevertheless seemed to enjoy the group. It was discovered that for many members transportation depended on family or friends who were often busy. The leader used this information to advocate on members' behalf with the local Office for the Aging. Eventually, a senior van was assigned to provide transportation for group members. In another instance, a worker built a coalition of members from various gay, lesbian, and bisexual support groups to bring political pressure on city officials to pass adequate antidiscrimination legislation.

Advocating for group members, within and outside the group, is especially important for populations and groups who experience prejudice and discrimination. Persons who are diagnosed with AIDS, for example, often have difficulty obtaining housing, health care, social services, and other community-based services to which they are entitled. Leaders of groups for members experiencing high levels of discrimination should be prepared to spend time outside group sessions to help members gain access to needed services.

Empowering Members

Group intervention can help empower members by raising their cultural consciousness and by developing mutual aid within the group (Chau, 1992; Hopps & Pinderhughes, 1999). Personal, interpersonal, and political power can be fostered by constructive dialogue among all members and by discussions that foster cultural identity and consciousness (Gutierrez & Ortega, 1991; Hopps & Pinderhughes, 1999). The leader can help members obtain a sense of personal power and self-worth by reinforcing positive feelings about their identity and encouraging all members to interact with each other. All levels of system intervention, including larger systems such as institutions and communities, should be included in these efforts. For example, a social support group sponsored by Centro Civico decided to sponsor a "senior expo" featuring the contributions of Hispanic elderly to the local community. The senior expo featured ethnic foods, arts and crafts, exhibitions, workshops, and volunteer opportunities. Two other important aspects of the senior expo were a voter registration drive and an opportunity for members of the community to discuss their concerns about public transportation and safety with city council members.

Using Culturally Appropriate Techniques and Program Activities

Culturally sensitive techniques and program activities value diversity within the group, acknowledge how members of minority groups have unique sets of experiences, and allow members to appreciate both minority and majority cultural contexts (Vasquez & Han, 1995). The use of culturally sensitive program activities and other intervention techniques helps members to develop mutual respect for each other. It has been noted, for example, that several curative factors at work in groups for women apply equally to members of other minority groups (Vasquez & Han, 1995). When members have ethnicity or some other characteristic in common, they often feel understood by each other and gain validation for a similar heritage and a similar experience. In addition, such groups help members have compassion for themselves, accept the reality of human frailty, and develop positive perceptions of others. Empowerment can also be a healing factor for members who have lacked power in their lives or who have been unable to act with power in their relationships.

Developing culturally sensitive intervention skills can be fostered by reviewing specialized formats reported in the literature for groups composed of members from specific cultures. Pearson (1991), for example, suggests that leadership skills need to reflect a more structured approach for some Asian and Asian American people. Adopting a traditional Western style, with less structure and reliance on members to take responsibility for group interactions, would cause discomfort for these types of members. In contrast, Rittenhouse (1997) suggests that feminist group work often encourages unstructured out-of-group contact, the minimization of the power distance between leader and member, and a focus on the societal and political factors that contribute to members' problems.

Other writers have also developed culturally sensitive formats for particular minority groups. For example, Gutierrez and Ortega (1991) report the success of ethnic identity groups and consciousness-raising groups in empowering Latinos. Lopez (1991) suggests that structured activity groups in which members work together on tasks can be helpful for Hispanic youth. Lewis and Ford (1990) describe how group leaders can help African American group members use social networks by incorporating traditional strengths of African American families into group work practice. Ashby, Gilchrist, and Miramontez (1987) demonstrate how incorporating traditional Native American "talking circles" into group meetings can be effective in group work with Native American adolescents. Similarly, Kim, Omizo, and D'Andrea (1998) present evidence that culturally consonant group work using a Native Hawaiian healing method and a culturally indigenous form of communication had a more beneficial effect on Native American adolescents' self-esteem than did group work that did not use this approach. Overall, Chau (1992) suggests that group interventions should be directed at helping members enhance ethnic consciousness and pride, develop ethnic resource bases and sources of power, and develop leadership potential. Recently, Hopps and Pinderhughes (1999) have developed a model for working with poor and oppressed populations from various racial and ethnic backgrounds.

Principles for Practice

The group leader has a dual responsibility with regard to diversity. The leader should differentiate among members and individualize each member's strengths but also universalize members' common human characteristics and goals. The leader should help to ensure cultural pluralism, that is, the right of persons from all cultures to adhere to their practices and worldviews. In addition, the leader should seek to promote harmony among members who are different from each other.

The research literature on working with persons from diverse backgrounds is characterized by suggestions for working with particular categories of persons. Group work practitioners can benefit from studying this body of knowledge and applying specific suggestions to their practice with particular groups of people. More broadly, however, the group leader should challenge the group to discover, acknowledge, and deal with its diversity. Often, members are the best source of teaching and learning about diversity. Although this should not be seen as the sole responsibility of members who are from different backgrounds, they can be invited to share their experiences.

To understand diversity and be sensitive to working with persons who come from different backgrounds, group workers should consider the following practice principles:

1. Some form of diversity is always present in groups. Workers should acknowledge the diversity in the groups they lead and help members to explore the differences they bring to the group experience.

2. Sensitivity to diversity is important for both leaders and members of groups. Leaders should begin by engaging in their own process of self-assessment and exploration of feelings about their own identity.

3. The process of becoming culturally sensitive is an ongoing obligation of all group leaders. Thus, leaders should continuously seek knowledge about how members define themselves and how the identities of members affect their participation in the group.

4. Being culturally sensitive requires an open mind. Leaders should be nonjudgmental about the differences they encounter among group members and should welcome the richness and positive potential that diversity offers to the group as a whole.

5. Persons from diverse backgrounds often have firsthand experience with prejudice, stereotyping, discrimination, and oppression. Leaders should understand and acknowledge the effects of these phenomena and help members to understand how such treatment can affect group participation.

6. Diversity and difference can have a profound effect on how groups function. Leaders should recognize that the dynamics of groups vary because of differences in the identities and backgrounds of their members and should consider how diversity is likely to effect the development of groups.

7. Member identity and background affects how members work toward their goals. A complete assessment—of group members, the group as a whole, and the group's environment—should consider the diverse characteristics of members and the cultural context in which they have developed.

8. Differences in communication styles and language affect the members' overall ability to communicate. Leaders should study the effects that language and communication have on the conduct of the group and attempt to understand how members from differing cultural groups communicate.

9. On the basis of their experiences with environments outside the group, certain members may lack power and may be denied access to society's resources. Leaders should seek to empower members, on both an individual and a communitywide basis, by using empathy, individualization, support, and advocacy.

10. Persons from differing backgrounds are sustained by their cultural and spiritual traditions. Leaders should acknowledge this and attempt to understand the place of spirituality as well as traditional concepts surrounding illness and healing and should use these factors as much as possible.

11. Members who stereotype each other or discriminate against each other should be challenged to confront their biases, prejudices, and stereotypes; they should not be allowed to continue these behaviors within the group.

12. There are a variety of specialized cultural formats appropriate for use in groups. Leaders should develop a repertoire of intervention techniques and program activities relevant to particular cultural groups with whom they are likely to work.

SUMMARY

This chapter focuses on leading task and treatment groups with members from diverse backgrounds. It is important for the group leader to develop a perspective from which to work effectively with members from differing backgrounds. The group leader should develop cultural sensitivity through a process of self-exploration. The leader can also benefit from exploring the identity of others and by gaining knowledge about differing cultural and ethnic groups. An important prerequisite to these activities is openness to differences exhibited by diverse cultures. In planning and composing groups, the leader should consider how persons of differing backgrounds will experience the group and how the group will be affected by their membership. The cultural backgrounds of members can have a profound effect on how members participate in the group. A complete assessment of the group and its members should consider the larger environmental context in which members live and how that context can influence group dynamics.

This chapter also discusses how leaders can intervene with sensitivity to diversity. Suggestions developed in this regard include using social work values and skills, emphasizing a strengths perspective, exploring common and different experiences among members, exploring meanings and language, challenging prejudice and discrimination, advocating for members, empowering members, and using culturally appropriate techniques and program activities. The chapter ends with a description of practice principles to assist leaders working with diverse groups of people.

LEARNING ASSIGNMENTS

1. Go to the library and find three articles on working with a specific ethnic or racial group. Extract and summarize five practice principles that would help you facilitate a group composed of individuals from this ethnic or racial group.

2. Form a small group. Have all members of the group, in turn, describe their ethnic backgrounds. Go around the group again and have all members describe how their ethnic heritages might influence participation in a group. Ask members of the group who do not strongly identify with a particular ethnic heritage to describe how a demographic variable such as age, gender, education, or socioeconomic status influences their behavior in groups.

3. Locate a cultural community different from your own. Learn when important community events are offered and attend one or two events. Afterward, record your observations, thoughts, and feelings. Share your record with one other member of your learning group.

4. Go to the video store and browse for a few videos that depict differing cultural groups. Invite some friends over and have a cultural movie festival. Serve popcorn and discuss the differences observed in language, values, roles, and other characteristics. End with a potluck supper featuring various types of ethnic foods.

5. Ask class members whether they would like to volunteer to discuss an incident in which they experienced prejudice or discrimination. Be sure to remind the class group that prejudice can occur because of many characteristics, such as age, sex, disability, or race. Ask other members of the class to react to the member's experience.

part II

The Planning Stage

chapter 6

Planning the Group

Planning the Group

PLANNING FOCUS

Planning marks the beginning of the worker's involvement in the group endeavor. The planning process has two distinct parts. The first is directed at forming the group, the aspect with which this chapter is primarily concerned. The second part of planning includes the ongoing adjustments and forward-looking arrangements that are made by the leader and the members as the group progresses through its beginning, middle, and ending stages.

In forming the group, the worker focuses on the individual member, the group as a whole, and the environment. In focusing on individual members, the worker considers each person's motivations, expectations, and goals for entering the group. The worker focuses on the group as a whole by considering the purpose for the group and the dynamics that may develop as a result of the members' interaction. The worker also focuses on the environment in which the group will function by considering the likely influence on the group of the sponsoring organization, the community, and the larger society.

The second aspect of planning is carried on throughout the life of the group. During the beginning stage, the worker and the members plan in more detail how to accomplish the overall group purpose. The worker carries out detailed assessments of individual members of the group. These assessments lead to additional planning activities in the middle and ending stages of the group. For example, in treatment groups, the worker and the members engage in an ongoing assessment of the extent to which the group is helping members accomplish their goals. This assessment, in turn, leads to the refinement, adjustment, and reformulation of treatment plans and to recontracting with individual members for modified treatment goals.

In task groups, the worker uses data collected during assessments to formulate procedures for accomplishing the group's work, such as developing session agendas, dividing labor and responsibility, and determining methods to be used in making decisions and solving problems. Information about this progressive aspect of the planning process is included in subsequent chapters.

Although this chapter emphasizes the need for pregroup planning, there are many instances in which the worker's ability to plan a group is constrained. It is common, for example, for the recruitment process to yield a pool of potential group members that is large enough to form only a single group. In this case, a worker faces the choice of accepting all applicants, delaying the group for additional recruitment, or screening out some applicants and beginning a group with few members. It is also common for workers to inherit leadership of existing groups or to form a single group from all clients of a particular program or residential setting.

The planning of task groups may be constrained for a variety of reasons. For example, recruitment may be constrained by organizational bylaws or dictated by administrative structure. Likewise, the members of a delegate council are often selected by the organizations who are represented by the council, thereby constraining pregroup planning about the composition of the group. Despite constraints, workers still have the responsibility to think carefully about how they will guide the group's development to ensure that it is productive and that it provides a satisfying experience for members. Workers should plan for the group as carefully as possible within any existing constraints. Such planning helps foster the achievement of positive group and member outcomes and avoids unanticipated difficulties later in the life of the group.

Elements of Treatment Group Planning

A number of models for planning treatment groups have been reported in the literature, and several elements of these models are similar (see, for example, Bertcher & Maple, 1977; Reid, 1997). One of the most important elements is establishing a group's purpose. Almost all models stress the importance of group purpose. Another frequently mentioned aspect of treatment group planning is the sponsoring agency and environment. Many writers stress worker actions needed for a good fit between the group and the agency. Most writers also mention assessing member characteristics so the group can be composed in a planned fashion.

In contrast, differences exist among many writers about how much emphasis to place on systematic member selection. Also, some writers emphasize such issues as group procedures, group size, and the number and frequency of meetings; others devote relatively little attention to these elements.

Elements of Task Group Planning

One common element of all task group planning models is the need for planning group goals. Almost all writers identify this element of planning as important (see, for example, Ephross & Vassil, 1988; Fatout & Rose, 1995). A second element commonly mentioned is planning for task group membership so that the necessary resources and levels of expertise are built into the group. A third element is preparing for meetings. Most writers suggest extensive use of program materials, specific meeting activities and procedures, and the use of a meeting agenda. Premeeting planning activities receive more emphasis in task group planning than they do in treatment group planning.

PLANNING MODEL FOR GROUP WORK

We have developed a model of planning that can be used for both treatment and task groups. This model includes the following:

1. Establishing the group's purpose
2. Assessing the potential sponsorship and membership of the group
3. Recruiting members
4. Composing the group
5. Orienting members to the group
6. Contracting
7. Preparing the group's environment
8. Securing financial arrangements
9. Preparing a written group proposal

The planning model describes an orderly set of procedures to guide workers. In actual practice, however, workers may not plan for the group in a step-by-step fashion. Instead, the worker may find that it is necessary to engage in several aspects of planning at the same time. For example, recruiting, contracting, and preparing the environment can occur simultaneously. Similarly, determining purpose and assessing potential membership can sometimes be done together. Carrying out one step may also influence how another step is handled. For example, in assessing the potential membership of a committee, the worker may realize that a budget item for travel is required for certain members of the group. Thus, the information gained in carrying out one procedure (assessing membership) influences action taken in another (securing financial arrangements).

Establishing the Group's Purpose

The first and most important question that can be asked about a proposed group is "What is the group's purpose?" A statement of the purpose should be broad enough to encompass different individual goals, yet specific enough to define the common nature of the group's purpose. A clear statement of purpose helps members answer the question "What are we doing here together?" It can help prevent a lack of direction that can be frustrating to group members and lead to an unproductive group experience.

A brief statement of the group's purpose generally includes information on the problems or issues the group is designed to address, the range of individual and group goals to be accomplished, and how individual members and the group as a whole might work together.

Some examples of statements of purpose follow.

- The group will provide a forum for discussing parenting skills; each member is encouraged to bring up specific issues about being a parent and to provide feedback about the issues that are brought up.

- The group will study the problem of domestic violence in our community, and each member will contribute to a final task force report on how to address the issue.

- The group will review and assess all proposals for improving services to youth from minority communities and decide what projects to fund.

These statements are broad, but they provide information that will help members understand the nature of the group endeavor. As discussed in Chapter 7, the members of the group usually discuss and clarify the group's purpose in early group sessions and produce more specific aims and goals through their interaction with each other and with the worker. It is nonetheless helpful for the worker to prepare for the early discussions by anticipating questions that members might raise, identifying potential agenda items, clarifying the roles that the members and the worker will play in the group, and identifying potential obstacles to effective group functioning.

The purpose of a group can frequently be clarified by considering how the idea for establishing the group was generated. The idea may have come from several sources, such as the group worker, agency staff members, potential clients, or the larger community. Frequently, a worker detects an unmet need for service or a population that might be underserved in an agency. In other cases, the worker collects data to verify a need for service or to identify a particular problem to be solved and uses this information as a basis for defining the purpose of a group. Staff members can also begin the process of planning for a group by suggesting that certain clients or certain tasks of the agency might best be served in a group. Potential group members can suggest that their personal needs or their need to accomplish certain tasks might be addressed most effectively in a group setting. Similarly, community leaders might identify a need they would like to see addressed in a group. The following examples illustrate how ideas for groups are generated.

Group-Worker-Generated

- The worker proposes an educational group for children on the basis of the worker's perception of the need for adolescent sex education.

- The worker proposes an advising delegate council in a hospital on the basis of a survey of employees' job satisfaction, which indicates the need for better communication among professional departments.

Agency-Staff-Generated

- Several agency caseworkers, concerned with rising rates of family violence, suggest that clients from their caseloads participate in a remedial group for child abusers.
- The chairperson of the agency board of directors requests that a committee be established to study and suggest alternative sources of funding for the agency.

Member-Generated

- The parents of children in a day-care center request a series of educational group meetings to discuss concerns about their children's behavior at home.
- Several clients receiving subsidized housing suggest to the director of the agency that a social action group be formed to combat poor housing conditions in a neighborhood.

Community-Generated

- A group of ministers representing community churches approach a community center about developing an afterschool program for children of the working poor.
- A coalition of community groups requests a meeting with the administrator of a community center to explore ways to reach out to young people before they are recruited by gangs.

Assessing Potential Sponsorship and Membership

Although assessment of potential sponsorship and membership for the group might be seen as separate, in reality, the agency and its clients are intrinsically linked. The worker must assess both the sponsoring agency and the potential membership base to plan for the group. Agency sponsorship determines the level of support and resources available to the group. The assessment of potential membership helps the worker make an early estimate of the group's potential viability.

Assessing Potential Sponsorship

In Chapter 1, it was noted that group work is carried out in conjunction with a system of service delivery, such as a social service agency. The nature of the sponsoring organization, its mission, objectives, resources, and clientele have a significant effect on the formation of the group. Hartford (1971) suggests that the purpose, focus, goals, and sanctions of the group service are conditioned by the setting and the clientele. Wilson and Ryland (1980) also emphasize the effect of the sponsoring organization, particularly its effect on task groups, and note that "whatever is defined as the purpose of the agency has a direct bearing on the decision-making process within the agency's constituent groups" (p. 172). For example, treatment groups rely on agency administrators and staff for sanctions, financial support, member referrals, and physical facilities. Similarly, task groups are intrinsically linked to the functioning of their sponsoring agencies and must continually refer to the agency's mission, bylaws, and policies for clarification of their task, charge, and mandate.

In assessing an organization as sponsor for the group, the worker should pay careful attention to the fit between the organization's policies and goals and the purpose of the proposed group. The proposed group should fit within the overall operating goals of the organization. If the group represents a new form of service or suggests a problem area or a population that has not been the focus of the potential sponsor, the worker will have to be prepared to justify the request to begin a group.

It is important to recognize that the worker's assessment of the sponsoring organization is carried out not only to determine the overall level of support for the proposed group service, but also to garner any additional support that may be needed to begin the group. Abramson (1983) has pointed out that it is essential to identify key areas of interest and perceived need within the entire organizational community. She suggests that it is often helpful to meet with line staff and program administrators to obtain their ideas about the need for a particular group service. In interdisciplinary settings, it is important to test the idea for a new group service beyond the social work staff. The idea for a new group service should be presented to staff from other disciplines by highlighting common perceptions of unmet needs and pointing out how the new group service could support and enhance the work of other disciplines. This process has the added benefit of breaking down interdisciplinary competition, fostering a sense of mutual mission, and developing a bond with staff on whom the new group program will ultimately depend for referrals.

The worker may also wish to carry out a needs assessment or gather data to document unmet needs. Administrators and boards of directors may be particularly interested in the costs and potential benefits of the proposed group service. A brief review of similar group work efforts can help clarify the possible costs or benefits associated with proposing a particular group program. In other situations, an organization may decide to offer the group service on a trial basis while conducting a cost analysis, such as the one described in Chapter 13.

It is also helpful to gather support for the idea for a new group service from the larger community. This can be done by encouraging consumers within a geographical region to express their interest in a new group service or by urging community leaders and others who have influence within community social service organizations to express their interest in and support for the new service.

The relevance of the proposed group program to the sponsoring organization's mission and the visibility it could bring to the organization should also be highlighted.

In some instances, the potential sponsoring organization may decide the proposed group is not central enough to its core mission. In a county-funded rape crisis center, for example, the worker may propose a group service for battered women who have been victims of family violence but who have not been raped. Such an expansion of services, although appropriate and related to the agency's purpose, may be viewed as beyond the scope of the agency's mission, beyond staff resources, or not reimbursable within the agency's current funding sources.

When workers encounter a lack of support or resistance to a proposed group service, they should determine whether the proposal could be modified to increase support and alleviate the concerns that have been expressed or whether a different sponsor should be sought. For example, with the previously mentioned domestic violence group, the worker might work with supervisors and other administrators within the agency to highlight the need for the group and to seek additional funding for the service. Alternatively, the worker might decide to explore the idea for the group service with a family service agency or a community center that has expressed interest in providing service for domestic violence victims.

When assessing potential sponsorship it is important to (1) identify the extent to which a resolution of the problem or issue addressed by the group is valued by the sponsor, (2) identify and include staff whose support will be crucial to the implementation of the program in the planning process, (3) identify and resolve any differences in perspective among staff that may lead to hidden agendas and thereby jeopardize the new group service, (4) obtain staff consensus about the goals of the program and the group work methods used to achieve them, and (5) assess the willingness of the sponsor to provide external supports, such as transportation, that may be crucial to the development of the group (Abramson, 1983). Overall, garnering support for the idea for a new group service both within and outside the organization helps ensure the success of the group when it is implemented.

Assessing Potential Membership

Along with assessing agency sponsorship and garnering support for a new group work endeavor, the worker should begin to assess the potential membership of a group. Such a beginning assessment does not involve extensive procedures, such as arriving at goals for members or agreeing on individual contracts. Rather, in this early assessment, the worker is thinking about who should be recruited to participate in a planned group.

When assessing the potential members of a treatment group, the worker can begin by collecting data about the extent of the problem and the need for a new group service. As potential clients are identified, the worker can collect data about them by direct observation, by personal or telephone interview, or by talking with collateral contacts such as family members or agency staff. The worker relates this information to the proposed group's purpose and decides whether the extent of the problem justifies the need for a new group service.

When planning task groups, the worker considers potential members according to their interest in the task, their expertise, and their power and position to help the group accomplish its purposes. Members might also be sought on the basis of their importance to the sponsoring agency, their status in the community, or their political influence.

An important aspect of assessing potential membership is determining whether potential members share the worker's perception of the tasks facing the group. Shared perceptions lead to group cohesion and increase members' satisfaction with group functioning. In addition, the worker spends less time overcoming obstacles and resistance to accomplishing the group's goals when members share similar perceptions of the concerns facing the group.

Information should be gathered about the extent to which potential members recognize the need for the group, its purpose, tasks, and goals. This process helps workers anticipate the degree of member commitment to the group. It also helps to coalesce divergent views of the purpose of the group and the methods used to accomplish the work of the group.

In groups in which the membership is culturally diverse, the worker may need to give particular attention to the differences in perception of the group's purpose. Members from differing backgrounds can have divergent opinions about the meaning of the group, and the purpose for meeting together.

It is also important to assess potential members' view of the sponsor. Is there any stigma attached to receiving service from a particular organization? Is the organization known to the potential client group? What is the organization's reputation with the group to be served? The worker should carefully consider what qualities of the potential sponsor are likely to attract clients and what obstacles may interfere with the successful initiation of a group program. For example, a family service agency may have the resources to sponsor a group for African American single mothers but may have difficulty recruiting members because potential members perceive the staff of the agency to be culturally insensitive. If the agency sponsoring the group is perceived to be unable to relate to particular segments of the community, it will encounter considerable resistance when trying to initiate a group service.

Often the worker must plan for leading a group of reluctant participants. The extent of reluctance can range from ambivalence about seeking assistance, to active resistance. The term *involuntary* is often applied to individuals who are ordered by the courts to receive treatment. Working with involuntary clients requires special expertise. During the planning stage, the worker should become thoroughly familiar with the legal statutes and ethical issues that apply and with the rights of individuals who find themselves in these situations (Rooney, 1992).

Workers may also be called on to plan groups for reluctant members who are given the choice between treatment and a negative alternative such as incarceration, probation, or the suspension of driving privileges. In these situations, the worker should become thoroughly familiar with the specialized methods developed to motivate clients to make productive use of the group experience. For example, Brekke (1989) describes the use of a five-session orientation group designed to prepare men who batter their wives for a more structured and lengthier cognitive behavioral group. Similarly, in a residential program for substance abusers, information and techniques to confront denial may be used in combination with powerful incentives such as the return of driving privileges. Within the residential setting, information about the damaging effects of alcohol, peer interaction focused on sobriety, and access to certain privileges may be combined to help members make productive use of a group program. More information about working with reluctant and resistant clients is presented in Chapters 7 and 9.

Workers planning a group for a new population are unlikely to have information at their fingertips about what strategies are most effective for working with individuals who have specialized problems. Gathering information by reviewing the literature and from practitioners experienced with the population can be invaluable in preparing for the group. Obtaining information about specialized groups is particularly important when planning groups for people from diverse cultural backgrounds and when the worker's background differs significantly from that of group members. Such information helps workers to recognize their own biases, develop tolerance for their own and others' perceptions, and enhance their abilities to accurately perceive clients' needs.

In assessing potential membership, the worker should consider the demographic differences and commonalities of potential members and how such characteristics will affect other steps in the planning process. For example, in assessing potential membership of a support group for Hispanic caregivers of elderly parents, the worker might learn that special recruiting techniques are indicated, such as printing announcements in Spanish, advertising in newspapers for speakers of Spanish, or contacting Hispanic community leaders.

To prepare for recruiting and orienting members in both voluntary and mandatory groups, it can be helpful to list the potential benefits of participating and to share them with potential members. Some workers are reluctant to describe the potential benefits of participating in a group because they fear they will be perceived as boasting about their own skills or because they fear raising the expectation for service among members of vulnerable groups. However, individuals who are considering whether to participate in a group welcome a clear description of the potential benefits of participation. A worker's enthusiasm and optimism can be contagious, increasing members' motivation to participate and their enthusiasm for what might be accomplished. Yalom (1995) refers to this process as the "instillation of hope."

When assessing membership, workers should also identify barriers, obstacles, and drawbacks to group participation. In their zest to recruit members, workers sometimes minimize the difficulties individuals might encounter in joining a group. Experience suggests that it is better to acknowledge disadvantages to participation and try whenever possible to resolve them so they do not prevent individuals from participating. Often, discussing disadvantages with potential members during an orientation interview and planning ways to resolve them can be helpful.

At other times, it may be necessary to find additional resources or to increase incentives from the sponsoring agency or the larger community. For example, practical barriers may be overcome if the sponsoring agency offers to provide transportation, child care, or a sliding fee schedule. Similarly, an organization in the larger community might offer a meeting site with less stigma or a group of organizations might lobby with a funding body to provide additional resources for a group program that has wide community support.

Recruiting Members

Recruitment procedures should ensure an adequate number of potential members for the group. In recruiting members, the worker considers sources from which potential members can be identified and referred to the group. Members can be recruited within the worker's agency or in other organizations or the community.

Within a social service agency, potential members can be identified from the caseloads of colleagues, from records, or from mailing lists. In some groups, current members may be able to identify potential members. Potential members might also introduce themselves to the worker, individually or in a group, to suggest that the agency initiate a particular group service. Finally, the worker might consider reviewing the agency's waiting list to determine whether any persons waiting for service would benefit from group treatment.

For certain treatment groups, such as for men who batter, the worker's own agency may not have a large enough potential membership base. In planning for these groups, the worker can contact other social service and health agencies to obtain referrals. In contacting other social service agencies for referrals, the worker may want to contact line staff with whom they are familiar. It is also helpful to contact supervisory and administrative staff to inform them of the purpose of the proposed group, to elicit their support, and to gain access to other line workers who can identify potential group members.

The worker also can assess the community to locate concentrations of potential members. Census data can be helpful in finding people with certain demographic characteristics (Toseland, 1981). The worker might also talk to community leaders, politicians, police officials, school teachers, or clergy.

For task groups, the type of group and its purpose often determine the best sources for recruiting members. For example, members of a committee to study an agency's employee benefit package can be recruited from employees of the agency and from the agency's board of directors. A task force to study the problem of refugee resettlement can recruit members from all agencies serving that population in the community.

Occasionally, membership recruitment is determined by the nature of the task group. The members of teams, for example, are selected for their specific expertise and professional background. Boards recruit members from community constituents because the board "stands in" for the community and is accountable to the community for the services the agency provides.

Methods of Recruiting Members

When the worker has identified recruitment sources, decisions must be made about how to reach them. A variety of recruitment techniques will help potential members understand the purpose of the group and help them decide whether to join. The techniques include (1) contacting potential members directly, (2) mailing and posting announcements, (3) preparing television and radio announcements and appearing on television and radio programs, and (4) issuing press releases and making appointments with feature writers of local newspapers.

Some evidence suggests that direct contact with potential clients is the most effective recruitment method (Toseland, 1981). When potential group members can be identified from agency records or from caseloads of colleagues, the worker may wish to set up initial appointments by letter or by telephone. The worker can then interview prospective members in the office or at home. However, person-to-person contact, particularly in-home contact, can be quite expensive in terms of the worker's time and therefore may not be feasible.

In some situations, the worker may recruit potential group members by contacting key people in the informal networks of a particular population. For example, in recruiting for a group composed of Native Americans, the worker may first discuss the idea with important Native American community elders to gain their acceptance for the group. When recruiting Chinese Americans, the worker might identify cultural associations that provide support for this population, which could provide the worker with a means for assessing the viability of the group and the potential for recruiting members. Since trust is a key issue when recruiting members of culturally diverse groups, workers also should spend time getting to know the community and to become known to its members before attempting to organize and lead a group.

Brief, written announcements also can be an effective recruitment tool. However, care must be taken to ensure that announcements are sent to the correct audience. To be effective, mailed and posted announcements must be seen by potential members or potential referral sources. Therefore, careful targeting of the pool of potential group members is essential. Too often, workers rely on existing mailing lists developed for other purposes or post announcements where they will not be noticed by the target group. Computerized record systems are becoming more widely available and can be useful in identifying and targeting individuals who may need a particular service.

If the worker has a list of potential members, announcements can be mailed directly to them. The worker may also mail announcements to workers in other social service agencies who are likely to have contact with potential group members. Experience suggests that a follow-up phone call to those who have received announcements increases the probability that referrals will be made.

Announcements can also be posted on community bulletin boards, in housing projects, public gathering places, and in local businesses. In rural locations, announcements can be posted at firehouses, church halls, schools, general stores, and post offices. Such locations are usually the best places to post announcements because people gather in those places to discuss information about their community. The worker also can ask that announcements be read at meetings of community service groups, church groups, business associations, and fraternal organizations.

The increase in computer literacy, the availability of local area networks, and the Internet has improved accessibility for potential members. Group announcements can be posted on local area networks or community computer bulletin boards or be sent to targeted users of particular computing services. It is also possible for organizations or nationally federated groups to create their own web pages that are accessible to millions of persons who may be interested in learning more about particular services.

Appendix C contains two examples of announcements for groups. An announcement should include a clear statement of the group's purpose. The proposed meeting place, dates, times, length and frequency of meetings, and any service fees should also be clearly specified. The sponsoring agency and the group leader's name should be listed along with telephone numbers for potential members to call for more information. It is sometimes helpful to list any special arrangements that are planned, such as child-care services, transportation, or refreshments.

The worker might also want to make information about the group available through public speaking and through local television or radio stations. Many civic and religious organizations welcome guest speakers. A presentation on the need for the group, its purpose, and how it would operate can be an effective recruitment tool. Commercial television and radio stations broadcast public service announcements deemed to be in the public interest, and the proposed group program might be eligible for inclusion in such broadcasts.

Commercial television and radio stations frequently produce their own local public interest programs, such as talk shows, public discussions, special news reports, and community news announcements. Although public access cable television channels generally have smaller audiences, they can also be used by the worker to describe a group service and to invite members to join.

Press releases and newsletter articles are another way to recruit members. Most newspapers publish a calendar of events for a specified week or month; brief announcements can be placed in the calendar. An article in the features section of a newspaper also can reach many potential members. Newspapers frequently publish stories about new group services or particular social problems. The worker should consider whether the group is newsworthy and, if so, contact a local editor and request an interview with a reporter. We have found that feature newspaper stories are the single most important source for recruiting new members to groups in community settings.

Composing the Group

After recruiting potential members, the worker should compose the group. In this process, the worker chooses members according to their needs and the requirements of the group as a whole. Group composition is carried out according to a set of established principles that the worker decides on beforehand. Several important principles of composition are

- A homogeneity of members' purposes and certain personal characteristics
- A heterogeneity of member coping skills, life experiences, and expertise
- An overall structure that includes a range of the members' qualities, skills, and expertise

In addition to these principles, the worker should consider the issues of diversity, group size, and whether the membership will be open or closed.

Homogeneity

The principle of homogeneity suggests that members should have a similar purpose for being in the group and have some personal characteristics in common. Homogeneity facilitates communication and bonding and helps members to identify and relate to each other's concerns.

Members should accept and identify with the major purpose for the group so they can use the meetings to their full advantage. The worker should assess the extent to which members' purposes coincide with one another and with the group's purpose as a whole. Without some common purposes for being in the group, members will have little basis for interacting.

Members should share some personal characteristics, such as age, level of education, cultural background, degree of expertise relative to the group task, communication ability, or type of problem. The worker should determine that all members have enough characteristics in common to facilitate the work of the group. The extent to which members should possess common characteristics varies with the type of group. In an educational group for new parents, it might be important that all members be able to read English at a sixth-grade level to understand program materials recommended for reading at home. In a program-oriented group for youngsters in a treatment center, the most important common characteristic may be their living situation. Groups of alcoholics, drug abusers, and delinquents all have a problem in common.

Heterogeneity

For most groups, there should be some diversity of members' coping skills, life experiences, and levels of expertise. It has been noted that the existence of differences in members' coping patterns "opens the eyes of members to options, choices, and alternatives, and makes it possible for them to learn from one another" (Klein, 1972, p. 6). In support groups, for example, it is helpful for members to learn what coping skills other members have found to be effective and what strategies they have used to solve problems.

In some groups, the worker chooses members with differing life experiences or diverse characteristics to foster learning among members. A growth group, for example, might be composed of members from different cultures, social classes, occupations, or geographic areas to expose individuals to the benefits of differing viewpoints and lifestyles. Differences among members can provide multiple opportunities for support, validation, mutual aid, and learning.

Workers should also consider building heterogeneity into the membership of task groups to ensure an adequate range of resources and provide an efficient division of labor when dealing with complex tasks. For example, agency boards of directors are usually composed of members who represent a variety of professions, agencies, and occupations. These members bring legal, financial, marketing, and other kinds of expertise to the board. Other task groups, such as delegate councils, are also often composed of members who represent differing constituencies with diverse interests and needs. For example, a coalition formed to study the problem of juvenile delinquency might be composed of members from diverse parts of a city, that is, members from the business district, the inner city, and suburban neighborhoods. Such heterogeneity can be an important asset to the group in accomplishing its tasks.

Group Structure

The worker structures a group by selecting members who are able to meet each other's needs and are able to accomplish the group's purposes. Guidelines include selecting members who

- Have the ability and desire to communicate with others in the group
- Can accept each other's behavior
- Can get along with each other despite differences of opinions, viewpoints, or positions
- Have some capacity to understand their own behavior
- Be motivated to contribute to and work in the group

A member who is grossly ineffective in communicating with peers could engender more antagonism than support from fellow members and is thus best excluded from group treatment. Similarly, people who cannot accept or use feedback and those who are highly opinionated and unwilling to consider other viewpoints are poor candidates for treatment groups. Ideally, it is helpful to have highly motivated members. Social workers, however, are often confronted with reluctant or involuntary clients. Methods to work with these clients are described in Chapters 7 and 9.

Guidelines for composing task groups have also been proposed. Likert (1961), for example, suggested that task groups be composed of members who are (1) skilled in various roles of membership and leadership, (2) attracted to the group, (3) highly motivated to abide by the group's values and to achieve group goals, and (4) strongly motivated to communicate fully and frankly all information that is relevant to the group's activity. Put more simply, Scheidel and Crowell (1979) suggest that members of task groups should "together possess all the information necessary to the performance of their task plus the ability to interpret and use it" (p. 122).

The worker should choose members who will be able to put the needs of the group or the requirements of the task before their own personal needs. Klein (1972) notes, for instance, that "committee productivity is curtailed when members use the committee for the meeting of personal needs rather than the fulfillment of group goals" (p. 335).

The worker also should seek members who demonstrate ability to cooperate with one another. No matter what the level of expertise or ability of members, task groups can be hampered by a lack of cooperative effort. Although it is not always possible to predict how people will work together, it is necessary to give this concept some consideration when composing a group.

Diversity and Demographic Characteristics

Although demographic characteristics alone are not predictive of successful group outcomes (Yalom, 1995), they are important to consider when composing a group. In selecting members, the worker usually considers three major characteristics: age, gender, and sociocultural factors.

It is not sufficient to consider only age when composing a group. The worker should seek members who are similar in their stage of development and their life tasks. The level of maturity, self-insight, and social skills can vary considerably within age groups. Neither children nor adults acquire these characteristics solely on the basis of age, but rather through multiple experiences with their environment, family, peer group, and culture. For example, in composing a children's group, it is helpful to consider the level of members' social and emotional development rather than age. Each potential member should be assessed to determine whether he or she has a common basis for interaction and communication with other members.

Research suggests that the behavior of members varies with the gender composition of the group (Forsyth, 1999). The worker should consider the purpose of the group, along with factors such as age range and level of maturity, to determine the most appropriate gender makeup of the group. In a men's or women's support group, for instance, an atmosphere of support and openness can often be created through homogeneity of composition. In a remedial group for children, a mixed-gender group may interfere with interaction because of the tendency of children at certain ages either to impress or ignore members of the opposite sex.

In other situations, mixed groups are more effective. For example, in a task group such as a teen-club planning meeting, a mixed group is most appropriate to help members of the opposite sex learn to relate to one another. Similarly, an assertiveness group might include both men and women so that members can realistically role play training exercises.

The sociocultural background of potential members can also have a profound effect on group processes and outcomes. The worker should assess differences and commonalities among members based on sociocultural factors and should be sensitive to the needs of each member as well as to the overall needs of the group. Hopps and Pinderhughes (1999) describe how groups can be effectively used to empower poor and oppressed individuals.

The level of support and interaction is often increased when members have a common sociocultural background. Support groups for foreign-born students in U.S. colleges, for example, are frequently based on the similar cultural backgrounds of the members. Thus, in some situations, the worker may decide that similar backgrounds will help members deal with certain problems or issues. For example, a worker may restrict membership in a cultural awareness group to members of a single ethnic group. Similarly, in a support group for parents of terminally ill children, the worker may restrict membership to people from the same cultural background to ensure that members will have similar belief systems and values about death, loss, and grieving.

In other instances, the worker may deliberately plan a group composed of members with diverse sociocultural backgrounds. Diversity can foster mutual understanding and learning among members. Socialization groups in neighborhood centers and youth organizations might be composed by the worker so they encourage members from different ethnic, cultural, and racial groups to interact. Sometimes differences among members can be a real source of strength. For example, in planning for a social action group concerned with increasing neighborhood police protection, membership drawn from people of different cultural backgrounds can demonstrate a broad base of support for the group's cause.

Size

There is no optimal size for treatment or task groups. The worker determines the size of the group according to several criteria. Bertcher and Maple (1985) suggest that size "depends on the objectives of the group and the attributes of its members" (p. 190). The group should be small enough to allow it to accomplish its purpose, yet large enough to permit members to have a satisfying experience.

Studies of committees have shown that the most common sizes are five, seven, and nine members (Brilhart, 1974). With the exception of large task groups, such as delegate councils, the optimal range for task groups appears to be from five to seven members. Bales (1954) suggests that five is the optimal number of members for task groups; for decision-making groups, Scheidel and Crowell (1979) suggest that seven members are desirable.

When determining the size of treatment groups, the worker should consider how the members will be affected. Will members feel satisfied with the attention given to their concerns or problems? This is an issue for the worker, because "as group size increases, the complexity increases rapidly; the number of interpersonal relationships increases geometrically as the number of members increases arithmetically" (Brilhart, 1974, p. 30).

Similar suggestions appear in the literature for the size of treatment groups. Bertcher and Maple (1985) suggest a range of more than 3 but less than 15 members. Klein (1972) notes, "Five to seven is often given as ideal . . . developmental groups of fifteen are viable" (p. 65). In general, the literature indicates that seven members are ideal (Garvin, 1997; Yalom, 1995). Despite suggestions about the ideal size for treatment groups, little empirical research has been conducted about the relationship between treatment group size and effectiveness.

When determining the size of task groups, the worker must consider how many members are needed to accomplish the tasks efficiently and effectively. Although smaller groups are not always best for accomplishing complex tasks, Thelen (1954) suggests that the worker compose the smallest group "in which it is possible to have represented at a functional level all the social and achievement skills required for the particular activity" (p. 187).

The worker should consider the advantages and disadvantages inherent in different group sizes. Larger groups offer more ideas, skills, and resources to members than do smaller groups (Douglas, 1979). In general, larger groups can handle more complex tasks (Bertcher & Maple, 1985). Members have greater potential for learning because of the presence of additional role models. Members have more opportunity for support, feedback, and friendship, yet there is also less pressure to speak or to perform. Members can occasionally withdraw and reflect on their participation. Also, in larger groups, fewer difficulties arise when one or more members are absent. There is less danger that the group will fall below the size needed for meaningful interaction (Yalom, 1995).

Larger groups also have disadvantages. The larger the group, the less individualized attention each member can receive. Close, face-to-face interaction is more difficult. There is more danger of harmful subgroups forming. Large groups also encourage withdrawal and anonymity by silent members. They create less pressure to attend because members' absence is less conspicuous than in smaller groups. Larger groups are also more difficult for the worker to manage. They frequently require more formalized procedures to accomplish their meeting agendas. Large groups have more difficulty achieving cohesiveness and more difficulty reaching consensus (Carron & Spink, 1995). Also, as size increases, task groups are less productive (Mullen & Cooper, 1994).

Overall, decisions about the number of members to include in a treatment or task group should be based on the purpose of the group, the needs of the members, their ability to contribute to the work of the group, practical considerations such as whether a potential member will be able to attend meetings, and any constraints imposed by the sponsor.

Open and Closed Membership

During the planning process, the worker should determine whether the group will be open or closed to new members. Open groups maintain a constant size by replacing members as they leave (Yalom, 1995). Members enter and terminate throughout the life of the group, ensuring the group's continuance. Closed groups begin and end with the same membership and frequently meet for a pre-determined number of sessions (Yalom, 1995).

Often the choice between open or closed membership is affected by the purpose of the group or by practical considerations. A treatment group based in a residential treatment facility, for example, adds members as they become residents. Similarly, a committee formed to study the deinstitutionalization of psychiatric patients might discover it needs to add representatives from local community group homes to make more comprehensive recommendations.

In some situations, closed groups are preferable to open groups. An educational group for those who wish to learn to be more assertive might find it helpful to begin and end with the same membership so that new members will not impede the progress of the original members. A closed group might also be helpful for teenage mothers learning parenting skills so that a prescribed curriculum that covers the content in a competency-based, step-by-step manner can be followed.

In other situations, open group membership is preferable. Many members of Alcoholics Anonymous (AA) report that they are comforted by the knowledge that they can, without notice, attend any open AA meeting in the community. Open-membership groups also can provide people who are experiencing crises in their lives with a timely alternative to treatment—they do not have to wait for a new group to form.

In many situations, open membership is the only practical alternative. Because of rapid patient turnover in hospitals, for example, workers would find it impractical to form a group and expect the same patients to attend a fixed number of meetings and then be discharged all together.

What modifications should the worker consider when planning for an open-membership group? If the worker can control when members begin and leave a group, the worker should consider during the planning process when it is optimal to add new members. For example, the worker may decide it is best to add new members during the first few sessions and then close group membership. Alternatively, the worker might plan to add no more than one or two new members in any given meeting.

In Chapter 3, it was mentioned that when membership change is frequent and extensive, group development is adversely affected. To cope with the effects of a changing membership, planners of open groups should consider ensuring that there is a well-publicized, fixed structure for every group meeting (Galinsky & Schopler, 1989; Schopler & Galinsky, 1984, 1990). Each meeting, for example, might feature a guest speaker followed by small-group discussion. It is helpful to publicize the topic for each meeting and to stress that meetings are open to new members. In groups with high turnover, each meeting should be independent;

that is, an individual should not need to have attended a previous meeting to understand or participate in a current meeting. Also, consideration should be given to rotating a cycle of topics in a fixed period of time so that all clients or patients who have an average length of stay in inpatient or outpatient programs can attend a full cycle of meetings before their discharge.

When workers have the opportunity to decide whether to form an open or a closed group, they should be guided by reviewing some of the following advantages and disadvantages of each membership option. Open membership allows new ideas and new resources to be brought to the group through new members. Hartford (1971) notes that the "influx of new ideas, beliefs, and values" (p. 135) can make open groups more creative than closed groups. New members can change the entire character of the group.

The difficulties involved in adding new members to an already functioning group are not insurmountable. Yalom (1995), for example, notes that members can join a group, learn the group norms, and participate in meaningful ways without requiring the group to regress to an earlier stage of its development.

There are, however, potential disadvantages to open group membership. Hartford (1971) suggested that "instability is the basic shortcoming of the open group, resulting from loss of leadership, turnover in personnel, exodus of members, loss of group identity" (p. 135). Adding new members can disrupt members' work and delay or arrest the development of the group as a whole (Galinsky & Schopler, 1989; Schopler & Galinsky, 1990). Members of closed groups may form a greater sense of cohesion because they have all attended the group since its beginning. There is often a greater stability of roles and norms in closed groups. The benefits of a stable membership include higher group morale, more predictability of role behaviors, and an increased sense of cooperation among members. The stability of membership also makes planning for group sessions easier.

A disadvantage of closed groups is that when members drop out or are absent, the number of members in the group may become too small for meaningful group interaction. Without the benefit of new ideas, viewpoints, and skills from new members, a closed group runs the risk of engaging in what Janis (1972) refers to as "group think," or what Kiesler (1978) calls "the avoidance of minority or outside opinions" (p. 322). Such avoidance can create an extreme form of conformity within the group that can reduce its effectiveness (Janis & Mann, 1977).

Orienting Members

After potential members have been recruited, the worker should screen them for appropriateness and orient them to the group. The primary orientation method for treatment groups is the intake interview. Generally, intake interviews are conducted individually. Intake interviews are important because they offer workers and members their first impressions of each other.

Alternatively, members of treatment groups can be oriented by listening to an audiotape of a group meeting, by viewing videotapes of a previous group, through didactic instruction, or by rehearsal of membership skills, such as how to effectively communicate one's thoughts and opinions. Role-induction strategies, often referred to as *pregroup training,* can take a single half-hour session or several sessions lasting several hours. Pregroup training can enhance group outcomes, reduce dropout rates, and increase members' satisfaction with the subsequent group experience (Bednar & Kaul, 1994; Kaul & Bednar, 1994).

Orientation for new members of task groups is sometimes done in small groups. For example, new board members may be asked to participate in a board training program that consists of several small group sessions on governance and the bylaws of the organization, fiduciary responsibilities, fundraising, and public relations.

Orientations may be designed for many purposes, but three primary ones are (1) explaining the purpose of the group, (2) familiarizing members with group procedures, and (3) screening members for appropriateness.

Explaining the Purpose of the Group

The worker should begin orienting members by stating the group's purpose. The statement should be specific enough to allow members to ask questions about the group and clarify what will be expected of them. However, the statement should also be broad enough and tentative enough to encourage input and feedback. This can help potential members discuss and work through any ambivalence they might have about participating in the group.

Familiarizing Members with Group Procedures

Group members frequently have questions about how the group will work. Through these questions, members try to understand some of the general rules of group functioning. During the orientation interview, it is helpful for the worker to explain procedures for member participation and for how the group will conduct its business.

Leaders of both treatment and task groups often establish routine procedures for meetings during either the planning stage or the beginning stage of the group. Some treatment group meetings, for example, use a short review period for the first few minutes to discuss the major points of the last session. Time is then allotted for identifying particular member concerns to be discussed during the current session. Some groups use the final few minutes to summarize, to discuss between-meeting assignments, or to talk about the group's progress.

Task groups frequently follow routine procedures such as reading the minutes of the previous meeting, discussing old business, and bringing up new business. Many of these procedures are decided on by the group in its early meetings, but discussion of group procedures during the planning stage helps members see how they can participate in and contribute to the group.

Screening Members for Appropriateness

During the orientation, the worker screens members to ensure that their needs are matched with the purposes of the group. The worker observes members and collects impressions and information about them. Workers also apply any criteria developed for inclusion or exclusion of potential members. Members with impaired functioning can often be identified during the orientation interview, which gives the worker a chance to decide whether their membership in the group is appropriate.

Factors that may render people inappropriate for group membership include (1) problems with scheduling transportation or other practical considerations; (2) personal qualities, such as level of social skills, that are extremely dissimilar to those of other group members; and (3) needs, expectations, or goals that are not congruent with those of the other group members. Such factors have been linked to members' dropping out of treatment prematurely (Yalom, 1995). In considering members' appropriateness for a group, Klein (1972) takes a pragmatic view, suggesting that members should have "the ability to communicate with each other, motivation to work on their problems, no behavior so bizarre as to frighten the others, and no wide differences that are personally or culturally beyond acceptance" (p. 60). Such a view is helpful because it focuses on behavior that is observed during the orientation process rather than on labels or classifications of disorders that are difficult to observe.

Contracting

During the planning stage, the worker begins the contracting process. Contracts usually result from the dynamic interaction of the worker and the members during the beginning stage of the group, but certain contracting procedures are initiated before the group begins.

Two forms of contracting take place during the planning stage: contracting for group procedures and contracting for individual member goals. The worker should make some preliminary decisions about group procedures before beginning. These decisions include the duration and frequency of group meetings, attendance requirements, procedures to ensure confidentiality, and other considerations such as time, place, and any fees for meetings. The worker should also begin the process of contracting for individual member goals although most of this type of contracting takes place during the beginning stage of group work.

A *contract* is a verbal or written agreement between two or more members of a group. In a legal contract, each party agrees to provide something, although what is provided by each does not have to be equal, and penalties are specified if either party does not fulfill the contract.

In most task and treatment groups, contracts are verbal agreements. For example, the leader of an educational treatment group for foster parents may agree to meet with the group for five two-hour sessions to explain the purposes of the agency. The leader may also agree to explain the help that the agency can offer and how the legal rights of foster children can be safeguarded. Members may agree to attend each session and to use the information that is provided to become better foster parents. Similarly, the leader of a treatment conference may verbally agree with group members about the procedures for reviewing cases, the responsibility of each staff member in the review process, and the ways in which the information presented during the meeting will be used in case planning.

At times, a written contract may be used. A written contract helps to clarify the group's purpose. It also helps members clarify expectations about the worker and the agency and allows the worker to specify what is expected of group members (Figure 6.1). A written contract can be referred to in group meetings if either the members or the worker needs to be reminded of the purpose, expectations, or obligations to which they agreed. Generally, written contracts specify ground

FIGURE 6.1 ■ *Example of a Treatment Group Contract*

As a group member I agree to:

1. Attend all group sessions.
2. Arrive on time for each group session.
3. Refrain from repeating anything that is said during group sessions to anyone outside of the group meeting.
4. Complete any readings, exercises, treatment plans, or other obligations that I agree to in the group before the next group session.
5. Participate in exercises, role plays, demonstrations, and other simulations conducted during group meetings.

As the group leader I agree to:

1. Be prepared for each group session.
2. Begin and end all group sessions on time.
3. Provide refreshments and program material needed for each session.
4. Discuss the group only with my colleagues at work and not outside of the work context.
5. Evaluate each group session to ensure that the group is helping all members resolve their problems and is personally satisfying to all group members.
6. Provide members with appropriate agency and community resources to help them resolve their problems.

_____   _____
Group member   Date

_____   _____
Group leader   Date

rules for participation that do not change during the life of the group. However, contracts can be renegotiated by mutual agreement at any time during the group's life.

Written contracts are rarely used in task groups. The meeting agenda and the bylaws or other governance structure under which the task group operates are usually the only written agreements binding group members. Ordinarily, task groups rely on verbal contracts about the tasks to be accomplished, the roles of group members, and the division of labor in the group.

Contracting for Group Procedures

The worker begins to determine group procedures by deciding on the duration and frequency of meetings. These decisions are closely related to the group's purpose and the needs of its members. In treatment groups, the optimal length of time for each meeting varies. Meetings of groups of individuals with dementia in a nursing home may last only 30 to 45 minutes, but meetings of outpatient support groups often last one to two hours. Some groups, such as encounter or sensitivity training groups, meet for longer time periods and within a short time frame to achieve high communication levels and reduce member defensiveness.

The frequency of group meetings should also be considered when contracting for group procedures. In general, weekly sessions are recommended for treatment groups, although this does not preclude meeting more often when needed. The frequency of task group meetings depends on the requirements of the task and any time limits or deadlines that need to be considered. The worker must also consider how much time each member can devote to the group.

Specification of other group procedures should also be considered. The worker can specify attendance requirements, confidentiality of discussions, or other rules governing behavior in the group, such as how discussions will take place and how decisions will be made. Additional details include the time and place for meetings, any attendance fees involved, and the monitoring and evaluation procedures to be used by the worker.

Contracting for Member Goals

During the planning stage, workers also begin contractual arrangements with individual members. During orientation meetings workers should help members to describe what they would like to accomplish through group participation. Workers should describe the broad goals they have for the group and invite members to do the same. Questions such as "What do you hope to accomplish through your participation in the group?" can stimulate members to think about their roles in a group, what goals they want to accomplish, and how the goals fit with the broad purposes described by the worker. Methods that can be used when contracting with members of both treatment and task groups are explained in more detail in Chapter 7.

Preparing the Environment

Two factors that should be considered when preparing a group's environment include the physical setting and making arrangements to accommodate members who have special needs. The extent to which the worker can control these factors is sometimes limited, but incorporating them into the planning process whenever possible enhances the chances for successful group development.

Preparing the Physical Setting

The setting for the group can have a profound effect on the behavior of group members and the conduct of group meetings. Room size, space, seating arrangements, furnishings, and atmosphere should all be considered. Difficulties encountered in early meetings, inappropriate behavior by members, and unanticipated problems in the development of the group can sometimes result from inadequate attention to the group's physical environment.

Room size can influence how active or involved members become with the business of the group. Generally, a small room engenders positive feelings of closeness among members and limits potential distractions. A large room can put too much distance among members and thus encourage some members to tune out. A small group of people meeting in a large room may be distracted by the open space around them and have difficulty concentrating on the group process.

On the other hand, a room may be too small and not allow enough space between members, which can lead to discomfort, irritability, anxiety, or acting out. Certain populations are particularly reactive to the size of the meeting room. Young children, for example, often benefit from a large, open area in which to engage in activities. Similarly, disabled older adults benefit from a room with wheelchair access; comfortable, high-back chairs that are not difficult to get in and out of; bright, glare-free lighting; and good acoustics (Toseland, 1995).

Comfortable seating should be available. Sometimes group members prefer to sit on the floor to create an informal atmosphere. Carpets, lamps, work tables, and other furnishings can also help create a comfortable atmosphere. A comfortable physical environment conveys a message to group members about the agency's regard for them as clients.

Overall, the worker should consider the total effect of the physical setting on a group's ability to accomplish its tasks. If a group is to engage in informal discussion, the worker can create an informal atmosphere with comfortable couches or pillows for sitting on the floor. If a group is to work on formal tasks, such as reviewing priorities for a five-year plan, the worker should create a more formal atmosphere. For example, a room in which the group can sit around a well-lighted table may be most appropriate.

Making Special Arrangements

The worker should be particularly sensitive to any special needs of group members and should be sure that special needs will not prevent members from being able to attend meetings. For example, when working with the physically challenged, the worker should plan a barrier-free location for meetings or should consider phone or computer groups as an alternative to face-to-face meetings. When planning a group for parents, the worker should consider child-care arrangements. For a children's group, the worker should discuss transportation arrangements and obtain parental consent for the children's involvement in the group. When working with individuals for whom English is a second language, the worker may wish to arrange for the services of an interpreter or may wish to co-facilitate the group with a bilingual worker.

TELEPHONE-MEDIATED GROUPS. In some situations, it is not possible for people who could benefit from social group work to meet face-to-face. For example, people who suffer from debilitating illnesses, such as the frail elderly and persons with terminal illnesses, often are not able to attend group meetings. In other situations, people may find it difficult to avail themselves of a group service because they live a long distance from the organization offering the service. For example, in rural communities, health and social service agencies often serve large geographic areas. Even in urban and suburban communities, some health and social service agencies, such as regional hospitals, serve the needs of special populations dispersed over a large area.

In recent years, technological advances have made it possible to have telephone conversations among a number of individuals. This is often referred to as *teleconferencing* or making a *conference call* (Kelleher & Cross, 1990). Until recently, the use of this technology was largely limited to task group meetings in large organizations with members who were geographically dispersed. Several pioneering individuals, however, have begun to use the technology to offer therapy and support groups to individuals who cannot meet face-to-face. For a review of the literature, see Schopler, Galinsky, and Abell (1997) or Schopler, Abell, and Galinsky (1998).

Galinsky, Rounds, Montague, and Butowsky (1993) and Bertcher (1990) have prepared manuals on how to set up and operate telephone groups. In addition, Bertcher is the editor of *Tell a Group Hotline,* an occasional newsletter published through the School of Social Work at the University of Michigan, copies of which can be obtained through the World Wide Web at address http://www-personal.umich.edu/~bertcher.

Some of the special considerations in setting up a telephone group are (1) teleconferencing capacity in the organization's telephone system, (2) a speaker phone if there will be more than one leader, (3) sufficient funds for teleconferencing, and (4) a willingness to call 15 minutes before the group and stay on the line until all members of the group are connected.

Because of the increased accessibility they afford, telephone groups are often planned for people with physical disabilities and those who live in rural areas. Although research on telephone groups is limited, some clinical evidence suggests that they have certain advantages over in-person interacting groups. The most obvious advantages are increased accessibility and convenience. In addition, telephone groups tend to reduce stigma because members can remain anonymous.

It has also been reported that there may be greater intimacy and cohesion in telephone groups than in in-person groups (Schopler, Galinsky, & Abell, 1997). Because members' identities are masked and because differences that are not salient to the purposes of the group are less likely to interfere with interaction, members are more willing to interact with one another and to share issues that are taboo in in-person groups.

At the same time, telephone groups have potential disadvantages. Perhaps the biggest disadvantage is cost, which in 1999 averaged more than $25 per person for an hour-long session set up by a leading teleconference provider. Other potential disadvantages include (1) difficulties in assessing members' needs and the impact of interactions without the benefit of facial expressions and other nonverbal clues; (2) the difficulty of including members with hearing problems; (3) distortions caused by technological problems, call waiting, or background noises from other persons in the household; (4) concerns about confidentiality because of a lack of privacy within callers' households; (5) changes in group dynamics caused by the lack of visual and nonverbal clues; (6) the difficulty of using program activities, flip charts, and other visual media; and (7) expressions of hostility or insensitivity that can sometimes be greater when members are not meeting face-to-face.

Some disadvantages in telephone groups are not inherent in the technology itself but rather in how it is used. For example, telephone groups that last over an hour can become disorganized and difficult to follow and can lead to fatigue, especially when members are frail (Stein, Rothman, & Nakaniski, 1993; Wiener, Spencer, Davidson, & Fair, 1993). For this reason, and because the amount of time for a telephone conference is often predetermined, leaders must be vigilant about preparing members properly for the ending of each meeting.

Another disadvantage of telephone groups is that they offer no informal time for members to get together with each other before or after the meeting (Rounds, Galinsky, & Stevens, 1991). With members' consent, swapping telephone numbers for between-session contact is one solution.

Because members lack visual cues during telephone meetings, the worker must be particularly attentive to tone of voice, inflection, silences, and other cues such as members' becoming less responsive or completely dropping out of the discussion over time. It is also helpful to (1) have members identify themselves each time they communicate, (2) help members to anticipate frustrations such as missed cues or interruptions during group meeting times while at the same time appreciating the benefits of the medium, (3) prompt members to clarify statements and to give clear feedback to each other, and (4) check on members' emotional reactions and make these clear to all group members (Schopler et al., 1997). In general, leaders of telephone groups should plan to be more active than in in-person groups, helping members to communicate effectively without visual cues.

Infrequently, the absence of face-to-face contact can lead to the development of fantasies, which in turn may lead to dissociation from reality, loss of control, and irrational responses (Stein et al., 1993). It can sometimes be difficult to determine whether these responses are the result of disease processes in frail group participants, such as dementia among end-stage AIDS patients, or because of the telephone group itself. Despite these limitations, telephone groups offer a promising alternative to face-to-face interacting groups for frail or isolated individuals. For more information about telephone groups see Kelleher and Cross (1990); Galinsky, Rounds, Montague, and Butowsky (1993); Kaslyn (1999); and the previously described website maintained by Bertcher at the University of Michigan.

COMPUTER-MEDIATED GROUPS. There has been a sharp increase in the popularity of computer-mediated groups in recent years. There are now computer-mediated groups for persons with many different types of health, mental health, and social problems. To access or develop a computer-mediated group, an individual must have access to a computer and an online service. The online service is used to access search services such as Excite or Netscape on the Internet, which are, in turn, used to find the desired site. For example, Alcoholics Anonymous groups can be accessed at http://www.stayingcyber.org.

Four ways that computer-mediated groups can be formed using the Internet are (1) chat rooms, (2) bulletin boards, (3) e-mail, and (4) listservs (Santhiveeran, 1998). Chat rooms are virtual spaces, opened during specified time periods, where individuals can post messages and receive feedback interactively in a short time frame. In contrast, bulletin boards are usually open 24 hours a day. They enable individuals to post messages that can be answered at any time. E-mail allows an individual to write messages to particular individuals who can respond at any time. Listservs allow a large group of individuals to present and receive information and news. Thus, some computer-assisted group meetings occur in real time; that is, everyone participates at a specific time and the discussion is interactive. Other group meetings require members to post messages to which other members can respond at any time. Sites on the Internet are also excellent sources of information and education for group members. For example, members of a computer-mediated, real-time support group for cancer patients might be encouraged to visit a site sponsored by a reputable source such as the National Cancer Institute or the University of Pennsylvania Medical School to obtain current information about diagnoses and treatment options.

Computer-mediated groups offer many advantages to participants. Like telephone groups, they offer a variety and diversity of support, especially for frail group members and persons with very specialized concerns who may not be sufficiently numerous in any one geographic area to form a group (Finn, 1995). They also offer the same anonymity as telephone groups but have particular appeal to those who enjoy written communication or the convenience of 24-hour access. Although they require an initial investment in hardware and software, online service charges are less expensive than telephone conference services. In addition, they eliminate time and distance barriers even more effectively than do telephone groups.

Weinberg, Uken, Schmale, and Adamek (1995) report that members of computer-mediated support groups experience instillation of hope, cohesion, universality, and other therapeutic factors commonly associated with face-to-face support groups. However, Finn and Lavitt, (1994) point out that computer-mediated groups often lack clear and accountable leadership and that this factor, in turn, has the potential to lead to destructive interactions, superficial self-disclosure, and the compounding of isolation by persons with interpersonal difficulties. In addition to a lack of formal facilitation by social workers and other helping professionals, there is a lack of professional standards regulating how to conduct these groups and how to bill for services that are rendered. Computer-mediated groups tend to limit access by individuals in lower socio-economic groups who have less access to computer hardware and software, and the service is not covered by medicare or medicaid.

It has been posited that computer-mediated groups might replace in-person support group services (Alemi et al., 1996). Although there is some evidence that current users of support groups substitute computer-mediated groups for attendance at some support group meetings, there is also evidence that the use of computer-mediated groups increases participation in in-person support groups by persons who have not previously attended in-person support group meetings (Bass, McClendon, Brennan, & McCarthy, 1998). More research on the benefits and limitations of computer groups needs to be conducted, however, before any definitive conclusions can be drawn about their effectiveness. More research and policy discussions are also needed about professional facilitation, professional standards and accountability, record keeping, and reimbursement rates for services rendered to online group members.

Securing Financial Support

The worker should be concerned about how the expenses associated with the group will be met. For this reason, the worker should explore the financing arrangements with the group's sponsoring agency, beginning with an assessment of the agency's total financial statement. The costs associated with treatment and task groups vary, but major items include the salary of the worker, the use of the meeting room, and the expense of supervision for the worker. Other expenses may include duplicating, telephone, mailings, refreshments, and transportation.

Using information about costs and income, the worker can determine what financial support must be obtained for the proposed group. Expenses such as the worker's salary and the meeting room are often routinely paid by the agency. For expenses requiring an outlay of cash, the worker should submit a budget request to the sponsoring agency. A petty-cash fund can provide a flexible means to cover expenses incurred by the group.

For some treatment groups, income may be generated by fees collected from members, or it may be produced from contracts or grants. Although most task groups do not usually generate income, some are formed specifically to generate money for new programs or to raise funds for the agency. Others generate financial savings for their sponsoring organization through creative problem solving or decision making.

Preparing a Written Group Proposal

In planning for a group, the worker might find it useful to prepare a written proposal. Such a proposal is sometimes required for obtaining agency sponsorship or for obtaining funding from various sources. A written proposal can also inform potential members about the group. Spending time to organize and write a group proposal can also aid the worker in preparing for meetings. For most groups, a brief summary of one or two pages, following the outline presented in Appendix D, is sufficient. Two sample proposals, one for a treatment group and one for a task group, are presented in Appendices E and F.

SUMMARY

This chapter stresses the need for planning in group work. Workers consider many variables and exercise control over as many of them as possible. The planning process should be guided by the purposes of the group, the needs of the members, and the requirements of the task.

The chapter presents a model for planning treatment and task groups. Steps in the model include (1) establishing the group's purpose, (2) assessing the potential sponsorship and membership, (3) recruiting members, (4) composing the group, (5) orienting members, (6) contracting, (7) preparing the group's environment, (8) securing financial arrangements, and (9) preparing a written group proposal. The model can be useful in planning for the many different types of groups a worker may lead. All planning models represent an idealized, step-by-step set of procedures that may vary, depending on the realities of agency practice, but following a logical planning model can assist workers in helping groups meet members' needs and accomplish established goals.

LEARNING ASSIGNMENTS

1. The local Alzheimer's Disease Association has asked you to convene a committee to advise them on how to reach out to African American and Hispanic American caregivers of frail elders with Alzheimer's disease. What issues would you consider when composing the group? What methods would you use to recruit members?
2. In a small group with your classmates, select a population in need of group services. Prepare a brief statement of the purpose of the group. Decide on inclusion and exclusion criteria for group members. Prepare an agenda for a group intake/orientation meeting.

3. Visit an agency that deals exclusively with a distinct population such as the elderly or the disabled. Interview a worker about what physical arrangements and special considerations would be needed to form a group for this population.

4. Your agency director has asked you to prepare a proposal for group services to help students at a local middle school cope with the recent suicides of two of their classmates. Use the outline in Appendix D and the example in Appendix E to help you prepare a written proposal.

CASE EXAMPLE

Cathy worked for a university counseling center that stressed preventive services. She perceived that there were an increasing number of women being referred to her by the university's health center with symptoms of depression and anxiety. Many had successfully raised children and were seeking further education to start a new career after their children had left home. In addition to having concerns about returning to school as nontraditional-age students, many did not receive much encouragement from their spouses or partners, rendering their efforts to seek a new career even more difficult. Cathy wondered if a support group would be the best way to help these women. She conveyed her plans for a possible group to her supervisor in the form of a group proposal and began planning for the group.

She talked with colleagues in the counseling center and the health center about their experiences with older students to assess the need for a support group. She found that they too had been seeing a number of women who were beginning second careers and who were in need of supportive services. To learn more about the types of problems older students might be encountering, she called the local community college and discussed the group with several academic advisors from Start Again, an educational program designed to assist nontraditional-age students. In addition, she spoke with a few women on her caseload to see if they shared her perception of the need for a support group. They seemed very interested. Cathy also spoke to her supervisor and discussed her preliminary ideas about the group. Her supervisor said that a support group would fit the mission and goals of the organization. She thought the group could help Cathy's clients with the transition back to school and prevent more serious psychological, social, and physical problems later, as the women pursued life changes associated with starting a second career.

Informed by her initial assessment, Cathy concentrated on defining the purpose of the group. She recognized that the initial statement of purpose should provide basic information that would help members understand the nature of the group and how it would work. She decided that the purpose would be "to bring women together to discuss issues about starting a second career, going to college as a nontraditional-age student, and dealing with family issues related to life changes." Members would share their experiences and support each other through discussion and social activities. Cathy hoped that the group would help eliminate or reduce members' depression and anxiety and increase their coping skills.

Cathy developed a two-pronged recruitment plan that she hoped would ensure the group had an adequate number of members. She described the purposes of the proposed group during weekly staff meetings in both the counseling center and the health center and asked her colleagues to refer potential members to her. In addition, she wrote a short article about the group for a monthly student newsletter that was widely distributed on campus. In it, she listed the purpose of the group and suggested that potential members call her at the office to discuss their interest in attending.

Despite these efforts, only a few persons contacted her about the group. In her telephone conversations with potential members, she learned that many felt overwhelmed by the demands of returning to school. Despite their perception that the group could be helpful, they seemed reluctant to commit their time to another new endeavor. Cathy suggested that potential members meet once to assess whether the group would meet their needs and be worth attending. Twelve women agreed to a first meeting, but the most convenient meeting time for the majority accommodated only nine women's schedules.

During the first orientation meeting, Cathy took notes on the women's individual situations. She noted that all potential members were over forty years old and all but one had children who were either in high school or college. All seemed to be having some difficulty balancing the academic demands of college with the time demands of their families. They displayed an interesting range of diversity based on income level as well as racial, ethnic, and cultural backgrounds. They also seemed to use differing coping strategies for dealing with their spouses' and partners' lack of supportiveness, suggesting that they could learn much from each other. Cathy also felt that all potential members were articulate, had good insight into their personal and family situations, and had potential for helping others in the group. Despite having only eight members attending the orientation session, Cathy felt that the composition of the group would promote the development of therapeutic group processes.

Cathy described the purpose of the group, answered members' questions about how the group would work, and helped members to discuss and shape how the group would function. After this discussion, members seemed genuinely interested in attending more sessions, and they seemed relieved to meet others who were experiencing similar life transitions. Cathy and the members agreed that the group could be an open one, adding members from time to time, but that the size of the group should not exceed eight members. In addition, members discussed some initial thoughts about attendance, confidentiality, length and time of meetings, and Cathy's role in the group. After this discussion, Cathy noted that they had started to form the elements of an informal contract that could be discussed more fully in the next meeting of the group. She added that in the early sessions, members could also begin to work on their individual goals and contracts with the group and with each other. Overall, the orientation session seemed quite successful.

Behind the scenes, Cathy made arrangements with the counseling center for supporting the new group. She identified a comfortable meeting space for the group, one that was accessible and private. Although members had no special child care or transportation needs, she asked the counseling center to provide some funds for refreshments.

The Group Begins

The beginning of a group is often characterized by caution and tentativeness. The members have certain expectations about the group because of experiences with other groups, previous relationships, and the role expectations and characteristic ways of interacting that they bring to the group. Usually, the participants realize that there is an important purpose for their face-to-face contact in the group. They may have met with the worker before the first group meeting or received information on the purpose of the group through other agency workers or from other group members.

Nevertheless, at the beginning of any group, members are not fully certain about its purposes. Members wonder about what will be expected of them and what the leader and the other members will be like. Thus, from the very first contact, participants assess each other, mainly on the basis of nonverbal cues such as dress and personal appearance. The first interchanges are often stereotyped conversations in which participants attempt to become familiar with one another through mutual interests in places, people, events, and common experiences (Hartford, 1971).

As the group meeting progresses, an approach-avoidance conflict becomes more evident (Garland, Jones, & Kolodny, 1976). Members approach each other in their striving to connect with one another, but they avoid getting too close because they fear the vulnerability that such intimacy implies. Members are concerned about the way they present themselves early in a group and often prefer to proceed with caution. Members often do not feel secure about what they can expect from the group or their own ability to perform in the group. Therefore, they are often cautious about what they reveal.

Discussion of emotionally charged issues can be detrimental in the beginning of a group. When a member self-discloses emotionally charged issues very early in the group's development, other members sometimes feel threatened and may disclose little for a time. This occurs because few norms have developed about how to behave, and members are unsure about how to respond. Members may feel threatened if they think they will be asked to self-disclose at similar levels.

They may not be ready to do so, or they may think others will not be receptive or supportive.

Through their initial interactions, members attempt to find their places within the group. As the group develops norms, members begin to find out what is acceptable and unacceptable behavior. The tentative interactions found at the beginning of most groups are a testing ground for developing relationships. Group members attempt to reach out to find who in the group they can trust with their thoughts and feelings and with whom they can form continuing relationships.

Members' past experiences can affect their reactions in a new group. A useful exercise that can be done early in the group's life is to have all members describe an experience they had in a previous group and emphasize how that group experience affects their participation in the current group.

Members react in different ways to the group situation. Some remain silent, taking a wait-and-see stance toward the other group members. Others try to reduce their anxiety by engaging in conversation or by asking questions to help them clarify their position in the group. Gradually, a pattern of relating develops within the group, and the pattern crystallizes as the group develops.

The worker needs to be aware of the patterns of relating as they develop. The worker can point out patterns of relating as they form and encourage the development of patterns that will help to accomplish group and individual goals. For example, the worker may want to model and reinforce open-interaction patterns that encourage all members to participate.

OBJECTIVES IN THE BEGINNING STAGE

The beginning stage is often considered, by both novice and experienced workers, to be a difficult stage of group work because members often seek direction about how to proceed but are ambivalent about following any suggestions. Members struggle to maintain their autonomy but, at the same time, fit in and get along with others in the group. The worker's primary goals are to help members to work together in a cooperative and productive manner and to feel that their unique contribution to the group is respected and appreciated. To accomplish these goals it is helpful to

1. Facilitate member introductions
2. Clarify the purpose and function of the group as it is perceived by the worker, the members, and the sponsoring organization
3. Discuss and clarify the limits of confidentiality within the group
4. Help members to feel that they are a part of the group
5. Guide the development of the group
6. Balance task and socioemotional aspects of the group process

 7. Set goals
 8. Contract for work
 9. Facilitate members' motivation and ability to work in the group
 10. Anticipate obstacles to achieving individual and group goals

In the following pages, these tasks and the corresponding skills necessary to carry them out are presented sequentially. In actual practice, of course, the group worker should be concerned about these tasks simultaneously.

Introducing New Members

When the participants have arrived and the group is ready to begin, the first task of the worker is to introduce members to one another. Introductions help members share their mutual concerns and interests and develop trust. The worker should decide which information is important for members to share with the group. Beyond each member's name, the information revealed by each member should depend on the purpose of the group. For example, if the group is an interagency task force to study the problem of battered women, members might be expected to share their position in their agency, their experiences with services to battered women, and their reasons for becoming involved in the task force. If the group is for parents with children who have behavior problems, in addition to information about themselves, parents might briefly describe their children and the behavior problems they are experiencing.

Introductions can give members a starting point for interaction. Therefore, the information that is shared should attempt to bring out commonalities. The worker can facilitate this process by noting common characteristics and shared concerns disclosed by different members. Rather than proceeding through the introduction mechanically, the worker should encourage members to discuss commonalities. This process helps members feel at ease with one another. It also helps develop group cohesion and demonstrates to members that they are not alone with their problems and concerns.

The opportunity for members to share common concerns and issues with one another is one of the unique aspects of social group work as a practice method. Yalom (1995) has called this phenomenon *universality*. People who come to treatment groups often believe that they are alone with their problems. In reality, although they may have been experiencing their problems in isolation, other people experience similar concerns. The first group meeting provides them with feelings of support and comfort as they realize they are not alone.

A similar process occurs in task groups. For example, workers from different community agencies often experience the same frustrations and problems in serving clients with particular social service needs. Alone, workers may think they can do little to make the system more responsive to clients. But together, in a task force, a treatment conference, or in any other task group, workers can share their concerns, coordinate their efforts, and work to change problematic situations.

Round Robin

The most common method of introducing members to one another is to have them speak in round robin fashion. If this method is used, it is helpful for the worker to go first. In the early stages of the group, members take many of their cues from the worker, who can serve as a model by disclosing personal characteristics. Once members hear the worker's introduction, they are likely to focus on the disclosures as they introduce themselves.

Sometimes, the worker may want members to disclose information about areas of concern that the worker does not share. For example, in a group of parents, the worker may not have children. Workers should note the absence of this characteristic in their own lives, state how it might affect their work in the group, and ask members to comment on this factor in their introductions. For example, the worker might say, "I don't have any children of my own, but I've worked with children in the past at summer camp, in foster care, and for the past four years in my current position."

When they introduce themselves, members rarely disclose more than the worker has disclosed. In fact, they initially tend to disclose to a lesser extent than the worker. Therefore, if workers expect a certain level of self-disclosure or want to foster disclosures in a certain area, their introductions should reflect what is expected. This is not to suggest that the introduction should call on members to reveal in-depth, personal life experiences. Pressing for such disclosures at the beginning of a group is likely to increase rather than decrease barriers to open communication.

Communication styles and expectations about self-disclosure are influenced by our cultural heritage. Pearson (1991) suggests, for example, that clients who identify with the cultural imperatives in Chinese society may believe that close, personal relationships are usually reserved for family and that high levels of self-disclosure are not as desirable as a "balance and restraint in the experience and expression of emotions" (p. 51).

Variations on Round Robin

Several variations on round robin may be useful in opening different types of groups. To increase interaction, for example, members can be divided into pairs. One member of each pair interviews the other for five minutes by asking for details specified by the worker. When time is up, members reverse roles and continue for another five minutes. When the group reconvenes, members introduce their partners to the group by recalling the facts learned during their conversation. In addition to helping members develop a relationship with a partner, group workers find that this method of introduction sometimes leads to a greater depth of self-disclosure than round robin because new group members are likely to reveal more about themselves on a one-to-one basis than when they face the entire group.

A variation on this opening is what Shulman (1999) has called "problem swapping" (p. 348). Members volunteer to discuss their problems or concerns openly before the group. This opening promotes group interaction, leads to the identification of shared problems and concerns, and helps members to consider how they might proceed.

An opening that is useful in growth-oriented groups is known as *top secret.* Members are asked to write down one thing about themselves that they have not or would not ordinarily reveal to new acquaintances. The leader collects the top secrets and reads them to the group. Members attempt to identify the person who made each revelation, giving a reason for their choice. This exercise can be repeated in a later group session to illustrate the extent to which trust and cohesion have increased in the group. Members often reveal more intimate or personal top secrets after they come to know and feel comfortable with the members of their group. Variations on this opening exercise are "my most embarrassing experience" and "my greatest success."

Another opening exercise that can help members to disclose something about themselves or their family of origin is called *my name.* Members can be asked to discuss how they got their names and what meaning the name has for them and for their family of origin. For example, a member might state that his father felt strongly that he should be named Samuel, after an uncle who had died. The member goes on to discuss the uncle and other facts about his family of origin. He might also mention that he disliked being called Sam by his parents and decided at age 13 to insist that his parents and friends call him by his middle name, Allen. This exercise can often lead to interesting discussions of members' feelings about themselves now and in the past. It also helps members learn each other's names, which is important for open and personal interaction.

Other openings such as *treasure hunt* can be useful. Members are asked to find out two or three facts about each of the other group members. This activity offers much structured, but informal, group interaction to help members overcome initial anxieties. The facts obtained are shared when the group reconvenes.

Program activities can also be used in opening a group. Such activities help members share important information about themselves while working on an assigned task or activity. In addition to increasing members' self-disclosure, program activities can build cohesion in the group. For example, in children's groups, members may be asked to pick an animal that represents them. When introducing themselves, members can name the animal they have selected and state what characteristics of the animal they identify with. Another program activity for children or adolescent groups is to have members stand in a circle and hold hands with two members who are not next to them. Members are then asked to untangle themselves and form a circle without letting go of each other's hands. Additional program activities that can be used to open a group can be found in Barlow, Blythe, and Edmonds (1999); Middleman (1982); or in the annual handbook on developing human resources by Pfeiffer and Goodstein (1984–1996) (published annually since 1984).

Variations in Group Beginnings

A number of factors can change the way a worker begins a group. Sometimes workers become involved with groups of people who have known each other since before the group was formed. This can occur when the members are clients of a neighborhood center, a residential treatment facility, or are friends in the community. Similarly, in task groups, members may be familiar with one another as coworkers in the same agency or as coworkers in a network of agencies working with similar clients or a similar social problem. When members know one another, the challenges for the worker are different from the challenges that occur in a group of strangers.

Members who have had previous contact with one another are more likely to relate in ways that are characteristic of their previously established patterns. Roles and relationships established earlier may be carried into the new group, regardless of their functional or dysfunctional nature in the current group situation. In groups in which only a few members know one another or in which previous relationships between members vary from friendly to neutral or unfriendly, subgroups are likely to develop more often than they would in groups composed of strangers. There is also a natural tendency for friends or acquaintances to interact with one another and exclude strangers.

When it is possible to obtain information about potential group members, the worker should try to find out about any relationships that may exist among potential members. This will give the worker some indication of what form members' relationships are likely to take as they begin the group. It also gives the worker an opportunity to plan strategies to intervene in dysfunctional relationship patterns. The worker may wish to use information about members' previous relationships to reconsider the composition of the group and to understand members' interactions as the group unfolds. For example, a worker in a group home might use knowledge about the relationships that have developed among residents when deciding how to intervene to change communication patterns in a governance group that has just been established within the facility.

Another common variation in beginning a group occurs when the worker becomes involved in a previously formed group. This can include a worker who (1) reaches out and works with a gang of adolescents, (2) is a consultant for a self-help group, (3) is asked to staff a previously formed committee, or (4) is asked to replace the leader of an intact treatment group. These situations are different from one in which all members are new to the group. Instead of members looking to the leader for direction, as in a new group, the worker in a previously formed group is the newcomer in a group with established patterns of relating. Members of previously formed groups are concerned with how the worker will affect the group, what they will have to do to accommodate the worker, and what the worker will expect of them. Members may also act on feelings resulting from termination with a previous worker.

In working with previously formed groups, the worker should become familiar with the group's structure and its current functions and processes. It is especially important that the worker become familiar with the formal and informal leadership of the group, with members' relationships with one another, and with the tasks that face the group. Information obtained from a previous leader or from agency records may offer some indication of how to approach the group. In working with gangs or other community groups for which little information is available, the worker may find it helpful to gather information about the group. Any information obtained before contact with the group should be considered tentatively, however, because it is difficult to predict how an ongoing group is likely to react to a new worker. The worker may also want to observe the group before attempting to intervene.

The worker's presence in a previously formed group will cause adjustments. A process of accommodation to the new worker and assimilation of the worker into the culture of the group will occur. In general, cohesive and autonomous groups that have functioned together for some time will find it difficult to accommodate a new worker and will expect the worker to become assimilated into the ongoing process of the group. For example, a worker from a neighborhood center who is interested in working with a closely knit gang of adolescents who grew up together may have to spend a considerable amount of time developing trust and rapport with the group before members will seriously consider participating in a recreational activity at the neighborhood center.

Defining the Purpose of the Group

Opening Statement

After the introduction, the worker should make a brief statement about the group's purpose and the worker's function in the group. When members are not clear about the purpose of the group or the motives of the worker, their anxiety increases and they are less likely to become involved in working on their concerns and problems. Tolson, Reid, and Garvin (1994) point out that when objectives are clearly specified, the group is more likely to achieve its goals. Evidence suggests that workers often fail to define the purposes of the group they are leading (Fuhriman & Burlingame, 1994). Even if the purpose has been explained to members during pregroup intake interviews, the worker should be sure to restate the purpose during the first meeting.

The group's purpose should be presented in as positive a way as possible. Frank (1961) and other cognitive psychologists have pointed out the importance of persuasion, expectancy, and placebo effects in psychotherapy. These factors are also present in group work practice. Presenting a positive, hopeful image of what can be accomplished in the group makes use of the beneficial effects of these cognitive expectancies. Rather than focusing on members' problems or concerns, the worker can express the group's purpose in terms of the goals to be accomplished. Thus, statements that focus on positive objectives and goals, such as "Through this group experience you can learn to . . . " "You can stop . . . " or

"Through all of our efforts in this task force we can . . . " are preferable to statements that focus on the negative aspects of problems or concerns.

If the worker has successfully led a previous group that focused on similar concerns, the worker can mention this success. In treatment groups, such a statement by the leader offers members the hope that the group will help them resolve their own concerns. In task groups, members are more likely to be motivated and to persist in goal achievement.

In open-ended treatment groups in which new members replace old ones, it is often helpful to have members who have been in the group for some time state how the group has been helpful to them. Professional group workers can learn from the way that self-help groups such as Alcoholics Anonymous and Recovery Incorporated rely on the testimony of successful members as a major component of their group program. In task groups, members who have had some experience in the group can be asked to orient new members.

The opening statement about the group's purpose should include a brief description of the functions of the agency sponsoring the group. In treatment groups, the opening statement should define the limits of service so that members will have a clear notion of what services they can expect and what services are beyond the scope of the agency. There is nothing more frustrating for both members and workers than members' implicit or explicit expectations that go unfulfilled. The opening statement should include a brief statement about how the worker intends to function in the group and the worker's role in helping the group meet members' needs and accomplish its goals.

In task groups, relating the agency's function and mission to the group's purpose helps members understand why they were called together to participate in the group. The opening statement allows members to see how the agency's functions are related to the group's task. It is not uncommon, for example, for members of task groups to ask about how and to whom the results of their work will be reported. Task group members may also be interested in the extent to which their group can make permanent changes in policies, procedures, and practices through its findings and recommendations.

Involving Members

The opening statement focuses the group on considering the purposes for meeting. It should be presented as a starting point for further discussion rather than as an immutable definition that is not open to negotiation, modification, or change. Attempting to impose a definition of the group without input from members tends to reduce members' commitment and motivation and to increase members suspicions that their autonomy is threatened.

The stated purposes and goals should be broad enough that members can formulate their own purposes and their own goals (Northen, 1969). This does not mean that the worker's opening statement should be so broad that almost any purpose or goal can be contained within it. Statements about improving members' social functioning or coping ability may be too abstract for members to comprehend. Opening statements should be presented in clear, jargon-free language. However, the leader should avoid being overly specific. Instead, the worker should solicit members' ideas and suggestions about how to operationalize particular purposes and goals.

Open communication, particularly when it may conflict with the purposes or goals articulated by the worker, is often difficult to achieve. In the beginning stage, members are reluctant to risk their own tentative position within the group or to express opinions that may differ from those expressed by the worker or other members. Therefore, in addition to providing members with opportunities to express their opinions and concerns regarding the group's purpose and goals, the worker should reach out for members' input.

This can be done in a variety of ways. First, the worker should state clearly that the group is meant to serve the needs of its members, who ultimately determine the group's purpose and goals. Members can then be asked to state their own purposes and goals and to comment on the broad purposes and goals articulated by the worker. During this process, workers can encourage feedback by taking comments seriously and praising the members for sharing their feelings and thoughts.

Members can sense whether the worker's call for feedback is genuine or perfunctory. If the worker makes a continuous effort to solicit feedback by encouraging all members to express their thoughts and feelings, members are more likely to feel that their input is welcome. For example, members can be asked to make a statement about how the group's purposes and goals meet their needs and to suggest how the group could be improved.

Confidentiality

In treatment groups and certain task groups, the worker should lead a discussion of issues of confidentiality during the opening portion of the group meeting. In treatment groups, members are often concerned about how information they share with the group will be used outside the group meeting by the worker and other group members. Members cannot be expected to disclose intimate concerns or develop a sense of trust unless they can be assured that discussions within the group will not be shared outside. It is often helpful to remind members about the confidentiality of meetings periodically throughout the life of the group. This is particularly important in residential settings because frequent interaction outside the group may promote violations of confidentiality. It is also important in children's groups and in groups for other populations that may have difficulty following confidentiality agreements made during a first meeting.

As mentioned in Chapter 1, in some cases, the worker may be obligated to share information discussed in the group with law-enforcement officials. Workers are also likely to share information with supervisors and with fellow staff members during treatment conferences. Therefore, workers have an ethical obligation to be clear about the limits of confidentiality and with whom and under what circumstances data may be shared.

Confidentiality is an important issue in many task groups. Members are often unsure about what issues, proposals, and facts can be shared with their colleagues. For example, a state-level task force designed to study ways to improve services to older people trying to be self-sufficient in the community might deliberate for six months on several proposals before issuing press releases and meeting with the governor's staff and members of the legislature in a coordinated effort to have its proposals implemented. Premature or partial release of information can hinder the work of the task force. The worker should make the issue of confidentiality clear from the beginning to avoid premature or unauthorized releases of information.

The time set aside for the discussion of confidentiality also provides an ideal opportunity for the worker to bring related value issues to the attention of the group. For example, the worker might engage the group in a discussion of how social group work values such as democratic participation, respect for the individuality of each member, self-determination, cooperation and mutual decision making, and the importance of individual initiative will be operationalized in the group.

It is helpful for the worker to assist the group in formulating a set of principles—a code of behavior for its operation—to which each member agrees to adhere. For example, members might agree to

- Listen without interruption when another group member is talking
- Avoid dominating the group discussion
- Be respectful of each other's thoughts and feelings
- Be sincere and honest when communicating their own thoughts and feelings
- Make positive, cooperative, helpful, and trustworthy contributions in response to each other's comments

Helping Members Feel a Part of the Group

When a group begins, there is little sense of belonging or cohesion. An important objective for the worker during the beginning stage is to help a diverse collection of individuals, who may be apprehensive and ambivalent, begin to identify themselves as a collective of supportive partners in a common enterprise. The worker aims to build cohesion while respecting individuality. To achieve this objective in early meetings, the worker should begin by helping members feel safe and comfortable in the group. Given a pregroup assessment of each member, the worker is in the best position to ensure that the demands of participating in a group do not exceed members' abilities. Thus, workers may tone down expectations for intimate disclosures suggested by a member or scale down unrealistic expectations about what can be accomplished in a given time frame.

To help members feel that they are a part of the group, it is a good practice to point out shared interests and common goals among members. Members are comforted by the familiar. Knowing that they are not alone with their concerns or issues helps them to feel closer to other participants in the group.

Pointing out commonalities does not mean the worker should overlook differences, however. The leader can use several techniques to help members acknowledge and begin to appreciate differences in the beginning stage of the group. The leader can point out the contributions that different backgrounds and different perspectives make to the group and can encourage members to explore differences and welcome new perspectives. The leader can ask nonthreatening, direct questions that help members explore, understand, and appreciate the different perspectives that are presented within the group.

The leader can also use program activities or exercises to help members explore differences in an entertaining and lively fashion. For example, a leader might help the group plan a dinner to which members would bring a dish representative of their culture, ethnicity, or nationality. Another activity is for each member to design a coat of arms that represents something about personal background and to present the coat of arms to the group for discussion. The leader might also ask each member to create a "self-disclosure collage" that artistically represents elements of themselves not known to other members in the group. Overall, differences among members in their backgrounds and life experiences should be neither magnified nor ignored. Instead, the worker's task is to help members appreciate and respect differences.

The worker also helps members feel that they are a part of the group by protecting them from injury. Thus, misinformation should be corrected, and personal attacks should not be condoned. Also, the worker should continually scan the group to ensure that the content of the meeting is not having an adverse emotional effect on members.

Guiding the Development of the Group

Different theoretical writings suggest a range of possibilities for guiding the development of a group. Some writers suggest that the worker should provide little or no direction at the beginning of a group and prefer an approach that encourages members of the group to struggle with purposes and goals until mutual agreements about them can be achieved (Klein, 1970). Unstructured approaches to group beginnings are often used in t-groups and other growth groups in which the purpose of meeting is to learn about group dynamics and one's own interpersonal interaction style. The process of struggling to develop purposes and goals without any direction from the leader, however, is often anxiety provoking. Therefore, workers should be cautious about using unstructured approaches with members who are not functioning at optimal levels, when time to achieve particular outcomes is limited, and when exploration of one's interpersonal style is not a primary goal.

Other writers suggest that techniques to guide the development of the group should be used only to empower members to make democratic decisions and to actualize the purposes and goals that members, rather than leaders, have agreed to accomplish (Hopps & Pinderhughes, 1999). For example, in describing a humanistic approach to group work, Glassman and Kates (1990) suggest that the workers use techniques "in shaping the group members' processes of interaction and self-expression" (p. 121), but take care not to manipulate, coerce, or control members. A humanistic approach to leadership during the beginning stage is especially appropriate in support groups, social action groups, and coalitions in which the empowerment of members and the mobilization of their collective energy and wisdom are primary goals. However, elements of a humanistic approach, such as respect for the dignity and individuality of each member and belief in each member's potential for growth and development, are essential in all group work efforts.

Writers within the humanistic tradition point out that techniques such as "directing" and making a "demand for work" can help members develop and implement mutually agreed-on purposes (Gitterman & Shulman, 1994; Glassman & Kates, 1990; Hopps & Pinderhughes, 1999; Shulman, 1999). Yet, few writers within the humanistic tradition spend time addressing issues of limit setting and socialization in groups of severely impaired individuals and in groups with members who have been ordered into treatment because of delinquent or criminal behavior. Clearly, however, there are many practice situations in which the sponsoring organization and the larger society expect that workers will use their authority to help members function as more productive members of society. Yalom (1983), for example, points out the need for limit setting and a clear structure when working with psychiatric inpatients. Similarly, Levine and Gallogly (1985) suggest methods for dealing with challenges to the worker's authority when working with groups of alcoholics in inpatient and outpatient settings.

Those who eschew workers' use of expertise and authority to structure the group also rarely address leadership issues in the beginning stage of time-limited treatment groups. In many practice settings, short-term groups, such as social skills and life skills training groups for psychiatric inpatients, groups to help new parents learn parenting skills, assertion training groups, and anger control groups, are offered because workers have specific information and specific skills they think will benefit members. In these groups, the worker is designated by society and the sponsoring organization as an expert who provides direction and structure so that the members can learn new skills. Of course, even in these groups, members want some opportunity to share their concerns and learn from one another, but they also want specific methods and directions that will help them cope with and alleviate pressing problems and concerns. Thus, other writers have developed methods that are particularly helpful for leaders working with time-limited groups. For example, Rose (1998) proposes that workers come to groups with relatively set agendas and concentrate their efforts on time-limited groups focused on specific problem areas rather than on long-term, less structured groups that do not limit the scope of problems dealt with by the group.

An example of a session agenda for a time-limited, structured, parenting group is presented in Figure 7.1. The agenda provides the organizing framework

FIGURE 7.1 ■ *Sample Session Agenda for a Time-Limited, Structured Parenting Group*

AGENDA

Date _____

Session I

Goals

By the end of this session, each parent will be able to

1. Describe the purpose of the group program
2. State how behavior is learned
3. Describe specifically one behavior of his or her child
4. State the behavior he/she will monitor during the next week
5. Describe how each behavior will be monitored

Agenda

1. Introduction
   A. Leader introduces self to group
   B. Each member introduces self to group (name, number of children, current problems you would like to work on)

2. Orientation to the group program
   A. Purpose of the group session
      1. Goals
      2. Why should parents be trained in parenting skills?
      3. Who is responsible for what?
   B. Group contracts—read, modify, sign

3. Introduction to behavior modification—lecture
   A. Behavior is learned
      1. Reinforcement
      2. Extinction
      3. Punishment
   B. Role-play demonstration

4. Break

5. Assessment
   A. Discussion of behavior checklist
   B. Describe one behavior of your child
   C. Develop monitoring plan: what, who, how, when

6. Buddy system
   A. Description
   B. Choose buddy, exchange numbers, arrange calling time

7. Assignment
   A. Monitor chosen behavior and begin to chart it
   B. Call buddy
   C. Read units 1 and 2 (exercises at the end of each chapter are optional)

8. Evaluation

---

for the first meeting. It indicates the goals for the session, the material to be covered during the group meeting, and the reading assignments and tasks required of each parent during the following week. Similar session agendas are prepared by the worker for each of the 10 sessions in the time-limited parenting group.

In structured, time-limited groups, it is quite common for the agenda to be developed before the group session. As compared with less structured, process-centered approaches, structured group approaches give the worker greater responsibility for group goals and the way the group conducts its work (Papell & Rothman, 1980). Although in process-centered approaches members are encouraged to take informal leadership roles and develop their own goals, agendas, and contracts, in time-limited groups the members' input is generally limited to modifying goals, agendas, and contracts that the worker has already developed.

Budman, Soldz, Demby, Davis, and Merry (1994); Drum and Knott (1977); McKay and Paleg (1992); Rose (1989, 1998); Shapiro, Peltz, and Bernadett-Shapiro (1998); and others describe a variety of time-limited, structured groups for acquiring skills, managing anxiety, coping with life transitions, and learning parenting skills. These groups usually meet for 6 to 16 meetings. Meetings usually contain a mixture of (1) educational material; (2) exercises, role play, and simulations to help members practice the material; (3) discussion of the material and the problems members are experiencing outside the group; (4) a brief period to go over weekly assignments for members to do outside the group; and (5) an evaluation of the meeting.

Because they focus on educating members and on providing emotional support, these groups are sometimes referred to as *psychoeducational* treatment groups. Psychoeducational groups are an increasingly popular and important source of help for many clients (Barth, Yeaton, & Winterfelt, 1994; Brennan, 1995; Hugen, 1993; Papell & Rothman, 1980; Pomeroy, Rubin, & Walker, 1995). Perhaps the greatest asset of these groups is that they provide a planned framework that can be replicated intact or modified and adapted to fit different types of client groups. For example, a worker who decides there is a need for a social skills training group in a particular setting can use the framework presented by Rose (1989) to lead this type of time-limited, structured group. Other agendas for psychoeducational groups appear in Drum and Knott (1977) and Asher-Svanum (1991).

In a series of studies on the efficacy of group work, groups with specific purposes, homogeneous concerns, clear agendas, and structured group meetings were found to be more effective than were groups with less structure (Budman et al., 1994; Toseland, 1977; Toseland, Kabat, & Kemp, 1983; Toseland & Rose, 1978). Members reported appreciating that the leader provided specific information and effective strategies to help them with their concerns. Thus, in a group program for patients recovering from bypass surgery, the leader can provide information about nutrition, diet, exercise, and other lifestyle changes and also provide members with an opportunity to discuss specific concerns and to learn stress reduction and other coping techniques.

Workers should keep in mind that members' concerns and needs are not always most appropriately served by a time-limited, structured group approach. In support groups, for example, a flexible structure that maximized member input was found to be more effective than was a structured approach in helping members to ventilate their concerns and to give and receive help from fellow group members (Toseland, Decker, & Bliesner, 1979; Toseland & Hacker, 1982; Toseland, Sherman, & Bliven, 1981). In these groups, members were encouraged to reach out to one another as much as possible. Goals and specific agendas for each meeting were determined on the basis of feedback and mutual agreement among all members during meetings.

It is unfortunate that there is not more dialogue between authors who promote short-term, structured, behavioral, and task-centered approaches to treatment groups and authors who promote long-term, process-oriented, humanistic approaches. Authors who promote one approach over another often fail to acknowledge the value of alternative approaches, actively dismiss important contributions of alternative approaches, and ignore the core skills that form the base for all group work. It is the thesis of this text that both approaches have much to offer and that social work practice situations fall along a continuum. At the ends of the continuum, pure approaches may be effectively applied, but in most practice situations, a blending of approaches makes the most sense. Structure should be viewed as a tool that should be used differentially in practice situations to help members and the group as a whole achieve agreed-on objectives.

Structure in Task Groups

Written agendas are frequently used in task groups to keep groups focused on the work that is to be accomplished. Figure 7.2 is an example of an agenda for a meeting of a delegate council. In this example, it is standard procedure to

- Approve the minutes of the previous meeting
- Receive reports from standing committees and administrative officers
- Work on current business
- Discuss any new business that might have been introduced earlier in the group meeting

Agenda items can be divided into three categories: information, discussion, and action. Often, agendas are accompanied by attachments to explain the agenda items. Agendas with their attachments are usually given to all group members several days before the meeting so they can become familiar with the business that will be discussed during the meeting.

In task groups, feedback is encouraged in several ways. Members might be encouraged to submit formal agenda items before group meetings. The items are then placed on the agenda. When the item is considered by the group, it is often

FIGURE 7.2 ■ *Sample Agenda for a Delegate Council*

Meeting date _____

CYPRUS HILLS DELEGATE COUNCIL

Order of Business

	Information	Discussion	Action
1. Call to order			X
2. Approval of the minutes of the previous meeting			X
3. Treasurer's report	X		
4. Program committee's report	X		
5. Director's report	X		
6. Emergency housing proposal		X	
7. Proposed changes in bylaws (see attachment A)			X
8. Election of members of the women's issues task force (see attachment B for slate of candidates)		X	
9. Proposal to develop an ad hoc committee on community health care		X	
10. New business		X	

helpful for the member who submitted the item to present it to the group. During meetings, members' feedback is usually limited to a discussion of the specific task or agenda item currently being discussed. Members have a chance to add new agenda items during a meeting only if the group's predetermined order of business can be concluded in time to discuss new business.

Task and Socioemotional Focus

Another objective of the worker in the beginning stage is to balance the task and socioemotional aspects of the group process. Through systematic observation of leadership training groups, committees, juries, classes, therapy groups, and labor relations teams, Bales (1950) established a set of 12 categories to describe group interactions. Half the categories are in problem-solving or task-focused areas, and the other half pertain to socioemotional areas. Bales' scheme for observing a group is instructive because it points out that in all groups the worker must be conscious of both the task and socioemotional aspects of group process.

In task groups, it has been found that about two thirds of group interactions are focused on task accomplishment and one third on socioemotional aspects, such as giving support and releasing tension (Bales, 1955). Evidence concerning treatment groups suggests that they often spend more time on socioemotional aspects than on task-focused discussion (Munzer & Greenwald, 1957). Despite the difference in emphasis, pioneering studies by Bales (1950, 1955) and more recent studies by other researchers (Forsyth, 1999) suggest that in both task and treatment groups, neither the task nor the socioemotional aspects of group process can be neglected. An exclusive focus on tasks in any group may lead to members' dissatisfaction with their social and emotional interaction in the group. Focusing exclusively on tasks can lead to conflict among members and may result in a less effective group.

An exclusive focus on the social and emotional aspects of group interaction leads to a group whose members will be satisfied with their relationships with one another but will be dissatisfied about what has been accomplished. Thus, a balance between the task and the socioemotional aspects of group process is essential. No magic formula exists for achieving the appropriate balance between task and socioemotional aspects of the group. Only through a careful assessment of the group needs and the members' needs, can the worker determine the appropriate balance and help the group achieve that balance (Tyson, 1998).

Goal Setting in Group Work

In the first few meetings, groups often spend a considerable amount of time discussing goals. When the worker discusses the group's purposes, the process of goal formulation begins. Goals continue to be defined and modified as the functioning of the group and its members are assessed.

Group workers differ in their opinions about who should take responsibility for formulating goals. Whereas Glassman and Kates (1990), Klein (1970), and Tropp (1968) suggest that members should set their own goals, Konopka (1983), Rose (1998), and Vinter (1985a) believe that, after careful assessment, the worker should formulate goals for the group. This text takes the position that goals in group work practice emerge from the interaction of individual members, the worker, and the system in which the group functions.

As professionals, workers set goals that are influenced by the values and aims of the social work profession. As members of social service organizations, workers are aware of the aims and the limitations of the services they provide. Workers should also be cognizant of their function in the larger society, which sanctions and supports their work. Workers' formulation of goals reflects what they believe can be accomplished with the support, resources, and limitations within which the group operates.

Workers' goals also are affected by what they know about the group members. In treatment groups, workers often have an opportunity to meet each member during the planning stage. Potential members are selected, in part, because of their compatibility with the purposes and goals developed for the group. Workers make preliminary assessments of members' needs and capacities and of the tasks that face each group member. Goals are formulated on the basis of the assessment process.

In task groups, a similar process occurs. Goals are formulated by the worker in relation to the charge to the group by the sponsoring organization and the capacities of members. For example, a worker who is leading a committee to examine problems of interdepartmental coordination would be reluctant to set a goal of changing agency procedures if none of the committee members were in policy-making positions in their departments. However, given the status and role of the members, the worker might help the group formulate a goal that includes making to respective department heads recommendations about steps that could be taken to improve coordination between departments. In this case, goal formulation is affected by the characteristics of the members who compose the group.

Goals are formulated by individual group members who have their own perspective on the particular concerns, problems, and issues that affect them and their fellow group members. In previously formed or natural groups, members have the advantage of knowing more than the worker does about the concerns of the other group members.

In formed groups in which members do not know each other before the first group meeting, members' goals are based on

- An assessment of their own needs
- Their previous attempts to accomplish a particular goal
- The environmental, social, and familial demands placed upon them
- Their assessment of their own capacities and capabilities
- Their impressions or experiences of what the social service agency sponsoring the group has to offer

Goals for the group are formulated through a process of exploration and negotiation in which the worker and the group members share their perspectives. In this process, members and the worker should communicate openly about the goals they have formulated individually.

The extent to which common goals can be developed for all group members varies from group to group. In some groups, members have one, overriding concern in common. For example, a group of cigarette smokers suffering from chronic lung disease may be able to move quickly to a discussion of a specific contract to reduce cigarette smoking. In groups that are more diverse, such as outpatients in a mental health setting, it is often more difficult to develop common goals. In these groups, common goals are often formulated on a general level, for example, to improve the interpersonal social skills of members. Goals for individuals in the group are formulated at a more specific level. For example, an individual goal might be "To improve my skills when confronting others about behaviors I find unacceptable."

The process of goal setting, therefore, is one in which the goals of the worker and the members are explored and clarified. Three types of goals emerge from this process: (1) group-centered goals that focus on the proper functioning and maintenance of the group; (2) common group goals that focus on the problems, concerns, and tasks faced by all group members; and (3) individual goals that focus on the specific concerns of each group member. In an educational treatment group for parents of young children, a group-centered goal might be to increase the group's attraction for its members. A common group goal might call for the parents to learn about the normal growth and development patterns of young children. An individual goal for the parents of one child might be to reduce their son's temper tantrums.

In task groups, three levels of goals can also be identified. For example, in a committee mandated to review intake procedures in a family service agency, a group-centered goal might be to establish open, member-centered interaction patterns. A common group goal might be to make several recommendations to the program director to improve admission procedures. An individual goal for a committee member might be to interview workers in two other agencies about different approaches to intake procedures that can be shared with the committee at the next meeting.

The worker should help members develop clear, specific goals. Early in the process, members formulate general goals they would like to achieve. Examples include statements such as "I would like to be less depressed" or "The group should try to reduce the paperwork involved in serving our clients."

After members have stated their goals for the group, workers should help clarify the goals and make them as specific as possible. This can be done by helping members identify objective and subjective referents of their goals and the criteria that will be used to evaluate them. For the goal statement "I would like to be less depressed," a member might define the referents of depression as sleeplessness, lack of appetite, and so on, and suggest criteria for improvement, such as sleeping seven hours each night and eating three meals a day.

Defining goals clearly helps both workers and members focus on what they are attempting to achieve in the group. Developing clear goals is a prerequisite for entering the middle stage of group work. Before goals can be prioritized and a contract between worker and members developed, goals should be stated as clearly as possible. All members should have input into the development of goals and an opportunity to influence the direction the group will take to accomplish them.

In previously formed groups, which have preexisting goals, the worker has a different role in goal formulation. In some groups, goals may not have been clearly defined, and the worker's task is to help members clarify their goals. This is often the case with groups of teenagers and children who have not carefully considered their goals. In other previously formed groups, clear goals may exist. The worker's task, then, is to become familiar with the goals and help the group achieve the goals that can be accomplished and modify or abandon those that are not likely to be achieved.

Sometimes a worker is asked to consult with a group when the group is blocked in its attempt to achieve its goals. The worker should help the group reassess its goals to ensure that they are clear and mutually agreed on by members, that they do not conflict with one another, and that they are achievable.

Achieving consensus about purposes and goals can be particularly difficult with involuntary members who are often pressured into participating in a group. Still, there is usually some common ground on which mutually agreed-on goals can be developed. For example, youthful offenders are sometimes given the choice of participating in group treatment or being sentenced through the juvenile court system. The worker can begin by stating the conditions and standards for continued participation and then encourage members to develop their own goals within these minimally acceptable conditions and standards. Trust takes longer to develop in such groups, but if the worker consistently shows interest in the members' goals, concerns, and aspirations, the group can be a useful treatment modality.

Contracting

In group work, *contracts* are mutual agreements that specify expectations, obligations, and duties. Most commonly, a contract is developed between group members and the worker who acts as the representative of the agency. However, contracts also can be developed between (1) the group as a whole and the agency, (2) the group as a whole and the worker, (3) the group as a whole and a member, (4) a group member and the worker, and (5) two or more group members. Although contracts involving the group as a whole are usually developed around group procedures, individual member's contracts are usually developed around individual treatment goals or individual task assignments.

The most common form of an individual-member contract is between a member and the worker. For example, a member may contract with the worker to stop smoking, to become more assertive, or to make more friends.

Contracts can also be developed between two or more group members to help each other achieve particular goals. For example, in an assertiveness training group, one member might decide to practice being assertive in two situations during the group meeting and in one situation during the week. The member may ask another member to praise her if she is assertive in the group and to telephone her during the week to see if she has been assertive in a situation outside the group. In return, she agrees to help the other member achieve a particular goal.

A third form of individual contracting occurs between a member and the group. The member, for example, can agree to obtain information about a resource for the group or can promise to report back to the group about the results of a particular meeting. In a cohesive group, member-to-group contracts can be quite effective because members do not want to let each other down by failing to follow through on the contract.

When contracting with individual members for goals or tasks, it is important to be as specific as possible in stating what is to be accomplished, who will be involved in the effort, and how success or failure will be determined. Bertcher and Maple (1977) refer to this process as formulating behaviorally specific outcome goals. Goals specified in a written or verbal contract should state briefly who will do what, under what circumstances, and how results will be measured. The following examples contain outcome goals for a treatment group and a task group:

Treatment Group (To help members stop smoking)

Who:	Mary Jane
Will do what:	will refuse the offer of a cigarette
Under what circumstances:	when it is offered at a social gathering
How will it be measured:	and will report this offer to the group.

Who:	John Franks
Will do what:	will smoke less than three cigarettes
Under what circumstances:	at home, during each day of next week
How will it be measured:	as reported by spouse.

Task Group (Committee to study juvenile crime)

Who:	Bill Evans
Will do what:	will interview the local family court judge
Under what circumstances:	prior to the next meeting
How will it be measured:	and prepare a written report for the committee.

Who:	Ann Murphy
Will do what:	will read five articles on juvenile crime
Under what circumstances:	within the next two weeks
How will it be measured:	and report significant findings to the committee.

Facilitating Members' Motivation

After an initial clarification of the broad purpose and goals of the group, the worker then helps members increase their motivation to begin accomplishing the purposes and goals that have been mutually decided on. Motivation is the key to the successful achievement of the group and member goals. To a large extent, such motivation is determined by members' expectations about (1) the worker's role in the group, (2) the processes that will occur in the group, and (3) what can be accomplished through the work of the group. Members bring a set of expectations to any group experience, and the expectations have a powerful influence on the way the members behave in the group. For example, if a member expects the worker to tell him or her how to proceed, it is unlikely that the member will take much initiative in the group. If the member has been involved in a previous group experience in which little was accomplished, the member's expectations and motivations to work hard to achieve individual and group goals are likely to be diminished.

As the worker and the members begin to explore how they can work together, the worker should help members identify their expectations and motivations. The worker can do this by asking members direct questions about what they think they can accomplish in the group and how they expect the group to function. It is surprising how often these questions uncover ambivalence about giving up old ways of doing things and fear about what new and unknown changes may bring.

Working through Ambivalence and Resistance

Sometimes members respond evasively to direct questions about their motivations and expectations, particularly when the worker has made an early and clear "demand for work" before assessing members' expectations and motivations (Schwartz, 1971, p. 11). The worker may find members reluctant to state ambivalent feelings about their ability to accomplish the goals for which they have contracted because they fear that the worker will disapprove. Before the worker states expectations about what members need to do to accomplish their goals, the worker should notice the overt and covert messages members give about accomplishing the group's work. If the worker picks up signals indicating a lack of motivation to accomplish goals, the worker should check the perception of the meaning of the message with the group members.

Ambivalent feelings about change are common and should not be viewed as an obstacle to accomplishing the group's work. It is rare for changes to be proposed and worked on without ambivalent feelings, and it is often difficult and painful to change problematic areas of one's life. At the very least, it requires giving up the security of old ways of doing things. Rather than ignoring, playing down, or attacking the ambivalence, workers should help members work through it. Acknowledging members' ambivalence is a helpful way to get members to recognize their reactions to change. A frank discussion of a member's ambivalence about change and the perceived ability to achieve a goal helps all members see that this is a common reaction to the changes they are planning to make. Also, a realistic appraisal of the chances for success is much preferred to covering up barriers to task achievement.

One exercise that can help uncover ambivalence is to have each member focus on a goal and list psychological, social, and environmental factors that hinder and promote its achievement. A variation on this exercise done with individual clients has been called "force field analysis" (Egan, 1998). In task groups, all members focus on one group goal. In treatment groups, it is more common for members to focus on one member's goal, but occasionally it is possible to select a common group goal on which to focus. The exercise can be done by all group members, in pairs, or at home between sessions.

In a force field analysis, the worker helps members list on paper or a blackboard the positive and negative aspects of attaining a goal and displays the results before all group members. This process facilitates an organized discussion of the factors that can help members achieve goals and the factors that may hinder them. Such a visual display helps members realize, often with surprise, that, despite their verbal assertions about achieving a goal, many factors may be detracting from their motivation.

An example of a list of positive and negative factors that could influence a group member's decision is shown in Figure 7.3. The decision involves whether the member should separate from her husband. An examination of a list of factors can help group members decide whether there are sufficient positive motivations for achieving a particular goal.

If a member reaches a decision to pursue a goal despite numerous factors that reduce motivation, the task of the worker and the other group members is

FIGURE 7.3 ■ *Analysis of Factors that Increase and Decrease the Motivation of a Member of a Treatment Group*

Problem: Whether to separate from my husband

Factors Increasing Motivation

1. Tom drinks too much.
2. Tom has been physically abusive twice in the last year.
3. There is almost daily verbal conflict between Tom and me.
4. Staying in the relationship causes me to feel angry and depressed.
5. My relationship is interfering with the quality of my work at my job.
6. Tom and I have infrequent sexual relations.
7. The kids are being affected by our constant fighting.

Factors Decreasing Motivation

1. Concern about what breaking up will do to the kids.
2. Worried about whether I can live on only my salary.
3. Wonder if I can care for three kids and keep working 40 hours a week.
4. Feeling as if I would be breaking my commitment to Tom.
5. I'll have to explain the separation to my parents, friends, etc.

to suggest ways to decrease the negative factors and increase the positive factors. For example, in the situation in Figure 7.3, the member decides to separate from her husband. To help the member change some of the factors that reduce her motivation, the group helps the member (1) overcome her fear about the effects of the separation on her children by suggesting that the children may be harmed more by seeing Mom and Dad constantly fighting than by experiencing their parents' separation; (2) examine her finances, her plans for child care, and other practical needs that she may have as she considers living independently; and (3) build her self-confidence and self-esteem by providing support and positive feedback during the separation process. Through this process, the group helps the member become motivated to achieve her goal with as little ambivalence, fear, and anguish as possible.

In some groups, workers encounter members who believe they have been coerced or manipulated into coming to the group. Instead of engaging in the work of the group, these members often spend valuable group time complaining about being forced to participate. In an excellent text on dealing with resistant group members, Edelwich and Brodsky (1992) suggest that, in such a situation, the worker can point out that the members chose to participate in the group. Although some individuals may have chosen to participate in the group to avoid other less desirable choices, that choice was an agreement made with a referring agency. For example, in the case of being found guilty of driving while intoxicated, the member may have agreed to participate in a group treatment program instead of losing his driver's license. The worker should acknowledge that the member may not want to be in the group, but also note that the person freely chose the group to an alternative. The worker should also state that members are free to terminate their participation at any time, but their decision to participate implies that they will adhere to the group norms and contractual obligations agreed to during the intake interview or the first group session.

As the group progresses, it may be necessary to remind members of the negative consequences of not participating, and that the member has the power to make additional choices that have positive consequences. It can also be helpful for the worker to use "I" statements while making a clear demand for work (Edelwich & Brodsky, 1992). For example, the worker might state:

> *I have a problem. Some of you don't seem to want to be here. If you don't want to be here, you don't have to be here. I don't want you to get the wrong impression—I'd rather you stay. But if you don't like being in the group, you can take it up with the agency that sent you and deal with the consequences of not continuing your participation. My job is to help you use your time in this group productively. Therefore, I would like those of you who choose to stay to think now about how you will use the group—what you want to accomplish. Think about the problems and issues in your life and what you'd like to work on in this group. I'll give you a few minutes. Then, let's go around and see what we can do together.*

Expectations about Role Performance

In addition to ambivalence about changing a way of doing things, members often are concerned at the beginning of the group that they will not be able to contribute in the way they think is expected of them. For example, members of a committee may think they will be asked to do too much to prepare for group meetings or they may fear they have nothing to contribute. Similarly, members of educational groups are often apprehensive about their ability to learn new material, and members of support groups are fearful that members will not understand or share their concerns. Because expectations about role performance can interfere with a member's participation in the group, it is helpful for workers to describe their expectations of members and solicit feedback and input. This process provides a forum for members to air their fears about the challenges they face. It also helps clarify any mistaken or distorted expectations that members may have and provides an opportunity for workers to modify or change their own expectations.

Authentic Communication about Purposes and Goals

Ambivalence about changing and fears about the demands that may be placed on them may lead members to be less than candid in early group meetings. Shulman (1999) points out that members of treatment groups may begin by sharing "near" problems "that do not bear directly on some of the more difficult and hard-to-talk-about issues" (p. 348). In task groups, members may bring up peripheral issues that could potentially sidetrack the group.

To increase authentic communication as the group develops, the worker can take several steps:

- Always treat members' suggestions and ideas about how to proceed with respect. The worker should not dismiss or ignore what a member says or treat it as a "smoke screen" or a "red herring." This will only alienate members and certainly will not encourage them to open up and reveal more meaningful issues. Instead, the worker should strive to understand the deeper issues implied by the member's message.

- Link the member's statements with the larger purposes of the group. The worker can do this by asking members how the suggestions or ideas fit in with the agreed-on purposes of the group.

- Place the relevant parts of the member's message in the context of themes or issues that have been previously discussed in the group.

- Support the initiative the member demonstrated by speaking up without endorsing the message. Statements such as "I'm glad to see that you are thinking about what you want to accomplish in the group" or "I'm happy to see that you care enough about the direction of the group to make that suggestion" let members know that their perspectives are welcome and valued without indicating that the worker supports the content of the message.

Anticipating Obstacles

In the beginning stage of group work, it is important for workers to help members anticipate the obstacles they may encounter as they work on specific goals and objectives. It is useful to ask members to describe the obstacles they foresee in accomplishing individual and group goals. Sometimes it is useful to encourage members to engage in a time-projection program activity. In this exercise, members are asked to imagine what it will be like for them at the end of the group when they have accomplished their goals. Members can be encouraged to discuss how changes brought about in the group are likely to be received by those around them and to focus on what might prevent accomplishments in the group from being implemented in settings outside the group. As members share potential impediments to long-term, meaningful change, the worker can facilitate a discussion about overcoming the impediments.

Experience suggests that when members and the leader are aware of potential obstacles, they can often plan ways to overcome them before the middle stage of the group. Chapter 9 describes a variety of methods that can be used during the middle stage of a group to help members overcome obstacles to accomplishing specific goals.

SUMMARY

Although all aspects of group work are important for the successful functioning of a group, the initial stage sets the tone for the group's future development. In the beginning stage, the worker's central task is to ensure that a group develops patterns of relating and patterns of task accomplishment that facilitate functioning as the group moves toward its middle stage of development.

To accomplish this, workers should focus on achieving certain objectives in the beginning stage of task and treatment groups. These include (1) introducing members of the group; (2) clarifying the purpose and function of the group as it is perceived by the worker, the members, and the sponsoring organization; (3) clarifying confidentiality issues; (4) helping members feel a part of the group; (5) guiding the development of the group; (6) balancing task and socioemotional aspects of the group process; (7) setting goals; (8) contracting for work; (9) facilitating members' motivation and ability to work in the group; and (10) anticipating obstacles.

Workers who are able to help their groups achieve these objectives in the initial stage will find themselves in a good position to help the group make a smooth transition to the middle stage of development. Any objectives that are not achieved early in the group's development will have to be reconsidered later as the group and its members encounter difficulties accomplishing agreed-on goals.

LEARNING ASSIGNMENTS

1. If you were asked to lead a group for elementary school children who exhibited acting out behavior in the classroom, what fears would you have about leading the group? How would you overcome these fears? Identify ways that you could structure group meetings to avoid acting-out behavior.

2. Form a small classroom group. Select three of the warm-up or introduction exercises described in this chapter. Use each exercise in your group. After you have completed all three, discuss the benefits and drawbacks of each. For what populations would each exercise be most appropriate?

3. Form a small classroom group. Have all members identify a study habit they would like to change. Have each member specify a change goal and the steps to achieve it. Using a format similar to the one shown in Figure 7.3, identify factors that would increase and decrease each group member's motivation for achieving the goal.

CASE EXAMPLE

At first, Drew felt enthusiastic about being assigned to lead a group called "the Lunch Bunch." His enthusiasm was tempered when his field instructor told him that it would be composed of 10 fourth- and fifth-grade boys who were suspended from the school lunchroom because of acting-out behavior. The purposes of the group were to help members learn acceptable ways of dealing with their peers and to reintegrate each member into the main lunchroom milieu.

In addition to having no control over the composition of the group, Drew was concerned about what might happen when all of the "offending parties" would come together for the first session. He interviewed each of the members assigned to the group to introduce himself, to learn about their expectations, and to begin to orient them to the group's purposes and goals. During the interviews he learned that various members were suspended from the lunchroom because they fought with other students and expressed their anger in inappropriate ways such as yelling, cursing, and throwing food. Most of the youngsters he met seemed to act appropriately during the initial interview and appeared enthusiastic about meeting with the Lunch Bunch.

On the day of the first session, Drew came prepared. In addition to a written agenda, name tags, art supplies, and some CDs for music, Drew brought chocolate chip cookies, hoping that after members ate their lunch, dessert would be an incentive for them to act appropriately until the group ended. As members entered, most seemed to know each other from classes. Drew chose to help members introduce themselves by playing a version of "Top Secret" in which each member wrote down something about himself that others would not ordinarily know. He read what each boy had written, and they had fun trying to figure out who had written each statement. Drew felt that this activity was moderately successful because it helped the members get involved with the group right away.

Next, Drew made an opening statement about the purpose of the group. He was careful to word the statement of purpose so that the boys could understand it and so that it gave them some guidance about what would happen in the group. He noted that the group's purpose was "to work together to learn safer ways of handling yourselves in the lunchroom, and to have fun while learning." Two of the members stated that they thought the group was like detention and was punishment for their behavior. Drew clarified that it was true that their behavior had gotten them referred to the group, but that the group was not punishment. He noted that both he and the members could plan some of the activities, and these would take into account what members wanted to do during group sessions. The boys seemed skeptical about this, so Drew asked for more discussion. He clarified that his role was to help them explore how to act with each other and to help them plan for activities in the group.

One of the most difficult discussions that took place early in the first session concerned confidentiality. One member wanted to know if Drew was going to tell the principal or his parents about what he might say or do in the group. Drew recognized that many of the boys frequently interacted with each other in settings outside the group, and this could easily compromise any promises of confidentiality. In addition,

Drew was responsible for reporting the progress of members to his field instructor and, ultimately, to the school principal. Drew mentioned these two issues to the members and suggested a few ground rules about confidentiality that the group might discuss at their next meeting. He suggested that it would be appropriate for members to discuss aspects of his participation with his parents, but members should not refer to group members by name. He emphasized that under no circumstances should members talk to other students about what went on inside the group. Finally, Drew said that he had to report on each member's progress to his field instructor, but that he would try to share what he would say with each boy individually before he discussed it with his field instructor.

After this, the group started to work on other rules for how the group should operate. During the first session, they agreed that they should all be good listeners, should wait their turn before speaking, and should try to help each other. Drew was satisfied that, in the time allotted, the group seemed to be making some progress on formulating a beginning contract. He suggested that members might think of other rules for the group and could bring these up in the next meeting.

Drew recognized that the time allotted for this first session was running out and he wanted to provide the members with a fun experience before they left to return to their classes. During the remaining time, they played some music from Drew's collection. Drew asked members what they felt after listening to each song. Some of this discussion was difficult for some of the members because they were not familiar with some of Drew's musical selections. Drew suggested that members could bring in some of their favorite music for the next session. The members received this news with enthusiasm. Drew said that when a member brought in a favorite musical selection, his responsibility would be to ask other members to identify what they felt after listening to it. Chocolate chip cookies for dessert tempered this early "demand for work."

c h a p t e r *8*

Assessment

Because of the complexity of human behavior and group dynamics, assessment is one of the most challenging aspects of group work practice. The worker makes assessments to understand particular practice situations and to plan effective interventions. For a complete and thorough assessment, the group worker considers (1) individual group members, (2) the group as a whole, and (3) the group's environment. Workers begin their assessments during the planning stage and continue to assess and reassess the group's work until the group ends.

Although assessments are made in all stages of a group's life, the process dominates a worker's time in the beginning phase of group work after the planning tasks (discussed in Chapter 6) are completed. It is at this time that the worker is most actively engaged in understanding the functioning of the group and its members.

DEFINITION OF ASSESSMENT

Siporin (1975) has stated, "assessment is both a process and a product upon which the helping process is based" (p. 219). As a process, assessment involves gathering, organizing, and making judgments about information. As a product, assessment is a verbal or written statement of the functioning of the group and its members, which is useful in the development of intervention plans.

There is little agreement in the literature on group work about assessment terminology or assessment focus. Some writers use the term *diagnosis* (Sundel, Radin, & Churchill, 1985), others use the term *assessment* (Rose, 1998), and still others prefer not to use either term (Schwartz, 1976). In this text, the term *assessment* rather than *diagnosis* is used because assessment is more compatible with a generalist approach to social group work practice. *Diagnosis* is a term borrowed from medicine. It refers to the identification of disease processes within an individual. In contrast, a thorough generalist assessment focuses on both the strengths and the problems encountered by individual group members and the group as a whole and carefully considers the effect of the larger social environment on the group and its members. Also, a holistic perspective focusing on the biological, psychological, social, cultural, spiritual, and environmental functioning of the members of the group is considered.

As with other aspects of social group work practice, assessment varies according to the type of group being conducted. In a treatment group, for example, the worker frequently focuses assessments on the problems experienced by individual members, but a task group leader's assessment is often focused on the ability of members to contribute to the group's productivity.

Despite differences in focus, there are many commonalities in the assessments made by workers leading different types of groups. For example, in both task and treatment groups, most workers assess the strengths and weaknesses of the group as a whole, the members, and the external environment in which the group and its members function. Commonalities also can be found in the assessment of different groups that are at the same stage of development. For example, in the beginning stage, workers make a systematic assessment of the functioning of the group and its members. During the middle stage, workers test the validity of their initial assessments and modify their intervention plans on the basis of the success of early interventions. In the ending stage of the group, the worker makes an assessment of the functioning of the group and its members to highlight accomplishments, to focus attention on areas that still need work, and to ensure that achievements accomplished during the group will be maintained after the group ends.

Relationship to Individual Assessment

Most readers are familiar with generalist social work practice approaches that rely on systems theory and take a holistic approach to assessment (Johnson, 1998; Kirst-Ashman & Hull, 1999). Using a generalist approach, group workers are supposed to assess individual members, the group as a whole, and the group in relation to its environment. In practice, however, there is a tendency for group workers to focus on individual members rather than on the processes of group interaction or the group in relation to its environment. This may be because many group workers were originally trained as caseworkers and have more experience working with individuals than with groups. Also, some workers do not have any formal education in group work. Data from analyses of the content and style of group leaders confirm the lack of focus on group dynamics (Hill, 1965; Toseland, Rossiter, Peak, & Hill, 1990). For example, Hill found that, on average, leaders spent less than 5 percent of their time on matters pertaining to dynamics of the group as a whole.

We strongly recommend that group workers be especially vigilant about spending time during each group meeting to discuss group processes. This can often be accomplished by making a conscious effort to point out processes in the here-and-now of group interaction. Sometimes, however, stopping the action to identify, clarify, or discuss group processes can be disruptive to the content being discussed. An effective alternative is to reserve a few minutes at the end of each group meeting for the worker and members to comment on and discuss the group processes. For example, a member might state that there seemed to be much member-to-member communication during the group meeting, that the discussion included only a few members, or that members did not seem to be considering the points of view of others. Similarly, the worker might comment on the norms developing in the group or the roles that members were playing. The members can then be encouraged to discuss what changes, if any, they would like to make in the group dynamics during future meetings.

If a separate time is set aside for discussing group process at the end of a meeting, care should be taken not to use the time to discuss content. It is easy to slip into discussions of content when group processes are being discussed. For example, during a discussion of group interaction patterns, two members might note that the entire session was spent focused on one member's problem. Another member might say, "John talked a lot because he is having a lot of problems with his wife." The worker should point out that the issue is not John's problem with his wife, but whether the group wants to spend an entire session focused on one member's concern. The worker can then guide the group to a discussion of the pros and cons of focusing on one member.

With the exception of social action groups and coalitions, workers often fail to pay much attention to the group's broader environment. Periodically throughout the life of a group, workers and members should take time to describe and discuss their perceptions of the relationship of the group to the sponsoring organization and to the larger community that sanctions the group's work.

Overall, assessment in group work is more complex than assessment in practice with individuals. In addition to assessing the functioning of individual group members, assessment in group work also means examining the processes that take place in the group as a whole and the support and opposition the group as a whole is likely to encounter in the larger social environment.

THE ASSESSMENT PROCESS

Fisher (1978) has aptly described assessment as a funneling process. In the early stages, the worker is confronted with amorphous and sketchy data about the group and its members. Initially, the worker fills in gaps by collecting missing data. As information is collected, the worker begins to sort through it and organize it systematically. The group members should be involved as much as possible in collecting and analyzing the data. This will help them to formulate goals and decide on targets for intervention.

Gradually, the assessment process narrows as data are collected and organized and judgments are made about how to intervene in, cope with, or alleviate a problem. In a group for people getting a divorce, for example, the worker might ask members to describe their feelings about their spouses. Information gathered from this preliminary assessment leads the worker to a further assessment of members' feelings of loss and anger toward their spouses. The worker then facilitates members' discussion of these feelings and helps them to make judgments about what interventions would be most helpful. Results of the assessment process are used to develop an intervention plan, which includes helping members express their feelings, share effective coping skills, and practice using coping skills to help them work through their feelings during and between group meetings.

How Much Information?

Several issues arise when workers assess the functioning of the group and its members. One of the most basic issues is how much information to collect. Although it is often recommended that workers collect as much information as possible (psychosocial histories for members of treatment groups or extensive information-gathering efforts in task groups), increasing information beyond a certain point may not lead to better interventions. Also, workers are sometimes confronted with urgent situations that preclude extensive data collection. In these situations, workers should be guided by goals formulated during the planning and the beginning stages of group work. Workers also should be as clear as possible about the relevance of the information being collected. Extensive data collection that has little relation to the group's goals is a violation of members' right to privacy and of dubious value for accomplishing group and individual member goals.

No matter how much information is collected, workers should suspend their judgments about a problematic situation until they have reflected on all the data they have time to collect. A widespread and potentially damaging mistake of novice workers occurs when they make judgments and offer suggestions concerning intervention strategies before they fully understand a problem or have found out what the member has already done to cope with the problem. When making premature suggestions, the novice is often confronted by a group member who says, "I tried that and it didn't work." The result is that the worker is at a loss as to how to proceed, and the member's faith in the worker's ability to help is shaken.

Some helpful principles to guide workers in their data-collection efforts include

- Use more than one mode of data collection whenever possible.
- Distinguish between the problem, concern, or task about which information is being collected and the source of the information.
- Obtain relevant samples of data from several sources.

- Structure data collection so that relevant information can be obtained quickly and efficiently.
- Develop a system that will not place overwhelming demands on persons who are collecting information or on persons who are asked for information.
- Avoid biasing data despite the selectivity and subjectivity that are inherent parts of any effort at data collection and assessment.
- Involve all group members in the assessment process so that multiple viewpoints can help overcome limitations of the worker's subjectivity.
- Discuss assessment data with a coleader or a supervisor between meetings.

Diagnostic Labels

Another issue that often arises when one makes assessments of the members of treatment groups is the use of diagnostic classification systems and labels. Diagnostic classification systems can be helpful in making differential assessments and arriving at effective treatment plans for group members. Classification systems such as the *Diagnostic and Statistical Manual of Mental Disorders* (DSM) are used in many mental health settings for assessment, intervention, and reimbursement purposes (American Psychiatric Association, 1994). Previous versions of the DSM were criticized as unreliable and irrelevant in relation to the selection of intervention procedures (Hersen & Bellack, 1976). However, the latest version (DSM-IV) appears to overcome many of the earlier problems.

Diagnostic labels can carry social stigma. Members of a group may be at risk for harmful stereotyping when diagnostic labels are used indiscriminately. Also, members may start to behave in ways that are consistent with the labels ascribed to them (Kirk & Kutchins, 1997). Therefore, group work practitioners should be wary of the indiscriminate use of diagnostic labels in mental health and other settings.

Although an in-depth examination of the applications of the DSM to group treatment is beyond the scope of this text, one example may help illustrate its usefulness. If not diagnosed properly, a confused 71-year-old could be diagnosed as having organic brain syndrome and be recommended for treatment in reality orientation and program activity groups to prevent further deterioration. Use of the criteria stated in the DSM, however, shows that the person's confusion may be diagnosed properly as a major depressive episode compounded by isolation and malnutrition. Given this diagnosis, a quite different form of group treatment would be recommended after the person's malnutrition had been treated. For example, the person might be encouraged to attend a therapy group for people suffering from problems of depression and be encouraged to expand personal friendship networks by becoming involved in an activity group at a senior center or a social group at a church or synagogue.

Assessment Focus

A third issue that often arises in making an assessment is how to focus data-collection efforts. Workers should avoid becoming locked into one assessment focus. Premature allegiance to a particular view of a situation can result in ignoring important data or attempting to fit all data into a particular conceptualization of the situation.

In focusing their assessments, workers should be guided by the unique needs and particular circumstances of each member and by the purposes of the group. In one group, for example, it may be important to focus on members' family situations, but in another group, it may be more beneficial to assess members' problem-solving skills. In other words, the focus of assessment should change with the changing needs of the group and its members.

To make an accurate assessment, workers should strive for objectivity. Although all observations contain some subjectivity, it is important to separate subjective impressions and opinions from more objective observations of behavior and events. Inferences should be based on logic and evidence.

It can also be helpful to share observations and inferences with group members. They can confirm the validity of the worker's observations and inferences and provide an alternative perspective. It is also helpful to check the validity of subjective inferences with supervisors. Obtaining alternative perspectives in this manner can help the worker make assessments and formulate intervention plans.

ASSESSING THE FUNCTIONING OF GROUP MEMBERS

During the assessment process, the worker should consider the current functioning of the members and, whenever possible, also examine members' functioning from a developmental perspective. A developmental perspective can help the worker assess whether a member's current functioning manifests itself in a transitory, acute pattern of behavior or a long-term, chronic pattern of behavior. It also helps the worker gain a greater understanding of the meaning of symptoms and their intensity, duration, and scope. Overall, assessments are more likely to be accurate and complete if they consider the developmental context in which members' problems have developed.

Workers should also assess how the personal characteristics of each member interact with functional abilities. Personal characteristics such as racial and cultural identity, gender, and age have an important influence on how members interact with one another in the group. For example, in working with groups of Native Americans, the worker should be aware of the cultural norm of withholding opinions about other people because of deep respect for the privacy of others and a tradition of noninterference (Good Tracks, 1973). When assessing members' behaviors and characteristics in a culturally sensitive way, a characteristic such as noninterference is viewed as a strength rather than as a limitation.

When making an assessment, workers should examine three broad aspects of members' functioning:

1. The intrapersonal life of the member
2. The interpersonal interactions of the member
3. The environment in which the member functions

In assessing members' intrapersonal lives, workers rely on their own observations, members' self-reports, and collateral reports. To examine members' intrapersonal functioning, the worker may focus on members' perceived health status; psychological and emotional well-being; and their cognition, beliefs, motivations, and expectations.

When assessing interpersonal functioning, workers focus on members' social skills, the extent and quality of their social support networks, and their role performance. The group provides a natural laboratory for the worker to observe the interpersonal functioning of each member, but it is also helpful to inquire about a member's interpersonal interactions with family and close friends because these relationships often have a significant effect on the member.

Workers should also examine the environmental context in which members function. Questions such as "Is the environment supportive or does it hinder members' ability to work on group and individual goals?" and "What resources can members draw on from their environment to help them achieve their goals?" are often pertinent.

In task groups, the worker may find it useful to assess the intrapersonal, interpersonal, and environmental functioning of members, though in a slightly different way. For example, leaders of task groups generally do not make in-depth assessments of members' physical, psychological, or emotional states. However, they are likely to examine a member's motivation for attending and the member's expectations about accomplishing the work of the group. Similarly, a task group leader would be unlikely to assess the extent to which members' families support their work in the group. The leader is more likely to consider what effect a controversial committee report might have on members' day-to-day interactions with their colleagues or on their interaction with the line staff they supervise.

Methods for Assessing Group Members

A variety of methods exists to help workers assess the functioning of group members. Among the most commonly used methods for assessing functioning are (1) members' self-observations, (2) worker observations, (3) reports by others who have seen the member function outside the group, and (4) standardized assessment instruments.

Self-Observation

Self-observation refers to members' examination and assessment of their own behavior. Usually, members simply recall and describe their own behavior, then examine and reflect on it with the help of the worker and other group members. Woods and Hollis (1990) referred to this process as "exploration-description-ventilation" (p. 115) and as "reflective discussion of the person-situation configuration" (pp. 124–134).

Retrospective self-observation and self-reflection are often helpful in developing insight about one's behavior, identifying patterns of behavior, and examining the effect of the environment. However, members' recollections may not be accurate; for a variety of reasons, recollections may be incomplete, vague, or distorted. Therefore, other methods of self-observation, such as self-monitoring, have been developed.

Because these methods are more intrusive and require more effort on the part of the member than simply recalling and reflecting on past behavior, workers should be sure that members are motivated to try the methods and have sufficient resources to implement them successfully. Workers should be aware that self-monitoring methods often presume members to be action oriented, insightful, and sensitive; thus, the methods may not be useful for all members.

SELF-MONITORING.   Rather than relying on memory of past events, members may examine their own behavior outside the group in a prospective and systematic fashion by collecting data on the frequency, intensity, and duration of a particular behavior and its antecedents and consequences. This process is often referred to as *self-monitoring*. An assessment of a particular behavior and its antecedents and consequences can be useful in determining how particular problematic behaviors are maintained.

Awareness of behavior patterns is a prerequisite for changing behavior. For example, an assessment of the antecedents of the anxiety that a member experiences in social situations may reveal that the statements the member tells himself about his lack of anything interesting to say trigger his anxiety.

Some evidence indicates that self-monitoring can be reactive; that is, the act of self-monitoring may by itself increase desired behaviors and decrease undesired behaviors (Stuart, 1977; Thoresen & Mahoney, 1974). However, self-monitoring can also have therapeutic and empowering benefits by heightening members' awareness of their current behavior patterns (Kopp, 1993).

To begin self-monitoring, the worker should be sure that members are motivated to examine their own behavior and to record it. Then the worker should help members decide exactly what they are going to monitor. It is often helpful to have members monitor behaviors they would like to increase as well as behaviors they would like to decrease. This process can help members to replace problematic behaviors with desired ones, rather than only reducing problematic behaviors.

In deciding what to monitor, workers should help members determine what is feasible and realistic, given their life circumstances. Members often want to collect data about several problematic behaviors at the same time. However, members are rarely able to follow through on such ambitious plans. Therefore, initially, members should be encouraged to develop realistic plans that they can readily accomplish. Later, they may wish to develop more ambitious monitoring plans.

In deciding on a realistic plan, it should be clear where, when, and under what conditions a particular behavior will be monitored. For example, it is unrealistic for a single parent with four children to expect to monitor the behavior of one child just before dinner or in the morning when the children are preparing for school. However, there may be time during the afternoon or evening when the parent can observe the child's behavior for a short period without being interrupted.

In most groups, members make a mental note of what they have observed between meetings, and they share their observations with other members during the next group meeting. Because it is sometimes difficult for members to accurately recall the data they have monitored, methods for recording self-monitored data have been developed. These methods include charts, logs, diaries, problem cards, and self-anchored rating scales.

Charting.   Some members find it useful to record monitored data on a chart because it provides an organized, visual display of the information. A chart allows members to see trends in the data—that is, whether a behavior is increasing or decreasing. It also may serve as a reminder for members to perform tasks that they agreed to complete between meetings.

Workers should help members be creative in designing charts. For example, in helping a parent develop a monitoring chart that will be shared with a young child, the worker can suggest using smiley faces, stars, or hearts instead of check marks to signify that a behavior was performed correctly.

The format of a chart depends on the method used to collect self-monitoring data. The simplest format uses a tally to measure the frequency of a behavior. More complicated formats are sometimes used to get an accurate assessment of the frequency of a behavior without having to count each occurrence. A chart divided into a number of time intervals can be used to count behaviors. For example, members can count the number of occurrences of a behavior in 10-minute intervals between 6 P.M. and 7 P.M. every evening. Charts can also be made that allow a member to record whether a behavior occurred at particular intervals during a designated period, such as at the beginning of every 30-minute time interval. For further discussion of methods to chart self-monitored data, see Bloom, Fisher, and Orme (1999) or Thoresen and Mahoney (1974).

Members sometimes fail to follow through on charting self-monitored behaviors. For some, charting may require too much organization. Others find it inconvenient to monitor and record their behavior immediately after it occurs.

Members sometimes prefer one of the methods described in the following sections.

Logs and Diaries.   Logs and diaries are often less accurate than monitoring charts because members rely on their memory of events to record behaviors at some convenient time *after* they occur rather than *as* they occur. However, because of their convenience, members sometimes prefer keeping a log or diary to keeping a chart.

Logs and diaries require members to record events in a descriptive fashion and can be a valuable source of qualitative data for the worker to gain valuable insights into the world of each member. Logs and diaries can also be used to help the worker understand other data reported in quantitative self-observations. To avoid logs and diaries that become too idiosyncratic, the worker can give members a clear indication of what data they are to record. For example, a worker may ask members to record problematic situations and their immediate cognitive, affective, and behavioral responses to situations. For examples of logs and diaries and more information about how to use them, see Bloom, Fisher, and Orme (1999).

Problem Card.   A variation on logs and diaries is the problem card (Flowers, 1979; Rose, 1981). Group members are asked to fill in one or more problem cards between meetings. On each card, the member is asked to describe briefly a problem experienced between sessions that is relevant to the group's theme. The member is also asked to choose from within the group a judge or rater who is willing to assess the member's progress. At intervals throughout the group's life, the judges are asked to rate group members' progress in ameliorating problematic behavior. Because of the evaluation component, the problem card procedure can be used for both assessments and evaluations.

Self-Anchored Rating Scales.   Members can also record their observations by using a self-anchored rating scale. This is a measurement device made by the worker and a group member specifically to record data about a problematic behavior that has been identified as the target of an intervention. To develop a self-anchored rating scale, the worker helps a group member identify behaviors, feelings, and thoughts that are associated with various levels of the problematic behavior. For example, in developing a scale to measure depression, a member suggests that severe depression occurs when he has suicidal thoughts and does not eat or sleep. Moderate depression occurs when he has thoughts that he is not a good father or husband, when he has little appetite and eats only one meal a day, and when he falls asleep only after lying awake for a long time. The member suggests that he is not depressed when he has a good appetite, can sleep well, and has thoughts that he is a good father and husband. An example of a self-anchored scale to rate depression is shown in Figure 8.1. For further information about developing self-anchored rating scales, see Bloom, Fisher, and Orme (1999).

FIGURE 8.1 ■ *Example of a Self-Anchored Rating Scale*

Very Depressed	**Moderately Depressed**	**Not Depressed**
1. Does not eat	1. Eats one meal a day	1. Has good appetite
2. Does not sleep	2. Has difficulty in	2. Sleeps well
3. Has suicidal thoughts	sleeping	3. Has thoughts about
	3. Has thoughts about	being a good father
	not being a good	and husband
	father or husband	

Worker Observation

Workers can assess the functioning of group members by observing them during meetings. In most practice situations, workers rely on naturalistic observations. However, specific activities such as simulations and program activities to assess members' functioning in a particular area can also be used.

NATURALISTIC OBSERVATION.   Workers can learn a great deal about members by observing their behavior in the group. Given free interaction within the group, members often display behaviors similar to behaviors exhibited outside the group. By scanning the group, the worker can stay aware of the reactions of all group members. The worker observes a member behaving in a certain manner, for example, and makes a mental note. Further observation, over time, helps the worker identify the member's behavior patterns and typical coping styles.

As the group develops, members can be asked to describe their behavior. This feedback can be used to determine whether members' self-perceptions are consistent with the worker's observations. The worker may also solicit other members' observations and reactions. The process of formulating an assessment on the basis of observations and perceptions of more than one individual is often referred to as *triangulation*. Triangulation can lead to assessments that are more accurate than assessments made by a single individual.

Although naturalistic observation offers the worker an opportunity to observe members' behavior in an unobtrusive fashion, its chief limitation is that group interaction may not offer the right opportunities to assess pertinent aspects of a member's behavior. For example, in a parenting skills group, a parent may describe how she sets limits on her child's behavior, but group interaction does not provide the worker with an opportunity to view the parent actually setting limits.

In addition, experience suggests that members may not always give accurate or sufficiently detailed accounts of their behavior. When the worker can actually observe the member engaging in a behavior such as limit setting, for example, the worker may find that the member does not set limits in the way that is stated. For example, the member's tone of voice or nonverbal cues may not match the description of the verbal behavior. Therefore, the worker may find other methods useful when observing members' behavior.

ROLE PLAYING.   Role playing, sociodrama, and psychodrama are as important for assessment as for intervention. They allow the worker and the other members of the group to observe a member acting out a situation. Role-play methods are described in detail in Chapter 13.

SIMULATIONS.   Simulations assess members' functioning in specific, role-playing situations. The worker asks for one or more volunteers to simulate a real-life situation. Members whose behavior is being assessed are asked to respond to the situation created by the volunteers as they would if they were confronted with the situation in their everyday lives. For example, in an assertion training group, three members might volunteer to role play standing in a line at a grocery store. The member whose behavior is being assessed is asked to stand at the end of the line. Then, another group member is asked to try to get ahead of the member at the end of the line. The worker and the remaining group members observe how the unassertive member handles the situation. Similarly, in a parenting group, a simulation may involve having two members play the role of siblings in an argument about who is to play with a toy truck. The parent whose behavior is being assessed is asked to act as he would if such a situation occurred at home.

Assessments of a member's behavior during a simulation can be made by all group members. Scales to rate a member's response can be developed specifically for the objectives and goals of a particular group. For example, in an assertiveness training group in which all group members are trying to reduce their anxiety and improve their responses, ratings may focus on (1) the anxiety level that a member demonstrates while making a response, and (2) the effectiveness of a response in asserting the member's rights in the situation.

Simulations have been developed for measuring the skills of several populations, including psychiatric inpatients (Clark, 1971; Goldsmith & McFall, 1975) and outpatients (Schinke & Rose, 1976), women (De Lange, 1977), the elderly (Berger, 1976; Toseland & Rose, 1978), social workers (Rose, Cayner, & Edleson, 1977), adolescents (Freedman, 1974; Rosenthal, 1978), the mentally challenged (Bates, 1978), and parents (Rose & Hanusa, 1980).

These simulations were developed by using the model described by Goldfried and D'Zurilla (1969), which includes (1) analyzing a problematic situation and developing several realistic situations that members are likely to confront in their daily lives, (2) enumerating possible responses to these situations, (3) evaluating the responses in terms of their efficacy in handling the problematic situation, (4) developing a measurement format, and (5) evaluating the measure's reliability and validity. Workers can use this model to create simulation tests for populations and problems for which simulation tests have not yet been developed.

Simulations have the potential limitation that group members know they are acting rather than performing in real-life situations. In most cases, however, members appear to forget that they are acting and perform as they would in real life.

PROGRAM ACTIVITIES.   Many different types of program activities can be used to assess the functioning of group members. The selection of appropriate activities depends on the type of group the worker is leading. In children's groups, the worker can have members participate in play activities and games. For example, the game Charades can be used to assess how members act out particular situations. Games requiring cooperation can be used to assess the extent to which members are able to negotiate differences.

In adolescent groups, a party, a meal, or a sports activity can often help the worker make an assessment of members' social skills and their level of social development. In adult groups containing moderately or severely impaired members, preparing a meal together or going on an outing can help the worker assess daily living skills. Program activities should be age-appropriate and should give members the opportunity to demonstrate behaviors that they would like to improve through their participation in a group.

When using role plays and program activities to assess members' behavior, it is important to keep in mind the influence of cultural heritage on members' performances. Role playing may not be a readily accepted form of group participation. For example, Lewis and Ho (1975) suggest that in group work with Native Americans, the use of certain techniques (for example, role plays) "are highly insensitive to the cultural orientation of Native Americans," and that Native Americans may "consider such group behavior to be false; it looks and sounds real but lacks genuineness, depth and real commitment" (p. 381).

The use of program activities can be a particularly effective means of assessing members of culturally diverse groups (Delgado, 1983). For example, Ashby, Gilchrist, and Miramontez (1987) reported the usefulness of cultural activities in reaching sexually abused Native American adolescents and suggested that program activities and techniques be culturally relevant to the needs of members. For more information about using program materials in groups, see the section on program activities in Chapter 9 and Appendix G.

Reports by Others

In addition to members' self-observations and workers' observations, leaders often rely on the reports of people who are familiar with members' behavior outside the group. When considering data reported by others, the worker should assess the data's reliability and validity, which can vary considerably from person to person and from one report to another. For example, some data may be based on rumors, assumptions, or the statements of unidentified third parties;

other data may come from direct observations. Obviously, the worker should place less confidence in rumors than in direct observations.

The worker should also consider the relationship of the person reporting the data to the member about whom data have been collected. Is the person reporting the data interested in the well-being of the group member or is the person motivated by ill feeling, personal gain, or rivalry? By examining a person's motivation for reporting data about a group member, the worker is in a better position to assess any potential bias in a report.

When a worker has an ongoing relationship with individuals who regularly report data about group members' behavior, such as mental health therapy aides, child care workers, and teachers, it is often worth the effort to help these individuals use reliable and valid data-collection systems. For example, a therapy group leader can offer to help a mental health therapy aide develop a chart to monitor the behavior of a group member at meals or during recreational activities. Similarly, a school social worker can offer an elementary school teacher assistance in using the Achenbach (1997) checklist, which is a standardized instrument to measure children's social behavior. In this way, the worker can build a relationship with persons who have daily contact with group members and ensure that accurate data are reported about members' behaviors outside the group.

Standardized Instruments

A fourth way that workers can assess the functioning of group members is by using standardized assessment instruments. Some instruments require lengthy personal interviews, but others are brief, paper-and-pencil measures known as *rapid assessment instruments*. The Beck Depression Inventory (BDI), for example, is a 21-item scale that assesses the presence and severity of depression. Levitt and Reid (1981) and Toseland and Reid (1985) found that rapid assessment instruments such as the BDI can be used by clinical social workers who have little training or previous experience in test administration.

Rapid assessment instruments can be used many ways in a group. For example, some members of an outpatient psychiatric group can be asked to spend a few minutes filling out the BDI during a group meeting or at home between meetings. Other members might be asked to fill out the Stait Trait Anxiety Inventory (Spielberger, Gorsuch, Lushene, Vagg, & Jacobs, 1983) or other instruments that assess the particular symptoms individual group members are experiencing.

Despite the usefulness of standardized assessment instruments for understanding the problems and concerns experienced by group members, it should be kept in mind that these instruments may not be appropriate for use with all populations. For example, when administered to members of specific sociocultural groups or to developmentally disabled persons, such instruments may not be valid or reliable. In fact, they may give the worker a distorted impression of members' strengths. Thus, when considering use of a standardized measure with a particular group of individuals, workers should check whether the description of the instrument includes information about its use with particular populations. If no information is available, workers should select another measure that has been found to be valid for use with the population of interest. A measure suspected of being culturally biased should never be used because even if caution is exercised in interpreting the results, others who have access to the results may draw erroneous conclusions.

Because rapid assessment instruments are focused on particular problem areas, the type of assessment instrument selected depends on the group's focus. Fisher and Corcoran (1994) present a variety of rapid assessment instruments for use with children, adults, couples, and families. They review, for example, nine scales developed by Hudson (1982) that assess (1) depression, (2) self-esteem, (3) marital discord, (4) sexual discord, (5) parent-child relationships, (6) child's relationship with mother, (7) child's relationship with father, (8) intrafamilial stress, and (9) peer relationships. These scales are also available as part of a computerized multiproblem screening inventory (Hudson, 1994).

Walls, Werner, Bacon, and Zane (1977) briefly describe more than 200 behavior checklists that can also be useful in assessing the problematic behaviors of children and adults, and Fisher and Corcoran (1994) describe measures for clinical practice. There are also texts that describe measures for specific populations. For example, Kane and Kane (1981) describe measures for assessing older adults; Ollendick and Hersen (1984) and Marsh and Terdal (1997) describe methods for assessing children. For additional information about available standardized assessment instruments, see Kramer and Conoley, 1992; Cone and Hawkins, 1977; Hersen and Bellack, 1976; Rauch, 1993; and Robinson and Shaver, 1973.

ASSESSING THE FUNCTIONING OF THE GROUP AS A WHOLE

Methods for assessing the group as a whole have been given less attention in the group work literature than have methods for assessing individual members (Fuhriman and Burlingame, 1994). In 1970, Klein proposed a schema for diagnosing and correcting group problems, and more recently, Fuhriman and Packard (1986) reviewed 26 ways of measuring group processes. Delucia-Waack (1997) also reviewed process and outcomes measures to encourage practitioners to evaluate their work with groups. The many different conceptualizations of group development mentioned in Chapter 3 are also attempts at assessing normal group functioning. In recent years, however, the group work literature has tended to emphasize assessing and treating the problems of individual group members within the group context and has de-emphasized methods to assess the functioning of the group as a whole. In assessing the group as a whole, the worker should be guided by the four major areas of group dynamics mentioned in Chapter 3. These are the group's

- Communication and interaction patterns
- Cohesion
- Social control mechanisms
- Group culture

Communication and interaction patterns are established early in the group. Therefore, the worker should be especially concerned about these patterns as they develop during the beginning stage. A careful assessment of communication patterns can alert the worker to potential problems and prevent them from becoming established as a routine part of group functioning. It can also help facilitate member-to-member communication and disclosure of important information that may be helpful in attaining group or individual member goals.

At the beginning of a group, too many member-to-leader interactions and too few member-to-member interactions may be of concern (Toseland, Krebs, & Vahsen, 1978). In newly formed groups, there is a natural tendency for members to look to the worker for direction. The worker may feel gratified by this and encourage it. Unfortunately, this pattern may undermine the mutual aid and group problem solving that occur when members direct their communication to everyone in the group rather than exclusively to the worker.

Other communication patterns that may also alert the worker to potential problems can develop in a group. For example, one member may attempt to dominate group discussion and thus prevent other members from interacting. Another potential problem is a lack of communication by a member. Although it is not unusual for some members to communicate less frequently than others, the worker should be aware of the potential for isolation when a member says little or nothing during the beginning stage of the group.

It is also important for a worker to understand what attracts members to the group. The worker should assess the group's attraction for its members to maintain and increase these forces and help the group become a cohesive unit in working toward group and individual goals.

The initial attraction of a group for its members may come from a variety of sources. In treatment groups, for example, attraction may come from members' hopes that the group will help them solve their problems, reduce their emotional distress, or teach them to perform new or more effective roles in their everyday lives. In task groups, it may come from the status or prestige associated with membership, the importance of the task on which the group is working, or a rare chance to share ideas with colleagues.

When workers assess group cohesion, they sometimes find that its development has not progressed satisfactorily. There are many indications that the group is not attractive to one or more of its members. Indicators include apathy or hostility toward group goals, the failure of members to listen to one another, and the growth of allegiances to other reference groups. By observing the indicators, the worker can gain much information about the attraction of the group for its members. Group cohesion can be measured by using a sociometric scale, the semantic differential, the Systematic Multiple Level Observation of Groups (SYMLOG) method, or by using scales specifically designed to measure group cohesiveness (Budman et al., 1987; Budman, Soldz, Demby, Davis, & Merry, 1993; Seashore, 1954). Some measures are described later in this chapter.

Workers should also assess the norms, roles, and status hierarchies that develop in newly formed groups. The norms that develop are extremely important because they define acceptable and unacceptable behavior in a group. Schopler and Galinsky (1981) found that norms have an important influence on members' satisfaction with their group experiences. Both members and observers indicated that inappropriate norms were more important than were cohesion, roles, goals, leadership, composition, or extragroup relationships in negative group experiences. Workers should help members modify norms that detract from individual and group goals and promote and protect norms that are beneficial for goal achievement.

Members' roles also begin to develop early in the group. According to Levine (1979), initial role taking in a group is a tentative process and may not reflect the roles members will occupy later in the group. Members try out roles and often vacillate among them, such as the socioemotional leader, task leader, dominator, and so on. During this stage of the group, the worker can point out the functional and dysfunctional characteristics of the roles to members and help the members develop role behaviors that will facilitate the group's functioning and their own functioning in the group.

Several typologies of role behavior have been developed to help workers assess member roles. Benne and Sheats (1948), for example, have classified roles into three broad categories: (1) group task roles that are related to helping the group decide on, select, or carry out particular tasks; (2) group building and maintenance roles that help the group function harmoniously; and (3) individual roles that are related to individual members' goals. Group task roles include the instructor, opinion seeker, information giver, elaborator, energizer, evaluator, procedural technician, and recorder. Group building and maintenance roles include the encourager, harmonizer, compromiser, gatekeeper, expediter, standard setter, group observer, and follower. Individual roles include the aggressor, blocker, recognition seeker, confessor, dominator, and help seeker.

Focusing on problematic roles, Shulman (1999) has identified the scapegoat, deviant member, gatekeeper, internal leader, defensive member, and quiet member. Most roles are not difficult for the worker to identify. The scapegoat, for example, receives much negative attention and criticism from the group because the member is blamed for a host of defects and problems. According to Shulman (1999), members attack the portion of a scapegoat's behavior that they least like about themselves. Although Shulman and others (Garland & Kolodny, 1967) mention that scapegoating is common, experience has shown it to be relatively rare.

When one or more members of a group assume dysfunctional roles, it is a signal that the group as a whole is not functioning at an optimal level. For example, when an assessment reveals that a member is functioning as a gatekeeper, that is, one who does not allow the group to discuss sensitive issues, the worker should help the group as a whole examine how to change its overall functioning rather than focus on the member who has assumed the dysfunctional role. The gatekeeper prevents the group as a whole from discussing difficult issues. A quiet member may signal difficulties in the communication and interaction patterns established in the group as a whole. It is rare that a problematic group role is an expression of one individual rather than of group dysfunction.

The status of individual group members and the power that the leader and other group members have at their disposal also affect the development of social control dynamics within the group. For example, although high-status members are likely to adhere to group norms and procedures, they are also much more likely to influence the development of a group than are low-status members. Members in the middle of the status hierarchy are likely to strive for greater status within the group by adhering to group norms and upholding the status quo (Forsyth, 1999). Low-status members are less likely to conform to group norms than either high-status or middle-status members (Forsyth, 1999). An accurate assessment of the status hierarchy in the group can help workers understand and anticipate the actions and reactions of members when the worker intervenes in the group.

An accurate assessment of the power bases that the worker and the members have at their disposal can be important in the beginning stages of group work. Workers who understand the limits of their influence over group members are able to use their power effectively and avoid trying to use it when it will be ineffective. An accurate assessment of the sources of members' power can also help the worker in planning strategies for intervening in the group as a whole and for helping members to form a mutual-aid network of shared resources within the group.

A fourth area that workers should assess when examining the functioning of the group as a whole is the group's culture. Ideas, beliefs, values, and feelings held in common by group members have a profound effect on the therapeutic benefits that can be achieved in the group. Just as some societal cultures promote the public expression of emotion and others do not, groups develop cultures that value certain ways of behaving.

In the beginning stage, the worker should examine the culture that is developing in a group. Does the culture help the group and its members achieve their goals? Because group culture develops more slowly than the other group dynamics, the worker's initial assessment of a group's culture should be viewed as a tentative indication about how the culture may develop. It is difficult to change a group's culture after it is well established, so the worker may wish to share initial impressions with members early. For example, in a group in which a worker observes that a negative, unsupportive culture is developing, it may be helpful to point out in the first or second meeting that most members' communications are problem oriented rather than growth oriented or that few supportive comments are made within the group. Methods to modify or change a group's culture are described in Chapter 9.

A number of methods to assess the group's culture have been developed. Some methods, such as the Hill Interaction Matrix and SYMLOG, were designed to assess a variety of types of groups along several different dimensions; others, such as the Group Atmosphere Scale (Silbergeld, Koenig, Manderscheid, Meeker, & Hornung, 1975), were designed to assess only the psychosocial environment of therapy groups. More information about the Group Atmosphere Scale is presented in Chapter 13.

Methods for Assessing the Group as a Whole

In most practice situations, workers reflect on group functioning between meetings and rely on their own subjective observations to assess the functioning of the group as a whole. But it also can be beneficial to involve the group as a whole in a more structured assessment. In addition to helping members become aware of and involved in improving the group's functioning, using one or more of the structured assessment methods described in the following pages can help confirm or disprove a worker's subjective impressions of group functioning.

There is no measure of group processes that is perfect for all situations. Therefore, it is important to examine measures carefully, thinking about which group-as-a-whole processes are of greatest interest and which measure is most likely to capture what is occurring in a particular group. Fuhriman and colleagues' (Fuhriman & Barlow, 1994; Fuhriman & Packard, 1986) reviews of group process measures are a helpful starting point.

Measuring Communication and Interaction

There are many ways to measure the meanings that underlie communications in the group. One widely used measure is the semantic differential. Using this method, members are asked to rate the meaning of an object or person on a series of seven-point bipolar attitude scales, such as good/bad, valuable/worthless, and so on. Three dimensions of attitudes that can be assessed by the semantic differential are individual group members' (1) evaluation; (2) perceptions of potency; and (3) perceptions of the activity of objects, concepts, or people being rated (Osgood, Suci, & Tannenbaum, 1957). An example of a semantic differential scale is shown is Figure 8.2.

By having members use the semantic differential to rate their fellow group members, the worker can begin to understand how members perceive one another. For example, using the activity scale, group members may rate one member as being particularly active and another member as being particularly inactive. Similarly, the scales can be used to obtain members' attitudes about specific concepts that may be relevant to group functioning, such as self-disclosure, communication, and leadership. The method can also be used to assess members' attitudes and perceptions about presenting problems or the group's task.

FIGURE 8.2 ■ *Example of a Semantic Differential Scale*

INSTRUCTIONS: On each of the scales below please place a check mark in the space that best describes how you feel about _____.

	7 Extremely	6 Quite	5 Slightly	4 Neither or In-between	3 Slightly	2 Quite	1 Extremely		
1. Large	___	___	___	___	___	___	___	Small	(Potent)
2. Worthless	___	___	___	___	___	___	___	Valuable	(Evaluative)
3. Fast	___	___	___	___	___	___	___	Slow	(Active)
4. Cold	___	___	___	___	___	___	___	Hot	(Active)
5. Happy	___	___	___	___	___	___	___	Sad	(Evaluative)
6. Weak	___	___	___	___	___	___	___	Strong	(Potent)
7. Good	___	___	___	___	___	___	___	Bad	(Evaluative)
8. Tense	___	___	___	___	___	___	___	Relaxed	(Active)
9. Tough	___	___	___	___	___	___	___	Soft	(Potent)
10. Active	___	___	___	___	___	___	___	Passive	(Active)
11. Heavy	___	___	___	___	___	___	___	Light	(Potent)
12. Fair	___	___	___	___	___	___	___	Unfair	(Evaluative)

$$A = \frac{}{3} + \frac{}{4} + \frac{}{8} + \frac{}{10} =$$

$$P = \frac{}{} + \frac{}{} + \frac{}{} + \frac{}{} =$$

$$E = \frac{}{} + \frac{}{} + \frac{}{} + \frac{}{} =$$

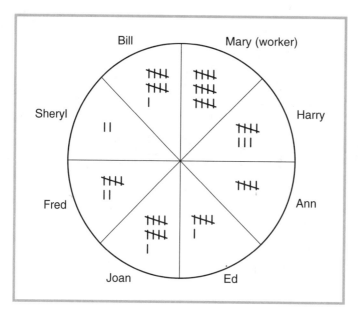

FIGURE 8.3 ■ *Chart for Recording the Frequency of Group Interaction*

Sometimes the worker may be less interested in the meaning of members' communications than in the distribution of communication within the group. An observer can use a chart such as the one shown in Figure 8.3 to record member-to-member and member-to-leader interactions.

To avoid observer fatigue, a sampling procedure may be used instead of continuous recording. Types of sampling procedures include

- Frequency recording—every time a behavior occurs it is recorded, for example, every communication in the group is recorded
- Interval recording—behavior is recorded for a specified interval of time, for example, the first two minutes of every five-minute time interval
- Time sample recording—behavior is recorded at a particular time, such as every 30 seconds

For ease of rating and to avoid the intrusiveness of live action ratings, group interaction can be videotaped or audiotaped, and observations can be made by replaying the tapes.

Measuring Interpersonal Attraction and Cohesion

Sociometry is a widely used method to measure interpersonal attraction. Originally developed by Moreno in the 1930s (Moreno, 1934), *sociometry* refers to the measurement of social preferences, that is, the strengths of members' preference or rejection of each other. Sociometric measures are obtained by asking about each member's preference for interacting with other members in relation to a particular activity (Crano & Brewer, 1973; Selltiz, Wrightsman, & Cook, 1976). They can also be obtained by having observers rate members' preferences for one another. Patterns of choices can differ significantly, depending on the activity on which members' preferences are being evaluated (Jennings, 1950). For example, in relation to the activity "playing together," a member of a children's group expressed great willingness to play with a particular member, but in relation to the activity "working on a project together," the member expressed less willingness to interact with the same member.

Sociometric ratings can be made concerning any activity of interest to a worker. For example, a worker may want to assess members' preferences for other members in relation to socializing between group meetings or choosing a partner to complete a task.

To obtain sociometric ratings, members are usually asked to write the names of the other members on one side of a sheet of paper next to a preference scale, for example, 1 = most preferred to 5 = least preferred. Members are then asked to rate everyone in the group except themselves in relation to a particular activity. For example, children in a residential treatment center might be asked, "If we were going on a day trip together, who would you like to sit next to during the bus trip?" and "Who would be your second choice?"

An index of preferences can be calculated for each member by dividing the total score a member receives from all group members by the highest possible score the member could receive. Members of attractive, cohesive groups have higher mean preference scores than do members of groups that are less cohesive and attractive.

Another way of presenting sociometric data is through a sociogram. As shown in Figure 8.4, solid lines represent attraction, dotted lines represent indifference, broken lines represent repulsion, and arrows represent the direction of preferences that are not reciprocal. For research purposes, sociometric data can be analyzed by more complicated methods such as multidimensional scaling (Gazda & Mobley, 1981).

Several other measures of the relationships between individual group members, and of overall group cohesion have been developed. Cox (1973), for example, developed the Group Therapy Interaction Chronogram, a graphic representation of interactions and relationships among group members that is similar to a sociogram but more complex. For assessments of the psychometric properties and utility of the Chronogram, see Fuhriman and Packard (1986) and Reder (1978).

To measure cohesion, Seashore (1954) suggests assessing the degree to which members (1) perceive themselves to be a part of the group; (2) prefer to remain in the group rather than to leave it; and (3) perceive their group to be better than other groups with respect to the way members get along together, the way they help each other, and the way they stick together. More recently, Budman and colleagues (1987, 1993) developed the Harvard Community Health Plan Group

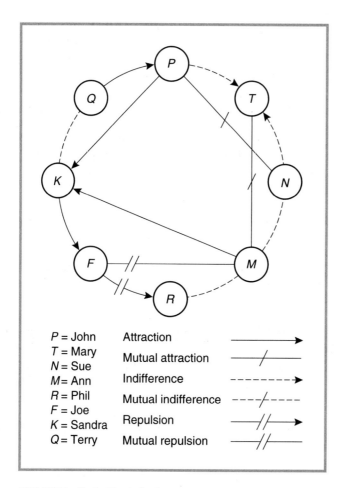

P = John   Attraction
T = Mary   Mutual attraction
N = Sue
M = Ann   Indifference
R = Phil   Mutual indifference
F = Joe
K = Sandra   Repulsion
Q = Terry   Mutual repulsion

FIGURE 8.4 ■ *A Sociogram*

Cohesiveness Scale, which can be used by trained clinical raters viewing half-hour, videotaped segments of psychotherapy groups.

Measuring Social Controls and Group Culture

The most fully developed method for assessing norms, roles, and other dimensions of a group as a whole is Bales' SYMLOG (Bales, 1980; Bales, Cohen, & Williamson, 1979). SYMLOG can be used as a self-report measure or as an observational measure.

As a self-report measure, members rate each other in relation to 26 behavioral descriptors, such as "dominant, talks a lot." Each descriptor is used to rate each member on a three-point scale from 0 = not often, to 2 = often, or it can be used as an observational measure in which independent raters assess group functioning. The product of a SYMLOG analysis of group functioning is a three-dimensional pictorial representation of group members' relationships to one another; it is called a SYMLOG field diagram.

In addition to assessing the functioning of groups, SYMLOG is useful in training novice group workers. Figure 8.5 is a SYMLOG field diagram made by Sharon, a member of an educational group for students learning how to lead treatment groups. The horizontal axis of Figure 8.5 represents the dimension friendly versus unfriendly, and the vertical axis represents the dimension instrumental versus emotionally expressive. The third dimension, dominant versus submissive, is represented by the size of the circles. Larger circles represent greater dominance and smaller circles represent greater submissiveness. For example, in Figure 8.5, Sharon perceives that Ann is the most dominant group member and Ed is the most friendly and emotionally expressive member.

Members rate all other members and themselves in relation to the three-dimensional SYMLOG space. In addition to rating overt behaviors, members can rate their values by evaluating which behavior they would avoid, reject, wish to perform, and think they ought to perform (see circles marked "avoid," "reject," "wish," and "ought" in Figure 8.5).

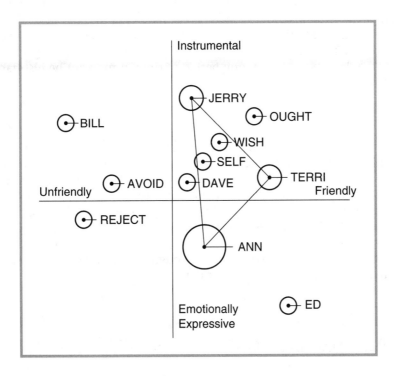

FIGURE 8.5 ■ *Sharon's SYMLOG Diagram of the Group*

SYMLOG field diagrams can be used for assessment in a variety of ways. One of the most basic ways is for members to compare their field diagrams. Are members' perceptions of the relationships among group members similar? Do individual members place themselves in the same position that other members place them?

A composite of group field diagrams can be made from the field diagrams of individual members. The composite can be used to analyze the functioning of the group as a whole. For example, who are the most dominant group members? Which members are included in the dominant subgroup (in Bales' terminology, "dominant triangle" as illustrated in Figure 8.5)? Which members are similar (spatially close) and which members appear to be dissimilar (spatially distant)? Who is the task (instrumental) leader and who is the socioemotional (emotionally expressive) leader? In this way, the SYMLOG procedure can be used to help members gain an understanding of how they are perceived within the group.

Particular roles of individual group members can also be identified. For example, Figure 8.5 shows Bill isolated in the unfriendly, instrumental quadrant of the field diagram. Is he an isolate or perhaps a scapegoat? Several more complicated and more sophisticated ways of interpreting field diagrams have been developed. For a detailed discussion of these methods, see Bales, Cohen, and Williamson (1979) and Bales (1980).

The SYMLOG method has two major limitations. First, the method is complex and takes time to learn before it can be used effectively. A more serious limitation is that a SYMLOG self-study takes about three hours to complete. Although this amount of time may be warranted for a team that functions together on a daily basis over a long period of time, it may not be justifiable for a short-term treatment group.

Other Methods of Assessing the Group as a Whole

Several other methods, including the Hemphill Index of Group Dimensions (Hemphill, 1956), the Hill Interaction Matrix (Hill, 1965, 1977), and the Group Rating Scale (Cooper, 1977), have been developed to rate dimensions of the group as a whole. For example, the Hill Interaction Matrix employs a 16-cell matrix to assess the content and style of group interaction. It has been used in a large number of published and unpublished studies to assess therapeutic processes in a wide range of therapy and support groups (Toseland, Rossiter, Peak, & Hill, 1990). Because these measures are used frequently to evaluate the functioning of a group, they are described in greater detail in Chapter 13.

ASSESSING THE GROUP'S ENVIRONMENT

The worker's assessment of the environment's influence on the functioning of the entire group should be distinguished from the assessment of environmental factors that affect individual group members. In both cases, however, the environment in which group members and the group as a whole function has an important effect on group work practice.

When assessing the influence of the environment on the group, the worker focuses on

- The organization that sponsors and sanctions the group
- The interorganizational environment
- The community environment

The emphasis on the influence of the environment is a distinctive aspect of social work practice and is not found to any great extent in the writing of group workers from other professional disciplines (Corey & Corey, 1997; Yalom, 1995).

Assessing the Sponsoring Organization

When assessing the influence on the group of the sponsoring organization, the worker examines how the group's purposes are influenced by the agency, what resources are allocated for the group's efforts, what status the worker has in relation to others who work for the agency, and how the agency's attitudes about service delivery influence the group work endeavor. Taken together, these factors can have a profound influence on the way the group functions.

As Garvin (1997) points out, an organization always has a purpose for sanctioning a group work effort. An organization's purpose may be stated explicitly or may be implied in the overall program objectives. The organization administration's purpose for encouraging the development of a group may not correspond to the worker's or the group members' ideas about a group's purpose. The extent to which the organization, the worker, and the group members can agree on a common purpose for the group will determine, in part, the extent to which the group will receive the support it needs to function effectively and the extent to which the group experience will be judged as beneficial by all concerned.

It is helpful for the worker to clarify the organization's purpose for sponsoring the group. A written group proposal, such as the one described in Chapter 6, can clarify the worker's intentions and provide the organization's administration with an opportunity to react to a written document.

During the process of clarifying the organization's purposes for the group, the worker can help shape the purposes proposed for the group. For example, a nursing home administrator may decide to sponsor a group to help the residents "fit in better" with the nursing home's rigid schedule of bathing, feeding, and housekeeping. The worker could help the nursing home staff and residents reformulate the group's purpose by considering the needs of both the group members and the organization. The purpose might be reformulated to improve the relationship between residents and staff by having them work together to find a way to meet staff's busy schedules while accommodating residents' needs for autonomy and individual preference.

An organization can also influence a group by its allocation of resources. As mentioned in Chapter 6, the worker should identify as early as possible the resources the group will need to function effectively. Once this is done, the worker can assess the likelihood that the organization will be able to allocate sufficient resources and can plan the best strategy to obtain any that may be needed. The worker's assessment may also include the extent to which resources, for example, a meeting room or some refreshments, can be obtained from alternative sponsors.

The worker's status in the sponsoring organization can also influence the group. If a worker is a low-status member of the sponsoring organization, there may be difficulty in obtaining resources for the group, in convincing the sponsor that the endeavor is a good use of his or her time, or in demonstrating that the group's purposes are consistent with the overall objectives of the organization. In this situation, the worker may want to consult with trusted colleagues who can give the worker some feedback about the feasibility of the proposed group. The worker might also ask these colleagues for their support for the development of the new group service.

The attitudes and practices of the sponsoring organization with regard to service delivery can have an important influence on the group work endeavor. The worker should assess whether the organization stresses individual or group work services. In some organizations, the stated commitment to teamwork is not matched by the resources and reward structure to support effective team functioning (Goodman et al., 1986; Hackman, 1990; Katzenbach & Smith, 1993). Where individual services are given priority, the worker may have to spend considerable time developing the rationale for the group and convincing the organization it is important to undertake such an endeavor (Hasenfeld, 1985).

The organization's policies regarding recruitment and intake of potential members also can affect a group. The worker should assess whether the clients are receiving services voluntarily or whether they have been ordered to attend the group. Mandated clients are likely to be hostile or apathetic about becoming members of the group. It is also helpful to gather information about the extent to which individuals are prepared by intake workers to receive group work services.

The organization's commitment to a particular service technology, such as practice theories, ideologies, and intervention techniques, may also influence the group work endeavor. For example, if the organization is committed to a long-term psychodynamic treatment model, it may oppose the development of a short-term, behaviorally oriented group. When the service technology planned for a particular group runs counter to an organization's preferred service technology, the worker should develop a convincing rationale for the particular service technology planned. For a treatment group, the rationale might include the effectiveness and efficiency of a particular method for treating a problem. In the case of a task group, the rationale might include the effectiveness or efficiency of a particular method for generating ideas or making decisions about alternative proposals.

To help ensure continued organizational support for the group, workers should take every opportunity to describe the group's progress to clinical supervisors and other administrative staff. This tactic provides an opportunity for the worker to mention the helpfulness of organizational support and any additional resources that are needed. For example, a worker leading a parenting group could discuss the progress made by members and the importance of transportation to and from group meetings but also note that problems in attendance could be reduced if the agency provided child-care services during group meetings. In the following chapters, guidelines are presented for choosing interventions and for formulating treatment plans on the basis of the needs of members and of the group as a whole.

Assessing the Interorganizational Environment

In assessing the group's environment, the worker should also pay attention to anything happening in other organizations that may be relevant to the group. The worker can make an assessment of the interorganizational environment by asking several questions: Are other organizations offering similar groups? Do workers in other organizations perceive needs similar to those that formed the basis for the worker's own group? Do other organizations offer services or programs that may be useful to members of the group? Would any benefit be gained by linking with groups in other organizations to lobby for changes in social service benefits?

Unless the worker or others in the organization are already familiar with what is being offered by all other organizations in the community, the worker's primary task in making an interorganizational assessment is to contact other organizations to let them know about the group offering. In addition to generating referrals and making other organizations aware of the group, the assessment may uncover needless duplication of service or, conversely, a widespread need that is not being met or is being met by uncoordinated individual efforts within separate organizations.

An example of a recent practice experience illustrates the importance of interorganizational assessments. An executive director of a small organization decided to do an interorganizational assessment after problems encountered in serving homeless people had been raised several times in monthly staff meetings. The director discovered a lack of sufficient space in shelters and a general lack of community interest in the welfare of the homeless. The worker called a meeting of professionals from several organizations to see what could be done. The interorganizational group contacted a local planning organization. In cooperation with the planning organization, the interorganizational group sought federal, state, local, and private funding to address the needs of the homeless. After much work, a social service program for the homeless was founded with a combination of federal, state, and local funding, and a new community shelter was opened.

Assessing the Community Environment

The worker should also assess the effect of the community environment on the group, the extent of support for the group from other community groups, and the community as a whole. When assessing the effect of the community on a group, the worker should focus on the attitude of the community concerning the problems or issues being addressed by the group. Within Hispanic and African American communities, for example, support groups for people with Alzheimer's disease are difficult to organize because of the stigma attached to the disease. These communities also attach great significance to handling such matters privately through family caregiving (Cox & Monk, 1990; Henderson, Guiterrez-Mayka, Garcia, & Boyd, 1993).

In treatment groups, if the problem is one that violates basic community values, members of the group are likely to be stigmatized. Lack of community acceptance and the resulting stigma attached to the problem may have other consequences, such as discouraging potential members from reaching out for help. It may also increase the level of confidentiality of group meetings and may affect procedures used to recruit new members. For example, because of the stigma attached to persons who abuse their children, Parents Anonymous groups generally have confidential meetings, and the recruitment process occurs on a first-name basis to protect members from people who may be more interested in finding out their identities than in attending meetings. Similar recruitment procedures are used in other professionally led and self-help groups that deal with socially stigmatized problems, such as spouse abuse, alcoholism, and compulsive gambling.

The worker should also make an assessment of the support for the group from other community groups and the community as a whole. For example, ministers, priests, and rabbis might be receptive to a group for abusive or neglecting parents, alcoholics, or spouse abusers. The worker can get referrals from these sources or obtain a meeting room such as a church basement. Similarly, a worker in a family service agency may find that several community groups—a women's civic organization, a battered women's shelter, a victim's compensation board, a council of churches, and a dispute resolution center—would welcome the development of a support group program for domestic violence victims. Workers who assess support from community groups are often in a better position to obtain new funding for a proposed group work service.

Group workers interested in building social action groups and coalitions need to be good at finding out the problems that are important to individuals in a community, which individuals have the capacity to make a change in a particular problem, and which individuals have the capacity to prevent or delay change. Information may be gathered from persons affected by the problem and those who have the capacity to affect it through a variety of means, such as (1) focused individual interviews, (2) focus groups, (3) community needs assessments, and (4) state and national survey data and reports.

The importance of unsolicited and unfocused information gathered while interacting with and forming alliances with community members, community leaders, politicians, and community activists should not be overlooked. It is essential for group workers who are interested in building social action groups and coalitions to get to know a community. To understand competing factions, uncover hidden problems, and form alliances often takes a considerable amount of time and commitment. Still, when the intent is to mobilize social action groups and coalitions, there is no substitute for taking the time necessary to get to know a community and to establish trusting relationships with as many different representatives of the community as possible.

A worker's assessment of the community environment may lead to a coalition of community forces to resolve a concern. According to Rubin and Rubin (1992), in assessing a community there "is the systematic gathering of information by people who are both affected by a problem and who want to solve that problem" (p. 156). There is also "a fact-gathering endeavor as people learn about the problem, a mobilization endeavor as people learn to share the problem, and a capacity-building endeavor as people work to solve the problem" (p. 156). For example, a community assessment may indicate that police officers have been asked increasingly to handle family disturbances. With the cooperation of the police force and local community leaders, a community organization might decide to reach out to persons experiencing family disturbances. In addition to casework service, these efforts could result in the development of several treatment groups, such as a couples communication group, a parenting group, and a recreational group for adolescents. It also might result in a task force of community leaders to work on issues of concern to families in the community.

LINKING ASSESSMENT TO INTERVENTION

In preparation for the middle stage of treatment groups, discussed in Chapter 9, workers should consider how they will use their assessment data to plan effective interventions. Few texts in group work or casework practice have addressed the way assessments are linked to intervention methods and treatment plans. This may, in part, account for findings from practice studies suggesting there is little correlation between workers' assessments or diagnoses and the interventions that are selected (Mullen, 1969; Stuart, 1970). Without guidelines about the interventions that are most appropriate for particular problems, workers will rely on interventions with which they are most familiar, regardless of their assessment of the group or its members.

Figure 8.6 illustrates a framework for developing treatment plans that result from an assessment of the individual group member, the group as a whole, and the group environment. Because problems are often multidimensional, several

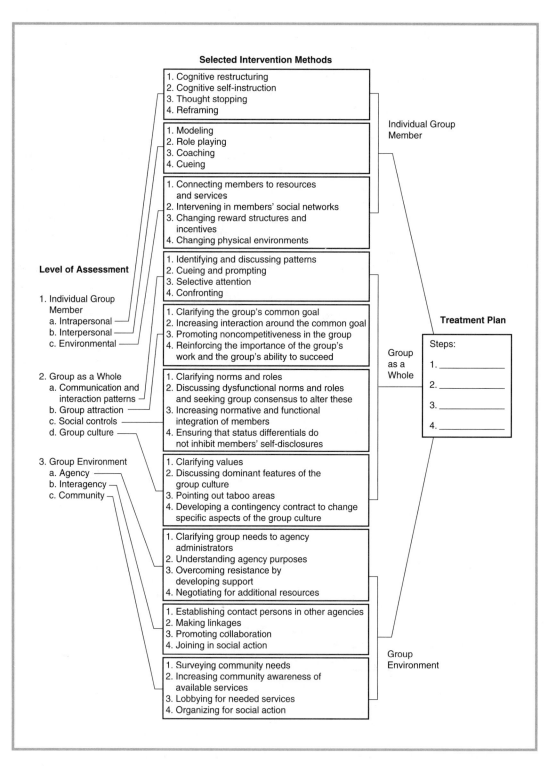

Selected Intervention Methods

1. Cognitive restructuring
2. Cognitive self-instruction
3. Thought stopping
4. Reframing

1. Modeling
2. Role playing
3. Coaching
4. Cueing

1. Connecting members to resources and services
2. Intervening in members' social networks
3. Changing reward structures and incentives
4. Changing physical environments

1. Identifying and discussing patterns
2. Cueing and prompting
3. Selective attention
4. Confronting

1. Clarifying the group's common goal
2. Increasing interaction around the common goal
3. Promoting noncompetitiveness in the group
4. Reinforcing the importance of the group's work and the group's ability to succeed

1. Clarifying norms and roles
2. Discussing dysfunctional norms and roles and seeking group consensus to alter these
3. Increasing normative and functional integration of members
4. Ensuring that status differentials do not inhibit members' self-disclosures

1. Clarifying values
2. Discussing dominant features of the group culture
3. Pointing out taboo areas
4. Developing a contingency contract to change specific aspects of the group culture

1. Clarifying group needs to agency administrators
2. Understanding agency purposes
3. Overcoming resistance by developing support
4. Negotiating for additional resources

1. Establishing contact persons in other agencies
2. Making linkages
3. Promoting collaboration
4. Joining in social action

1. Surveying community needs
2. Increasing community awareness of available services
3. Lobbying for needed services
4. Organizing for social action

Level of Assessment

1. Individual Group Member
   a. Intrapersonal
   b. Interpersonal
   c. Environmental

2. Group as a Whole
   a. Communication and interaction patterns
   b. Group attraction
   c. Social controls
   d. Group culture

3. Group Environment
   a. Agency
   b. Interagency
   c. Community

Individual Group Member

Group as a Whole

Group Environment

Treatment Plan

Steps:

1. _____

2. _____

3. _____

4. _____

FIGURE 8.6 ■ *Linking Assessment and Intervention in Treatment Groups*

different interventions may be selected to become part of a comprehensive treatment plan. For example, in a couples group, the worker and each member may select specific interventions to meet individual needs. One member decides to use a cognitive restructuring intervention to help her stop getting defensive when confronted by her husband. As part of his treatment plan, another member decides to join Alcoholics Anonymous. At the same time, the worker helps the first member change her interaction patterns in the group and helps the second member stop avoiding confrontation in the group.

SUMMARY

This chapter has suggested that the worker assess three areas of the functioning of individual group members, four areas of the functioning of the group as a whole, and three areas of the environment in which the group functions. Chapters 9 through 12 describe a variety of interventions that the worker can use when assessment indicates an intervention is warranted.

This chapter examines in detail the process of assessment. Although assessments are made throughout all stages of a group's development, they are often concentrated in the latter portions of the beginning stage and the initial portions of the middle stage. This is the time when the worker and the group members are planning intervention strategies to achieve the goals they have agreed on in the planning and beginning stages of the group.

In making assessments, the worker examines the functioning of individual group members, the group as a whole, and the group's environment. When assessing individual members, the worker examines intrapersonal, interpersonal, and environmental areas of each member's functioning. In addition, the worker examines each member's functioning in relation to what the member can contribute to the group, what needs the member brings to the group, and what intervention plans are most likely to be successful in helping the member alleviate concerns and problems. A number of methods that can be used separately or in combination for assessing the functioning of individual members are presented in this chapter.

To assess the group as a whole, the worker focuses on the four areas of group dynamics described in Chapter 3. These are (1) interaction and communication patterns; (2) the attraction of the group for its members; (3) social controls such as roles, norms, and status hierarchies; and (4) the group's culture. Several methods for assessing the group as a whole are described.

Because group work practice occurs within the context of a larger service delivery system, it is important to consider the effect of the group's environment on its functioning. To make a thorough assessment of the group's environment, it is suggested that the worker assess the sponsoring organization, the interorganizational environment, and the larger community environment in which the group functions. After explaining the potential effects of each of these aspects of the environment on the group, the chapter describes the linkage between assessment and intervention.

LEARNING ASSIGNMENTS

1. Imagine you are leading a group of parents of young children. Three of the parents mention they are having difficulty handling their children's temper tantrums. What steps would you take to help the parents develop a chart to monitor their children's behavior? How would you encourage other group members to assist in this process? Prepare a monitoring chart that you could use as an example in the group.

2. Using Figure 8.3, observe a committee meeting or other task group and record the frequency of interaction among members. Were you able to identify distinct subgroups? Did your observations help you identify task and socioemotional leaders within the group? Was there a scapegoat? On the basis of your observations, speculate on why some members spoke more frequently than others.

3. Interview the executive director of a social service agency. Inquire about the mission and goals of the agency and the types of group services offered to the agency's clients. How do the group work services that are offered reflect the mission and goals of the agency? Ask the director what types of group services would be considered as outside the mission and goals of the agency. Ask about the extent of influence of the agency's board of directors on the group work services that are offered. Also, inquire about the effect of any formal or informal interagency service arrangements and the influence of the larger community on group work services in the agency.

4. Choose a group in which you are currently involved. Prepare a written assessment that focuses on a problem experienced by (1) one member of the group, (2) the group as a whole, and (3) the group in interaction with its environment. Using Figure 8.6, select appropriate interventions to address each level of problems and prepare a treatment plan.

CASE EXAMPLE

Jody conducted a Banana Splits group for fourth graders whose parents were in the process of separating or divorcing. The group had been meeting for four weeks. Its purpose was to help the children discuss their concerns about their changing family situation and to assist them in finding support from each other. The beginning phase of the group was going well. Members were becoming more comfortable with Jody and with each other. They seemed to be opening up a little more about their concerns. Jody used a number of program materials to help members get to know each other and identify their feelings.

As she conducted the group, Jody recognized that she was beginning to gather information about each of the members and about how the group was working as a unit. She was also learning a good deal about how important it was to work with others in the group's environment, such as teachers, guidance counselors, and school administrators. It was time to take some of this information and prepare a more formal assessment that would be useful for her future work with the members of the group. Also, she wanted to become more systematic in her understanding of the dynamics in the group as a whole because she recognized that the group's environment played an important part in the success of the group process. She designed several methods for collecting additional data to help her begin the formal assessment process.

She began by assessing the needs of the individual members of the group. The membership was fairly homogeneous—all the students were fourth graders and came from the same school district. Yet, she noted that members had very different home situations that could affect how they were coping with their changing family situations. She used several sources to collect data about how students were coping with their family situations. First, she contacted the parents of each child. She asked each parent to fill out a short rating scale on the child that identified eating, sleeping, and study habits while the child was at home. Second, she asked each child's teacher to write a paragraph that described the child's behavior in the classroom. Specifically, she asked each teacher to comment on his or her observations of the child's social interaction, school performance, and overall mood in the classroom. Third, Jody recorded her own observations of each child during group sessions, carefully documenting her observations by using excerpts from the child's dialogue in the group. She also recorded the major concerns that surfaced for each member during group sessions.

She organized this information in individual files for each member and added to the information as the group progressed. As she collected more data, Jody synthesized them and wrote a summary assessment of each member's situation that included information about the home environment, adjustment to the separation process, class behavior, connections to other members in the group, socialization patterns at school, and grades. She planned to use this information to work with each member in formulating individual goals to be worked on during later group sessions.

Although Jody observed that the group seemed to be progressing well, she decided to explore the dynamics in the group and more formally to assess how the group was functioning. She began by taking careful notes on the patterns of communication and interaction between members. She noticed that the group had several small cliques that had formed, and she wondered if this dynamic was reinforced by interaction among subgroup members that took place outside of the group. She administered a short sociometric exercise to the members to more fully assess interaction within the group. On further investigation, she learned that subgroups seemed to form based on how classes were organized for the fourth grade students at the school. She also learned through observing the group that many members were communicating more to her than to other members. As a group goal for future meetings she planned to promote member-to-member communication by encouraging students to talk to each other rather than to her. One way Jody assessed the group's cohesion was by asking members to end each meeting with a short statement about how they felt the group session went. She noted that many members were positive in their comments after each session. She also noted that the members were becoming more independent and responsible for deciding things in the group, and she felt that the group's culture was developing adequately for this stage of the process.

Jody also took a good deal of time planning for this group, especially by preparing the organizational environment. She felt it was a good time to reassess aspects of the group's environment, particularly in relation to how the group was being perceived by teachers, administrators, and parents. She designed a short evaluation instrument and sent it to these constituencies, asking for their perceptions and feedback about the Banana Splits group. In addition, she interviewed the principal to share information about the group and to assess how important the group was to members of the school. On interviewing the principal, Jody learned that the school board was interested in replicating Jody's group with students in other classes. To avoid behavior problems and school violence that might occur if family problems were not addressed, the board currently seemed to favor early intervention and increased services to children whose parents were separating or divorcing. As a goal, Jody planned to make a presentation to the school board about expanding group work services to students experiencing turbulent family environments.

The Middle Stage

chapter 9

Treatment Groups: Foundation Methods

During the middle stage, groups are focused on accomplishing the objectives, goals, and tasks developed earlier in the life of the group. It is assumed that by the middle stage, workers have already discussed the group's purposes; developed a group contract concerning confidentiality, attendance, and number of sessions; and developed individual contracts with particular treatment goals for each member. It is also assumed that the group as a whole has developed an initial set of dynamic processes, including a pattern of communication and interaction; a beginning level of interpersonal attraction and group cohesion, norms, roles, and other social control mechanisms; and a group culture. The primary task of the worker during the middle stage is to help members accomplish the goals they have contracted to achieve, which is accomplished by (1) helping members overcome obstacles to goal achievement in their own lives, (2) facilitating group dynamics that support members' efforts, and (3) helping the organization and larger community respond to members' efforts.

MIDDLE-STAGE SKILLS

The middle stage of treatment groups is characterized by an initial period of testing, conflict, and adjustment as members work out their relationships with one another and the larger group. Contracts are negotiated and renegotiated, members establish their positions in relation to one another, and the group develops a niche within the sponsoring organization.

The testing, conflict, and adjustment that occur in the group are signs that members are becoming comfortable enough to assert their own needs and their own vision of the group. During this period, members demonstrate their independence and abilities to engage in leadership activities. They may question the purposes and goals of the group or the methods that have been proposed to accomplish them. They may also express contrary opinions and concerns about group processes or their interactions with the leader or certain members. In the beginning stage, members are often glad to have the worker structure the group, but testing and conflict often signify that members are vying for ownership of the group (Henry, 1992).

In most circumstances, acknowledging members' issues and concerns, giving a nondefensive response, and fostering a group discussion about how to handle the concern is all that is needed to help the group continue to function in a smooth and satisfying manner. In some situations, however, conflicts may escalate. In these situations, the conflict resolution skills and strategies presented in Chapters 4 and 11 can be quite useful in helping to satisfy members' needs while accomplishing group goals.

Although some elements of testing and conflict will continue to emerge as a normal part of the life of a group, after an initial period of adjustment, the main focus of the middle stage turns to goal achievement. Members work together to achieve the goals expressed in the contracts they have made with the group's leader, other group members, and the group as a whole. During the middle stage, the worker makes modifications to these contracts based on and in relation to the assessment of the group's development, the changing needs of members, and the changing demands of the social environment in which the group functions.

Although every group has a unique developmental pattern that calls for different leadership skills, workers are often expected to perform six broad activities during the middle stage of all treatment groups. These activities include the following:

1. Preparing for group meetings
2. Structuring the group's work
3. Involving and empowering group members
4. Helping members to achieve goals
5. Working with reluctant and resistant group members
6. Monitoring and evaluating the group's progress

Preparing for Group Meetings

During the middle stage, the worker should continuously assess the needs of the group and its members and plan to meet identified needs in subsequent meetings. The cycle of assessment, modification, and reassessment is the method by which the leader ensures continued progress toward contract goals.

In structured, time-limited groups, the worker spends a considerable amount of time between meetings preparing the agenda for the next group meeting. For example, for the fourth session of an educational group for prospective foster parents, a worker might prepare (1) material on helping children develop values, (2) a brief handout on value clarification, (3) an exercise to illustrate some concepts about helping children develop their own value system, and (4) questions that will help to organize the group's discussion of values. In preparing for the meeting, the worker would select material that will lead to a stimulating and interesting discussion and estimate the time needed to cover the material in relation to the time available for the meeting.

Less structured, process-oriented groups also require preparation. A worker leading a group for residents of an adolescent treatment center prepares for the next meeting according to her assessment of the efficacy of previous group meetings and the current functioning of each group member discussed in weekly treatment review meetings. For example, after discussion with members, the worker may decide to focus the next meeting on helping members improve how they express anger. In preparing for the group, the worker gathers examples of how anger has been expressed in the past by residents and uses these examples to prepare role-play exercises designed to improve members' expression of anger. The worker models more appropriate methods of expressing anger and helps members practice the new methods.

Preparation is also required when workers use program materials to achieve group goals. Middleman (1980) points out that the use of program materials has had an important place in the history of group work. *Program materials* are activities, games, and exercises designed to provide fun, interesting experiences for members while achieving particular goals. Workers sometimes make the mistake of thinking that program activities such as arts and crafts or preparing for a dance are not appropriate group work activities because they are not focused solely on therapeutic verbal interactions. However, when carefully selected, program activities can be very therapeutic.

Program activities provide a medium through which the functioning of members can be assessed in areas such as interpersonal skills, ability to perform daily living activities, motor coordination, attention span, and ability to work cooperatively. Program activities can also be used as a part of specific treatment interventions. In addition to achieving specific goals such as improving skills in interpersonal functioning, leadership, problem solving, and activities of daily living, program activities help build group cohesion, prosocial group norms, and a group culture that fosters continued member participation. Program activities can also be used to make the group more attractive for its members. For example, in a children's group, the worker may place a program activity, such as charades, between group discussions to maintain members' interest.

Choosing appropriate program activities requires a careful assessment of the needs of group members. Characteristics of members should be matched with the characteristics of potential program activities. Vinter (1985b) has developed a scheme for rating program activities on their prescriptiveness, control, movement, rewards, competence, and interaction. Similarly, Middleman (1982) has attempted to point out some of the particular benefits of more than one hundred program activities, and Henry (1992) has attempted to categorize program activities that are especially useful for members at different stages of a group's development.

Because of the great number of possible program activities for children, adolescents, adults, and the elderly, workers should keep a resource file of catalogued activities to draw on as they are called on to work with different types of groups. Such a resource file can be an asset in selecting specific program activities during the life of a group. Appendix G lists a variety of sources for program activities that can be used in groups for children, adolescents, and older adults.

Figure 9.1 presents a procedure for evaluating program activities for specific group needs. Selection should be made on the basis of (1) the objectives of the program activity; (2) the purposes and goals of the group; (3) the facilities, resources, and time available for the activity; (4) the characteristics of the group members; and (5) the characteristics of particular program activities.

The procedure suggested in Figure 9.1 can be used to help workers select program activities for any type of treatment group. For example, when choosing activities for an inpatient group whose purpose is to help prepare members for community living, the worker should consider activities that stimulate members' interest in the outside world. In addition to the group's purpose and the objectives of particular program activities, the worker should consider the other factors shown in Figure 9.1. For example, an inpatient group meets in an occupational therapy room equipped with kitchen facilities, tables, blackboards, arts and crafts, and toys. All members are more than 70 years old and have poor physical and mental health. Their interests include gardening, nature, travel, and cooking. The worker selects a program activity that stimulates members both physically and socially to prepare them for living in a community residence.

Using Figure 9.1 as a guide, the worker ruled out activities such as a discussion of current events and selected an activity in which each member helped prepare a meal to be shared by all. Afterward, the worker reconvened the group around the meal and asked members to share their feelings. Questions such as "Did the activity remind you of when you lived at home?" and "How do you feel about living on your own and having to prepare meals?" were used to stimulate a therapeutic discussion based on the program activity.

The therapeutic benefit of any program activity depends on how the activity is used by the worker. Activities provide little benefit if careful attention is not given to making sure they are directed toward therapeutic purposes. In the example above, the program activity of preparing the meal stimulated the sensory awareness of members. During the activity, the worker encouraged social interaction. At the end of the meal, a discussion of the thoughts, feelings, and behaviors that members experienced during the activity was used to stimulate members' interest and desire to return to the community.

To prepare for meetings, workers should also review recordings of previous meetings and data from other monitoring devices. Making effective use of feedback about the progress of a group is essential during the middle stage. The worker can use observations collected in summary recordings, for example, as the basis for determining that the interaction pattern of the previously described in-

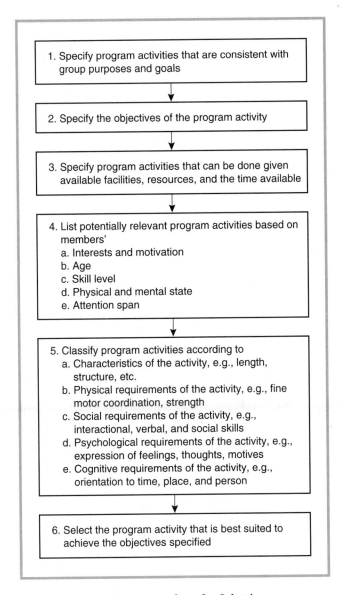

FIGURE 9.1 ■ *A Procedure for Selecting Program Activities*

patient group should be changed to encourage participation from several members who have not been active in group discussions. In another case, data about members' satisfaction with the previous meeting of a single-parent support group suggested that information about educational opportunities for adult students should be included in future meetings.

Preparation for the next group meeting may also include visualizing how the meeting should be conducted and, if necessary, rehearsing intervention procedures or techniques. This strategy is particularly important when a worker is using a new or unfamiliar procedure or exercise.

In recent years, an increased awareness of the benefits of clear contracts and specific goal statements has highlighted the need for careful preparation between meetings. For example, Rose (1989) has suggested that specific written agendas be distributed at the beginning of each meeting. Such agendas are appropriate for structured, short-term groups that are focused on a single concern or problem. Other treatment groups may have broader concerns that are not easily anticipated or addressed by a written agenda for each meeting. However, regardless of whether a written agenda is used, workers should be sufficiently prepared so they are clear about their objectives for each meeting and their plans for achieving the objectives.

Structuring the Group's Work

Structuring the work of treatment groups has been recognized as a necessary ingredient of social work treatment for many years (Perlman, 1970). Recently, managed care has given greater impetus to short-term structured approaches (Budman, Simeone, Reilly, & Demby, 1994; MacKenzie, 1995; Murphy, DeBernardo, & Shoemaker, 1998). *Structure* refers to the use of planned, systematic, time-limited interventions and program activities. Highly structured interventions rely on the guidance and direction of the worker, but less structured approaches encourage members to take full responsibility for the purpose, goals, and interventions used in the group.

In general, structure encourages the rapid learning of new responses. Therefore, one advantage of structured groups is that they provide an efficient means for members to learn new skills. The appeal of the Minnesota Couples Communication Program (Miller, Nunnally, & Wackman, 1972), Parent Effectiveness Training (Gordon, 1975), Positive Peer Culture (Vorrath & Brendtro, 1985), Systematic Training for Effective Parenting (Dinkmeyer & McKay, 1990), and similar approaches testifies to the popularity of structured group programming for certain types of problems.

Structure is essential in multicomponent treatment programs, sometimes referred to as *psychoeducational* groups. For example, an assertion-training group may include a brief lecture and group discussion about what it means to be assertive, followed by role playing, modeling, rehearsal, reinforcement, and cognitive interventions—all activities are designed to help members practice becoming more assertive. As the number of treatment components grows, the need for careful structuring of the entire intervention program increases.

During the middle stage of treatment groups, the worker can perform a variety of activities to structure the group's work. One of the most basic activities is to let members know that each meeting will begin and end on time. Except for the first meeting, openings should not be delayed in anticipation of late members. Starting meetings late only reinforces members' future tardiness.

The worker should also structure the end of a meeting to summarize and conclude interactions rather than to begin new agenda items. New items should not be introduced near the end of a session. Sometimes a group member will wait until the end of the meeting to disclose an important piece of information or to voice an important concern. Because these "doorknob" communications (Shulman, 1999) cannot be dealt with adequately in the short time remaining, the worker should ask the member to hold the new material until the next meeting. If the member's concerns cannot wait until the next group meeting, the worker may want to schedule an individual meeting.

One of the best ways for a worker to structure a group's time is by setting agendas. Whether verbal or written, a clear agenda helps focus attention on what will be covered during the meeting and makes members aware of how much time is available for exercises, role plays, presentations, and discussions. When preparing and presenting agendas, workers should encourage members to share their ideas about what direction the group should take.

The worker also can structure a group by establishing and maintaining orderly communication and interaction patterns. The structure of the interaction process should give all members an opportunity to participate. Some members, however, may receive more attention in one meeting and less in others. For example, in a remedial group in which members have individualized treatment contracts, the worker may decide to focus on one member at a time to help each one work on the personal treatment contract for an extended period. In other situations, such as an educational group, the worker may decide to present didactic material and then encourage all members to discuss the material. The worker may decide to structure the discussion so that each member is encouraged to participate and no member is allowed to talk for longer than several minutes at one time. In either case, the worker will have made a planned effort to structure the group's use of communication and interaction patterns.

The worker structures a group's communication and interaction patterns by helping the group determine how much time should be spent on a particular issue or problem and by guiding members' participation in role plays, exercises, and other group activities. In these efforts, the worker balances the socioemotional needs of individual members and the needs of the group as a whole to accomplish specific goals. The worker also should strive to foster members' initiative and leadership but should prevent the group from being dominated by a single individual or a subgroup.

Sometimes workers are reluctant to assert themselves, for example, by guiding the group from a discussion of one issue to another or directing role plays or program activities. Workers should be aware, however, that group members expect them to provide guidance and leadership, particularly when the group is having trouble staying focused on its stated objectives. Workers are expected to use their professional knowledge and skills to guide members' progress toward the goals that have been set without dominating or suppressing members' initiatives. When the worker is unsure about whether the group needs more time to work on an issue or an exercise, the worker should ask members a direct question about their needs.

When guiding group activities, the worker should ensure that the transition from one activity to another is as smooth as possible. This can be done by summarizing what has been said, recommending how the group might pursue unresolved issues, and suggesting that the group move on to remaining issues.

Time is an important factor in structuring the work of a group. Time-limited, structured group work methods have been shown to be effective for children, adolescents, and adults experiencing a variety of problems (Barth, Yeaton, & Winterfelt, 1994; Brennan, 1995; Hugen, 1993; McKay & Paleg, 1992; Pomeroy, Rubin, & Walker, 1995; Rose, 1989; Rose & Edleson, 1987; Shapiro, Peltz, & Bernadett-Shapiro, 1998). Despite the evidence for the effectiveness of time-limited approaches to group work, some needs are clearly better served in long-term groups. For example, the popularity of self-help groups indicates that they provide important support through life transitions and life crises (Powell, 1987; White & Madara, 1998). It may also be preferable to address other needs in groups that do not emphasize a time-limited structured format. For example, when members seek help in changing established personality characteristics, long-term rather than short-term group treatment approaches are often recommended (Frances, Clarkin, & Perry, 1984; Seligman, 1998).

Focusing is another way to structure the work of a group. In any treatment group, the focus of an intervention, sometimes referred to as the level of an intervention, can be either the individual member, the group itself, or the group's external environment. The focus of the group should change with the changing needs of the group. For example, a worker leading a group for men who have battered their wives makes an assessment that the group has failed to encourage members to express feelings of anger, and that this problem is inhibiting the group from achieving its objective of preventing further domestic violence. The worker decides to select the group as the target of an intervention designed to help members talk about feelings. The worker has each member express two feelings about being a member of the group. Other exercises used in later group sessions help members learn to identify their feelings of anger and intervene before they escalate into violent outbursts. At the end of the first exercise, the group leader changes the focus of the group and concentrates on helping members work on individualized treatment plans. In a subsequent group meeting, the leader again suggests a change of focus by asking group members whether they would like to invite their partners to a meeting. The leader explains that this will help members appreciate the devastating effect that domestic violence has had on their partners. By suggesting changes of focus, the leader helps the group to obtain new perspectives on problems and to tackle problems in multidimensional ways that add variety to the type of work that is done in the group. For more information about groups for men who batter see Browne, Saunders, and Staecker (1997); Edleson and Tolman (1992); Gondolf (1997); Pence and Paymar (1993); Saunders (1996); Sonkin (1995); and Williams (1994).

Degree of Structure

Reviews of the effectiveness of group interventions (Budman et al., 1994; MacKenzie, 1990) indicate that structured interventions are effective in helping clients to achieve treatment goals. MacKenzie (1994), for example, indicates that early group structure has a variety of beneficial effects on group processes and outcomes, such as reducing members' fears and anxieties, promoting members' involvement and self-disclosure, and increasing group cohesion and positive feelings about the group.

Considerable controversy exists, however, about how *much* structure is useful for treatment groups. It has been argued, for example, that substantial structure may not be beneficial because it prevents members from exercising their own initiative (Glassman & Kates, 1990). Too much structure may decrease members' commitment to the group because they may feel structure has been imposed on them rather than selected by them to help them achieve their own self-monitored goals. Lieberman, Yalom, and Miles (1973) found that structured exercises did not facilitate group development or successful outcomes in the groups they observed.

Although much available evidence indicates that structured, short-term interventions are at least as effective as less structured, longer-term interventions (Budman et al., 1994; MacKenzie, 1990, 1994), highly structured interventions may be more appropriate for some problems than for others. For example, although a highly structured, multicomponent group treatment program was found to be more effective than a less structured program for helping older people increase their social skills (Toseland & Rose, 1978), a less structured, process-oriented approach that was focused on facilitating group members' determination of their own purposes and goals was found to be more effective than a structured approach in developing mutual support groups for older people (Toseland, Sherman, & Bliven, 1981).

Similarly, short-term, highly structured approaches may not be best for clients who are mandated to attend group treatment. These clients take time to develop relationships and to build trust in workers' efforts to help them. On the other hand, clients who are in crisis may need less time to build relationships with the worker and other members and therefore can profit from short-term treatment.

The nature of clients' problems and needs should be carefully considered when deciding how to structure a group. For example, work with antisocial adolescents, clients in residential treatment centers, severely impaired psychiatric patients, and street gangs often occurs in long-term groups. These groups focus on specific, narrowly defined concerns and objectives only in the context of broader, long-term objectives and goals. For example, a short-term goal for a group of psychiatric inpatients might be for the patients to learn specific social skills. This goal may be accomplished in a short-term social skills group. However, the long-term goal for each member—to live independently in the community—may best be accomplished through a program that includes a series of short-term groups focused on specific skills and a long-term group integrating what is learned in the brief, focused groups. Short-term, structured approaches such as task-centered practice seem to recognize long-term treatment needs by suggesting that successive short-term contracts can be developed for certain clients, such as antisocial adolescents, who may need long-term treatment (Reid, 1997).

In some situations, it may be best to strive for a group structure that encourages members to use their own resources when carrying out intervention plans. A group for parents of children with Down syndrome, for example, may be most successful if members are encouraged to share their mutual concerns and diverse efforts at being effective parents for their disabled children. Such a structure encourages the formation of a mutual support network among the parents.

In other cases, it may be best if interventions are highly structured by the worker. For example, a worker leading a group to teach children to resolve conflict may have a specific outline for each group session that includes didactic material about resolving conflict, reviewing homework assignments, role playing, observing and recording observations about the role play, making suggestions and giving feedback about the role play, modeling a new response, reviewing the new response, and assigning tasks to be done before the next session (Rose, 1998).

In both the parents' group and the children's group described above, the worker is clear about how the structure of the group has contributed to goal achievement. The worker selected an intervention method by assessing the specific problems facing members and the needs of the group as a whole. The worker did not apply a familiar intervention plan without regard to the situation. Overall, no simple guidelines can be provided about the "right" amount of structure for a group. Instead, workers should carefully assess the needs and desires of members before deciding on how to structure a particular group.

Involving and Empowering Group Members

Another important activity in the work stage of treatment groups is to help members become fully involved in the work of the group. The ultimate goal of the process is to empower members so they can take charge of their lives both inside and outside the group. Workers who are insecure about their position often make the mistake of being overly directive or even manipulative. Instead of doing their utmost to help members take as much responsibility as they are able to for the direction of the group, insecure workers often think they have to be in control at all times. This view is often counterproductive and leads members to become rebellious or passive-aggressive.

An important first step in the process of involving and empowering group members is for workers to show their belief in members' strengths. Statements that express confidence in members' motivation and tenacity, point out their abilities, and describe their previous accomplishments help to foster members' resolve to accomplish particular goals.

Expressing belief in members' strengths does not mean that the worker should be unrealistic and ignore impediments to goal achievement. Thus, a second step in the process of empowering group members is to acknowledge the difficulties and obstacles members encounter as they attempt to reach particular goals and objectives. It is also important to recognize their efforts to overcome obstacles. Statements such as "Ann, I really admire that you're not giving up—that you continue to confront this difficult issue with your daughter" or "Expressing yourself about this painful issue really shows your courage, Charlie" affirm and validate members' efforts to take charge of their own lives, even when the work is difficult.

A third way to empower group members is to help them know that they have a stake in the content and direction of the group. Statements such as "This is your group—what do you want to see happen in it?" help members overcome a tendency to expect the worker to take full responsibility for group content and process.

A fourth step to encourage involvement and empowerment is to praise members for reaching out to help each other. Statements such as "I really liked the way you shared how you felt about Ann's situation" or "This group is really making progress—it's wonderful to see how supportive you are of each other" demonstrate support of members' self-help efforts and foster the continued development of cohesion in the group as a whole. Vannicelli (1992) found that similar statements help foster cohesion in groups for substance abusers and their families.

A fifth way to empower group members is to encourage them to try out new behaviors and actions both within and outside the group. Members should be encouraged to begin by taking small action steps and carefully observing the results. Members can then report the results of their efforts to the group. They should be encouraged to acknowledge each other's accomplishments and to support each other when obstacles are encountered.

Program activities can also be used to involve and empower group members. Activities should involve as many members as possible, and members should be encouraged to take leadership roles and support each other's efforts. Members also should be encouraged to adapt program activities to suit their needs. Rigid adherence to particular ways of conducting program activities should be de-emphasized.

Involving and empowering members does not mean that the worker stops providing direction and guidance. However, when guiding group interaction, workers should solicit members' input and feedback and make sure their suggestions are given serious consideration. For example, the worker might state, "Jane, I'm glad you expressed your feeling that we may be moving too fast. How about others in the group? What is your opinion about how fast we have been moving today?"

Helping Members Achieve Their Goals

During the middle stage of the group, workers should concentrate on helping members achieve the goals they have agreed to accomplish. Contracting for treatment goals is an evolving process. A tentative agreement or contract is usually discussed while interviewing potential members during the planning stage of a group. The contract is reaffirmed and made more concrete and specific during the beginning stage of the group as members interact with one another for the first time. Although much of a treatment group's work during the middle stage is devoted to carrying out contracts developed during the beginning stage of the group, contracts continue to evolve as the group progresses during the middle stage.

Croxton (1985) notes that secondary contracts may be developed to refine initial contracts. For example, a member of a group for recently separated people might contract to reduce her angry feelings and violent outbursts toward her former spouse when he picks up their children. A secondary contract might involve the member in discussing her feelings of anger with another member outside the group and reporting back to the group what she has learned about how to handle angry feelings. A variety of different secondary contracts could be used to help the member achieve the goals specified in her primary contract. Thus, secondary contracts evolve as group members progress toward their treatment goals.

Although a portion of a treatment group's work should be devoted to maintaining a group's optimal functioning, most of an effective group's time during the middle stage should be focused on helping members achieve their goals. This can be accomplished by helping members (1) maintain their awareness of their goals, (2) develop specific treatment plans, (3) overcome obstacles to members' work on treatment plans, and (4) carry out treatment plans.

Awareness of Goals

The first step in helping members to achieve their goals is to maintain their awareness of the goals they identified and agreed to work on in earlier group meetings. Workers should not assume that members continue to be aware of these goals as the group progresses. Reconfirming members' commitment to the goals they decided to achieve in earlier meetings serves several purposes. It lets members know the worker remains interested in their progress. It checks for a continued mutual understanding of the contract. It helps ensure that the worker and members remain focused on the same issues. Confirming goals helps avoid confusion and promotes members' organized and systematic efforts to work on contracts. Periodically confirming goals also gives the worker an opportunity to check whether any changes need to be made in the contract, and it gives members a chance to share their feelings and thoughts about what has been accomplished and what remains to be done. For example, the contract for a group of parents waiting to adopt children might include attending group meetings on (1) child development, (2) legal proceedings for adoption, (3) special issues and concerns of adopted children, and (4) supportive resources and services available for adoptive parents and their children. During each meeting the worker might ask members whether the content of the meeting is useful. Members can be given the opportunity to express their reactions to what has occurred and to make suggestions for improving future meetings or continuing the meetings as originally planned.

Maintaining members' awareness of and commitment to contract goals is essential in treatment groups that focus their work on individual contracts. At times, the worker may spend a considerable amount of time helping one member work toward a particular goal. For example, in a group for alcoholics, the worker might spend 30 minutes working with one member in relation to a secondary contract to help the member improve his methods of expressing anger. As a result, during the two-hour group meeting, only three or four members may have an opportunity to work intensively on their treatment goals. When this occurs, it is particularly important to generalize work with an individual to other members so that everyone feels involved in the group. For example, members can be asked whether they use ways of coping with stressful situations similar to the ways described by the member being given the group's attention. The worker can also encourage other members to share experiences that may be helpful to the member. Such interventions help to establish a norm for mutual helping among members.

If extensive time is spent with only a few members during one meeting, the worker should spend a brief period of time checking on other members' progress. Members who did not have an extensive opportunity to participate in a meeting should be encouraged to participate more during the next meeting. This strategy helps prevent repeated and prolonged attention to a few members and reduces the possibility that some members will avoid working on their contracts.

During the middle stage, the worker should also help members to develop a process for reviewing their treatment goals and contracts. Although the review process may be idiosyncratic to the needs of a particular group, the worker should avoid haphazard or constantly changing review procedures. Without a clearly defined process that all members can expect, there is the danger that some members' progress will be carefully monitored but that of others will not. When monitoring is haphazard, members who are assertive and highly involved are more likely to be monitored, but members who are less assertive and those who are resistant will not receive the attention they require. One method that is widely used is to facilitate a brief go-round during the beginning of each meeting in which all members, in turn, spend a few minutes describing their goal, what they accomplished since the last meeting, and what they plan to accomplish before the next meeting.

With unsystematic monitoring procedures, tasks that are to be completed between meetings might not receive proper follow-up. There is nothing more frustrating and disconcerting for members than to complete a task between meetings and then not be given the opportunity to report the results during the next meeting. In addition to creating an ambiguous demand for work, failure to follow up on tasks often gives members the impression that the worker is disorganized and that there is little continuity from one meeting to the next.

Once a systematic procedure for monitoring is established, the worker rarely needs to remind members to report their progress to the group. The expectation of weekly progress reports helps maintain members' motivation to work toward contract goals between sessions and reduces the need to remind members of their contract agreements. It also helps members gain a sense of independence and accomplishment as they assume responsibility for reporting their own progress.

Developing Treatment Plans

A second way to help members achieve contract goals is by facilitating the development of specific, goal-oriented treatment plans. When all members are working on the same contract goal, the worker develops and implements plans with the group as a whole. For example, in a weight-loss group, a medical social worker might help members prepare a method for monitoring their daily caloric intake, present material on good nutrition, and introduce methods for modifying eating habits. The worker may then help individual members discuss their special needs and help them modify what has been presented to fit their specific circumstances.

When helping a member develop and implement an individual treatment plan, the worker should enlist the support of all group members. The worker should use every available opportunity to make connections among members, to point out parallel issues and concerns among members' situations, and to encourage all members to participate. As members become involved as helpers, the group's cohesion increases and members feel satisfied that they have something to contribute. Known as the *helper-therapy principle* (Lieberman & Borman, 1979), this strategy works in such a way that members who help others often benefit as much as those who are helped.

Before deciding on a treatment plan, the worker helps members explore and gather facts about their situations. A guided group discussion on the specifics of a situation, the alternatives that have been tried, and the possibilities that have not been explored is often sufficient to help members develop intervention plans. Sometimes, however, members try to grab at potential solutions without exploring alternatives, particularly when members are experiencing a great deal of stress or psychic pain from their problems. The worker should encourage members to explore alternatives thoroughly before deciding on an action plan.

An exploration of the situation may reveal a need for additional information. The member, with or without the help of the worker, might be asked to spend time between sessions gathering data. The process of members' monitoring their own behavior and gathering additional facts about their situation is essential to the development of effective treatment plans.

After group discussion and data gathering, a treatment plan may become apparent. For example, information gathered by a depressed member of an outpatient psychotherapy group might suggest that negative, self-deprecating thoughts and self-statements are maintaining his depression. The thoughts and self-statements persist despite the member's adequate performance in job- and family-related responsibilities. The treatment plan developed as a result of this information would focus on helping the member replace negative thoughts and self-deprecating statements with realistic thoughts and self-statements about his abilities, accomplishments, and positive qualities. The member would contract with the group to make a list of positive self-statements to be repeated each time an obtrusive, negative self-statement occurs. Secondary contracts, such as having the member ask other group members to describe how they perceive him during interactions in the group and having the member get positive feedback from significant others, can also be used to help the member overcome his depression.

Sometimes exploration of the problem may not immediately lead to a clear plan of action. The worker should help members consider alternatives before deciding on a final plan of action. Because of their professional training and knowledge, workers are often the primary generators of alternative intervention plans. Although the intervention plan that is selected may have been originally generated by the worker or another group member, members should be encouraged to refine alternatives and select the most appropriate plans for their own needs. They should not look at a plan as imposed by someone else. Members who experience their action plans as self-selected are more likely to follow through on them.

A treatment plan can be quite complex. It may involve a sequence of actions suggested by different members of the group. These different sequences of actions occur simultaneously. A complex plan should be divided into a series of discrete steps that are defined as clearly and specifically as possible. For example, to become more assertive, a member might (1) clarify the difference between aggressiveness and assertiveness through group discussion and reading a book on assertiveness, (2) decide in which situations to become more assertive, (3) practice being more assertive in the group during role plays and group discussion, (4) practice being assertive outside the group with family members or a friend, and (5) practice being assertive in a real-life situation.

Ideally, each step of the treatment plan should specify (1) who, (2) does what, (3) when, (4) where, (5) how often, and (6) under what conditions (Maple, 1977). It is especially important to be clear and specific when there are several people responsible for different aspects of a comprehensive treatment plan. Treatment plans often require the involvement of the worker, the client, other agency personnel, and the client's family. The effective worker should make sure that all persons who are a part of the treatment plan are clear about their roles, their responsibilities, and their expected contributions.

In some groups, all work is completed during meetings, but it is often helpful to encourage members to complete tasks between meetings. Many different tasks can be developed to help accomplish treatment plans between meetings. According to Wells (1994), there are (1) observational or monitoring tasks to gather information or to increase awareness of behaviors, emotions, or beliefs; (2) experiential tasks to arouse emotion and to challenge beliefs or attitudes; and (3) incremental change tasks to stimulate change step by step. Other types of tasks include mental or cognitive tasks to help group members change cognition and belief systems and paradoxical or two-sided tasks that result in changes no matter how they are carried out. For example, the treatment plan of a nonassertive group member includes the paradoxical task of having the member assert her right in a situation in which she would normally remain passive. If the member does the task, she is learning to be more assertive. If she does not do it, she is showing that she can assert herself in reference to her treatment plan.

Tasks can be individual, reciprocal, or shared (Tolson, Reid, & Garvin, 1994). For example, an individual task for a member in a smoking-cessation group may be to keep a log of the number of cigarettes smoked each day. Workers may also agree to perform individual tasks. A worker in a rural county welfare agency, for example, might agree to find out whether there are any transportation services available to enable teenage parents to attend a parenting skills group.

In a reciprocal task, if one person does something, another person will also do something. For example, if a member of an adolescent group does his assigned chore in his community residence each day for one week, the worker will help the member to obtain a pass to see his parents the next weekend.

A third type of task is shared by two or more people. For example, members of the group may form a buddy system (Rose, 1989), also referred to as consulting pairs (Garvin, Reid, & Epstein, 1976), in which each member is expected to remind the buddy to work on a specific task between group meetings.

In developing treatment plans and specific tasks, the worker should proceed by making sure that members are able to carry out each step successfully. It is especially important for members to have a successful experience in carrying out the first task they agree to accomplish. If they are successful with their first task, they are much more likely to successfully complete a second task.

Successfully completing an initial task gives members a sense that their goals are reachable. It also helps build self-confidence, feelings of self-efficacy, and a sense of control and mastery over the problem the member is attempting to alleviate. As members begin to feel self-confident, they are more likely to persist in their attempts at solving problems and concerns and are therefore more likely to be successful than when feelings of inadequacy limit their attempts to solve problems (Bandura, 1977). In this way, feelings of self-efficacy are reinforced and enhanced, which in turn can result in more effective and persistent problem solving in the future.

In developing treatment plans, the worker should assess a member's competencies and work with the member to plan an initial task that can be accomplished without an extraordinary amount of effort. Novice workers often develop treatment plans that are unrealistic. Members may agree to a treatment plan to please a worker or another group member, only to find that they are not prepared to undertake the tasks contained in the plan. The worker should also attempt to ensure that tasks are paced appropriately so that they become progressively more difficult as the member gains confidence and skill.

The worker can intervene to reduce the possibility that a member might have considerable difficulty in completing a task. Simulations, role plays, and other exercises can be performed in the group before the member tries the task at home, in the community, or in any other less hospitable environment. Rose (1989) suggests that members can be prepared for unreceptive or hostile environments by simulating these conditions in the group. One of the advantages of group treatment is that members can practice with other members of the group before they attempt to perform a task in the natural environment. Acting out roles also helps members become more aware of their own roles in a situation. An entire treatment method known as *psychodrama* is based on the benefits of acting out life experiences with others (Blatner, 1996).

Members should be encouraged to tackle one task at a time. In treatment planning, it is surprising to find how many clients with multiple problems suggest working on several different problems and their resulting tasks simultaneously. Although members often have good intentions in the group session, when they return home they have less motivation to follow through on the multiple tasks they have agreed to accomplish. It is better to start with one or two concrete, carefully planned tasks than to encourage a member to work on a variety of tasks simultaneously. When a member has completed the initial tasks, he or she can take on more difficult ones. If a member does not perform a task satisfactorily, the worker should help the member to view this as a learning experience rather than as a failure. A task that can be completed on the basis of the information and feedback gained from the initial experience can then be planned.

At the end of a session, the worker should ask members to review the tasks that were agreed on during the session. It is not uncommon for members or the worker to forget tasks that were agreed to one or two hours earlier in the midst of an active and interesting group session. A review can eliminate confusion, misconceptions, or discrepancies about specific tasks. At this time, members should also be encouraged to remind each other of any tasks or portions of tasks that have not been mentioned. This process ensures that everyone leaves the group with a clear notion of what has to be done before the next meeting. A recording form such as that shown in Figure 9.2 can be used to help the worker and the group members keep track of the tasks they have agreed to complete.

Overcoming Obstacles to Members' Work

It is important to help members to work on their treatment goals when they encounter obstacles. Members need help to work on their goals because making changes in habituated behavior patterns can be difficult. For example, a member of a psychotherapy group who has contracted to stop drinking alcohol might begin drinking again after only two days of abstinence. In a different group, a member who has contracted to become independent of her parents might make excuses about why she has not had time to explore alternative living arrangements.

FIGURE 9.2 ■ *A Group Task Recording Form*

Member's Name	Task	When	Where	How Often	Under What Circumstances

Date: _____

Session #: _____

Group: _____

In both cases, members encountered obstacles to achieving their goals. First, the worker should check with the member to find out whether the member also acknowledges that he or she has encountered an obstacle. Shulman (1999) suggests that the worker should also make a clear and specific "demand for work." The initial demand for work is a gentle reminder to the member that the worker and the other group members are interested in helping that member achieve personal goals. The demand for work should be accompanied by an offer to help the member overcome any obstacles to goal achievement.

With a member's agreement, the worker can encourage the member to explore what has been happening to prevent or block work on treatment goals. The worker can also involve the group as a whole by having members participate in the analysis of the factors that may be inhibiting a member's goal achievement. This technique can help both the member who is having difficulty following through on a treatment contract and other members, who can practice overcoming ambivalence and resistance in their own change efforts.

Obstacles interfering with members' abilities to work toward treatment goals may be the result of an inappropriate contract. A careful analysis of the contract may indicate that it was poorly designed and should be renegotiated. A contract can be inappropriate for several reasons, including the following:

- Goals in the contract are vaguely defined or too global to be achieved.
- Goals are too difficult to achieve at the current stage of treatment.
- The worker and the member focused on long-term goals rather than on more immediate, short-term goals that have a higher probability of being accomplished in a shorter period of time.
- There is a misunderstanding between the member and the worker about the nature of specific contract goals.
- Inappropriate goals were set without careful assessment of the member's situation.
- Changing problems and situations necessitate modifications in the treatment goals developed for a contract made earlier in the group's development.

For all these reasons, helping members work toward treatment goals often means helping them clarify, redefine, or renegotiate contracts.

Working toward goals also involves increasing members' motivation to take action to overcome the obstacles they have encountered. If a member agrees that action is important, the worker's task is to help the member believe that change is possible. Many group members are willing to act but refuse to do so because they do not believe in their own ability to change their situation. In such cases, self-instructional training (Meichenbaum, 1977), described in Chapter 10, may be useful in increasing a member's willingness to attempt a new behavior. It can also be helpful to ask other members to share their experiences regarding behavior change. They often serve as convincing role models who inspire and motivate reluctant members.

When the lack of motivation is severe, the worker should consider renegotiating a contract, focusing the new contract on helping the member increase motivation to work on a specific issue or concern rather than to work on the concern itself. Such a contract may involve helping the member examine factors that affect motivation to work on a particular goal and to examine any potential consequences of not working toward the goal.

When helping members overcome obstacles, workers should not ask "why" questions because these have been found to be unproductive in helping members work toward treatment goals (Flowers, 1979). Group members often do not have the answers to "why" questions, and if they do, the explanation may attribute causes to incorrect sources, which further complicates the problem. Instead, the worker should ask members "how" or "what" questions that encourage members to describe cognitive, affective, behavioral, or environmental circumstances that may be diminishing their ability to work on treatment goals.

"How" questions and "what" questions keep members focused on current behaviors that lead to or exacerbate existing problems. For example, the worker might ask, "What occurred just before you became angry?" or "How did you feel when _____ happened?" Such questions tend to elicit actual behavior and events, but "why" questions, if they can be answered at all, tend to elicit the opinion or judgments of members on the basis of their interpretations of information. Thus, "how" questions are more likely than are "why" questions to elicit information that will help members make active behavior changes and achieve their treatment goals.

The final step is to help members decide what actions to take to overcome obstacles and renew their progress toward treatment goals. In making the plan, the worker helps members to get support for their efforts from as many sources as possible. For example, the worker asks the member who returned to drinking after two days to go around the group and tell each of the other group members that he will not drink until the next group meeting. Members are encouraged to support this member by making replies such as "I'm happy for you—I admire your determination to work on your problem." Group members can also help the member by suggesting interventions such as changing his cognitive self-statements and modifying his home environment by removing all alcohol from his house. The worker can ask several members to give the member a call during the week to help him follow through on his verbal commitment. To enlist the help of his family and friends, the worker can ask the members' permission to contact them to gain their support and encouragement for the member's decision not to drink. To provide continued support during evening hours, the member can be referred to an Alcoholics Anonymous group. In this way, the member receives support for working toward contract goals from a variety of sources within and outside the group.

In summary, helping members work toward treatment goals is an important activity for any worker who plans to lead effective treatment groups. All treatment groups require effort from members if they are to be successful in achieving their goals. The worker's task is to help members mobilize their resources and maximize their use of the group to help them accomplish their goals. The worker should be constantly vigilant and point out inertia, ambivalence, and other psychological, social, and environmental barriers that block members' progress in the group. Because inertia, ambivalence, and reluctance to change are common even among highly motivated clients, the strategies and techniques on working with reluctant and resistant group members, presented later in this chapter, may also be useful in helping members to work on their treatment plans.

Helping Members Carry Out Treatment Plans

Workers can use five intervention roles to help members carry out their treatment plans. These roles are (1) enabler, (2) broker, (3) mediator, (4) advocate, and (5) educator. Although other roles have been identified as appropriate for helping members carry out their treatment plans, these five roles are the most important and most frequently assumed by workers leading various types of treatment groups.

ENABLER ROLE.   The enabler role is the most basic of all intervention roles. As Shulman (1999) points out, the enabler reaches out to members and lets them know that their ideas, opinions, and feelings are valued. The worker encourages members to express their concerns and feelings regarding their treatment plans. The worker monitors members' reactions to the work occurring in the group and encourages members who appear to have something to contribute to share their thoughts with the group. As obstacles are encountered, the difficulty of making changes in established behavior patterns is acknowledged. In this way, the worker shows empathy for members who are confronted with difficult life situations. At the same time, the worker helps members use their own skills to identify, confront, and remove obstacles that detract from their ability to carry out treatment plans.

As the group progresses, members are praised for their contributions and encouraged to continue their participation. The worker helps the group develop a supportive culture in which members can count on one another for mutual aid in overcoming difficult problems. As an enabler, the worker helps members revitalize and mobilize their strengths and resources to cope with difficult problems (Compton & Galaway, 1999).

BROKER ROLE.   In the broker role, the worker identifies community resources that may help clients carry out their treatment plans. In most communities throughout the United States, there is a complex and often confusing network of community services and resources that group members often know little about. As a broker, the worker helps members become aware of appropriate services, eligibility criteria, and other conditions for using a service. For example, a member of a group may be experiencing great distress in caring for her elderly mother. As part of a plan to help reduce this distress, the worker suggests that the member contact a local home health-care agency. First, though, the worker discusses eligibility criteria for receiving home health aid, the availability of third-party reimbursement, the duration and extent to which services can be expected, and whether services are available 24 hours a day. After this discussion, the worker refers the member to a specific contact person in the home health-care agency. To avoid frustration, disappointment, and unmet expectations, the worker also prepares the member for barriers that may be encountered, such as a one-month delay in processing reimbursement claims for home health-care services.

To help workers perform broker functions adequately, agencies should keep an up-to-date listing of community resources, with brief, pertinent information about contact people, access points, eligibility requirements, and other requirements for receiving services. In some communities, directories are prepared by a planning agency and made available. Workers who may not be thoroughly familiar with all community services available in their area can refer to a community resource directory for information.

MEDIATOR ROLE.   As a mediator, the worker helps to resolve disputes, conflicts, or opposing points of view within the group or between a member and some other person or organization. For example, in a group for adolescents in a residential treatment center, the worker might help two members resolve a conflict about their participation in a recreational activity. In another group, the worker might help a member resolve a conflict with a child-care worker.

To be an effective mediator, Compton and Galaway (1999) suggest that a worker should help members in conflict recognize the legitimacy of each other's interests. The worker identifies and works toward common values and interests, helps the members avoid situations in which winning and losing are paramount, attempts to get at the specifics of the conflict, and helps the members recognize that their ongoing relationship is more important than winning or losing a specific conflict.

As a mediator, the worker resolves disputes by helping members arrive at a settlement or an agreement that is mutually acceptable. It is essential for workers to avoid taking sides in a dispute. Workers should also avoid making judgments about disputes on the basis of their own positions or values. The mediator role is based on an assumption of neutrality and on the ability of disputing parties to work together through constructive, open communication. More information about conflict resolution skills is provided in Chapter 11.

ADVOCATE ROLE.   In some cases, a worker's efforts to act as a broker and refer members to needed services and resources may not succeed. The referral source may not be sympathetic to members' needs, or there may be no appropriate services or resources available. In these situations, the worker advocates on behalf of group members to help them obtain services or resources. As an advocate, the worker represents members' interests and needs.

The worker can negotiate to obtain needed services on behalf of one or more group members. For example, in negotiating with a community service center to plan more activities for adolescents, a worker might offer to supervise the youth worker or volunteer who is to lead one of the new activities. In other cases, the worker might use persuasion to obtain voluntary acceptance of a change. According to Pincus and Minahan (1973), voluntary acceptance of a change comes about because the target of the change realizes that the worker's request is correct, just, and legitimate and recognizes and accepts the worker's professional expertise and judgment.

In attempting to gain what is needed for members of a group, the worker may also assume an adversarial role. As an adversary, the worker challenges the validity of the status quo. The worker may appeal a ruling, lobby for a change in rules, organize a rally, or in countless other ways work for changes in systems that affect members of the group. For example, in a group for nursing home residents, one member's treatment plan included having him take part in a regularly scheduled activities program. The member missed the program several times because the clock in his room had been stolen, and the activities director had a policy that residents must be responsible for getting to the program by themselves. The worker advocated for the member by speaking to the activities director, explaining the situation, and working out a plan whereby the member was notified by the director one hour before the program began. In the same group, the worker also advocated for members by requesting that nurses' aides change their order of serving dinner so that residents who took part in the group did not have to eat cold food.

When services or resources to address particular needs are not available, advocacy efforts include making others aware of the unmet needs and establishing services to address them. For example, in an activities group in a board-and-care facility for older adults, members expressed a variety of concerns about their lack of control over their living conditions. The worker met with the director of the facility to advocate for patients' rights to self-determination. Through these efforts, the worker obtained the permission of the director to form a residents' council to advise the administrative staff on issues affecting residents. Members of the activity group served as the nucleus for the residents' council, which continued after the 12-week group ended.

The worker's advocacy efforts may, therefore, include helping develop new services and resources. The worker acts as an advocate by helping others understand the importance, intensity, and extent of a particular problem. By demonstrating how a need is relevant to the objectives and goals of an agency and by making their own expertise and knowledge available, workers can actively participate in developing new services for group members.

EDUCATOR ROLE.   One of the most important roles assumed by workers in helping members achieve their treatment goals is that of the educator. As an educator, the worker presents new information to help resolve members' concerns; demonstrates and models new or improved behaviors; and suggests role plays, simulations, and in vivo activities to help members practice new or different ways of behaving in problematic situations. Unlike the enabler role, in which the worker helps members use their own resources, the educator draws on professional knowledge about changing or modifying behavior patterns and adds to members' existing knowledge and skills.

In educating group members, it is often helpful to use visual and motor modes of teaching, as well as the more common didactic mode. Learning can often be enhanced, for example, by visual displays on newsprint and by graphs, charts, or other media. Videotape and audiotape recordings can provide members with feedback about their behavior in a group.

Novice workers sometimes assume that simply mentioning a new piece of information or discussing how to perform a new behavior is sufficient to help members learn it. Experience suggests that members are frequently unable to perform behaviors described verbally. Therefore, it is important to have members practice new behaviors before trying to perform them in real-life situations, particularly for complex skills. Sometimes a series of steps involving modeling the new behavior, practice, feedback, coaching, and additional practice is necessary to help a member perfect a new skill.

Working with Reluctant and Resistant Group Members

In some situations, workers will be called on to work with members who do not want to be in the group. Rooney (1992) notes that involuntary groups are often formed either through external legal pressure or by nonlegal external pressure from family or other referral sources.

When working with involuntary group members, it should be kept in mind that members always have the right to refuse to participate. It is important, however, for the worker to point out the consequences of refusal, and to clarify non-negotiable aspects of participation if involuntary members choose to participate in the group. Nonnegotiable aspects may include rules about attendance and participation, such as coming on time and not coming to the group intoxicated or high on drugs. It is also important to clarify members' rights and choices. The worker should attempt to maximize members' freedoms within the constraints of the legal and nonlegal pressures they are experiencing to be in the group and to change behaviors.

Behroozi (1992) points out that not all involuntary group members are alike. Individuals in involuntary groups resist goal setting for many reasons. Some perceive their problems to be too embarrassing to work on them in a group. Some are angry that they have been considered incapable of handling their own problems. Some view themselves as failures or as incompetent and consequently find their personal problems too daunting to tackle. Some deny problems because to admit them would throw their view of themselves into chaos.

One of the first tasks of the worker, therefore, is to develop a nonjudgmental, accepting, and safe group environment in which members can feel free to express their own views of their problems. As members express their views, it is important for the worker to assess members' motivation for being in the group and to identify how the group can be helpful to them (Rooney, 1992).

As members express their views, it is helpful to adopt a position that maximizes members' sense of control and expertise. Acknowledging that members can help the leader understand what it is like to be in their shoes and that members are in the best position to help themselves demonstrates respect and can do much to help the worker join with members in their fledgling attempts to express and work on their concerns.

It is also essential to acknowledge members' feelings and reactions to being in the group. Authentic and direct communication helps members to express their feelings rather than hide them. Sometimes, paradoxical interventions can be combined with authentic and direct communication to help members to express and begin to deal with their feelings of resistance (Milgram & Rubin, 1992). For example, the worker might state that he or she is aware that the members were ordered to attend the group or face more severe consequences and that they are not interested in what the group has to offer. This can sometimes have a paradoxical result in that often one or more members react by talking about how the group might be helpful.

It can also be helpful to reframe resistance as the members' way of communicating their feelings about being forced to attend. The worker should not try to prevent members from venting their anger. Instead, the anger should be acknowledged. After everyone has had an opportunity to ventilate, the worker should point out that, because members have chosen to attend or else face other consequences, they might as well use the group to their advantage rather than waste their own time. The worker should ask members to put aside the goals imposed on them from outside the group and to think about what goals they would like to achieve.

The worker should try to uncover the feelings and thoughts that underlie members' resistant behavior. For example, are members scared or hurt? Are they trying to control the situation or to avoid confronting issues that they experience as too difficult to face? Kottler (1992) points out that, once the underlying meaning of resistant behavior has been figured out, the worker is in a much better position to offer therapeutic assistance.

It can also be helpful to dramatize naturally occurring consequences (Edelwich & Brodsky, 1992). The worker should avoid talking about abstract consequences and, instead, focus on the natural consequences that have occurred because members failed to confront their problems. For example, the worker might say, "You almost lost your license for driving while you were drunk. What would you do if they took away your license? How would you get to work? In what other ways would not being able to drive affect you?"

The worker should avoid moralizing or blaming. Problem behaviors should be presented in a direct, factual way and, whenever possible, members should be asked to describe in their own words the negative consequences that have resulted from problem behaviors. For example, the worker might divulge what members' blood-alcohol levels were at the time of their arrests for driving while intoxicated and ask them to describe what consequences they have had as a result of the arrest.

Workers should encourage resistant members to make "I" statements. Instead of allowing members to project blame onto someone else, "I" statements help members take responsibility for their feelings, thoughts, and actions.

Confrontation is often necessary to help members overcome their resistance (Kottler, 1992). It is better for members to confront each other, rather than for the leader to confront members (Edelwich & Brodsky, 1992; Milgram & Rubin, 1992). The latter approach can lead members to coalesce against the leader. Also, because members' confrontations are based on members' experiences, their confrontations are often more powerful than workers' confrontations.

The leader should strive to build a group culture that encourages confrontation of members' motivation to work in the group. However, because resistant members avoid taking responsibility for their actions, it is unrealistic to expect them to confront each other initially. The worker must first model constructive confrontation.

According to Edelwich and Brodsky (1992), constructive confrontations should be (1) solicited rather than imposed, (2) done gently and with caring, (3) descriptive rather than evaluative, (4) specific and concrete, (5) presented in an atmosphere of trust, and (6) timed so that the member is able to hear and experience the full effect of the interaction. Constructive confrontations should include a descriptive statement, an "I" statement, and a reference to natural consequences (Edelwich & Brodsky, 1992). For example, the worker might say, "You say that you didn't do anything and you can't understand why you're being singled out. But if I had been caught driving with a blood alcohol level as high as yours, I would have been given the same choice as you: lose my license or come here. And if I kept avoiding the consequences of my behavior, I'd have problems on the job, at home, and with the law—as you are having."

To build a group culture in which confrontation of resistance and avoidance of problems is normative among members, rather than solely emanating from the leader to members, it can be helpful to include former members or members with greater longevity in the group. Members who have already confronted and grappled with their own resistance can discuss their initial reluctance to participate in the group and how the group enabled them to work through their resistance and confront their problems. For example, it is helpful to have more experienced members talk about how avoiding problems does not help and how facing up to problems is the first step to doing something about them.

To create empathy and to help members take responsibility for their actions, as Rooney (1992) points out, it can be helpful to invite victims to group meetings. These individuals can talk about the experience of victimization and its impact on them.

Even though constructive confrontations can help overcome members' resistance to working in the group, it is important to remember that reluctant and resistant members will continue to experience obstacles to goal achievement as they attempt to develop and implement treatment plans. These obstacles can reduce their motivation, which makes them reluctant to continue to work to accomplish specific goals. Reid (1992), for example, points out that beliefs about change and obstacles encountered in the external environment reduce members' motivation to engage in tasks to resolve particular problems. Methods designed to help members change their beliefs and to make the external environment more responsive are described in Chapter 10.

Although all the tactics mentioned can be helpful when working with resistant clients, the most important thing the worker can do is maintain a therapeutic stance. In a wonderful book on working with difficult clients, Kottler (1992) points out that it is essential for workers to avoid personalizing oppositional behavior. Also, one must avoid retaliating, threatening, and levying punitive sanctions. Instead, the worker should be patient and compassionate, keep a sense of humor, and avoid feeling omnipotent, that is, believing that one can help anyone, all the time.

Monitoring and Evaluating the Group's Progress

Monitoring and evaluating progress provides feedback for workers and members, which is useful in developing, modifying, and changing treatment plans. It also is helpful in maintaining the functioning of the group as a whole. Monitoring and evaluating are important ongoing processes that should occur throughout the life of a group.

One of the most common methods of obtaining feedback from members during the middle stage of a group's development is to give members a session evaluation form (such as that shown in Chapter 13, Figure 13.3) at the end of each group session. Although the format of session evaluation questions (closed-ended, Likert-type questions and open-ended questions) remains fairly standard from group to group, the content of questions varies. Changing the content of questions provides workers with the specific information they need about a particular group's work.

How frequently should session evaluation forms be administered? In some groups, they can be used at the end of each session. Workers who are not familiar with using session evaluation forms sometimes wonder how they will be received by members, but brief forms that take only a few minutes to fill out are not a burden for members to complete. In fact, members often enjoy the chance to let the worker know what they like and dislike about the group.

In other groups, workers may prefer to evaluate the group's progress after every second or third session. The exact frequency of monitoring and evaluating ultimately depends on the need for ongoing feedback about the group's development. Verbal evaluations are often used as a substitute for written evaluations, but anonymous written evaluations may offer better feedback because they can offer a measure of confidentiality not available through verbal evaluations.

Other frequently used methods of monitoring and evaluating include having members self-monitor their behaviors and having others who are familiar with members' concerns (such as other workers or family members) report progress to the worker. These and other monitoring and evaluation methods are described in Chapters 8 and 13. The actual methods used for obtaining feedback are, however, not as important as whether the feedback is systematically solicited, collected, and acted on. Obtaining feedback allows workers to fine-tune a group as it progresses through the middle stage. It also is a signal to members that their opinions are valued and that their ideas and concerns will be analyzed and acted on. For these reasons, monitoring and evaluating a group's progress is an essential worker activity during the middle stage of group development.

SUMMARY

The middle stage of treatment groups is the period in which members focus on the goals they have contracted to achieve in the group. This chapter focuses on six foundation activities that all workers perform while leading treatment groups during their middle stage. The section about preparing for group meetings includes a discussion of how to select program activities. The section on structuring the group's work includes a discussion of the optimal amount of structure to meet members' needs. The section about involving and empowering group members includes building on members' strengths and their commitment to the group as a whole. The section on helping members achieve contract goals includes techniques for (1) keeping members aware of goals they have contracted for, (2) developing treatment plans, (3) overcoming obstacles to members' work on treatment plans, and (4) helping members carry out their treatment plans. The section about working with reluctant and resistant group members includes a discussion of constructive uses of confrontation. The chapter concludes with the foundation activity of monitoring and evaluating the group's progress.

LEARNING ASSIGNMENTS

1. You are preparing to lead a socialization group in an afterschool program for third and fourth graders. Develop three program activities that are age appropriate. Prepare a list of materials that you would need to have on hand to conduct the activities. Write a paragraph describing the benefits of each of these activities for members. Describe a *variation* on one of the activities (or an additional program activity) that would help members develop problem-solving skills. Describe a *variation* that would help members develop expressive skills.

2. Develop a written session agenda for an educational group for individuals who want to be foster parents. Develop a written agenda for the meeting of a task group in which you participate.

3. Identify a social action group in your community. Observe the extent to which members are involved and active. To what extent do the leaders and other active participants help all members feel empowered to work toward a particular group goal? If you were the leader, how would you have run the meeting differently to help empower members?

4. Develop a written group contract for outpatients meeting in a community mental health center. In addition, give an example of a contract that one member might make with (1) the group as a whole, (2) the group's leader, and (3) another member.

CASE EXAMPLE

As Jim planned for the middle stage of his group for men who were physically abusive to their partners, he grew increasingly concerned about how he was going to help overcome their resistance to participating in the group. As a condition of their probation, members were mandated to attend a 10-session group that had both an educational and a rehabilitative focus. Jim's responsibility was to conduct the group and write individual progress reports for the probation department.

During the initial two meetings, members spent a great deal of time objecting to being mandated to attend the group. Several members noted that although the probation department required them to be there, they felt little obligation to participate in discussions. Others stated that they were thinking of dropping out. Jim knew that these statements represented initial resistance to being mandated for treatment. Jim also recognized that these members, who once exercised control over their relationships through violence, were now in a position of being controlled through the legal process. Because domestic violence often involves power and control, the involuntary status of the membership was particularly difficult for members to accept.

During the first session, Jim allowed members to express their feelings and to ventilate. He also pointed out their ambivalence about dealing with the problems that had caused their situation. He hoped that by doing this he could overcome some of the initial resistance and help members accept the purpose of the group. Although this helped somewhat, several members continued to demonstrate verbal and nonverbal expressions of resentment and anger about being required to attend the group. However, Jim asked members to talk about what the consequences of nonattendance might be. This discussion helped reinforce and make more vivid members' recognition that, if they chose not to attend, they would have their probation revoked and be jailed. Through discussing possible consequences, members seemed to become more resigned to their attendance, although they continued to show some resentment about having to discuss what they considered to be private matters.

During the second session, Jim helped some members to overcome resistance by reframing their situations. Jim assured the members that they had rights and choices about attending the group. He suggested that although they were ordered by the court to attend, they had also actively chosen to obey this mandate. He gave them positive feedback for making this choice, and suggested that now that they had made this decision, they might as well decide to make the best possible use of the group. By avoiding threats, moralizing, and blaming, Jim secured the initial participation of the members.

As the group entered the middle stage, Jim sensed that the men were beginning to accept their involuntary status as members. However, when he suggested that members begin to discuss what individual goals they might want to accomplish in the group, he was again met with silence and nonverbal communications that suggested to him that members were not willing to move into the middle (i.e., work) phase of the group. A few members eventually noted that they felt that they could handle their problems by themselves and were reluctant to discuss their personal situations with other members. Jim stated that sometimes he thought that, as a man, he was expected always to be in control of his feelings and be competent enough to handle his own problems. He asked members if they sometimes felt this way too. One member agreed that this seemed to be true for him, and then several other members nodded in agreement. This led to some meaningful discussion about role expectations but did not seem to help members identify individual goals for changing their feelings and behaviors.

By modeling nonjudgmental and accepting behavior, Jim helped members talk briefly about their relationships with their partners. Jim noted that most of the members verbalized a strong need for having power and control in their relationships with their partners. He wondered out loud whether members were reluctant to have their assumptions about relationships challenged. He acknowledged members' feelings and beliefs, but at the same time, he challenged members to rethink how they viewed their relationships. He speculated that this might be one of the reasons that members were unwilling to discuss individual goals for themselves. Although some members still blamed their partners for the violence, for the most part, they responded well to Jim's honest and authentic confrontations.

Jim used two techniques that gradually helped members respond to his demand for work. First, he gave members a copy of the "Power and Control Wheel," which illustrates how domestic violence centers around power and control. He discussed some of the theoretical aspects of the cycle of domestic violence. It took some discussion for members to understand the point of view expressed in this material, but Jim could see that it was sinking in. Second, he discussed how he had helped members of other groups like this to have more satisfying relationships with their partners. He noted that success and better relationships were both possibilities if members committed themselves to working hard in the group. He again assured members that he would be supportive of their efforts, but that they needed to take the first step by thinking about their individual goals. The introduction of new information that challenged members' beliefs, accompanied by the instillation of hope, eventually overcame members' resistance to moving into deeper aspects of their problems. By the end of the fourth session, members had developed individual goals they could work on for the rest of the group sessions. In later sessions, resistance re-emerged again. For example, some members had great difficulty accepting that they needed to change some of their thoughts and behaviors. Other members had difficulty at work or in other environments that contributed to their resistance to investing themselves in change efforts.

The sessions were difficult ones because of the different types and levels of resistance in the group. Nevertheless, Jim's understanding about involuntary group members and about resistance within the group helped him to avoid taking the resistance he encountered personally. Jim continued to struggle, however, both with his own strong feelings about violence and working with men who had dysfunctional beliefs about relationships and with the group's constant testing of his ability to be accepting and nonjudgmental. He discussed these feelings, and how he was handling them, with his supervisor.

Treatment Groups: Specialized Methods

This chapter focuses on specialized intervention methods for individual group members, the group as a whole, and the group's external environment. Even though this chapter sequentially presents interventions at the three levels, in actual practice, interventions at one level often affect other levels. As the group unfolds, the skilled worker moves easily among all the levels by combining interventions for the individual member, the group as a whole, and the group's environment to help members reach their treatment goals.

INTERVENING WITH GROUP MEMBERS

When intervening with individual group members, the worker may select from

1. Intrapersonal interventions that focus on members' cognition and affects, that is, their thoughts, beliefs, values, feelings, sensations, and emotions
2. Interpersonal interventions that focus on members' relationships with others within and outside the group
3. Environmental interventions that seek to change or modify the psychosocial and physical space in which members function

Intrapersonal interventions are particularly appropriate when an assessment has determined that a member's bio-psychosocial development may have helped to contribute to dysfunctional or irrational belief systems. Interpersonal interventions are particularly useful when an assessment has determined that members need further development of their skills in relating to others. Environmental interventions are particularly useful when an assessment determines that a member lacks material resources to ameliorate a problem or when the environment is impeding a member's ability to accomplish a goal.

Intrapersonal Interventions

Since the beginnings of group work practice, workers with psychodynamic orientations have focused most interventions in treatment groups on the intrapersonal aspects of group members' behavior. In recent years, there has also been a growing interest in techniques to intervene in the covert, intrapersonal lives of group members using cognitive and cognitive-behavioral approaches to practice (Beck, 1995; Klosko & Sanderson, 1998; Leahy, 1996; Rathus & Sanderson, 1998; Rose, 1998; Sheldon, 1995; Smucker, Dancu & Foa, 1999; Stern & Drummond, 1991).

Before using specific techniques, group workers should be aware of the overall process of helping members make intrapersonal changes. This process includes helping members to

1. Identify and discriminate among thoughts, feelings, and behaviors
2. Recognize associations between specific thoughts, feelings, and behaviors
3. Analyze the rationality of thoughts and beliefs
4. Change distorted or irrational thoughts and beliefs

Identifying and Discriminating

The first step in any intrapersonal intervention is to help members accurately identify thoughts, feelings, and behaviors and to discriminate among them. Some members have great difficulty putting their subjective thoughts and feelings into words. But without clearly identifying a member's thoughts and feelings for the rest of the group, it is not possible to help members cope with or change these covert processes.

In helping members identify and discriminate behavior from thoughts and feelings, members should be encouraged to describe their behavior in specific, observable terms as if a camera were taking a picture of the event and the member were a bystander observing the behavior. Sometimes, members have a difficult time describing feelings. It is common for group members to respond to a question about what they are feeling with a description of a behavior or a thought. This response is particularly true of men, who are taught as they are growing up that expressing feelings is a feminine, not masculine, trait. For example, in response to a question about what he was feeling, an obviously angry group member stated, "I'm not feeling anything." When the worker responded that people are always feeling something, no matter how slight, the member said, "I'm feeling that your interpretation of my behavior is not correct." This statement is, of course, a thought, not a feeling.

To help members who have difficulty discriminating feelings from thoughts, the worker can have the member get feedback from the group. In the previously described situation, for example, the member went around the group and asked the other members how they perceived he was feeling. Responses expressing that he appeared to be angry gradually indicated to the member that he was not in touch with his feelings. Sometimes it is necessary to have members practice discriminating thoughts from feelings in several situations inside and outside the group before they are able to identify and separate them correctly.

Recognizing Associations

The second step in intrapersonal interventions is to help members recognize that there is an association among thoughts, feelings, and behaviors. For example, if a man thinks someone is deliberately following him as he walks home one evening, he is likely to feel apprehensive and to behave accordingly. He may look over his shoulder or walk on the well-lighted side of a street. Similarly, if a woman thinks she is not skillful at a particular task, she is likely to feel incompetent and is less likely to continue to work on the task if she encounters difficulty than if she thinks that she can perform the task adequately.

For members to alter associations among thoughts, feelings, and behaviors, they must be aware of their existence. Awareness can be accomplished through a self-monitoring process. Members are asked to monitor particular thoughts and the feelings and behaviors that occur immediately following them. The group helps members look for patterns of association among particular thoughts, feelings, and behaviors. Sometimes members may clearly remember specific thoughts and their associated feelings and behaviors, and it may not be necessary to spend time monitoring them before reporting them to the group. This is often the case with automatic thoughts that constantly recur to members (Beck, 1995; Beck et al., 1990; Smucker et al., 1999).

Data about thoughts, feelings, and behaviors collected either prospectively or retrospectively should be discussed in the group. Such a discussion usually reveals that specific thoughts are exacerbating or maintaining unwanted feeling states and behavior patterns. For example, an anxious group member may find that her thoughts are focused on her "inability to do anything right" and that she would not be able to complete her work assignments on time. By discussing her thoughts in the group, she became aware that the thoughts led to her fears and her anxiety about her performance on the job and, in turn, tended to distract her from her work, which led her to feel more anxious. Both consequences were reinforcing her beliefs that she would not be able to complete her assignments, that she could not do anything right, and that she was a failure.

The previous example suggests that thoughts lead to feelings and behavior, but it is also possible that particular cues or signals can lead to thoughts, which can, in turn, lead to feelings and behavior. For example, a cue for an anxiety-producing thought might be the approach of a person of the opposite sex in a singles bar. The approach signals the person who begins to think anxiety-producing thoughts, such as "I hope he doesn't come over here" and "I won't know what to say." The thoughts can then lead to feelings of anxiety and to avoidance behavior. Such a sequence of events can become habituated, and thus a particular cue or even the thought of the particular cue can lead to the entire sequence of dysfunctional thoughts, feelings, and behaviors.

The second step in the process of intrapersonal interventions, therefore, also includes helping members become aware of internal cues, such as muscle tension or butterflies in the stomach, and external cues, such as the approach of a person, that trigger a sequence of events. In long-term treatment focused on personality change, workers may want to help members gain insight into the historical determinants of the cues. Once members are aware of the cues that trigger an association between thoughts, feelings, and behavior, they are ready to move to the next step in the process.

Analyzing the Rationality of Thoughts and Beliefs

The third step in intrapersonal intervention is to help members analyze the rationality of the thoughts and beliefs that maintain or exacerbate dysfunctional feelings and behavior patterns. Epictetus wrote in *The Enchiridion:* "Men are not disturbed by things but by the views taken of them." According to many cognitive psychologists, dysfunctional and irrational thoughts and beliefs arise from erroneous or misleading interpretations of events (Ellis, 1962; Freeman, Pretzer, Fleming, & Simons, 1990; Klosko & Sanderson, 1998; Mahoney, 1974; Meichenbaum, 1977; Stern & Drummond, 1991). Group members may

- Overgeneralize from an event
- Selectively focus on portions of an event
- Take too much responsibility for events that are beyond their control
- Think of the worst possible consequence of future events
- Engage in either-or dichotomous thinking
- Assume that because certain events have led to particular consequences in the past they will automatically lead to the same consequences if they occur in the future

Sometimes corrective information and feedback are sufficient to change thoughts and beliefs based on incomplete or incorrect information. For example, some teenage girls believe that they will not become pregnant if they have sexual intercourse only once or twice. With proper information, however, beliefs about the result of sexual activity can be changed.

Ellis (1962) and others (Beck, 1995; Leahy, 1996; Sheldon, 1995; Smucker et al., 1999; Stern & Drummond, 1991; Yost, Beutler, Corbishley, & Allender, 1985) have suggested that faulty interpretations occur because of irrational beliefs and ideas people have about the way things should operate in their world. For example, members may believe that they must be thoroughly "competent, adequate, and achieving in all possible respects if they are to consider themselves worthwhile" (Ellis, p. 63). Ellis lists 11 common irrational ideas that affect members' interpretations of events. These beliefs are usually based on absolutist thinking, rather than on well-reasoned, logical interpretations or elaborations from factual evidence. Words such as *should, ought,* and *must* are cues to the existence of absolutist thinking, which may lead to irrational or erroneous interpretations of events. For example, a group member might believe that to consider himself worthwhile he must be competent in all possible respects. When his performance falls short of his unrealistically high standards, he becomes depressed.

Changing Thoughts, Beliefs, and Feeling States

The fourth step in intrapersonal interventions is to help members change irrational or distorted thoughts, beliefs, and associated feeling states. Several techniques that have been developed for this purpose are listed here along with a brief description of their use in group treatment.

COGNITIVE RESTRUCTURING. *Cognitive restructuring* is a term first used by Mahoney (1974) to refer to a group of techniques such as rational emotive therapy and misattribution therapy. These techniques are designed to expose faulty logic in group members' thought patterns and to help them replace the irrational thought processes with logical, rational patterns of thought. Yost, Beutler, Corbishley, and Allender (1985), for example, report using cognitive restructuring techniques effectively when working with groups of depressed older adults.

More recently Mahoney (1995a, 1995b) has pointed out that belief systems are formed through the course of development as individuals interact with their social environment. Thus, beliefs may not be "faulty" or "irrational" but constructed from the unique social experiences and the processing of these experiences that continually occurs within each individual. Smucker et al. (1999), for example, describe how childhood trauma experiences can affect adult survivors. Group work can help members become more aware of the factors that shape and maintain belief systems and how these factors might be modified through new experiences within and outside the group.

The worker can help members change belief systems by doing the following:

1. Having members examine the experiences on which thoughts and beliefs are based
2. Helping members examine the way past experiences were construed
3. Helping members consider the impact of their construction of experiences in their current lives
4. Helping members get feedback from others in the group about alternative ways of construing and responding to experiences
5. Practicing new ways of responding both cognitively and behaviorally that will enhance members' current coping abilities

Through a combination of group discussion, analysis, and action, members help each other gain insight into their attributions concerning previous events and the effects of their construction of events on their current lives. Cognition and behaviors that result from the attributions are replaced with thoughts, beliefs, and behaviors that are more functional for coping with events in their current lives. Smucker et al. (1999) refer to this as *imagery rescripting and reprocessing.*

COGNITIVE SELF-INSTRUCTION.   Cognitive self-instruction refers to helping members use internal dialogues and covert self-statements for solving problems and coping with difficult life events. Children and adults can use the technique to replace dysfunctional internal dialogues with self-statements that help them to solve a problem. For example, instead of a member's saying to herself, "I can't do this," she can learn to say, "I'll try to do it the best I can" or "I'll bet my answer is as good or better than anyone else's," and "First I'll examine all the data and then I'll think of the possible solutions."

Also referred to as stress inoculation training (Meichenbaum & Fitzpatrick, 1993), cognitive self-instructions can be used to prepare for a particular situation or to help a member perform effectively during a situation. For example, to prepare for a situation, a member might say, "When I talk to Sally, I'll tell her directly that I can't do it. If she tries to persuade me, I'll just repeat that I've decided not to do it." While in a particular situation, a member might say, "I'm in control" or "I can do this."

It has been found by D'Zurilla and Goldfried (1971) and Meichenbaum (1977) that internal dialogues are important mediators of effective problem solving. Poor problem solvers tend to repeat dysfunctional self-statements, which make them give up more quickly and get blocked more easily in problem-solving efforts than persons whose self-statements encourage active problem-solving efforts. Research evidence and clinical experience confirms that this procedure is an effective intrapersonal intervention for members who engage in dysfunctional internal dialogues (Beck, 1995; Leahy, 1996; Sheldon, 1995).

THOUGHT STOPPING.   Some group members have difficulty controlling maladaptive or self-defeating thoughts and internal dialogues. The thought-stopping technique is a way to help members reduce these thoughts (Davis, Eshelman & McKay, 1998). While the member is concentrating on a thought, the worker suddenly and emphatically says, "Stop." This procedure is repeated several times. The member gradually begins to think "Stop" and to remember the worker's voice saying "Stop" whenever the obtrusive thought occurs. Variations of the technique include having members pinch themselves when obtrusive thoughts occur, having them replace obtrusive thoughts with covert dialogues and images that are not self-defeating, and having members meditate on a particular scene or phrase when obtrusive thoughts occur.

REFRAMING.   Reframing is a cognitive technique used to help group members see situations or problems from another point of view. It means "to change the conceptual and/or emotional setting or viewpoint in relation to which the situation is experienced and to place it in another frame which fits the facts of the same concrete situation equally well or even better, and thereby changes its entire meaning" (Watzlawick, Weakland, & Fisch, 1974, p. 95).

For example, a member who complains that he is afraid to ask a coworker to dinner might be helped to reframe the situation as one in which he is sparing himself and his coworker from possible romantic entanglements that may interfere with job performance. In another case, a single parent who is angry at her former husband for encouraging their child to fight back when teased may be helped to reframe the situation as one in which her former husband is helping the child develop and maintain a male identity.

Once a member experiences a problem from a new perspective, the positive aspects of the situation are highlighted and the negative aspects of the situation have a better chance of being changed. The woman, for example, may then thank her former husband for staying involved with their child and suggest some other ways that the husband might help the child, such as how to settle disputes without fighting. The male group member may develop a platonic friendship with his coworker.

Reframing can also be used to help a member experience a problem or concern as an asset (Yost et al., 1985). For example, in a situation in which a member's spouse does not want to have sexual relations, the problem can be viewed as a helpful sign that something is wrong in their relationship.

COGNITIVE IMAGERY TECHNIQUES.   Flooding and implosion are two cognitive imagery techniques used to extinguish excessive and unproductive reactions to feared or anxiety-provoking events (Masters, Burish, Hollon, & Rimm, 1987; Shipley & Boudewyns, 1980). In *implosion,* the member is asked to imagine the most extreme version of a feared event or stimulus within the protected environment of the group. Thus, if a group member experiences anxiety when thinking about asking someone for a date, the member would be asked to imagine that person saying no and making a disparaging remark such as "I wouldn't go out with someone like you" or "You're not sophisticated enough for me." Because the member will not experience any horrible consequences from such a rebuff, he or she will overcome the fear associated with the possible consequences of asking for a date. Members often react to this technique with comments such as "That wasn't so bad" or "I didn't like the reaction I received, but I learned that I could live with it. I won't be so afraid of the consequences the next time."

Flooding is a procedure similar to implosion except that the member is asked to imagine the actual feared event rather than an extreme or exaggerated version of it. Feedback from other group members can be used to help the member see that although reactions may, at times, be unpleasant, they can be handled without great difficulty. The member learns how others cope with unpleasant reactions and develops personal methods for coping.

Research evidence on flooding and implosion suggests that in vivo exposure to the situation or event is more successful than imagined exposure (Masters,

Burish, Hollon, & Rimm, 1987). In group treatment, a role-play exercise may be used to expose a member to the feared situation. When the member practices handling the situation in the group, the member can then be assigned the task of experiencing the situation outside the group. Because duration of exposure is also associated with treatment outcome, the member should be encouraged to practice coping with the situation several times inside and outside the group.

A variety of other cognitive imagery techniques can be used effectively in groups. Kottler (1992) suggests that rational imagery can be used effectively to help members challenge irrational beliefs and assumptions and to act effectively in anxiety-producing situations. For example, in a group for agoraphobics, members could be asked to imagine themselves walking in a beautiful outdoor setting on a sunny, autumn day.

When using imagery techniques, the worker should ensure that members remain in a relaxed state and that they are able to imagine the situation vividly. Members should be instructed to signal the worker immediately if their anxiety increases or if the cognitive image they are visualizing fades. To help produce vivid imagery, the worker should recite a richly detailed image while members are in a relaxed state with their eyes closed.

PROGRESSIVE MUSCLE RELAXATION.   This technique combines cognitive instructions with physical activities to relieve stress and help group members overcome anxiety. The premise is that muscle tension is related to anxiety and stress. Helping members reduce muscle tension, therefore, helps relieve anxiety.

With members seated in comfortable chairs or reclining on the floor, the worker explains the entire procedure to them. Members should be as comfortable as possible throughout the procedure. In a calm, hypnotic voice, the worker (or an audiotaped voice) repeats the relaxation instructions, which include tensing and relaxing each major muscle group in the body. For example, the worker might say, "Stretch your arms out next to you [or on your lap, if seated]. Make a fist with both hands as hard as you can. Feel the tension and tightness in your hand. Keep your hands clenched [10 seconds]. Now relax. Just let your hand rest against the floor [or on your lap, if seated]. Notice how the tension and tightness are leaving your hands. Notice how the feelings of tension are being replaced by warm feelings of relaxation and comfort. Notice how your hands feel now compared with when you were tensing them."

Each muscle group is tensed and relaxed in this manner. Instructions for the entire relaxation procedure are not given here, but they are available in several excellent sources (Bernstein & Borkovec, 1973; Davis et al., 1998; Lehrer & Woolfolk, 1993). Records and audiotape cassettes are also available with complete instructions (Bernstein & Borkovec, 1973).

Although progressive muscle relaxation is most often conducted in individual treatment, it can be used effectively in group treatment (Rose, 1989). The major drawback in using this technique in group treatment is that it requires cooperation from every member. One member who distracts the group can ruin the effect of the procedure for everyone else. Sometimes the distraction may be unintentional, such as when a member falls asleep and begins to snore. In other situations, the distraction may be intentional. For example, a member who is not motivated may laugh or joke during the first tension-release cycle and thereby distract other group members.

To use relaxation effectively, the entire procedure should be explained before beginning. To reduce intentional distractions, members should have the opportunity to voice any questions or any reluctance about using the procedure before beginning. To reduce unintentional distractions, members should be given a signal to let the group leader know if they are having a problem. For example, a member might not be able to relax or, in rare cases, may become more tense. The member can signal the worker and the worker can give that member individual attention.

The relaxing nature of the procedure, dim lights, and comfortable position sometimes causes members to fall asleep. However, the regular breathing or snoring of a sleeping member can be distracting to other group members. Such unintentional distractions can be reduced if the worker explains that sleeping members will be awakened by a touch on the hand or arm.

Other relaxation procedures can be used as a substitute for progressive muscle relaxation. Some workers prefer meditation, bioenergetics, hypnosis, rolfing (deep muscle massage), or jogging. Although each procedure was developed from differing theoretical orientations, they all can achieve a similar result: a relaxed group member.

SYSTEMATIC DESENSITIZATION.   The technique of systematic desensitization can be particularly effective for treatment groups composed of members with phobias. With this technique, the worker helps members construct a hierarchy of situations or scenes that are feared. Starting with the least feared situations and progressing to the most feared situation, members are asked to imagine each situation while they are in a state of deep relaxation induced by progressive muscle relaxation.

A hierarchy of situations should consist of at least 10 scenes in which the member experiences gradually increasing levels of anxiety. For example, a hierarchy for a member who has been too fearful to date consists of (1) thinking about a prospective dating partner, (2) considering asking that person for a date, (3) planning where to go on the date, (4) planning how to ask the person for a date, (5) approaching the person to ask for a date, (6) starting a conversation, (7) asking the person for a date, (8) driving to the person's house, (9) walking up to the person's home, and (10) going out with the person.

Depending on the extent and the intensity of the anxiety, hierarchies may contain many more scenes. Scenes should not jump too quickly from a low to a high level of anxiety. For very fearful members, it is often necessary to construct hierarchies with as many as 20 or 30 scenes.

Once the members are helped to construct their own hierarchies (even if each member has the same phobia, individual hierarchies differ), the progressive muscle relaxation technique is used to induce a state of relaxation. The members are then asked to imagine the first scene on their hierarchy as if they were actually involved in it for about 10 seconds. If members experience anxiety, they are instructed to signal by raising a finger. Members experiencing anxiety are told to stop imagining the scene and helped to return to their former state of relaxation. When they are fully relaxed, they can imagine the scene again.

At this point, desensitization proceeds at the pace of the slowest group member unless some provision is made for members to complete their hierarchies at their own pace. One method to overcome this problem is to have members work in pairs to help each other work through the hierarchy each has developed (Rose, 1989). The worker should not allow members to work on their hierarchies for more than 30 minutes because the desensitization procedure is quite demanding, both in terms of continuously visualizing scenes and in remaining in a deeply relaxed state. If members do not complete their hierarchies during one meeting, they can begin the next meeting with the next to last scene they completed successfully in the previous meeting.

Interpersonal Interventions

Group work is an especially appropriate modality for dealing with interpersonal problems. Used effectively, the group can become a natural laboratory for examining and improving the relationships members have with one another. Unlike individual treatment, a group offers members the opportunity to demonstrate their interpersonal skills and to receive feedback from a variety of people. Members can serve as models of particular interpersonal skills and can play various roles in situations acted out in the group.

Interpersonal behaviors can be learned indirectly by listening to others describe how to behave in a situation. But behaviors are more effectively learned (1) vicariously, by watching what other people do or say, and (2) directly, by repeating and practicing new behaviors. When learned directly, a new behavior is usually performed on a trial-and-error basis until it is performed appropriately.

Learning a new behavior by hearing it described is often imprecise and is fraught with potential misinterpretation. Therefore, behavior is most adequately taught by having a member watch someone else perform it correctly and having the member practice the new behavior in a role-play exercise.

Many workers tend to allow the group to spend too much time discussing how to behave without actually helping members practice new behaviors, perhaps because of the contrived nature of role-play situations, the initial resistance of some members to role playing, and the extra instructions and direction the worker must provide to make role play successful. The learning that occurs from watching a model and rehearsing a new behavior, compared with merely talking about how to perform a new behavior, suggests that both modeling and role-play techniques should be used more frequently by workers helping members learn new or improved interpersonal behaviors.

Learning by Observing Models

Several factors affect the extent to which behaviors are learned by observing others (Bandura, 1977). Workers should understand the process underlying observational learning so that they can use modeling to help members solve interpersonal problems and learn new interpersonal skills.

Figure 10.1 illustrates the major components of observational learning. Performance of the modeled behavior depends on

- The level of attention or awareness of the observer
- The extent to which the observer retains what is seen
- The observer's abilities to perform the observed behavior
- The extent to which the observer is motivated to perform the behavior

The attention of a member who observes a model is important because, although behavior may be learned without one's awareness, attention is always selective

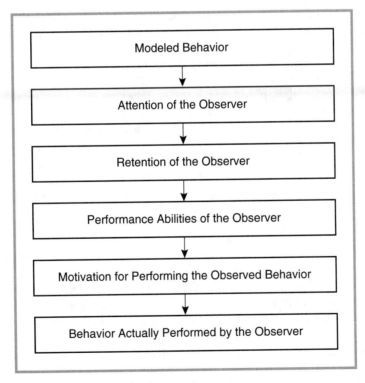

FIGURE 10.1 ■ *The Process of Observational Learning*

and is greatly facilitated by focusing on what is being observed. The worker can help focus awareness by calling members' attention to particular aspects of a model's behavior. For example, a member who is learning to be more assertive may be asked to pay particular attention to the facial expressions, body positions, and voice tones of a member who is modeling an assertive response. Attentional processes are also enhanced by the attractiveness of the model. For example, a member is more likely to pay attention to a group member who is held in high regard than to a member who has low status in the group. Members are also likely to be more attentive to models who are similar to themselves. Thus, workers should try to match the characteristics of models to the members who are observing them.

Retentional processes are also important in learning an observed behavior. In addition to developing images of the behavior that can be easily retrieved from a member's memory, retention is often facilitated if the model explains the covert and overt processes he or she goes through before performing a behavior. Explanations help the member develop a cognitive structure in which to organize perceptual images. When modeling an assertive behavior, the worker may, for example, explain the cognitive process occurring before the assertive response. Internal dialogues such as "I say to myself, 'I have a right to tell that person . . . '" can be helpful to members observing someone modeling a behavior.

The model may also explain general principles. For example, in making an assertive response, the member modeling the behavior might explain, "In general, I am always direct—I explain my needs to the person and I make a direct request for the person to change his behavior." Explaining general principles also provides an organizing framework that the member can use in different situations encountered in the future.

The member's ability to perform the modeled response is a critical component of observational learning. The member may pay careful attention to the way a model performs a behavior and retain details of the performance but may not be able to respond in a similar fashion. The best way to ensure that a member is able to perform a behavior correctly is to have the member perform the behavior in the group and receive feedback about the performance. If it is available, videotape feedback of the member's performance can also be effective in teaching new interpersonal behaviors.

Group members may know how to behave in interpersonal situations but may not be motivated to do so. What factors increase motivation? According to Bandura (1977), behaviors are more likely to occur if the observer sees others being rewarded for similar performances. Conversely, if an observer sees others being sanctioned for a given behavior, the observer is less likely to behave in a way that may result in similar sanctions.

A member, however, may not have to observe someone being sanctioned to not perform a new behavior. New behaviors are often difficult to perform until they are well learned. Difficulties associated with learning a new behavior, along with the absence of strong incentives, are frequently a sufficient disincentive for members considering performing new behaviors. Therefore, observational learning is selective. In daily living, for example, we often do not repeat a new behavior that we see performed by someone else.

To ensure that group members learn new behaviors by observing the worker or other members, several factors should be present. Members' attention should be carefully focused on how the behavior is being performed. Members should be helped to retain cognitive images of observed behavior by developing a set of organizing principles—a cognitive framework—that explains why a model responded in a particular manner. To build their capacity to respond, members should practice responses and receive feedback about the quality of their performances. Members' motivation for performing observed behaviors can be increased by demonstrating to them that the incentives sufficiently outweigh the disincentives for performing a particular behavior.

Learning by Role Playing

Role playing is an enactment of a social role in an imagined social situation. Role playing can be used for (1) assessment, (2) simulation, (3) understanding, (4) decision making, or (5) behavior change (Etcheverry, Siporin, & Toseland, 1987). Role playing is a powerful tool for any of these purposes. As shown in Table 10.1, role-playing techniques increase members' awareness and understanding of their interpersonal skills and produce behavior changes by providing members with corrective feedback and the opportunity to practice improved responses in the sheltered environment of the group.

Role-playing techniques can be structured or unstructured. Structured procedures use predetermined scripts or vignettes developed by the leader, and members act out prescribed roles believed to be important by the leader. For example, in an assertiveness training program group members may be asked to role play a number of common situations requiring assertive responses, such as dealing with someone who has cut into a line, returning damaged merchandise, or turning down a request to borrow an item. Structured role plays are not spontaneous, but they have the advantage of ensuring that the worker is ready with an effective response.

Unstructured role-play procedures are listed in Table 10.1. The procedures are developmental and open ended to allow spontaneous, emerging processes of learning and problem solving. Unstructured role-play procedures can be further divided into primary and secondary procedures. Primary role-play procedures can be used alone to accomplish particular purposes; secondary procedures are used in conjunction with primary procedures to extend their effect and widen their scope (Etcheverry et al., 1987).

Primary Role-Play Procedures

OWN ROLE.   In the own-role procedure, a member uses his or her experiences and plays the protagonist. Other roles are played by the worker or other group members, who may represent people, feeling states, thoughts, or objects. The

TABLE 10.1 ■ *Uses of Unstructured Role-Play Procedures*

Procedure	Awareness/Understanding	Behavior Change
A. Primary Role-Play Procedures		
1. Own role	Demonstrates and clarifies members' behavior, their role in interpersonal interactions, and their concerns and problems Facilitates members' insight into their own feelings, thoughts, and behaviors Identifies situational cues to facilitate differential responses Identifies members' problems and concerns	Allows members to practice new behaviors Reduces members' performance anxiety Prepares members for obstacles and setbacks
2. Role reversal	Stimulates empathy for another person whose role is being enacted by the protagonist Increases members' awareness of cognitive and affective aspects of other people Objectifies and clarifies the situational context of members' own behaviors	Encourages spontaneity and participation Facilitates changes in members' expectations of others Facilitates change in members' behavior Improves empathic skills
3. Autodrama/ monodrama/ chairing	Same as for own role and role-reversal procedures Identifies and clarifies members' own feelings at deeper levels than own role or role-reversal procedures Increases members' awareness of their own self-talk	Same as for own role and role-reversal procedures Facilitates learning of adaptive self-talk Enables changes on deeper, more complex levels than own role or role-reversal procedures
4. Sculpting/ choreography (Action sociogram)	Stimulates members' awareness and discussion of their own behavior and the group's interaction patterns	Facilitates changes in members' attitudes, behaviors, and interaction patterns

TABLE 10.1 ■ *Continued*

Procedure	Awareness/Understanding	Behavior Change
B. Supportive Role-Play Procedures		
1. On-the-spot interview	Identifies and clarifies members' thoughts and feelings while they are in a role Connects thinking and feeling to behaviors in a role	Provides practice in self-awareness and self-talk
2. Soliloquy	Same as on-the-spot interview procedure but less structured	Same as on-the-spot interview procedure
3. Doubling	Helps members verbalize and express covert thoughts, feelings, and behaviors Same as on-the-spot interview procedure Identifies new behaviors for acquisition	Same as on-the-spot interview procedure Gives permission and support for members' owning their own thoughts, feelings, and behaviors Facilitates expression of feelings Promotes members' skill in using feelings as cues for appropriate responses Allows members to practice their self-expression skills
4. Mirror	Promotes members' knowledge of the consequences of their own behavior on others Enables self-confrontation	Provides members the opportunity to practice new behaviors Enables feedback and reinforcement when learning new behaviors
5. Sharing	Universalizes members' experiences Models self-disclosure	Provides support and confirmation of members' experiences, abilities, etc. Facilitates learning of self-disclosure skills

own-role technique is particularly useful in assessing a member's interpersonal skills because it allows the worker and other group members to observe how the protagonist acts in a particular situation. The own-role procedure is also helpful as a means for members to practice new behaviors. Supportive procedures such as the soliloquy, on-the-spot interview, or doubling can be used to increase a member's awareness of behavior while performing the role of protagonist.

ROLE REVERSAL.   In role reversal, a group member acts as the protagonist by taking on the role of another person. For example, a husband may act in the role of his spouse. The procedure enables a member to experience a situation from another's point of view. Role reversal is particularly useful for teaching empathy, especially if it is used with doubling or soliloquy. It helps to clarify situations and to increase members' self-awareness. It also increases the spontaneity, flexibility, and openness of the member playing the protagonist's role. Variations of this procedure include substitute role playing (playing a symbolic, substitute role) and role distance (playing an emotionally distant role).

AUTODRAMA, MONODRAMA, AND CHAIRING.   A procedure in which a group member plays multiple roles is variously called autodrama, monodrama, and chairing (Blatner, 1996). The multiple roles represent the different ways members view themselves or the different ways others view a member. The procedure is usually conducted using one or more empty chairs, each representing a role, a character part, or a personality aspect. The member switches from one chair to another in changing roles. When occupying each chair, the person initiates and maintains a dialogue with the other chairs, which represent other aspects of the person's self.

The technique is particularly useful in helping members become aware of the various roles they play and their effects on each other. It is also useful in helping members assess internal dialogues and self-talk, such as irrational beliefs and devaluating self-statements. Therefore, the procedure can be used effectively in cooperation with cognitive restructuring procedures to practice adaptive self-statements and self-instructions that aid effective problem solving. Self-role and double chairing are other names for this procedure.

SCULPTING AND CHOREOGRAPHY.   Also called action sociogram, variations of the sculpting and choreography technique are psychodrama and sociodrama (Blatner, 1996; Moreno, 1946). In this procedure, a member, as protagonist, is directed to sculpt or position himself or herself and other group members in a drama that represents a symbolic or real situation in the member's life. The protagonist explains each person's role, and the worker directs the action, which can last for an extended period of time.

The dramatic enactment is designed to expose intense feelings and conflicts in a member's life and thus it can be used as an assessment device by the worker. Another benefit of the technique is that it immerses the whole group in intense participatory involvement leading to in-depth self-disclosure and enactment of crucial concerns and issues. In addition to the self-awareness this technique produces, the procedure helps the protagonist understand the importance of others in personal life situations. Although there is little empirical evidence for the efficacy of the technique, clinical reports and experience suggest that the cathartic experience and heightened awareness that result from participating in a dramatic enactment can lead to changes in members' thoughts, feelings, behaviors, attitudes, and interaction patterns.

The psychodrama variation of the technique focuses on the internal, psychological status of the actors. The sociodrama variation emphasizes the social and environmental aspects of the protagonist's situation. For an excellent, in-depth explanation of these procedures, see Blatner (1996).

Supplementary Role-Play Procedures

ON-THE-SPOT INTERVIEW.   On-the-spot interviewing involves stopping the role-play action before it is finished and interviewing one or more actors. The worker asks specific, detailed questions designed to elicit particular thoughts and feelings at that point in the role play. The procedure is designed to increase a member's awareness of cognitive, affective, and behavioral aspects of a role performance. It identifies self-statements and self-talk that are dysfunctional and self-devaluating. It also teaches self-observation and enhances self-awareness.

SOLILOQUY.   The soliloquy procedure involves stopping the role-play action and asking an actor to disclose what he or she is thinking or feeling. Unlike the on-the-spot interview, in which the actor is asked specific, closed-ended questions, soliloquy questions are open ended and encourage the member to engage in a monologue that discloses in-depth thoughts and feelings. The procedure is particularly useful for increasing a member's self-awareness.

DOUBLING.   The doubling procedure uses a group member to act as the alter ego or inner voice of the protagonist. To emphasize identification with the protagonist, the double is required to speak in the first person, for example, saying, "I feel . . . " or "I think . . . " Variations on the procedure are the "divided double" and the "multiple double." In the divided double, the alter ego speaks for different parts of the protagonist's inner self. The multiple double calls for two or more actors to speak for different aspects of the protagonist's self. To validate the truth of a double's statements in offering inferences, interpretations, or alternative reactions, the protagonist is sometimes asked to repeat and accept or reject the double's statements.

The doubling procedure can serve several important functions. It helps make role plays more dramatic and produces more in-depth experiences. It facilitates understanding and self-awareness of the protagonist's behavior. In addition to fostering insight, it gives permission for the protagonist to acknowledge repressed or taboo thoughts and feelings. It also increases the emotional sensitivity and self-expression of the protagonist. The procedure is often used in conjunction with own-role, chairing, and sculpting procedures.

MIRROR.   In the mirror procedure, a group member re-enacts a role-played performance for the protagonist. Other members can verify the accuracy of the replay. The procedure may also be used in an exaggerated, amplified, and stereotypical manner to emphasize particular aspects of the protagonist's behavior.

The procedure is useful as a confrontational technique to help the protagonist gain awareness of behavior. It is an excellent substitute for videotape feedback when videotape equipment is unavailable. The procedure is particularly useful in conjunction with modeling, coaching, and prompting to provide feedback to a member attempting to learn a new behavior. It is also a way of involving other group members in a member's situation to facilitate their empathy and their skills in self-expression.

SHARING.   The sharing procedure is often used at the close of role-play action. Group members give members who have role-played feedback about their performances. The procedure is designed to provide supportive feedback to the member who risked himself or herself in revealing a difficult situation by acting as the protagonist in the role play. It also enables members to share their own reactions and feelings to the role play.

Environmental Interventions

Environmental interventions help members to modify or change the psychosocial and physical situations in which they live. Environmental interventions consist of

- Connecting members to concrete resources
- Expanding members' social networks
- Modifying the contingencies that result when members perform desired behaviors
- Planning physical environments to facilitate members' goal achievement

Connecting Members to Concrete Resource

To connect clients to concrete resources, the worker first identifies the member's need and then assesses the member's ability and motivation to follow through and obtain the resource. For a highly motivated, well-functioning group member, the worker may be able to act as a broker to identify a contact person at the appropriate resource and give the member general information about what to expect when contacting the resource. The worker verifies that the member has obtained the needed resource at the next group session.

In some treatment groups, such as those composed of severely impaired psychiatric patients or older people with organic brain disorders, workers may have to take additional steps to ensure that members obtain the resources they need. For example, it may take some time to prepare members for a referral because of their lack of motivation or their failure to recognize their need for services. It may also be necessary to contact family members or guardians to help prepare them for a referral. In addition, medical impairments may limit or prevent members from contacting resources without assistance. Transportation may have to be arranged and the worker, an aide, or a volunteer may have to accompany the member to the resource. It may also be necessary to teach members the skills necessary to obtain a needed resource. For example, an unemployed group member might need to learn interviewing and resume-writing skills before beginning a job search.

Expanding Members' Social Networks

Another type of environmental intervention consists of helping socially isolated members expand their social networks by gaining needed support from others (Biegel, Tracy, & Corvo, 1994; Haring & Breen, 1992; Tracy & Biegel, 1994). The first step in expanding a member's social network is to analyze the member's current social relationships. Figure 10.2 illustrates the social network of Tom, a socially isolated member of a support group for people who have recently separated. The diagram indicates that Tom has only two active social relationships. Tom's other network relationships are inactive. He no longer plays with the softball team; he no longer sees Jean or Bob, with whom he used to be friendly; and because his brother lives nearly 1000 miles away, they rarely see one another.

Diagramming a member's social network on a flip chart or blackboard can stimulate group discussion about ways to expand the network (Tracy & Whittaker, 1990). For example, after examining the chart in Figure 10.2, several group members suggested that Tom renew former network relationships that lapsed after his marriage. To do this, Tom rejoined the softball team and renewed his friendships with Jean and Bob. Tom also was encouraged to join Parents Without Partners, a self-help group that sponsors many social, recreational, and educational events in his community.

Analyzing one group member's social network can stimulate other members to consider their own networks. Examining Figure 10.2 might cause members to become aware that they could also benefit from expanding their own social relationships. For example, after confirming that group members wanted to become more involved with one another, the worker suggested that members exchange telephone numbers and choose one person to call during the week. By scheduling one meeting at a member's home and supporting members' suggestions that they get together informally after the meeting, the worker encouraged

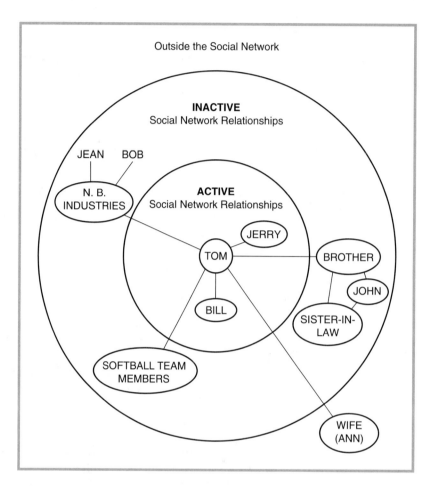

FIGURE 10.2 ■ *A Social Network Chart*

the members to form a supportive social network for one another. As the members began to meet regularly, it became apparent that child care responsibilities limited many of the members' abilities to socialize, so members with children decided to help each other with child care, thereby freeing each other to engage in social activities. Thus, through a worker's intervention efforts and the mutual-aid properties of the group, members' social networks were expanded.

Contingency Management Procedures

So that members can maintain their successes between group sessions, it is often necessary to modify or change the rewards and punishments they receive for behaving in ways that are not consistent with their treatment goals. This procedure is sometimes called *contingency management* because the rewards or punishments that are contingent on the performance of a behavior are modified to increase or decrease the probability that a behavior will be performed in the future (Sheldon, 1995).

Contingencies that increase the probability that a member will perform a behavior are called *reinforcers*. Typical positive reinforcers include social rewards that are verbal, such as praise, and nonverbal, such as a smile, a pat on the back, and similar signs of approval. Positive reinforcers also include tangible rewards such as money and food.

Negative reinforcers also increase behaviors. But unlike positive reinforcers that increase behavior through rewards, negative reinforcers increase behavior through aversive means. Negative reinforcers include yelling, nagging, and the silent treatment. Workers should emphasize the use of positive reinforcers that members enjoy receiving rather than negative reinforcers that are unpleasant and often result in deleterious side effects such as anger.

Unless a behavior is self-reinforcing, it will decrease if rewards are not received for performing it. Therefore, ignoring a behavior will tend to extinguish it if the behavior is not self-reinforcing to the member. Social disapproval, confiscation of tangible rewards, and physical punishment also decrease behaviors.

In general, workers should encourage the use of positive reinforcers and extinction procedures rather than negative reinforcers or punishment procedures. Often, it is sufficient to reward a desired behavior and ignore an undesirable behavior. Although positive reinforcers are preferred whenever possible, in some circumstances punishments may be imposed for failure to comply with group rules. For example, the members of a children's group decided that those who came late to group meetings would clean up after snacks were served.

Rose (1989) points out that the undesirable side effects of punishment procedures are avoided when members impose their own punishments, sometimes referred to as *response costs*. Thus, punishment procedures should not be imposed unilaterally by the worker. The group as a whole should decide on a policy, that is, the type of punishment (social disapproval or removal from the group) and the circumstances in which sanctions will be applied. The resulting policy should be applied uniformly.

The worker should help the group develop a realistic policy that is not too severe. Sometimes members develop unrealistically harsh rules to govern behavior in the group. William Golding's novel, *Lord of the Flies,* is a literary example of how groups can decide on punishments that are too severe. It is common, for example, for members of children's groups to develop group rules that, left unchallenged, lead to severe punishment. For example, in one group, members decided that anyone caught laughing should be thrown out of the group. In such cases, the worker should intervene and help the group develop less severe sanctions for misbehavior.

When using contingency management procedures, the worker should begin by helping members identify the rewards and punishments they receive for performing desired and undesired behaviors. Contingencies are identified by monitoring the consequences resulting from the performance of a particular behavior. If contingencies do not act to increase desired behavior and decrease undesired behavior, the worker can help the member modify them. Sometimes members may be able to administer their own rewards and punishments. For example, members may be encouraged to praise themselves for performing a certain behavior—to take themselves out for a good meal or buy a new piece of clothing. Such self-reinforcement procedures have been shown to be effective in helping members control their own behaviors and feel better about themselves (Yost et al., 1985).

It can also be helpful to involve other group members or significant others in members' lives in modifying the contingent rewards and punishments members receive for performing desired and undesired behaviors. Family members and friends can help provide an environment that promotes therapeutic goals. For example, a wife or husband may compliment the spouse for positive changes. A mother or father may praise their daughter for helping her little brother with his homework.

To formalize an agreement about what behaviors to reinforce, a verbal or written contingency contract can be developed. Such a contract specifies (1) what specific behaviors will be performed, (2) who will perform the behavior, (3) how the behaviors will be reinforced, and (4) who will administer the reinforcement. For example, the father of an adolescent group member may agree to take his son on a fishing trip if his son agrees to attend classes without misbehaving for two weeks. Although developing a written contingency contract may strike some individuals as too rigid or formal, it should be recognized that written agreements have the advantage of avoiding confusion later when individuals may have different recollections of the nature of an agreement.

There are many different types of contingency contracts. As mentioned, members may administer their own rewards and punishments in self-administered contingency contracts. Contracts may be made between the group member and significant others, between two group members, or between all group members and the worker. Contracts may also be reciprocal; that is, parties to the contract reward each other for performing desired behaviors. Reciprocal contracts are particularly useful in couples' groups because spouses can reinforce each other for performing desired behaviors.

By using contingency management procedures, the worker helps members perform desired behaviors by changing the environmental consequences that result when a behavior is performed. Too often, workers intervene effectively in the group to help members reach desired goals but fail to pay attention to what will happen when members try to perform desired behaviors outside the group. Contingency management procedures are a useful way to extend therapeutic interventions beyond the boundaries of group sessions. Yost et al. (1985), for example, described how contingency management procedures can be used to help group members who are depressed.

Some individuals react negatively to contingency contracts because they perceive them as manipulative, artificial, or as relying exclusively on extrinsic rather than intrinsic motivation. It is important to remember that contingency contracts are *voluntary* and *explicit* agreements between two or more parties. Co-ercive, exploitative, and underhanded attempts to control behavior have no place in the design or the execution of contingency contracts. It is true that con-tingency contracts specify artificial arrangements of rewards and punishments, but they should be prepared with consideration of the naturally occurring con-sequences that will sustain the behavior over the long term. For example, in the situation described previously, although the father will not be able to take his son on a fishing trip each time the son behaves well for a two-week period in school, it is anticipated that by behaving well, the son will stop receiving negative feed-back from teachers, administrators, and peers and will start enjoying school. Therefore, the artificial arrangement of contingencies will be replaced with nat-urally occurring contingencies such as praise from the teacher and good report cards. The extrinsic rewards for behaving well will be replaced, over the long term, by intrinsic rewards such as feeling competent, well liked, or self-confident.

Planning Physical Environments

Helping members modify their physical environments is another type of envi-ronmental intervention. Although often given little consideration, the physical environment has a profound effect on the problems and concerns that members experience. Environmental stimuli can make it easier or more difficult for a member to accomplish treatment goals. For example, members of a weight-loss group find that it is more difficult to lose weight if their refrigerators are stocked with fattening foods than if their refrigerators contain only those items that are a part of the diet that members agreed on. Similarly, it is difficult for a member of an inpatient psychotherapy group who is about to be discharged to learn in-dependent living skills in an institutional environment that does not allow the person to cook, clean, or shop.

To the extent possible, workers should help members modify physical envi-ronments so they promote goal achievement. In general, physical environments should give members the opportunity to practice the skills they are learning in the group. Members who are learning skills for independent living, for example, should have the opportunity to practice as many of the skills as feasible in the institutional setting in which they live. Physical environments should reduce bar-riers that are likely to impede a member's attempts to accomplish a goal. For ex-ample, a member who is attempting to stop drinking should remove all alcohol from her home.

Environmental interventions should be proactive as well as reactive; that is, in addition to ensuring that an environment does not provide unwanted stim-uli, the worker should help members modify environments so that they en-courage goal-directed behavior. A member who is attempting to lose weight may, for example, place a calorie chart on his refrigerator door to help him plan meals. A member of a parenting group may place a monitoring chart in her child's room.

Each time the child behaves correctly, gold stars are placed on the chart. When a certain number of stars accumulate, they can be redeemed for a trip to the zoo or extra play time with Mom or Dad. In both cases, modifications of the environment stimulate efforts toward goal achievement.

In inpatient settings, environmental modifications can include a restructuring of the entire milieu. Wright, Thase, Beck, and Ludgate (1993), for example, describe how cognitive therapy with inpatients can be enhanced by developing a cognitive milieu that permeates the entire residential unit.

INTERVENING IN THE GROUP AS A WHOLE

Workers select the group as a whole as the focus of interventions when they decide that the group process should be altered to help members achieve their goals. In this way, the group becomes the means as well as the context of treatment. As discussed in Chapter 3, four areas are critical to the effective functioning of any group: (1) communication and interaction patterns, (2) cohesion, (3) social controls, and (4) culture. These are the primary areas in which the worker intervenes when selecting the group as a whole as the focus of interventions.

Because most group dynamics have developed before the middle stage begins, the worker's task during this stage is to maintain and enhance dynamics that are contributing to the group's success and intervene to change dynamics that are interfering with the group's development. Experienced workers realize the power that group dynamics have in leading to successful group outcomes. In comparing 10 different methods of leading encounter groups, Lieberman, Yalom, and Miles (1973) found that "group characteristics" such as norms, cohesiveness, and climate had an important effect both on members' satisfaction with their experience in different groups and on the overall outcomes achieved by the groups. Similarly, in a study comparing methods of working with antisocial boys in groups, Feldman, Caplinger, and Wodarski (1983) also found that group dynamics had a powerful mediating effect on outcome, regardless of the type of treatment modality used. In the following sections, some suggestions are made about how group dynamics can be modified to achieve therapeutic purposes.

Changing Communication and Interaction Patterns

The worker may intervene to change the frequency, duration, distribution, or content of the communication and interaction patterns occurring in a treatment group. The frequency of interactions a member initiates in a group is important because it is difficult, if not impossible, to assess and treat a member who remains relatively silent throughout the group. Members must actively participate if they are to benefit from group treatment.

Shulman (1999) points out that what silent members really fear is being confronted with their silence. Therefore, it is more helpful to prompt such members to speak with statements such as, "What do you think about what _____ is saying?" or "You have some experience with this _____ , what do you think?" rather than to confront the members with data that suggest they are not participating frequently enough.

Another way to increase participation is to praise members when they add to the group's discussion. Positive comments such as "That was really helpful" or "I see that you understand what _____ is saying" can be used to show quiet group members that their contributions are valued. Positive reinforcement procedures have been demonstrated to be effective in several studies that have examined methods to increase members' participation in groups (Rose, 1989). Other techniques to increase the frequency of communication include asking members to lead the group discussion on a certain topic and going around the group and eliciting members' thoughts and comments on a particular topic.

Workers also may wish to change the duration of a member's communications in the group. This is particularly true for verbose members who dominate the group's discussions. Sometimes simply pointing out that other members of the group need time to participate is sufficient to limit the member's communications. For others, it is necessary to develop a contingency contract in which members agree to ignore the talkative member when the member talks for more than a specified length of time. Alternatives to this procedure include interrupting the member after he or she talks for a certain amount of time as well as reminding the member with a nonverbal cue that he or she is talking too much.

Workers may also want to change the distribution of communication and interaction patterns. Ideally, each member of the group should have an opportunity to participate. Although some group members may be more involved in a particular discussion than other members, communications should be distributed fairly evenly among all members over the course of several meetings. Workers should prevent situations in which they are doing most of the communicating or situations in which members direct most of their comments to the worker rather than to each other. Workers may also want to intervene when members of subgroups interact primarily with one another rather than with everyone.

As in efforts to change the frequency and duration of members' communication patterns, the most successful interventions for changing the distribution of communication patterns include cues to help members remain aware of their inappropriate communications, accompanied by prompts and positive reinforcement to help them change these patterns. For example, Toseland et al. (1978) reported that an intervention consisting of cues, verbal prompts, and reinforcement was successful in reducing the number of member-to-leader communications and increasing the number of member-to-member communications in a parenting skills group.

The content of the messages sent and received in the group is just as important as the frequency, duration, and distribution of group members' communications. Workers should be particularly concerned about the task orientation and the tone of the messages communicated in the group. Workers should intervene when most communications are not task relevant or when they are excessively negative.

Of course, some group discussion will not be task relevant. Joking, small talk, and interesting but irrelevant stories often make the group more attractive. Members have a need to express their own identity in the group. However, task-irrelevant discussions should not be allowed to take much of the group's time. Members come to treatment groups for particular purposes, and too much irrelevant conversation interferes with their ability to achieve goals, which ultimately leads to their dissatisfaction with the group.

Usually, it is sufficient to point out excessive digressions to the group and call the group's attention back to the session's agenda and the goals that should have been briefly mentioned at the beginning of the meeting. In some cases, however, such intervention may not be sufficient to help the group return to a task-centered discussion. The group's digression may signify a test or a challenge to the worker's authority, dissatisfaction with the content outlined in the session agenda, or an indication that group members are too fearful or anxious to discuss a particular topic. In such cases, it is helpful for the worker to point out a personal hypothesis about the reasons for the group's digression. Through discussion and feedback, the worker can help members to decide on how best to renew their focus on the group's goals. This process may make members aware that they are avoiding a difficult issue that they need to discuss. In other cases, it may lead to changes in the worker's style or the session's agenda.

Workers should also be concerned about the tone of the messages conveyed in the group. Frequent put-downs; excessive negative comments without suggestions for improvement; and infrequent occurrences of supportive, warm, or reinforcing comments make the group unattractive for its members. To change the tone of messages being communicated in the group, workers can act as models by making supportive comments whenever possible. Workers can also show their disapproval of negative comments by ignoring them or by suggesting that the member who makes the negative comment accompany it with a positive comment. Exercises designed to help members give positive feedback can also be helpful. For example, a worker might say, "I've noticed we make a lot of comments about what a person does wrong during our role plays. How about for the next role play, each member will identify at least one thing that the person does well."

Changing the Group's Attraction for Its Members

There is a consensus in group work literature (see Chapter 3) that cohesiveness and interpersonal attractions have many beneficial effects on group functioning. Group cohesion is built in a warm, caring, and empathic group environment. The worker can foster the development of this type of environment by actively listening to members, validating their experiences, and affirming their attempts to cope with the situations confronting them. By modeling genuine concern and interest in each member's experiences, the leader encourages members to tune in to each other's needs and to reach out in supportive, mutually helping interactions.

Cohesion and interpersonal attraction can also be stimulated by acknowledging members' efforts to support each other and by praising members for their active and constructive participation in the group. Thus, in addition to modeling concern and interest, the leader should take an active stance in guiding the group to increased cohesion and intimacy. Appropriate self-disclosures and revelations that deepen the group experience and make it more meaningful and more profound should be encouraged. Similarly, gentle and caring confrontations that encourage members to get in touch with their strengths or realize overlooked possibilities and alternative perspectives should be invited.

Physical arrangements can also make a difference in building group cohesion. Groups tend to be more cohesive and attractive when they are relatively small and there is plenty of interaction that is distributed fairly evenly throughout the group. In small groups in which there is considerable interaction, members have the feeling that their ideas are being heard and considered; in large groups and groups with poorly distributed communication patterns, members who are not a part of the "inner circle" of decision makers often feel that their ideas and suggestions are not being given sufficient attention. Suggestions for redistributing communication patterns can also be helpful to make a group more attractive.

Simple creature comforts can also make a difference in the attractiveness of the group. Refreshments such as coffee and doughnuts can be offered, and socializing over coffee during a break in a long session or immediately after a short session helps reduce the exclusive problem focus of groups and allows members to get to know each other as ordinary people rather than as clients. In addition, for some group members, refreshments and snacks can be strong incentives for participating in a group, particularly for children and psychiatric inpatients because their access to snacks is often limited.

Other ways to increase the attractiveness of a group include dispensing rewards such as a weekend pass as an incentive for participation in a group, planning interesting program activities and outings for the agenda of future group meetings, encouraging members to select topics for group discussion, and ensuring that members continue to make progress toward their treatment goals.

As the group becomes more cohesive, some members may fear becoming overly dependent on the group. The leader should encourage members to talk about these feelings and ease their concerns by indicating that such feelings are commonly experienced in groups when cohesion and intimacy increases. Acknowledging the support and security that the group provides and also acknowledging members' efforts to maintain their autonomy and their ability to function independently can help allay members' fears.

Fears about becoming overly dependent sometimes have their roots in problems with members' ability to develop intimate relationships. Intimacy implies vulnerability. When members disclose personal, emotionally charged issues that they may not have been able to talk about with others, they are exposing their vulnerability to the group. Members may have had previous unsatisfactory experiences in revealing emotionally charged issues to persons with whom they felt intimate. Thus, it is natural for members to feel ambivalent about sharing personal issues with the group. It is helpful for the leader to point this out so that all members of the group will be more likely to respond in a sensitive and caring way to fledgling attempts to self-disclose personal issues. Leaders should also make clear that they will protect members by blocking critical, insensitive comments and by encouraging supportive and caring interactions.

There are times when a worker does not want to increase a group's cohesion. For example, cohesion should not be increased in groups in which antitherapeutic norms have been established. Research by Feldman, Caplinger, and Wodarski (1983), for example, found that in groups composed solely of antisocial boys, *interpersonal integration,* defined as the reciprocal liking of the boys in a group for one another, was negatively associated with treatment outcomes. In these groups, cohesion apparently resulted in peer pressure to conform to antitherapeutic group norms. Thus, antisocial behaviors were reinforced rather than extinguished by group treatment.

Using Social Controls Effectively

The social controls exerted in a group can enhance the functioning of the group as a whole or they can lead to the demise of the group. Social controls exerted through norms, roles, status hierarchies, and the various power bases from which the leader draws authority are important forces within the group. As mentioned in Chapter 3, without social controls, group interaction would become chaotic and unpredictable, and the group would soon cease functioning. But in groups in which social controls are too strong, members soon feel restricted and coerced. They tend to rebel against the control or refuse to attend future meetings.

Social controls are applied most effectively by workers who command the admiration and respect of group members. Personal characteristics such as an empathic and warm demeanor; a sense of humor; sensitivity; insight; and the ability to remain calm, collected and professional in difficult situations encourage members to follow the worker's guidance and leadership. Similarly, specialized knowledge and the judicious use of wisdom gained from personal and professional experience help to increase the potency of the worker. Potent workers are self-confident but able to admit mistakes. They lead by example, not by applying social sanctions or by attempting to control, dominate, or manipulate the group. They tend to ignore rather than to sanction deviant behavior exhibited by group members, preferring instead to acknowledge and praise positive contributions and to set a tone and an atmosphere that encourage members to support and uplift one another.

During the middle stage of treatment groups, the effective worker helps the group develop social controls to integrate members' activities for goal achievement. Both normative integration (members' acceptance of group norms) and functional integration (members' assuming roles and activities that contribute to the group's work) are positively associated with beneficial group outcomes (Feldman, Caplinger, & Wodarski, 1983). One step that can help members to become normatively and functionally integrated into a group is to prevent domination of the group by one or more members who have a great deal of social power and who do not use it for therapeutic purposes. It has been found, for example, that socially dominant members in groups for youth with antisocial behavior problems often tend to ignore or subvert therapeutic group norms and resist efforts to promote prosocial behavior change (Feldman et al., 1983).

When facilitating normative integration, potent workers help members adhere to therapeutic group norms and change norms that are interfering with the group accomplishing its goals. For example, in a group that has developed a norm that members are not to be verbally abusive with one another, a member who becomes verbally abusive may be asked to leave the group until he or she can regain control.

In other cases, the worker may encourage and protect members who are deviating from antitherapeutic group norms. For example, a worker supports and encourages a member of a couples' group who begins to describe problems in the couple's sexual relations, a topic that has not been previously discussed by group members. In another group, the worker encourages a member to talk about the scapegoating of a member who is intensely disliked by other group members.

Workers should also help members become functionally integrated in the group. As mentioned in Chapter 8, some members take on deviant group roles such as the "group jester" or the "isolate." It is the worker's responsibility either to help the member assume a more functional role or to help the group modify its processes to find a useful role for the member. For example, the jester might be encouraged to take on a more functional role, such as helping members express feelings and concerns about a particular problem.

Changing Group Culture

Another aspect of group dynamics that workers should consider during the middle stage of treatment groups is the culture that has developed in the group. Does the culture help the group achieve its goals? If not, one way to change the group's culture is to challenge commonly accepted beliefs and ideas held by members. For example, in a group for abusive parents, the worker wanted to change a group culture that discouraged the expression of intense feelings and emotions. First, the worker pointed out that feelings were rarely expressed during group sessions. Next, the worker invited the group to discuss this observation. Several members indicated that they were afraid they might lose control of their actions if they showed their feelings. The worker suggested a series of role-play exercises designed to help the members gradually express more intense emotions and learn that they could express feelings without losing control. As the group progressed, members acknowledged that allowing feelings to build up inside until they exploded was much less healthful for themselves and their families than was learning to express feelings appropriately as they experienced them.

Another way workers can change the existing group culture is to point out its dominant features and areas that appear to be taboo or not able to be discussed. When this is done, members often indicate that they had wanted to discuss taboo areas in previous group meetings but feared the group would not be receptive. These members can then be encouraged to express their thoughts and feelings on the taboo subject. In other instances, role-play exercises can be used to stimulate the group's consideration of an area that was formerly taboo.

A third way to change the culture established in a group is for the worker to develop a contingency contract with members. This procedure was used successfully in working with adolescents in a group home. The contract specified that if a member was supportive and helpful to other members who disclosed personal problems and concerns during three of five group meetings each week, the member would have access to special rewards such as a trip to a sports event or tickets to a movie. The contract helped change the group culture from one in which members were ridiculed for expressing personal issues to one in which members supported and encouraged personal disclosures.

A similar procedure was used in a children's group. Peer pressure had created an environment in which members were teased for participating in role play and program activities. The worker developed a contingency contract using a point system. Points accumulated for participating in role plays could be used at the end of the group meeting to obtain special refreshments, games, or small toys. The incentive system was effective in encouraging the children to participate in role-play exercises designed to teach them problem-solving skills.

CHANGING THE GROUP ENVIRONMENT

The material resources provided for group work services, the types of clients eligible for services, and the service technologies and ideologies endorsed by the agency all have a bearing on the services the group worker offers. Group services are also influenced by interagency linkages and by the community's response to the problems and concerns of persons who seek group treatment. In this section, suggestions are made about ways to

- Increase social service agency support for group work services
- Develop links to interagency networks
- Increase community awareness of social problems that could be treated through group work services

Increasing Agency Support for Group Work Services

Before intervening to increase support for group work services, workers must first have a thorough understanding of their agencies. Like people, agencies have unique histories that influence their continued growth and development. It is often helpful to trace the development of clinical services within an agency to learn about the changes and innovations that have taken place over time. This process can help the worker understand the rationale for current clinical services, the agency's responsiveness to proposals for change, and the ways in which previous proposals for change were incorporated into the agency's structure.

A historical perspective helps the worker avoid making a proposal for increased support for group work services on the basis of a rationale that has been rejected in the past. It also helps to give the worker an understanding of the long-term development of the agency, an understanding that is likely to be shared by administrators whose support for innovations in clinical programming is essential.

Before proposing an increase in support for group work services, the worker should have a sound grasp of the current needs and future development plans of the agency. A proposal for group work services should be structured in such a way that it clearly shows how new or increased services will meet the current needs and future developments anticipated by the agency's administrators and board members. The proposal should emphasize the distinct advantages of group work services. For example, it may be possible to show that treatment groups are a cost-effective alternative to individual treatment services (see the cost-benefit analysis example in Chapter 13). Because most agencies want to get the most out of their resources by serving as many clients as possible for as little cost as possible, group treatment services may be an attractive alternative to individual treatment services.

A well-developed proposal itself is not enough to guarantee that an agency will increase its support for group work services. Workers also should know how to proceed within their agencies to get proposed changes accepted. Patti (1974) suggests that workers be aware of several organizational factors that help to predict the degree of resistance that can be expected to a change proposal. These factors include

- The extent of the proposed change
- The value orientation and decision-making style of the administrator responsible for deciding whether to accept the proposal
- The administrative distance between the practitioner and the decision maker
- The agency's investment in the status quo

The worker can, for example, expect greater resistance to a proposal for a basic change in the agency's services, such as a change from individual treatment to group treatment in all clinical programs, than to a modest proposal for group services to a specific client group.

The rationale for a proposal is also important in terms of the resistance it will encounter. An administrator who is concerned about saving money will probably be less inclined to accept a proposal that requires new funding than a proposal that is expected to reduce costs. Whenever possible, workers should try to present multiple rationales for group work services. For example, the worker might cite relevant research about the type of group being proposed, suggest how desired individual and group outcomes might be achieved, and describe how the group work service may reduce agency costs or increase reimbursement for clinical services.

The more levels of approval—that is, the further a proposal must go from the originator to final administrative approval—the greater the likelihood of resistance. If a group worker's proposal requires approval from administrators who are at a much higher level in the bureaucratic structure, the worker will have to elicit the support of supervisors who can argue for the proposal when it reaches higher levels of review. Even with support from supervisors, proposals are more likely to be altered the higher they go in the bureaucracy.

Resistance may also be encountered if the worker is proposing changes that reverse or negate program components or services that have received substantial support in the past. Agencies are not likely to abandon funded commitments in favor of a new proposal unless the proposal can be proved to be quite exceptional.

Once the worker has anticipated the resistance a proposal may encounter, support to overcome this resistance can be developed. Brager and Holloway (1978) suggest involving resistant coworkers in the proposal's development. Because they have had a hand in shaping the proposal, initially reluctant coworkers can usually be counted on for support in later negotiations. It is especially important to allow administrators who will be deciding whether to accept the proposal and persons who will be responsible for carrying out the proposal to have input into its development. During its development, a proposal may be revised several times to gain the support of critics who have reservations about the proposed changes. By the time it is ready for final consideration, the proposal is likely to have gone through several levels of review in which important participants have become sensitized to its benefits and their own questions or concerns have been addressed.

Links with Interagency Networks

Interventions in a group's environment include establishing links between agencies. Interagency links can be established by identifying and contacting workers in other agencies who work with similar populations or deal with similar social service problems. After informal telephone discussions are initiated, a planning meeting should be scheduled.

Interagency links can have several benefits. When other agencies are aware of particular types of group services offered by an agency, they may refer clients for treatment. For example, if a worker at a community agency is aware that a battered women's shelter offers support groups for women, the worker can refer women who would otherwise not receive services to this agency.

Agency networks help identify needs for particular services. In a meeting of workers from several agencies, for example, it became apparent to a group worker from a family service agency that no services existed for treating men who battered their wives. After carefully documenting the need in other agencies, a group work service was established for this population by the family service agency.

Interagency networks also help avoid duplication of services. Competition between agencies can be avoided by preventing the development of duplicate services existing elsewhere in the community and by facilitating the development of services when gaps in service delivery exist. Workers who cultivate interagency links can share the knowledge and practice experience they have gained from working with specific client groups and learn from the experiences of group workers in other agencies. In this way, knowledge can be pooled and mistakes made by one worker can be avoided by others.

Interagency networks are useful in lobbying for new group work services. For example, in a meeting of workers from a number of community agencies, it became apparent that additional services were needed to prevent criminal activity among unemployed youths. Although no worker was able to do anything about this problem alone, together they put enough pressure on the city's youth services program to obtain funding for a half-time group worker for the local community center.

Increasing Community Awareness

Ultimately, group work services depend on the support of local community residents. Residents' awareness of the social problems that exist in their communities and their belief that group work services can help maintain adequate social functioning and alleviate social problems are essential. Group workers have a responsibility to bring community problems to the attention of local officials and civic organizations and to make them aware of how group work services can help to alleviate their problems.

A variety of methods can be used to raise a community's awareness of social problems and increase its commitment to group work services. Needs assessments (see Chapter 13) are especially effective for documenting the need for additional services. Agency statistics about the number of clients not served because of a lack of resources or a lack of available services can also be useful. To call attention to community problems, workers can testify at legislative hearings, they can become members of local planning bodies, or they can help to elect local officials who are supportive of the community's social service needs. Only through such efforts will group work services remain available to persons who need them.

A group worker's skills can also be used to organize clients so that they can lobby on their own behalf for needed services. For example, an outpatient group in a community mental health center in a poor urban area was composed entirely of women who were receiving Aid to Families with Dependent Children (AFDC) benefits. It became apparent that many of the women's problems were tied to the subsistence-level benefits they received as well as to the environmental conditions in which they lived. The worker informed the women of a national welfare rights coalition and helped them form a local rights group. Although this effort did not make a tremendous or immediate change in their life circumstances, it did give the women a constructive way to voice their complaints and lobby for changes in their community. It helped them to overcome what Seligman (1975) called "learned helplessness."

SUMMARY

This chapter focuses on specialized intervention methods that can be used during the middle stage of treatment groups. The methods are commonly used to intervene at the level of (1) the group member, (2) the group as a whole, and (3) the environment in which the group functions. Interventions at the level of the group member can be subdivided into those that deal with (1) intrapersonal, (2) interpersonal, and (3) environmental concerns. Interventions in the group as a whole can be subdivided into those that focus on (1) communication and interaction patterns, (2) attraction for its members, (3) social control mechanisms, and (4) culture.

The chapter concludes with an examination of interventions to change the environment in which a group functions, an important, but often neglected, area of group work practice. Discussion of interventions in this portion of the chapter includes ways to (1) increase agency support for group work services, (2) develop links to interagency networks, and (3) increase community awareness of social service problems that can be alleviated by group treatment.

LEARNING ASSIGNMENTS

1. Form a small group and choose a leader. Have each member identify one situation that causes anxiety. Have the leader help each member construct a hierarchy of situations related to the source of anxiety. Using the progressive muscle relaxation technique, have the members achieve a relaxed state. Then have them visualize each item in the hierarchies they have created. Encourage members to

go at their own pace and to return to a less anxiety-provoking situation as soon as they become anxious.

2. Design and make your own audiotape or videotape to help you and other group members achieve positive cognitive imagery and a relaxed state. Choose relaxing music, sounds, or scenes from nature that you think would help someone relax. Play your tape for members of the group. What images did your composition evoke?

3. How would you design a session for the middle phase of a social skills group for children? What interventions or program activities would you use to increase the quantity and quality of social interactions among the members?

4. Form a small group of members who are willing to experiment with role playing. Have each member spend a few moments writing a short case scenario that illustrates a client problem. Choose some scenarios, assign roles to members of the group, and role-play the situations. Have members discuss how they felt about playing the roles.

5. Assume you are leading a support group for women who have recently been widowed. Describe three ways you would help the members develop new social relationships. Refer to Figure 10.2, and diagram an example of a social network for one member. How could you help this member expand her social network? How could you encourage the group to assist in this process?

6. For a group of your choice, design three activities or interventions to increase group cohesion.

7. You are leading a structured educational group with a lot of content to be covered. During the sessions, you note that there is much leader-to-member interaction but little member-to-member interaction. How could you increase member-to-member interaction in the group?

8. Describe three strategies for working with a too-talkative male member in a mixed group for recently separated people.

9. Assume you have been running an open group in an agency of your choice. The group has had some difficulties getting referrals, and you are concerned that you will not have enough members to run a viable group. What interventions could you carry out to increase agency support for the group? What interventions could you carry out to increase support for the group in other organizations or in the community?

CASE EXAMPLE

Diana instituted several innovative groups as part of the Mental Health Association's Assertive Community Treatment Program. The mission of this program was to actively reach out to persons who lived in the community and experienced a variety of severe and persistent mental health problems, particularly schizophrenia. In working with this population, Diana and the association found that helping persons with severe mental health problems find meaningful employment had a very positive effect on their functioning in the community. Employment, with accompanying case management and family support counseling, was strongly associated with successful treatment outcomes.

One of Diana's most successful groups was aimed at empowering members by helping them build the interpersonal and problem-solving skills necessary for successfully finding and keeping employment. The group also served as a support system for members as they attempted to find and keep jobs in the community. The members of the group were adult men and women who lived in either the association's community residences or at home with their families.

The group had been together for several weeks. Members had worked through the beginning stage of group development, despite a difficult "storming" period during which several members had expressed some discomfort with the level of disclosure in the group. Following this, Diana was successful in helping each member articulate and set individual goals to work on during the group. During the middle stage of the group, members began to focus on their individual goals. In addition, Diana encouraged them to help each other and the group as a whole to achieve the goals they had agreed to accomplish.

Diana guided the group in its middle phase by introducing some structure into meetings. She divided work done during group meetings into two time periods. During the first part of the meeting members engaged in structured role plays and program activities aimed at increasing their readiness for seeking employment. These activities helped members learn new skills that would help them do job searches and make initial contacts with employers. They also practiced interpersonal skills by doing mock employment interviews with each other. After each interview, members gave and received feedback from each other and from Diana. They also learned to use modeling and rehearsal to develop better interviewing skills. During the second part of the meeting members had open discussion time, when they could share their successes and concerns about securing and maintaining employment. During this part of the group session members were able to provide mutual aid and support to each other. Diana found that structuring the time during sessions and using exercises and role plays were helpful for reinforcing job readiness skills. These activities also bolstered members' confidence in the effectiveness of the group.

Diana also recognized that it was important to help members get fully involved in the group. She often gave individual attention and encouragement to members and expressed her belief in their strengths and capacities. She helped members feel that the group validated them as individuals and as members. Getting members involved in the group also meant helping them to feel they had a stake in the work of the group. Often, for example, she would ask the group as a whole to plan activities they thought would be helpful. She also encouraged them to fully participate in these activities, and to try new experiences in the protective environment of the group.

Diana also helped remind members of their individual goals by utilizing individual contracts between members and the group. For example, one of the members mentioned that she had difficulties in working with older persons in her previous work environment. As part of her individual contract, this member agreed to talk to three older persons in her neighborhood and report back to the group about her experiences. Another member who had a history of being late for previous jobs was asked to keep track of when he woke up and to make notes about his morning routine. These notes were used during group problem solving to make suggestions about how this member could become more organized and punctual.

As each session began, Diana had a brief check-in period during which members reviewed what they had done between sessions and reported on any homework they had to complete from the previous session. She asked members to talk about how they were progressing in meeting their individual goals. She also discussed and demonstrated ways for them to monitor their progress. She used effective modeling skills to show members how to give each other positive reinforcement when they made progress on their goals.

Work with the group was not always easy. Often, Diana found herself helping members deal with setbacks that stemmed from interpersonal difficulties. Some of these obstacles to achieving goals were related to difficulties members had in forming mutually supportive relationships. Diana helped the group discuss how best to achieve good social relationships with others. She also helped members to see how some of their social behaviors might interfere with their job search efforts. Discussion with members about these issues proved useful in helping her to design role plays and rehearsals to build members' social and interpersonal skills.

c h a p t e r *11*

Task Groups: Foundation Methods

This chapter focuses on the foundation skills, procedures, and methods used in task groups during their middle stage. After a brief discussion of the importance of task groups in social service and health agencies, the first section of the chapter describes nine activities that workers commonly engage in during the middle stage of task group development.

The second section of this chapter describes a six-step model for effective problem solving in groups. The model includes a discussion of the practice skills workers use during each step of the process.

THE UBIQUITOUS TASK GROUP

It has been said that U.S. citizens are involved in committees and other task groups more than any other people (Tropman, 1996). Participation in the decisions that affect lives is characteristic of a democratic society. Every day millions of meetings take place throughout the United States. Social service agencies could not function without committees, treatment conferences, teams, boards, and other work groups.

Social workers and other helping professionals are often called on to chair committees, teams, and other task groups. For example, social workers are frequently designated team leaders in interdisciplinary health-care settings because social work functions include coordination, case management, and concern for the bio-psychosocial-cultural functioning of the whole person. Workers also are asked to staff task groups (Tropman, 1996). In general, the staff person plays a supportive role in helping the group clarify its goals and carry out its work. Acting under the direction of the task group's leader, the staff person reports directly to the group. The duties and roles of a staff person are quite varied and can include serving as a resource person, consultant, enabler, analyst, implementer, tactician, catalyst, and technical adviser. Despite the importance and widespread use of task groups in social service agencies, with a few notable exceptions (Brill, 1976; Ephross & Vassil, 1988; Fatout & Rose, 1995; Toseland & Ephross, 1987; Tropman, 1996), the human services have paid little attention to how task groups work.

Although task groups can be useful, they can be a source of frustration for their participants when they function ineffectively. For example, Napier and Gershenfeld (1993) describe the "incredible meeting trap" in which little is accomplished and members leave feeling frustrated by the group process. Similarly, Edson (1977) suggests that committee meetings are often dominated by "narrowminded, pigheaded, sly, opinionated, bigoted manipulators" (p. 224). Edson's comments are strongly stated, but they make the important point that many workers are dissatisfied with task group meetings and indifferent to or suspicious about their outcomes. Meetings that are not well run are boring and unsatisfying. They suffer from a lack of participation and corrective feedback from members, who lose interest.

Although task group meetings are often seen as a chore to be endured by members for the good of the organization,[1] well-run meetings can be a positive experience. They help draw people together by creating effective teamwork in which ideas are shared, feelings are expressed, and support is developed for group members and for the decisions made by the group. There are few experiences in the workplace to equal the sense of cohesion, commitment, and satisfaction that members feel when their ideas have been heard, appreciated, and used in resolving a difficult issue and arriving at a decision. The next sections of this chapter describe methods that can help workers lead task groups effectively.

LEADING TASK GROUPS

Although workers perform many similar activities in task and treatment groups during the middle stage, there is a greater emphasis on certain activities because of the differing foci of task and treatment groups. Task groups, for example, are more concerned than are treatment groups with creating new ideas, developing plans and programs, solving problems that are external to the group, and making decisions about the organizational environment.

To lead task groups effectively during their middle stage, it is important to stay focused on the purposes and functions that the group is expected to accomplish. In his classic text on leading task groups, Maier (1963) suggests that

[1]See the film *Meeting in Progress*, Round Table Films, 113 N. San Vincente Blvd., Beverly Hills, CA 90211, for a vivid example of task group members who are ready to end a meeting as soon as a decision is reached.

the primary purposes of task groups are problem solving and decision making. He goes on to describe methods designed to increase task groups' problem-solving and decision-making abilities.

Although problem solving and decision making are important, several other functions of task groups have been identified in the literature (Napier & Gershenfeld, 1993; Scheidel & Crowell, 1979). Sometimes task groups perform only one function, but usually they attempt to perform several functions simultaneously. These functions may include keeping members informed and involved, empowering members, and monitoring and supervising their performance. For example, in a community agency serving homebound older people, paraprofessional outreach workers might meet weekly with their supervisor to discuss common problems in obtaining psychological, social, and medical services for their clients. Because workers spend so much time away from the office, a secondary objective of the group might be to help workers identify with the organization for which they work. To accomplish primary and secondary objectives during the middle stage of task groups, workers are called on to help with a variety of activities including the following:

1. Preparing for group meetings
2. Sharing information, thoughts, and feelings about concerns and issues facing the group
3. Involving members and helping them feel committed to the group and the agency in which they work
4. Facilitating fact finding about issues and concerns facing the group
5. Dealing with conflict
6. Making effective decisions
7. Understanding the political ramifications of the group
8. Monitoring and evaluating the work of the group
9. Problem solving

Preparing for Group Meetings

During Meetings

At the beginning of a meeting, the worker is responsible for several tasks. The worker begins by introducing new members and distributing handouts not included with the material distributed before the meeting. Before working on agenda items, the worker should make a brief opening statement about the purpose of the meeting. In this statement, the worker may want to call members' attention to previous meetings and to the mandate of the group as a way to indicate that the meeting will undertake a necessary and important function. Making members aware of the salience of the agenda items to be considered is important for maintaining members' interest and willingness to work during the meeting.

The worker should seek members' approval of written minutes that were distributed before the meeting and request that members raise any questions, changes, or amendments they would like to enter into the minutes. After the minutes are approved, the worker should make announcements and call on group members to make designated reports. Reports should be brief and to the point. Members should verbally summarize written reports that have been circulated with the agenda rather than reading them verbatim because reading lengthy reports can be boring and result in loss of interest and attention of other members.

During the middle portion of the meeting, the worker's task is to help the group follow its agenda. Whatever the purpose of a specific meeting, the middle portion is the time when the group accomplishes much of its most difficult work. To avoid getting stuck on one item of business in meetings that have extensive agendas, details of particular items should be worked out before the meeting. If this is not possible, Tropman (1996) points out, the group can agree "in principle" on overall objectives and goals about a particular task and a subcommittee or an individual group member can be charged with working out the details and bringing them back to the group later.

The worker should model the behavior that is expected of all members. A worker who shows respect, interest, integrity, and responsibility will convey these feelings to members. By encouraging equitable participation, the expression of minority-group opinions, and an appreciation of all sincere contributions to the group's work, the worker sets a positive example for group members to follow.

Jay (1977) suggests that the worker should act more as a servant of the interests of the group as a whole than as a master who imposes his or her will on the group. According to Jay, the worker's self-indulgence is the "greatest single barrier to the success of a meeting" (p. 263). By demonstrating that the good of the group as a whole is foremost when conducting the group's business, the worker gains the respect of members. Authority, control, and discipline should be used only to reduce threats to the group's effective functioning, not to impose the worker's wishes on the group. As members perceive that the worker is committed to accomplishing the group's common objective, the worker will gain the cooperation and the admiration of group members.

The worker should ensure that the pace of the meeting leaves enough time to accomplish the items specified in the agenda. Workers should not rush through important decisions because they are pressed for time at the end of a meeting. Members also become frustrated when they are expected to present or discuss ideas but have no time to do so because the group has spent too much time on earlier agenda items. Part of the responsibility of an effective worker in preparing for a meeting is making sure that the number of agenda items is manageable. Items sometimes take longer to discuss than anticipated, so it is good practice to plan extra time into an agenda. When too many agenda items are submitted for a meeting, the worker should rank the items for importance. Items that are assigned a low priority should be postponed to a later meeting.

Before adjourning, the worker should

- Summarize the meeting's accomplishments
- Praise members for their efforts
- Identify issues and agenda items that need further attention
- Mention where the meeting has placed the group in terms of its overall schedule
- Mention major topics for the next group meeting
- Summarize as clearly as possible the tasks that members agreed to accomplish before the next meeting

These strategies help to clarify responsibilities, reduce confusion, and increase the probability that members will complete assignments that were agreed to during earlier portions of the group's discussion.

Between Meetings

Two major tasks to accomplish between meetings are (1) seeing that decisions and tasks decided on at the previous meetings are carried out, and (2) preparing for the next meeting. The worker can do the first task by reading the minutes of previous meetings. Properly kept minutes include summaries of actions taken, tasks that were assigned, and the time frame for reporting back to the group. It is also helpful for the worker to make brief notes during a meeting or soon after the meeting ends about any decisions made that need to be followed up before the next meeting.

In seeing that the decisions agreed on by the group are carried out between meetings, Tropman (1996) suggests that a worker ensure that members work on and complete reports and other assignments that are necessary for the next group meeting. This does not mean that the worker takes over these tasks, but rather encourages and facilitates the progress of members assigned to carry out particular tasks. For example, the worker might meet with subcommittees of the larger group to provide information or guidance as they carry out their functions.

Between meetings, the worker should also develop and maintain close contacts with administrative staff, governing bodies, and other constituencies that may be affected by the group's work. As spokesperson for the group, the worker should keep in mind that he or she represents the group's public image. A worker should express the officially accepted opinions of the committee, not personal views. The worker should not enter into private agreements or commit to decisions or positions that have not been discussed and accepted by the group. In all but emergency situations, the worker should convene the group and consult with it before making decisions. The only exception is when the group, the agency, or a regulatory body has empowered the worker to act independently without first consulting with the group.

The second major task of the worker between meetings is to prepare for the next group meeting. When there is a written agenda for each meeting, the worker or the member designated as the group's secretary should send a memo to each group member soon after a meeting to request agenda items well ahead of the next meeting. This process allows enough time for the agenda and background or position papers to be completed and sent to members so they can be read before the next meeting. Meeting agendas should be established to facilitate discussion. One effective framework is the following:

1. Examine and approve (with any corrections) brief, relevant minutes from the last meeting
2. Make information announcements
3. Vote to include special agenda items
4. Work on less controversial, easier items
5. Work on difficult items
6. Break
7. Work on "for discussion only" items
8. Consider any special agenda items if there is sufficient time
9. Summarize
10. Adjourn

In preparing for the next meeting, the worker should also organize opening remarks and administrative summaries to be presented. Special care should be taken in preparing for meetings that do not have a written agenda. In such instances, the worker should be clear about how to direct the meeting, what tasks the group will work on, and what goals are to be achieved.

Part of the worker's responsibility in preparing for a meeting is assessing the group's functioning. Questions such as "What is the group's relationship with its outside environment?" "Has the group been functioning smoothly?" "What norms, roles, and interaction patterns have developed in the group?" can stimulate the worker to consider how best to prepare for the next meeting.

In many task groups, the worker acts as both the leader and staff person. However, if a separate staff person is available to a task group, that person can prepare background reports and memos that analyze the group's options, develop resources, set up the meeting arrangements, and attend to other group needs.

Sharing Information

Another important activity of the leader during the middle stage is to help members share information, thoughts, and feelings with one another. For example, medical social workers from different community hospitals organize into an informal support group. Once each month, the leader and the group meet to share information about their work and new techniques for working with people in medical settings.

Teams, committees, delegate councils, and boards use group meetings as a means for members to share their concerns, their experiences, their perspectives, and their expertise. This is an important activity because, as a result of highly differentiated work roles, contact among workers in many agencies is infrequent. Job assignments such as individual treatment sessions and home visits limit opportunities for communication among workers.

Social issues and problems often affect several agencies, and task groups can bring workers from different agencies together. A group meeting is a convenient way for them to share unique viewpoints and differing perspectives on issues, problems, or concerns they face in their own agencies. By providing a forum for sharing knowledge and resources, interagency task groups encourage cooperative and coordinated problem solving.

Open communication and unimpeded sharing of information are prerequisites for task groups to accomplish their objectives. Vinokur-Kaplan (1995) suggests that effective communication within the group and between the group and the organization are key elements of effective teamwork. Empirical findings regarding group productivity and group process confirm that how information is communicated and used in a group has an important effect on the quality and the quantity of a group's productivity (Forsyth, 1999).

Task group participants make differential use of the information and resources possessed by various group members, depending on how members' expertise relates to the issues and tasks facing the group. During the middle stage of group work, the worker should help the group develop open channels of communication that can be used appropriately as members have contributions to make during the meeting.

The first step in aiding effective communication and sharing information is to ensure that all members have a clear understanding of the topic being discussed and the task facing the group. To stimulate all members' participation in the discussion, the topic must be relevant. If members have little interest in the topic and no stake in the outcome, there is little reason for them to participate. In many groups, members become bored, disinterested, and dissatisfied because they do not understand the importance of a particular topic. The leader should help each member see the relevance and importance of issues as they are brought before the group. When it is clear that a discussion topic is relevant to only a few members of a task group, the worker should consider forming a subgroup to meet separately from the larger group and have the subgroup provide a brief report of its deliberations and recommendations at a later meeting of the entire group.

To focus interest, promote task-relevant discussions, and reduce confusion among members, it is often helpful to develop clear procedural steps such as the six-step, problem-solving model presented later in the chapter. Summarizing and focusing skills can also help the group remain on task. Summarizing can be used to check understanding, to review previously discussed subjects, to go back to items that were not fully discussed, to help separate a problem or issue into several parts, and to bring members' attention to a particularly important aspect of the discussion.

Focusing can be accomplished by suggesting that the group discuss one issue at a time, by pointing out that the group has digressed from the discussion topic, and by making task-relevant statements. Jay (1977) points out that effective workers often have self-imposed rules limiting their communications early in group meetings to allow members the maximum opportunity to participate in the discussion. Often, a few brief summaries and comments that focus the discussion are all that is needed early in the group's work.

Another method of establishing open communication channels and promoting information sharing among all group members is to ensure equitable participation in the group. According to Huber (1980), equitable participation "is the level of participation that is in keeping with the individual's information, knowledge, or other contribution to the group's effort" (p. 185).

The worker can help the group develop a standard of fairness in participation by encouraging the development of rules for participation. Members may agree to keep their comments brief, be attentive to the communication of others when they are speaking, and encourage silent members to participate. The worker can help members follow the rules that are established. The worker can invite participation by asking other members for feedback about the proposal. The worker can also interrupt long speeches, ask members to summarize their comments briefly, or suggest that members give others a chance to reply.

In some cases, it is helpful to structure the discussion by using a round robin procedure or the rules of parliamentary procedure. In a round robin procedure, each member is asked to present one idea or one piece of information. Going around the group, members take turns presenting one piece of data. This procedure is continued, and each member takes as many turns as needed. Members who do not have any additional ideas or information simply pass during their turn. The cycle is completed when all ideas have been shared by all members.

The round robin procedure has several advantages over unstructured, interactive communication procedures. All members have an equal opportunity to participate. Because only one idea is presented at a time, the procedure avoids the boredom that often results when one member enumerates several ideas one after another. By continuing to go around the group until all ideas are heard and by asking members to pass if they do not have any new information to present, a norm is established for sharing as many ideas as possible.

In large task groups, however, round robin procedures are often too time-consuming. Unless the group is divided into subgroups, the procedure is not useful. To facilitate equitable participation in large groups, the worker should consider using parliamentary procedures (Gulley, 1968; Maier, 1963; Scheidel & Crowell, 1979) following *Robert's Rules of Order* (Robert, 1970). These procedures, which have been developed over the past 600 years in meetings in business, industry, and political bodies in Britain and the United States, provide for orderly and structured participation in large group meetings.

Group workers should be aware that parliamentary procedures are subject to manipulation by members who are familiar with their complexities. By trading favors for votes before a meeting and calling for votes with few members present, parliamentary procedures can be used to subvert majority rule. Despite these disadvantages, *Robert's Rules of Order* can be helpful in ensuring equitable participation in large meetings. A brief description of parliamentary procedures is included in Chapter 12.

Enhancing Involvement and Commitment

A third important activity during the work stage of task groups is to help members feel that they are a vital part of their agency and the task groups that it sponsors. Because much of any organization's work is done by individuals, there is a danger that staff can become isolated and alienated from an organization. Task groups provide support for their members and a sense of belonging that reduces alienation. For example, a worker in an outreach program for the frail elderly spends much time working with the frail elders who comprise the caseload. Monthly team meetings with other outreach workers provide support and recognition for the worker who is faced with the difficult, often emotionally charged, task of working with the frail older adults.

Helping members become involved through their participation in a task group benefits both the organization and its employees. Task groups provide an organized means of developing, implementing, and getting employees to follow policies, procedures, and goals of the agency. They allow employees an opportunity to influence the policies and procedures developed by the agency, which, in turn, helps to make the agency responsive to the needs of its workers. Task groups also help to organize, coordinate, and channel employees' input by clearly delineating how a task group fits into the overall structure of an agency—to whom the group reports and what authority and power the group has to develop or change agency policies. Employees' input can be organized and channeled appropriately.

Several steps can be taken to help task group members feel their input is vital to the agency's sound functioning. First, workers should help members understand the importance of the group's work, its relationship to the agency's purpose, and how the group fits into the agency's administrative structure. This can be accomplished by clearly stating the group's purpose, using flow charts to explain how the group fits into the agency's administrative and decision-making structure, and clarifying the duties, responsibilities, authority, and power that result from membership in the group. Members find this information helpful as they prepare reports and make recommendations or decisions that affect the organization and its consumers.

Second, workers should assign members specific roles in the group. Roles that encourage members to depend on one another for task accomplishment and roles that place them in the position of representing the group to a larger constituency help members feel that they are part of a collective effort that is of vital importance to effective agency functioning.

A third method of enhancing members' involvement and commitment is to invite their input into the agenda and the decision-making processes of the group. This can be done by encouraging members to develop and submit agenda items for future group meetings. Circulating the agenda and any background papers before a meeting can help members prepare their thoughts and concerns before a meeting and increase the chances that they will participate by sharing their views during the meeting. It has been shown that the greater a member's effort and sacrifice in preparing for and working on a task, the more likely the member is to stay involved and committed to the group (Kiesler, 1978). Therefore, asking members to prepare for a meeting by reading background papers, collecting information, and submitting agenda items tends to increase involvement and commitment to the group and the larger organization.

A fourth method of helping members become involved is to encourage them to participate in the decision-making process to the extent possible (Scheidel & Crowell, 1979). Shared decision making has been found to increase motivation (Kiesler, 1978), increase acceptance and understanding of decisions (Bradford, 1976), increase the information available for decision making (Huber, 1980), and help in processing complex information (Carnes, 1987).

Although some writers suggest that decision making should always be shared among members (Bradford, 1976), there are potential disadvantages to giving members decision-making authority. According to Huber (1980), the disadvantages are (1) the great amount of personnel time spent in group decision making, (2) the tendency for groups to produce decisions that are not acceptable to management, (3) expectations that future decisions will also be made through group participation, (4) the tendency for groups to take longer than individuals to reach decisions, and (5) the possibility that group decision making could cause conflict among group members who may have to work together every day. Thus, the decision to delegate decision making to groups should be made only after carefully considering both its advantages and disadvantages in a particular situation. When the advantages of group decision making are questionable, it is often possible to have the group make several recommendations but leave the final decision to one person.

Developing Information

A fourth activity of the worker during the middle stage of task groups is to help members generate information and develop creative alternatives for responding to difficult issues and problems facing the group. Although task groups are often thought to be particularly effective for sharing information and developing creative ideas, the available evidence suggests that ordinary interactive group discussions inhibit rather than increase the disclosure of information, ideas, and creative solutions (Hare, Blumberg, Davies, & Kent, 1995).

Reasons that group processes may inhibit information sharing and the development of creative ideas include the following:

- Status-conscious group members feel intimidated by members with higher status. Lower-status members tend to share less information and avoid making suggestions that offend higher-status members.
- Norms and social pressures for conformity tend to limit the expression of new and creative ideas.
- Groups have the advantage of the variety of opinions and knowledge offered by all members, but group members may censor controversial opinions.
- Covert judgments are often made but not expressed openly in groups. Members, therefore, become concerned about the effects their self-disclosures will have on future interactions with group members.
- Interacting groups tend to reach premature solutions without considering all available evidence.

The worker can help in several ways to improve group members' opportunities to present new ideas, combine information, and generate creative solutions in interactive groups. First, the worker must clearly indicate to all members that their input is welcome, which means that the worker must be able to address the members' concerns about sanctions that may result from expressing sensitive or controversial ideas in the group. If the worker cannot guarantee freedom from sanctions, he or she should try to be as clear as possible about the boundaries of the discussion. For example, it might be possible for committee members to discuss new policies regarding service delivery, but it might not be acceptable for them to criticize existing supervisory staff who have to follow current policy guidelines. When sanctions are possible from individuals outside the group, the worker can encourage the group to consider keeping their discussions confidential. If lower-status members fear reprisals from higher-status members, the worker can discuss the use of sanctions with higher-status members before the group meeting and gain their cooperation in refraining from applying them. The worker can also suggest that higher-status and lower-status members discuss this issue in the group.

Feedback can both help and hinder the group's development of information and creative solutions. It is commonly thought that all feedback is useful because it helps group members detect and correct errors in information processing (Argyris, 1977; Bowers & Franklin, 1976; Nadler, 1977), but this is not true in all circumstances. In the early phase of developing information and forming creative solutions, evaluative feedback can have the effect of suppressing further suggestions (Nadler, 1979; Van de Ven, 1974). Members fear their ideas may be evaluated negatively and that this will reflect on their competence and their status in the agency. Under these circumstances, few members risk making suggestions, giving opinions, or volunteering information that will not be readily accepted. To encourage free discussion, creative ideas, and new insights about a problem or issue, the worker should ask members to refrain from evaluating ideas early in the group's discussion.

Several other steps can also be taken to help the group develop information and creative ideas to solve a problem. The worker can

- Encourage the group to develop norms that promote free discussion of ideas
- Point out group pressures that inhibit members' free discussion
- Model an open exchange of ideas by presenting creative, controversial, and thought-provoking ideas
- Encourage members to continue to share unique ideas by praising those who present innovative suggestions
- Encourage lower-status members, who often find it difficult to present their ideas, to share their ideas as early as possible in the group's discussion
- Help the group separate information and idea-generating steps from decision-making steps

When these suggestions are implemented, interacting groups can develop more creative solutions than they would under ordinary conditions.

Dealing with Conflict

It is unlikely that all members of a task group will immediately agree on all aspects of the work of the group. Thus, it is important for workers to realize that conflicts occur even in effective task groups (Napier & Gershenfeld, 1993; Wittman, 1991). Conflict often emerges at the end of the beginning stage or beginning of the work stage of the group. Earlier in the life of a group, members are just getting to know one another and are less likely to express conflicting viewpoints.

Although some view all conflict as a problem that should be prevented or resolved (Smith & Berg, 1997), most theoreticians and practitioners now make a distinction between what has been called instrumental or substantive conflict and what has been called affective or social conflict (Guetzkow and Gyr, 1954; Wittman, 1991). *Substantive conflict* is based on members' differing opinions about ideas, information, and facts presented during the task group's work. This type of conflict is often helpful to the development of the group because it stimulates healthy dialogue, the development of solutions that encompass different points of view, and the careful analysis of proposed solutions.

Affective conflict is based on the emotional and interpersonal relationships among members within and outside of the group because it pits members against each other. This type of conflict is rarely helpful to the development of the group. In general, affective conflict is more difficult to resolve than substantive conflict because it is resistant to persuasive reasoning.

Certain personality characteristics have also been associated with productive and nonproductive conflict. For example, a win-win orientation is often associated with productive conflict, whereas zero-sum orientation is often associated with nonproductive conflict (Wall, Galanes, & Love, 1987; Wall & Nolan, 1987). Similarly, rigidity is associated with conflict escalation, and flexibility is associated with the ability to change perceptions and to accommodate differing points of view (Wall & Nolan, 1987).

Timely intervention into group processes can often help to defuse conflicts. For example, the worker leading a treatment conference in a mental health center might notice that a subgroup of members is not participating as expected. The worker comments on this and discovers that subgroup members are quiet because they disagree with the opinions of a vocal, controlling member. The worker helps the subgroup and the individual member resolve their differences by pointing out the conflict and helping the members confront it. The worker also acts as a mediator to help the subgroup and the member negotiate differences.

Some workers have difficulty dealing with conflict. They avoid, ignore, or minimize it, hoping it will go away. These strategies are generally counterproductive. Avoiding conflict rarely leads to satisfying and meaningful dialogue about the issues facing the group. Most often, when conflicts are avoided, members get the message that they should not express their true feelings and that an honest sharing of information and opinions should be sacrificed so that the group can function "harmoniously." When conflicts are ignored, they sometimes smolder until a particular interaction or event causes them to intensify and erupt. At other times, conflicts subside, but one or more group members are left feeling they have lost the battle. Neither outcome is desirable.

How can the worker handle conflict in a productive and satisfying manner? Substantive and affective conflicts can be reduced by the following procedures:

1. View conflict as a natural and helpful part of group development.
2. Help members recognize the conflict.
3. Encourage group norms of openness and respect for others' viewpoints.
4. Encourage group members to suspend judgment until they have listened to the entire group discussion.
5. Encourage members to view issues in new ways, to understand situations from other members' vantage points, and to be flexible in their own views of a situation.
6. Help members avoid focusing on personality conflicts or personal differences. Instead, help members express the facts and preferences underlying their alternative viewpoints and opinions.
7. Emphasize factors that promote consensus in the group discussion.

8. Develop information and facts about the situation and seek expert judgments to help resolve conflicting information.

9. Follow orderly, preplanned steps for considering alternatives and deciding on solutions.

10. Use decision criteria that are mutually agreed on by group members.

11. Clarify and summarize the discussion frequently so that all members have a similar understanding of what is being discussed and the decision criteria that will be used.

12. Be sensitive to members' personal concerns and needs in developing solutions and arriving at a decision.

13. Remain neutral in the conflict and ask questions that seek clarification whenever possible.

In the classic text *Getting to Yes,* Fisher, Ury, and Patton (1997) suggest that the worker should help members (1) separate the person from the issue or problem being addressed, (2) focus on interests or attributes of the problem rather than on members' positions on the issue, (3) generate a variety of possible options before deciding what to do, and (4) insist that the decision about how to proceed be based on some objective standard.

Probably the single most important step in dealing with conflicts in a group is to help members view disagreements as opportunities to gather information and to share views and opinions, rather than as personal attacks or as threats to authority or position. Cooperative processes involve recognizing the legitimacy of others' interests (Ephross & Vassil, 1988). Thus, it is important for the leader to welcome differing viewpoints and to encourage the members to do the same. Also, it is helpful to

- Ask members to elaborate on the thinking that led to their viewpoints.
- Suggest that other members listen carefully and ask questions before they react.
- Highlight points of consensus and mutual interest as they arise.

Another step in dealing with conflict involves helping members to avoid turning conflicts into personal attacks. The worker should ask members to keep their comments focused on the issues rather than on members' personal characteristics and should encourage members to make "I" statements and to avoid "you" statements that attack other members or subscribe motives to their behavior. The worker should not react to outbursts and should not encourage members to defend their positions. Instead, the worker should help members in a conflict describe their interests, values, fears, and their goals or objectives.

How this method of dealing with conflicts makes a difference can be seen in the following situation. First, the member attempts to defend a position by saying, "I don't want my staff to take on this new program because they are already overworked. We were asked to take on more work last meeting. I don't think it's fair to ask us again. What about Joe's department? Why can't they handle this?" By using alternative wording, however, the member could express her interests, fears, and objectives with "I" statements such as "My interests are in ensuring that the workers in my department don't get too overloaded with work. I appreciate your faith in my department, but I fear that my already overworked staff will become overwhelmed. My objective is to ensure that the workers in my department don't get so overloaded that they can't do a good job, and also that they don't get so burned out that they just throw up their hands and stop trying to do a quality job." The second statement lends itself to negotiation. For example, the leader might ask the member to describe the workload of her department and any changes in it over the past year. If the workload has increased and concerns about an overload are warranted, the leader might help the group to explore options for getting the work accomplished.

Another useful procedure for dealing with conflict is to help members look beyond their particular positions on an issue and to understand what others hope to accomplish. The worker should encourage members who are having a conflict to state their concerns and their priorities as concretely as possible, but discourage them from defending their positions. Instead, the worker can encourage members to ask questions of each other and to put themselves in each other's positions. The worker should point out shared interests and mutual gains. For example, the worker might point out that all department heads have a stake in ensuring that the members of one department do not become so overloaded that they cannot do a good job.

The worker can help members to reach consensus by agreeing in principle to mutually acceptable goals. As many solutions as possible for achieving the goals should be generated. The worker should ask members to express their preferences for particular options. If a single option is not preferred by all parties, the worker should negotiate a solution by combining options that include some gains and some sacrifices on the part of all parties to the conflict.

Making Effective Decisions

Facilitators of task groups are often called on to help members make effective decisions. For example, a board president helps the board of directors decide whether to expand their agency's geographical service area. A community organizer helps a neighborhood association decide whether to establish a neighborhood watch group to address the crime rate in the community. The leader of an executive council helps the group determine who will be promoted within the organization.

Although groups are often used to make decisions, evidence about their effectiveness is mixed. Groups are better than individuals in influencing opinions and obtaining commitments from members (Kelley & Thibaut, 1969; Lewin,

1948). Napier (1967) found that groups are better at integrating complex perceptual and intellectual tasks because members can rely on one another for assistance. However, for other types of problems, groups may not be any more effective than individuals, and sometimes may be less efficient than individuals working alone (Campbell, 1968; Rotter & Portugal, 1969). In summarizing the literature that has compared the problem-solving activities of task groups with the activities of individuals, Hare and colleagues (1995) drew the following conclusions:

- Groups are superior to individuals in solving manual problems such as puzzles, particularly when the problem can be subdivided so that each person can use personal expertise to work on a problem component. The superiority of groups has been less consistently documented when the task to be accomplished is of a more intellectual nature, such as a logic problem.

- Although groups are better than the average individual, they are not better than the best individual. Therefore, a group of novices may perform worse than one expert.

- Groups have the advantage of the variety of opinions and knowledge offered by the members, but group members may censor controversial opinions.

- Part of the superiority of group problem solving results from the pooling of individual judgments to converge on a group norm. For some problems, similar accuracy may be achieved by averaging the decisions of noninteracting individuals.

- When groups solve intellectual tasks, members' rational, information-processing orientation may be impeded by socioemotional concerns.

- Because task groups require members to deliberate until they reach a decision, the decisions made in task groups may be more costly than decisions made by one or more individuals working alone.

To improve group decision making, workers should help members avoid the phenomenon known as *group think,* which is mentioned in earlier chapters (Janis, 1972). Group think occurs when group contagion takes over and members fail to express their own thoughts and feelings. Instead, they go along with the predominant sentiment of the group. This phenomenon has been recognized for years. For example, more than 80 years ago, LeBon (1910) referred to *group mind,* a state in which members allow an emotion generated from their participation in a group to dominate their intellectual powers. Similarly, more than 70 years ago, Freud (1922) wrote about the power that the group has over an individual's ego.

Before 1960, it was generally thought that problem-solving groups make more conservative decisions than do individuals. Experiments by Stoner (1968) and Ziller (1957), however, indicated that groups make riskier decisions than individuals. Stoner (1968) called this phenomenon the *risky shift.* As evidence began to accumulate, it became clear that the shift may be toward greater or lesser risk. Riskier decisions are made when a group's members approve of risk taking (Teger & Pruitt, 1967; Wallach & Wing, 1968), when persuasive information is presented (Ebbesen & Bowers, 1974), when the responsibility for the decision is shared among group members (Myers & Arenson, 1972; Zajonc, Wolosin, & Wolosin, 1972), or when the leader approves of a risky decision (Myers & Arenson, 1972). On the other hand, risk taking is discouraged in some groups, and members are rewarded for developing conservative solutions (Stoner, 1968).

Several steps can be taken to help members avoid group think and risky shifts. Norms and a group climate that encourages free and open discussion of ideas tend to discourage conformity and to decrease group think. Procedures that clarify how a group will use information and arrive at a decision also tend to reduce conformity. For example, in a family service agency, a personnel committee deciding between many qualified applicants for a clinical position might develop decision criteria. Criteria for making decisions should include all the factors that group members consider to be essential in making a good judgment. Thus, the personnel committee develops decision criteria calling for an applicant who has clinical experience and supervisory skills, speaks Spanish, and is familiar with the use of psychotropic medications in outpatient mental health settings.

To avoid a lack of clarity and later disagreements, the worker should allow the group to discuss the rationale behind each decision criterion. It is often helpful to ask members about their understanding of each criterion and to use examples to illustrate how each one would be applied in rating alternative solutions. After developing and clarifying the criteria, the group should rate their relative importance so that the group can decide between alternative solutions. Referring to the previous example, group members may decide that clinical competency and supervisory experience are twice as important as the other criteria for the position. They would then use those criteria to review each job applicant's folder to select the best candidate. A more detailed explanation of developing and using decision criteria in task groups is presented in the section on social judgment analysis in Chapter 12.

To arrive at a final group decision, a procedure for choosing among alternatives is needed. Most groups make their final decisions using consensus, compromise, or majority rule. In certain situations, each procedure can result in quite different decisions. To avoid the suspicion that a particular decision-making procedure is being chosen to influence a decision about a particular issue, a method of choosing among alternatives should be agreed on as early as possible in a task group's deliberations.

Consensus is often considered the ideal way to select among alternatives because all group members commit themselves to the decision. When reviewing conditions for effective work with groups, Whitaker (1975) suggests that helping a group achieve consensus reduces conflict within the group and makes the group more effective. Consensus does not, however, necessarily imply agreement on the part of all group members. Napier and Gershenfeld (1993) point out that consensus requires that individuals be willing to go along with the group's predominant view and carry it out in good faith.

Although other decision-making procedures are quicker, reaching consensus often brings considerable support for a decision because members are more likely to cooperate in implementing decisions that they have thoroughly discussed and agreed on. Consensus is sometimes difficult to achieve in groups. It can be time-consuming and tension-provoking because each alternative must be discussed thoroughly along with dissenting viewpoints. Also, there is the danger that members will acquiesce and decision quality will be sacrificed to arrive at a solution that is acceptable to all group members (Napier & Gershenfeld, 1993). Nevertheless, reaching consensus rather than deciding by majority rule builds group cohesion and member satisfaction.

When issues are controversial and there is much dissenting opinion, it is often possible to reach consensus by modifying original proposals. To develop amendments to proposals that are acceptable to all group members, the discussion of each alternative should focus on the reasoning behind members' objections to the alternative. This process helps all group members identify the acceptable and unacceptable parts of each alternative. After a discussion of all the alternatives, the acceptable parts of several alternatives can often be combined into one solution that is acceptable to most, if not all, members.

Majority rule is a frequently used procedure to decide between alternatives in task groups because it is less time-consuming than consensus or compromise procedures, and when the vote is done by secret ballot, it protects the confidentiality of members. Majority rule is an excellent procedure for deciding routine and relatively minor questions. However, because a significant minority may not agree with the final outcome, majority rule is a less appealing procedure when the issue is important and when the support and cooperation of the entire group are needed for successful implementation. For important decisions, a two-thirds majority vote is an alternative to simple majority rule. A two-thirds majority vote ensures at least substantial support for a decision made by the group.

Simple mathematical procedures have also been recommended to achieve majority rule (Delbecq, Van de Ven, & Gustafson, 1975; Huber, 1980). For example, each member of a task group can be asked to rate alternative solutions on a five-point scale from 5 = best alternative to 1 = worst alternative. The group's leader or staff person tabulates the vote on each alternative solution. Because this procedure is easily done without identifying a member's individual rating, it also preserves anonymity during the decision-making process. Another mathematical procedure is to have all members rank alternative solutions. Ranks are tallied, and the mean of the ranks is calculated for each alternative. The nominal group technique discussed in Chapter 12 uses this procedure for selecting among alternatives.

Understanding Task Groups' Political Ramifications

Although much of this chapter and the next are focused on problem solving and decision making, task groups also have political functions that are frequently overlooked or ignored by group workers because they are uncomfortable with the notion of behaving in a political fashion. Levinson and Klerman (1973) recognized this stance when they said the cultivation of power is viewed by many professions, including social work, "as vulgar, as a sign of character defect, as something an upstanding professional would not be interested in or stoop to engage in" (p. 66). Yet, politics are an important part of the dynamics that govern the functioning of task groups during the middle stage.

An essential step in becoming more aware of the political functions of task groups is to develop an orientation that views political behavior as an essential ingredient of all task groups. Gummer (1987) points out that rather than viewing political behavior as symptomatic of a character defect, it may be better viewed "as the quest of the mature personality for the resources needed to affect increasingly larger areas of one's world" (p. 36).

Gummer suggests that task groups should be analyzed and understood in terms of how they are used to exercise and enhance the power of the members who participate in them. Although the overt exercise of power is generally frowned on in our society, there are many symbolic ways that task groups help managers exercise their power and position within an organization. In a power-oriented analysis of task groups, Gummer (1987) focused on four elements: (1) the physical setting, (2) membership, (3) the agenda, and (4) procedural rules.

In regard to the physical setting, Gummer suggests considering the symbolic meaning of the meeting location. For example, is the meeting taking place in a neutral place, or in a place that is "owned" by the leader or a particular member? Is the meeting taking place in a symbolic setting such as an outreach office or a new building to symbolize the importance of the setting? Gummer also suggests analyzing the symbolism attached to how the meeting room is arranged. For example, does the setting promote work or comfort? Are chairs set up around a table with paper, pencils, overhead projectors, and other work-oriented aids? Or is the setting filled with couches, soft chairs, food, and other items that convey a relaxed, informal atmosphere?

Who is invited to participate in a meeting is also important from a political perspective. Participation in meetings is the organizational equivalent of enfranchisement. Gummer (1987) says "whether an organization is run along autocratic, oligarchic, or democratic lines, whatever rights members are entitled to are accorded by their inclusion in certain organizational groups. Conversely, limits on one's organizational position are established by exclusion from certain groups" (p. 30).

Determining who can participate is an important source of power because it "organizes into attention" the interests and positions associated with the included individuals (Forester, 1981). For example, the character of a task group might be changed when consumers are included on advisory boards. Similarly, the substantive deliberations of a committee examining staffing ratios and workloads almost certainly changes when both nonprofessional and professional staff are included in the meetings.

Meeting agendas can also be used for political purposes. Bachrach and Baratz (1962) suggested that power can be exercised by confining the scope of decision making to relatively safe issues. The ordering of items on the agenda may also be used for political purposes. For example, the leader or certain members may take a long time to discuss several trivial issues at the beginning of a meeting as a way to leave little time to work on issues that they would rather not address. Similarly, how agenda items are presented often has political ramifications. Gummer (1987) suggests that politically oriented individuals who want certain items tabled, defeated, or changed encourage their proponents to present their issues in the broadest terms possible so that the specifics of the issue are not discussed, and thus the specifics become confused or obfuscated by a general discussion of the philosophical principles of the organization. Conversely, items that these members would like to see acted on and accepted by the group are presented as specifically and noncontroversially as possible.

Procedures governing how the group conducts its business can also be developed with political purposes in mind. In democratic organizations it is expected that, at a minimum, procedural rules should (1) provide task group members with sufficient time to deliberate the issues the group is charged to address and (2) provide for adequate representation of minority opinions. However, procedural rules can be manipulated by politically minded individuals. For example, important decisions may be deferred to the executive committee of a board rather than taken up during a full board meeting. Similarly, the membership of a nominating subcommittee or a finance subcommittee may be stacked to favor the wishes of the board chairperson or a certain subgroup of powerful members.

Monitoring and Evaluating

The worker is also often called on to help task groups structure monitoring and evaluation efforts. Task groups may monitor and evaluate their own functioning or be called on to monitor and evaluate other systems. For example, an outpatient mental health team may monitor and evaluate its own performance by reviewing recidivism data on all former clients at three-month, progress-review meetings (Vinokur-Kaplan, 1995).

Task groups may also monitor and evaluate the functioning of other entities. For example, the board of a social service agency is responsible for monitoring and evaluating the functioning of the agency. Because boards are ultimately responsible and legally liable for the proper conduct of social service agencies, monitoring and evaluating functions are a critical component of an effective board's work (Chait, Holland, & Taylor, 1993; Wolf, 1990).

For effective monitoring and evaluation during the middle stage, task groups must be clear about their mandate from the agency and the ethical, moral, and legal obligations as expressed by regulatory agencies, professional societies, legislative bodies, and the larger society. Sometimes these items are clearly specified in the bylaws of the sponsoring organization. Often, however, it is the responsibility of the task group to develop a set of standards, rules, or guidelines that can be used to monitor and evaluate performance. For example, a large, private social service agency decided to encourage evaluations of several of its service programs.

To ensure that the research would serve a useful purpose, protect the rights and the confidentiality of their clients, and meet state and federal rules and regulations, an institutional research review board was formed. The first meeting of this group focused on reviewing the procedures of similar review boards at other agencies and examining state and federal regulations. The group then prepared guidelines governing its own operation and guidelines for researchers to use when preparing proposals to be reviewed by the board. The guidelines were, in turn, modified and ratified by the executive staff and the board of the social service agency.

To fulfill their monitoring and evaluating functions adequately, task groups develop feedback mechanisms to help them obtain information about the results of a decision and take corrective actions when necessary (Nadler, 1979). The type of feedback useful to a task group depends greatly on the group's mandate and the monitoring and evaluating required in the particular situation. A board, for example, may require periodic reports from the agency director, the director of clinical services, the agency executive, and the coordinator of volunteer services. In addition, the board may review program statistics, quarterly financial statements from a certified accountant, and reports from funding sources about the performance of the agency. In other cases, a task group may use formal data-gathering procedures to perform its monitoring and evaluation functions. A discussion of these methods is presented in Chapter 13.

Problem Solving

Problem solving has been given more consideration in the group work literature than any other functions of task groups. Task groups spend much time performing other functions, but problem solving is often seen as a task group's major function. Although separate from sharing information, involving others, and making decisions, problem solving incorporates many of the functions of task groups. Thus, problem solving is best viewed as a complex set of functions that vary with the type of problem facing the group. The next section describes a generic, six-step, problem-solving model that can be used effectively in a variety of task groups.

A MODEL FOR EFFECTIVE PROBLEM SOLVING

The effectiveness of problem-solving efforts depends on the extent to which an optimal solution is developed and implemented. Effective problem solving involves six steps:

1. Identifying a problem
2. Developing goals

3. Collecting data
4. Developing plans
5. Selecting the best plan
6. Implementing the plan

As shown in Figure 11.1, the steps are not discrete. In practice, they tend to overlap. For example, preliminary goals are often discussed during problem identification, and goals are modified and refined as data collection continues. Similarly, data collection often continues as the group begins to develop plans for problem resolution.

Problem solving can take as little as 5 or 10 minutes or as long as several months. The length of any problem-solving process depends on many factors, such as the nature of the problem, the structure and function of the group, and the opportunity, capacity, and willingness of the group members to solve problems. Problem-solving processes are often described as if they occur once, which may be true for groups convened to solve a single problem, but that is not always true. Problem-solving processes are generally used repeatedly by groups as they

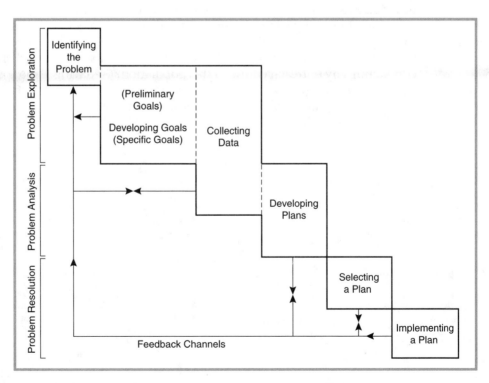

FIGURE 11.1 ▪ *The Problem-Solving Process in Task Groups*

conduct their business. A task group may have to use two or more cycles of a problem-solving process to accomplish a single task. The process is represented in Figure 11.2. An adult protective service team, for example, may spend three meetings developing a plan for emergency evening coverage for all clients on team members' caseloads, and the plan might be implemented for a two-month trial period. After the trial period, the team may reconsider aspects of the plan. Using the problem-solving process a second time, the team may decide on a modified version of the plan that proves effective in ensuring adequate emergency evening coverage. Thus, over the course of several months the team is involved with two problem-solving cycles to accomplish its task.

Identifying a Problem

How a problem is identified and defined is crucial to effective problem solving. It affects what data will be collected, who will work on the problem, what alternatives will be considered, and who will be affected by the problem's resolution. When they are first identified, problems are often unclear and muddled. They appear to be unsolvable, complicated mazes of tangled or disjointed components. Even when problems appear to be fairly well delineated, there is often a need for further clarification. For example, the staff of a social service agency may perceive a problem in serving a large group of Mexican Americans who live in the area. Although at first glance this appears to be a fairly clear problem, it could be defined in several ways, including (1) not having Spanish-speaking workers, (2) not conducting any outreach efforts to this population, (3) having a poor public image with Mexican Americans in the community, (4) not having the financial resources to develop programs, and (5) providing the wrong services to meet the needs of the population.

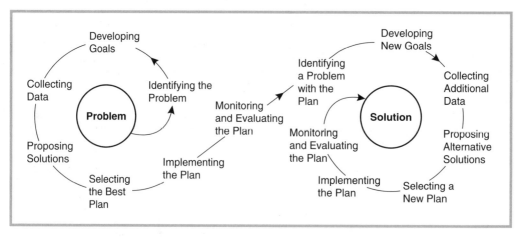

FIGURE 11.2 ■ *Two Cycles of a Problem-Solving Process*

Several steps can be taken to help a group define a problem to promote problem solving:

1. Clarify the boundaries of the problem.
2. Seek out members' perceptions of the problem and their expectations about how it will be solved.
3. Develop a problem-solving orientation.
4. Define a solvable problem.
5. Specify the problem as clearly as possible.

Clarifying Boundaries

The first issue that confronts workers and members as they define the boundaries of a problem is how to handle large problems that may have several interrelated components. Groups are often confronted with large problems that seem to be unmanageable and unsolvable. In other cases, a vague concern or problem expressed by a group member may emerge as a large problem as members begin to discuss the issues. One method of handling a large problem is to partialize the problem. Several manageable, solvable problems, for example, can be developed from a large problem that at first seems unsolvable, unmanageable, or overwhelming.

When the group partializes a problem, it must decide on which aspect of the large problem to work on first. Some guidelines suggest that groups should work first on a problem that

- Is clearly under the group's legitimate authority
- Is a pressing problem
- Is potentially under the group's control
- Will have far-reaching, beneficial effects when solved
- Is meaningful enough so that a solution is important to group members and to others outside the group
- Has a good chance of being resolved successfully

Boundaries refer to the extent and scope of a problem or issue facing the group. Defining clear boundaries helps problem solvers focus and clarify their thoughts and suggestions about a problem, which leads to more effective solutions (D'Zurilla & Goldfried, 1971). When setting boundaries, the worker is in a delicate position. On the one hand, an effective worker does not want to hamper the group's creative problem-solving ability. The worker should encourage the group to consider all the relevant options for problem resolution. On the other hand, the worker is often in a better position than is any other group member to recognize what is politically, economically, and organizationally feasible. For example, in a group working on ways to increase services for Mexican Americans, it would be helpful to inform members that solutions to the problem should not commit the agency to new services that require additional funding because no new money is available during the current fiscal year. The worker could explain that although the solution should not require new funds, the group might consider making recommendations to the agency's administrative staff about seeking additional funding during the next fiscal year.

Whenever possible, the boundaries of the problem-solving process should be as broad and as flexible as possible so as not to stifle creative problem solutions. The worker should point out members' freedom within the boundaries and the importance of accomplishing the task within specified limits. The group should be given a convincing rationale for limiting the scope of a problem and the scope of the efforts used to resolve it. Without guidelines, the group may arrive at a solution that is unacceptable to persons who must implement it. Members who spend their time and energy developing a solution that is not feasible will feel frustrated and disappointed when they realize their recommended solution was not implemented.

An example of the delicate balance the worker should strike in suggesting boundaries for problem solving occurs in the following statement by the leader of the hypothetical task group addressing the needs of Mexican Americans:

> *The needs assessment we have just completed confirms our suspicions—we are not doing enough to serve Mexican Americans in our catchment area. As we discuss the problem and decide what to do, we should keep in mind that we have just entered a new fiscal year and the agency's budget does not allow for new programming that requires additional funding. The executive director has informed me that within this constraint she will actively pursue any solutions that you suggest for improving service to this population. She is ultimately responsible for presenting solutions we suggest to the board and getting the solutions implemented in the entire agency. In discussing the problem, we should consider ways that existing services could be redirected or applied differently to the clients we serve. Eligibility requirements and other issues related to access might also be explored. We may also want to consider using regularly scheduled, in-service training and supervision to increase our awareness of the problem and to enhance our skills in dealing with this population. What are your thoughts about tackling this problem?*

This example illustrates that the worker has set some broad guidelines for problem solving and has made some tentative suggestions to the group about what aspects of the problem might be worth exploring. The worker has given the group some indication of what is feasible within the budget constraints of the agency and has clarified who is responsible for implementing potential solutions. By asking for members' thoughts about the problem, the worker is inviting them to define the boundaries of the problem within these broad guidelines.

Members' Perceptions and Experiences

Members' perceptions of problematic situations and their expectations about how the situations should be resolved determine the way the members approach a problem. If the members of a group are to be satisfied with the group's problem-solving process and committed to the solution that is reached, the members' views about problems facing the group must be respected. There is no better way to show respect than to solicit their views and ensure that they are given a fair hearing by all members. Failure to clarify members' expectations and perceptions about a problem often leads to difficulties later in the group's problem-solving process. Hidden agendas can develop, in part, because unclarified expectations are acted on by members.

Clarifying boundaries and helping members express their perceptions and expectations of the problem-solving situation can be helpful techniques in arriving at a common understanding of the problem. An open discussion usually causes a modification of all group members' perceptions and expectations. Common perceptions and expectations form the basis for mutually agreed-on goals.

Careful consideration of the views of individual group members does not mean that every opinion or bit of information should be treated as equally correct or important. Although there is a tendency to associate equality of ideas with equal treatment of group members, the concepts should not be confused (Kiesler, 1978). Members should be treated equitably in the group process, but the importance of their contribution changes as the work of the group changes.

Problem-Solving Orientation

During the process of identifying a problem it is important for the worker to help members develop a problem-solving orientation (D'Zurilla & Goldfried, 1971). Such an orientation includes

- Minimizing irrational beliefs about problematic situations
- Recognizing and being willing to work on problems as they occur
- Inhibiting tendencies to respond prematurely on the first impulse or do nothing

Irrational beliefs about "how the world should be" can inhibit members from recognizing problematic situations and can also interfere with problem resolution (Ellis, 1962). Irrational beliefs can lead to primitive solutions that can have detrimental consequences for the group as a whole. It is important for the worker to encourage all members to challenge irrational beliefs and to encourage rational approaches to problem solving. Members should be helped to use evidence, logic, and sound reasoning as they identify and define a problematic situation (Barker, 1979; Gouran, 1982; Harnack & Fest, 1964; Stattler & Miller, 1968).

An effective problem-solving orientation also includes recognizing problems that need attention and being willing to work on them. It is sometimes difficult for task groups to confront and work on problems facing them. For example, a team in a psychiatric hospital may avoid discussing problems in its own functioning for fear that the discussion will be viewed as an attack on individual members. In this case, the team leader should help by facilitating the development of a group climate that encourages problems to be viewed as shared concerns whose resolution will benefit all team members.

In developing a problem-solving orientation within the group, it is important to help members reduce their tendency to make immediate and automatic responses (Toseland, 1977). Frequently, members suggest solutions without carefully considering the problem. It has been found that less effective problem solvers are impulsive, impatient, and quick to give up (Bloom & Broder, 1950). Therefore the workers should encourage members to stop to think about the problem, collect data, and analyze alternative solutions before deciding what to do (Dollard & Miller, 1950).

There should be sufficient time during a meeting agenda to grapple with difficult problems. According to Tropman (1996), difficult items should be placed in the middle third of the agenda. At this point, members are at the peak of their (1) psychological focus, (2) physiological awareness, (3) attention, and (4) attendance. Easier items should be placed earlier in the agenda. Because they require less energy, items for discussion only can be placed at the end, when members have little energy for problem solving.

Defining a Solvable Problem

Groups are sometimes blocked in their problem-solving ability because they fail to frame the problem correctly (Maier, 1963). Group members may fail to identify the correct actors, the correct systems, or the correct obstacles that constitute the problem situation. In the early stages of problem solving, the group should be tentative and flexible with its problem definition so that the definition can be modified when new data are collected.

How problems are stated can affect the entire problem-solving process. The worker can use several techniques to improve the group's ability to define a solvable problem. Maier (1963) suggests that, whenever possible, problems should be stated in institutional rather than personal terms. For instance, in the example presented earlier, a definition that attributed the problem of lack of services for Mexican Americans to an inept director of clinical services would have alienated the director of clinical services and thus have made the problem more difficult to solve. However, identifying the problem as a lack of service hours for Mexican Americans would have opened possibilities for modifying service delivery patterns. Similarly, defining the problem as a lack of knowledge and expertise about Mexican American clients would have suggested that the committee consider assessing members' willingness to learn more about the Mexican American population.

To help the group obtain a new perspective on a problem, the worker can use the reframing technique described in Chapter 10. An exercise that can help members reframe a problem is to ask them to imagine themselves experiencing the problem as another might experience it. For example, members of a program committee who have reservations about making efforts to improve services for Mexican Americans could be asked to imagine themselves going to an agency in which no one speaks English and in which most clients and all workers have a different cultural and ethnic background from their own. The exercise encourages members to reconsider their stand on the question of whether something should be done to improve services for the Mexican American population.

Reframing may also be done by focusing on the positive aspects of a problem. For example, a problem that is experienced as anxiety provoking may be reframed as one that motivates the group to improve a situation. In these ways, members' motivation to solve problems can be increased.

Specifying the Problem

Having a clearly defined and mutually understood problem is essential if members are to work effectively together. When problems are first expressed in a meeting, they are often stated as partially formulated concerns. For example, a committee member might say, "I get a sense that some of our staff may be having difficulty with the new record-keeping system." Many terms in this statement are vaguely defined. Terms such as "get a sense," "some of our staff," and "difficulty" can have different meanings for each member of the group.

As concerns are raised by members, the worker should help them clarify vague or ambiguous terms. The statement above, for example, could be clarified to indicate that three members of the community team and one member of the day treatment team expressed concerns that the new record-keeping forms took too long to fill out. Further, the phrase "took too long to fill out" should be clarified so that it becomes clear what it is the group is being asked to consider. For example, "took too long to fill out" could mean "cannot complete the case record in the 15 minutes allocated for that purpose," or could mean "being asked to collect data that are not needed to work with clients." Sometimes members of the task group may find that they cannot specify the problem further without collecting additional information.

After the group has clarified the problem, the worker should summarize it in a clear, brief statement. Ideally, the problem should be defined in objective terms that have similar meanings for all members. Objective terms with clear, observable referents help members arrive at a common understanding of the situation. When summarizing, the worker should restate the boundaries of the problem and the group's authority and responsibility so that members have a clear idea of their role in resolving the problem.

Developing Goals

The second step in the problem-solving process is goal setting. Goal setting does not occur only once in the problem-solving process. Tentative goals are formulated soon after the problem has been identified and aid in data collection because they help shape the scope of the information to be collected. Goals are often modified and specified as information is accumulated. Initial goals may sometimes be abandoned entirely, with new goals developed on the basis of the data accumulated.

The procedures for developing goals for specific problems are similar to the goal-setting procedures described in beginning a group. Through a process of exploration and negotiation, the worker and the members share their perspectives about the goals the group should achieve relative to a particular problem. The emphasis should be on formulating goals that are mutually acceptable.

Like problem statements, goal statements should be as clear and specific as possible. Desired changes in problem situations should be stated as objective tasks. For instance (referring again to the previous example), goals to increase services to Mexican Americans might include (1) providing eight hours of training for each outreach worker during the next six months, (2) increasing the number of Mexican Americans served by the agency from an average of three per month to 15 per month by the next fiscal year, (3) translating program brochures into Spanish within three months, and (4) printing 400 bilingual Spanish-English brochures at the beginning of the next fiscal year. Each goal is specific and easily understood.

Group workers can use several other principles for developing effective goals, including the following:

- Goals should be directed at the mutual concerns of all members.
- Goals should be consistent with the group's mandate, its overall objectives, and the values that have been agreed on by the group as a whole.
- Goals should be attractive enough to gain the commitment, cooperation, and investment of all group members.
- Goals should be realistic and attainable through the resources available to the group and its members.
- Goals should be time limited.
- The goal-setting process should set a supportive, encouraging climate for goal attainment.

At the end of the goal-setting process, members should be clear about the tasks they must perform to achieve the goals. It is important for the worker to summarize the goals that have been decided on by the group and to review each member's role in their achievement. This process avoids misunderstandings about who is responsible for what during a specified time period. Members should be clear about the time frame for accomplishing goals and about the mechanisms for reporting their achievements to the group.

It is often helpful to partialize large goals into a series of smaller ones that can be accomplished in a short time period, particularly in newly organized groups whose members may be overwhelmed by the enormity of a task and unsure about the group's ability to accomplish the task. Partializing goals gives members a sense of accomplishment as they reach subgoals. The sense of accomplishment increases the attractiveness of the group and helps ensure highly motivated members for future problem-solving efforts.

Collecting Data

Data collection is the third step in the problem-solving process. This step begins as soon as a problem is identified by a group and continues as broad goals are defined and refined and as plans are developed. As a process, data collection is concerned with the generation of ideas and should be kept separate from analyzing facts and making decisions because these procedures are evaluation techniques and may inhibit idea generation. Data collection relies on creative, imaginative thinking; data analysis relies on evaluative thinking. Groups sometimes arrive at hasty, ill-conceived solutions because they rush to implement initial ideas without carefully exploring the situation, the obstacles to problem resolution, and the ramifications of a proposed solution.

Areas of information that are important for groups to obtain include

* The history of the problem
* Previous attempts to resolve the problem
* Facts about the situation, such as who is involved and where, how, and when the problem occurred
* Characteristics of the problem, such as its duration, intensity, scope, and importance
* The psychosocial context of the problem
* Organizational and societal rules and regulations that impinge on the problem

The group should have as much information as possible about the problem as it analyzes data and prepares alternative solutions. Knowing the history of the problem helps the group develop a longitudinal perspective on the problem's development and course. Comparing the state of affairs before and after a problem has occurred can often point to potential causes and possible solutions. While gathering data about the history of the problem, the group should become familiar with previous attempts to solve it. This information can help the group avoid repeating past failures.

The worker should help members pinpoint as many facts about the situation as possible. To help members separate facts from opinions and feelings, the worker should encourage members to describe the situation. After the facts of the situation are described, members should be encouraged to share their views of the problem. Scheidel and Crowell (1979) list five conditions that help to create a group climate that encourages members to share information and views about a problem:

- Maintaining the group's openness to speculation
- Encouraging an open search for all pertinent data
- Encouraging all group members to present their ideas
- Demonstrating genuine appreciation of differences
- Refraining from evaluation

A supportive group climate reduces the need for members to defend their positions. Gibb (1961) points out that communications should be expressed (1) non-judgmentally, (2) genuinely, (3) without the intent of controlling others, (4) with tentativeness rather than certainty, and (5) as an equal rather than as a superior contribution. Facilitating this type of communication in a group increases problem exploration and contributes to high-quality solutions.

Members occasionally can become stuck in the ways they explore and review a problem (Napier & Gershenfeld, 1993). To develop new approaches, members should be encouraged to (1) view problems flexibly, (2) expand the way information is collected and combined, (3) recognize and fill gaps in available information, (4) generate new ideas by viewing situations from alternative perspectives, and (5) use both lateral and vertical thinking processes.

Vertical thinking processes are often associated with rational problem-solving strategies. *Vertical thinking* relies on inductive and deductive reasoning. Evidence and reason are used in a logical fashion until a solution is reached. Solutions are grounded in facts that are built one on another in an orderly, systematic, and linear fashion.

Lateral thinking processes are particularly useful when vertical thinking processes have not yielded a creative solution. Lateral thinking helps free ideas that have been blocked by stale, routine ways of conceptualizing a problem and its potential solutions. Instead of relying on an orderly, linear combination of facts, *lateral thinking* is characterized by the use of analogies, metaphors, similarities, contrasts, and paradoxes. Seemingly disparate facts, thoughts, and ideas are put together in new and creative ways. Analogies, for example, help bring out similarities between objects or situations that were previously considered to be different. For example, solutions found to be helpful in analogous situations might be tried by group members in their current problem-solving situation. For further information about the lateral thinking process, see De Bono (1968, 1971, 1972).

Developing Plans

Data collection encourages divergent thinking processes, but preparing plans for problem resolution encourages convergent thinking processes (Scheidel & Crowell, 1979). The worker calls on members to organize, analyze, and synthesize facts, ideas, and perspectives generated during problem exploration. Figure 11.1 shows that plans should be developed during the analysis portion of problem-solving efforts.

The first step in analyzing information generated during data collection is to display the data for all members. It is difficult for members to keep a large amount of information in mind as they attempt to develop alternative solutions. Displaying information on newsprint or a blackboard helps to ensure that all members are aware of the full range of information shared during a discussion.

The next step is to order and clarify the information generated by the group. Useful techniques include

- Separating relevant from irrelevant facts
- Combining similar facts
- Identifying discrepancies
- Looking for patterns across different facts
- Ranking facts from most important to least important

During the process of organizing data, members should be encouraged to discuss the logic behind their reasoning, not their particular ordering of information. Members should be encouraged to give each other a chance to explain why they see things the way they do, rather than to defend their own choices. Defending choices often entrenches group members' opinions. A discussion of how members think information should be used often brings out commonalities and similarities in their views of the situation.

After the information is ordered, it is helpful to redefine the problem, specifying, refining, and, if necessary, reframing it in view of the facts, ideas, and perspectives that have been discussed. It is also helpful to re-examine the group's goals by comparing the problem situation with the outcomes the group would like to achieve by resolving the problem. Once a common definition of the problem is reached and a valued end state is specified, the group should have little trouble developing a plan to solve the problem.

Before making a decision, members should be encouraged to develop as many alternative solutions as possible. Because critical and evaluative comments tend to inhibit the production of creative ideas, workers should caution members not to criticize each other's solutions as they are presented. When members generate alternative solutions, they should also keep in mind that their strategies and plans must begin to specify the action system and the tasks, as well as the time, energy, and resources necessary for implementing the solution.

Selecting the Best Plan

After all members have presented their alternatives, the group should review each one. The review serves several purposes. It helps ensure that all members understand each alternative. Misunderstandings at this point can cause conflict and reduce the chances for achieving closure in the problem-solving process. Reviews can be used to clarify the objectives and goals of each alternative plan.

When reviewing each alternative, members can be encouraged to discuss how they would overcome obstacles and challenges likely to be encountered if the alternative were implemented. For large or costly decisions, task groups sometimes recommend that one or more alternatives be tested in pilot programs before full-scale implementation of one plan.

Members are then ready to choose among alternative plans. When selecting among alternatives, members should be encouraged to consider the overall likelihood that a plan will resolve the problem in a manner that is valued by all group members. For this purpose, it is helpful for members to develop criteria that can be used to judge each plan. Rational methods based on multiattribute utility analysis (see Chapter 12) have been developed to help members develop decision criteria. Although much has been written about these methods (Baron, 1994; Clemen, 1996; Watson & Buede, 1987), they have not been widely applied in the human services. (For exceptions, see Dalgleish, 1988; Milter and Rohrbaugh, 1988; and Toseland, Rivas, and Chapman, 1984.)

Sometimes groups rely on decision criteria developed by experts. For example, a task group formed by the U.S. Department of Health and Human Services was charged with distributing funds for health maintenance organizations in medically underserved areas. By using panels of experts, the committee developed four criteria for deciding among programs that applied for funds in medically underserved areas. These criteria were (1) the number of physicians per 1000 people, (2) the percentage of families in the area with less than $5000 annual income, (3) the infant mortality rate in the area, and (4) the percentage of the area's population over age 65 (Health Services Research Group, 1975).

In most situations, groups rely on the expertise of their own members to develop decision criteria. This is frequently done by having members rate the advantages and the disadvantages of each alternative. Alternatives may be combined or modified to maximize advantages and minimize disadvantages. As members decide among alternatives, they should keep in mind the group's mandate, its goals, and the ideal situation they would like to see result if the problem were resolved successfully. Members may also want to consider other factors, such as the benefits and costs of implementing alternative solutions, the comfort and ease with which particular solutions are likely to be implemented, and the political ramifications of alternative solutions. The most effective solution to a problem may not be the most desirable solution if it is too costly or if it is likely to offend, inconvenience, or otherwise upset persons who will be asked to implement it.

Implementing the Plan

Excellent decisions can be worthless if they are not implemented properly. Effective problem solving requires that a task group actively oversee the implementation of its plan.

Input from persons who will be influential in implementing the plan should be solicited as early as possible in the problem-solving process. Once a solution is decided, members should begin to gain support for the decision from constituencies outside the group. Members should seek the support of persons with authority to implement the decision and those who will be accountable for the decision. For example, the committee that decided to improve outreach efforts to Mexican Americans by training staff and publicizing agency programs in the community sought the cooperation of the board of directors, the agency's executive director, the directors of programs responsible for implementing staff training and publicity campaigns, all direct service staff who were going to be involved in the program, and leaders of the Mexican American community.

When seeking the support of others, members may have to educate people about the value of a new approach to a problem. Motivating people to cooperate with the implementation of a decision is not an easy task. However, motivation is important because passivity during the implementation stage of problem solving can mean the demise of a promising solution. In gaining cooperation, individual members or the group as a whole may also use persuasion, lobbying, or other tactics to gain the support of others (Rothman, Erlich, & Tropman, 1995).

Once the receptivity of persons responsible for implementing the decision is ensured, the group can begin to organize and supervise the plan's implementation. With a large plan, a division of labor is often helpful—each member may be assigned specific responsibilities. There may also be a need for training to educate persons who will implement the plan.

It is often helpful to delineate steps in the implementation sequence. Objectives can be specified for each step, which allows the group to obtain periodic feedback about the plan's implementation. A time line can be attached to the implementation sequence to clarify how much time is needed for each step during the implementation stage.

Implementing the proposed solution also includes identifying, contacting, and utilizing available resources. A heterogeneous group can be advantageous in this process because of the available resources a diversity of members can bring to the group. It is also important to prepare members for opposition. Obstacles may include inertia, passive resistance, or active attempts to block implementation of a proposed solution.

As Figure 11.1 shows, feedback is essential in the problem-solving process. When planning for the implementation of a decision, group members should establish feedback channels to keep the group apprised of a solution's utility in terms of its expected outcome. Feedback can be used to overcome obstacles, stabilize change, and meet the challenges of a continually changing environment.

SUMMARY

This chapter focuses on the foundation skills, procedures, and methods needed to work effectively with task groups. Task groups have an important place in all human service organizations. Each day, meetings take place that have an important effect on what services are provided and how they are delivered. Social workers and other helping professionals are frequently called on to chair or staff committees, teams, and other task groups. When meetings are well run, members become a satisfied and cohesive team committed to achieving its objectives. Poorly run meetings, however, often lead to boredom and frustration.

During the work stage of task groups, the worker often is called on to engage in the following activities: (1) preparing for group meetings, (2) helping members share information, (3) helping all members get involved in the work of the group, (4) helping members develop ideas and information, (5) dealing with conflict, (6) helping members make effective decisions, (7) understanding the political ramifications of task groups, (8) monitoring and evaluating, and (9) problem solving.

Problem solving is probably the single most important function of task groups. The chapter concludes with a six-step, problem-solving model: (1) identifying a problem, (2) developing goals, (3) collecting data, (4) developing plans, (5) selecting the best plan, and (6) implementing the plan. In practice, these steps overlap and they are interconnected by feedback channels. Task groups repeat variations of problem-solving processes during the life of the group as they perform their functions and work on the tasks that confront them.

LEARNING ASSIGNMENTS

1. You have been asked to chair a committee charged with the task of making recommendations about whether it would be feasible for the large social service agency in which you work to provide child care for employees. Describe how you would prepare for the first meeting of the committee. Prepare a written agenda.

2. Observe a task group meeting. After the meeting, evaluate the effectiveness of the leader. What are the strengths and weaknesses of this individual's leadership style? Did the leader appear to be well prepared for the meeting? What changes would have helped make the meeting more productive?

3. You are leading an organizational decision-making group charged with deciding how to expand its services to an underserved minority community. As the deliberations of the group proceed, there appear to be wide differences of opinion and conflict among the members. As the group's leader, what strategies could you employ to help the members of the group resolve their conflicts and decide on a plan?

4. Conduct separate interviews with the leader and a member of an interdisciplinary team. Ask them to describe how well members of the team get along with each other. Ask specifically about role boundaries and role ambiguity among the members of the team. Also ask about how conflicts and professional rivalries are handled. Compare and contrast the responses of the two individuals you interviewed.

5. Observe a meeting of a community group or organization. How did the group solve problems? How did the group make decisions? How did the leader involve the members in group problem-solving procedures? When faced with alternative solutions, what procedures were used to decide among alternatives?

CASE EXAMPLE

Lola's supervisor thought it was time to review her accomplishments as a group leader. Two years ago Lola was assigned to chair the organization's long-range planning committee. Lola felt she had been an active group leader. Lola lived in a rural part of West Virginia called Blair County. She worked for Join Together, an outreach and community development organization. The organization's long-range planning committee was composed of representatives from all levels of the organization, including administration, client services, program development, and finance. Over the course of her tenure as leader, the group had achieved a high level of functioning. Lola's supervisor identified several activities and skills that helped the group to function effectively and achieve its purpose.

Lola spent a good deal of time preparing for group meetings. In addition to reviewing and monitoring the work of subcommittees, she researched issues for future meetings, prepared an agenda, and made numerous personal contacts with group members. Lola hoped that her level of activity between meetings served as a model for all members. After evaluating the amount of work done by members outside of meetings, Lola's supervisor concluded that her modeling behavior had helped to establish a group norm of hard work.

One of the most impressive aspects of the group meetings was the sharing of information that occurred among members. Lola encouraged all members to keep the group updated on existing programs and ideas for new services. Between meetings Lola shared important information with all members of the committee. At the beginning of each meeting, members shared updates and suggestions with each other. Lola's supervisor noted to herself that through this process, the group had achieved a high level of communication and interaction. Members were familiar and comfortable with the roles they played in the group. Her assessment was that these factors fostered group cohesiveness and raised the productivity of group members.

Lola also helped the group develop a clear structure for the monthly meetings. She helped establish clear procedures for developing information, solving problems, and making decisions. She encouraged members to participate actively during meetings by modeling good member skills such as listening, asking good questions, and giving support. She also helped members feel that their feedback and recommendations were taken seriously by the organization. Lola worked carefully with the administrators to ensure that group deliberations would be influential on the future directions of organizational policy and programs. Group members felt empowered by this knowledge.

Lola's organizational skills helped the group adopt a clear structure for solving problems and making decisions. She helped the group decide on a standard format for problem solving. For example, when faced with having to decide how to find funding for a new volunteer outreach program in the local school, the group followed the steps of identifying the problem, setting goals, collecting data, developing plans, and selecting and implementing the plan. The group learned and relied on this format in many of its problem-solving discussions. During decision-making activities, Lola suggested clear guidelines about how to proceed. These were discussed, modified, and adopted by the group. She encouraged the group to develop decision criteria and procedures before making important decisions. Although this took some time, Lola's organizational skills helped the group decision-making process become easier and more systematic. Lola was also good at helping the group build consensus by finding common interests and points of agreement. Consensus building helped members be more committed to the group decision.

Lola spent time monitoring and evaluating the group. She devoted a regular portion of each meeting agenda to discussions of members' efforts and their effectiveness. She also developed a survey form to obtain members' feedback about her leadership skills and for gathering suggestions about how the group could be improved. Lola shared the results of the survey with members and incorporated members' suggestions into the work of the group.

The long-range planning committee had some history of disagreements and conflicts. Several of the members had strong personalities. Others felt that their departments should have more control over the projects chosen for future funding and implementation. Lola's greatest difficulty was her ability to deal with the conflicts that arose in the group. Her supervisor noted that she seemed uncomfortable with conflict in the group. She suggested that Lola listen carefully to both sides of discussions and remain neutral in the face of pressure to agree with one side or the other. Lola helped the group recognize that some disagreements about issues were healthy for group discussions. Lola's supervisor suggested that she help the group differentiate these substantive conflicts from affective conflicts, in which members personalized conflicts with other members. At different times, Lola helped the group resolve both types of conflicts. Still, she worked hard to more fully develop her skills of listening, mediating, negotiating, and compromising.

As Lola's supervisor reflected on the group's accomplishments, she noted that Lola had guided the group by providing it with many of the elements it needed to function effectively. Lola felt a sense of pride in knowing that she had used her talents and skills to guide the development of an effective task group. Through her efforts, the group identified several service needs and helped to implement programs for persons living in rural West Virginia.

Task Groups: Specialized Methods

This chapter describes specialized methods for helping organizational and community groups accomplish their goals during the middle stage. The first section is divided into two parts describing methods for helping small and large organizational groups accomplish their objectives. The second section describes specialized methods for helping community groups accomplish their objectives. A brief introduction of each method is followed by a description of the procedures necessary to implement the method, its recommended uses, and evidence about its effectiveness.

Most methods described in this chapter have been used successfully in social service organizations and in business. However, methods such as quality circles, focus groups, and social judgment analysis have received wider attention in business and industry and are only now being adopted in social service organizations. For a comprehensive review of these and other structured problem-solving techniques, see VanGundy (1988).

SMALL ORGANIZATIONAL GROUPS

Brainstorming

Brainstorming is probably the best known of the specialized methods presented in this chapter. The primary purpose of brainstorming is to increase the number of ideas generated by members. Elements of brainstorming, such as suspending judgment of ideas, have long been recognized as effective techniques, but Osborn (1963) was the first to develop a systematic set of rules for generating creative ideas, which he called *brainstorming*.

During brainstorming, total effort is directed toward creative thinking rather than to analytical or evaluative thinking. Analytical and evaluative thinking can reduce ability to generate creative ideas. Members are concerned about their status in a group, and if they expect critical judgments about their thoughts and ideas, they are not likely to express them. Analytical and evaluative thinking can also serve as a social control mechanism. Members who continue to present ideas that are viewed critically are likely to be sanctioned. Members may also screen out potentially creative, but controversial, ideas before they are ever expressed. By attempting to reduce analytical and evaluative thinking, brainstorming encourages free disclosure of ideas.

Four rules are used to manage the group's interaction during brainstorming:

1. *Freewheeling* is welcomed. Members are encouraged to express all their ideas, no matter what they are. Members should not hold back on ideas that might be considered wild, repetitious, or obvious.

2. Criticism is ruled out. Members are asked to withhold analyses, judgments, and evaluations about any ideas presented during the idea-generating process. Members should not try to defend or explain their ideas.

3. Quantity is wanted. According to Osborn (1963) and Clark (1958), the more ideas suggested in the allotted time, the better the quality of ideas. Quality occurs by itself if enough ideas are generated.

4. Combining, rearranging, and improving ideas are encouraged. Often called *hitchhiking,* this technique calls on group members to build on ideas that have already been expressed. Members can combine or modify ideas and suggest how other members' ideas can be improved.

Procedures

Brainstorming can be conducted in any size of group, although large groups may inhibit idea generation and reduce a member's ability to participate in the allotted time. Because brainstorming encourages the generation of creative and unique ideas, a heterogeneous membership representing many points of view facilitates the process. The procedure can be conducted in a short period of time (15 minutes), but longer meetings may produce more quality ideas because ideas presented in the last third of a group's meeting are often of a higher quality than ideas produced during the first two thirds of the meeting (Stattler & Miller, 1968).

At the beginning of the meeting, the worker explains the problem to be brainstormed and the four basic rules of brainstorming. A warm-up period of 10 to 15 minutes can be used to familiarize members with the procedure and to help them learn to express and hear ideas without criticizing them. During this time, the worker can model appropriate behavior and make some suggestions about procedures such as lateral thinking that may increase creativity. Even when some members of the group have used brainstorming procedures previously, the warm-up time gives all members an opportunity to prepare to change routine patterns of analyzing and evaluating ideas. It also allows them to become acclimated to freewheeling idea generation.

During the brainstorming procedure, the leader or coleader writes the members' ideas on a flip chart or a blackboard. Having a coleader record ideas is particularly helpful during warm-up sessions because it is difficult for the leader to train members, record ideas, and model appropriate behavior at the same time. Ideas should be recorded by using the words of the speaker as much as possible. Key words should be abstracted so suggestions fit on a sheet of newsprint or a blackboard.

The interaction pattern in the group should encourage the free flow of ideas. Members should be asked to offer one idea at a time and to allow everyone to have a turn presenting ideas. Occasionally, it is necessary to limit talkative members by encouraging members who have not contributed extensively to express their ideas. In large groups (more than 15 members), it has been recommended that members raise their hands before they begin to speak (Scheidel & Crowell, 1979). This procedure also makes it easier to record ideas because they can be clarified more quickly when the recorder's attention is focused on the speaker.

Sometimes groups run out of ideas or repeat similar ideas without pursuing new or alternative thinking patterns. At this point, instead of closing a session, the worker should read ideas from the list to stimulate thinking, focus the group's attention on unexplored areas of the problem, or pick out one or two ideas around which the group may want to generate additional ideas. Throughout the process, the worker should (1) express interest in the ideas as they are presented, (2) urge members to continue to produce creative ideas, and (3) help the group elaborate on ideas that have already been presented.

The worker should not try to have the group evaluate ideas immediately after the brainstorming procedure. Waiting a day or longer allows members to think of new ideas to add to the list and allows time for them to return to an analytical way of evaluating ideas. Once the meeting has ended, the worker should ensure that members are not blamed or sanctioned for the ideas they have expressed. If they are, brainstorming will not succeed in future meetings.

Uses

Brainstorming procedures are useful under certain conditions. Brainstorming should be done in groups that have already defined a problem. In many respects, brainstorming can be used as a substitute for the methods described in the Developing Plans section of the problem-solving model described in Chapter 11. Brainstorming procedures are particularly appropriate if the problem the group is working on is specific and limited in range (Scheidel & Crowell, 1979). It has been shown that the quality of solutions improves in groups that have been instructed to focus on specifically defined problems rather than on broadly defined problems (Davis, Manske, & Train, 1966). Parnes (1967) suggests using *limited critical thinking* rather than *free associating* as recommended by Osborn (1963). This process ensures that group members focus their ideas by making them relevant to a specific situation being examined by the group.

Brainstorming can be used in both groups and organizational settings. For example, when a board of directors of a social services agency begins a search for a new executive director, the board president decides to involve line staff in the hiring process. The president convenes a diverse group of agency staff members to brainstorm ideas about what qualities a new executive director should demonstrate. Members of the brainstorming group are encouraged to think of as many positive qualities as they can, and each is asked to contribute creative ideas. The board president, acting as group leader, prepares a list of ideal qualities or attributes the staff have contributed and presents the list to the board of directors for consideration during the search for the new executive director.

Brainstorming methods are useful when the group wants to generate as many ideas as possible. Brainstorming, therefore, should not be used when the group faces a technical problem that requires systematic, organized thinking. Implicit in the brainstorming approach is the notion that the problem can have many solutions (Scheidel & Crowell, 1979). In many situations, groups confront problems that can be solved several ways, but sometimes problems have only one right answer. In these situations, brainstorming is not appropriate. Other rational, structured problem-solving methods such as social judgment analysis or the nominal group technique are more likely to help a group produce the best solution (Toseland & Rivas, 1984).

Effectiveness

Most evidence for the effectiveness of brainstorming is based on anecdotal accounts of its use in business meetings (Clark, 1958; Osborn, 1963), but the method has been investigated through empirical research (Bayless, 1967; Maltzman, Simon, Raskin, & Licht, 1960; Taylor, Berry, & Block, 1958). Although the Taylor study is often cited to disclaim the effectiveness of brainstorming, the study did not compare brainstorming and nonbrainstorming conditions. Taylor, Berry, and Block (1958) found that brainstorming produced better results when it was done by individuals working alone than by individuals in a group. Findings from the study suggest that nominal group brainstorming is better than interacting group brainstorming but do not suggest whether group brainstorming is better than a group meeting without brainstorming.

Other studies show that when brainstorming is used in a group context, the results are positive (Bayless, 1967; Maltzman et al., 1960). Groups that use brainstorming produce more ideas of a higher quality than groups that do not use this approach (D'Zurilla & Goldfried, 1971). Nominal brainstorming, in which members generate as many ideas as possible without interacting, may be even more effective than brainstorming in interactive groups. In a more recent study, it was found that members of brainstorming groups were more satisfied, felt their groups used a more effective process, and felt they communicated more effectively than members of groups who were not trained in the procedure (Kramer, Kuo, & Dailey, 1997). These important outcomes have been neglected in previous research on brainstorming. Thus, brainstorming may have some positive unintended consequences that are unrelated to the goal of generating more and higher-quality ideas.

Brainstorming generates ideas from a wide base because it encourages all group members to participate fully. The method also tends to establish members' commitment to the idea that is ultimately decided on because members have helped shape the idea that is selected. Napier and Gershenfeld (1993) have listed other benefits of brainstorming in groups, including the following:

- Dependence on a single authority figure is reduced.
- Open sharing of ideas is encouraged.
- Members of highly competitive groups can feel safe.
- A maximum output of ideas occurs in a short period of time.
- Members' ideas are posted immediately for everyone to see.
- Ideas are generated internally rather than imposed from outside the group, which increases the feeling of accountability.
- Brainstorming is enjoyable and self-stimulating.

Despite its benefits, brainstorming is not without drawbacks. It is not easy to achieve an atmosphere in which ideas are generated freely. Brainstorming can initially cause discomfort to members who are not used to freely sharing their ideas (Collaros & Anderson, 1969; Hammond & Goldman, 1961; Vroom, Grant, & Cotton, 1969). The brainstorming procedure breaks norms that ordinarily protect members from making suggestions that may result in overt or covert sanctions (Bouchard, 1972b).

Other factors also may reduce the efficacy of brainstorming procedures. For example, although the warm-up period is essential for optimal performance during brainstorming, warm-ups require time, which may not be available. Inertia may also interfere with brainstorming because the technique requires a change from ordinary group procedures. The worker may not feel justified in imposing the procedure on reluctant or skeptical members who are unaware of its benefits. Although brainstorming has many potentially beneficial effects, if it is to be used effectively, members must be made aware of its usefulness and workers must apply it correctly.

Variations on Brainstorming

Reverse Brainstorming

First proposed by Richards (1974), reverse brainstorming is a procedure that can be used to list the negative consequences of actions quickly and thoroughly.

Group members are asked, "What might go wrong with this idea?" Reverse brainstorming is useful after a variety of ideas have been generated. Members should first use a scanning procedure, such as the one suggested by Etzioni (1968), to reduce a long list of ideas to several alternatives. Members then brainstorm about the consequences of carrying out each alternative. When the group is aware of potential obstacles to solving the problem, the worker then can ask members to suggest ideas for overcoming the obstacles.

Trigger Groups

The trigger group procedure uses the findings of Taylor, Berry, and Block (1958) and Dunnette, Campbell, and Joastad (1963), who discovered that brainstorming is more effective when it is done by individuals working alone than by individuals interacting in groups. In a trigger group, each individual works alone for 5 to 10 minutes to develop a list of ideas and suggestions (Richards, 1974). Members then read their lists to the group. The group takes about 10 minutes to clarify, add to, or combine ideas that each member has presented. As in brainstorming, suggestions are made without criticism. After all members have presented their ideas, the group decides together on criteria for evaluating the ideas. Ideas are then screened by the group, one at a time, to arrive at a single solution to a problem.

   This approach allows members to work independently to develop ideas without verbal or nonverbal evaluative comments from other group members. Also, as each member reads, it focuses the attention of the entire group on the ideas of one individual, which gives members a feeling that their ideas are heard, understood, and carefully examined and gives each member an opportunity to receive constructive comments from all group members. Trigger groups are best when conducted with five to eight members because the time necessary to develop ideas, to brainstorm, and to critically evaluate each individual's ideas can be prohibitive in larger groups.

Synectics

Synectics is a method for generating creative ideas during problem solving. *Synectics* is a Greek word that means the joining of different and seemingly irrelevant elements. Gordon (1961) developed synectics after years of exploring methods to increase creativity. Prince (1970) added to Gordon's ideas and expanded the method for use in group problem solving.

   A synectics meeting lasts about three hours and includes five to eight members with diverse interests and experiences. Much of the meeting follows an ordinary problem-solving sequence. A problem is introduced by the worker, and members are encouraged to present their ideas about it. To avoid coercion and intimidation, the worker should not be someone with influence or power over other group members. The worker also should have a neutral view of the problem. A major goal of synectics is to develop a climate of trust in which all ideas are valued. During the preliminary discussion, the problem is clarified and specified. The worker's job is to help members reframe the problem by sepa-rating it from its usual context, help members present unique ideas without crit-icism, and help the group refrain from making premature decisions.

As the problem-solving process continues, the worker may notice that mem-bers are making predictable, noncreative responses to a problem. At a timely point during this discussion, the worker can suggest that the group go on an excursion (Napier & Gershenfeld, 1993). An *excursion* is a method of using analogies to stim-ulate new ideas. For members who have not participated in synectics meetings before, the worker should begin with a direct analogy that is easy to develop.

A direct analogy is an analogy to something in the environment. The worker might ask a question such as "What is there about this problem that's like what is often found in nature?" Other types of analogies include the following:

- Personal analogy—"How would you feel if you were this problem?"
- Symbolic analogy—"What object or thing do you associate with this problem?"
- Fantasy analogy—"Imagine that you could control time; how would you use time to help resolve this problem?"

Such questions can help members develop creative ideas about a problem (Gor-don, 1961).

Synectics is an interesting alternative to rational problem-solving approaches, such as social judgment analysis. Although there have been several anecdotal ac-counts of the effectiveness of synectics (Prince, 1970), only one study confirms assertions that groups using this method develop more creative ideas than they would if they used ordinary problem solving or brainstorming (Bouchard, 1972a). Therefore, more research is needed on synectics and other creative problem-solving methods, such as lateral thinking, to ascertain whether they are viable ways for generating creative ideas and effective solutions to problems.

Focus Groups

Focus groups are designed to collect in-depth, qualitative information about a particular service or topic of interest to the managers of an organization. The em-phasis is on facilitating members' discussion of a subject until points of agree-ment and disagreement become clear. The strength of focus groups is their ability to explore topics and generate hypotheses through the explicit use of group in-teraction (Morgan, 1997). They may also be used to clarify and enrich data col-lected during surveys or other research methods. Focus groups are often associated with marketing research in which they are used to solicit opinions and reactions to new or existing products. However, within the social sciences, they were used as early as World War II to examine the effectiveness of wartime pro-paganda (Merton & Kendall, 1946). Since that time, focus groups have been used by health and social service organizations as a qualitative research method to collect information about a variety of topics, but especially to assess clients' satisfaction and opinions about particular services.

Procedures

Focus group meetings consist of a semistructured group interview and discussion with 6 to 12 group members. Meetings typically last one to two hours. The worker's task is to gently direct the group to discuss items of interest to the sponsor of the group, probe superficial answers, and encourage the group to move on when a particular topic appears to be exhausted.

Aaker, Kunar, and Day (1998) have presented four key elements to the success of a focus group: (1) planning a specific agenda, (2) recruiting and screening appropriate participants, (3) effective moderation during meetings, and (4) clear and detailed analysis and interpretation of the results. Planning the agenda begins by carefully considering the purpose for the group and the topics to be covered. Because focus groups are meant to encourage in-depth discussion, it is important to maintain the focus by not exploring too many topics. Next, the worker should develop a series of relevant questions for which responses are sought. From these questions, a discussion guide is prepared. The guide is an outline that helps ensure that specific issues are covered. The discussion guide should proceed in a logical order from general to specific areas of inquiry. Although all topics should be covered, the guide is not meant to be a rigid template for the conduct of group meetings. If a question does not generate useful, nonrepetitive information, the facilitator should move on to the next question or probe. Similarly, new or interesting ideas that emerge from the interaction between members should be pursued.

Careful screening of participants is crucial to the success of a focus group. Focus group participants should be interested in and have opinions about the topic to be discussed. They should have enough characteristics in common so that they will feel comfortable interacting. To get a broad, in-depth understanding of a subject, it is important to select individuals with a wide range of experience and diverse opinions. Because individuals who have participated in previous focus groups may dominate the discussion, they are generally excluded from participation. Also, it is preferable to recruit individuals who do not know one another. Relatives, friends, and neighbors tend to talk to each other rather than to the whole group, and, because of the presence of individuals they know, they are sometimes less open about their true opinions.

Because positive, freewheeling group interaction can help reticent participants express in-depth opinions and discuss all aspects of a particular topic, effective leadership is essential in focus groups. Leaders should be familiar with the topic to be discussed and sensitive to the verbal and nonverbal cues given off by participants. Aaker, Kunar, and Day (1998) suggest that focus group leaders should have the ability to (1) establish rapport quickly, (2) listen carefully to each member's opinions, (3) demonstrate a genuine interest in each member's views, (4) avoid jargon and sophisticated terminology that may turn off members,

(5) flexibly implement the discussion guide, (6) sense when a topic is exhausted or when it is becoming threatening, (7) know what topic to introduce to maintain a smooth flow of the discussion, and (8) facilitate group dynamics that encourage the full participation of all members and avoid domination by talkative members.

Focus groups often yield a wealth of disparate comments and opinions. To prepare reports and to do qualitative analyses of the data derived from a focus group meeting, it is useful to have an audiotape or videotape of group meetings. Reports of focus group meetings should capture the diverse opinions that are expressed as well as any consensus that is achieved. It is also useful to categorize members' comments in a manner that relates the comments to the specific hypotheses or questions that the focus group was intended to address.

Uses

Focus groups can be used for many purposes (Kinnear & Taylor, 1996; Lehmann, 1989). Major purposes include

- Generating hypotheses about the way individuals think or behave that may be tested quantitatively at a later point
- Obtaining in-depth information about a topic
- Generating or evaluating impressions and opinions about the services an organization offers or plans to offer
- Overcoming reticence to obtaining personal views and opinions
- Generating information to help develop client-satisfaction questionnaires and other types of questionnaires
- Providing in-depth analysis and interpretation of previously collected data and the findings of previously reported studies

Focus groups are particularly well suited for gathering in-depth data about the attitudes and cognition of participants (Morgan, 1997). For example, a community mental health agency might be concerned about its effectiveness in reaching Native Americans within its service area and decide that one of the agency outreach workers should recruit a focus group composed of local Native American community leaders to explore community perceptions of the mental health center and its services. Following a carefully planned agenda and using a structured interview guide, the group leader would help the focus group members identify their perceptions of the agency and its strengths and weaknesses. The group leader would use information gained during the focus group meeting to design a larger needs assessment research project and to make preliminary recommendations to the agency director for improvements in service delivery procedures.

Although the information derived from focus groups is excellent for developing hypotheses and for exploring issues in-depth, caution should be exercised when using the information as the sole basis for making important decisions affecting large groups of individuals. Because a limited number of participants can be included in focus groups, the data derived may not be as representative of a larger population as data derived from a well-designed survey.

Effectiveness

Many data about the effectiveness of focus groups are based on case examples and anecdotal data (Dillon, Madden, & Firtle, 1994). According to Kinnear and Taylor (1996), compared with other procedures for soliciting attitudes and cognition, focus groups have the following advantages: (1) synergism, resulting from interacting group members who produce a wider range of information, insight, and ideas than do individuals who are interviewed alone; (2) snowballing, resulting from group members' stimulating each other to share their ideas and opinions and express their feelings; (3) security, resulting from having others express similar opinions and feelings; and (4) speed, resulting from interviewing several individuals together.

Swenson, Griswold, and Kleiber (1992) indicate that focus groups can have a positive effect on participants. For example, 67 percent of the participants of the focus groups in their study reported continuing to think about the topics raised in the meetings, 67 percent reported that the discussion during the groups affected their thinking, and about 27 percent reported discussing and following up on the issues raised in the focus groups after the meetings had ended. Fern (1982) also found that individual interviews produced more ideas than did focus groups. Byers and Wilcox (1991) and Lederman (1989) found that focus groups were not suitable to many types of data collection but did generate rich qualitative data and hypotheses for future exploration.

Most experts agree that the effectiveness of focus groups depends heavily on the moderator's ability to facilitate the discussion. As with any group, the effectiveness of a focus group can be limited by group think, domination by a talkative member, and a host of other problems with group dynamics described in earlier chapters. The interpretation of data from focus groups can also present problems because the small sample of individuals makes it unclear whether the opinions expressed are representative. Also it can be difficult to interpret sharp discrepancies in group members' views of a particular situation.

Despite these limitations, with adequate preparation and a skillful moderator, focus groups can provide an effective and efficient method for collecting in-depth, qualitative data about the thoughts and opinions of consumers of health and social services. For more information about conducting focus groups, see Krueger (1994, 1997, 1998) or Stewart and Shamdasani (1990), and for more information about using focus groups as a qualitative research method, see Morgan (1997).

Nominal Group Technique

The nominal group technique (NGT) is different from traditional interacting approaches to solving problems in task groups. The technique was developed in the late 1960s by Andre Delbecq and Andrew Van de Ven as they studied program planning groups in social service agencies and the operation of committees and other idea-aggregating and decision-making groups in business and industry (Delbecq, Van de Ven, & Gustafson, 1975). Since its development, the technique has been used extensively in health, social service, industrial, educational, and governmental agencies as an aid to planning and managing programs.

Procedures

An NGT meeting should have six to nine group members. Larger groups should be separated into two or more smaller groups. Because participants are required to write and because ideas are presented on a flip chart, group members should be seated around a U-shaped table. A flip chart with newsprint should be placed at the open end of the U. Supplies that are needed include a flip chart, a felt-tip pen, a roll of tape, index cards, worksheets, and pencils.

Before an NGT meeting, the worker should develop a clear statement of the problem. According to Delbecq, Van de Ven, and Gustafson (1975), the agency is responsible for deciding on the group's purpose and the problem to be addressed before the meeting. At the beginning of the group, the worker states the purpose of the meeting. Then the worker hands out lined paper with the problem statement written at the top, reads the problem statement, and asks all members to take five minutes to list their ideas or responses to the problem. Ideas and responses should be written in brief phrases, without verbal or nonverbal communication with other group members. To give the members some notion of what types of responses are being asked for, workers may want to prepare some sample ideas or responses as models. While group members are working, the leader also writes ideas in silence and ensures that members of the group do not interact with one another.

The next step is a round robin recording of ideas generated by each group member. The ideas are listed on a flip chart that is visible to all group members. The worker asks one member for an idea, writes it on the flip chart, and then goes around the group by asking each person in turn for one idea. Members are encouraged to *hitchhike,* that is, use ideas already on the chart to stimulate their thinking and add on their worksheets ideas that they did not think of during the silent period. When a member has no new ideas, the member passes and allows the next group member to present an idea until everyone is finished.

The ideas should be recorded as rapidly as possible in members' own words. During the round robin, members should not critique, elaborate on, or defend ideas. Completed sheets from a flip chart should be taped to a flat surface in view of all group members.

The third step is a serial discussion to clarify the ideas that have been presented. Items from the flip chart are taken in order and discussed for two or three minutes. Each member who expressed an idea is encouraged to explain briefly the evidence and the logic used in arriving at it. At this point, members are free to express their agreement or disagreement with the idea and to discuss its relative importance. Although evaluative comments are welcome, the group should not be allowed to focus on any one idea for a long period of time or to get into a debate over the merits of a particular idea.

The fourth step is a preliminary ordering of the importance of the ideas that have been listed. Each member is asked to work independently in selecting from the list a predetermined number of the ideas with the highest priority. The number of items selected varies, depending on the length of the list, but should include about one quarter to one half the original ideas on the list. Members write their choices on index cards and hand them to the worker. The number of votes that each idea receives from all members is recorded next to the item. This process helps individual members obtain feedback about ideas that are highly regarded by their fellow members.

Each member is then asked to choose five highest-priority ideas from the narrowed-down list. The members rank the ideas on a scale of 5 = highest priority to 1 = lowest priority. The idea and its rank order are then placed on an index card. One index card is used for each idea. The cards are collected and the rank orders are tallied by writing them next to their corresponding ideas on the flip chart. After all ranks have been tallied, the mean rank for each idea is determined by adding the numbers (ranks) next to each item and dividing by the number of group members.

Delbecq, Van de Ven, and Gustafson (1975) suggest that the group may want to discuss the ranks when (1) there are large discrepancies among members' rating patterns or (2) items that are obviously rated too high or low (in the worker's opinion) appear when the items are tallied. These writers claim the resulting discussion and second vote often increase the judgmental accuracy of the group. It is usually the worker or a powerful group member who calls aspects of preliminary votes into question, but this action may be viewed by less powerful group members as a way to manipulate the group process. Therefore, it is recommended that before beginning NGT, the group as a whole should decide under what circumstances a second vote will be taken.

Uses

The NGT technique was created to "increase rationality, creativity, and participation in problem-solving meetings associated with program planning" (Delbecq et al., 1975, p. 1). In a brief review of the literature on small groups, Van de Ven and Delbecq (1971) identified eight inhibiting influences on the performance of interacting groups:

1. A focus effect in which interacting groups pursue a single thought pattern for long periods
2. Members' participation only to the extent that members feel equally competent to other members

3. Covert judgments made but not expressed as overt criticism

4. The effect of status differentials within a group

5. Group pressure for conformity resulting from sanctions by "expert" group members

6. Influence of dominant personalities on the group

7. Too much time and energy spent on maintaining the interacting group rather than working on the task

8. Members' tendencies to reach quick decisions without fully exploring the problem

By combining the positive aspects of noninteracting nominal groups and interacting problem-solving groups, Delbecq, Van de Ven, and Gustafson (1975) developed NGT. According to Van de Ven and Delbecq (1971), NGT does the following:

• Stimulates activity through the presence of others and by everyone's working in silence

• Avoids evaluative comments when the problem dimensions are being formed

• Provides members an opportunity to search their own thought processes

• Avoids dominance by strong personalities

• Prevents premature decision making

• Encourages all members to participate

• Allows minority opinions to be expressed

• Tolerates conflicting and incompatible ideas that are written in silence before they are presented to the entire group

• Eliminates hidden agendas

• Gains members' cooperation in achieving a solution

• Structures the process so that members feel obligated to work on the problem

As an example of the effective use of NGT, consider the case of a multiservice agency facing a financial crisis. The executive council charged with tightening the budget uses NGT to generate ideas for saving money. The executive director leads her executive council in this effort by first asking that each member work alone and write down creative ideas for saving money in the budget. In round robin fashion, each member presents one idea at a time to the group until all ideas are presented and recorded on a flip chart. Next, the executive director leads a limited discussion of the suggested savings measures, discussing the pros and cons of each suggestion. After this process, she asks each member again to work independently to rank each item in order of its value to the savings effort. Selecting the most frequently mentioned suggestions, she asks members to choose the five best alternatives. She computes the five highest-priority suggestions and uses them to initiate plans for budget savings at the agency.

The NGT method can be used to create a long list of ideas or alternative solutions to a problem. Scheidel and Crowell (1979) suggest that it produces more ideas than any other idea-generating and problem-solving techniques they reviewed. It can also be used as a consensus-building technique because each group member is given an equal opportunity to express ideas and participate in reaching a decision. By structuring the interaction, NGT reduces the domination of a few members and makes full use of the creative capabilities and pooled wisdom of all group members. This, in turn, helps to ensure a broad base of support for any decision made by the group.

Effectiveness

The NGT procedure is based on social science findings about task groups that have been accumulated over decades of research. Each step is designed to make use of these findings. Delbecq, Van de Ven, and Gustafson (1975) reported that research findings indicate the following procedures increase judgmental accuracy in decision making:

1. Having members make independent judgments
2. Expressing judgments mathematically by ranking or rating items
3. Using the arithmetic mean of independent judgments to form the group's decision
4. Having members make decisions anonymously
5. Using feedback about preliminary judgments for final voting

The NGT technique uses these research findings in its decision-making step by taking the mean rating of independent rank-order judgments that have been placed on anonymous index cards. Similarly, scientific evidence is the basis for each step in the NGT procedure. Reliance on scientific evidence in developing NGT has apparently worked. Overall, the empirical evidence supports contentions that NGT is more effective than interacting group methods for idea generation, problem solving, and consensus building (Toseland, Rivas, & Chapman, 1984; Van de Ven, 1974), and members are more satisfied with their participation in NGT groups than in untrained groups (Kramer, Kuo, & Dailey, 1997).

However, NGT does have drawbacks. The method is cumbersome. It takes a considerable amount of time (at least one and one half hours), which may not be available to a task group that must complete its work in a short time, especially for routine decisions that may not require the precision afforded by this method. Also, the worker has to be trained in the method and equipped with the necessary supplies to conduct an NGT meeting.

A seemingly inconsequential, though often important, drawback of NGT is that the group process is highly structured, which some members may find unpleasant. One study found that members of NGT groups were less satisfied than members of less structured groups using a problem-solving approach (Toseland et al., 1984). Initially members may be suspicious that they are being manipulated. Aspects of NGT tend to exacerbate rather than quell these fears. For example, having the worker rather than group members define the problem, and having the worker or a powerful group member influence voting procedures by calling for a second vote may feel constricting or even manipulative to members who are used to more freedom during problem solving and decision making. Despite these drawbacks, NGT groups are more satisfying to members than groups in which no structure is provided (Kramer et al., 1997), and the procedure can help task groups generate ideas and solve difficult problems more effectively than in groups where no training is provided.

In recent years, computers have been increasingly used to enhance brainstorming in groups. Rather than write ideas on paper as in NGT, group members are seated in a computer-supported meeting room with their own computer keyboards and screens. Participants enter their ideas with their keyboards (often anonymously) and can see what others are writing simultaneously on their screens. Evidence suggests that such computer support can significantly increase the creativity of a group in comparison to a traditional NGT process (Jessup & Valacich, 1993; Valacich, Dennis, & Connolly, 1994). With greater access to the Internet and the World Wide Web, groups are beginning to engage in brainstorming from their individual workplaces using electronic meeting support tools available on local area or wide area networks. For example, the group leader might ask a question through e-mail and ask participants to reply electronically with all their ideas (Schuman & Rohrbaugh, 1996).

Multiattribute Utility Analysis

Although NGT structures the method used in problem-solving groups to maximize beneficial group dynamics, multiattribute utility (MAU) analysis focuses on the content of the interactions in a group. An MAU method structures the group only to the extent that participants are given a method for using information about a problem. An MAU model uses decision rules to specify the relationships between attributes of a problem. The decision rules are used to increase the utility of decisions made by task groups.

Procedures

A group's use of an MAU model may begin by having each member work alone, either in individual meetings between each member and the worker or in a nominal group meeting in which all members work separately on instructions given by the worker. During this time, the problem and its alternative solutions are explained to members. For example, members are informed that their group has been appointed to decide among applicants for the position of assistant program director. The worker helps group members clarify their thinking about the problem. Specifically, the worker helps each member determine the attributes that are thought to be relevant to making a decision. For example, a member might decide that the attributes she considers important for the position of assistant program director include (1) amount of supervisory experience, (2) amount of clinical experience, (3) level of management skills, and (4) extent that the candidate likes to develop new and innovative service programs. Alternatively, the attributes might be developed through a brainstorming or NGT process.

The worker also helps each member specify the levels of each attribute by specifying minimal criteria for the solution, any constraints on the solution, and the functional form of each attribute. For example, members might decide that minimal criteria for the assistant program director's position include three years of supervisory experience and five years of clinical experience. The members also decide that the candidate must have an MSW or an MPA degree.

The utility function of an attribute specifies the attribute's functional relationship to the overall solution—that is, how levels of an attribute are related to the utility of choice of a particular solution. Figure 12.1 gives one member's utility functions for the four attributes mentioned previously. The utility functions indicate that as the amount of supervisory experience increases, satisfaction with the candidate (the utility of choosing a particular candidate) increases until the candidate has more than 10 years of experience, at which time the member's satisfaction with the candidate declines. At this point, the member thinks a candidate may have too much supervisory experience for the position.

For the clinical experience attribute, a similar utility function occurs, except that satisfaction with a candidate increases until the candidate has more than 15 years of clinical experience. For the management skills attribute, a straight linear relationship exists, which suggests that the higher the score on a management skills test and interview, the higher the satisfaction with the candidate. In the case of developing innovative programs, a curvilinear relationship is present; that is, candidates who are either low or high on this attribute are less preferred than candidates who have moderate inclination to develop new programs.

Figure 12.1 also shows the weight that a group member gave to each attribute. Weights can be assigned by dividing 100 points among all attributes in a manner that reflects the relative importance of each in proportion to the others. In Figure 12.1, the management skills attribute is assigned a weight of 40, making it four times as important as clinical experience, which has been assigned a weight of 10.

The procedure of establishing minimal criteria, constraints, and attributes with their weights and functional forms is the basis of a member's decision rule, that is, how a group member will use information about a problem to make a judgment. Members develop their own decision rules. When all members have completed this task, they share their decision rules with each other. It is helpful for the worker to post each member's decision rules side by side on a flip chart or blackboard so that all members can see how their decision rules compare.

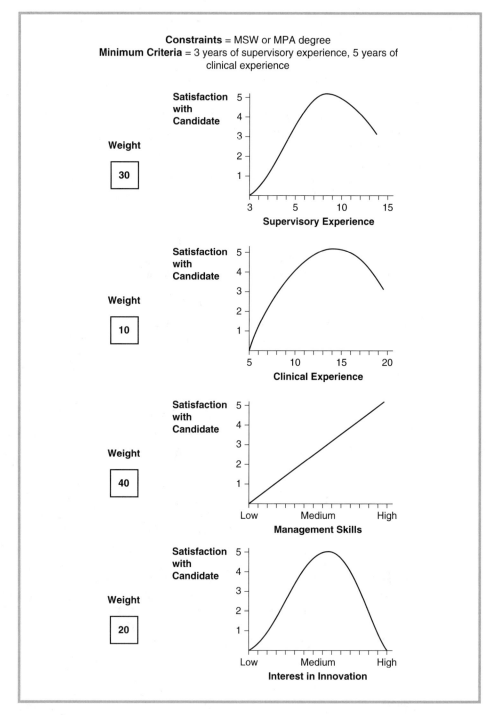

FIGURE 12.1 ■ *A Group Member's Decision Rules for Choosing among Applicants for Assistant Program Director*

The next step in an MAU process is to have members discuss the logic behind their decision rules. During this unstructured discussion, the only rule is to focus on the reasoning behind the choice of attributes, weights, and functional forms (Edwards, 1977; Huber, 1980). For example, members should not discuss individual candidates for the position, but would be encouraged to discuss why a member gave management skills four times the weight of clinical experience when considering candidates for this particular job.

Members discuss the decision rules until they agree on a common group rule that satisfies all members. Consensus is usually not difficult to reach because members find it easier to agree on how information will be used than on specific alternatives. Once a group decision rule has been decided, it is a routine procedure to see how each alternative is ranked on the basis of the decision rule. First, alternatives that do not meet the criteria or the constraints set up by the decision rule are eliminated. The next step is to calculate each alternative's score on the decision rule. Each score is multiplied by that attribute's weight, and the total score is summed across each attribute. A total score on each alternative is calculated. The alternative (in this case, a candidate) that is rated the highest based on the decision rule is the one selected by the group as its final decision.

An Alternative Approach

In some groups, members may feel uncomfortable when asked to express their preferences so explicitly and analytically as is required to construct an MAU model with weights and utility functions. Social judgment analysis (SJA) offers an alternative approach for identifying members' decision rules. The SJA technique can be less demanding on the group but somewhat more difficult for the worker. The SJA method is used with increasing frequency in problems of group judgment and choice (Brehmer & Joyce, 1988; Cooksey, 1996).

To use SJA, a number of alternatives (often called *cases*) are presented to a group. The cases depict different levels of performance on the multiple criteria (often called *cues*) at issue. For example, one candidate might have 10 years of supervisory and clinical experience with low management skills and low interest in innovation. Another candidate might have 20 years of clinical experience, 3 years of supervisory experience, a moderate level of management skills, and high interest in innovation. Group members would be asked to independently express their overall satisfaction with each candidate by using a single judgment scale, such as a rating that ranges from 0 = not satisfactory to 10 = highly satisfactory. Typically, 20 to 30 cases might be evaluated in this way.

With a statistical technique called *multiple regression,* a worker using SJA can compute the weights and function forms that the group members appear to be using to make their judgments about the cases under review. One software package commonly used for this purpose is called POLICY PC (Executive Decision Services, Albany, NY). Sometimes a worker may decide to use both MAU and SJA to allow a group to compare and contrast results as a way to better inform their discussion. There is some evidence that the use of both MAU and SJA in group settings can significantly improve the quality of group judgment (Reagan-Cirinicione, 1994).

USES.   The MAU and SJA methods are used primarily as decision-making techniques for choosing among distinct alternatives or for ranking numerous cases by priority. These approaches are not used for generating ideas. Both MAU and SJA have been used in a variety of settings, such as business, industry, urban planning, health, and mental health organizations (Cooksey, 1996; Kleindorfer, Kunreuther, & Schoemaker, 1993; Winterfeldt & Edwards, 1986). In the future, it is likely that an increasing number of large human service organizations, particularly at the state and national level, will use computer-based group support systems, sometimes called *electronic brainstorming* or *electronic group decision support systems* to enhance group creativity as well as group decision making. For more information about electronic brainstorming and computer-assisted group decision support systems see Jessup and Valacich (1993).

An SJA approach appears to be better than other group methods in achieving consensus and in enhancing commitment and support for decisions made by the group (Rohrbaugh, 1979, 1981; Reagan-Cirinicione, 1994), which is particularly important in groups that face difficult choices between alternatives. By providing for a thorough discussion of each individual's decision rules instead of a more traditional discussion of alternative choices, the group achieves consensus about how information will be used to make a decision. This type of discussion also helps eliminate the polarization that often takes place when members try to defend their choices of alternative solutions.

Once the group decides on a decision rule, all alternatives are rated according to that rule. Because members have had a chance to influence the decision rule, the choice that is made by the group reflects the input of all members and, therefore, is likely to have the cooperation and commitment of all members when it is implemented.

Effectiveness

The SJA approach is the most rational and technical method discussed in this chapter for leading task groups. It attempts to order and systematize information by assigning each piece of information a weight and a functional relationship to the overall decision. Empirical evidence about this approach (Edwards, 1977; Harmon & Rohrbaugh, 1990; Huber, 1980; Rohrbaugh, 1979, 1981) suggests that it can be helpful as an analytical tool in making decisions based on the information available in a problematic situation. Rohrbaugh (1979, 1981) also found that SJA is more effective than both interacting group methods and NGT in developing group consensus and commitment to a decision, and research by Toseland, Rivas, and Chapman (1984) suggests that SJA is better than NGT or problem solving in producing consistent, high-quality decisions. Still, inspirational leadership is essential for the effective use of SJA and other computer-assisted group decision support systems (Sosik, Avolio, & Kahai, 1998).

The primary drawback to SJA is that it is a complicated method limited to making decisions between clear, established alternatives. When decisions between clearly delineated alternatives are crucial and consensus is important, SJA should be considered the method of choice for problem-solving groups. However, SJA should be used only by a trained worker who has both conceptual and practical experience in developing decision rules. In addition, SJA is not useful for generating ideas or alternative solutions but can be used after alternatives have been developed by other methods (Rohrbaugh, 1984).

Quality Circles and Quality Improvement Teams

Although quality circles (QCs) and quality improvement teams (QITs) are associated with business and industry, they are now used widely in social service mental health and health organizations (Al-Assaf & Schmele, 1997; Gummer & McCallion, 1995; Schmidt & Finnigan, 1993; Sluyter & Mukherjee, 1993). Quality circles are small groups of line employees from the same department who get together voluntarily, elect a leader, and identify and solve problems they have in completing their work assignments. In the United States, the idea behind QCs is to encourage line workers to get together and use both their brains and their hands to produce a quality product (Robson, 1988). Management intent, however, was not only to improve quality but also to prevent workers from becoming alienated from the process and place of their work.

The use of QITs is a newer concept that has evolved from total quality management (TQM). In contrast to QCs, QITs frequently consist of employees from different organizational levels and a variety of departments or functions within the organization. Members are often selected by management, and membership on the team is required. Also, the project the team works on is often selected, and almost always approved, by management (Berry, 1991).

There are frequent misconceptions about the origins of quality circles and their original purposes. Although they are often associated with Japanese business, the U.S. quality control expert W. E. Deming taught statistical quality control techniques and the value of cooperation to workers during World War II (Walton, 1990). The concept was not received well in the United States. However, after World War II, Japanese business became increasingly interested in statistical quality control and found Deming's ideas appealing. Later, when his ideas were reintroduced in the United States during the 1970s, less emphasis was placed on statistical quality control and more emphasis was placed on the socioemotional and participatory aspects of QCs (Cole & Tachiki, 1983; Seely & Sween, 1983). Today, however, QCs and QITs are encouraged to rely on data from statistical quality control procedures (Kinlaw, 1992; Shuster, 1990).

Procedures

An organization generally has a coordinator for all QC activities. This individual's role is to ensure that (1) training is provided, (2) there is coverage when facilitators are sick or take personal leave, and (3) each circle has a way of communicating suggestions about problem solving to top-level management.

Each QC consists of six to eight employees who meet for about one hour each week to identify and solve problems facing their department or work group. A facilitator is selected by the membership. Often this individual is a mid-level manager who serves as the link between the QC and upper management. To ensure that QCs run smoothly and effectively, facilitators should be trained in group dynamics and leadership skills. During meetings, the facilitator uses group dynamics, problem solving, brainstorming, and other procedures to facilitate an in-depth discussion and analysis of the topic or issue being addressed by the group.

There are few specific procedures for the operation of QCs. Rather, QCs operate on the basis of core principles, including

- Commitment from top-level management to the process
- A commitment to providing training for staff in QC, problem-solving, and statistical control procedures
- Voluntary membership in QC groups
- A focus on problems identified by workers rather than by management
- The selection of leadership and the ownership of the QC process by line staff
- A focus on data-based problem solving
- A focus on solving problems in ways that benefit both line workers and management

According to Kinlaw (1992), QITs use the following steps for quality improvement:

1. Understanding the opportunity or problem
2. Defining the specific target for improvement
3. Designing strategies to reach the target
4. Designing data-acquiring strategies
5. Designing a process to use the data
6. Determining how the project will be managed

Quality circles are often used for idea generation and for improving the work environment, but QITs emphasize systematic, data-based, problem-solving strategies for improving the quality of services delivered by an organization.

Uses

The primary purpose of QCs and QITs is to improve the quality of the service or product delivered to consumers. Thus, QCs and QITs are two ways for management and line staff to demonstrate their commitment to delivering health and social services in the most effective manner. For example, in a multiservice agency serving developmentally disabled adults, staff members may become increasingly aware that clients often have multiple service providers and that problems arise in the coordination of service plans. In QIT meetings, staff would decide to review a selected number of cases to obtain data about the number of providers and how services are currently coordinated. The QIT group would use these data as the basis for recommendations about the design of a new case management system.

In addition, QCs and QITs have several other benefits. They encourage workers to solve problems that interfere with job satisfaction and their performance, and they help workers gain a greater sense of control and autonomy. In turn, workers may have more sense of responsibility and commitment to their work.

Effectiveness

Many writers have claimed that QCs improve productivity, quality, and employee attitudes. For example, Goldstein (1985) suggests that in addition to quality improvements, QCs have been reported to have

> *increased productivity, raised level of morale, increased employee motivation, improved communication, changed the emphasis from fire fighting to prevention, enhanced the commitment to job and organization, reduced reliance on authority to get things done, reduced costs, reduced delivery times, developed people, trained leaders and supervisors, introduced an orientation toward learning, enhanced the coordination of work, and reduced vertical and horizontal demarcations over ownership of problems. (p. 514)*

Despite these assertions, findings about the effectiveness of QCs and QITs are equivocal. Although some studies have found a strong correlation between participatory management systems and the quality and quantity of the work produced, other studies have found little correlation (Gummer, 1988; Gummer & McCallion, 1995). In reviews of studies of QC performance, Adam (1991) and Barrick and Alexander (1987) found that most studies revealed that quality circle programs resulted in improved quality and efficiency of services and the reduction of production costs and unpleasant working conditions. However, with some noticeable exceptions (Marks, Mirvis, Hackett, & Grady, 1986), QCs were not effective in improving employee's attitudes or in reducing staff turnover, absenteeism, or tardiness. Overall, therefore, Adam (1991) tentatively concluded that QCs are effective in improving services but are not effective in improving worker attitudes and morale.

Despite positive findings about the improved efficiency of services, Lawler and Mohrman (1985) report that managers' initial enthusiasm for quality circles is often dampened when they try to document savings from early quality circle ideas. To avoid QCs and QITs becoming fads that end after initial enthusiasm wanes, Lawler and Mohrman (1985) suggest the approaches might best be viewed as part of a larger organizational effort to move toward a more participatory management system.

Also, for QCs and QITs to have a lasting effect on an organization, there must be a commitment to them from all levels of management and they must be compatible with the organization's work culture (Gummer & McCallion, 1995). For example, in a study of the use of QCs in state government, Denhardt, Pyle, and Bluedorn (1987) concluded that, in many departments, employees had never been asked to consider how their work processes might be improved. Smith and Doeing (1985) point out that, in contrast to U.S. managers, Japanese managers often take a longer-term perspective on the development of employees. Thus, making a meaningful shift to participatory management styles that include QCs or QITs is a slow process that takes long-term and concerted commitment at all levels of an organization.

LARGE ORGANIZATIONAL GROUPS

Parliamentary Procedure

Parliamentary procedure is a framework for guiding decision making and problem solving in large task groups. It has been developed over time in many different settings to meet the needs of a variety of task groups. Although there are some commonly accepted rules, there is no single body of laws that is universally accepted as parliamentary procedure.

Parliamentary procedure originated in 1321 in the English Parliament as a set of rules called *modus tenedia Parlia-mentarium* (Gray, 1964). From these roots, Thomas Jefferson developed a *Manual of Parliamentary Practice* in 1801 for use in Congress, and in 1845, Luther Cushing formulated a manual for use in lay, as well as legislative, assemblies (Robert, 1970). *Robert's Rules of Order* was initially published in 1876 and has had many subsequent revisions and printings. Today, *Robert's Rules of Order* is the set of parliamentary procedures most frequently followed by task groups.

Procedures

In parliamentary meetings, the activity of the group is determined by motions brought by group members. Motions fall into one of four classes:

1. *Privileged motions* deal with the agenda of the group meeting as a whole. They do not have a relationship with the business before the group and include motions such as adjournment and recess.
2. *Incidental motions* are concerned with procedural questions relating to issues *on the floor*. Some examples are a *point of order* and a *point of information*.

3. *Subsidiary motions* assist in the handling and disposal of motions on the floor. Motions to table, postpone, or amend are subsidiary motions.

4. *Main motions* introduce the central, substantive issues for group consideration. There can be no pending motions when a main motion is proposed. Examples of main motions are reconsideration of an issue previously disposed of and resuming consideration of a tabled motion.

All motions made from the floor follow procedures governing the introduction of that type of motion. It is the chairperson's job to ensure that the rules and procedures are followed. Although the chairperson is supposed to remain neutral during group deliberations, the person can influence the group's work in a variety of ways. Group members must be recognized by the chair before they can make a motion. The chairperson rules on questions of procedure that arise during a meeting and also organizes the meeting by ordering the agenda items and specifying the amount of time available to discuss each item.

Although the rules of parliamentary procedure are not universally standardized, that is, groups often modify a set of procedures such as *Robert's Rules of Order,* there is a method of prioritizing motions that is adhered to by most groups conducting parliamentary meetings. Table 12.1 shows the priority that each motion takes during a meeting. Although main motions contain the essential business of the parliamentary meeting, they receive the lowest priority because privileged motions govern how all agenda items are considered, and incidental and subsidiary motions are always made in reference to a main motion. Therefore, these motions are given a higher priority than that for main motions. For further information about parliamentary meetings, see *Robert's Rules of Order* (Robert, 1970).

Uses

Parliamentary procedure is often used in large groups because it provides a well-defined structure to guide group process. The rules of parliamentary procedure help ensure a high level of order and efficiency in task group meetings when many agenda items are discussed. Order and efficiency are achieved through rules that demand consideration of one issue at a time. The rules prescribe the way in which issues are brought before the group, processed by the group, and disposed of by the group. In a meeting of a delegate council composed of representatives from many social service agencies, for example, parliamentary procedure can be used to lend order to how representatives interact. Thus, with many members representing the diverse interests of several agencies, meetings are run in a formal manner, and members are generally guaranteed a structured means by which they can bring their interests, motions, and agenda items to the large group.

Parliamentary procedure is especially useful for considering well-developed agenda items that need some discussion and debate and a relatively speedy decision by an entire task group (Gulley, 1968). Parliamentary procedure is of limited value, however, when a problem or issue facing the group has not been

TABLE 12.1 ■ *Procedures for Acting on Motions during a Parliamentary Meeting*

Type of Motion	Priority of the Motion	Can the Speaker Be Interrupted?	Does the Motion Need a Second?	Is the Motion Debatable?	Can the Motion Be Amended?	Vote Needed to Adopt the Motion
Privileged Motions						
Set the time of adjournment	1	N	Y	N	Y	Majority
Call for adjournment	2	N	Y	N	N	Majority
Call for recess	3	N	Y	N	Y	Majority
Question of privilege	4	Y	N	N	N	Chair's decision
Call for prescheduled items of business	5	Y	N	N	N	No vote
Incidental Motions						
Point of order	6	Y	N	N	N	Chair's decision
Request for information	6	Y	N	N	N	No vote
Call for a revote	6	N	N	N	N	No vote
Appeal the chair's decision	6	Y	Y	N	N	Majority
Object to consideration of a motion	6	Y	N	N	N	2/3
Call to suspend the rules	6	N	Y	N	N	2/3
Request to withdraw a motion	6	Y	Y	N	N	Majority

TABLE 12.1 ■ *Continued*

Type of Motion	Priority of the Motion	Can the Speaker Be Interrupted?	Does the Motion Need a Second?	Is the Motion Debatable?	Can the Motion Be Amended?	Vote Needed to Adopt the Motion
Subsidiary Motions						
Table a motion	7	N	Y	N	N	Majority
Call for immediate vote	8	N	Y	N	N	2/3
Limit/extend debate	9	N	Y	N	N	2/3
Postpone the motion	10	N	Y	Y	Y	Majority
Refer the motion to a subcommittee	11	N	Y	Y	Y	Majority
Amend the motion	12	N	Y	Y	Y	Majority
Postpone the motion indefinitely	13	N	Y	Y	N	Majority
Main Motions						
General main motion	14	N	Y	Y	Y	Majority
Reconsider a motion already voted on	14	Y	Y	Y	Y	2/3
Rescind a motion under consideration	14	N	Y	Y	Y	2/3
Resume consideration of a tabled motion	14	N	Y	N	N	Majority
Set a special order of business	14	N	Y	Y	Y	2/3

clearly defined, when sufficient data have not been gathered about the problem, or when alternative solutions have not been explored and developed for consideration during decision making. Thus, these procedures should not be used as a substitute for problem solving done by subcommittees of the larger task group.

Effectiveness

The long history of using parliamentary procedure in important decision-making bodies throughout the Western world testifies to its usefulness in providing a structure for task group meetings. By limiting and focusing the deliberations of a task group to one solution at a time, discussion and debate are facilitated, and motions are dealt with expeditiously. Clearly specified rules lead to an orderly and systematic consideration of each agenda item. Rules that remain consistent throughout the life of a group assure members that there is an established order that they can rely on for fair and equitable treatment when sensitive or controversial issues are presented.

Parliamentary procedure also protects the rights of the minority. For example, it takes only two members to introduce a main motion, one to state the motion and another to second the motion. Some motions can be made by a single member. Every group member is given an equal opportunity to participate. Majority rights are also protected because a quorum is needed to conduct a meeting, and majority rule is relied on for all decisions.

Parliamentary meetings have several disadvantages. Meetings are subject to manipulation by members who are familiar with parliamentary procedures. Members who are less familiar with the procedures may be reluctant to speak or be unsure of when or how to raise an objection to a motion. Another limitation is that private deals may be made outside a meeting to gain a member's support for an agenda item in a forthcoming meeting. Private deals circumvent the intent of parliamentary procedure, which is based on openly debating the merits of a proposal. Private deals also tend to enforce the will of powerful members who offer attractive incentives to members who support their positions on particular agenda items.

Parliamentary meetings have other limitations. The procedure encourages debate, which can lead to polarization of members' opinions. Also, members often try to defend their positions rather than understand the logic behind opposing viewpoints. Perhaps the most important limitation of parliamentary procedure is that it is not well suited for problem solving, especially when the problem is complex, muddled, or not fully understood. A large task group using parliamentary procedure does not usually attain the level of interaction, the depth of communication, or the flexibility necessary to explore alternative solutions that may be necessary to resolve difficult problems. Large task groups should conduct most problem-solving efforts in subcommittees that report back to the larger group. The larger group can then debate the merits of a proposed solution and reach a decision based on majority rule.

Phillips' 66

Phillips' 66, or *buzz group,* as the method is often called, was developed to facilitate discussion in large groups (Phillips, 1948). Originally, Phillips' 66 referred to a technique of dividing a large group or audience into groups of six and having each group spend six minutes formulating one question for the speaker. The method has been expanded to include many different ways to facilitate communication in large groups. For example, Maier and Zerfoss (1952) suggest using multiple role-playing strategies for training staff in large groups. Members of the larger group are asked to form smaller groups and role-play the same or similar situations. Each group designates a recorder, who reports a summary of group members' experiences when the large group reconvenes.

Other variations have also been developed. Bradford and Corey (1951) have suggested organizing audience listening teams in which each team is asked to listen to, discuss, and report back to the larger group about an aspect of the speaker's presentation. They have also suggested selecting individuals from the audience to serve on an *audience representational panel* to react to the speaker. All these techniques are modifications and expansions of the basic principles of Phillips' 66.

Procedures

Phillips' 66 should be used only after clear instructions are given to members about what they will be doing during the procedure, especially because once the large group has broken down into smaller groups, the sudden change from the structure and control of a large group meeting can cause confusion. If the groups are not clear about their direction, they may flounder or begin to work on something other than what was assigned by the leader.

To reduce the chances for confusion, the worker should ensure that each group is clear about the problem or task it is facing. Problem statements, tasks, and goals should be specific. When they are broad and nonspecific, the small groups have to spend time refining them, which may lead to work that is quite different from what the worker had intended. Members should also be clear about their assignments. They should understand what subgroup they belong to, what the group is supposed to do, what should be contained in the recorder's report, how much time they have, and where and when the subgroup is supposed to meet.

The size of the subgroups and the amount of time each subgroup spends together depend on the situation. The original design for Phillips' 66, six-member groups meeting for six minutes, may be appropriate in some situations but not in others. Generally, at least 20 to 30 minutes are required for a large group to break down into smaller groups and accomplish any meaningful work. Subgroups should be separated so members can hear each other and conduct their work. However, in a large meeting room, it is not necessary to ask members to talk quietly. The noise and activity of other groups can be contagious and thus spur all groups to work harder (Maier, 1963).

In very large meetings, having each subgroup report back to the larger group may be monotonous and time-consuming. Alternatives include limiting the reporting time to a few minutes for each subgroup, having each subgroup report on a portion of the discussion, and having each subgroup prepare a brief written report that can be shared after the meeting.

Phillips' 66 can be combined with a procedure known as *idea writing* (Moore, 1994). When participants break into small groups, each member can be given a sheet of paper with a triggering question or item to which the member should respond in writing. After approximately five minutes, members place their sheets in the center of the group. Each member then selects another member's sheet and responds in writing for approximately five to ten minutes to the initial idea prepared by the first member. This process is repeated until all members have prepared written responses on every idea sheet. Members may react by writing what they like and dislike about the previous ideas and reactions and can offer suggestions for improvement. After this process is completed, members find their original sheets and read their ideas and other members' reactions to it. The members of the small group then discuss the ideas that emerge from the written interaction, and the group facilitator summarizes the discussion on a flip chart. When the larger group reconvenes, the small-group facilitator can use information on the flip chart to present a summary of the small group's ideas.

Uses

Although most problem-solving activities take place in small task groups, occasionally there is a need for large groups, such as members of a social agency or a delegate assembly, to engage in problem-solving discussions. Parliamentary procedure, in which the chair must recognize individual speakers from the floor, is not designed for large problem-solving discussions. It is designed for debating the merits of proposals and voting on alternatives that are already well developed. Phillips' 66 can be used as an alternative method for problem solving in large task groups. For example, during an in-service training program covering management skills, the group trainer asks the large group to divide into smaller groups and answer the question "What makes a good manager?" Members of the small groups work to develop a short list of answers to the question within a limited period of time. When the large group reconvenes, each group reports its answers, and the material is used by the trainer in the didactic presentation and in group discussion following the presentation.

Although Maier (1963) suggests that a skillful, self-confident worker can conduct large problem-solving discussions by using techniques such as summarizing and posting alternatives, the obstacles to large-group interaction tend to make such discussions difficult. For example, it can be difficult to hold the attention of all members when individual members are speaking. It is also difficult to encourage shy members to express themselves, particularly if they have minority opinions.

Using Phillips' 66, the worker can involve all members in a group discussion. The small size of individual buzz groups makes it easier for shy members to express themselves. Also, members can choose to participate in buzz groups that are focused on topics of particular interest to them. Reporting ideas generated by individual buzz groups back to the larger assembly ensures that input from all members is considered in the problem-solving process. Overall, Phillips' 66 is a useful method that overcomes the limitations of parliamentary procedure when large groups are called on to solve problems.

Effectiveness

Phillips' 66 is a practical, commonsense procedure for facilitating discussion and problem solving in large groups. Its effective use has been reported in a variety of sources (Gulley, 1968; Maier, 1963; Stattler & Miller, 1968). When applied correctly, Phillips' 66 can be used in a variety of situations. However, poor planning, confused or nonspecific instructions, or a muddled explanation of the goals of the procedure can turn a large task group meeting into disorganization and chaos.

METHODS FOR WORKING WITH COMMUNITY GROUPS

Work with community groups such as social action groups, coalitions, and delegate councils involves many of the methods and skills described throughout this text. For example, community groups frequently use brainstorming and other problem-solving methods to generate ideas and address issues during meetings. Work with community groups is distinguished from other forms of group work practice by special emphasis on the following: (1) mobilizing individuals to engage in collective action, (2) building the capacity of the group and its members to effect community change, and (3) planning and organizing social action strategies. The remainder of this chapter focuses on these three aspects of practice with community groups.

Mobilization Strategies

Whether working with social action groups, coalitions, or delegate councils, a primary task of the worker is to mobilize individual members to action. The worker is a catalyst to stimulate interest in community problems and motivate members to work together. When engaging in mobilization efforts, the worker identifies and works with several constituencies, including the individuals who are experiencing the problem, community leaders, informal and formal community groups and organizations, and larger social institutions. For example, to mobilize a coalition to prevent domestic violence, a worker meets with victims of domestic violence, women's groups, the staff of domestic violence shelters, dispute resolution centers, police departments, family courts, and departments of social services, as well as with ministers, priests, rabbis, and local politicians.

An important initial step in any mobilization effort is to become familiar with the perceptions of community members about the issues the community group will attempt to address. It is often helpful to begin by meeting with civic and religious leaders and with community activists. These individuals can provide a helpful overview of the community's past responses to the issue and to similar issues. However, it is also essential to meet with as many community residents as possible.

Kahn (1991) notes that person-to-person contact with community residents helps build community groups and organizations in which each member feels valued. When meeting with community residents, the worker should avoid telling residents why they should be concerned about a particular issue or problem. A more effective strategy is to ask them to describe their problems and concerns and validate and affirm the issues they raise by mentioning how their views are consistent with views of other community residents. In this way, community residents begin to get a sense that it is their issues, not the worker's issues, that will be addressed through collective action.

As the worker becomes familiar with the community, the worker should identify individuals, community groups, and organizations that might be willing to help with mobilization efforts. To determine the extent to which individuals, groups, and organizations can help, the worker should evaluate their positions within the power structure of the community. The worker should then consider how forming a partnership with particular individuals and groups may help or hinder mobilization efforts. Often, the worker decides to form partnerships with a wide range of individuals, community leaders, and organizations. However, the worker should also be careful about involving individuals or organizations who do not share compatible goals or who have such a negative reputation in the community that they might damage the group's effort.

Mobilization involves consciousness raising. Working with individual citizens, community leaders, and formal and informal organizations, the worker attempts to bring a single issue or a group of related issues to greater public awareness. Consciousness raising may be done several ways, including

- Meeting with community residents
- Making presentations to civic and religious organizations
- Testifying at public hearings
- Publicizing the issue through local newspapers and radio and television stations
- Demonstrating, picketing, and boycotting

The goal of consciousness-raising efforts is to encourage community members to gain a renewed sense of individual and community pride and to join forces to improve their community.

Mobilization to action involves helping members understand the power of collective action against injustices and inequities. Helping individuals vent their frustration and anger "through public declarations, and by acting against those causing the problem" (Rubin & Rubin, 1992, p. 69) can sometimes resolve individual problems. However, individual actions are easily ignored, dismissed, or punished by persons in power. Therefore, the goal of the worker should be to help individuals understand the value of pooling their efforts so they can exert sufficient influence to effect change.

One way to accomplish this goal is to highlight the incentives for collective action. Individuals become actively involved in a community group if they think they have something to gain, if they think they can contribute, and if they believe in the goals of the group. According to Rubin and Rubin (1992), the worker can highlight a variety of incentives such as "material incentives like improved income or better housing, solidarity incentives such as the enjoyment of belonging to the group, and expressive incentives including the excitement and satisfaction of articulating opinions and values" (p. 211).

Mobilization to action also involves *bootstrapping,* that is, engaging in action projects that build interest and commitment in a community (Rubin & Rubin, 1992). A good way to begin bootstrapping is to identify a project or activity that is relatively easy and leads to an immediate success. For example, a social action group, a coalition, or even a delegate council might sponsor a community forum to which they invite local politicians and the news media. Similarly, a "community education day" might be planned at a shopping mall, a "teach-in" might be scheduled at a school, or a rally might be organized in a public square. Later, when members have experienced the initial successful completion of a project, they can be encouraged to tackle larger projects, such as a community survey or an extensive lobbying effort, that require more effort and resources.

Capacity-Building Strategies

Capacity building means helping community groups develop the ability and the resources to successfully tackle one issue or a set of issues. The worker plays the role of coordinator in helping members gather data and build resources. A first step in capacity building is to help group members become as knowledgeable as possible about the issues they are addressing. Workers should facilitate exchanges of information among members about the issues facing the group and about ways to accomplish particular objectives.

In many instances, the worker and the members will not have enough information about a problem. In these situations, the worker should encourage the group to gather data before proceeding. Original data can be gathered through community surveys or focused interviews with key informants. The worker might also help members gain access to public records and reports. For example, in helping to organize a neighborhood association, (1) city building department files could be used to gather data on building-code violations, (2) police department records could be used to collect data on the number and type of crimes in a particular neighborhood, (3) the county clerk's office could be used to gather data on property ownership, and (4) the department of public welfare or the local community development agency could be used to obtain estimates of poverty rates.

A second step in capacity building involves helping the group become familiar with the structures within a community that can aid change efforts. It is important to identify individuals with the power to bring about needed changes within a community and determine to whom these individuals report. The worker also can help the group identify and contact religious and civic organizations that may be interested in joining forces to work on a particular issue, analyze the strengths and weaknesses of opponents to change, or decide what tactics might be used to change opponents' minds. For example, would a landlord be most vulnerable to a rent strike, to moral pressure from a church group, or to having housing code violations strictly enforced?

A third step is to help the group learn how to influence local government. The worker can help group members identify policy makers and bureaucrats who might support group efforts to have existing laws enforced or introduce new legislation to address a particular issue. The worker can help the group develop a clear position on the issues with as much supporting documentation as available. To the extent possible, the group might form a partnership with legislators and bureaucrats so they can collaborate on the change effort. Rubin and Rubin (1992) note that legislators are receptive to ideas that make them look active, creative, and effective. The worker can help legislators and bureaucrats place the issue on the agenda by testifying at public hearings and by using lobbying efforts.

A fourth step in capacity building is to help the group make an inventory of its existing resources and identify resources needed to accomplish particular goals. For example, the group may find it needs legal advice. Can a lawyer be identified who would be willing to work with the group? Similarly, the group may want to publish a fact sheet or a brochure for a lobbying effort. Can a business or community organization that would be willing to help the group design or print the brochure be identified? An important role of the worker is to help the group locate resources to accomplish its objectives.

Social Action Strategies

A variety of social action strategies can be used to help community groups accomplish their objectives during the middle stage. The techniques include political action strategies, legal strategies, and direct action strategies (Rubin & Rubin, 1992). Many forms of political activity are available to community groups, such as

- Organizing voter registration drives
- Nominating and working on the campaigns of public officials

- Developing and supporting referendums, propositions, and other grass-roots efforts to bypass legislators and get proposals directly on the ballot
- Lobbying and advocating positions
- Participating in public hearings
- Monitoring compliance with laws by bureaucratic and regulatory agencies

Although political action strategies are designed to get persons in power to pay attention to the goals of a community group, legal action strategies are designed to force politicians and bureaucrats to take action on issues supported by a community group or a coalition of community groups. Political action strategies can have sweeping and binding effects, but they are often expensive and time-consuming. Sometimes, the threat of legal action by a single counsel on retainer can create some action. More often, however, legal action requires a professional staff, a large budget, and a great deal of patience. Although coalitions of community groups and community groups affiliated with national organizations can use legal strategies effectively, political action strategies and direct action strategies are often preferred.

Direct action strategies include rallies, demonstrations, marches, picketing, sit-ins, vigils, blockades, boycotts, slowdowns, strikes, and many other forms of nonviolent and violent protest. Direct action strategies allow members to ventilate frustration and anger, but they can be counterproductive. Negative publicity, fines, physical injury, and time lost at work are just a few of the possible consequences. Thus, direct action strategies should not be undertaken without careful thought and preparation, and then only if it is clear that safer political and legal strategies are unlikely to achieve the desired objective. It is also important to keep in mind that the threat of direct action is often as terrifying as the action itself. Therefore, if a community group is serious about engaging in a direct action strategy, it is often wise to publicize the group's intent and the specific steps that an opponent can take to avoid the action.

In his text, *Rules For Radicals,* Alinsky (1971) developed a number of pragmatic rules for choosing among different action strategies. For example, he suggested picking a direct action strategy that enjoys wide support among members. He also suggested picking a strategy that emphasizes the weaknesses of the opponent. Thus, a rally that gets widespread news coverage might be particularly effective against an opponent concerned about negative publicity, but an economic boycott might be more effective against a corporation under pressure from shareholders to increase profits.

When selecting a social action strategy, there is a generally accepted protocol that social workers and other professionals should adhere to when carrying out their work with community groups. Less intrusive and more cooperative strategies should be tried before disruptive or conflict-oriented strategies are engaged. It has been suggested that when a social action strategy is considered, collaboration or negotiation should be employed before conflict (Pincus & Minahan, 1973). Collaboration means that in attempting to effect some change in a target system, the worker tries to convince the target system that change is in the best interests of all involved. In negotiation, the worker and the target system both give and receive something in the process of change. The process of bargaining involves a good faith quid pro quo arrangement and assumes that each party will make some change desired by the other.

Should collaboration and negotiation fail to achieve a desired change, the group may be forced to engage in conflict strategies. In any case, the worker should always help group members use each of the three strategies in a constructive and an ethical fashion. The worker should carefully guard against a group choosing conflict as an initial strategy because of the perception that the strategy will result in change more quickly and easily because members may be used to solving problems through conflict or because members wish to carry out personal retribution against a target system.

SUMMARY

A variety of methods have been developed in industry, business administration, and human service organizations to help task groups accomplish their goals during the middle stage. This chapter examines some of the most widely used methods: (1) brainstorming, (2) reverse brainstorming, (3) trigger groups, (4) synectics, (5) focus groups, (6) the nominal group technique, (7) social judgment analysis, (8) quality circles, and (9) quality improvement teams. The chapter also includes descriptions of methods such as parliamentary procedure and Phillips' 66 that can be used to lead large task groups.

The second section of the chapter describes specialized methods for helping community groups accomplish their objectives during the middle stage. This section focuses on three methods for helping community groups achieve their objectives: (1) mobilizing individuals to engage in collective action, (2) building the capacity of the group and its members to effect community change, and (3) social action strategies.

LEARNING ASSIGNMENTS

1. Form a small group. Using the brainstorming procedures described in this chapter, come up with as many creative ways as possible to learn group leadership skills.
2. You have been asked by the director of Catholic Charities in your area to help the Committee on Children and Youth plan a series of focus groups in several parishes in the diocese. The focus groups are designed to gain a better understanding of parishioners' views of the most pressing problems and needs of

teenagers in the diocese. Develop an agenda and a specific series of questions that might be used during focus group meetings. What suggestions would you make to the committee to help ensure that appropriate participants are recruited? How would you help the committee ensure that there was effective moderation during meetings?

3. Locate and interview a manager of a for-profit, private sector organization. For example, select a production or service industry, a large corporation, or a small business. How does the organization involve its employees in organizational decision making? Are there group formats for employees to contribute to the management of the company? To what extent are managers, supervisors, or line employees expected to be group leaders?

4. A family shelter for victims of domestic violence has recently received a large grant to be used to expand its services. The board of directors has suggested three discrete ways that the money could be used: (1) initiate a group services program for men who abuse their wives, (2) expand the shelter's services, or (3) begin a new program to provide treatment to children who live in abusive homes. Form a small group. Use the nominal group technique or the social judgment analysis procedure described in this chapter to decide on one alternative for how the money should be spent.

5. Seek permission to attend a board meeting or the meeting of some other group that uses parliamentary procedure. How knowledgeable did the chairperson appear to be about the rules of parliamentary procedure? To what extent were parliamentary procedures used? Do you think that a different level of adherence to the rules of parliamentary procedure would have affected the meeting? Why?

6. Identify a social action group or organization in your community. Interview a leader of the group. Ask the leader to describe how the group originally formed. How were individuals mobilized to engage in collective action? What obstacles had to be overcome? What strategies were used to build the capacity of the group and its members to effect community change? What types of social action strategies have been used by the group? What types of strategies would not be used by the group? Why?

CASE EXAMPLE

Funding sources for the AIDS Outreach Association were so impressed with Nora's research and documentation that they approved a budget allocation for hiring four people to fill newly created case management positions. Because of the importance of this new initiative, Nora wanted to have input from all constituencies within the organization. Therefore, she formed an ad hoc committee composed of supervisors, program directors, and two consumers to assist in the recruitment and selection procedures and processes.

During the first meeting of the committee, Nora discussed the development and implementation of the purpose of the group and its charge. She noted that the group would be responsible for deciding what skills would best fit the position and for rating and ranking job candidates. During this first session, the group discussed the tasks, activities, and services that case managers would be providing to consumers. The first session ended with a list of potential duties that could be assigned to the new employees.

One week later, Nora convened the group for the second time. The group members tried to design a procedure for screening candidates but were unable to focus on what criteria would guide the selection process. There were lots of ideas, but the group could not seem to keep track of them. Nora suggested that the group take a short break. When group members returned, Nora placed a flip chart at the head of the table. She suggested that members use brainstorming techniques to generate ideas about the skills and attributes needed for the job. She explained that in brainstorming, members should develop as many ideas as possible without evaluating the importance of the ideas. In other words, members were asked to come up with as many ideas as possible and not to critique any ideas until the idea-generation phase of the process was complete. As each member contributed an idea it was recorded on the flip chart. At the end of the brainstorming session, Nora took all the criteria that had been listed and rearranged them into a comprehensive list. She was amazed at the number of criteria the group had generated.

Armed with many creative ideas for how to rate candidates, the group now faced the task of reducing the list to the most important set of criteria. Nora suggested that the group use elements of the nominal group technique (NGT) in carrying out this activity. She guided the group members in a review of the list of criteria, and she asked members to write their top choices on a piece of paper, ranking their choices from highest to lowest. During this process members were asked to refrain from discussing their choices with each other. Next, Nora asked members to present their highest-ranked ideas in round robin fashion, going around the group until all members had contributed their choices for the five highest criteria. Nora used this list to sort criteria into categories. She then asked members to take turns discussing their choices with the rest of the group. Following the discussion, Nora asked members to vote on a consolidated list of criteria by assigning values to their top five choices. After this was done, Nora tallied up the numerical ratings and listed the top five criteria as determined by the vote of each group member. These included amount of experience working with persons with AIDS, knowledge about AIDS, knowledge of the service system, interpersonal skills, and potential for developing new programs. The group agreed that these would be the criteria that they would use to screen and rank job applicants. They ended the group meeting by developing a position description using the criteria and directed Nora to advertise the position in two local newspapers.

Some weeks later, Nora convened the group to discuss their next task. Since the last meeting, the positions had been advertised and a number of applications had been sent to the organization. The group's next task was to screen the candidates and to rate them according to the criteria the group had established.

At first, members rushed into the task of discussing individual candidates without establishing ground rules for how to proceed. Nora suggested that the group use a more organized approach to the process, namely, multiattribute utility (MAU) analysis. This required the group to review and specify the criteria they had previously decided on to rank candidates, to specify minimum and optimum levels of qualifications for the job, and to systematically rate candidates according to the decision criteria. Although some members were skeptical in the beginning of this procedure, they soon experienced satisfaction to see that by using this form of group analysis they were able to more systematically review each job candidate. At the close of this procedure, members were able to rank the top candidates for the open positions. To ensure that consensus about the ranking of the top candidates was achieved, a final round of discussion followed the group's ranking process. The committee ended its work by presenting the chief executive officer of the AIDS Outreach Association with a ranked list of candidates to be interviewed for the new positions.

part *V*

The Ending Stage

chapter *13*

Evaluation

Evaluation is the process of obtaining information about the effects of a single intervention or the effect of the total group experience. Workers can use informal or formal measures to obtain such information. In conducting an informal evaluation, a worker might ask the members of a group to evaluate how the group is progressing. To complete a formal evaluation, a worker might collect information systematically using preplanned measurement devices before, during, or after the group has met. In either case, the worker uses the information to evaluate the group. This chapter explores many ways to obtain information about a group and guides the worker in deciding what evaluation methods will be most useful in various situations.

THE PRACTITIONER'S DILEMMA

Increasingly in social work and allied disciplines, there has been a push toward accountability and empirically validated practice. Workers have been urged to become practitioner-researchers to improve their work as they practice (Thomas, 1990). The push for evaluating practice has occurred even though group workers sometimes fail to keep adequate records, let alone perform systematic evaluations of their practice.

The dilemma for many practicing group workers is that other demands of practice seem to be more pressing than evaluations, which require valuable time and energy. Further, many practitioners find it difficult to understand the logic of evaluation methods or their day-to-day usefulness. It has been proposed that practitioners (1) leave research to researchers, (2) become consumers of research, and (3) concentrate on developing experience and expertise as group leaders (Trotzer, 1977). However, Trotzer and most others urge group workers to evaluate their own practice whenever possible.

The push toward accountability and empirically validated group work practice has made a difference. In a review of the literature in 1986, Feldman (1986) found that compared with a review completed 20 years before (Silverman, 1966), the number of research studies had more than doubled. However, Feldman noted that the number of research studies was still small and that much needed to be done before group workers could claim that their practice is well grounded in scientific research.

WHY EVALUATE? THE GROUP WORKER'S VIEW

When considering whether to evaluate their work with a particular group, workers will need to

1. Determine their reasons for conducting an evaluation
2. Assess the ability of their agencies to provide the encouragement and resources necessary for evaluating their own practice
3. Determine the time they have available for an evaluation
4. Match their information needs and available time with an appropriate method for evaluating their practice

Reasons for Conducting Evaluations

Workers' reasons for wanting information about a group depend on how they believe they can use the information. Some of the benefits of evaluation for group workers include the following:

- Evaluations can satisfy workers' curiosity and professional concerns about the effects of specific interventions they perform while working with a group.
- Information from evaluations can help workers improve their leadership skills.
- Evaluations can demonstrate the usefulness of a specific group or a specific group work method to an agency, a funding source, or society.
- Workers can assess the progress of group members and see whether the group is accomplishing agreed-on purposes.
- Evaluations allow group members and others who may be affected to express their satisfactions and dissatisfactions with a group.
- Workers can gather knowledge that can be shared with others who are using group methods for similar purposes and in similar situations.
- Workers can systematize and make overt the covert hypothesis-generating and hypothesis-testing processes they routinely engage in as they practice.

Organizational Encouragement and Support

To evaluate their practice with a group, workers should begin by assessing the willingness of the organization for whom they work to provide the resources to conduct an evaluation. Some organizations do little or nothing to encourage evaluations and may even penalize the worker for attempting one. Agency norms, peer pressure, or administrative directions may suggest to workers that other tasks are more important than evaluating their practice. In other cases, high caseloads may inhibit workers' abilities to evaluate their practice.

Without active encouragement by an organization's administrators, workers are left to rely on their own motivations for evaluating their work with a group. Organizations can increase workers' opportunities for evaluation by including evaluation tasks as a part of workers' practice responsibilities, by providing the time for practice evaluations, and by encouraging workers to discuss evaluations during regularly scheduled staff meetings. Rather than requiring workers to fill out forms and records that they do not use and often do not see again after administrative processing, organizations can instead help by developing and implementing information systems that can be used by workers to evaluate their practice. A well-designed information and evaluation system can provide feedback for group work practitioners as well as for agency administrators.

Time Considerations

Workers should consider how much time they have available to conduct an evaluation. Most workers collect some information about the groups they lead, and this information can often be the basis for an evaluation if it is collected appropriately. Little additional time is needed for evaluation beyond the time necessary to make modifications in the original data-collection system.

In other situations, workers may want information that is not routinely collected. They should estimate the amount of time it will take them to collect, process, and analyze the additional information. They can then compare the time needed for the evaluation with the time they have available and decide whether the evaluation is feasible.

When workers have valid reasons for evaluating their practice, they may be able to persuade their organization to allow them sufficient time to conduct the evaluation, particularly when a worker is developing a new, innovative program to achieve the goals the organization has set as a priority for service delivery.

Selecting an Evaluation Method

After determining how much time is available for an evaluation, workers should consider how to match their information needs and available time to an appropriate evaluation method. This chapter reviews the major types of evaluations. Each evaluation method is discussed in terms of its strengths and weaknesses, time requirements, and flexibility.

Workers must also decide what data-collection instruments they will use in conjunction with a particular evaluation method. The major types of data-collection instruments used by group workers include the following:

- Progress notes
- Self-reports or personal interview data from workers, members, and observers
- Questionnaires
- Analysis of reports or other group products
- Review of audiotapes and videotapes of group meetings
- Observational coding schemes
- Role play or in vivo performance tests
- Reliable and valid scales

These data-collection instruments can be used with any of the major types of evaluation methods. Some measures, however, are frequently associated with one type of evaluation. For example, progress notes are often used in monitoring evaluation methods; reliable and valid scales are more frequently used in effectiveness and efficiency evaluations. As each type of evaluation method is reviewed, the methods of collecting data that are often associated with each method are described.

EVALUATION METHODS

Workers can use four broad types of evaluation methods to obtain data: evaluations for (1) planning a group, (2) monitoring a group, (3) developing a group, and (4) testing the effectiveness and efficiency of a group method. Workers can use any of the evaluation methods to obtain information about the process or the outcome of a group. Process evaluations focus on the interaction in a group; properties of a group such as cohesion, norms, roles, and communication patterns; how the group is being conducted; or other aspects of the functioning of a group. Outcome evaluations focus on the products or tasks achieved by individual members or the group as a whole.

Regardless of the type of evaluation employed or whether the evaluation focuses on processes or outcomes, workers should be able to use evaluations to receive feedback about their practice. Instead of viewing practice evaluations as useless administrative requirements, workers should see them as a way to help them become more effective, and as a way to develop new knowledge that can be shared with other group workers.

EVALUATIONS FOR PLANNING THE GROUP

Evaluations used for planning a group are seldom mentioned in the group work literature. This section discusses two important evaluation methods for planning: (1) obtaining program information, technical data, and materials for specific groups that the worker is planning to lead and (2) conducting needs assessments to determine the feasibility of organizing a proposed group.

Obtaining Program Information

The worker can often benefit from information about methods previously used in working with similar groups. Workers may be able to obtain some information from colleagues or from workers in other agencies in which similar groups have been conducted. Workers may also find it useful to

- Examine records from previous groups that focused on similar concerns
- Review relevant journals[1] or texts using computerized or manual search procedures
- Attend workshops and conferences where group workers share recent developments in the field

Library literature searches have been made much easier and much less time-consuming in recent years by the availability of online CD-ROM computerized databases. Two databases that are particularly relevant to social group workers are Social Work Abstracts Plus and PSYCLIT (psychology). Also, group workers in health settings may find MEDLINE (medicine) useful; group workers in school settings may find ERIC (education) useful; and group workers in forensic settings may find NCJRS (National Criminal Justice Reference Service) useful.

When planning a task group it is also helpful to

- Read the minutes of previous group meetings
- Read the bylaws of the sponsoring organization
- Read any operating procedures that may exist from previous meetings of the task group
- Be clear about the charges and responsibilities of the group
- Obtain information about how similar objectives and goals were accomplished in other organizations and by other task groups
- Attend meetings of groups working on similar concerns

[1]Some of the most important journals that focus on specific groups and specific group work methods are *Group and Organization Management, The Group, International Journal of Group Psychotherapy, Journal for Specialists in Group Work, Small Group Research,* and *Social Work with Groups.*

Needs Assessment

Workers might also find it useful to have some information about potential members of a proposed group. This information might include (1) potential members' willingness to attend the group, (2) their motivations for attending, and (3) their capabilities for helping the group achieve its purposes. In treatment groups, workers may want to conduct a needs assessment by asking other workers whether clients with whom they work might be appropriate for the group or whether workers have received requests for a particular group service they have been unable to meet.

Data from community needs assessments designed for multiple purposes can be useful in obtaining information about potential group members. Contacting people or organizations in the community may also provide access to potential members. When workers have identified the clients, they can contact them directly by a personal interview, a telephone call, or a letter. Toseland (1981) has described methods of reaching out to clients in more detail.

In some task groups, membership may result from elections, appointments, or the person's position in an organization. A planning evaluation can familiarize a worker with rules and regulations governing a task group's composition and operation. Planning evaluations can also help a worker collect information and assess the potential contributions that members can make in helping the group achieve its objectives (Rothman, 1974). For more information about conducting planning evaluations, see Polansky (1960) or Rossi, Freeman, and Wright (1979).

EVALUATIONS FOR MONITORING A GROUP

Monitoring refers to keeping track of the progress of group members and group processes. Monitoring is discussed in Chapter 8 as an assessment device, but it can also be used to evaluate group work practice. Monitoring methods have received more attention in the group work literature than has any other type of evaluation method. Monitoring is the least demanding and most flexible of the evaluation procedures described in this chapter. It can be useful for obtaining information for process or outcome evaluations.

Monitoring Methods

The first step in the monitoring process is to decide what information to collect. For example, persons who work with remedial groups designed for clients with psychological disorders may be interested in monitoring changes in individual members over the course of the group on the five axes presented in the *Diagnostic and Statistical Manual of Mental Disorders* (American Psychiatric Association, 1994). A worker asked to lead an interdepartmental committee of a large public welfare agency may be interested in monitoring the extent to which individual committee members complete assigned tasks.

Whatever information group workers decide to collect, they must be clear about how they define it so it can be monitored with appropriate measures. Concepts that are ambiguous, obscure, or unspecified cannot be measured accurately.

The next step in monitoring is to decide how the needed information will be collected. Data can be collected by administering questionnaires; asking for verbal feedback about the group; or by recording information about the group through written records, tape recordings, or video recordings of group sessions.

In treatment groups, members may be asked to record information about their own behavior or the behavior of other group members. Self-monitoring methods include (1) counting discrete behaviors; (2) keeping a checklist, a log, or a diary of events that occur before, during, and after a behavior or a task that is being monitored; and (3) recording ratings of feeling states on self-anchored rating scales. These types of monitoring methods are described in Chapter 8 because they are often used for assessment. As illustrated in the following sections, in the monitoring process, collecting data can be the task of the worker or of the group members.

Monitoring by the Group Worker

One of the easiest methods of monitoring a group's progress is to record during or after each meeting the activities that occur. This form of record keeping involves writing or dictating notes after a meeting (Wilson, 1980). The worker may use a process-recording method of monitoring or a summary-recording method. Process recordings are narrative, step-by-step descriptions of a group's development. Wilson and Ryland (1949) noted that process recordings can help a worker analyze the interactions that occur during a group meeting. However, process recordings are time-consuming and, therefore, rarely used by experienced group workers. They are, however, useful in the training and supervision of beginning group workers because they provide rich detail and give trainees an opportunity to reflect on what occurs during group meetings.

Summary recording is less time-consuming, more selective, and more focused than process recording. Summary recording focuses on critical incidents that occur in a group and involves using a series of open-ended questions. The questions are most frequently used for monitoring a group's progress after each group session, although they may be used at less frequent intervals during a group's development. Figure 13.1 is an example of a summary recording form used to record a meeting of a family life education group for foster parents.

When using either summary or process recordings, it is important for the worker to record the information as soon as possible after the meeting so that events are remembered as accurately as possible. The meaning of the open-ended summary-recording questions should be as clear as possible so that workers' recordings are consistent from group to group. Ambiguous questions open to several interpretations should be avoided. The amount of time required for summary

FIGURE 13.1 ■ *Group Recording Form*

Group name: _____   Beginning date: _____

Worker's name: _____   Termination date: _____

Session number: _____   Date of session: _____

Members present: _____

_____

_____

_____

Members absent: _____

_____

_____

Purpose of the group: _____

_____

Goals for this meeting: _____

_____

_____

Activities to meet these goals: _____

_____

_____

_____

Worker's analysis of the meeting: _____

_____

_____

_____

_____

Plan for future meetings: _____

_____

_____

_____

_____

recordings depends on the number of questions to which the worker responds and the amount of analysis each question requires.

The open-ended questions of summary-recording devices sometimes fail to focus or define the recorded information sufficiently, especially when the worker wants similar information about all clients. Summary-recording devices are usually not designed to connect the group worker's activities to specific goals and outcomes.

Recording systems such as the problem-oriented record (Kane, 1974), have been designed to overcome this problem. In the problem-oriented record-keeping system, problems to be worked on by the group are clearly defined, goals are established, and data are collected and recorded in relation to each specified problem. The system enables workers to show how group work interventions designed to accomplish a certain goal are connected to a specific assessment of the problem.

In task groups, the minutes of a meeting serve as the record of the group's business. They are often the official record of the proceedings of a group. Minutes are prepared from notes taken during the meeting by a person designated by the worker or elected by the group's membership. A staff person, the secretary of the group, or another person may take notes regularly. Sometimes, members rotate the task. The minutes of each meeting are usually distributed to members before the next meeting and are approved by members, with any revisions, during the first part of the next meeting.

Workers may also want to use audiotape or videotape recorders to obtain information about a group. Recordings have the advantage of providing an accurate, unedited record of the meeting. In remedial groups, audiotapes provide immediate feedback about members' verbal behavior. Members may want to replay a segment of the tape if there is a discrepancy about what was said during some portion of the meeting.

In educational and other groups, videotapes can be used to demonstrate appropriate behavior and critique inappropriate behavior. Videotaping is especially useful during program activities, such as role playing, that are designed to increase skills or change behavior patterns. Video feedback helps members review their behavior during role-play practices to discuss alternative ways of behaving. For example, members of an assertion training group might watch videotapes of themselves in a situation requiring an assertive response. They may analyze voice tone, facial expressions, body posture, and the verbal interactions that occurred. Audiotapes and videotapes provide the worker with a permanent record that can be shared with the group, with supervisors, or in educational workshops.

There are some disadvantages to taping a group. Because of recording's absolute quality, group members are not able to make statements off the record, which may inhibit the development of trust in the group. The worker may not find it necessary or even desirable to have the level of detail provided by a tape. The worker may have to spend too much time reviewing irrelevant portions of a tape to find information that could have been obtained quickly if brief, summary recordings had been used instead. However, if a worker is interested in monitoring the group's interaction patterns in a thorough and precise fashion or if an entire transcript of the group session is needed, audio or video recordings are ideal.

Sometimes it is desirable to use specialized coding systems to obtain reliable and valid data from tape-recorded group sessions, particularly when the worker wishes to obtain a detailed and accurate picture of group processes for research. Coding systems can be used by one or more raters of the tapes to determine the frequency and content of a group's interactions. Coding systems described by Bales (1950), Bales, Cohen, and Williamson (1979), Budman et al. (1987), Hill (1977), and Rose (1989) are examples of methods that can be used to analyze specific group interactions. Other coding systems are described in comprehensive reviews of group process instruments prepared by Fuhriman and colleagues (Fuhriman & Packard, 1986; Fuhriman & Barlow, 1994).

Monitoring by Group Members

The most common use of monitoring by group members occurs in treatment groups in which individual members keep a record of their behavior between group meetings and report back on the behaviors during the next meeting. An illustration of the steps in the self-monitoring procedure appears in Figure 13.2. During this procedure, the worker and the group members together decide (1) what data to collect, (2) when to collect the data, (3) how much data to collect, (4) how to collect the data, and (5) when the information collected by members should be analyzed by the group. As these questions are discussed and answered, the worker reviews each member's monitoring plan.

Members can also monitor a group's progress at the end of each meeting or at intervals during the life of the group. Members may use a short questionnaire devised for this purpose or they can discuss the group's performance orally with the worker. Monitoring of this type encourages members to provide periodic feedback that can be used by workers to improve their practice throughout the life cycle of a group.

Group members also benefit from self-monitoring procedures. Members can share ideas about the group's performance and how it might be improved, which gives them a sense of control and influence over the group's progress and increases their identification with the group's purposes. Also, members who believe their ideas are valued, respected, and listened to are more likely to feel satisfied with their participation in the group.

Verbal evaluations of a group's performance do not provide a permanent record. An evaluation form consisting of closed-ended, fixed-category responses and open-ended items can be used if the worker, group members, or the agency wants written feedback about the group. Figure 13.3 shows a session evaluation form developed by a worker leading a group for single parents. The form contains several easily understood closed- and open-ended questions. The closed-ended questions are Likert-type scales that require respondents to record their opinions on an ordered scale. Because the same scale values are used for all group mem-

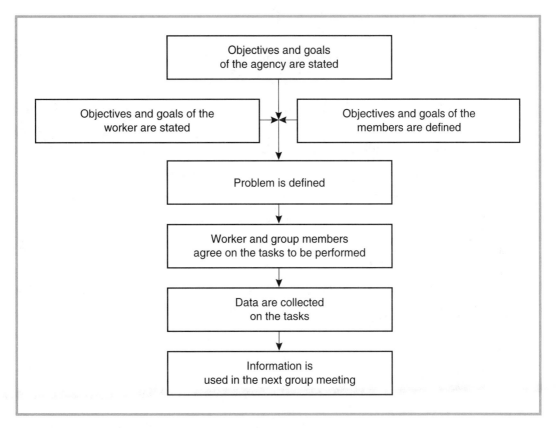

FIGURE 13.2 ■ *The Self-Monitoring Process*

bers, responses made by each member can be compared with one another. Open-ended items are designed to allow each member to reply uniquely; responses may vary considerably from member to member.

In task groups, members often make oral reports of their progress. Although the reports are often not considered to be evaluation devices, they are an important means by which the worker and the members monitor the group's work. At the completion of a task group, minutes, documents, final reports, and other products that result from the group's efforts can also be used to evaluate the success of the group.

In treatment groups, an important indicator of the group's performance is the completion of contracts that individual members make with the group or the worker about tasks to be done during the week to resolve a problem or change a particular behavior. Another indicator is the completion of between-session tasks. Rose (1989) calls the completion of between-session tasks the "products of group interaction." He suggests that the rate of completion of tasks is an important indicator of the success of the group.

FIGURE 13.3 ■ *Session Evaluation Form*

Was the information presented about child development helpful to you in
understanding your child's behavior?

4	3	2	1
Very Helpful	Somewhat Helpful	A Little Helpful	Not at All Helpful

What information did you find most helpful? _____

_____

_____

Rate the effectiveness of the leader in this group session.

4	3	2	1
Very Helpful	Somewhat Helpful	A Little Helpful	Not at All Helpful

What did you find most helpful about the group during this session?_____

_____

_____

What did you find least helpful about the group? _____

_____

_____

Overall, rate your satisfaction with today's group meeting.

4	3	2	1
Very Helpful	Somewhat Helpful	A Little Helpful	Not at All Helpful

Additional comments: _____

_____

_____

EVALUATIONS FOR DEVELOPING A GROUP

A third method of evaluating group work practice, developmental evaluation, is
useful for the worker who is interested in preparing new group work programs,
developing new group work methods, or improving existing group programs. Developmental research, as it has been called by Thomas (1978), is similar to re-

search and development in business and industry. It allows practicing group workers to create and test new group work programs.

The process of developmental evaluation includes developing, testing, evaluating, modifying, and re-evaluating intervention methods as new groups are offered. Developmental evaluations are especially appealing for workers who offer the same or similar group programs repeatedly because the evaluations require workers to evaluate group programs in a sequential manner. A developmental evaluation occurs as successive group programs are offered.

Unlike monitoring evaluations, which are relatively easy for group workers to conduct, developmental evaluations are rather complex. They require careful thought, planning, and design by the worker. The process of conducting a developmental evaluation consists of

- Identifying a need or problem
- Gathering and analyzing relevant data
- Developing a new group program or method
- Evaluating the new program or method
- Modifying the program or method on the basis of the data obtained

As shown in Figure 13.4, the process may be conducted several times as new group programs are offered and evaluated by the worker. Although developmental

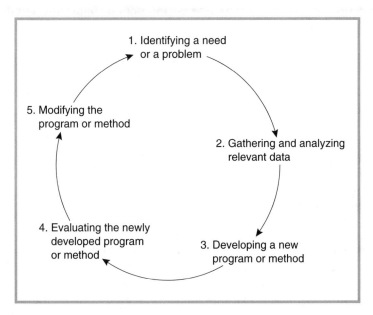

FIGURE 13.4 ■ *Steps in the Developmental Research Process*

research requires careful thought as well as time and energy, it yields improvements in programs and methods that can make group work practice more effective and more satisfying.

In developing and evaluating a new group program or a new group method, the worker can select from a variety of research designs, depending on the type of program or method being developed and the context in which the evaluation will occur. Single-system methods and case study methods are particularly useful for developmental evaluations. Although quasi-experimental design methods are also frequently used in developmental research, in this chapter the methods are described in relation to effectiveness and efficiency evaluations because they are also frequently used in evaluations of group outcomes. For a more thorough discussion of the issues involved in choosing an appropriate method for developmental research, see Bailey-Dempsey and Reid (1996), Fortune and Reid (1998), Rothman and Tumblin (1994), and Thomas and Rothman (1994).

Single-System Methods

Single-system methods (often called single-subject designs) have been developed to evaluate data collected over time from a single system such as a group. The data obtained by using single-system designs may include information about a single group member or the group as a whole. Single-system methods compare baseline data to data collected when an intervention is made in the group. The baseline period occurs before the intervention period. Data collected during the preintervention or baseline periods are intended to represent the functioning of the group as a whole or a group member on a particular variable. After the baseline period, an intervention occurs, which may cause a change in the data collected during the baseline period.

As shown in Figure 13.5, a change in level or in slope of the data collected may occur after the intervention. Observations before and after the intervention are compared to see how the change has affected what the group worker is measuring. For example, after collecting baseline data and finding that members of a group were talking almost exclusively to the worker rather than to each other, the worker may intervene by discussing the issue with the group, prompting members to talk with one another more frequently, and praising them when they initiate conversation with one another.

After the intervention, communications between members and the worker decrease, and communications between members increase. Figure 13.6 graphs the results of such an intervention. The single-system method illustrated in Figure 13.6 is often called an *AB design,* in which A is the baseline period before intervention and B is the postintervention, data-collection period.

Various single-system designs are multiple baseline, withdrawal, reversal, and changing criterion. These types of single-system designs are more complicated to apply for the practicing group worker than is the AB baseline-intervention design,

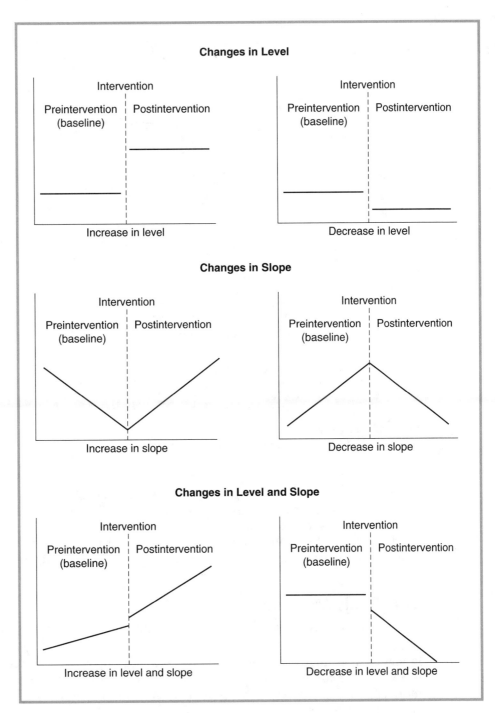

FIGURE 13.5 ■ *Changes in Baseline Data after an Intervention in a Group*

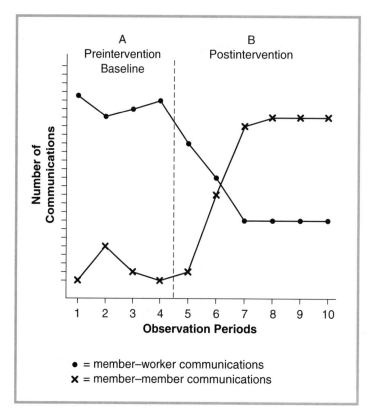

FIGURE 13.6 ■ *Graphed Data from a Single-System Evaluation*

but they are also more effective than the AB design in reliably evaluating practice outcomes. They are especially useful when workers have the time, energy, interest, and resources to test the efficacy of a new or alternative intervention to improve practice with future groups working on similar problems. For additional information about single-system methods, see Bloom, Fisher, and Orme (1999).

Case Study Methods

Case studies rely on precise descriptions, accurate observations, and detailed analyses of a single example or case. Case studies were developed by researchers interested in qualitative research methods. Because group workers are accustomed to keeping records and analyzing their work in detail, these methods may have more appeal for some group workers than the quantitatively oriented, single-system research methods.

As with single-system methods, case study methods are based on intensive analysis of a single case. Therefore, the data collected may not be as internally or externally valid as data collected using classic control-group designs. Nevertheless, the strengths of case studies are that they can provide a clear, detailed, vivid description of the processes and procedures of a group in action, and they are often more feasible to apply in practice settings than in control-group designs.

Case study methods include participant and nonparticipant observation (Johnson, 1975; Patton, 1990), case comparison methods (Butler, Davis, & Kukkonen, 1979), ethnographic methods (Scheneul, Lecompte, Nastasi, & Borgatti, 1998), and focus group interviews (Greenbaum, 1998; Krueger, 1994; Morgan, 1997). For example, a group worker who is considering leading a preventive health group for cardiac patients may find it useful to personally observe a group being conducted at another hospital or to have the group session recorded for playback and analysis. The worker could use case study methods to analyze the content of the recordings or notes made from observing the group and use the information to change group work methods or develop new group programs in the worker's own setting.

Using a case comparison method, a worker who has developed a group program for alcoholics may want to compare the program with similar programs, perhaps those offered by Alcoholics Anonymous and a county alcoholism program. A comparison of the three programs along prespecified dimensions created by the worker to answer specific information needs could lead to innovations in the worker's program. The worker may also want to conduct focus group interviews with individuals who have participated in each program to determine the most- and least-valued features of each program. These features could then be evaluated for their efficacy, as described in the process shown in Figure 13.4.

Group workers might also want to use case study methods in working with task groups. For example, a worker might want to use nonparticipant observation to compare the methods that other day-treatment mental health agencies use when reviewing clients in treatment-team meetings.

Both single-system methods and case study methods offer workers the opportunity to continually develop and improve their practice. Rigorous application of these methods requires that workers spend time designing and implementing evaluation methods and collecting data that are not routinely available. The worker must decide whether the extra effort spent in organizing and carrying out a developmental evaluation is worth the new or improved programs that may result.

EVALUATIONS FOR DETERMINING EFFECTIVENESS AND EFFICIENCY

Effectiveness evaluations focus on the extent to which a group accomplishes its objectives. They give workers the opportunity to gain objective feedback about the helpfulness of the methods being used. Efficiency evaluations compare the benefits of a group program with its cost. They attempt to place a monetary value on the outcomes of a group and to compare this cost with the costs incurred by conducting a group.

Effectiveness and efficiency evaluations rely on experimental and quasi-experimental designs, reliable and valid measures, and statistical procedures to determine the significance of an intervention on the outcome of task or treatment groups. Compared with the other types of evaluations mentioned in this chapter, effectiveness and efficiency evaluations are less flexible, more technically complex, and more difficult to conduct. Because of the nature of the methods employed and the precision and rigor necessary to apply them, a flexible and cooperative setting is needed to conduct effectiveness and efficiency evaluations. The sponsoring agency must be willing to supply the needed resources and the technical assistance necessary for conducting such evaluations.

One method for evaluating outcomes that is less difficult to apply than many other effectiveness evaluation methods is called *goal attainment scaling* (Kiresuk & Sherman, 1968). Using this method, the worker can obtain information about the achievement of goals by individual group members or the group as a whole. An example of goal attainment scaling is shown in Figure 13.7.

Members and the group leader can work together to develop outcome measures for each scale level. For example, a group may decide that the most unfavorable outcome for the problem of depression is suicide. Similarly, the group may decide that the most favorable outcome for loss of appetite is to eat three meals a day and to snack between meals. After work on the problem areas is completed, goal attainment can be measured by using the scales that have been developed for each problem area. In the example in Figure 13.7, goal attainment is indicated by a box around the actual outcome. For the problem of anxiety, the outcome was one self-rated occurrence of feeling anxious each day. This outcome was given a score of 4.

As shown in Figure 13.7, it is possible to weight each scale differentially so that attaining more important goals receives greater emphasis in the overall evaluation than does attaining less important goals. Thus, the goal attainment score of 4 obtained for the problem of anxiety is multiplied by its weight of 5 to yield a goal attainment score of 20. Even though the goal attainment score on the problem area of depression is a 3, after it is multiplied by its weight (25), the weighted goal attainment score for the problem of depression (75) is much greater than that obtained on the problem of anxiety (20). Goal attainment scores on each scale can be added together to form a composite score for individual or group goal attainment.

Statistical procedures have been developed to compare goal attainment scores across individual group members and across groups (Garwick, 1974). Although goal attainment scaling has received some methodological criticism (Seaberg & Gillespie, 1977), the procedure remains an important tool for group workers to consider when conducting effectiveness evaluations.

A variation on goal attainment scaling that has been used successfully in several studies of the effectiveness of group treatment is the pressing problem index (Toseland, Labrecque, Goebel, & Whitney, 1992; Toseland, Rossiter, & Labrecque,

FIGURE 13.7 ■ *Example of Goal Attainment Scaling*

	Problem Areas		
Scale Levels	**Anxiety**	**Depression**	**Loss of Appetite**
1. Most unfavorable expected outcome	Four or more self-rated occurrences of feeling anxious each day	Suicide	Refuses to eat any daily meals
2. Less than expected outcome	Three self-rated occurrences of feeling anxious each day	One or more attempts at suicide	Eats one meal each day
3. Expected outcome	Two self-rated occurrences of feeling anxious each day	No attempts at suicide, discusses feelings of depression	Eats two meals each day
4. More than expected outcome	One self-rated occurrence of feeling anxious each day	No attempts at suicide, discusses possible causes of depression	Eats three meals each day
5. Most favorable expected outcome	No self-rated occurrence of feeling anxious each day	No attempts at suicide, identifies two causes for depression	Eats three meals a day and snacks between meals
Weight	5	25	5
Goal Attainment Score	4	3	3
Weighted Goal Attainment Score	20	75	15

1989). During the intake interview, potential group members are asked to describe several problems they would like to work on in the group. These problems, plus any other problems known to commonly affect the individuals targeted for the intervention, are listed in an inventory of pressing problems. Before meeting and again at the end of the group, participants are asked to rate the stress caused by each pressing problem and their efficacy in coping with the problem. Change in stress and efficacy in coping with the pressing problems are assessed by adding up the responses to all pressing problems at each time of measurement.

Effectiveness evaluations rely on experimental and quasi-experimental designs to determine whether a group accomplishes its objectives. A true experimental design employs random assignment of participants to treatment and control groups. It compares the treatment and control groups on specific outcome variables to measure differences between treatment and control group subjects.

In *quasi-experimental designs,* participants cannot be randomly assigned to treatment and control groups. It is often difficult to assign subjects randomly to treatment and control groups in practice settings. Therefore, quasi-experimental designs are often used in effectiveness evaluations even though they are subject to possible biases because nonrandomly assigned subjects are more likely to be nonequivalent on important variables that may affect the outcome variables being measured (Toseland, Kabat, & Kemp, 1983).

It is especially difficult to conduct adequate effectiveness evaluations in group research projects. To do valid statistical analyses of data from experimental designs, the observations or measures on each unit of analysis must be independent. Researchers testing the effectiveness of group treatment sometimes assume that individual group members are the unit of analysis. However, individual members are not independent of one another in a group setting because they are affected by other members of the group. For example, while members are taking a questionnaire, a lawn mower might go past the window and disturb all members of the group. Members' scores are not totally independent of one another; that is, the lawn mower affects all members in a similar manner. One way to overcome this problem is to ensure that all evaluation instruments are given to group members on a one-to-one basis outside of the group meeting.

The requirement for independent observations is also violated by researchers interested in group-level phenomena such as cohesion and leadership. Glisson (1986) has pointed out that some statistical procedures such as analysis of variance (ANOVA) are not robust to this violation, which can lead to serious overestimates of the effectiveness of group procedures (Eisenhart, 1972). Because there must be a relatively large number of units of analysis to obtain valid statistical comparisons of a group-level phenomenon, effectiveness evaluations of group work practice require that a relatively large number of groups be conducted. Evaluating large numbers of groups is often difficult to do in practice settings because of the limitations on resources, group participants, and competent group leaders. For these reasons, alternatives to using the group as the unit of analysis have been proposed (Burlingame, Kircher, & Honts, 1994; Hoyle & Crawford, 1994).

Efficiency evaluations can be complex and time-consuming, but they can also be useful to persons who want to assess whether their programs are cost-effective. For example, a nonprofit health agency employs a group worker to conduct a smoking-cessation group program. The worker conducts an effectiveness evaluation and finds that 60 percent of the group members become nonsmokers after the group program. The worker also collects data about the costs of the program and the costs to employers who have employees who smoke. These data provide the basis for the worker's efficiency evaluation.

Figure 13.8 shows the worker's calculations and illustrates that at a success rate of 50 percent, the smoking-cessation group program saves the employer $220 each year, beginning one year after the program ends. Savings to the employer last for as long as the employee remains with the company as a nonsmoker. Because the smoking-cessation program has a success rate of 60 percent, employers who have long-term employees are likely to save more than $220 each year for each employee who participates in the smoking-cessation program. This information would be helpful to the nonprofit health agency in motivating large employers whose workers' average length of employment exceeds one year to offer smoking-cessation group programs to their employees.

A description of the methodology for effectiveness evaluations can be found in Babbie (1999), and a description of efficiency evaluations can be found in Drummond, Stoddart, and Torrance (1987) or Gold, Siegel, Russell, and Weinstein (1996). Group workers should have a basic understanding of these methods to be able to assess the efficacy of their own practice and to be able to critically evaluate methodologies used in published reports about the effectiveness and efficiency of group work methods and group programs.

FIGURE 13.8 ■ *An Efficiency Evaluation of a Group Program for Smoking Cessation*

Costs of Smoking to the Employer per Employee per Year*	
Insurance:	
Health	$220.00
Fire	10.00
Workers' Compensation and other accidents	40.00
Life and disability	30.00
Other:	
Productivity	166.00
Absenteeism	100.00
Smoking effects on nonsmokers	110.00
Total cost of smoking	$660.00
Per Employee Cost of the Smoking-Cessation Program	
Smoking-cessation program	$120.00
Employee time to complete the program	100.00
Total Cost for Each Employee	$220.00
Total Cost of Achieving One Nonsmoker (based on a projected success rate of 50%)	$440.00
Savings to Employers	
Total cost of smoking	$660.00
Total cost of the smoking-cessation program	–440.00
	$220.00

*Cost figures taken from Marvin Kristein, "How Much Can Business Expect to Earn from Smoking Cessation," presented at the Conference of the National Interagency Council on Smoking and Health, Chicago, Illinois, January 9, 1980.

EVALUATION MEASURES

The four broad types of evaluation methods provide a framework that workers can use to collect information for planning, monitoring, developing, or assessing the efficacy or efficiency of their practice with a group. In applying these methods, workers can choose from a variety of measures to collect the necessary information for an effective evaluation. Numerous measures have been developed for evaluating group work practice; some specifically focus on properties of the group as a whole, and others may be useful to the worker in evaluating changes in members of specific groups. Decisions about which measures to use depend on (1) the objectives of the evaluation, (2) properties of the measures being considered for use, (3) the form in which the data will be collected, and (4) what constructs will be measured.

Choosing Measures

The first and most essential step in choosing appropriate measures is to decide on the objectives of the evaluation. Clarifying the information that is needed, what the information collected will be used for, and who will use the information can help the worker choose the appropriate measures for the evaluation. For example, if the worker is interested in obtaining feedback from members about their satisfaction with a particular group, the worker may be less concerned about the reliability and validity of a measure than about the difficulties members might experience in providing the information. The worker may also be concerned about members' reactions to the evaluation and the time needed to administer it, particularly if the worker has a limited amount of group time available for conducting an evaluation.

The worker should be familiar with two properties of measures that govern the quality of the data to be collected. *Reliability* refers to the extent to which an instrument measures the same phenomenon in the same way each time the measure is used. A reliable measure is consistent. When measuring the same variable, it yields the same score each time it is administered. *Validity* refers to the extent to which a data-collection instrument measures what it purports to measure. A valid measure is one that yields a true or actual representation of the variable being measured. The ideal situation is for a group worker to use a reliable and valid measure that has already been constructed. When such measures exist, they are generally superior to measures developed quickly by the worker without regard to reliability or validity.

Constructing reliable and valid measures takes a considerable amount of time. Workers should decide what level of measurement precision and objectivity is needed when deciding how much time to spend constructing and validating a measure. For additional information about constructing reliable and valid measures, see Hopkins (1998), Nunnally (1994), or Sax (1996).

Another consideration in choosing appropriate evaluation measures is to decide what form of data collection would be most useful to the group worker and most convenient for group members. Data can be collected by interviewing members, by written response to a questionnaire, or by audio or video recordings. The data-collection form that will be most helpful to the worker depends on how the data will be used and the extent to which group members are willing and able to cooperate with the data-collection procedures used. In evaluating group work with children, older people, and disabled people, for example, audiotaped responses can often overcome any difficulties the individuals might have in making written responses.

Finally, the worker must decide how a particular property or concept will be measured. For example, after deciding that the objective of an evaluation is to test the effectiveness of a particular group, the worker must decide whether information is sought about changes in the behavior, cognition, or the affect of individual group members. In task groups, the worker may want to measure both the extent to which a group completes its tasks and the quality and the quantity of the products or tasks achieved.

When one conducts evaluations, it is often helpful to have multiple measures of the property being measured. When measuring the effectiveness of a group program for drug abusers, for example, the worker might want to measure reductions in drug intake, changes in self-concept, and changes in beliefs about the effects of drug abuse. Multiple measures, such as blood tests, attitude scales, and a questionnaire concerning information about drug use, might be useful in assessing the group's effectiveness in helping members become drug free.

Types of Measures

A wide variety of reliable and valid measures are available for group workers to use when they are evaluating interventions with specific groups (Fisher & Corcoran, 1994; Kramer & Conoley, 1992; Robinson & Shaver, 1973). These sources include self-report measures, observational measures, and measures of the products of group interaction. In the description of each type of measure, the text indicates particular measures that have often been used in evaluations of group work.

Self-Report Measures

Perhaps the most widely used evaluation measures are written and oral self-reports, in which group members are asked to respond to questions about a particular phenomenon. Although they may focus on any phenomenon, self-report measures are particularly useful in measuring intrapersonal phenomena such as beliefs or attitudes, which cannot be measured directly by observational measures. Group workers can also construct their own self-report measures for specialized situations in which no published self-report measures exist. However, it is difficult to construct a reliable and valid self-report measure. Fortunately, a variety of published self-report measures are available, including measures of anxiety, depression, assertiveness, self-concept, and locus of control. Four published measures that may be of particular interest to group workers are the Group Atmosphere Scale (Silbergeld, Koenig, Manderscheid, Meeker, & Hornung, 1975), Hemphill's Index of Group Dimensions (Hemphill, 1956), the Hill Interaction Matrix (Hill, 1977), and Yalom's Curative Factors Scale (Lieberman, Yalom, & Miles, 1973; Stone, Lewis, & Beck, 1994).

The Group Atmosphere Scale (GAS) was designed to measure the psychosocial environment of therapy groups. It consists of 12 subscales: (1) aggression, (2) submission, (3) autonomy, (4) order, (5) affiliation, (6) involvement, (7) insight, (8) practicality, (9) spontaneity, (10) support, (11) variety, and (12) clarity. Each subscale contains 10 true-false items. The GAS has been assessed to have acceptable reliability and validity (Silbergeld et al., 1975).

Hemphill's Index of Group Dimensions measures 13 properties of groups: (1) autonomy, (2) control, (3) flexibility, (4) hedonic tone, (5) homogeneity, (6) intimacy, (7) participation, (8) permeability, (9) polarization, (10) potency, (11) stability, (12) stratification, and (13) viscidity. The measure consists of 150 items to which group members respond on a five-point scale from definitely true to mostly false.

The Hill Interaction Matrix (HIM-A, HIM-B, HIM-G) is a self-report measure in which a group leader, a group member, or an observer responds to 72 items about group process. The measure is designed to discriminate between types of group interactions on two dimensions: the content discussed and the level and type of work occurring in the group.

Yalom's Curative Factors Scale is a widely used, 14-item measure that assesses 12 therapeutic dimensions in treatment groups: (1) altruism, (2) catharsis, (3) cohesiveness, (4) existentiality, (5) family re-enactment, (6) guidance, (7) hope, (8) identification, (9) interpersonal input, (10) interpersonal output, (11) self-understanding, and (12) universality. Stone, Lewis, and Beck (1994) have reported some psychometric properties of the instrument.

Observational Measures

Unlike self-report measures that rely on the accuracy of a respondent's memory, observational measures use independent, objective observers to collect data as they occur or as they are replayed from video or audio recordings. Although observational measures are less susceptible to biases and distortions than are self-report measures, observational measures are used less frequently than self-report measures because they require the availability of one or more trained observers to collect the data. The observers code discrete group interactions into categories that are mutually exclusive and exhaustive; that is, during each observation period, only one observation is recorded and it can be recorded in only one category.

The most well-known observational measure for groups is called Bales' Interaction Process Analysis (Bales, 1950). This observational index consists of 12 categories. Interactions are coded by assigning each person a number. For example, when an interaction occurs from member 1 to member 4 or from member 3 to member 1, the interaction is marked 1-4 or 3-1 in the appropriate category. With well-trained observers, Bales' Interaction Process Analysis can be a useful tool for the evaluation of group interactions.

More recently, Bales (1980) and Bales, Cohen, and Williamson (1979) have developed a new measure called Systematic Multiple Level Observation of Groups (SYMLOG). As explained in Chapter 8, SYMLOG is a method for analyzing the overt and covert behaviors of group members. With SYMLOG, a three-dimensional graphic presentation or field diagram of the interaction of group members is made. Through the field diagram, group members can analyze the way they interact with one another to improve the ability of the group to accomplish its tasks. An example of the use of SYMLOG for assessing group functioning can be found in Chapter 8. As an evaluation tool, SYMLOG can be used to measure several variables affecting both the socioemotional and the task aspects of members' behavior in groups.

Other observational measures have also been used for evaluating changes in a group over time. For example, Moreno's (1934) scales of sociometric choice and sociometric preference, described more fully in Chapter 8, assess relationships among members of a group by having each member rank other members on certain dimensions such as their preference for working with other group members or their liking for other group members.

Products of Group Interaction

A worker may be able to measure the products of group interaction in a simple and straightforward manner. In task groups, products of the group's work are often tangible. For example, a team may develop a written document that governs how services will be delivered to clients. The work of a delegate council may be evaluated by the number of agenda items it acts on during its monthly meeting. In both instances, group products can be used for purposes of evaluation. In treatment groups, products of group interaction may also be useful measures. Rose (1989) suggests that measurable products of group interaction include behavior change, the number of between-meeting tasks generated at a group meeting, and the number of tasks actually completed.

Evaluation measures from which workers can choose when evaluating their practice with a group range from measures consisting of a few open-ended questions made by a worker who wants to get some feedback from group members to sophisticated observational measures requiring highly trained observers. Workers develop or select measures in relation to the evaluation design they are going to use and, ultimately, in relation to the information they hope to obtain. Although selecting appropriate measures and implementing effective evaluations is time-consuming for the practicing group worker, it is often well worth the effort because it may result in improved service and in new and innovative group programs.

SUMMARY

Evaluation is the method by which practitioners obtain information and feedback about their work with a group. In the current age of accountability and fiscal constraints by which difficult program choices are made, evaluation methodologies are useful tools for practitioners. This chapter discusses some reasons that group workers may choose to use evaluation methods in their practice.

Practitioners are often faced with a dilemma when considering whether to evaluate their practice. They must decide whether the demands of serving clients are compatible with developing and conducting evaluations. This chapter describes the strengths and weaknesses of a number of evaluation methods that may be used in differing practice situations and settings.

Four broad types of evaluation methods are evaluations for (1) planning a group, (2) monitoring a group, (3) developing a group, and (4) testing the effectiveness and efficiency of a group. These methods are used with a variety of evaluation measures to help practitioners develop, test, and implement more effective group work methods. Evaluation methods can also be combined with knowledge accumulated from practice experiences (sometimes referred to as *practice wisdom*) to improve the methods used by group workers to meet a variety of needs in diverse practice settings.

LEARNING ASSIGNMENTS

1. Schedule an interview with an administrator in a social service agency and ask the following questions: What requirements do funding agencies have for evaluating the group work services offered by the agency? Have these requirements changed in recent years? What additional efforts, if any, are made to evaluate the quality of the services offered by the agency? What incentives and disincentives do workers have for evaluating their practice?

2. Form a classroom group and identify a population that you think may be in need of group work services. Prepare a questionnaire that could be used to assess the needs of this population. Make sure to include items that assess the barriers that may interfere with this particular population's use of existing group work services.

3. Locate a social service agency offering group work services. How are group work services monitored? Is there a standardized format for recording information on each group session? Is a summary form used periodically or at the end of a group? Are clients asked to provide feedback about their satisfaction with the group work services that are offered? If you were called in as a consultant to this agency, how would you change the way services are monitored?

4. Select a target population or problem for a group work service. Conduct a literature search using a computerized online database such as Social Work Abstracts

Plus. Find the articles that appear to be most relevant. How helpful was the computer search in planning for the group?

5. If you are the leader or a member of a task or treatment group, ask members to fill out the Session Evaluation Form presented in Figure 13.3 at the end of a meeting. Prepare a written analysis of the responses of the group members to each question. What conclusions can you reach about the helpfulness of the meeting, the satisfaction of the members, and the effectiveness of the leader? How could the group be more helpful and satisfying to the members? How helpful was the measure in providing feedback about the effectiveness of the group?

6. Locate a published assessment instrument that could be used to evaluate the effectiveness of a treatment group. Review the items in the assessment instrument and comment on the extent to which you think they would help you assess the effectiveness of your work. Prepare six additional items that might be particularly pertinent when assessing the effectiveness of a group work service for this population.

CASE EXAMPLE

Despite telling his group work students always to monitor and evaluate their practice with groups, Bob knew that they would be caught in the classic practitioner's dilemma. The demands of service delivery would make it difficult for them to spend the time and resources needed to formally evaluate their work with groups. He was surprised, however, when a former student returned with good news about research funding and a request for help. Maureen had been awarded a demonstration grant of $5000 to develop an evaluation of her violence reduction group. In addition, the state's education department suggested that if her research project was successful, Maureen could apply for a much larger grant to implement and evaluate additional groups. She hoped that Bob could give her some helpful ideas for a research design.

Maureen's violence reduction group was aimed at sensitizing elementary students to the types of violence in their school environment and helping them find nonviolent ways of behaving. It had an educational component that consisted of a series of standardized lessons about violence. In addition, it had a growth component in which members learned new ways of handling themselves when confronted with anger from their peers.

Based on her conversations with Bob, Maureen decided to use the Achenback Child Behavior Checklist (Achenback, 1991) in her evaluation because it had been found to be a reliable and valid measure of children's behavior by researchers who had examined its psychometric properties. Although there is both a parent and a teacher version of the Achenback Child Behavior Checklist, she decided to use only the parent form because she was concerned that teachers were too busy to spend the time to fill out the form for each student involved in the project. Instead, she designed a short questionnaire aimed at collecting feedback from teachers about students' behaviors in the classroom.

Maureen decided to use a partial-crossover control group design to evaluate the impact of the group. She would start a new group from the waiting list and use some of the students who were still on the waiting list as a control group. In partial-crossover design, after the intervention is conducted with the experimental group, the control group is then offered the intervention.

Although the design would provide good information about the effectiveness of the group, it posed several ethical issues. First, Maureen had to secure written permission from the parents of the children who would participate in both the experimental and control groups. Second, Maureen had to discuss and justify the use of the waiting list as a control group with parents of the involved children and with school administrators. Confidentiality and voluntary participation were also issues. As a result of her discussions with students, parents, and administrators, Maureen secured permission to proceed with the research.

To help ensure the equivalence of the experimental and control groups, Maureen randomly assigned students on the waiting list to either of the two groups. When the groups were composed, she asked the parents of children in both groups to fill out the behavior checklist. This measurement served as a pretest for both the experimental and control groups and provided important baseline information. She triangulated these data with information obtained from teachers who filled out the short questionnaire she had developed. Maureen then conducted the violence reduction sessions with the experimental group. At the end of the group, she again administered the Achenback checklist to parents of children in the experimental and control groups and again collected data from teachers. She then compared the pretest and posttest results for both groups. Students in the experimental group achieved positive movement on their checklist scores whereas scores for the control group members did not change significantly. Using the control group scores as a second pretest, Maureen then ran the violence reduction group for the members of the control group. Posttest scores for this crossover group were significantly higher than their pretest scores.

The parents of students who participated in Maureen's violence reduction groups reported fewer incidents of acting out behavior of a violent nature, especially related to school. In addition, teachers reported that students who participated in the violence reduction groups had more control over their feelings of anger and used more positive measures for mediating their personal disputes in the classroom.

Maureen spent a good deal of time preparing a final report on her research project. She made sure to document both the results of her findings as well as the nature of the intervention that took place within the violence reduction groups. School administrators were pleased at the outcome of her evaluation efforts. With a sense of pride and gratefulness, Maureen sent a copy of the final report to her former research teacher with a note of thanks for helping her with the project. She later learned that her research report was the highlight of the state education department's review panel's deliberations on funding new initiatives aimed at reducing violence in schools.

Ending the Group's Work

The ending stage, a critical part of group work practice, has been given increasing attention in recent years.[1] The skills workers use in the ending stage determine, in part, the success of the entire group experience. In this stage, workers and members form their lasting impressions of the group. An otherwise satisfying and effective group can be ruined by a worker who is not skillful in closing the group.

During the ending stage, the group's work is consolidated. In task groups, the decisions, reports, recommendations, and other products of the group as a whole are completed, and consideration is given to how the results of the work can best be implemented. In treatment groups, the changes made by individual group members are stabilized, and plans are made for maintaining these gains after the group ends. In groups in which members' self-disclosure has been high, it is necessary to help members work through their feelings about terminating their relationships with the worker and with each other. It is also a time when workers confront their own feelings regarding ending their work with a particular group. This chapter examines the tasks and skills involved in ending individual group meetings and closing the work of the group as a whole.

FACTORS THAT INFLUENCE GROUP ENDINGS

Endings vary depending on whether a group has an open or closed membership policy. In closed groups, unless there are unplanned terminations, all members end at the same time. In these groups, the worker can help all members to deal with common issues and feelings that arise as the group draws to a close. Open groups

---

[1]See, for example, the *International Journal of Group Psychotherapy* (1995) 46(1), which is mainly devoted to the process of termination.

present a more difficult challenge for the worker. Some members may be experiencing reactions to termination, but others may experience reactions common to the beginning stage of the group. In open groups, the worker should individualize work with each member. However, because each member will eventually experience disengagement from the group, the worker can use the reactions of members who are terminating to help members who will experience similar reactions in the future.

Endings also vary according to the attraction of the group for its members. In groups that members find attractive, endings may not be viewed as a positive event. Conversely, if group meetings are viewed as something to be endured, news of the last meeting may be received with relief.

In addition, endings vary depending on whether the group is a treatment group or a task group. In many therapy groups and support groups, for example, members reveal intimate details of their personal lives. They let down their defenses and become vulnerable as they share concerns and issues that are important to them. In these types of groups, mutual aid and support develop as members deepen relationships with one another and the worker. They come to trust each other and to rely on the therapeutic advice and suggestions given by the worker and fellow group members.

THE PROCESS OF ENDING

In therapy, support, and growth groups, termination may be accompanied by strong emotional reactions. However, in educational and socialization groups, termination rarely results in the expression of strong emotional reactions.

Terminating the relationships that may have influenced the members of treatment groups is quite different from terminating the relationships formed in task groups. In task groups, members' self-disclosure is generally at a relatively low level. Because the focus of these groups is on a product, such as a report or the development of a plan of action, members often look forward to the end of a group with a sense of accomplishment or with relief that their work is finished. Because they have not let down their defenses or shared their personal concerns to any great extent, there is rarely an intense emotional reaction to ending. Also, members of task groups may work together again on other committees, teams, or councils. Therefore, the endings of task groups do not have the same sense of finality as do endings of treatment groups.

In the task group literature, with the notable exception of Keyton (1993), the focus is on the skills the leader uses to end individual group meetings rather than on how the leader ends the entire group experience (Tropman, 1996). This focus contrasts sharply with treatment group literature, which generally focuses on ending work with the group rather than ending work in a particular meeting.

PLANNED AND UNPLANNED TERMINATION

At the beginning of closed, time-limited groups, workers and members decide how many times the group will meet. Northen (1969) points out, "Ideally, termination occurs when a person or a group no longer needs the professional services" (p. 223). Fortune and colleagues (Fortune, 1985; Fortune, Pearlingi, & Rochelle, 1991) found that few social workers considered terminating with a client unless they considered that their work together had been successful. The most important criteria for termination were improved coping in the environment, improved intrapsychic functioning, the client's wish to terminate, meeting initial goals, and changes in therapeutic content (Fortune et al., 1991).

Member Termination

Sometimes members stop attending before the planned ending date. Unplanned termination of membership is a relatively common experience. Review studies have found unplanned termination rates of about 30 percent (Connelly & Piper, 1984; Connelly, Piper, DeCarufel, & Debbane, 1986). Unplanned termination varies with the length of the group. For example, unplanned termination rates of 5 percent to 20 percent have been reported for short-term, structured, psychoeducational groups in outpatient settings (Budman, Simeone, Reilly, & Demby, 1994; Labrecque, Peak, & Toseland, 1992; Toseland, 1995; Toseland, Labrecque, Goebel, & Whitney, 1992). In contrast, Fieldsteel (1996) reported unplanned termination rates of 28 percent to 78 percent in psychoanalytic group therapy.

In treatment groups in which participation is voluntary, a reduction in membership sometimes occurs after the first or second meeting of a group. After the initial drop, groups often develop a stable core of members who continue until the group ends.

When leading groups, workers sometimes find themselves asking rhetorically, "What have I done to cause members to fail to return to the group?" In follow-up contacts with members who terminated prematurely, many workers find they did not cause premature termination. For example, in a group for separated and divorced persons, three people did not return to the second group meeting. When they were contacted, it was found that one person lived 40 miles from where the group met and, after driving home on foggy rural roads after the first group meeting, had decided not to return. Another member's job had unexpectedly changed and required the person to be at work during the group's meeting times. It was learned from the third person's employer that one of his children had experienced a serious accident. The member called two weeks later to explain that "I have been running between the hospital and my responsibilities to the other two [children]."

Similarly, in evaluating a smoking-cessation group treatment program, it was found that members left treatment prematurely for a variety of reasons

(Toseland, Kabat, & Kemp, 1983). Several were dissatisfied with their group or their group's leader, but others left for reasons unrelated to their treatment experience. Although it is commonly assumed that dropouts are treatment failures, in evaluating eight smoking-cessation groups, it was found that one of seven dropouts left treatment prematurely because he had stopped smoking and believed he no longer needed treatment. Another dropout quit smoking before a follow-up evaluation. Thus, it is important to realize that unplanned termination of members may be the result of their lack of interest or motivation, particular life circumstances, or other factors beyond the control of the worker that have little or nothing to do with a worker's leadership skills. Toseland and colleagues (1997), for example, found that attendance at group meetings by older adults in nursing homes was greatly affected by their health status.

Yalom (1995) lists nine factors that may cause group members to drop out of treatment prematurely. Yalom points out that some members leave because of faulty selection processes. Factors causing dropouts include the following:

1. External factors, such as scheduling conflicts and changes in geographical location
2. Group deviancy, such as being the richest group member, the only unmarried member, and the like
3. Problems in developing intimate relationships
4. Fear of emotional contagion

Other premature terminations are the result of flawed therapeutic technique (Yalom, 1995), such as

1. Inability to share the worker's time
2. Complications arising from concurrent individual and group therapy
3. Early provocateurs
4. Inadequate orientation to therapy
5. Complications arising from subgrouping

Workers should not, however, assume that members' decisions to terminate prematurely have nothing to do with the group's process or its leadership. Sometimes members drop out as a result of their dissatisfaction with the group or its leader. For example, in therapy and growth-oriented groups in which confrontation is used as a therapeutic technique, members occasionally become so angry when confronted with an emotionally charged issue that they threaten to terminate. To prevent premature termination, MacKenzie (1994) suggests use of a careful pregroup screening interview to select members who have the capacity to benefit from the group. It is not always possible, however, to screen out members whose defensiveness, anger, and impulsivity may cause them to abruptly leave a group. Therefore, some workers also specify in the initial contract that members must give two weeks' notice before leaving the group so that members have a chance to rethink their decisions.

Pregroup training has also been found to be an effective way to prevent premature dropouts from therapy groups (Bednar & Kaul, 1994; Kaul & Bednar, 1994). For example, Piper, Debbane, Bienvenu, and Garant (1982) found a reduction of 13 percent to 30 percent in the dropout rate attributed to the successful management of anxiety and the development of interpersonal bonds that resulted from a pregroup training program.

When workers take the time to explore members' reasons for terminating, the data gathered can help reduce premature terminations in subsequent groups. Sometimes, for example, workers learn that arranging for child care while the group is in session helps reduce the number of dropouts. Arranging transportation to and from the group may also help. At other times, workers may find that there are ways they can improve their own skills to prevent members from dropping out of the group. For example, they may learn to be more gentle or tentative when they use confrontation methods.

Occasionally, an entire group may end prematurely. Just as there are many reasons for the premature termination of individuals, there are also many reasons for the premature termination of groups. A group that begins with a small number of members may lose several members and thus be unable to continue functioning effectively (Hartford, 1971). Groups may not receive sufficient support from their sponsoring agencies to continue functioning, or groups may be unable or unwilling to respond to external pressure to change their functioning.

Groups may also end prematurely as a result of internal dysfunction. For example, communication and interaction patterns may be maldistributed and cause subgrouping, scapegoating, or domination by a few members. The group may lack sufficient attraction for its members and, therefore, may fail to coalesce or function as a cohesive unit. Social controls such as norms, roles, status hierarchies, and power may cause severe tension and conflict when some members rebel against the control of the worker or other members. Lack of appropriate social controls may cause chaos or an aimless drift that eventually leads to dissolution of the group as a whole. Members may also have great difficulty deciding on common values, preferences, ways of working together, or other aspects of the group's culture.

Whenever workers confront the possibility that a group may end prematurely, they should carefully examine the factors that are contributing to the problem. It is often possible to trace a group's dysfunction back to the planning stage. Careful examination of the factors that contributed to a group's demise can help workers avoid such pitfalls in future groups.

Worker Termination

Although rarely mentioned in the literature, there are many instances in which workers have to terminate their work with a group. Probably the most common reason for worker termination is that students leave at the end of their field placements, but change of employment or shifting job responsibilities also lead to worker termination. In a study of two groups in which workers terminated their participation, Long, Pendleton, and Winter (1988) found that the termination of the worker led to testing of the new worker and to a reorganization of the group's processes and structures.

Several steps can be taken to reduce the disruption that can be caused by worker termination in an ongoing group:

- Group members should be told as early as possible when termination will occur.
- The reasons for termination should be shared with the group, and members should be encouraged to discuss their feelings frankly.
- Unfinished business should be completed.
- The new worker should be introduced to the group and, if possible, colead the group for a while with the terminating worker.

ENDING GROUP MEETINGS

Scheidel and Crowell (1979) list four generic worker tasks in ending group meetings: (1) closing the group's work, (2) arranging another meeting, (3) preparing a summary or report of the group's work, and (4) planning future group actions. In preparing to close, the worker should help the group keep to its agenda. The worker should ensure that all items of business and all members' concerns are given sufficient attention, but the group should not be allowed to spend too much time discussing one item of business or one member's concerns. To move the group along, the worker can do the following:

- Keep members focused on the topic of discussion
- Limit the time that each member has to discuss an issue
- Summarize what has been said
- Obtain closure on each issue or concern as it is discussed

In closing the group's work, the worker should avoid bringing up new issues, concerns, or items of business. Despite efforts to use structure to reduce discussion of important issues at the end of a meeting, Shulman (1999) points out that members occasionally raise "doorknob" issues just before ending. If consideration of these issues can be postponed, they are best handled during the next meeting when they can be given fuller consideration. When discussion of an important issue cannot be postponed, the worker should ask group members whether they prefer to continue the discussion for a brief period. If not, the issue may be taken up outside the group by the worker and any interested members.

In closing the group's work, the worker should also help members to resolve any remaining conflicts. Resolving conflicts helps members to work in harmony for the decisions reached by the group as a whole. In addition, the worker may want to discuss the strengths and weaknesses of the working relationship that has developed among members during the group meeting, particularly if the group will work together in the future.

During the ending minutes, the worker should help the group plan for future meetings. When considering whether to meet again, it is helpful to review and summarize the group's work. A summary of the group's activities during the meeting clarifies issues that have been resolved and points out issues that remain unresolved. A clear summary of the group's progress is a prerequisite for arranging another meeting. Summaries also remind members of the activities or tasks they have agreed to work on between meetings and help the worker become aware of items that should be included in the agenda for the next meeting.

If a group has completed action on a particular task, the final minutes can also be used to ensure that all members understand and agree to the oral or written information that will be presented at the conclusion of a group's work. Some task forces may prepare extensive written reports of their findings and conclusions. In these groups, it is not productive to prepare the report during the group meeting. The closing minutes can be used to formulate and highlight the major conclusions to be enumerated in the report, to assign members responsibility for preparing major sections of the report, and to develop a mechanism for obtaining approval from members before disseminating the report.

The endings of group meetings can also be used to plan future group actions. However, because planning action steps is time-consuming, plans are usually developed during the middle of a group meeting. At the ending of a meeting, plans are summarized, and members select (or are assigned) tasks to carry out.

The worker should help members maintain their motivation, commitment, and responsibility to implement and carry out the tasks they have agreed to complete between meetings. To help members maintain their motivation, the worker should praise members for their work in the group and for their willingness to commit themselves to tasks outside the meeting. The worker may also want to mention any benefits that will accrue to members for maintaining their commitment to the plans and activities they have agreed to complete.

ENDING THE GROUP AS A WHOLE

A variety of tasks are associated with ending a group as a whole:

- Maintaining and generalizing change efforts
- Reducing group attraction and promoting the independent functioning of individual members

- Helping members deal with their feelings about ending
- Planning for the future
- Making referrals
- Evaluating the work of the group

With the exception of evaluating the work of the group, which is discussed in Chapter 13, the remaining portion of this chapter examines each ending task and the skills and techniques the worker can use to facilitate the effective ending of a group. Many of these tasks may be carried out simultaneously. The specific order in which each task is completed depends on the specific group the worker is leading.

Maintaining and Generalizing Change Efforts

After treatment plans have been developed and carried out, workers should ensure that the changes that have been achieved are maintained and generalized to other important aspects of members' lives. Evaluations of results of therapeutic interventions suggest that positive changes are often difficult to maintain over time. For example, in an evaluation of two different group intervention programs for caregivers of the frail elderly, it was found that some of the positive changes found immediately after group intervention were not sustained at one year (Labrecque, Peak, & Toseland, 1992; Toseland, 1990).

Positive changes are even harder to maintain in group treatment programs that are focused on individuals with addictive disorders. For example, in an evaluation of a group treatment program for smokers, it was found that although more than 60 percent of members who attended the program initially stopped smoking, the cessation rate had dropped to 36 percent after three months (Toseland, Kabat, & Kemp, 1983). Results obtained for a variety of other addictive disorders, such as narcotics use, alcohol use, and overeating, show similarly high relapse rates (Chiauzzi, 1991; Marlatt, 1996; Marlatt & Barrett, 1994; Vaillant, 1995). Maintenance is also difficult to achieve in working with antisocial group members such as juvenile delinquents and in working with group members who have severe psychological disorders.

Both novice and experienced workers often mistakenly believe that changes in specific behaviors can be taken as a sign of generalized improvement in a member's level of functioning. These workers do little to ensure that specific behavior changes generalize to related, but untreated, behaviors. Results of a variety of different treatment programs have shown, however, that therapeutic changes occurring in specific behaviors do not always generalize to similar behaviors performed by a member in other contexts (Masters, Burish, Hollon, & Rimm, 1987). For example, an unassertive group member may learn to be assertive in a particular situation but may continue to be nonassertive in other situations. Similarly, a parent may learn how to reduce a child's temper tantrums, but this success may not affect the parent's ability to help the child play cooperatively with other children.

Although some people seek group treatment only for changes in specific behaviors, most people enter group treatment with the expectation that there will be a generalized improvement in their life situations. Therefore, it is important for workers to help members generalize changes achieved in specific behaviors and performed in particular situations to related behaviors performed in other contexts.

With the notable exception of Rose (1989, 1998), little has been written about these topics in group work. Almost all the theoretical and clinical work on maintenance and generalization of change has come from the literature on behavior modification and learning theory. The literature suggests several things workers can do to help members maintain and generalize the changes they have achieved, including the following:

- Helping members work on relevant situations
- Helping members develop confidence in their abilities
- Using a variety of different situations and settings in helping members learn new behaviors
- Using a variety of naturally occurring consequences
- Extending treatment through follow-up sessions
- Preventing setbacks in an unsympathetic environment
- Helping members solve problems independently by providing a framework for organizing data and solving problems that can be used in many different situations

Relevant Situations

To achieve long-lasting changes that will generalize to similar situations in members' lives, the concerns and issues worked on in the group should be a relevant and realistic sample of concerns and issues experienced by members in their daily lives. Sometimes members become distracted by issues that are not central to their concerns, a possible sign that the members are avoiding difficult issues and the changes they necessitate. The worker can help by drawing members' attention back to the central concerns that brought them together as a group.

In other cases, the situations discussed may be highly specific and individual. Although it is important to be as specific and concrete as possible when developing treatment plans, it is also important to ensure that situations that are relevant to all group members are included in the group's work so that members are prepared for situations they are likely to encounter in the future.

Although group meetings should provide a protected environment in which members receive support, encouragement, and understanding, the group should also be a place in which members can get honest feedback about how their behavior is likely to be seen outside the group. Members should be encouraged to try out new behaviors in the group, but they should not be misled into thinking they will receive the same level of support and encouragement for trying new behaviors outside the group. In short, although the group should provide a supportive and caring atmosphere in which to work, the group should help members to understand, cope with, and prepare for reactions likely to be experienced outside the group.

Helping Members Develop Confidence

Many treatment groups spend much time discussing members' problems and concerns as well as their inappropriate ways of handling situations. Although ventilating thoughts and feelings may be therapeutic, Lee (1997) points out that too much time in treatment is often spent on the negative aspects of members' problems and not enough time is spent empowering members and building their self-confidence. Lee suggests that emphasis on negative thoughts, feelings, and experiences reinforces the members' tendency to continue to express these problems outside the group.

As the group progresses, workers should encourage members to focus on adaptive alternatives to the problematic situations they are experiencing. If members dwell on poor performances and inhibiting thoughts in the group, they are less likely to feel confident about their abilities to cope with or resolve the problems they experience in their daily lives. Although it is not possible or desirable to avoid discussions of problems in treatment groups, workers should help members become more aware of their own abilities. Members should be encouraged to use their abilities and their resources to resolve the problematic situations that they encounter as they prepare for leaving the group. Program activities, role plays, and exercises are particularly useful in helping members to become more aware of their strengths and to build confidence in their ability to solve problems. This process, in turn, will help members gain confidence in their abilities to continue to function adaptively after they leave the group.

Using a Variety of Situations and Settings

Another aspect of maintaining and generalizing change is preparing members for different situations that may interfere with their abilities to maintain the changes they have made. Although preparations for maintaining changes are emphasized during ending-stage meetings, such activities should be given attention throughout members' participation in a group. Issues and concerns brought to group treatment are rarely, if ever, confined to one situation or setting in a member's life. A member who experiences communication difficulties, for example, often experiences them in many situations with different people. Therefore, it is often helpful in treatment groups to have members practice responses with different members in a variety of situations. Because of the availability of group members who will respond differently from one another, group treatment is ideally suited for this purpose. Bandura's research (1977) confirms that the use of multiple models (group members) promotes generalization of treatment effects.

Easier situations should be role-played before more difficult situations. What constitutes an easy or a difficult situation varies from person to person, so the worker should assess each person's needs when developing a hierarchy of situations to work on in the group. Once a member demonstrates the ability to handle a variety of situations in the group, the member should be encouraged to get additional practice by trying new ways of behaving between meetings.

Program activities can also be used to simulate situations that may be encountered outside the group. For example, children referred to a group because they have difficulty playing with classmates can be encouraged to participate in team sports in which cooperative play is essential; long-term psychiatric patients may be encouraged to prepare and participate in a group dinner as a way of practicing skills that will help them when they are placed in a community residence.

Using Naturally Occurring Consequences

Although it is often difficult to make changes initially, changes are maintained and generalized by the resulting positive consequences. For example, although losing weight is initially uncomfortable, loss soon results in positive compliments from peers and feeling better about oneself. To maintain and generalize behavior changes, the worker should help group members experience the positive consequences of changes as soon as possible and maintain the positive consequences for as long as possible.

One method is to help members focus on positive rather than negative consequences. For example, a member who decides to stop smoking should be encouraged to seek out the reactions of family members, friends, and group members who no longer have to put up with the smell of stale cigarettes and smoke-filled rooms. The member should also be encouraged to replace urges to smoke with thoughts about the soon-to-be-experienced positive effects of not smoking, such as increased lung capacity and greater vitality and endurance. The worker can also contact significant others in the member's life and ask that they continue to reinforce the ex-smoker's resolve not to smoke after the group ends.

Another way to enhance naturally occurring contingencies is to help members modify environmental consequences so that behavior change is more readily maintained and generalized. For example, a buddy system may be established so that group members receive positive feedback for changes between group sessions. Group members may be asked to modify friendship patterns, social activities, or their home environment in ways that provide positive consequences for changes they have made through their efforts in the group. By enhancing and highlighting naturally occurring positive consequences and by reducing negative consequences, initial changes can be maintained and generalized.

Follow-Up Sessions

Another way to help ensure that treatment results are maintained and generalized is to provide members the opportunity to meet together for follow-up sessions after the completion of a formal group treatment program. For example, a time-limited, outpatient psychotherapy group might meet for 12 weekly sessions and then for six follow-up sessions at one-month intervals. After this time, two quarterly meetings during the rest of the year might complete the treatment contract.

Although follow-up sessions are infrequently used by professionals, they make self-help groups appealing to participants. The popularity of self-help groups can, in part, be attributed to the flexible, open-ended, long-term membership that is encouraged in many of these groups. Self-help groups often have a small group of members who regularly attend meetings, along with many other members who attend as needed (Toseland & Hacker, 1982). For self-help group participants who have attended sessions regularly in the past, occasional attendance at future meetings can maintain treatment gains and gradually reduce dependency on the group.

Follow-up sessions reinforce members' commitment to maintaining changes. They remind members of the changes that have taken place in their lives since they began treatment. Members can share similar experiences about their difficulties in maintaining changes and trying to generalize changes to new situations and new life experiences.

Follow-up sessions are generally not used to introduce members to new material. Instead, they are used as an opportunity for members to share their experiences since the previous meeting. Members should be encouraged to discuss new problem situations they have encountered and to describe how they have handled these situations. The emphasis should be on helping members identify the coping skills they have developed to maintain changes achieved during treatment.

Follow-up sessions are particularly helpful for members who have difficulty maintaining treatment gains. Members can discuss the circumstances surrounding particular relapses and consult the group worker and other members about how to best handle these occurrences. The additional support provided by follow-up sessions is often sufficient to help members overcome brief relapses that might otherwise turn into treatment failures.

Preventing Setbacks in Unsympathetic Environments

Even when careful attention has been given to the environment that a member faces outside the group, the support, trust, and sharing found in well-functioning treatment groups is rarely duplicated in the members' home or community environments. Members should be prepared to face possible setbacks in the unsympathetic environment they are likely to experience outside the group. Rose (1989) suggests that the experiences of the worker in leading previous groups, as well as the experiences of former group members, are useful in developing vignettes that describe realistic and typical situations group members are likely to encounter outside the group. During the final few group sessions, members should discuss how to respond to such situations and practice responses with one another by using modeling, role play, rehearsal, and coaching.

Because members are likely to experience situations that threaten their treatment gains soon after changes are initiated, members should be encouraged to describe such situations in the group. In this way, all group members become exposed to a variety of situations and reactions to changes, and they can learn to handle reactions before the situations occur in their own lives. Meichenbaum (1977), for example, reported that a stress inoculation treatment program in which members were taught to anticipate negative reactions and ways to cope with the reactions was effective in helping members maintain treatment gains.

Members may encounter difficult situations any time of the day or night. Because the group worker may not be available to members at those times, the worker should inform members about how to contact on-call workers, emergency hot lines, and other 24-hour services.

The difficulty of maintaining changes among members with drug, alcohol, and other addictive behavior problems suggests a need for intensive and extensive treatment. One way to augment group treatment with a professional worker is to link members to self-help groups. Alcoholics Anonymous groups, for example, often meet each evening, or at least several times each week, and can provide members with an alternative to spending their evenings in a neighborhood bar or drinking alone at home. These groups also encourage recovering alcoholics to form close relationships with new members, which provides new members with models of sobriety and encourages the development of a network of supportive relationships. Similarly, organizations such as Recovery, Inc., Parents without Partners, Parents Anonymous, and Gamblers Anonymous help members with other types of problems and concerns to become involved with a network of people to whom they can turn at particularly difficult times.

Members of task groups can also benefit from preparing for an unsympathetic environment. Plans, reports, and other products of a task group's work may encounter resistance as they are considered by others outside the group. Resistance is especially likely when the products of a task group are controversial or have negative implications for a particular program, an entire organization, or a social service delivery system. Also, resistance is more likely to be encountered when proposals must go through several levels of review before they are approved (Brager & Holloway, 1978). Therefore, it is important for task group members to anticipate resistance to implementing the group's work and to plan strategies to counteract the resistance.

Helping Members Solve Problems Independently

No matter how many different situations are discussed and practiced within a group, it is not possible to cover the full range of situations that members may experience outside a group. Therefore, during the group, members should be learning how to solve their own problems independently to gradually lessen the need for continued treatment. This process should begin as early as possible in the group experience and be given particular emphasis in the last few meetings of the group.

Throughout the group treatment process, workers can support independent functioning by building members' confidence in their existing coping skills and by helping members develop and rely on new coping skills. Workers should also teach members the principles underlying the intervention methods used in the group. Workers sometimes fail to teach members the underlying therapeutic principles of an intervention because they think professional knowledge should not be shared with clients, that group members may not be able to understand therapeutic principles, or that members may misuse the information they receive. Most group members who enter treatment voluntarily are eager to learn more about ways to cope with their concerns. For example, having members of an assertion-training group read *Your Perfect Right* (Alberti & Emmons, 1995), having members of a parent-training group read *Parents Are Teachers* (Becker, 1971), or having members of a weight-loss group read *Slim Chance in a Fat World* (Stuart & Davis, 1972) helps them to learn basic principles that they can use as they encounter situations not discussed in the group.

Some treatment approaches, such as Eric Berne's *transactional analysis* (Berne, 1961) and Albert Ellis' *rational-emotive therapy* (Ellis, 1962, 1992), encourage workers to help members understand the basic principles underlying their treatment approaches. Workers who use other treatment approaches should also consider spending time teaching members the basic principles underlying therapeutic interventions. When teaching members, workers should translate technical terms into jargon-free explanations, especially if members use English as a second language.

Having members summarize what they have learned in the group and deduce general principles from the summaries are other effective ways to help members see how principles can be applied to other situations. For example, in summarizing what they have learned, members of a couples' group became aware of general principles regarding communication, such as maintaining eye contact to show that they are listening, summarizing core content of messages to ensure understanding, and using "I" messages to communicate their feelings and thoughts.

Reducing Group Attraction

In addition to helping members maintain and generalize the changes they have made in a group, the ending stage should help members become less dependent on the group. This goal can be achieved by helping members rely on their own skills and resources as well as on sources of support outside the group. Planning for termination should begin with workers' awareness of their own feelings about terminating with individual members and with the group as a whole. Particularly in support groups and therapy groups, it is not uncommon for workers to become emotionally attached to individual members or to the group as a whole. Workers should be careful not to foster dependence. They should carefully assess whether they are being overly protective of members or covertly or overtly undermining members' efforts to function without the group. Supervision can be useful in helping workers examine their feelings about terminating.

To ensure that members are prepared for ending, it is good practice to begin discussions of termination at least four sessions before the planned termination date. Members should be fully involved in planning for termination. Program activities can be used effectively at the end of a group to help members prepare for termination (Henry, 1992; Mayadas & Glasser, 1981; Wayne & Avery, 1979). Workers should describe the ideas they have about program activities for ending the group, solicit members' feedback, and ask for additional suggestions. Appropriate program activities for ending a group are activities that

- Demonstrate or encourage reflection about the skills members have learned in the group
- Encourage members to express their feelings about the group and each other
- Focus on future activities
- Encourage both individual and group participation

For example, getting together for a dinner is a program activity that is commonly used at the ending of a group. Planning for a dinner encourages both individual and group-oriented participation. During the dinner, members often discuss the things they have learned in the group, their feelings about ending, and their plans for the future.

Endings are often marked by ceremonies. Program activities, such as having a party or a potluck dinner, awarding certificates of merit, or having each member say or write something special about other members, can be viewed as ceremonies that signify the end of the group.

Used creatively, ceremonies can also help maintain and generalize changes made by members. For example, in the next-to-last session of a weight-loss group, members were asked to write themselves two letters, each containing (1) their feelings about being overweight, (2) how good it felt to be losing weight, and (3) a reiteration of their commitment to continue losing weight. The self-addressed letters were mailed by the worker after the group had ended at three-week intervals as a reminder to members of their commitment to losing weight and maintaining weight losses.

Group attraction can be reduced in other ways. Members can be encouraged to summarize their accomplishments and discuss why they no longer need the group. Meetings can be scheduled less frequently or for shorter periods of time to reduce the importance of the group for members. Workers can encourage members to become involved in outside activities that compete with the group for members' time and energy. Such activities also can support members and help them maintain changes.

Feelings about Ending

The feelings that members and workers have about ending are related to the relationships that have developed in the group. The feelings that members and workers have about ending their participation in a group depend on a number of factors, including whether the group is planned to be time limited or open ended, how long the group meets, the nature of the group's work (e.g., primarily task or socioemotional), the intensity of the relationships that develop among members, and the extent to which the ending is associated with a sense of progress, achievement, or graduation (Germain & Gitterman, 1996). After examining reactions to termination, Fortune and colleagues (Fortune, 1987; Fortune, Pearlingi, & Rochelle, 1992) concluded that the strongest reactions were positive affect, positive flight to constructive outside activities, and objective evaluations of treatment goals and processes.

Many positive feelings can result from a skillfully facilitated group ending:

- A feeling of empowerment and potency as members realize they are capable of accomplishing goals
- A feeling of independence resulting from being in greater control of their own lives
- A sense of satisfaction and pride in successfully completing the group experience
- A feeling of usefulness resulting from helping other members during group interaction
- A feeling of confidence that problems can be coped with or solved

At the same time, however, members may experience negative feelings about the ending of a group. A common reaction is denial (Levine, 1979). Not wanting to show that they will miss the worker or others in the group, members sometimes ignore workers' attempts to prepare them for ending by changing the topic of discussion or by indicating that they are looking forward to ending. Other common reactions are feelings of disappointment, powerlessness, abandonment, or rejection (Brabender & Fallon, 1996). Members may act out these feelings by becoming angry or hostile. In other cases, they may engage in regressive behavior that exhibits the symptoms or problems they had when they first entered the group (Malekoff, 1997). Other reactions include emotional or psychological clinging to the worker, acting out, and devaluing the group experience or the skill of the worker (Levinson, 1977; Malekoff, 1997).

More often, members simply wish they could continue with the warm, supportive relationships they have found in the group. Therefore, they may experience a sense of loss and accompanying sadness at the ending of the group. Members may also question their ability to maintain changes without the help of the group.

As mentioned earlier, workers are not immune to reactions to ending a group. In a study of practitioners' reactions to termination of individual treatment, Fortune, Pearlingi, and Rochelle (1992) report that the practitioners' strongest reactions are

- Pride and accomplishment in the client's success
- Pride in their own therapeutic skill
- A renewed sense of therapeutic process
- Sadness, sense of loss, or ambivalence about no longer working with the client
- Doubt or disappointment about the client's progress or ability to function independently
- A re-experiencing of their own losses
- Relief, doubt, or guilt about their therapeutic effectiveness

According to Levine (1979), workers should be aware of their own reactions to ending to fully appreciate the difficulties that members may be experiencing. If workers are not aware of their own feelings, they may withdraw emotionally or they may encourage the dependence of members and prolong treatment beyond what is needed. Workers also may want to share their reactions as a way of helping members identify and express their own feelings and reactions.

It is helpful to begin termination several meetings before the end of the group. As members begin to react to ending, the worker can point out that conflicting or ambivalent feelings during this stage are common. Members should be encouraged to discuss their conflicting and ambivalent feelings.

Workers can help members with their negative emotional and behavioral reactions to ending by developing increased awareness of the connection between their feelings and behaviors and the termination process. It is also helpful to encourage members to discuss the coping abilities and other gains they have achieved as a result of being in the group. The worker can prepare members for ending by clarifying what the role of the worker and the sponsoring agency will be in helping members maintain gains after the group ends.

Planning for the Future

In time-limited groups, some members may wish to contract for additional services. When considering new services, the worker should help members clarify (1) their continuing needs, (2) the goals they hope to achieve, (3) the duration of the new service period, and (4) any appropriate modifications of the original contract. Recontracting should occur when there is a clear need for additional services and when members are highly motivated to achieve additional goals or to continue work on original goals that they have only partially completed. Occasionally, all members of a group may express interest in continuing to meet. In such cases, the worker may recontract for additional meetings with all members or may encourage members to meet on their own without the worker.

When workers encourage members to continue to meet on their own, they are participating in the development of a self-help group. The worker helps groups continue to meet by developing natural leadership and by helping with any resources that may be needed (Toseland & Coppola, 1985). Rather than total independence, many new self-help groups prefer continuing contact, guidance, and leadership from the worker until the new group has been firmly established. Many existing self-help groups have been started by professional workers in this manner (Toseland & Hacker, 1982). The worker can continue to assist self-help groups after they have developed by (1) providing material support to maintain the group, (2) referring clients to the group, and (3) acting as a consultant to the group.

In rare instances, the members of a group may wish to continue meeting because they are unable to terminate the group in a positive and responsible fashion. The group may develop a culture that supports members' dependency rather than preparing them for independent functioning in the environment outside the group. When this occurs, the worker should explore the situation with the group and, in a supportive manner, help the members end the group experience by using activities as discussed in this chapter. Klein (1972) has referred to this process as a worker's skill in letting go of the group.

Sometimes the ending of a group may result in no further contact with members. However, workers are rarely sure that members will not need services in the future. Changing life situations, new crises, or relapses may cause members to seek help again. The worker should discuss how members can seek additional services if they are needed. In some agencies, the worker may explain that he or she has an open-door policy, so that members who need additional services can contact the worker directly. In other agencies, the policy may be for former clients to apply for services in the same manner that new clients apply. Taking this step clarifies the position of the worker and the agency with regard to how members can obtain any additional services that may be needed.

The worker should plan for the future with each member. Plans should include the support systems and resources that will be available after the group ends. Workers should also encourage members to use their own skills, resources, and strengths to meet their needs by expressing confidence in members' abilities, encouraging them to try new skills outside the group, and repeating successful skill-building activities and role plays so members develop feelings of mastery and self-confidence.

In some situations, preparation for the future may involve planning with others for continuing treatment for members. For example, in preparing for the ending of the children's group, the worker should contact the children's parents to review each child's progress and to plan for additional services. In groups in which members are participating in other agency services such as individual counseling, the worker should contact the member's case manager or primary worker to evaluate the member's progress in the group and to plan for additional services. Similarly, in residential and inpatient settings, the ending of a group may not signify the end of service. The worker should meet with other staff, perhaps in a case conference or team meeting, to report progress and to plan for the future needs of members.

Members who prematurely terminate from groups should not be forgotten when plans for future service needs are made. Without follow-up contact, dropouts may feel abandoned. Their failure to continue with a particular group may signify to them that their situation is hopeless. Therefore, dropouts from treatment should be contacted whenever possible. One of the primary objectives of a follow-up contact is to motivate persons who terminate prematurely to seek further treatment if it is needed. The worker can inquire about difficulties the former members may be having in continuing to attend group meetings, and may suggest ways to overcome these impediments. During this process, the worker should identify any needs that former group members have for continuing service and refer them to appropriate resources and services.

Making Referrals

During the ending stage of group work, workers frequently connect members to other services or resources. In some cases, members may be transferred to workers in the same agency. In other cases, referrals may be made to workers in other agencies.

A referral should be made only after the worker and the member have appraised the member's need for additional services or resources. If the member is motivated to seek additional services, the referral can proceed. If the member is not motivated to seek additional services, but the worker's assessment suggests that additional services may be beneficial, the worker should proceed by helping the member explore reasons for resistance.

Whenever possible, the member should be helped to use informal, natural helping systems. If these types of systems are unavailable or are judged to be inadequate, the member should be referred to professional helping resources. Before making a referral, the worker should discuss the reasons for the referral with the member and answer any questions the member has. It is often helpful to find out whether the member has had any prior contact with the referral source or has heard anything about the source. Members' impressions and previous experiences with particular referral sources can be influential in determining whether members will follow through and use the resources to which they are referred.

In preparing to make effective referrals, workers should become familiar with available community resources. They should also get to know a particular contact person in frequently used referral sources. It is also helpful to be familiar with basic information about referral sources to share with members who are being referred, such as information about eligibility requirements, the waiting time for service, the business hours of the agency, and the type of service provided. Such information will prepare the member for what to expect when contacting the referral source and will avoid members' developing expectations that will not be met. Because it may be difficult for workers to be familiar with all community resources that are available in an area, agencies should maintain up-to-date files with basic information about such resources and services.

When making a referral, the worker should write the name of the agency, the contact person, and the agency's address on a card to give to the member. In some cases, referral sources may have forms that have to be filled out before a member can be seen. Often, release forms need to be signed by the member so that information in a member's file can be sent to the referral source.

Because many people never reach the resources or services to which they were referred (Craig, Huffine, & Brooks, 1974; Weissman, 1976), it is helpful for the worker to call the contact person while the member is with the worker to emphasize that the member is expected at the referral source for a particular appointment. The worker should also ensure that the members

- Know how to get to the agencies to which they have been referred
- Have a means of transportation or know how to use public transportation
- Are capable of getting to the referral sources

Members who are severely impaired may need help in getting to referral sources. The worker, a volunteer, or a case aide may have to accompany the member during the first visit.

The worker should check to ensure that members have reached the referral source and have received the needed service. In addition, members should be instructed to contact the worker if they fail to get what they need from the referral sources. A referral may fail for a number of reasons, including the following:

1. The referral source has had a change in policy; for example, eligibility requirements may have become more stringent.
2. The member lacks motivation.
3. The member lacks the skill necessary to obtain the needed resources.
4. The worker has given the member incorrect information or insufficient help to contact the referral source.

Follow-up contacts allow workers to assess why members did not obtain needed services or resources. They also allow workers to plan with members about how to obtain needed resources and services in the future.

SUMMARY

The ending stage is a critical time in the life of a group. During the ending stage, the work of the group is consolidated and lasting impressions are made about the efficacy of the entire group experience. Endings can either be planned or unplanned. Unfortunately, in many voluntary groups, unplanned terminations are fairly common. This chapter makes suggestions about how to facilitate planned endings and what to do when members terminate before the planned ending of a group.

Procedures for facilitating endings vary, depending on the type of group being led. In task groups and treatment groups in which members have not been encouraged to self-disclose or form supportive relationships, endings are less emotionally charged than are endings in groups in which considerable self-disclosure has taken place and in which members depend on one another for help with their personal concerns and problems. Other variations in group endings depend on whether the group has an open or closed membership policy, is short-term or long-term, and is attractive or unattractive to its members.

Major tasks in ending a meeting of a group include (1) closing the work, (2) arranging another meeting, (3) preparing a summary or a report of the group's work, and (4) planning for future group actions. Major tasks in ending the group as a whole include (1) maintaining and generalizing change efforts, (2) evaluating the work of the group, (3) reducing group attraction and promoting independent member functioning, (4) helping members with their feelings about ending, (5) planning for the future, and (6) making effective referrals. This chapter examines the skills and strategies needed to carry out each task.

LEARNING ASSIGNMENTS

1. Interview an experienced group worker. Ask the respondent to discuss personal experiences with members who drop out of treatment groups. Make a list and rank the reasons for unplanned termination of members. What might the group worker have done to reduce the number of unplanned terminations?

2. You have been leading a short-term social skills group designed to help psychiatric inpatients live independently in the community. In preparing for ending the group, describe four strategies that you could use to help members maintain their newly acquired skills.

3. How would you assist a member of a residential group who started acting out when she learned that she would be leaving the facility after a one-and-a-half-year stay for foster placement? What effects might her acting out behavior have on other members of the residence? How would you help the residents deal with these effects?

4. Imagine that you work in an intensive outpatient alcoholism rehabilitation program that relies on group treatment as the primary therapeutic modality. How would you help prepare the members of your group to maintain sobriety after they leave the program?

5. Design three program activities that would be useful for the ending stage of a treatment group. Describe the purpose of each activity. How would each activity help members end their group experience on a positive note? How would each activity help group members resolve their feelings about ending?

CASE EXAMPLE

As the facilitator of a staff support group for hospice workers, Carla was familiar with the needs of the group members. She had been hired two years ago to conduct weekly sessions of the group so that the staff could have an opportunity to discuss their feelings and the stress associated with working with the terminally ill. But Carla faced a new challenge when Nick, the new executive director, informed her that the group would have to be discontinued because of cost constraints. Although Nick had insisted that she give the group only one week's notice before it ended, Carla had been able to negotiate for three more group sessions.

Carla pondered the group's situation and wondered how the members would take the news. As hospice workers, the group members faced endings with their clients every day. Now, the group members would have to deal with the ending of the group and the dissolution of an important support system. Although group members had achieved high levels of cohesiveness and mutual aid in the group, Carla feared that ending the group would detrimentally affect staff morale and the quality of their work.

Carla outlined some of the goals she hoped to accomplish in the next three sessions. She wanted to present the news about discontinuing the group in as positive a way as possible. Members would need time to adjust to the idea of ending the group, so she planned on telling the group during the next meeting. She also wanted to help members maintain some of the gains they had accomplished through the group, particularly those that helped them deal with the stress of their work. At the same time, she wanted to help members reduce their reliance on the group for formal support and find sources of support outside of the group. Finally, she hoped that the members would be able to spend time evaluating the effectiveness of the group. These were formidable goals for the group's last sessions.

The ending of the group was announced at the next meeting. Carla took a supportive but matter-of-fact approach to making the announcement. Despite her own feelings about the actions of the new executive director, she refrained from blaming him for ending the group. By doing this she hoped to redirect some of the members' energies into accomplishing as much as they could in the next three sessions. However, members spent a good deal of time expressing strong feelings about ending the group. Several were angry and others expressed a sense of sadness and loss. Some members wondered how they would be able to deal with the stress of their jobs without the support of the group. Carla allowed a good deal of time for members to ventilate.

As members came to accept the ending of the group, Carla made some suggestions about how to proceed. She challenged group members to discuss how the group had helped them. Despite some early resistance, members were able to discuss the benefits they had obtained by participating in the group. Several were quite articulate about how, as a result of their group participation, they had accomplished personal changes that helped them deal with the emotional impact of their work. Carla used the discussions to encourage members to maintain these changes after the group ended. She then suggested that members come to the next group session prepared to discuss how they could get personal and emotional support from sources outside the group. Members accepted this homework assignment and the session ended.

During the next session, members began by revisiting their reactions to the ending of the group. Members expressed feelings of anger, loss, grief, and frustration. Carla again allowed them time to ventilate and work through these feelings. She pointed out that in a symbolic way, the ending of the group would mirror the dying, death, and grief process so familiar to the members in their everyday work at the hospice. She observed that members needed time to work though their own sense of loss over ending the group.

Later in the session, Carla reviewed each member's suggestions about how to find support outside of the group. As a result of this discussion, the group decided to develop a buddy system in place of the weekly group. Relying on this system, members could systematically exchange feelings and experiences related to their work. Carla suggested that the support system would allow members to become more independent from the group and more focused on other sources of support. She emphasized that the development of the buddy system demonstrated members' ability to create a new way to obtain support. Then, as the meeting ended, she reviewed and reinforced some of the capacities and skills members had demonstrated during previous group sessions when describing how they coped with emotionally challenging patient care situations.

Carla was totally surprised by the group's last meeting. She had expected that the beginning of the last session would be somber because of the strong emotional bonds among members and the feelings they had expressed about ending. On her arrival, however, she was greeted with a chocolate cake, refreshments, and a nicely wrapped present from the group. Members expressed their gratitude to Carla for her strong leadership and support. Carla gratefully accepted the members' comments and asked if the group could finish its formal discussions and then move on to its party.

Members mentioned that they were more resigned to ending the group. They expressed fewer feelings of anger and more feelings of sadness during this last session. Members also discussed their favorite memories of the group and how the group had benefited them. Finally, Carla asked members to evaluate the effectiveness of the group by completing a short questionnaire with open-ended questions. After completing the questionnaire, members discussed plans for the future. Although the last session went well, it was a bittersweet experience.

Case Examples

Although case examples are useful in the teaching and learning of group work practice, there is a dearth of examples illustrating practice with treatment and task groups. This chapter presents two case examples. The first example, a caregiver support group, illustrates work with a treatment group. The second example, a community coalition helping people with AIDS, illustrates work with a task group.

A CAREGIVER SUPPORT GROUP

The case example selected to illustrate practice with treatment groups describes a support group for family members who are providing care for frail elderly relatives. It illustrates the blending of supportive, educational, and psychotherapeutic interventions in a single group. It also illustrates a blending of a relatively structured group format with relatively unstructured follow-up meetings.

The leader of the group is a professional social worker who has had extensive clinical experience working with individuals and family members with chronic disabilities. The group met for eight weekly two-hour sessions and then decided to continue to meet monthly. During the first eight meetings, the group agreed to use a structured approach that included support, education, coping skills, and problem solving. Monthly follow-up meetings were less structured, with members reporting in turn what had transpired since the last meeting and seeking support and assistance as needed.

The Support Component

Although specific time was set aside during each meeting for the educational, problem-solving, and coping-skills components, support interventions were used throughout each group meeting. Supportive interventions included (1) ventilation of stressful experiences in an understanding and supportive environment, (2) validation and confirmation of similar caregiving experiences, (3) affirmation of members' abilities to cope with their situations, (4) praise for providing high-quality care, (5) support and understanding during difficult situations, (6) hopefulness about the future, and (7) mutual aid. The worker took the lead in modeling supportive interventions and encouraged members to be supportive of each other.

The Educational Component

The educational component occurred during the first 30 to 40 minutes of each of the initial eight meetings. A different topic was covered each week:

- Session 1 provided an introduction to the support group.
- Session 2 focused on caregivers' emotions and feelings.
- Session 3 focused on care receivers' reactions to illness.
- Session 4 focused on how caregivers could take care of themselves but still do positive things with their frail parent.
- Session 5 focused on communication between the caregiver and care receiver and between the caregiver and other family members.
- Session 6 focused on community resources.
- Session 7 focused on medical needs, pharmacology issues, and the nursing home placement process.
- Session 8 focused on home management techniques and strategies and on resources for environmental modifications including specialized home-care appliances and devices.[1]

After a brief presentation by the leader or a guest speaker, members were encouraged to ask questions, share information, and discuss issues related to the weekly topic presented by the leader.

The Coping-Skills Component

This part of the program was conceptually linked to Lazarus and Folkman's (1984) model of stress and coping based on Stress Inoculation Training (SIT), developed by Meichenbaum and colleagues (Meichenbaum, 1977, 1985; Meichenbaum & Cameron, 1983). SIT involves multiple strategies such as didactic

[1]A number of manuals are available that describe topics for caregiver support group meetings and provide useful background material. Three of these manuals are *Caregiver's Support Group Facilitator's Manual,* Department of Veterans Affairs, Central Office, Social Work Service (122), 810 Vermont Avenue NW, Washington, DC 20420; Montgomery, R. (Ed.). (1985). *Helping Families Help.* Seattle: University of Washington Press; and *Practical Help: Guide for Course Leaders,* New York State Office for the Aging, 2 Empire State Plaza, Albany, NY 12223.

teaching, relaxation training, cognitive restructuring, self-monitoring, and self-instruction. Instead of teaching a single stress-management technique, the leader introduced members to several techniques and encouraged members to use the techniques that worked best for them. Although the leader's goal was to cover specific coping skills during each meeting, the contents of the coping-skills component were incorporated flexibly into the first eight sessions according to the needs of the members and the pressing problems members expressed during discussions in the educational component and during the problem-solving component (Everly, 1989).

Session 1 of the coping-skills component was focused on assuring caregivers that their reactions to their family members' health problems were normal. The session also focused on acquainting members with the concepts of stress, appraisal, and coping (Lazarus & Folkman, 1984). At the end of the session, members were given the opportunity to discuss their reactions to their family members' illness, their illness-related appraisals, and the coping strategies they had been using to deal with their reactions.

Session 2 focused on helping members identify and label their emotional and bodily coping responses to their family members' physical and mental condition and to their role as a caregiver. The leader reinforced effective coping skills and encouraged members to work toward changing ineffective coping skills. As in previous successful group intervention programs for caregivers of the chronically ill (McCallion, Toseland, & Diehl, 1994; Toseland & Rossiter, 1989), members were encouraged to recognize their own specific emotional and bodily reactions to stress and to identify situations that provoked stress and characteristic coping responses. They were also taught to better recognize early signs of stress and their typical cognitive appraisals and coping reactions. To facilitate the learning process, members were asked to keep a diary between group meetings to record the stressors they experienced during the week and their cognitive and behavioral responses to the stressors. Practice in recognizing stressors and identifying typical appraisals and coping reactions continued during remaining sessions.

During sessions 3 and 4, two relaxation techniques were introduced and practiced by members as a means to creatively counteract the negative effects of strain associated with caregiving and to cope with other, unavoidable life stresses. First, a deep breathing technique was introduced and practiced (Toseland, Labrecque, Goebel, & Whitney, 1992). The technique, which is easily learned, provided members with an effective strategy to moderate their typical reactions to stress by interrupting their habituated responses and slowing down their cognitive processes, thereby increasing the likelihood that more planned and effective coping reactions could be chosen.

Second, progressive muscle relaxation (Jacobson, 1978) was introduced and practiced. Members were given an audiotape containing muscle relaxation instructions and encouraged to practice at home between sessions. The tape contained two sets of instructions, a complete, 45-minute set of instructions on side 1, and, for individuals who had mastered side 1, a shorter version of the same instructions on side 2. Members' experiences with the relaxation tape were reviewed during subsequent sessions.

Sessions 5 through 8 focused on cognitive restructuring strategies, including self-talk, perspective taking, and cognitive self-instruction strategies (Meichenbaum, 1985; Meichenbaum & Cameron, 1983). Building on exercises presented in session 2, members were taught how to use early stress cues as signals to activate more effective appraisals and coping strategies. In particular, members were taught how to use the method of *inner dialogue* (coping self-talk) to plan coping reactions that were more effective and gratifying for them. Members were asked to identify their typical and preferred coping self-talk phrases and to reflect on the usefulness of the phrases.

In addition, members were introduced to the concept of coping imagery and asked to identify coping images they preferred. Between meetings, members were asked to continue to note stressful events in their diaries and also record what self-talk and cognitive imagery strategies they had used to cope with stressful events. Entries in their diaries were discussed during each group meeting. During session 8, members' use of cognitive restructuring strategies was reviewed, and potential problems were addressed.

The Problem-Solving Component

A problem-solving model similar to the one described in Chapter 11 was introduced during session 1 as a device to help members move beyond ventilation of experiences and emotional reactions to using methods for improving their coping skills. Each week, members were encouraged to take turns working on their individual concerns by using the problem-solving model, which was displayed on two flip charts for easy viewing. Frequently, the problem-solving component was combined with the coping-skills component. Sometimes, members learned a new skill and then practiced it on a pressing problem that they were experiencing. At other times, members shared a problem they were having and the group leader or another member suggested a coping skill that might help.

It should be noted that because the members of the caregiver support group had a tremendous need to ventilate pent-up emotions and to share their experiences and concerns with each other, the problem-solving model was not always carried out in a linear, step-by-step fashion. Still, by using the model, the leader was able to help all members address at least one pressing problem during the eight-week group, and many members addressed several problems.

Session 1

During the first session, members shared information about themselves. The leader, Mrs. S, spoke first. She modeled the level of self-disclosure she hoped members would engage in when they introduced themselves. She described her professional experience, her own caregiving experience, some positive experiences she had in previous caregiver groups, and what she hoped would be some beneficial outcomes of participating in the support group. Next, she asked members to introduce themselves one by one. They shared the following information about themselves and the person for whom they were caring:

Mrs. Z: Mrs. Z has four children and is 54 years old. Because she married late in life, two of her four children are teenagers and living at home. Mrs. Z's mother, age 81, lives alone, has diabetes, is extremely overweight, has been widowed twice, and is depressed. Although married and working full time, Mrs. Z still manages to see her mother almost every day. She does her mother's shopping and supervises her mother's medication.

Mrs. B: Mrs. B is a 61-year-old widow with one child who lives in another state. Mrs. B cares for her mother-in-law, age 86, who came to live in Mrs. B's home seven years ago after suffering a stroke. Three years ago, Mrs. B's husband died. Since his death, her mother-in-law, who is a diabetic, has been totally dependent on Mrs. B and is home alone all day while Mrs. B works as a legal secretary.

Mrs. A: Mrs. A is caring for her bedridden mother, who has heart disease and Parkinson's disease and has lived with Mrs. A and her husband for five years. Mrs. A's mother has also been recently diagnosed with cancer. An aide comes in three times a week for four hours a day, but the remaining burden of care is left to Mrs. A.

Miss G: Miss G is 28 and works part-time as a clerk in a neighborhood store. Miss G's 76-year-old mother, a fiercely independent woman, lived alone until she suffered a stroke six months before the first group meeting. She now lives next door to Miss G in a duplex that Miss G bought with her mother's help.

Mrs. H: Mrs. H's father, age 87, has lived with her for 10 years. Mrs. H is an only child, divorced, with no children. Her father has a heart condition, arthritis, wears a hearing aid, and is argumentative.

Mrs. L: Mrs. L's mother, age 83, has Alzheimer's disease and diabetes. Mrs. L's husband resents his mother-in-law's presence and would like Mrs. L to place her mother in a nursing home.

Miss O: Miss O has been taking care of her mother for 13 years since her father died. Her mother, age 74, lives next door. Miss O's own health is poor because of arthritis and open heart surgery three years ago.

Mrs. M: Mrs. M's mother, age 77, lived alone until four years ago when she had a series of strokes. Her physician did not think she should be home alone when released from the hospital. She has since been living with Mrs. M.

Mrs. T: Mrs. T is a 36-year-old married woman with three children ages 4, 7, and 12. Mrs. T had planned to go back to work when her youngest child entered first grade, but she is not sure that she can manage this now because her mother has come to live with the family. Mrs. T is caring for her 71-year-old mother, who is suffering from manic depression and high blood pressure. Mrs. T's mother has been in the United States for 45 years and has lived with Mrs. T since being released from a state psychiatric institution three-and-a-half years ago. Mrs. T's mother had worked as a house cleaner but is now retired. She has had mental health problems for many years and has been in and out of the psychiatric units of local hospitals. She takes medication to control her psychiatric symptoms and her high blood pressure.

Notice that all members of the group are women and that all are caring for parents or parents-in-law. Having done some research before leading her first caregiver group, the leader, Mrs. S, was aware that the two most common groups of caregivers of the frail elderly are spouses and adult children. In a previous group that Mrs. S conducted for caregivers, she found that adult child caregivers had concerns and issues that were different from issues of spouse caregivers. For example, she found that adult children were more concerned about the effect of caregiving on their relationships with their spouses and their own children. They were also more concerned about work-related issues and about the responsibilities and duties of a child to a parent.

Mrs. S also found that women and men react differently to caregiving and have different concerns and issues. She observed, for example, that women were less comfortable discussing their relationships with their husbands and in discussing their roles as wives, mothers, and caregivers when men were present in the group. She also realized that many daughters-in-law shared the same concerns as daughters. Therefore, Mrs. S decided to limit participation in this particular group to daughters and daughters-in-law.

After the introductions, norms for group participation were discussed and agreed to by all members. Emphasis was placed on the confidential nature of the group discussions. Because problem solving was a major focus of the group, the eight-step problem-solving model was presented in some detail by Mrs. S. She also tried to incorporate problem solving into each of the weekly educational topics. For example, when the group discussed feelings that caregivers typically experienced, the focus was not only on group sharing of emotions such as anger or guilt, but also on problem-solving techniques that could help members to cope better with these feelings outside the group.

Session 2

By the second session, members were beginning to feel comfortable with each other. Cohesion and trust were beginning to build. The following dialogue occurred during the problem-solving component of the session:

Mrs. T: My husband really has a hard time dealing with my mother. I can understand his feelings. She is hard to live with. But I'm caught in the middle—I'm the only daughter she has.

Mrs. L: I know what you mean. You know, my mother has Alzheimer's disease. In the past two years it's gotten a lot worse. My husband says it's about time that

I think about putting Mom in a nursing home. I *do* think about it, but I just can't bring myself to do it.

Mrs. T: [looking at Mrs. S] What should I do? I feel like I'm trapped.

Mrs. S: Both of you are in a difficult situation. [She looks at Mrs. T.] Is there one thing that your mother does that is particularly bothersome?

Mrs. T: [pause] When Mom refuses to take her medication, her mood swings really get out of hand. At that point, even I have trouble with her.

Mrs. S: Is there any pattern to your mom's refusal to take her medication?

Mrs. T: It seems she does it when we try to get away. We have a summer camp on Lake Jones. [pause] We've been going up there on weekends for years. It's only been the past few years when Mom has gotten so frail that going to camp has become a real problem. We have a neighbor that we met at church look after her when we go now, but I think she resents us leaving her alone.

Mrs. S asks Mrs. T to elaborate on her relationship with her mother. After gathering additional information, several possible solutions to the problem are suggested by members.

Mrs. L: Why don't you take her when you go?

Mrs. T: We've tried that. The trip is too much for her. She gets exhausted. Besides, she really doesn't like it up there. You know, it's a pretty primitive camp. TV and radio reception isn't very good, and the place is small—only three rooms. That's the way they were built years ago.

Mrs. H: Maybe you could put the medication in her favorite beverage and leave it for her in individual containers in the refrigerator.

Mrs. T: I don't think that will work. My mother insists on taking her own medication.

Miss G: How about using that respite service up at St. Peter's (hospital). We used it, and it was good. They could give her medications.

Mrs. T: Mother would never go for that.

Mrs. S: Remember about step 2 of the problem-solving model [pointing to the flip chart and turning to Mrs. T]. Don't judge the solutions before hearing what everyone has to say. Okay?

Mrs. T: Oh, right. I forgot.

Miss G: What does her psychiatrist say? Why don't you ask him what to do?

Mrs. M: What about having a home health aide come in when you're gone?

Mrs. S: Anybody else have any suggestions?

Miss O: You have a brother, don't you?

Mrs. T: Yes, I do.

Miss O: Does he live in town?

Mrs. T: Yes, he does. We've always been close.

Miss O: What about asking him to take your mother, or to sit with her when you want to go away?

Mrs. S: Anybody else? [She scans the group for suggestions.] Okay, then, let me go over what has been suggested.

Mrs. S recaps the suggestions. Mrs. T says that asking the psychiatrist is the suggestion she is most comfortable with. Mrs. T describes what she will ask the psychiatrist, and the group helps her figure out how she will respond if he does not address her questions appropriately. Mrs. S suggests that Mrs. T role-play the situation, but Mrs. T is reluctant. Mrs. S models a response with Mrs. Z playing the psychiatrist. The group laughs as Mrs. Z pretends she has a Viennese accent and introduces herself as Dr. Freud. Next, Mrs. T practices her response. At the end of the role play, Mrs. T also says she might ask her brother to help out. She explains that she has not wanted to trouble him because "he is very busy with his own family." She also explains that he has offered to help out in the past. During subsequent sessions, Mrs. S tries to reinforce problem-solving skills and to focus group discussion in that direction.

The following dialogue, which occurred at the end of the group meeting, illustrates how Mrs. S tries to help group members become more aware of group processes, and how she encourages members' input.

Mrs. S: Gee, I don't know where the time goes, but we're almost out of time. As you know, I like to spend a few minutes at the end of each meeting talking about what I've observed and getting some feedback from you. I noticed today that you are really becoming comfortable with each other. I like the way you're connecting with each other, the way you share with each other and support each other.

Miss G: You mean you can't get a word in! [laughter from the group]

Mrs. S: It's good to see. What about the rest of you? What are your feelings about the group? [She scans the group.]

Mrs. T: So far, it's been great. I really look forward to coming.

Miss O: I wish I had joined a group a long time ago. It's really helping me to see how others are managing.

Mrs. A: I really like it, too. If I had one suggestion, I guess it would be that I'd like to get a little more specific information.

Mrs. S: Specific information?

Mrs. A: Well, my mother's doctor really didn't tell me much about what I should expect. I mean, I'd like to find out more about Parkinson's disease.

Mrs. S: I see. I won't be able to get too specific during meetings because of all the different problems you're coping with. [She scans the group.] But what I can do is to identify resources where you can find out more information. How would that be?

Mrs. A: I'd really appreciate that.

Mrs. L: If it's possible, I'd like to find out more about Alzheimer's disease.

Mrs. S: Okay, on the way out write down what illnesses, or what things you'd like more information about. During the week, I'll do a little investigating and see if I can't find out where you can get more information.

Session 3

The following dialogue from the third session illustrates how the coping-skills component was implemented.

Mrs. B: I feel really sorry for my mother-in-law. I have to work and she's home alone all day. She really misses Tom [her son]. She keeps saying she can't understand why he died and she's still alive. She says she wants to die.

Mrs. S: That's really hard.

Mrs. B: The thing is, there's nothing I can do. She just keeps repeating the same things. Sometimes, you know, I get really frustrated. Then I feel guilty because I know she can't help it.

Mrs. S: What's the feeling like?

Mrs. B: I can feel myself getting tense just before I get home. I think I'm anticipating hearing her say how much she misses Tom and that she wishes she was with him. Sometimes, I feel like pulling out of the driveway and not walking in. But I know that's not realistic.

Mrs. S: What about the deep breathing exercise we just practiced? Do you think that might help calm you down? You could practice that while you're still out in the car before you come in.

Mrs. B: Yes, I could try that. I'll try anything at this point. Sometimes, my stomach really starts to churn when I start driving down my street. Maybe if I take a few deep breaths and remind myself that I'm doing the best I can for her, then it won't get to me so much.

Miss G: Yeah, I know that when Mother drives me crazy it helps me to disappear into another room for a few minutes. Anything that will get me to stop and think before I snap at her might help. Maybe the deep breathing will help me not to lose it—if you know what I mean.

Mrs. H: I sure do. Sometimes, I could strangle my father. You know, it's funny. I would never say that in front of anybody else. They'd think I was a terrible person, a terrible daughter.

Miss O: I think we all feel like that sometimes. [Several group members nod.] How can you help it! I love her [Miss O's mother], but sometimes it just gets to me, it's so constant.

Mrs. S: [looking at Miss G, Mrs. H, and Miss O] It's a real struggle but you can really be proud of how much you are doing. Well, maybe the deep breathing will help. Try it and let me know what you think next week. Okay?

During session 3, a brief sample of dialogue also illustrates how the support component of the group has a positive effect.

Mrs. L: I feel better than I did before coming here. The situation hasn't become any easier, but I've begun thinking about various alternatives [for her mother]. You [looking at Mrs. S and then around the group] really understand what I'm going through deciding if it's time to put her in a home. I think that somehow that has given me the courage to really begin to explore options. I feel like I'm not an awful person.

Mrs. Z and others: Of course you're not! You've done so much for her, more than what a lot of others would have done. But, sometimes it's time. It may be better for her and for you.

Mrs. L: Before I came here I really felt like I was going crazy. Like I was the only one in this kind of a situation. But I'm not. Some of you have it a lot worse than me.

Miss O: Jean [Mrs. L], I just wanted you to know that you're an inspiration to me. Sometimes, when I'm down and I think about giving up, I think of you. I'm sure whatever you decide about your mom, it will be for the best.

Mrs. L: I hope so, I'm trying to do what's right.

Mrs. Z: We're all trying our best, it's just so hard!

Session 4

The following dialogue, taken from a discussion after the educational component of session 4, illustrates that it is possible for more than one member of a group to derive benefit from the discussion of a particular topic.

Mrs. H: Does anybody feel that their parent is manipulative in their caregiving situation?

Mrs. A: I think manipulation gains advantage.

Mrs. S: I don't understand quite what you mean, why don't you give us an example?

Mrs. H: When my father says he really doesn't feel good, I think he is really telling me that I shouldn't go out and leave him [alone]. I feel like my life is out of my control—that I'm being manipulated by him. If I leave him, and something happens while I'm out, I'd feel terribly guilty for not being there. But when I stay home, I really resent having to give up my plans, my life.

Mrs. S: Maybe he needs to be reassured that he's still as important to you as you are to him.

Mrs. T: You know the need to be reassured could explain my mother's behavior, too.

Mrs. S: Do you see a connection between your mother's medication problem and feeling manipulated?

Mrs. T: Well, yes, when she doesn't take her medicine she becomes the center of attention. It's almost like she believes it will distract us from going to our camp without her on weekends.

Mrs. H: Your mother won't take her pills just to feel that you still love her and will not abandon her?

Mrs. T: It sounds like that could be, don't you think so? [She looks at Mrs. S.]

Mrs. S: [scanning the group] What do you think?

Mrs. L: Even if it's true, what can she do about it?

Mrs. Z: You know, I've found it helps to let them know you know they are manipulating you. Sometimes if you lay your cards on the table, you can be in a better position to prevent the manipulation.

Mrs. B: That's fine, but it's not easy to do. My mother-in-law would just say I was overreacting.

Miss O: You have to remember that you have rights, too. You have to stand up for yourself. Remember the topic for today's meeting, taking care of yourself.

Mrs. S asks Mrs. T if she has any other thoughts. Mrs. T brings up her worries about vacation plans for the upcoming summer season.

Mrs. T: If my husband and I can't handle her intrusion into our weekend trips, what would she do if we tried to go on a longer vacation? I thought I was going to go back to work now that my children are getting older. But even having company over is a problem. Mental illness is not like physical illness. I can't even take a short vacation without worrying. How will I ever be able to go back to work?

The group members respond with empathy. They agree that mental illness is potentially more embarrassing because of the unpredictable nature of some psychiatric symptoms.

Mrs. T: And you know, I'm darn tired of hearing, "I don't know how you do it" from family and friends. I'm not looking for meaningless praise.

Mrs. B: I know exactly what you mean. Occasionally, I'd like to hear an offer of help, rather than being praised for what I'm doing all by myself!

Miss G: What's the use? I have four brothers and they expect me to do everything. It's always been that way. When I complain to my mother, all she does is stick up for them. She makes excuses for them. She says they are busy with their own families, that if they could help out they would. But, what about me? What about my life? Don't I deserve a break?

Mrs. S: It's frustrating, isn't it?

Miss G: It sure is. But at least I can share some of my feelings here. Before, I had no one I could talk to.

Mrs. T: It does help to talk about it. My husband commented the other day that the group meetings seem to help me have a little more patience with the children and with my mother.

Mrs. S: [scanning the group] I'm glad to hear you're getting something out of the group. You deserve it. And I'm glad you're here for each other. There's nothing like sharing and giving and getting ideas and suggestions from each other. [Members nod and there is a pause.] Well, what about a break? When we come back, I'll go over a strategy that may help you cope with your frustration, and then during problem solving we can think of ways that may help us get family more involved.

Miss G: Sounds good to me.

Mrs. B: Me too.

Session 6

The original group contract was for members to meet for eight weekly sessions (no monthly follow-up meetings), so during session 6, Mrs. S brings up the issue of group termination. She mentions that another group she conducted had continued to meet. She also mentions that group members could be a resource for each other by keeping in regular phone contact, which leads to a general discussion by group members about the benefits of the support group.

Miss O: On the way over here tonight I was worrying about what I would do when the group ended. You know, friends don't really understand. They mean well, but unless they are doing it too, they just don't know what it's like to be tied down like this and not know when it's going to end. Sometimes, I think my mother will go on forever and I will die first.

Mrs. Z: You're right, how many friends can you discuss the differences between Depends and Attends [different brands of adult diapers], which ones to use, and what store has the best prices?

Mrs. M: Yeah, even if you have a good friend, you might drive her away if you talk about what's really on your mind. Can you tell your friend you think about what it would be like if your mother died? Your friend will think you're a monster and tell you that you should be grateful your mother is still alive. I don't know what I would do without the group.

Mrs. T: You know, ever since I started coming here I've been more patient with my mother. I think it's because I know I can let it all out here. I really look forward to coming here because I know you all understand what I'm going through.

Mrs. S: I take it, then, from all your comments that you're not sure if you want to end. Why don't you all give it some thought? We'll discuss this again next week. Okay?

Session 7

During the problem-solving component, Mrs. T admits to still feeling manipulated.

Mrs. T: I'm playing her game, playing into her hands, and I can't take it anymore. I finally got a chance to speak to Dr. L about my mother's medication. He mentioned an apartment where they have staff 24 hours a day, run by the county mental health center. I think he called it the Supportive Living Program.

Mrs. S: How do you feel about the suggestion from the doctor?

Mrs. T: Terrible. I can't even bring myself to dial the phone numbers to find out more about it. I want to, but I feel like I'd be abandoning her.

Mrs. Z and Mrs. H both say that even if she feels uncomfortable considering this move, Mrs. T has still come a long way since session 1. However, other members confront Mrs. T and remind her it takes two to continue the manipulative pattern.

Mrs. B: Nobody can manipulate you unless you let them.

Mrs. M: That's right, it takes two, you know. You must be letting her do this to you or she wouldn't be able to do it.

Mrs. B: By not going [on weekends] you give your mother a tremendous sense of power and control.

Mrs. T: But even her psychiatrist says he never dealt with someone like her before.

Mrs. M: Do you find that reassuring?

Mrs. T: Yeah, wouldn't you?

Mrs. S: I think that the other members of the group are trying to point out that you are the one who is responsible for your own happiness, not Anna [Mrs. T's mother]. They are trying to convey that it's up to you to take control of this situation, and that you can do it.

Mrs. T: I know I have to do it, I have to do something.

Member-to-member confrontation in the context of mutual aid and mutual support helps members to gain new perspectives and become motivated to handle problems in new ways.

During the seventh session the following dialogue occurred:

Mrs. T: I have some good news. I finally got up the courage to ask my brother. He spoke to his wife and they agreed to team up and help out. They said they would take care of Mom anytime we went away, as long as we let them know in advance, and that's not a problem. Jack [her husband] was real happy about that, so he hasn't bothered me one bit about Mom being in our house recently. In fact, he's been a big help lately.

Mrs. S: That's wonderful. [Other members nod and there is a pause.]

Mrs. L: I've been thinking maybe it's time to find a place [nursing home] for Mom. But, every time I do, I get to feeling so guilty.

Mrs. S: [speaking to Mrs. L and the entire group] Remember the self-talk coping skills we learned earlier; part of guilt is what you tell yourself.

Mrs. Z: Give yourself credit for time served, look at what you have done, and have tried to do already. That's what I do, that and read the Bible.

Mrs. S: [speaking to the entire group] Mrs. Z says positive things to herself and reads the Bible. What about the rest of you? What things have you found that help you cope?

During the seventh group meeting, the members also decided to continue to meet once a month and to stay in contact with each other by telephone between meetings.

A Follow-Up Session

During a follow-up meeting almost one year after the eight weekly group meetings, Mrs. L reported the following news.

Mrs. L: As some of you already know, Mom is now at Eaton Park [a skilled nursing facility]. She took a turn for the worse about a month ago. She had to be sent to St. Peter's [hospital] for over a week. I didn't know what to do [pause] about taking her back. I mean, I still wanted her home. I know that's what she would have wanted. But she was so bad she didn't even recognize me anymore. I thought about what you had said to me [during the meetings], how I shouldn't feel guilty when it was time to have her go to a home, how much I had done for her over the years. It meant a lot to me.

Mrs. S: You've meant a lot to us.

Mrs. L: I just couldn't keep taking care of her. I had to watch her every minute, afraid she'd walk out of the house and get lost—or worse, burn down the house or something. I had lunch with Beatrice [Mrs. M] while my mother was in the hospital, and Mary and Sarah [Mrs. W and Mrs. Z] called. That helped give me the courage to go ahead with what I had to do. You know, without the support of the group, I think I would have fallen apart.

A COMMUNITY COALITION

This case example describes a group work effort to bring together representatives of several community service agencies to help establish a community residence for people with AIDS. The case was selected because it portrays how the group worker plans and implements a strategy for community change by using a range of group work skills during several sessions of the group. The case also illustrates that members of coalitions have varied special interests and political concerns that require the worker to assess and intervene both within the group and within larger systems outside the group, such as the community.

The group worker, Ms. C, is an experienced social worker employed by the United Services Association (USA), a small, multiservice agency in River Falls, a city of about 250,000. River Falls has a well-developed social service system, several hospitals and health facilities, and a number of community residences for the mentally ill and the developmentally disabled. However, there are no community residences for people with AIDS, perhaps because the AIDS crisis has never been fully acknowledged by community residents and leaders.

The chief executive of USA asked Ms. C to compose a group to help the agency establish a community residence for people with AIDS. The executive had recently been contacted by representatives of two local hospitals. They urged him to involve the agency in community residence programming for people with AIDS. The hospitals were receiving more AIDS cases, but few had discharge-planning options for patients who no longer required hospitalization but who were unable to return home.

The state had recently announced funding for community residences for people with AIDS, and the executive director had completed the agency's grant application for the project. The agency expected a response to its application in about two months. Meanwhile, the executive director thought the coalition group could begin to discuss how they could assist in establishing the residence and its services. The cooperative effort of the agency representatives was an important factor in establishing the community residence because the agency would provide a wider resource base in support of such an effort and might help overcome the anticipated negative reaction to the residence from members and leaders of this conservative community.

The Planning Stage

Several planning considerations needed resolution before the coalition could be established:

1. Ms. C was assured of the support of the USA organization in planning for and financing the new residence, but she was concerned about how other social service agencies would perceive the organization's intentions. In establishing other community residences for the developmentally disabled, the agency had encountered resistance from other agencies, which USA assessed as "turf issues." It would be necessary to involve these agencies early in the planning effort to help avoid similar resistance.

2. However, Ms. C noted that she had several important contacts in local social service and community organizations and that these people could probably be counted on to support the plan and work together.

3. Ms. C would need to identify potential members and assess their organizations' willingness to align with the purpose of the coalition (planning and supporting the community residence). In addition, she would need to assess potential differences of opinion and inform potential coalition-group members about how the coalition could help USA in its efforts.

4. In recruiting for the coalition, a diverse group of members representing a variety of service issues relevant to people with AIDS would be sought. Ms. C would seek coalition members who displayed a homogeneity of attitude about support for people with AIDS and who had heterogenous talents and resources that were needed for the group to achieve its purpose.

5. Although the coalition could start out as a small group, it would probably be necessary to add members as other agencies important to the project were identified. Thus, the coalition would function as an open group.

6. Because of the potential for interagency turf issues and because of the likelihood of community resistance to the proposed residence, the coalition would need to meet in a neutral community setting. The setting would also have to accommodate larger numbers of community people when public testimony and discussion were sought by the coalition.

It was arranged for meetings to take place every other week in the meeting room of the local Episcopal church. The church had adequate space, and outreach workers from the church's volunteer service committee had a strong history of serving people with AIDS in River Falls. Ms. C made a list of potential members, visited several of them, and telephoned others. Briefly orienting the potential members to the purpose of the group, she was able to secure promises of weekly attendance from the following people, who would represent their organizations:

The Rev. and Mrs. W: Codirectors, River Falls Episcopal Street Ministry

Mr. S: Manager, River Falls City Housing Authority

Ms. P: Director, The Fallsview Homeless Shelter

Mr. L: Outreach worker, The Gay and Lesbian Community Center

The Rev. G: Pastor, Our Lady Star of the Sea, Roman Catholic Church

Mr. A: AIDS educator, AIDS Council of River Falls

Dr. J: Chief of staff, River Falls General Hospital

Mrs. B: Social worker, St. Mary's Hospital of River Falls

Mr. Z: Support group coordinator, Families of PWA

Ms. T: Director of social services, River County

Mr. R: Professor of social work, River College

The Beginning Stage

Ms. C arranged a mutually agreeable time for all potential members to meet in the Episcopal church's meeting room. Before the first session, she reviewed the purpose of the coalition as she envisioned it. To help members fully identify with the goals of the group, she prepared a short statement that included recognition that the members might want to discuss the group's purpose in the early sessions.

> *The purpose of this group is to discuss the need for community residence planning for people with AIDS in River Falls. The USA organization is prepared to sponsor a community residence for people with AIDS and is interested in securing planning assistance and support from this coalition. Of particular importance is how to secure community acceptance for this new type of community residence. As a group, I think it would be really helpful for us to discuss how we might attempt to gain community acceptance and support for the residence.*

The First Session

Members arrived on time and appeared to be enthusiastic. Ms. C noted that members greeted each other eagerly and broke into groups of two or three to discuss topics of mutual interest and exchange small talk. For several members who knew each other from telephone conversations or who had heard of each other before, this was their first face-to-face contact, so the mood of the group took on a festive tone. Ms. C called the group to order, and members gathered chairs in a circle. The following dialogue occurred:

Ms. C: I want to thank all of you for coming today. I noticed that several of you have finally seen faces of people you have only known from the telephone. This is a great way to start this group, and it suggests that we need to find other ways of getting together more often. [She pauses.] As I discussed with each of you, the USA organization is interested in exploring the possibility of starting a community residence for persons with AIDS. I have been asked to convene a coalition group of experts in this work to assist in this project. Your initial reaction to our proposal has been quite positive, and the next step is for us to meet and discuss the project. I am distributing a statement that I envision as a beginning purpose for this group. [She hands out a copy of the statement of purpose.] I would appreciate it if you would take a minute and read this. [Members read silently.] Having read the statement, perhaps this would be a good time to introduce ourselves. Would each of you introduce yourself, and give the group some feedback about the statement of purpose?

The Rev. W: I'll start, since it is our pleasure to host all of you today in our community meeting room. My wife and I have long been supporters of services to people with AIDS, and we have a special program in our street ministry that offers support and emergency assistance to people with AIDS and their families. We see the need for housing for these folks, and we are pleased to offer any support we can.

Mr. S: I agree. The Housing Authority supports the idea of community residences for people with AIDS, although I would add that many of our elected officials would rather see them treated in larger facilities in other communities. There is a housing shortage in River Falls, and I don't see it getting any better. I would suggest that we proceed carefully so we can overcome some of the stereotypes about people with AIDS and convince other community leaders that this project is a worthy one.

Ms. P: I believe there are several people with AIDS residing on a temporary basis in our homeless shelter. We have been offering shelter to several people who are in the process of testing and treatment for AIDS, but we can offer little help other than our shelter, which is not particularly well equipped for dealing with people who have difficult health problems. Our organization recognizes the need for a more specialized facility, but we are skeptical about whether such a residence would be accepted in any of River Falls' neighborhoods.

Mr. L: The Gay and Lesbian Community Center has offered some support to people with AIDS, but we are not equipped for dealing with some of their difficult health concerns. It would seem to us that any community residence for people with AIDS should have a strong health or medical services orientation. We see the major issue here as overcoming the strong homophobic reaction of community leaders and residents, even though many persons with AIDS are heterosexual.

Mr. A: The AIDS Council is prepared to contract with the USA organization to provide health and medical services for residents of the proposed residence. We also think we can be valuable in educating the public about AIDS, as this is part of our mission. Any proposal such as this would need to have a strong component of community education; this is the only way to overcome the usual resistance to dealing with AIDS.

The Rev. G: It is a shame that our community has such narrow ideas about people with AIDS. I agree with what has been said so far. I can't speak for our parish, but our priests recognize the need to minister to people with AIDS—we need assistance in learning more about how to be helpful. This is why I am here.

Dr. J: The River Falls General Hospital has been seeing more patients who have been diagnosed as HIV-positive, and has been treating increasing numbers of people with serious opportunistic infections related to AIDS. Some of these people remain in the hospital for extended periods, but when they are ready to be discharged, they find that they have no place to go. Many lose their housing because they can't afford to keep up mortgage or rent payments. Many also lose their jobs, and, as you know, this means they lose their health insurance. It is a very difficult situation, and I'm not sure that the County Social Services Department is doing its share to help these people.

Mrs. B: Our experience in the social services department of St. Mary's Hospital is very similar. I agree with Dr. J.

Ms. T: I don't think that last statement is an accurate one. The county has emergency funds to help people with some of the costs for temporary housing, but we are not equipped to serve the increasing numbers of homeless people in this county. I'm not sure that the hospitals are taking enough responsibility in these matters.

Mr. Z: The support groups we run for families of people with AIDS have many similar themes. We think a community residence would assist people in transition from hospital to more permanent housing. In some cases, people with AIDS will never return to a place they call home.

Mr. R: I am here because River College, particularly the social work program, is interested in lending support and perhaps student assistance to this effort to plan for people with AIDS. Last semester, my students and I did a preliminary needs assessment in cooperation with the Department of Health, and what we found may surprise you. I brought copies of our report today and I will gladly discuss our findings with this group.

Ms. C noted that all members had spoken and contributed their organization's initial reaction to the USA proposal. Although there appeared to be support expressed for the idea of a community residence, she noted tension between the director of the County Social Services Department and representatives of the local hospitals. She decided not to address the tension at this time. Instead, she decided to summarize some of the major points of the previous discussion.

Ms. C: I appreciate your candid comments. Several themes have emerged; let me try to summarize them. The problem of housing for people with AIDS seems to be verified based on most of your comments. Another important issue identified by some of you is the potential reaction of community residents to housing for individuals who are HIV-positive. Several of you commented on local reaction, in general, to the AIDS crisis. In addition, some of you suggested services for people with AIDS, as well as health and medical services and the need for community education about AIDS. How does that summary sound to you? Is it a fair portrayal of our first conversation together?

The summary of the initial comments helped the group review some of the overt agendas of the individual members and their agencies. Ms. C thought it important to let the group know that the USA organization was in the process of applying for state funding and was prepared to take action on establishing the community residence within the next few months if funding were received. The agency also wanted to make it clear at the first meeting that it would be the actual service provider, with autonomy and control over the operation of the residence. Ms. C stated the USA's agenda and solicited feedback from the group:

Ms. C: I need to speak briefly on behalf of my own agency. My executive has asked me to make clear our intentions to carry out this project. While we intend to do most of the work of establishing funding, finding a location, and applying for housing permits and other regulatory requirements, we need your help in two ways. First, we recognize the collective expertise in this room today. We hope to use many of the services your organizations offer. We may contract for services with some of you and ask others for guidance in this effort to provide services to people with AIDS. Second, we recognize that, as many of you have suggested, there is potential for a great deal of community resistance to this project. We hope that you will assist us in challenging potential resistance and help us mediate conflicts that could occur. I'd like to get some feedback from you about our intentions and how we can cooperate in this important endeavor.

Dr. J: I appreciate your openness, and I think my organization can support your intentions.

Mr. Z: I'm not sure how I can help, but perhaps we can find that out as we go along.

Ms. C: Thank you. Are there other comments from members? [She scans the group.]

Mr. R: I have discussed the need for community residence programming with students at River College and they are interested in helping. Could a student representative of the Social Work Club attend our meetings?

Ms. C: How would everyone feel about that? [Members nod in agreement.]

The Rev. W: It looks to me as if most of us here think this is a good idea. It also appears that most of us support the idea of USA taking the lead in this project.

Ms. C: Can I ask if there are concerns about the project that any of you have?

Ms. T: I personally support this project. However, I think it's important to recognize that many of our local leaders and politicians in River Falls might not feel the same way. They may also think the Department of Social Services should not be involved. Since our funding is somewhat controlled by our community leaders, our agency may have some difficulty in participating.

The Rev. W: I appreciate what you are saying, and you might count on some of us talking to our politicians about the project if you think it will help.

Mr. L: We can't forget politics here. Many of our political leaders are not in favor of services that make them or their constituents uncomfortable.

Ms. C: Can you elaborate on this for us?

Mr. L: I just think there is a lot of resistance to acknowledging that our community has a problem with AIDS. I think we should start discussing this and how we can overcome the resistance. [Members verbalize agreement.]

Ms. C: It is easy to see, from all of your reactions to [Mr. L's] comment, that you think River Falls should acknowledge the AIDS crisis. This seems to be a recurring theme in our discussions so far. Do others want to comment on this?

Ms. P: I would suggest that this group concentrate on helping the community learn about AIDS. This would allow the USA to do what it does best—namely, work on establishing community residences.

Mr. L: This seems reasonable.

The Rev. G: You're suggesting we establish some sort of educational effort to get information about AIDS to the community?

Ms. P: Yes, that's a possibility. If the public could see us working together to do this, they might take this information more seriously.

Mr. L: Then perhaps community residence programming might go more smoothly.

Ms. P: Exactly!

This interaction demonstrates how group discussion helped the group come to a fuller understanding of the group's purpose. Although Ms. C stated the general purpose for the group (assisting in establishment of a community residence), the group started to define and modify the purpose through its initial discussions. Ms. C realized that modifying the group purpose was an important step to building group cohesion and was necessary before the group could be productive.

In the next interaction, Ms. C probed the group for potential obstacles to group consensus on purpose, including differences of opinion about the work of the group. She recognized that groups often mask their differences in the beginning stage and that the illusion of unanimity among members can hide obstacles to productive work.

Ms. C: Most of us appear to be in favor of helping the community accept the AIDS crisis, but I wonder if we all mean the same thing? How do you think the group might approach this task of community education?

Mr. S: I hope this doesn't mean that we want to have a demonstration or picket the city offices! I could lose my job.

Ms. C: Could you elaborate on that?

Mr. S: Well, you might have read last week in the papers, there was an organization called ACT-UP demonstrating at the Center City Commissioner's office. They were trying to get the attention of some local politicians and were hoping to get them to appropriate money for support of persons with AIDS. They made the commissioner and themselves look bad.

Mr. L: ACT-UP demonstrations are only one way to educate the public, but sometimes that type of strategy is necessary.

Mr. S: I can't be part of anything like that. I'm a city employee!

Mr. L: I can understand that; maybe there are other ways you can contribute.

Mr. Z: Most of the members of our support group for families do not agree with ACT-UP's philosophy and tactics. Many of our members have a need for anonymity and confidentiality. I doubt they would support that kind of experience.

Ms. C: Perhaps we need to consider some ideas about how to go about our task. Planning a demonstration or using conflict as a strategy are only two ways to approach our task; let's discuss other ways.

Two members expressed their mutual concern about how the group would achieve its goals. Although Ms. C encountered potential obstacles to the group working together, she recognized that the concerns were part of a normally functioning group in its beginning stage. She facilitated work on how the group would achieve its goals. During the first session, the group agreed to consider possible strategies for carrying out a community education project to help USA in its efforts to establish a community residence.

The Second Session

The second session focused on the content of the planned educational presentation—how group members could gather general information about AIDS and specific information about its prevalence in River Falls. The group decided to divide into two subcommittees, one to collect resources such as videotapes, written material, and names of possible speakers, and the other to collect specific information on how many cases of AIDS have been diagnosed in River Falls. Each member volunteered for a particular subcommittee depending on what expertise was needed. Each subcommittee was to bring its information back to the next meeting.

The Third Session

In the third session, each subcommittee presented its findings, and the session was educational for all. Discussions centered on how the group would use the findings to teach members of the community about AIDS. The group discussed how to design the educational effort. Ms. C led the group in a brainstorming exercise to generate as many ideas as possible about how to teach members of the community about AIDS. The group then had a freewheeling discussion of all options, and members were asked to rank their top three choices. The choices with the most votes were listed on a flip chart, and members were again asked to discuss the top few choices. Although the group was asked to vote one more time to choose the best options, it decided to try to reach consensus without a formal vote. The following dialogue took place:

Mr. R: It appears that we have a few good ideas about how to inform the public about AIDS. I prefer a general educational meeting, open to the public.

Ms. C: [scanning the group] What are other members' preferences?

Mrs. B: I have been impressed with the work done by Mr. A and the AIDS Council. I wonder if the council would take major responsibility for presenting a program open to the public?

Mr. R: I was wondering the same thing. It seems this type of educational program should be done by experts, who have the most up-to-date information.

Mr. A: Our agency would be glad to take the lead.

Ms. C: How would other members feel about that?

Ms. P: This seems like a logical choice. Still, we should be involved in the effort to provide support and to suggest that we are all in this together.

Mr. R: I suggest we all be available to be discussion leaders, perhaps divide into smaller groups to discuss questions.

Ms. P: I agree. We need to be part of all of the strategies to get this information to the public. Let's decide where and when.

Ms. C: I just want to make sure that we are all in agreement. Can I ask all of you if an open educational presentation is your first choice? [All members indicate their support.] Then we have reached consensus on this issue.

The Middle Stage

The group met for its fourth and fifth sessions to plan the details of the educational meeting with the public. Room and space arrangements were made, refreshments were purchased, and members of the group took responsibility for advertising and encouraging community leaders to attend. One day before the presentation, the local television news ran a story about the coalition and its work, which gave much-needed publicity to the educational effort. Despite a small group of community residents who expressed their opposition to the event, the presentation was well attended and well received, and community residents had opportunities to ask questions in small group discussions.

The coalition had a debriefing session at a local restaurant, and Ms. C announced that the community residence proposal had received the grant and the project was ready to proceed. The next step was to find a suitable location with room to house five to eight people with AIDS. She reported that a house had been found in a neighborhood near a hospital and that discussions were taking place between the owners of the house and the USA agency. Ms. C asked the group to convene again to discuss further planning for the project.

The Sixth Session

The sixth session of the group was supposed to focus on plans to open the community residence. The USA agency was taking the responsibility for many of the details involved in opening the residence, but the executive director wanted the group to help plan how some of the health, counseling, transportation, and other services could be provided.

However, as news of the proposed residence spread throughout the community, opposition to the chosen location began to grow. Community political leaders, responding to pressures from residents, threatened to pass zoning legislation that could exclude the USA from opening the residence in the chosen area. Ms. C convened the group to discuss the new development. After Ms. C's opening remarks, the group started a discussion of a newspaper feature story about local reaction to the idea of opening a community residence for people with AIDS and the threatened zoning change by the River Falls City Council.

Ms. C: As we all know, our plans for a community residence are well under way, and we need to consider what steps the group can take to make this residence a reality. But I have some bad news to announce. It now appears that some members of the River Falls City Council are opposing our efforts. I have been informed by my agency's director that soon the City Council will attempt to rezone the area we have chosen for the residence to prevent us from opening a multiple-resident dwelling. Our agency is prepared to go to court to prevent this, but I was wondering if the group had some suggestions for a different strategy?

Ms. P: I think the coalition can do several things. For one thing, we all know some of our City Council members—we could meet with them individually and try to persuade them to change their minds.

Ms. C: How do you suggest we go about that?

Ms. P: There are any number of ways, but I wonder if some of us could make individual appointments with some of them, perhaps to discuss the proposal and find out what their objections are.

The Rev. G: I agree. At least we could show up, identify ourselves, and ask for a public meeting or hearing to discuss the residence.

Ms. C: This strategy sounds very good. We have an important perspective to offer here. Any other ideas?

Dr. J: I can provide all of us with our latest figures on new cases of AIDS among River Falls residents. Some of this information might suggest that our City Council members need to start making plans for these people rather than ignore them.

Ms. C: I think we can all agree that we have more information than the council members do and that we need to get the information to them before they vote to rezone.

Mr. L: I think they would lose a case in court. They are clearly discriminating against people with AIDS, which is against federal and state antidiscrimination laws.

Mr. S: I share that opinion, but I wonder if an adversarial position is the first strategy we should use?

Mr. R: I'm afraid they're the ones taking the adversarial position. However, I'm in favor of working with them rather than against them.

Mr. S: I don't like this whole idea of going against the City Council. I have to remind you again that I am a city employee, and it would look pretty bad if I were involved in a group that supported a court action against the city.

Mr. L: I'm sorry to hear you say this, because I think eventually we will have to take sides here.

In addition to dealing with the crisis precipitated by the threatened actions of the City Council, Ms. C now faces conflict within the group. The opposing viewpoints of two of the members pose a threat to the cohesiveness of the group. The outside threat—the possible actions of the City Council—brought the group together, but the internal conflict threatens to split the group into opposing sides.

Ms. C: I think it is good that we are open and honest about our reactions here. I appreciate your position, Mr. S, and I wonder if others wish to comment on what you have said?

Mr. Z: I support taking the more conservative approach. As I mentioned before, many members of the support groups my agency sponsors wish to keep their anonymity, and others are not inclined to challenge their City Council members.

Mr. L: I respect what you are saying, but eventually, when things can't be worked out, we will have to challenge them. Perhaps we need to discuss this possibility.

Ms. C: The group seems to be struggling here. I suggest we discuss how we can work out our differences before they interfere with our important efforts to make the residence a reality. Each of you has a valid point. How can we come together on this?

Mrs. B: I think we should consider taking it one step at a time. I was always taught to consider collaboration before conflict. It seems to be more effective for some situations.

Mr. L: Our agency is often forced into conflict with public officials around their continuing homophobia. As you remember, the City Council recently failed to pass antidiscrimination legislation for gay men and lesbian women. I am becoming accustomed to having to fight for the rights of our organization's members.

Ms. C: And you think their opposition to the residence is a similar problem?

Mr. L: Well, no. I guess there are some similar issues here, but I think the City Council might respond positively if we contacted them and discussed the residence and the incidence of new cases of AIDS in our hospitals.

Ms. C: Do others feel the same way? [The group members appear to agree.] So if we agree that our first strategy should be talking and collaborating, can the group work together to accomplish this?

Mr. S: I have no problem with this. I just want us all to agree as a group before we try any other strategy.

Ms. C: You're suggesting that we discuss and reach a consensus on each strategy before we try it?

Mr. S: Yes, this will guarantee we all work together.

Mr. L: We should present a united front and work together whenever we can.

Ms. C: Can the group agree on a rule of consensus when deciding which strategies to employ? [The group orally indicates agreement.]

In this interaction, Ms. C attempted to mediate differences among the members. She remained neutral in the discussion, recognized the validity of opposing viewpoints, and used the resources of the group to support a solution. In addition, Ms. C recognized the necessity of processing group dynamics with the members when the group appeared to be struggling, which had the eventual effect of helping members agree on the rule of consensus that became a norm for the group's future deliberations.

The Seventh Session

The strategy of meeting individually with City Council members was successful. Members divided into subgroups of three and met with council members to share information and make recommendations. The concerted effort of the coalition helped persuade the council to support the project. Two members of the council who were particularly supportive of the community residence were invited to join the group and help implement the project.

The following excerpt is from a group discussion on how to obtain some of the necessary support services for the community residence. Ms. C told the group members they could help USA by suggesting how services could be arranged and financed. The climate of the group was positive because the group had resolved the crisis posed by the threat of rezoning and had added new members who supported the purpose of the group.

Ms. C: I wanted to let you know that progress is being made on the community residence. We have a signed contract with the seller, and we are planning renovations. Our time line is about ten weeks. We have also begun to identify potential staff for the residence. Do any of you have suggestions about how to find additional staff who might be interested in working in the residence?

The Rev. G: I wanted to know if volunteers would be used. Some of our parishioners are interested in donating items, cooking meals, being companions.

Mr. R: I'm proud of the fact that some of our social work students are interested in volunteering to work at the residence.

Ms. C: The USA organization briefly discussed the use of volunteers, but we didn't reach any conclusions. Are other members in touch with possible sources of volunteers?

Mr. A: The AIDS Council has a Buddy Program—a volunteer is paired with a person with AIDS. We could also provide volunteers to help with shopping and transportation and to provide companionship.

Mrs. W: Our church has a volunteer committee, and if some group members could make a short presentation to them, they might be helpful in providing volunteers.

Ms. C: Are there any suggestions about how to proceed on the volunteer possibility?

Mr. R: I would be glad to take responsibility for studying the volunteer idea, talking to those of you who are interested in helping provide volunteers. Would that be agreeable? [Mr. R looks around at the other members.]

Ms. C: It looks like we have a lot of support for this idea. [She looks at Mr. R.] Can you form a subcommittee and get back to us at our next meeting?

Mr. R: Sounds good!

Ms. C: Any other ideas about staffing?

Ms. P: We have several applications for employment in our shelter, and we don't have any openings right now.

Ms. C: I don't think we could have access to applications without violating confidentiality and informed consent, could we?

Ms. P: No problem. If you develop a short employment announcement, we can send it to people whose applications we have. Just don't read it to any of our current staff. [The group laughs.]

Ms. C: I promise!

This excerpt illustrates how the members developed a system of mutual aid during the middle stage of the group's development. Frequent intervention on the part of the group leader was not as necessary as it was in earlier sessions when the group processes included organizing, norm development, and conflict resolution. Members took more responsibility for the business of the group by playing important leadership and task accomplishment roles.

The work of the group continued, which supported the eventual opening of the USA community residence for people with AIDS. Several members of the coalition helped develop a service plan for the residence. The AIDS Council provided educational services for families of the residents. Visiting social workers from the two hospitals were assigned to the residence as part of the discharge planning process for some of the residents. A volunteer program was initiated with the cooperation of several agencies, and oversight of the program was assigned to Mr. Z, the support group coordinator of the Families of People with AIDS organization. Eventually, the coalition changed its focus from providing support for the community residence to carrying out a community needs assessment for further community residences for people with AIDS.

The Ending Stage

The coalition continued to meet during the implementation phase of the new community residence. The residence had a waiting list of many potential residents, and this troubled the coalition. The following excerpt illustrates how the coalition agreed to change its focus and reformulate its goals.

Ms. C: It has been over a year since we started this group. I think we have accomplished quite a bit. This might be a good time to evaluate what we have done as a group. How do you feel about this?

Mr. Z: It seems to me we have achieved our initial goals. I think there is more work to be done in establishing other community residences.

Dr. J: I think we have learned a lot about community residence programming. We have helped educate the community about AIDS, and we have gained support from some important community leaders. We should continue to meet and think about what other tasks we can accomplish.

Ms. C: Do other members feel this way?

Mr. R: I agree. It might be possible for the group to continue but change its focus slightly.

Ms. T: What do you have in mind?

Mr. R: I have been doing some research on the number of new cases of AIDS treated at the local hospitals. I am concerned that the residence only serves a few people, and many more need this service. Perhaps we should study this problem and try to come up with some recommendations to solve it.

Ms. C: I agree with your observations. Would other members be interested in continuing?

Mrs. B: I would be very interested in continuing, especially if we can develop some additional resources for people with AIDS. At the hospital, we are very concerned about developing new discharge planning options.

Ms. C: I notice that many of you appear receptive to the idea of continuing the group. If we agree to continue meeting, we should reformulate our goals. Perhaps we can brainstorm for a while and try to develop some new ideas.

Mr. A: This is a good strategy. We have worked well together and accomplished a lot. I think we should discuss this further.

In its ending stage, the group attempted to evaluate its effectiveness in accomplishing its goals. Although the community residence was operational, and other important tasks had been accomplished by the group, several members identified additional possible tasks. Members felt that it was important to continue the work of the group by doing further research on the needs of people with AIDS in River Falls.

SUMMARY

This chapter presents two cases that illustrate group work practice in a treatment group and a task group. The first case deals with a support group for family members who are providing care for frail elderly relatives. The case illustrates four different components of the group: support, education, developing coping skills, and problem solving. The dialogue concentrates on how members support each other and how they solve problems by developing a system of mutual aid.

The second case illustrates a coalition of community organizations who work together to open a community residence for people with AIDS. The case illustrates how task groups are used in the community and how members with different interests and approaches can work together to accomplish the group's goals.

The two case examples do not necessarily illustrate the ideal processes or outcomes for such groups. The examples were developed to help readers improve their abilities to analyze group work and to apply group work theory to practice situations. It is hoped that the case examples will encourage readers to develop and analyze their own case material.

LEARNING ASSIGNMENTS

Caregiver Support Group

1. Consider the information shared by the group members during the first session of the group. Construct a chart that illustrates the heterogeneous as well as the homogeneous characteristics of the members. Using this chart, write a summary statement of what members have in common and how they are different. If you were the worker, what other member characteristics would you have sought during the group's composition?

2. Prepare a session agenda addressing one of the topics listed in the educational component of this group. How would you foster member discussion during the educational component of the session?

3. Prepare a short statement of purpose that could be used to orient members during the first meeting. What rules of group behavior would you suggest for members? How would you introduce norms to the members?

4. Choose two of the sessions illustrated in the case example. Write a statement that Mrs. S could have used to summarize the work that had been done in each session.

5. If you were asked to lead this type of support group, how would you handle the following situations that might surface in the group?

   a. One member continually shows up late for meetings.
   b. One member monopolizes the conversation.

    c. One member violates the norm of confidentiality by talking to a neighbor about someone in the group.

    d. One member refuses to allow the group to move into deeper and more sensitive areas of discussion.

    e. The group uses a quiet member as a scapegoat.

    f. The group appears sluggish and does not want to discuss difficult issues common to members.

    g. The group develops two subgroups that dominate the session discussions.

    h. The group wants to become independent from the leader, hold meetings at the homes of different members, and invite new members to participate.

6. The agency director has asked you to evaluate the effect of this group on the individual members and on the larger community. Design evaluation strategies for each purpose.

7. What else could Mrs. S have done to plan for the termination of the group? How could she have helped ensure that the gains members made during the group were maintained?

Community Coalition

1. Although six planning considerations are listed in this case, what other planning issues might be involved in forming this coalition? How would you use homogeneity and heterogeneity of members' characteristics in composing the group? What special community or environmental considerations would you consider if you were the worker?

2. Choose five situations, issues, or social problems for which a community coalition might be an effective means of gaining community support. Choose one issue and identify 5 to 10 organizations in your community that might be particularly important to include in the coalition. Write a short statement of purpose that could be used to begin the first session of the group.

3. During the first and sixth sessions of the group, Mr. S and Mr. Z expressed concern about how the group might carry out its purpose. If you were the worker, how would you have handled this potential source of conflict within the group? What techniques would you have used to increase group cohesion?

4. The purpose of the coalition was tested when the community political leaders threatened to pass legislation to preclude the opening of the community residence. How would you have handled this situation? How would you have used the coalition to achieve the desired support from community political leaders?

5. In the middle stage of the group, several members engage in a process of mutual aid, which assists the group in achieving its purpose and helps the members get their own needs met. Identify three situations in which members worked together to achieve the goals of the group. How could the worker have increased mutual aid among the members?

6. Identify the bond that helped members continue the community coalition after the group had accomplished its goals. If you were the worker, what actions would you suggest to help the group change its goals?
7. How would you have arranged a systematic evaluation of the process and outcomes of this group? Construct a follow-up questionnaire that could be used to obtain data about the effectiveness of the group.

Guidelines for Ethics

American Group Psychotherapy Association, Inc.[1]

INTRODUCTION

The American Group Psychotherapy Association is a professional multidisciplinary organization whose purpose is to "provide a forum for the exchange of ideas among qualified professional persons interested in group psychotherapy and to publish and to make publications available on all subjects relating to group psychotherapy; to encourage the development of sound training programs in group psychotherapy for qualified mental health professionals; to encourage and promote research on group psychotherapy and to establish and maintain high standards of ethical, professional group psychotherapy practice."

Membership in the American Group Psychotherapy Association presumes strict adherence to standards of ethical practice. As a specialty organization, AGPA supports the ethical codes of the primary professional organizations to which our members belong. Providing guidelines for the ethical behavior of group psychotherapists serves to inform both the group psychotherapist and public of the American Group Psychotherapy Association's expectations in the practice of group psychotherapy.

GENERAL GUIDELINES

Ethics complaints about AGPA members will be directed to the primary professional organization of the members. AGPA's response as to sanctions will parallel

[1]Reprinted with the permission of the American Group Psychotherapy Association, Inc., 25 East 21st Street, 6th Floor, New York, NY 10010, Telephone: (212) 477-2677.

that of the primary organization. For example, if the primary organization concludes that an individual's membership should be suspended for one year, AGPA will suspend membership for one year. Should an ethical complaint be received regarding a member of AGPA who does not belong to a primary professional organization, the complainant will be directed to the state licensing board and/or the state or federal legal system. If the member is found guilty, AGPA's sanctions will parallel the sanctions of the state licensing board, other governmental agencies or courts of law as to the person's ability to practice; the AGPA cannot parallel such sanctions as fines, penalties or imprisonment.

For those members of the American Group Psychotherapy Association who are psychiatrists, the principles of ethics as applied by the American Psychiatric Association shall govern their behavior; members who are clinical psychologists shall be expected to comply with the principles of ethics laid down by the American Psychological Association; members who are clinical social workers shall be expected to comply with the ethical standards established by the National Federation of Societies for Clinical Social Work; members who are clinical specialists in nursing shall be expected to comply with the principles of ethics of the American Nurses' Association; members who are pastoral counselors shall be expected to comply with the ethical standards of the American Association of Pastoral Care; and members of other professional disciplines having published principles of ethics shall follow those principles. Members of the Association who do not belong to one of the above professional groups having a published standard of ethics shall follow the principles of ethics laid down by the American Psychological Association.

GUIDELINES OF GROUP PSYCHOTHERAPY PRACTICE

The following guidelines of group psychotherapy practice shall serve as models for group therapists' ethical behavior.

Responsibility to Patient/Client

1. The group psychotherapist provides services with respect for the dignity and uniqueness of each patient/client as well as the rights and autonomy of the individual patient/client.

    1.1 The group psychotherapist shall provide the potential group patient/client with information about the nature of group psychotherapy and apprise them of the risks, rights, and obligations as members of a therapy group.

    1.2 The group psychotherapist shall encourage the patient/client's participation in group psychotherapy only so long as it is appropriate to the patient/client's needs.

    1.3 The group psychotherapist shall not practice or condone any form of discrimination on the basis of race, color, sex, sexual orientation, age, religion, national origin, or physical handicap, except that this guideline shall not prohibit group therapy practice with population specific or problem specific groups.

2. The group psychotherapist safeguards the patient/client's right to privacy by judiciously protecting information of a confidential nature.

    2.1 The group shall agree that the patient/client as well as the psychotherapist shall protect the identity of its members.

    2.2 The group psychotherapist shall not use identifiable information about the group or its members for teaching purposes, publication, or professional presentations unless permission has been obtained and all measures have been taken to preserve patient/client anonymity.

3. The group psychotherapist acts to safeguard the patient/client and the public from the incompetent, unethical, illegal practice of any group psychotherapist.

    3.1 The group psychotherapist must be aware of her/his own individual competencies, and when the needs of the patient/client are beyond the competencies of the psychotherapist, consultation must be sought from other qualified professionals or other appropriate sources.

    3.2 The group psychotherapist shall not use her/his professional relationship to advance personal or business interests.

    3.3 Sexual intimacy with patients/clients is unethical.

    3.4 The group psychotherapist shall protect the patient/client and the public from misinformation and misrepresentation. She/he shall not use false or misleading advertising regarding her/his qualifications or skills as a group psychotherapist.

Professional Standards

The group psychotherapist shall maintain the integrity of the practice of group psychotherapy.

1. It is the personal responsibility of the group psychotherapist to maintain competence in the practice of group psychotherapy through formal education activities and informal learning experiences.

2. The group psychotherapist has a responsibility to contribute to the ongoing development of the body of knowledge pertaining to group psychotherapy whether involved as an investigator, participant, or user of research results.

3. The group psychotherapist shall accept the obligation to attempt to inform and alert other group psychotherapists who are violating ethical principles or to bring those violations to the attention of appropriate professional authorities.

Ethical Guidelines for Group Counselors[1]

Association for Specialists in Group Work[2]

ETHICAL GUIDELINES

1. **Orientation and Providing Information:** Group counselors adequately prepare prospective or new group members by providing as much information about the existing or proposed group as necessary.

2. **Screening of Members:** The group counselor screens prospective group members (when appropriate to their theoretical orientation). Insofar as possible, the counselor selects group members whose needs and goals are compatible with the goals of the group, who will not impede the group process, and whose well-being will not be jeopardized by the group experience. An orientation to the group (i.e., ASGW Ethical Guideline #1) is included during the screening process.

3. **Confidentiality:** Group counselors protect members by defining clearly what confidentiality means, why it is important, and the difficulties involved in enforcement.

4. **Voluntary/Involuntary Participation:** Group counselors inform members whether participation is voluntary or involuntary.

5. **Leaving a Group:** Provisions are made to assist a group member to terminate in an effective way.

[1]Reprinted with the permission of the Association for Specialists in Group Work, a Division of the American Counseling Association, 5999 Stevenson Avenue, Alexandria, VA 22304.

[2]These guidelines were approved by the Association for Specialists in Group Work (ASGW) Executive Board, June 1, 1989.

6. **Coercion and Pressure:** Group counselors protect member rights against physical threats, intimidation, coercion, and undue peer pressure insofar as is reasonably possible.

7. **Imposing Counselor Values:** Group counselors develop an awareness of their own values and needs and the potential effect they have on the interventions likely to be made.

8. **Equitable Treatment:** Group counselors make every reasonable effort to treat each member individually and equally.

9. **Dual Relationships:** Group counselors avoid dual relationships with group members that might impair their objectivity and professional judgment, as well as those which are likely to compromise a group member's ability to participate fully in the group.

10. **Use of Techniques:** Group counselors do not attempt any technique unless trained in its use or under supervision by a counselor familiar with the intervention.

11. **Goal Development:** Group counselors make every effort to assist members in developing their personal goals.

12. **Consultation:** Group counselors develop and explain policies about between-session consultation to group members.

13. **Termination from the Group:** Depending upon the purpose of participation in the group, counselors promote termination of members from the group in the most efficient period of time.

14. **Evaluation and Follow-Up:** Group counselors make every attempt to engage in ongoing assessment and to design follow-up procedures for their groups.

15. **Referrals:** If the needs of a particular member cannot be met within the type of group being offered, the group counselor suggests other appropriate professional referrals.

16. **Professional Development:** Group counselors recognize that professional growth is a continuous, ongoing, developmental process throughout their career.

Standards for Social Work Practice with Groups[1]

Association for the Advancement of Social Work with Groups, Inc., an International Professional Organization (AASWG)

These standards reflect the distinguishing features of group work as well as the unique perspective that social workers bring to their practice with groups. Central to social work practice with groups is the concept of mutual aid. The group worker recognizes that the group, with its multiple helping relationships, is the primary source of change. The group worker's role is one primarily of helping members work together to achieve the goals that they have established for themselves.

By design, these standards are general, rather than specific. They are applicable to the types of groups that social workers encounter in the full range of settings in which they practice. Further, the standards allow the individual practitioner to apply a variety of relevant group work models, within the more general mutual aid framework.

Section I identifies essential knowledge and values that underlie social work practice with groups. In Sections II through V, worker tasks in the pre-group, beginning, middle, and ending phases of the group are identified, as is specific knowledge that may be needed by the worker in each phase.

[1]Reprinted with the permission of AASWG.

I.   Core Knowledge and Values

A.   Familial, social, political, cultural context of member identity, interactional style, and problem
   • members are viewed as citizens
   • members are capable of change and capable of helping one another

B.   Attention to the whole person
   • systems perspective used in assessment and intervention
   • person and environment
   • bio-psycho-social perspective
   • member-in-group
   • group-in-community

C.   Competency-based assessment
   • emphasis on member strengths as well as deficits

D.   Mutual aid function
   • group consists of multiple helping relationships
   • worker's primary role is one of helping members to help one another

E.   Groups characterized by democratic process
   • members are helped to own the group
   • equal worth of members and worker
   • worker is not all powerful "expert"
   • worker to group and worker to members
   • relationships characterized by egalitarianism and reciprocity

F.   Emphasis on empowerment
   • group goals emphasize individual member growth and social change
   • group worker promotes individual and group autonomy

G.   Worker's assessment and interventions characterized by flexibility and eclecticism

H.   Small group behavior
   • group as an entity separate and distinct from individual members
   • phases of group development foster change throughout the life of the group
   • recognition of how group process shapes and influences individual member behavior

I.   Groups formed for different purposes and goals
   • group type (e.g., education, problem-solving, social action) influences what worker does and how group accomplishes its goals

J. Monitoring and evaluation of success of group in accomplishing its objectives through observation and measurement of outcomes and/or processes

II. Group Work in the Pre-Group Phase

Tasks:

A. Identify common needs of potential group members

B. Plan and conduct outreach, recruitment of members

C. Secure organizational support and sanction for group, if needed

D. Address organizational resistance to groups, if needed

E. Screen and prepare members for group, when appropriate

F. Secure permission for members' participation, when needed

G. Develop compositional balance, if appropriate

H. Select appropriate group type, structure, and size

I. Establish meeting place, time, etc., that promotes member comfort and cohesion

J. Develop and articulate verbally and/or in writing a clear statement of group purpose that reflects member needs and, where appropriate, agency mission

K. Develop and articulate clear statement of worker role that reflects the group's purpose

L. Use preparatory empathy to tune into members' feelings and reactions to group's beginning

Knowledge Needed:

A. Organization's mission and function and how this influences nature of group work service

B. Social and institutional barriers which may impact on the development of group work service

C. Issues associated with group composition

D. Human life cycle and its relationship to potential members' needs

E. Cultural factors and their influence on potential members' lives and their ability to engage in group and relate to others

F. Types of groups and their relationship to member needs

G. Specific types of individual and social problems that lead to a need for group

III. Group Work in the Beginning Phase

Tasks:

A. Provide clear statement of group (and, if necessary, agency) purpose and worker role

B. Elicit member feedback regarding perception of needs, interests, and problems

C. Encourage members to share concerns and strengths with one another

D. Facilitate connections between members and members and worker

E. Encourage awareness and expression of commonalities among members

F. Monitor group for manifestations of authority theme and, when needed, respond directly

G. Assess impact of cultural differences between members and between members and worker and address directly when needed

H. Assist group in establishing rules and norms that promote change and growth

I. Use of self to develop cohesion among members and comfort with worker

J. Assist members in establishing individual and group goals

K. Clarify link between individual and group goals

L. Help members to establish a beginning contract which provides clarity and direction to their work together

M. Promote individual autonomy and empowerment of members

N. Create and maintain environment of sociocultural safety

Knowledge Needed:

A. Group dynamics in beginning stage of group

B. Causes/manifestations of resistance to change among members and in external environment

IV. Group Work in the Middle Phase

Tasks:

A. Point out commonalities among members

B. Reinforce connection between individual needs/problems and group goals

C. Encourage and model supportive, honest feedback between members and between members and worker

D. Use here and now/process illumination to further group's work

E. Help members use role playing, behavioral rehearsal, and other verbal and non-verbal activities to accomplish individual and group goals

F. Monitor norms that govern group's work

G. Assess group's progress toward its goals

H. Re-contract with members, if needed, to assist them in achieving individual and group goals

I. Identify obstacles to work within and outside group's boundaries and deal with directly

J. Clarify and interpret communication patterns between members, between members and the worker, and between the group and others external to the group

K. Identify and highlight member conflict, when needed, and facilitate resolution

L. Summarize sessions

Knowledge Needed:

A. Group dynamics in the middle phase

B. Role theory and its application to members' relationships with one another and with worker

C. Communication theory and its application to verbal and non-verbal interactions within group and between group and others external to group

D. Member interactions as manifestations of sociocultural forces of race, class, gender, sexual orientation, etc.

E. Member interactions as manifestations of psychodynamic factors

F. Purposeful use of verbal and non-verbal activities

V. Group Work in the Ending Phase

Tasks:

A. Identify and point out direct and indirect signs of members' reactions to ending

B. Share worker's ending feelings with members

C. Assist members in sharing their feelings about endings with one another

D. Help members identify gains they have made and changes that have resulted from their participation in the group

E. Assist members in applying new knowledge and skills to their daily lives

F. Encourage member feedback to worker

G. Help members honestly reflect on and evaluate their work together

H. Develop plans for continuation of service or referral of members, as needed

I. Assess individual member and group progress

J. Evaluate impact of group experience on individual members and external environment

Knowledge Needed:

A. Group dynamics in the ending phase

B. Formal and informal resources which maintain and enhance members' growth

C. Influence of past losses and separations in lives of members and worker on group's ending

Films and Videotapes

Len Brown. *Problem Solving*. Rutgers University, School of Social Work, 536 George Street, New Brunswick, NJ 08903.

Len Brown. *Termination*. Rutgers University, School of Social Work, 536 George Street, New Brunswick, NJ 08903.

M. R. Carroll. *Group Work: Leading in the Here and Now*. American Counseling Association, 5999 Stevenson Avenue, Alexandria, VA 22304-3300.

Tom Casciato. *Circle of Recovery, with Bill Moyers*. Circle of Recovery, Box 2284, South Burlington, VT 05407.

Center for Psychological Issues in the Nuclear Age. *Meetings That Lead to Action*. Center PINA, 475 Riverside Drive, New York, NY 10115

Edmund S. Muskie Institute of Public Affairs. *Mattering . . . A Journey with Rural Youth*. The Clearinghouse, Muskie School, PO Box 15010, University of Southern Maine, Portland, ME 04112.

Naomi Feil. *Looking for Yesterday*. Edward Feil Productions, 4614 Prospect Avenue, Cleveland, OH 44103.

Naomi Feil. *The More We Get Together: How to Form a Validation Group*. Edward Feil Productions, 4614 Prospect Avenue, Cleveland, OH 44103.

Mel Goldstein. *Reflections on Group Work: The Video Curriculum to Teach Social Group Work*. School of Social Work, State University of New York at Stony Brook, Health Sciences Center, Stony Brook, NY 11794.

Insight Media. *Groups and Group Dynamics*. Insight Media, 121 West 85th Street, New York, NY 10024.

William Lauzon. *Staff Groups: Wellness in the Workplace*. Office of Television and Radio, Building 4048–Kilmeer, Rutgers University, New Brunswick, NJ 08903.

Walter Lifton. *Just Like a Family*. University Film Service, University at Albany, State University of New York, 1400 Washington Avenue, Albany, NY 12222.

Andrew Malekoff. *A Sense of Alienation or Belonging: Building Bridges through Group Involvement*. Institute for Group Work with Children & Youth, 480 Old Westbury Road, Roslyn Heights, NY 11577-2215, Attn: Jane Yazdpour.

Edward Mason. *Chrysalis '86: The Development of a Therapeutic Group*. Penn State AudioVisual Services, 1127 Fox Hill Road, University Park, PA 16803.

Robert Pasick. *Men in Therapy: Men's Issues and Group Treatment*. AGC United Learning, Menninger Video Productions, 1560 Sherman Avenue, Suite 100, Evanston, IL 60201.

William Piper. *Helping People Adapt to Loss: A Short-Term Group Therapy Approach*. Guilford Publications, Catalog #2498, 72 Spring Street, New York, NY 10012.

Public Broadcasting Video. *Frontline: The Color of Your Skin*. PBS Video, 1320 Braddock Place, Alexandria, VA 22314. No. Fron-9211K. (This is not a film about group work, but a film showing group dynamics at the U.S. Army's Defense Equal Opportunity Management Institute. This film can be used to discuss sensitivity training or race relations in groups.)

Sheldon Rose. *The Best of the Children's Groups.* School of Social Work, University of Wisconsin–Madison, 425 Henry Mall, Madison, WI 53706.

Sheldon Rose. *Common Problems in Parent Training Groups.* School of Social Work, University of Wisconsin–Madison, 425 Henry Mall, Madison, WI 53706.

Sheldon Rose. *The Golden Eagles.* School of Social Work, University of Wisconsin–Madison, 425 Henry Mall, Madison, WI 53706.

Sheldon Rose. *Problem Solving in Groups.* School of Social Work, University of Wisconsin–Madison, 425 Henry Mall, Madison, WI 53706.

Round Table Films. *Meeting in Progress.* Round Table Films, 113 North San Vincente Boulevard, Beverly Hills, CA 90211.

Saul Scheidlinger & Cary Sandberg. *Reunion with the Mother of Abandonment: A Group Fantasy.* Insight Media, 121 West 85th Street, New York, NY 10024.

Lawrence Shulman. *Skills of Helping: Leading a First Group Session.* Instructional Communication Center, McGill University, Montreal, Quebec, Canada H3A 2K6.

Lawrence Shulman. *Skills of Helping: The Married Couples Group.* Instructional Communication Center, McGill University, Montreal, Quebec, Canada H3A 2K6

Rosemary Snead. *Skills and Techniques for Group Counselling with Youth.* Research Press, 2612 North Mattis Avenue, Champaign, IL 61821.

David Spiegel & Pat Fobair. *Supportive-Expressive Group Therapy for People with Cancer and Their Families.* Center for Media and Independent Learning, University of California Extension, 2000 Center Street, 4th Floor, Berkeley, CA 94704.

David Spiegel & Pat Fobair. *Tape I, The Process of Forming a Support Group and Detoxifying Death; Tape II, Taking Time and Fortifying Families; Tape III, Dealing with Doctors and Controlling Pain through Self-Hypnosis; Tape IV, A Model Session.* Center for Media and Independent Learning, University of California Extension, 2000 Center Street, 4th Floor, Berkeley, CA 94704.

Roberta Starzecpyzl. *Shooting Stars.* Dragon Rising Productions, P. O. Box 629, Village Station, New York, NY 10014.

Irving Yalom. *Understanding Group Psychotherapy.* Center for Media and Independent Learning, University of California Extension, 2000 Center Street, 4th Floor, Berkeley, CA 94704.

Irving Yalom. *Outpatients.* Center for Media and Independent Learning, University of California Extension, 2000 Center Street, 4th Floor, Berkeley, CA 94704.

Irving Yalom. *Inpatients.* Center for Media and Independent Learning, University of California Extension, 2000 Center Street, 4th Floor, Berkeley, CA 94704.

Irving Yalom. *Yalom: An interview.* Center For Media and Independent Learning, University of California Extension, 2000 Center Street, 4th Floor, Berkeley, CA 94704.

OTHER FILM RESOURCES

Interviews of Saul Bernstein, Giesela Konopka, Helen Northen, Helen Phillips, Mary Lou Sommers, and Gertrude Wilson as well as other films are available in VHS format from David Klaassen, Social Welfare History Archives, University of Minnesota, 1012 Walter Library, 117 Pleasant Street, SE, Minneapolis, MN 55455.

Group Announcements

SUPPORT GROUP FOR NEW PARENTS

You are invited to join a support group of parents who have children ages 6 months to 2 years. The group will discuss concerns identified by its members including such possible issues as infant care, sharing household responsibilities, disciplining your child, toilet training, and child-care resources.

Sponsor

Greenwich Community Mental Health Center
49 Cambridge Avenue
Greenwich, NY
(212) 246-2468

Group Leaders

George Oxley, ACSW, clinic director
Marybeth Carol, BSW, clinic social worker

Membership

Open to all parents with children from ages 6 months to 2 years

Dates and Times

March–April–May, Thursday evenings from 7:30 to 9:30 P.M.

Child Care

Parents are encouraged to bring their children to the center. Child care will be available from human service interns of Hudson Center Community College.

499

Cost

Enrollment fee for the three-month group, total $90.00 per couple, payable monthly

For further information, call Mr. Oxley or Ms. Carol at (212) 246-2468.

 # YOUTH CENTER INTEREST MEETING

The residents of the Johnsonville, Pittstown, and Valley Falls area are invited to discuss the proposed establishment of a youth center for these communities. Issues to be discussed include cost of service, fundraising, need for service, and support for such a service.

Sponsor

Rensselaer Council of Community Services

Meeting Place

Johnsonville Firehouse

Date and Time

Thursday, March 25, from 7 to 9 P.M.

Further Information

Call Jim Kesser, ACSW
(212) 241-2412

Refreshments will be served.

Outline for a Group Proposal

Treatment/Task

Abstract

Short statement summarizing major points of group

Purpose

Brief statement of purpose
How the group will conduct its work
Job description of the worker

Agency Sponsorship

Agency name and mission
Agency resources (physical facilities, financial, staff)
Geographic and demographic data on agency

Membership

Specific population for the group
Why population was chosen

Recruitment

Methods to be used

Composition

Criteria for member inclusion/exclusion
Size, open or closed group, demographic characteristics

Orientation

Specific procedures to be used

Contract

Number, frequency, length, and time of meeting

Environment

Physical arrangements (room, space, materials)
Financial arrangements (budget, expense, income)
Special arrangements (child care, transportation)

An Example of a Treatment Group Proposal

ADOLESCENT DISCHARGE GROUP

The Children's Refuge Home

Abstract

This is a proposal for a social skills training group for adolescents who are about to be released into the community from the children's refuge home.

Purpose

The group will discuss what each member expects to be doing on release to the community. The group will reinforce social learning that has taken place during the residential placement and will help members learn new social skills that will be needed to successfully relate to parents, siblings, teachers, and employers. Role playing, behavior rehearsal modeling, and reinforcement will be employed as methods of teaching social skills.

Agency Sponsorship

The Children's Refuge Home, a residential treatment facility for delinquent youth, serves teenage boys who cannot live at home because of law-breaking activities. About 200 boys reside here in 15 cottages. The agency has a 200-acre campus with an on-campus school. Staff ratio is about one staff member per four boys; direct-care staff include child care workers, social workers, nursing staff, psychologists, psychiatrists, and clergy.

Membership

Approximately 10 boys are released to the community each month. The discharge group will be composed from a population of boys for whom discharge is planned within the next three months.

Recruitment

Because this group represents a new service for the institution, members will be recruited by asking cottage parents for volunteers from their respective cottages. An announcement will be printed and delivered to the senior cottage parents for all cottages. In addition, teachers and social workers will be contacted to suggest possible candidates for the group.

Composition

The group will be composed of six to eight boys from 12 to 14 years old who anticipate discharge from CRH within the next three months. In addition, this first group will include only children who will be returning to natural parents or relatives rather than to foster care or group homes. The group will be closed and will not add new members because it is important that social skills be learned in a gradual and cumulative fashion.

Orientation

Each member will be interviewed by the leaders. During this interview, the members will view a videotape on group treatment for children, and the details of the tape will be discussed to demonstrate how group meetings will be conducted.

Environment

The ideal location for this group is the diagnostic classroom within the campus school. Proximity to videotaping equipment is necessary so group members can tape and view role plays. A small budget is required ($120) for proposed field trips, charts, and materials for listing skills and posting individual and group progress, and for refreshments after meetings. Additional expenses include two color videotapes ($60). Special arrangements will have to be made so that each member's afterschool recreation schedule is free for Monday afternoon meeting times.

appendix F

An Example of a Task Group Proposal

TASK FORCE ON RESEARCH UTILIZATION IN PROBATION

Abstract

This is a proposal for establishing an interagency task force to study how research and research procedures are used in three county probation offices. The group will issue a report with recommendations for increasing research use in probation settings.

Purpose

This group will be formed to study the use of research in county probation offices. The group will meet to discuss the results of surveys taken on each probation office regarding the extent to which probation workers use published research to inform their practice and the extent to which they conduct research in conjunction with their practice. The group will be convened by Robert Rivas, ACSW, at Siena College.

Agency Sponsorship

The task force will be sponsored by the tri-county consortium of probation agencies. The Rockwell County agency will provide physical facilities for meetings. Financial costs will be shared by all county agencies.

Membership

Each county agency will nominate three representatives to attend meetings to ensure equal representation among agencies.

Recruitment

Mailings will be sent to all agency directors. Members of the tri-county association will be informed by an announcement in the newsletter. Each agency director will be requested by letter to appoint three representatives to the task force.

Composition

The task force will require that each agency appoint one representative from each of the following categories: probation administrator, probation supervisor (or senior officer), and probation officer. The task force will include nine representatives from agencies and two research consultants from local colleges. All members of the task force should have some knowledge about research methods. This will be a closed group, although interested people may attend specific meetings after obtaining permission from the group's leader.

Orientation

The group will be given several research reports to read to prepare for discussions. The group leader will contact each member individually to get ideas for composing an agenda.

Contract

The task force will meet once a month for six sessions. Meetings will last for three hours and will take place every fourth Monday of the month from 9 A.M. to noon. The group will be required to compose and issue a preliminary report on research use within one month after the final meeting.

Environment

The Rockwell County agency will provide the use of its staff meeting room, which is equipped with tables and blackboards, for the group's work. Copying facilities will be provided by Rockwell County, and each county will be billed for one third the expenses (limit $30.00 per county). About $100 will be required to prepare and distribute the task force's final report and recommendations (contributed by the county association). Agency directors for each county have been requested to provide travel allowance (25 cents a mile) for all travel in conjunction with the work of the task force.

Suggested Readings on Program Activities

PROGRAM ACTIVITIES FOR GROUPS OF CHILDREN AND ADOLESCENTS

Allen, J. S., & Klein, R. J. (1996). *Ready, set, relax: A research-based program of relaxation, learning, and self-esteem for children.* Watertown, WI: Inner Coaching.

Borba, M., & Borba, C. (1978). *Self-esteem: A classroom affair.* Minneapolis, MN: Winston Press.

Carrell, S. (1993). *Group exercises for adolescents: A manual for therapists.* Newbury Park, CA: Sage Publications.

Cartlege, G., & Milbrun, J. F. (Eds.). (1980). *Teaching social skills to children.* Elmsford, NY: Pergamon Press.

Duncan, T., & Gumaer, J. (1980). *Developmental group for children.* Springfield, IL: Charles C. Thomas.

Ehly, S., & Dustin, R. (1989). *Individual and group counseling in the schools.* New York: Guilford Press.

Ferrara, M. (1992). *Group counseling with juvenile delinquents: The limit and lead approach.* Newbury Park, CA: Sage Publications.

Goldstein, A. P., Sprakin, R. P., Gerhaw, N. J., & Klein, P. (1980). *Skill streaming the adolescent. A structured learning approach to teaching prosocial skills.* Champaign, IL: Research Press.

Hazel, J. S., Schumaker, J. B., Sherman, J. A., & Sheldon, J. (1981). *A social skills program for adolescents.* Champaign, IL: Research Press.

Kaufman, G., & Lev, R. (1990). *Stick up for yourself: Every kid's guide to personal power and positive self-esteem.* Minneapolis, MN: Free Spirit.

Mandell, G., & Damon, L. (1989). *Group treatment for sexually abused children.* New York: Guilford Press.

Mannix, D. (1993). *Social skills activities for special children.* West Nyack, NY: The Center for Applied Research in Education.

McElherne, L. M. (1999). *Jumpstarters: Quick classroom activities that develop self-esteem, creativity and cooperation.* Minneapolis, MN: Free Spirit.

McGinnis, E., & Goldstein, A. P. (1984). *Skill streaming the elementary school child: A guide for teaching prosocial skills.* Champaign, IL: Research Press.

McGinnis, E., & Goldstein, A. P. (1990). *Skill streaming in early childhood.* Champaign, IL: Research Press.

Middleman, R. (1982). *The non-verbal method in working with groups: The use of activity in teaching, counseling, and therapy.* An enlarged edition. Hebron, CT: Practitioners Press.

Morganett, R. (1990). *Skills for living: Group counseling activities for young adolescents.* Champaign, IL: Research Press.

Norem-Hebeisen, A. A. (1976). *Exploring self-esteem.* New York: National Humanities Education Center.

Payne, L. M. (1994). *Just because I am: A child's book of inspiration.* Minneapolis, MN: Free Spirit.

Payne, L. M. (1994). *We can get along: A child's book of choices.* Minneapolis, MN: Free Spirit.

Pfeiffer, J. W., & Goodstein, L. (Eds.). (1984–1998). *The annual: Developing human resources.* San Diego, CA: University Associates, Inc.

Pope, A. W., McHale, S. M., & Craighead, W. E. (1988). *Self-esteem enhancement with chil-dren and adolescents.* New York: Pergamon Press.

Rathjen, D. P., & Foreyt, J. P. (Eds.). (1980). *Social competence: Interventions for children and adults.* Elmsford, NY: Pergamon Press.

Rose, S., & Edleson, J. (1991). *Working with children and adolescents in groups.* San Francisco: Jossey-Bass.

Smith, M. A. (1977). *A practical guide to value clarification.* La Jolla, CA: University Associates.

Teolis, B. (1998). *Ready-to-use conflict resolution activities for elementary students.* West Nyack, NY: Center for Applied Research in Education.

Wells, H. C., & Canfield, J. (1976). *One hundred ways to enhance self-concept in the classroom.* Englewood Cliffs, NJ: Prentice-Hall.

Whitehouse, E., & Pudney, W. (1996). *A volcano in my tummy: Helping children to handle anger. A resource book for parents, caregivers, and teachers.* Gabriola Island, BC: New Society.

PROGRAM ACTIVITIES FOR GROUPS OF OLDER PEOPLE

Beisgon, B. (1989). *Life enhancing activities for the mentally impaired elderly.* New York: Springer.

Birren, J., & Deutchman, D. (1991). *Guiding autobiography groups for older adults.* Baltimore: John Hopkins Press.

Booth, H. (1986). Dance/movement therapy. In I. Burnside (Ed.), *Working with the elderly: Group processes and techniques* (2nd ed., pp. 211–224). Boston: Jones and Bartlett.

Clark, P., & Osgood, N. J. (1985). *Seniors on stage: The impact of applied theater techniques on the elderly.* New York: Praeger.

Clements, C. (1994). *The arts/fitness quality of life activities program: Creative ideas for working with older adults in group settings.* Baltimore: Health Professions Press.

Dickey, H. (1987). *Intergenerational activities.* Buffalo, NY: Potentials Development for Health & Aging Services.

Fisher, P. (1989). *Creative movement for older adults.* New York: Human Sciences Press.

Flatten, K., Wilhite, B., & Reyes-Watson, E. (1988). *Exercise activities for the elderly.* New York: Springer.

Flatten, K., Wilhite, B., & Reyes-Watson, E. (1988). *Recreation activities for the elderly.* New York: Springer.

Foster, P. (Ed.). (1983). *Activities and the "well elderly."* New York: Haworth Press.

Fry, P. (1983). Structured and unstructured reminiscence training and depression among the elderly. *Clinical Gerontologist, 1*(13), 15–37.

Goodwin, D. (1982). *Activity Director's bag of tricks.* Chicago: Adams Press.

Helgeson, E., & Willis, S. (Eds.). (1987). *Handbook of group activities for impaired older adults.* New York: Haworth Press.

Hennessey, M. (1986). Music therapy. In I. Burnside (Ed.), *Working with the elderly: Group processes and techniques* (2nd ed., pp. 198–210). Boston: Jones and Bartlett.

Houten, L. (1990). *Moving for life: Movement, art & music.* Buffalo, NY: Potentials Development for Health & Aging Services.

Hurley, O. (1996). *Safe therapeutic exercise for the frail elderly: An introduction* (2nd ed). Albany, NY: Center for the Study of Aging.

Ingersoll, B., & Goodman, L. (1983). A reminiscence group for institutionalized elderly. In M. Rosenbaum (Ed.), *Handbook of short-term therapy groups* (pp. 247–269). New York: McGraw-Hill.

Ingersoll, B., & Silverman, A. (1978). Comparative group psychotherapy for the aged. *The Gerontologist, 18*(2), 201–206.

Jacobs, R. (1987). Older women: Surviving and thriving. Milwaukee, WI: Family Service America.

Kamin, J. (1984). How older adults use books and the public library: A review of the literature. Occasional papers number 165 (ERIC Document Reproduction Service No. ED 247954).

Karras, B. (1994). *Say it with music: Music games and trivia.* Mt. Airy, MD: Eldersong Publications.

Killeffer, E., Bennett, R., & Gruen, G. (1985). *Handbook of innovative programs for the impaired elderly.* New York: Haworth Press.

King, K. (1982). Reminiscing psychotherapy with aging people. *Journal of Psychosocial Nursing and Mental Health Services, 20*(2), 21–25.

Lesser, J., Lazarus, L., Frankel, R., & Havasy, S. (1981). Reminiscence group therapy with psychotic geriatric in-patients. *The Gerontologist, 21*(3), 291–296.

Lewis, M., & Butler, R. (1974). Life review therapy: Putting memories to work in individual and group psychotherapy. *Geriatrics, 29*(11), 165–173.

Lowman, E. (1992). *Arts & crafts for the elderly.* New York: Springer.

McMorde, W., & Blom, S. (1979). Life review therapy: Psychotherapy for the elderly. *Perspectives In Psychiatric Care, 17,* 292–298.

Schlenger, G. (1988). *Come and sit by me: Discussion programs for activity specialists.* Owings Mills, MD: National Health Publishing.

Schulberg, C. (1979). *The music therapy sourcebook.* New York: Human Sciences Press.

Sherman, E. (1987). Reminiscence groups for the community elderly. *Gerontologist, 27*(5), 569–572.

Sherman, E. (1990). Experiential reminiscence and life review therapy. In G. Lietaer, J. Rombauts, & R. Van Balen (Eds.), *Client-centered and experiential psychotherapy in the nineties.* Leuven, Belgium: Leuven University Press.

Suchan, C. (1985). *Edible activities.* Buffalo, NY: Potentials Development for Health & Aging Services.

Thurman, J., & Piggins, C. (1996). *Drama activities with older adults: A handbook for leaders.* New York: Haworth Press.

Toseland, R. (1995). *Group work with the elderly and family caregivers.* New York: Springer.

Wilson, M. (1977). Enhancing the lives of aged in a retirement center through a program of reading. *Educational Gerontology, 4*(3), 245–251.

Wolcott, A. (1986). Art therapy: An experimental group. In I. Burnside (Ed.), *Working with the elderly: Group process and techniques* (pp. 292–310). North Scituate, MA: Duxbury Press.

Zgola, J. (1987). *Doing things: A guide to programming activities for persons with Alzheimer's disease and related disorders.* Baltimore: Johns Hopkins Press.

Aaker, D., Kunar, V., & Day, G. (1998). *Marketing research* (6th ed.). New York: John Wiley & Sons.

Abels, P. (1980). Instructed advocacy and community group work. In A. Alissi (Ed.), *Perspectives on social group work practice* (pp. 326–331). New York: The Free Press.

Abramson, J. (1983). A non-client-centered approach to program development in a medical setting. In H. Weissman, I. Epstein, & A. Savage (Eds.), *Agency-based social work* (pp. 178–187). Philadelphia: Temple University Press.

Abramson, J. (1989). Making teams work. *Social Work with Groups, 12*(4), 45–63.

Achenbach, T. (1991). *Manual for the Child Behavior Checklist: 4–18 and 1991 Profile.* Burlington, VT: University Associates in Psychiatry.

Achenbach, T. (1997). *Child Behavior Checklist.* Burlington, VT: University Medical Education Associates.

Adam, E. (1991). Quality circle performance. *Journal of Management, 17*(1), 25–39.

Addams, J. (1909). *The spirit of youth and the city streets.* New York: Macmillan.

Addams, J. (1926). *Twenty years at Hull House.* New York: Macmillan.

Al-Assaf, A., & Schmele, J. (Eds.). (1997). *The textbook of total quality in healthcare.* Boca Raton, FL: St. Lucie Press.

Alberti, R., & Emmons, M. (1995). *Your perfect right* (8th ed.). San Luis Obispo, CA: Impact Press.

Alemi, F., Mosavel, M., Stephens, R., Ghaderi, A., Krishnaswamy, J., & Thakkar, H. (1996). Electronic self-help and support groups. *Medical Care, 34,* OS32–OS44.

Alinsky, S. (1971). *Rules for radicals.* New York: Random House.

Alissi, A. (Ed.). (1980). *Perspectives on social group work practice.* New York: The Free Press.

Allport, F. (1924). *Social psychology.* Boston: Houghton Mifflin.

American Association of Group Workers. (1947). *Toward professional standards.* New York: Association Press.

American Psychiatric Association. (1994). *Diagnostic and statistical manual of mental disorders* (4th ed.). Washington, DC: Author.

Anderson, J. (1979). Social work practice with groups in the generic base of social work practice. *Social Work with Groups, 2*(4), 281–293.

Anderson, J. (1997). *Social work with groups: A process model.* New York: Longman.

Aponte, J., Rivers, R., & Wohl, R. (1995). *Psychological interventions and cultural diversity.* Boston: Allyn and Bacon.

Argyris, C. (1977). Organizational learning and management information systems. *Accounting, Organizations and Society, 2,* 113–123.

Aronson, H., & Overall, B. (1966). Therapeutic expectations of patients in two social classes. *Social Work, 11,* 35–41.

Asch, P. (1957). An experimental investigation of group influences. In Walter Reed Army Institute of Research, *Symposium on preventive and social psychiatry.* Washington, DC: Walter Reed Army Institute of Research.

Ashby, M., Gilchrist, L., & Miramontez, A. (1987). Group treatment for sexually abused Indian adolescents. *Social Work with Groups, 10*(4), 21–32.

Asher-Svanum, H. (1991). *Psychoeducational groups for patients with schizophrenia.* Gaithersburg, MD: Aspen.

Association for the Advancement of Social Work with Groups. (1998). *Standards for social work practice with groups.* Akron, OH: AASWG.

Atkinson, D., & Lowe, S. (1995). The role of ethnicity, cultural knowledge, and conventional techniques in counseling and psychotherapy. In J. Ponterotto, J. Casas, L. Suzuki, & C. Alexander (Eds.), *Handbook of multicultural counseling* (pp. 387–414). Thousand Oaks, CA: Sage.

Axelson, J. A. (1999). *Counseling and development in a multicultural society* (3rd ed.). Pacific Grove, CA: Brooks/Cole.

Babbie, E. R. (1999). *The basics of social research* (8th ed.). Pacific Grove, CA: Brooks/Cole.

Bachrach, P., & Baratz, M. S. (1962). Two faces of power. *American Political Science Review, 56,* 947–952.

Back, K. (1951). Influence through social communication. *Journal of Abnormal and Social Psychology, 46,* 9–23.

Bailey, D., & Koney, K. M. (1996). Interorganizational community-based collaboratives: A strategic response to shape the social work agenda. *Social Work, 41,* 602–611.

Bailey-Dempsey, C., & Reid, W. J. (1996). Intervention design and development: A case study. *Research on Social Work Practice, 6*(2), 208–228.

Bales, R. (1950). *Interaction process analysis: A method for the study of small groups.* Reading, MA: Addison-Wesley.

Bales, R. (1954). In conference. *Harvard Business Review, 32,* 44–50.

Bales, R. (1955). How people interact in conference. *Scientific American, 192,* 31–35.

Bales, R. (1980). *SYMLOG: Case study kit.* New York: The Free Press.

Bales, R., Cohen, S., & Williamson, S. (1979). *SYMLOG: A system for the multiple level observations of groups.* New York: The Free Press.

Balgopal, P., & Vassil, T. (1983). *Groups in social work: An ecological perspective.* New York: Macmillan.

Bandura, A. (1969). *Principles of behavior modification.* New York: Holt, Rinehart & Winston.

Bandura, A. (1977). *Social Learning Theory.* Englewood Cliffs, NJ: Prentice-Hall.

Barker, L. (1979). *Groups in process: An introduction to small group communication.* Englewood Cliffs, NJ: Prentice-Hall.

Barlow, C., Blythe, J., & Edmonds, M. (1999). *A handbook of interactive exercises for groups.* Boston: Allyn and Bacon.

Baron, J. (1994). *Thinking and deciding* (2nd ed.). New York: Cambridge University Press.

Barrick, M., & Alexander, R. (1987). A review of quality circle efficacy and the existence of positive-findings bias. *Personnel Psychology, 40,* 579–593.

Barth, R. P., Yeaton, J., & Winterfelt, N. (1994). Psychoeducational groups with foster parents of sexually abused children. *Child and Adolescent Social Work Journal, 11*(5), 405–424.

Bass, D., McClendon, M., Brennan, P., & McCarthy, C. (1998). The buffering effect of a computer support network on caregiver strain. *Journal of Aging and Health, 10*(1), 20–43.

Bates, P. (1978). *The effects of interpersonal skills training on the acquisition and generalization of interpersonal communication behaviors by moderately to mildly retarded adults.* Unpublished doctoral dissertation, University of Wisconsin, Madison.

Baugh, S., & Graen, G. (1997). Effects of team gender and racial composition on perceptions of team performance in cross-functional teams. *Group & Organization Management, 22*(3), 366–383.

Bayless, O. (1967). An alternative pattern for problem solving discussion. *Journal of Communication, 17,* 188–197.

Beck, A., & Freeman, A. (1990). *Cognitive therapy of personality disorders.* New York: Guilford.

Beck, J. (1995). *Cognitive therapy: Basics and beyond.* New York: Guilford.

Becker, W. (1971). *Parents are teachers.* Champaign, IL: Research Press.

Bednar, K., & Kaul, T. (1994). Experimental group research: Can the cannon fire? In A. Bergen & S. Garfield (Eds.), *Handbook of psychotherapy and behavior change* (4th ed., pp. 631–663). New York: John Wiley & Sons.

Behroozi, C. S. (1992). A model for social work with involuntary applicants in groups. *Social Work with Groups, 15*(2/3), 223–238.

Bell, J. (1981). The small group perspective: Family group-therapy. In E. Tolson & W. Reid (Eds.), *Models of family treatment* (pp. 33–51). New York: Columbia University Press.

Benne, K., & Sheats, P. (1948). Functional roles of group members. *Journal of Social Issues, 4*(2), 41–49.

Berger, R. (1976). *Interpersonal skill training with institutionalized elderly patients.* Unpublished doctoral dissertation, University of Wisconsin, Madison.

Berger, R. (1996). A comparative analysis of different methods of teaching group work. *Social Work with Groups, 19*(1), 79–89.

Berne, E. (1961). *Transactional analysis in psychotherapy.* New York: Ballantine Books.

Bernstein, D., & Borkovec, T. (1973). *Progressive relaxation training: A manual for the helping professions.* Champaign, IL: Research Press.

Berry, T. (1991). *Managing the total transformation.* New York: McGraw-Hill.

Bertcher, H. (1990). *Tell-a-group: How to set up and operate group work by telephone*. Unpublished manuscript, University of Michigan, School of Social Work, Ann Arbor.

Bertcher, H. (1994). *Group participation: Techniques for leaders and members* (2nd ed.). Newbury Park, CA: Sage.

Bertcher, H., & Maple, F. (1977). *Creating groups*. Newbury Park, CA: Sage.

Bertcher, H., & Maple, F. (1985). Elements and issues in group composition. In M. Sundel, P. Glasser, R. Sarri, & R. Vinter (Eds.), *Individual change through small groups* (2nd ed., pp. 180–203). New York: The Free Press.

Biegel, D., Tracy, E., & Corvo, K. (1994). Strengthening social networks: Intervention strategies for mental health case managers. *Health and Social Work, 19*(3), 206–216.

Bion, W. (1991). *Experiences in groups and other papers*. London: Routledge.

Blatner, H. (1996). *Acting-in: Practical applications of psychodramatic methods* (3rd ed.). New York: Springer.

Blau, P. (1964). *Exchange and power in social life*. New York: John Wiley & Sons.

Blazer, D. (1978). Techniques for communicating with your elderly patient. *Geriatrics, 33*(11), 79–84.

Bloom, B., & Broder, L. (1950). *Problem-solving processes of college students*. Chicago: University of Chicago Press.

Bloom, M. (1996). *Primary prevention practices*. Newbury Park, CA: Sage.

Bloom, M., Fisher, J., & Orme, J. (1999). *Evaluating practice: Guidelines for the accountable professional* (3rd ed.). Boston: Allyn and Bacon.

Boatman, F. (1975). *Caseworkers' judgments of clients' hope: Some correlates among client-situation characteristics and among workers' communication patterns*. Unpublished doctoral dissertation, Columbia University, New York.

Bouchard, T. (1972a). A comparison of two group brainstorming procedures. *Journal of Applied Psychology, 56*, 418–421.

Bouchard, T. (1972b). Training, motivation and personality as determinants of the effectiveness of brainstorming groups and individuals. *Journal of Applied Psychology, 56*, 324–331.

Bowers, D., & Franklin, J. (1976). *Survey-guided development: Data-based organizational change*. Ann Arbor, MI: Institute for Social Research.

Bowman, L. (1935). Dictatorship, democracy, and group work in America. In *Proceedings of the National Conference of Social Work* (p. 382). Chicago: University of Chicago Press.

Boyd, N. (1935). Group work experiments in state institutions in Illinois. In *Proceedings of the National Conference of Social Work* (p. 344). Chicago: University of Chicago Press.

Boyd, N. (1938). Play as a means of social adjustment. In J. Lieberman (Ed.), *New trends in group work* (pp. 210–220). New York: Association Press.

Brabender, V., & Fallon, A. (1996). Termination in inpatient groups. *International Journal of Group Psychotherapy, 46*(1), 81–99.

Brackett, J. (1895). The charity organization movement: Its tendency and its duty. In *Proceedings of the 22nd National Conference of Charities and Corrections*. Boston: G. H. Ellis.

Bradford, L. (1976). *Making meetings work: A guide for leaders and group members*. La Jolla, CA: University Associates.

Bradford, L., & Corey, S. (1951). Improving large group meetings. *Adult Education, 1*, 122–137.

Brager, G., & Holloway, A. (1978). *Changing human service organizations: Politics and practice*. New York: The Free Press.

Brehmer, B., & Joyce, C. (1988). *Human judgment: The SJT view*. New York: North-Holland.

Brekke, J. (1989). The use of orientation groups to engage hard-to-reach clients: Model, method and evaluation. *Social Work with Groups, 12*(2), 75–88.

Brennan, J. W. (1995). A short term psychoeducational multiple family group for bipolar patients and their families. *Social Work, 40*(6), 737–743.

Breton, M. (1994). On the meaning of empowerment and empowerment-oriented social work practice. *Social Work with Groups, 17*(3), 23–37.

Breton, M. (1995). The potential for social action in groups. *Social Work with Groups, 18*(2/3), 5–13.

Brilhart, J. (1974). *Effective group discussion* (2nd ed.). Dubuque, IA: William C. Brown.

Brill, N. (1976). *Team-work: Working together in the human services*. Philadelphia: J. B. Lippincott.

Brill, N. (1998). *Working with people: The helping process* (6th ed.). New York: Longman.

Brown, A., & Mistry, T. (1994). Group work with mixed membership groups: Issues of race and gender. *Social Work with Groups, 17*(3), 5–21.

Brown, B. M. (1995). A bill of rights for people with disabilities in group work. *Journal for Specialists in Group Work, 20*, 71–75.

Brown, L. (1991). *Groups for growth and change.* New York: Longman.

Browne, K., Saunders, D., & Staecker, K. (1997). Process-psychodynamic groups for men who batter. *Families in Society, 78,* 265–271.

Browning, L. (1977). Diagnosing teams in organizational settings. *Group and Organization Studies, 2*(2), 187–197.

Budman, S., Demby, A., Feldstein, M., Redondo, J., Scherz, B., Bennett, M., Koppenall, G., Daley, B., Hunter, M., & Ellis, J. (1987). Preliminary findings on a new instrument to measure cohesion in group psychotherapy. *International Journal of Group Psychotherapy, 37*(1), 75–94.

Budman, S., Simeone, P., Reilly, R., & Demby, A. (1994). Progress in short-term and time-limited group psychotherapy: Evidence and implications. In A. Fuhriman & G. M. Burlingame (Eds.), *Handbook of Group Psychotherapy* (pp. 319–339). New York: John Wiley & Sons.

Budman, S., Soldz, S., Demby, A., Davis, M., & Merry, J. (1993). What is cohesiveness? An empirical examination. *Small Group Research, 24*(2), 199–216.

Burlingame, G., Kircher, J., & Honts, C. (1994). Analysis of variance versus bootstrap procedures for analyzing dependent observations in small group research. *Small Group Research, 25*(4), 486–501.

Burwell, N. (1995). Human diversity and empowerment. In H. W. Johnson et al. (Eds.), *The social services: An introduction* (4th ed., pp. 357–370). Itasca, IL: Peacock Press.

Butler, H., Davis, I., & Kukkonen, R. (1979). The logic of case comparison. *Social Work Research and Abstracts, 15*(3), 3–11.

Byers, P. Y., & Wilcox, J. R. (1991, Winter). Focus groups: A qualitative opportunity for researchers. *The Journal of Business Communication, 28*(1), 63–77.

Cabral, R., Best, J., & Paton, A. (1975). Patients and observer's assessments of process and outcome in group therapy: A follow-up study. *The American Journal of Psychiatry, 132,* 1052–1054.

Campbell, J. (1968). Individual versus group problem solving in an industrial sample. *Journal of Applied Psychology, 52,* 205–210.

Carletta, J., Garrod, S., & Fraser-Krauss, H. (1998). Placement of authority and communication patterns in workplace groups. *Small Group Research, 29*(5), 531–559.

Carnes, W. (1987). *Effective meetings for busy people.* New York: IEEE Press.

Carron, A., & Spink, K. (1995). The group size-cohesion relationship in minimal groups. *Small Group Research, 26*(1), 86–105.

Cartwright, D. (1951). Achieving change in people. *Human Relations, 4,* 381–392.

Cartwright, D. (1968). The nature of group cohesiveness. In D. Cartwright & A. Zander (Eds.), *Group dynamics: Research and theory* (3rd ed., pp. 91–109). New York: Harper & Row.

Cartwright, D., & Zander, A. (Eds.). (1968). *Group dynamics: Research and theory* (3rd ed.). New York: Harper & Row.

Chait, R., Holland, T. P., & Taylor, B. E. (1993). *The effective board of trustees.* Phoenix, AZ: Oryx Press.

Chau, K. (1992). Needs assessment for group work with people of color: A conceptual formulation. *Social Work with Groups, 15*(2/3), 53–66.

Chiauzzi, E. J. (1991). *Preventing relapse in the addictions: A biopsychosocial approach.* New York: Pergamon Press.

Clark, A. (1998). Reframing: A therapeutic technique in group counseling. *Journal for Specialists in Group Work, 23*(1), 66–73.

Clark, C. H. (1958). *Brainstorming.* New York: Doubleday.

Clark, K. (1971). *Evaluation of a group social skills training program with psychiatric inpatients: Training Vietnam era veterans in assertion, heterosexual dating, and job interview skills.* Unpublished doctoral dissertation, University of Wisconsin, Madison.

Clemen, R. T. (1996). *Making hard decisions: An introduction to decision analysis* (2nd ed.). Belmont, CA: Duxbury Press.

Cohen, M. B., & Mullender, A. (1999). The personal in the political: Exploring the group work continuum from individual to social change goals. *Social Work with Groups, 22,* 13–31.

Cole, R., & Tachiki, D. (1983, June). A look at U.S. and Japanese quality circles: Preliminary comparisons. *Quality Circles Journal, 6,* 10–16.

Collaros, R., & Anderson, L. (1969). Effects of perceived expertness upon creativity of members of brainstorming groups. *Journal of Applied Psychology, 53*(2), 159–164.

Compton, B., & Galaway, B. (1999). *Social work processes* (6th ed.). Pacific Grove, CA: Brooks/Cole.

Cone, J., & Hawkins, R. (Eds.). (1977). *Behavioral assessment: New directions in clinical psychology.* New York: Brunner/Mazel.

Connelly, J. L., & Piper, W. (1984). *Pretraining behavior as a predictor of process and outcome in group psychotherapy.* Paper presented at the 15th Annual Meeting of the Society for Psychotherapy Research, Lake Louise, Alberta.

Connelly, J. L., Piper, W., DeCarufel, F., & Debbane, E. (1986). Premature termination in group psychotherapy: Pretherapy and early therapy predictors. *International Journal of Group Psychotherapy, 36*(1), 145–152.

Conrad, W., & Glenn, W. (1976). *The effective voluntary board of directors: What it is and how it works.* Chicago: Swallow Press.

Cooksey, R. W. (1996). *Judgment analysis: Theory methods and applications.* New York: Academic Press.

Cooley, D. (1909). *Social organization.* New York: Charles Scribner's Sons.

Cooper, C. (1977). Adverse and growthful effects of experimental learning groups: The role of the trainer, participant, and group characteristics. *Human Relations, 30,* 1103–1129.

Cooper, L. (1976). Co-therapy relationships in groups. *Small Group Behavior, 7*(4), 473–498.

Corey, M., & Corey, G. (1997). *Groups: Process and practice* (5th ed.). Pacific Grove, CA: Brooks/Cole.

Counselman, E. F. (1991). Leadership in a long-term leaderless women's group. *Small Group Research, 22,* 240–257.

Cox, C., & Monk, A. (1990). Minority caregivers of dementia victims: A comparison of black and Hispanic families. *Journal of Applied Gerontology, 9*(3), 340–354.

Cox, E. (1988). Empowerment of the low income elderly through group work. *Social Work with Groups, 11*(4), 111–119.

Cox, E., & Parsons, R. (1994). *Empowerment-oriented social work practice with the elderly.* Pacific Grove, CA: Brooks/Cole.

Cox, M. (1973). The group therapy interaction chronogram. *British Journal of Social Work, 3,* 243–256.

Coyle, G. (1930). *Social process in organized groups.* New York: Richard Smith.

Coyle, G. (1935). Group work and social change. In *Proceedings of the National Conference of Social Work* (p. 393). Chicago: University of Chicago Press.

Coyle, G. (1937). *Studies in group behavior.* New York: Harper & Row.

Craig, T., Huffine, C., & Brooks, M. (1974). Completion of referral to psychiatric services by inner-city residents. *Archives of General Psychiatry, 31*(3), 353–357.

Crano, W., & Brewer, M. (1973). *Principles of research in social psychology.* New York: McGraw-Hill.

Croxton, T. (1985). The therapeutic contract in social treatment. In M. Sundel, P. Glasser, R. Sarri, & R. Vinter (Eds.), *Individual change through small groups* (2nd ed., pp. 159–179). New York: The Free Press.

Dalgleish, L. I. (1988). Decision making in child abuse cases: Applications of social judgment theory and signal detection theory. In B. Brehmer & C. R. B. Joyce (Eds.), *Human judgment: The SJT view.* New York: North-Holland.

Davis, F., & Lohr, N. (1971). Special problems with the use of co-therapists in group psychotherapy. *International Journal of Group Psychotherapy, 21,* 143–158.

Davis, G., Manske, M., & Train, A. (1966). An instructional method of increasing originality. *Psychonomic Science, 6,* 73–74.

Davis, I. (1975). Advice-giving in parent counseling. *Social Casework, 56,* 343–347.

Davis, L., Galinsky, M., & Schopler, J. (1995). RAP: A framework for leadership of multiracial groups. *Social Work, 40*(2), 155–165.

Davis, L., & Proctor, E. (1989). *Race, gender and class: Guidelines for practice with individuals, families and groups.* Englewood Cliffs, NJ: Prentice-Hall.

Davis, L., Strube, M., & Cheng, L. (1995). Too many blacks, too many whites: Is there a racial balance? *Basic and Applied Social Psychology, 17*(1/2), 119–135.

Davis, L., & Toseland, R. (1987). Group versus individual decision making. *Social Work with Groups, 10*(2), 95–105.

Davis, M., Eshelman, E., & McKay, M. (1998). *The relaxation and stress reduction workbook* (4th ed.). Oakland, CA: New Harbinger.

De Bono, E. (1968). *New think: The use of lateral thinking in generation of new ideas.* New York: Basic Books.

De Bono, E. (1971). *Lateral thinking for management.* New York: American Management Associations.

De Bono, E. (1972). *Lateral thinking: Productivity step by step.* New York: Harper & Row.

De Lange, J. (1977). *Effectiveness of systematic desensitization and assertive training with women.* Unpublished doctoral dissertation, University of Wisconsin, Madison.

Delbecq, A., Van de Ven, A., & Gustafson, D. (1975). *Group techniques for program planning: A guide to nominal group and delphi processes.* Glenview, IL: Scott Foresman.

Delgado, M. (1983). Activities and Hispanic groups. *Social Work with Groups, 6,* 85–96.

Delucia-Waack, J. (1997). Measuring the effectiveness of group work: A review and analysis of process and outcome measures. *Journal for Specialists in Group Work, 22,* 277–292.

Denhardt, R., Pyle, J., & Bluedorn, A. (1987). Implementing quality circles in state government. *Public Administrative Review, 47*(4), 304–309.

Devore, W., & Schlesinger, E. (1999). *Ethnic-sensitive social work practice* (5th ed.). Boston: Allyn and Bacon.

Dienesch, R. M., & Liden, R. C. (1986). Leader-member exchange model of leadership: A critique and further development. *Academy of Management Review, 11,* 618–634.

Dies, R. (1994). Therapist variables in group psychotherapy research. In A. Fuhriman & G. M. Burlingame (Eds.), *Handbook of Group Psychotherapy* (pp. 114–154), New York: John Wiley & Sons.

Diller, J. (1999). *Cultural diversity: A primer for the human services.* Belmont, CA: Wadsworth.

Dillon, W., Madden, T., & Firtle, N. (1994). *Marketing research in a marketing environment* (3rd ed.). Burr Ridge, IL: Irwin.

Dinges, N., & Cherry, D. (1995). Symptom expression and use of mental health services among ethnic minorities. In J. Aponte, R. Rivers, & J. Wohl (Eds.), *Psychological interventions and cultural diversity* (pp. 40–56). Boston: Allyn and Bacon.

Dinkmeyer, D., & McKay, G. (1990). *Systematic training for effective parenting* (Rev. ed.). New York: Random House.

Dion, K., Miller, N., & Magnan, M. (1970). Cohesiveness and social responsibility as determinants of risk taking. *Proceedings of the American Psychological Association, 5*(1), 335–336.

Dluhy, M. (1990). *Building coalitions in the human services.* Newbury Park, CA: Sage.

Dodge, K., Gilroy, F., & Fenzel, L. (1995). Requisite management characteristics revisited: Two decades later. *Journal of Social Behavior and Personality, 10,* 253–264.

Dolgoff, R., & Skolnik, L. (1992). Ethical decision making, the NASW code of ethics and group work practice: Beginning explorations. *Social Work with Groups, 15*(4), 99–112.

Dollard, J., & Miller, N. (1950). *Personality and psychotherapy.* New York: McGraw-Hill.

Douglas, T. (1979). *Group process in social work: A theoretical synthesis.* New York: John Wiley & Sons.

Drum, D., & Knott, J. (1977). *Structured groups for facilitating development: Acquiring life skills, resolving life themes and making life transitions.* New York: Human Science Press.

Drummond, M., Stoddart, G., & Torrance, G. (1987). *Methods for the economic evaluation of health care programmes.* Oxford, UK: Oxford University Press.

Dunnette, M., Campbell, J., & Joastad, K. (1963). The effect of group participation on brainstorming effectiveness for two industrial samples. *Journal of Applied Psychology, 47,* 30–37.

D'Zurilla, T., & Goldfried, M. (1971). Problem solving and behavior modification. *Journal of Abnormal Psychology, 78,* 107–126.

Early, B. (1992). Social work consultation with the work group of the school. *Social Work In Education, 14*(4), 207–214.

Ebbesen, E., & Bowers, R. (1974). Proportion of risky to conservative arguments in a group discussion and choice shift. *Journal of Personality and Social Psychology, 29,* 316–327.

Edelwich, J., & Brodsky, A. (1992). *Group counseling for the resistent client: A practical guide to group process.* New York: Lexington Books.

Edleson, J., & Syers, M. (1990). The relative effectiveness of group treatments for men who batter. *Social Work Research and Abstracts, 26,* 10–17.

Edleson, J., & Tolman, R. (1992). *Intervention for men who batter.* Newbury Park, CA: Sage.

Edson, J. (1977). How to survive on a committee. *Social Work, 22,* 224–226.

Edwards, W. (1977). How to use multiattribute utility measurement for social decision making. *IEEE Transactions on Systems, Man and Cybernetics, 7,* 326–340.

Egan, G. (1998). *The skilled helper* (6th ed.). Pacific Grove, CA: Brooks/Cole.

Eisenhart, C. (1972). The assumptions underlying the analysis of variance. In R. Kirk (Ed.), *Statistical issues* (pp. 226–240). Pacific Grove, CA: Brooks/Cole.

Elliott, H. (1928). *Process of group thinking.* New York: Association Press.

Ellis, A. (1962). *Reason and emotion in psychotherapy.* Secaucus, NJ: Lyle Stuart.

Ellis, A. (1992). Group rational-emotive and cognitive-behavior therapy. *International Journal of Group Psychotherapy, 42*(1), 63–82.

Empey, L., & Erikson, M. (1972). *The Provo experiment: Impact and death of an innovation.* Lexington, MA: Lexington Books.

Emrick, C. D., Lassen, C. L., & Edwards, M. T. (1977). Nonprofessional peers as therapeutic agents. In A. Gurman & A. Razin (Eds.), *Effective psychotherapy: A handbook of research* (pp. 120–161). New York: Pergamon Press.

Ephross, P. H., & Vassil, T. (1988). *Groups that work.* New York: Columbia University Press.

Etcheverry, R., Siporin, M., & Toseland, R. (1987). The uses and abuses of role playing. In P. Glasser and N. Mayadas (Eds.), *Group workers at work: Theory and practice in the 1980s* (pp. 116–130). Lanham, MD: Littlefield, Adams & Company.

Etzioni, A. (1961). *A comparative analysis of complex organizations on power, involvement and their correlates.* New York: The Free Press.

Etzioni, A. (1968). *The active society: A theory of societal and political processes.* New York: The Free Press.

Evans, C., & Dion, K. (1991). Group cohesion and performance. *Small Group Research, 22*(2), 175–186.

Evans, R., & Jaureguy, B. (1981, Winter). Group therapy by phone: A cognitive behavior program for visually impaired elderly. *Social Work in Health Care, 7,* 79–91.

Everly, G. S. (1989). *A clinical guide to the treatment of the human stress response.* New York: Plenum.

Ewalt, P., & Kutz, J. (1976). An examination of advice giving as a therapeutic intervention. *Smith College Studies in Social Work, 47,* 3–19.

Falck, H. (1988). *Social work: The membership perspective.* New York: Springer.

Fatout, M., & Rose, S. (1995). *Task groups in the social services.* Thousand Oaks, CA: Sage.

Feldman, R. (1986). Group work knowledge and research: A two-decade comparison. *Social Work with Groups, 9*(3), 7–14.

Feldman, R., & Caplinger, T. (1977). Social work experience and client behavior change: A multivariate analysis of process and outcome. *Journal of Social Service Research, 1*(1), 5–33.

Feldman, R., Caplinger, T., & Wodarski, J. (1983). *The St. Louis conundrum: The effective treatment of antisocial youth.* Englewood Cliffs, NJ: Prentice-Hall.

Feldman, R., & Wodarski, J. (1975). *Contemporary approaches to group treatment: Traditional, behavior modification and group-centered.* San Francisco: Jossey-Bass.

Fern, E. (1982). The use of focus groups for idea generation: The effects of group size, acquaintanceship, and moderator on response quantity and quality. *Journal of Marketing Research, 19,* 1–13.

Festinger, L. (1950). Informal social communication. *Psychological Review, 57,* 271–282.

Fiedler, R. (1967). *A theory of leadership effectiveness.* New York: McGraw-Hill.

Fieldsteel, N. D. (1996). The process of termination in long-term psychoanalytic group therapy. *International Journal of Group Psychotherapy, 46*(1), 25–39.

Finn, J. (1995). Computer-based self-help groups: A new resource to supplement support groups. In M. Galinsky & J. Schopler (Eds.), *Support groups: Current perspectives in theory and practice* (pp. 109–117). New York: Haworth.

Finn, J., & Lavitt, M. (1994). Computer-based self help groups for sexual abuse survivors. *Social Work with Groups, 17*(1/2), 21–46.

Fisher, J. (1978). *Effective casework practice: An eclectic approach.* New York: McGraw-Hill.

Fisher, J., & Corcoran, K. (1994). *Measures for clinical practice: A sourcebook* (2nd ed.). (Vol. 1, Couples, Families, and Children & Vol. 2, Adults). New York: The Free Press.

Fisher, R., Ury, W., & Patton, B. (1997). *Getting to yes: Negotiating agreement without giving in* (2nd ed.). London: Arrow Business Books.

Flowers, J. (1979). Behavior analysis of group therapy and a model for behavioral group therapy. In D. Upper & and S. Ross (Eds.), *Behavioral group therapy, 1979: An annual review* (pp. 5–37). Champaign, IL: Research Press.

Forester, J. (1981). Questioning and organizing attention: Toward a critical theory of planning and administrative practice. *Administration and Society, 13*(2), 181–205.

Forsyth, D. (1999). *Group dynamics* (3rd ed.). Belmont, CA: Wadsworth.

Fortune, A. (1979). Communication in task-centered treatment. *Social Work, 24,* 390–397.

Fortune, A. (1985, December). Planning duration and termination of treatment. In A. Fortune (Ed.), *Social Service Review* (pp. 648–661). Chicago: University of Chicago Press.

Fortune, A. (1987). Grief only? Client and social worker reactions to termination. *Clinical Social Work Journal, 15*(2), 159–171.

Fortune, A., Pearlingi, B., & Rochelle, C. (1991, June). Criteria for terminating treatment. *Families in Society: The Journal of Contemporary Human Services, 72*(6), 366–370.

Fortune, A., Pearlingi, B., & Rochelle, C. (1992). Reactions to termination of individual treatment. *Social Work, 37*(2), 171–178.

Fortune, A., & Reid, W. J. (1998). *Research in social work* (3rd ed.). New York: Columbia University Press.

Frances, A., Clarkin, J., & Perry, S. (1984). *Differential therapeutics in psychiatry: The art and science of treatment selection.* New York: Brunner/Mazel.

Frank, J. (1961). *Persuasion and healing: A comparative study of psychotherapy.* New York: Schocken Books.

Freedman, B. (1974). *An analysis of social behavioral skill deficits in delinquent and undelinquent adolescent boys.* Unpublished doctoral dissertation, University of Wisconsin, Madison.

Freeman, A., Pretzer, J., Fleming, J., & Simons, K. (1990). *Clinical applications of cognitive therapy.* New York: Plenum.

French, J., & Raven, B. (1959). The bases of social power. In D. Cartwright (Ed.), *Studies in social power.* Ann Arbor: Institute for Research, University of Michigan.

Freud, S. (1922). *Group psychology and the analysis of the ego.* London: International Psychoanalytic Press.

Fuhriman, A., & Barlow, S. (1994). Interaction analysis: Instrumentation and issues. In A. Fuhriman and G. M. Burlingame (Eds.), *Handbook of Group Psychotherapy* (pp. 191–222). New York: John Wiley & Sons.

Fuhriman, A., & Burlingame, G. (1994). Group psychotherapy: Research and Practice. In A. Fuhriman and G. M. Burlingame (Eds.), *Handbook of Group Psychotherapy* (pp. 3–40). New York: John Wiley & Sons.

Fuhriman, A., & Packard, T. (1986). Group process instruments: Therapeutic themes and issues. *International Journal of Group Psychotherapy, 36*(3), 399–525.

Galinsky, M., Rounds, K., Montague, A., & Butowsky, A. (1993). *Leading a telephone support group for persons with HIV disease.* Chapel Hill: University of North Carolina Press.

Galinsky, M., & Schopler, J. (1977). Warning: Groups may be dangerous. *Social Work, 22*(2), 89–94.

Galinsky, M., & Schopler, J. (1980). Structuring coleadership in social work training. *Social Work with Groups, 3*(4), 51–63.

Galinsky, M., & Schopler, J. (1989). Developmental patterns in open-ended groups. *Social Work with Groups, 12*(2), 99–114.

Garland, J., Jones, H., & Kolodny, R. (1976). A model of stages of group development in social work groups. In S. Bernstein (Ed.), *Explorations in Group Work* (pp. 17–71). Boston: Charles River Books.

Garland, J., & Kolodny, R. (1967). Characteristics and resolution of scapegoating. In National Conference of Social Welfare, *Social Work Practice* (pp. 198–219). New York: Columbia University Press.

Garvin, C. (1997). *Contemporary group work* (3rd ed.). Boston: Allyn & Bacon.

Garvin, C. (1998, October). *Potential impact of small group research on social group work practice.* Paper presented at the 20th Annual Symposium of the Association for the Advancement of Social Work with Groups, Miami, Florida.

Garvin, C., Reid, W., & Epstein, L. (1976). A task-centered approach. In R. Roberts & H. Northen (Eds.), *Theories of social work with groups* (pp. 238–267). New York: Columbia University Press.

Garwick, G. (1974). *Guideline for goal attainment scaling.* Minneapolis: Program Evaluation Project.

Gazda, G., & Mobley, J. (1981). INDS-CAL multidimensional scaling. *Journal of Group Psychotherapy, Psychodrama and Sociometry, 34,* 54–72.

Gebhardt, L., & Meyers, R. (1995). Subgroup influence in decision-making groups: Examining consistency from a communication perspective. *Small Group Research, 26*(2), 147–168.

Gentry, M. (1987). Coalition formation and processes. *Social Work with Groups, 10*(3), 39–54.

Germain, C., & Gitterman, A. (1996). *The life model of social work practice* (2nd ed.). New York: Columbia University Press.

Getzel, G. (1998). Group work practice with gay men and lesbians. In G. P. Mallon (Ed.), *Foundations of social work practice with lesbian and gay persons.* (pp. 131–144). New York: Harrington Park Press.

Gibb, C. (1969). Leadership. In G. Lindzey & E. Aronson (Eds.), *The handbook of social psychology* (2nd ed., pp. 205–273). Reading, MA: Addison-Wesley.

Gibb, J. (1961). Defensive communication. *The Journal of Communication, 11,* 11–148.

Gibbs, L., & Gambrill, E. (1998). *Critical thinking for social workers.* Thousand Oaks, CA: Pine Forge Press.

Giordano, J. (1973). *Ethnicity and mental health.* New York: Institute of Human Relations.

Gitterman, A., & Shulman, L. (Eds.). (1994). *Mutual aid groups, vulnerable populations, and the life cycle* (2nd ed.). New York: Columbia University Press.

Glassman, U., & Kates, L. (1990). *Group work: A humanistic approach.* Newbury Park, CA: Sage.

Glisson, C. (1986). The group versus the individual as the unit of analysis in small group research. *Social Work with Groups, 9*(3), 15–30.

Gold, M., Siegel, J., Russell, L., & Weinstein, M. (1996). *Cost-effectiveness in health and medicine.* New York: Oxford University Press.

Goldfried, M., & D'Zurilla, T. (1969). A behavioral-analytic model for assessing competence. In C. D. Spielberger (Ed.), *Current topics in clinical and community psychology* (Vol. 1, pp. 151–196). New York: Academic Press.

Goldsmith, J., & McFall, R. (1975). Development and evaluation of an interpersonal skill training program for psychiatric inpatients. *Journal of Abnormal Psychology, 84,* 51–58.

Goldstein, A., Keller, K., & Sechrest, L. (1966). *Psychotherapy and the psychology of behavior change.* New York: John Wiley & Sons.

Goldstein, H. (1983). Starting where the client is. *Social Casework, 64,* 267–275.

Goldstein, H. (1988). A cognitive-humanistic/social learning perspective on social group work practice. *Social Work with Groups, 11,* 9–32.

Goldstein, S. (1985). Organizational quality and quality circles. *Academy of Management Review, 10*(3), 504–517.

Gondolf, E. (1997). Batterer programs: What we know and need to know. *Journal of Interpersonal Violence, 12,* 83–98.

Goodman, P., et al. (1986). *Designing effective work groups.* San Francisco: Jossey-Bass.

Good Tracks, J. (1973). Native-American noninterference. *Social Work, 18,* 30–34.

Gordon, T. (1975). *P.E.T.* New York: Plume Books.

Gordon, W. (1961). *Synectics: The development of creative capacity.* New York: Harper & Row.

Gouran, D. (1982). *Making decisions in groups: Consequences and choices.* Glenview, IL: Scott Foresman.

Graen, G., & Schiemann, W. (1978). Leader-member agreement: A vertical dyad linkage approach. *Journal of Applied Psychology, 63,* 206–212.

Gray, G. (1964). Points of emphasis in teaching parliamentary procedure. *The Speech Teacher, 13,* 10–15.

Grayson, E. (1993). *Short-term group counseling* (3rd ed.). Washington, DC: American Corrections Association.

Green, J. (1999). *Cultural awareness in the human services: A multi-ethnic approach* (3rd ed.). Boston: Allyn and Bacon.

Greenbaum, T. (1998). *The handbook for focus group research* (2nd ed., Rev.). Thousand Oaks, CA: Sage.

Guetzkow, H., & Gyr, J. (1954). An analysis of conflict in decision-making groups. *Human Relations, 7,* 368–381.

Gulley, H. (1968). *Discussion, conference and group process* (2nd ed.). New York: Holt, Rinehart & Winston.

Gully, S., Devine, D., & Whitney, D. (1995). A meta-analysis of cohesion and performance: Effects of level of analysis and task interdependence. *Small Group Research, 26*(4), 497–520.

Gummer, B. (1987). Groups as substance and symbol: Group processes and organizational politics. *Social Work with Groups, 10*(2), 25–39.

Gummer, B. (1988). Post-industrial management: Teams, self-management, and the new interdependence. *Administration in Social Work, 12*(3), 117–132.

Gummer, B. (1991). A new managerial era: From hierarchical control to "collaborative individualism." *Administration in Social Work, 15*(3), 121–137.

Gummer, B. (1995). Go team go! The growing importance of teamwork in organizational life. *Administration in Social Work, 19*(4), 85–100.

Gummer, B., & McCallion, P. (Eds.). (1995). *Total quality management in the social services: Theory and practice.* Albany: State University of NY, University at Albany, School of Social Welfare, Professional Development Program of Rockefeller College.

Gutierrez, L., & Ortega, R. (1991). Developing methods to empower Latinos: The importance of groups. *Social Work with Groups, 14*(2), 23–43.

Hackman, J. (Ed.). (1990). *Groups that work (and those that don't).* San Francisco: Jossey-Bass.

Halpin, A. (1961). *Theory and research in administration.* New York: Macmillan.

Halstead, L. (1976). Team care in chronic illness: A critical review of the literature of the past 25 years. *Archives of Physical Medicine and Rehabilitation, 57,* 507–511.

Hammond, L., & Goldman, M. (1961). Competition and non-competition and its relationship to individuals' non-productivity. *Sociometry, 24,* 46–60.

Hare, A. P. (1976). *Handbook of small group research* (2nd ed.). New York: The Free Press.

Hare, A. P., Blumberg, H. H., Davies, M. F., & Kent, M. V. (1995). *Small group research: A handbook.* Norwood, NJ: Ablex.

Haring, T., & Breen, C. (1992). A peer-mediated social network intervention to enhance the social integration of persons with moderate and severe disabilities. *Journal of Applied Behavior Analysis, 25,* 319–334.

Harmon, J., & Rohrbaugh, J. (1990). Social judgement analysis and small group decision making: Cognitive feedback effects on individual and collective performance. *Organizational Behavior and Human Decision Processes, 46,* 35–54.

Harnack, R., & Fest, T. (1964). *Group discussion: Theory and technique.* New York: Appleton-Century-Crofts.

Hartford, M. (1962). *The social group worker and group formation.* Unpublished doctoral dissertation, University of Chicago, School of Social Service Administration, Chicago.

Hartford, M. (Ed.). (1964). *Papers toward a frame of reference for social group work.* New York: National Association of Social Workers.

Hartford, M. (1971). *Groups in social work.* New York: Columbia University Press.

Hasenfeld, Y. (1985). The organizational context of group work. In M. Sundel, P. Glasser, R. Sarri, & R. Vinter (Eds.), *Individual change through small groups* (2nd ed., pp. 294–309). New York: The Free Press.

Hazel, J. S., Schumaker, J. B., Sherman, J. A., Sheldon, J. (1981). *A Social Skills Program for Adolescents.* Champaign, IL: Research Press.

Health Services Research Group. (1975). Development of an index of medical underservedness. Health Service Research, 10, 168–180.

Heap, K. (1979). *Process and action in work with groups.* Elmsford, NY: Pergamon Press.

Hemphill, J. (1956). *Group dimensions: A manual for their measurement.* Columbus: Monographs of the Bureau of Business Research, Ohio State University.

Henderson, J., Guiterrez-Mayka, M., Garcia, J., & Boyd, S. (1993). A model for Alzheimer's disease support group development in African-American and Hispanic populations. *Gerontologist, 33,* 409–414.

Henry, S. (1992). *Group skills in social work: A four-dimensional approach* (2nd ed.). Itasca, IL: F. E. Peacock.

Hersen, M., & Bellack, A. (1976). *Behavioral assessment: A practical handbook.* Elmsford, NY: Pergamon Press.

Hersey, R., & Blanchard, K. (1977). *Management of organizational behavior: Utilizing human resources* (3rd ed.). Englewood Cliffs, NJ: Prentice-Hall.

Hersey, R., Blanchard, K., & Natemeyer, W. (1979). Situational leadership, perception and the impact of power. *Group and Organization Studies, 4*(4), 418–428.

Herzog, J. (1980). Communication between co-leaders: Fact or myth. *Social Work with Groups, 3*(4), 19–29.

Hill, F. (1965). *Hill interaction matrix* (Rev. ed.). Los Angeles: Youth Studies Center, University of Southern California.

Hill, W. (1977). Hill interaction matrix (HIM): The conceptual framework, derived rating scales, and an updated bibliography. *Small Group Behavior, 8*(3), 251–268.

Hogan-Garcia, M. (1999). *The four skills of cultural diversity competence: A process for understanding and practice.* Belmont, CA: Wadsworth.

Homans, G. (1950). *The human group.* New York: Harcourt Brace Jovanovich.

Homans, G. (1961). *Social behavior: Its elementary forms.* New York: Harcourt Brace Jovanovich.

Hooyman, N., & Kiyak, H. (1996). *Social gerontology: A multidisciplinary perspective* (4th ed.). Boston: Allyn and Bacon.

Hopkins, K. (1998). *Educational and psychological measurement and evaluation* (8th ed.). Boston: Allyn and Bacon.

Hopps, J., & Pinderhughes, E. (1999). *Group work with overwhelmed clients.* New York: The Free Press.

Horne, A., & Rosenthal, R. (1997). Research in group work: How did we get where we are? *Journal for Specialists in Group Work, 22*(4), 228–240.

Howe, F. (1998). *Fund-raising and the nonprofit board member* (2nd ed.). Washington, DC: National Center for Nonprofit Boards.

Hoyle, R., & Crawford, A. (1994). *Use of individual-level data to investigate group phenomena: Issues and strategies, 25*(4), 464–485.

Huber, G. (1980). *Managerial decision making.* Glenview, IL: Scott Foresman.

Hudson, W. (1982). *The clinical measurement package.* Homewood, CA: Dorsey Press.

Hudson, W. (1994). *MPSI: The MPSI technical manual*. Tempe, AZ: Walmyr.

Hugen, B. (1993). The effectiveness of a psychoeducational support service to families of persons with a chronic mental illness. *Research on Social Work Practice, 3*(2), 137–154.

Hula, K. (1999). *Lobbying together: Interest group coalitions in legislative politics*. Washington, DC: Georgetown University Press.

Jacobsen, B., & Jacobsen, M. (1996). The young bears. In R. Rivas & G. Hull (Eds.), *Case studies in generalist practice* (pp. 14–21). Pacific Grove, CA: Brooks/Cole.

Jacobson, E. (1978). *You must relax*. New York: McGraw-Hill.

Janis, I. (1972). *Victims of group think*. Boston: Houghton Mifflin.

Janis, I. (1982). *Groupthink* (2nd ed.). Boston: Houghton Mifflin.

Janis, I., & Mann, L. (1977). *Decision making: A psychological analysis of conflict, choice and commitment*. New York: The Free Press.

Janssen, P. (1994). *Psychoanalytic therapy in the hospital setting*. London: Routledge.

Jay, A. (1977). How to run a meeting. In F. Cox, J. Erlich, J. Rothman, & J. Tropman (Eds.), *Tactics and techniques of community practice* (pp. 255–269). Itasca, IL: F. E. Peacock.

Jennings, H. (1947). Leadership and sociometric choice. *Sociometry* (10), 32–49.

Jennings, H. (1950). *Leadership and isolation* (2nd ed.). New York: Longman.

Jessup, L., & Valacich, J. (1993). Support group systems. [Special issue]. *Small Group Research, 24,* 427–592.

Jette, A. (1996). Disability trends and transitions. In R. Binstock & L. George (Eds.), *Handbook of aging and the social sciences* (4th ed., pp. 94–116). San Diego, CA: Academic Press.

Johnson, D. W. (1997). *Reaching out: Interpersonal effectiveness and self-actualization* (6th ed.). Boston: Allyn and Bacon.

Johnson, J. (1975). *Doing field research*. New York: The Free Press.

Johnson, L. (1998). *Social work practice: A generalist approach* (6th ed.). Boston: Allyn and Bacon.

Johnson, S., & Bechler, C. (1998). Examining the relationship between listening effectiveness and leadership emergence: Perceptions, behaviors, and recall. *Small Group Research, 29*(4), 452–471.

Kadushin, A., & Kadushin, G. (1997). *The social work interview: A guide for human service professionals* (4th ed.). New York: Columbia University Press.

Kahn, S. (1991). *Organizing: A guide for grassroots leaders*. Silver Spring, MD: NASW.

Kane, R. (1974). Look to the record. *Social Work, 19,* 412–419.

Kane, R. (1975a). The interprofessional team as a small group. *Social Work in Health Care, 1*(1), 19–32.

Kane, R. (1975b). *Interprofessional teamwork*. Syracuse, NY: Syracuse University School of Social Work.

Kane, R., & Kane, P. (1981). *Assessing the elderly: A practical guide to measurement*. Lexington, MA: Lexington Books.

Kart, G., Metress, E., & Metress, J. (1978). *Aging and health*. Reading, MA: Addison-Wesley.

Kaslyn, M. (1999). Telephone group work: Challenges for practice. *Social Work with Groups, 22,* 63–77.

Katz, A. H., & Bender, E. I. (1987). *The strength in us: Self-help groups in the modern world*. Oakland, CA: Third Party Associates.

Katz, A. H., Hedrick, H., Isenberg, D., Thompson, L., Goodrich, T., & Kutscher, A. (Eds.). (1992). *Self-help: Concepts and applications*. Philadelphia: Charles Press.

Katzenbach, J., & Smith, D. (1993). *The wisdom of teams*. Boston: Harvard Business School Press.

Kaul, T., & Bednar, R. (1994). Pretraining and structure: Parallel lines yet to meet. In A. Fuhriman and G. M. Burlingame (Eds.), *Handbook of Group Psychotherapy* (pp. 155–188). New York: John Wiley & Sons.

Keith, R. (1991). The comprehensive treatment team in rehabilitation. *Archives of Physical Medicine and Rehabilitation, 72,* 269–274.

Kelleher, K., & Cross, T. (1990). *Teleconferencing: Linking people together electronically*. Norman: University of Oklahoma Press.

Keller, T., & Dansereau, F. (1995). Leadership and empowerment: A social exchange perspective. *Human Relations, 48*(2), 127–146.

Kelley, H., & Thibaut, J. (1969). Group problem solving. In G. Lindzey & E. Aronim (Eds.), *Handbook of social psychology* (2nd ed., pp. 1–101). Reading, MA: Addison-Wesley.

Kephart, M. (1951). A quantitative analysis of intragroup relationships. *American Journal of Sociology, 60,* 544–549.

Keyton, J. (1993). Group termination: Completing the study of group development. *Small Group Research, 24*(1), 84–100.

Kiesler, S. (1978). *Interpersonal processes in groups and organizations.* Arlington Heights, VA: AHM.

Kim, B., Omizo, M., & D'Andrea, M. (1998). The effects of culturally consonant group counseling on the self-esteem and internal locus of control orientation among Native American Adolescents. *Journal for Specialists in Group Work, 23*(2), 143–163.

Kinlaw, C. D. (1992). *Continuous improvement and measurement for total quality: A team-based approach.* San Diego, CA: Pfeiffer & Co.; Homewood, IL: Business One Irwin.

Kinnear, T., & Taylor, J. (1996). *Marketing research: An applied approach* (5th ed.). New York: McGraw-Hill.

Kiresuk, T., & Sherman, R. (1968). Goal attainment scaling: A general method for evaluating comprehensive community mental health programs. *Community Mental Health Journal, 4*(6), 443–453.

Kirk, S. A., & Kutchins, H. (1988). The business of diagnosis *DSM-III* and clinical social work. *Social Work, 33*(3), 215–220.

Kirk, S. A., & Kutchins, H. (1994). The myth of the reliability of DSM, *The Journal of Mind and Behavior, 15*(1/2), 71–86.

Kirk, S. A., & Kutchins, H. (1997). Making us crazy. *DSM: The psychiatric bible and the creation of mental disorders.*

Kirk, S. A., Siporin, M., & Kutchins, H. (1989). The prognosis for social work diagnosis. *Social Casework, 70*(5), 295–304.

Kirst-Ashman, K., & Hull, G. (1999). *Understanding generalist practice* (2nd ed.). Chicago: Nelson Hall.

Klein, A. (1953). *Society, democracy and the group.* New York: Whiteside.

Klein, A. (1956). *Role playing.* New York: Associated Press.

Klein, A. (1970). *Social work through group process.* Albany: School of Social Welfare, State University of New York at Albany.

Klein, A. (1972). *Effective group work.* New York: Associated Press.

Klein, M. (1997). *The American street gang* (2nd ed.). Oxford, UK: Oxford University Press.

Kleindorfer, P. R., Kunreuther, H. C., & Schoemaker, P. J. H. (1993). *Decision sciences: An integrative perspective.* New York: Cambridge University Press.

Klosko, J., & Sanderson, W. (1998). *Cognitive behavioral treatment of depression.* Northvale, NJ: Jason Aronson.

Knottnerus, J. (1994). Social exchange theory and social structure: A critical comparison of two traditions of inquiry. *Current Perspectives in Social Theory* (Suppl. 1), 29–48.

Kolb, J. (1997). Are we still stereotyping leadership? A look at gender and other predictors of leader emergence. *Small Group Research, 28*(3), 370–393.

Kolodny, R. (1980). The dilemma of co-leadership. *Social Work with Groups, 3*(4), 31–34.

Konig, K. (1994). *Psychoanalytic group therapy.* Northvale, NY: Jason Aronson.

Konopka, G. (1949). *Therapeutic group work with children.* Minneapolis: University of Minnesota Press.

Konopka, G. (1954). *Group work in the institution.* New York: Association Press.

Konopka, G. (1983). *Social group work: A helping process* (3rd ed.). Englewood Cliffs, NJ: Prentice-Hall.

Kopp, J. (1993). Self-observation: An empowering strategy in assessment. In J. Rauch (Ed.), *Assessment: A sourcebook for social work practice* (pp. 255–268). Milwaukee, WI: Families International.

Koss-Chioino, J. (1995). Traditional and folk approaches among ethnic minorities. In J. Aponte, R. Rivers, and J. Wohl (Eds.), *Psychological interventions and cultural diversity* (pp. 145–163). Boston: Allyn and Bacon.

Kottler, J. (1992). *Compassionate therapy: Working with difficult clients.* San Francisco: Jossey-Bass.

Kramer, J., & Conoley, J. (1992). *Eleventh mental measurement yearbook.* Lincoln, NE: Buros Institute of Mental Measurements.

Kramer, M., Kuo, C., & Dailey, J. (1997). The impact of brainstorming techniques on subsequent group processes. *Small Group Research, 28*(2), 218–242.

Krueger, R. (1994). *Focus groups: A practical guide for applied research* (2nd ed.). Thousand Oaks, CA: Sage.

Krueger, R. (1997). *Analyzing and reporting focus group results.* Thousand Oaks, CA: Sage.

Krueger, R. (1998). *Developing questions for focus groups.* Thousand Oaks, CA: Sage.

Kurtz, L. (1997). *Self-help and support groups: A handbook for practitioners.* Thousand Oaks, CA: Sage.

Labrecque, M., Peak, T., & Toseland, R. (1992). Long-term effectiveness of a group program for caregivers of frail elderly veterans. *American Journal of Orthopsychiatry, 62*(4), 575–588.

Lakin, M. (1991). Some ethical issues in feminist-oriented therapeutic groups for women. *Inter-*

national *Journal of Group Psychotherapy, 4,* 199–215.

Lang, N. (1972). A broad range model of practice in the social work group. *Social Service Review, 46*(1), 76–84.

Lang, N. (1979a). A comparative examination of therapeutic uses of groups in social work and in adjacent human service professions: Part I— The literature from 1955–1968. *Social Work with Groups, 2*(2), 101–115.

Lang, N. (1979b). A comparative examination of the therapeutic uses of groups in social work and in adjacent human service professions: Part II—The literature from 1969–1978. *Social Work with Groups, 2*(3), 197–220.

Lauffer, A. (1978). *Social planning at the community level.* Englewood Cliffs, NJ: Prentice-Hall.

Lawler, E., III, & Mohrman, S. (1985, Spring). Quality circles after the fad: There are benefits for managers and employees—and there are limitations. *Public Welfare, 43*(2), 37–44.

Lazarus, R. S., & Folkman, S. (1984). *Stress, appraisal, and coping.* New York: Springer.

Leahy, R. (1996). *Cognitive therapy: Basic principles and applications.* Northvale, NJ: Jason Aronson.

LeBon, G. (1910). *The crowd: A study of the popular mind.* London: George Allen & Unwin Ltd.

Lederman, L. C. (1989). *Assessing educational effectiveness: The focus group interview as a technique for data collection.* Paper presented at the meeting of the Speech Communication Association, San Francisco.

Lee, J. (Ed.). (1990). *Group work with the poor and oppressed.* New York: Haworth.

Lee, J. (1997). The empowerment group: The heart of the empowerment approach and an antidote to injustice. In J. Parry (Ed.), *From prevention to wellness through group work* (pp. 15–32). Binghamton, NY: Haworth Press.

Lehmann, D. (1989). *Market research and analysis* (3rd ed.). Homewood, IL: Irwin.

Lehrer, P., & Woolfolk, R. (Eds.). (1993). *Principles and practice of stress management* (2nd ed.). New York: Guilford.

Leszcz, M. (1992). The interpersonal approach to group psychotherapy. *International Journal of Group Psychotherapy, 42*(1), 37–62.

Levine, B. (1979). *Group psychotherapy: Practice and development.* Englewood Cliffs, NJ: Prentice-Hall.

Levine, B. (1980). Co-leadership approach to learning group work. *Social Work with Groups, 3*(4), 35–38.

Levine, B., & Gallogly, V. (1985). *Group therapy with alcoholics: Outpatient and inpatient approaches.* Newbury Park, CA: Sage.

Levinson, D., & Klerman, G. (1973). The clinician-executive: Some problematic issues for the psychiatrist in mental health organizations. *Administration in Mental Health, 1*(1), 52–67.

Levinson, H. (1977). Termination of psychotherapy: Some salient issues. *Social Casework, 58*(8), 480–489.

Levitt, J., & Reid, W. (1981). Rapid assessment instruments for social work practice. *Social Work Research and Abstracts, 17*(1), 13–20.

Lewin, K. (1946). Behavior as a function of the total situation. In L. Carmichael (Ed.), *Manual of child psychology* (pp. 791–844). New York: John Wiley & Sons.

Lewin, K. (1947). Frontiers in group dynamics. *Human Relations, 1,* 2–38.

Lewin, K. (1948). *Resolving social conflict.* New York: Harper & Row.

Lewin, K. (1951). *Field theory in social science.* New York: Harper & Row.

Lewin, K., & Lippitt, R. (1938). An experimental approach to the study of autocracy and democracy: A preliminary note. *Sociometry, 1,* 292–300.

Lewin, K., Lippitt, R., & White, R. (1939). Patterns of aggressive behavior in experimentally created "social climates." *Journal of Social Psychology, 10,* 271–299.

Lewis, E., & Ford, B. (1990). The network utilization project: Incorporating traditional strengths of African-American families into group work practice. *Social Work with Groups, 13*(4), 7–22.

Lewis, H. (1982, October). Ethics in work with groups: The clients' interests. In N. Lang & C. Marshall (Chairs), *Patterns in the mosaic.* Symposium conducted at the Fourth Annual Meeting of Social Work with Groups, Toronto.

Lewis, R., & Ho, M. (1975). Social work with Native Americans. *Social Work, 20,* 379–382.

Lieberman, M. (1975). Groups for personal change: New and not-so-new forms. In D. Freedman & J. Dyrad (Eds.), *American handbook of psychiatry* (pp. 345–366). New York: Basic Books.

Lieberman, M., & Borman, L. (Eds.). (1979). *Self-help groups for coping with crisis.* San Francisco: Jossey-Bass.

Lieberman, M., Yalom, I., & Miles, M. (1973). *Encounter groups: First facts.* New York: Basic Books.

Lighthouse, Inc. (1995). *The Lighthouse National Survey on vision loss: The experience, attitudes and knowledge of middle-aged and older Americans.* New York: The Lighthouse.

Likert, R. (1961). *New patterns of management.* New York: McGraw-Hill.

Likert, R. (1967). *The human organization.* New York: McGraw-Hill.

Lippitt, R. (1957). Group dynamics and the individual. *International Journal of Group Psychotherapy, 7*(10), 86–102.

Loewenberg, F., & Dolgoff, R. (1996). *Ethical decisions for social work practice* (5th ed.). Itasca, IL: Peacock Press.

Lonergan, E. C. (1989). *Group intervention* (3rd ed.). Northvale, NJ: Jason Aronson.

Long, K., Pendleton, L., & Winter, B. (1988). Effects of therapist termination on group processes. *International Journal of Group Psychotherapy, 38*(2), 211–223.

Lopez, J. (1991). Group work as a protective factor for immigrant youth. *Social Work with Groups, 14*(1), 29–42.

Luft, J. (1984). *Group processes* (3rd ed.). Palo Alto, CA: Mayfield.

Lum, D. (1996). *Social work practice and people of color: A process-stage approach* (3rd ed.). Pacific Grove, CA: Brooks/Cole.

MacKenzie, K. R. (1990). *Introduction to time-limited group psychotherapy.* Washington, DC: American Psychiatric Press.

MacKenzie, K. R. (1994). Group Development. In A. Fuhriman and G. M. Burlingame (Eds.), *Handbook of Group Psychotherapy* (pp. 223–268). New York: John Wiley & Sons.

MacKenzie, K. R. (Ed.). (1995). *Effective use of group therapy in managed care.* Washington, DC: American Psychiatric Press.

MacKenzie, K. R. (1996). Time-limited group psychotherapy. *International Journal of Group Psychotherapy, 46*(1), 41–60.

MacLennon, B. (1965). Co-therapy. *International Journal of Group Psychotherapy, 15,* 154–166.

Maguire, L. (1991). *Social support systems in practice: A generalist approach.* Silver Spring, MD: National Association of Social Workers Press.

Mahoney, M. J. (1974). *Cognitive and behavior modification.* Cambridge, MA: Ballinger Books.

Mahoney, M. J. (Ed.). (1995a). *Cognitive and constructive psychotherapies: Theory, research and practice.* New York: Springer.

Mahoney, M. J. (Ed.). (1995b). *Constructive psychotherapy.* New York: Guilford.

Maier, N. (1963). *Problem-solving discussions and conferences: Leadership methods and skills.* New York: McGraw-Hill.

Maier, N., & Zerfoss, L. (1952). MRP: A technique for training large groups of supervisors and its potential use in social research. *Human Relations, 5,* 177–186.

Malekoff, A. (1997). *Group work with adolescents.* New York: Guilford Press.

Maloney, S. (1963). *Development of group work education in social work schools in U.S.* Unpublished doctoral dissertation, Case Western Reserve University, School of Applied Social Science, Cleveland.

Maltzman, I., Simon, S., Raskin, D., & Licht, L. (1960). Experimental studies in the training of originality. *Psychological Monographs, 7* (493).

Maluccio, A. (1979). *Learning from clients.* New York: The Free Press.

Maple, F. (1977). *Shared decision making.* Newbury Park, CA: Sage.

Marks, M., Mirvis, P., Hackett, E., & Grady, J. (1986). Employee participation in a quality circle program: Impact on quality of worklife, productivity, and absenteeism. *Journal of Applied Psychology, 71,* 61–69.

Marlatt, G. (1996). Taxonomy of high-risk situations for alcohol relapse: Evolution and development of a cognitive-behavioral model. *Addiction, 91* (supplement), S37–S49.

Marlatt, G., & Barrett, K. (1994). Relapse prevention. In M. Galanter & H. D. Kleber (Eds.), *The American Psychiatric Press textbook of substance abuse treatment* (pp. 285–299). Washington, DC: American Psychiatric Press.

Marsh, E., & Terdal, L. (Eds.). (1997). *Behavioral assessment of childhood disorders* (3rd ed.). New York: Guilford.

Marsiglia, F., Cross, S., & Mitchell-Enos, V. (1998). Culturally grounded group work with adolescent American Indian students. *Social Work with Groups, 21*(1), 89–102.

Masters, J., Burish, T., Hollon, S., & Rimm, D. (1987). *Behavior therapy: Techniques and empirical findings* (3rd ed.). San Diego, CA: Harcourt Brace Jovanovich.

Mayadas, N., & Glasser, P. (1981). Termination: A neglected aspect of social group work. *Social Work with Groups, 4*(2), 193–204.

Mayer, J., Soweid, R., Dabney, S., Brownson, C., Goodman, R., & Brownson, R. (1998). Practices of successful community coalitions: A multiple case study. *American Journal of Health Behavior, 22*(5), 368–369.

Mayer, J., & Timms, N. (1970). *The client speaks: Working class impressions of casework.* New York: Atherton Press.

McCallion, P., Toseland, R., & Diehl, M. (1994). Social work practice with caregivers of frail older adults. *Research on Social Work Practice, 4,* 64–68.

McCaskill, J. (1930). *Theory and practice of group work.* New York: Association Press.

McClane, W. (1991). The interaction of leader and member characteristics in the leader-member exchange model of leadership. *Small Group Research, 22,* 283–300.

McCorkle, L., Elias, A., Bixby, F. (1958). *The highfields story: An experimental project for youthful offenders.* New York: Holt.

McDougall, W. (1920). *The group mind.* New York: G. P. Putnam's Sons.

McGee, T., & Schuman, B. (1970). The nature of the co-therapy relationship. *International Journal of Group Psychotherapy, 20,* 25–36.

McGrath, J. (1984). *Groups: Interaction and performance.* Englewood Cliffs, NJ: Prentice-Hall.

McGrath, J. (1992). Time, interaction, and performance (TIP): A theory of groups. *Small Group Research, 22,* 147–174.

McGrath, P., & Axelson, J. (1999). *Accessing awareness & developing knowledge: Foundations for skill in a multicultural society* (3rd ed.). Pacific Grove, CA: Brooks/Cole.

McKay, M., & Paleg, K. (Eds.). (1992). *Focal group psychotherapy.* Oakland, CA: New Harbinger.

McLaughlin, R., White, E., & Byfield, B. (1974). Modes of interpersonal feedback and leadership structure in six small groups. *Nursing Research, 23*(4), 207–318.

McLeod, P., Lobel, S., & Cox, T. (1996). Ethnic diversity and creativity in small groups. *Small Group Research, 27*(2), 248–264.

Meichenbaum, D. (1977). *Cognitive-behavior modification: An integrative approach.* New York: Plenum.

Meichenbaum, D. (1985). *Stress inoculation training.* New York: Plenum.

Meichenbaum, D., & Cameron, R. (1983). Stress inoculation training: Toward a general paradigm for training coping skills. In D. Meichenbaum & M. E. Jaremko (Eds.), *Stress reduction and prevention* (pp. 115–154). Norwell, MA: Plenum.

Meichenbaum, D., & Fitzpatrick, D. (1993). A constructivist narrative perspective on stress and coping: Stress inoculation applications. In L. Goldberger & S. Breznitz (Eds.), *Handbook of stress: Theoretical and clinical aspects* (2nd ed., pp. 706–723). New York: Free Press.

Merenda, D. (1997). *A practical guide to creating and managing community coalitions for drug abuse prevention.* Alexandria, VA: National Association of Partners in Education.

Merton, R., Fiske, M., & Kendall, P. (1956). *The focused interview.* Glencoe, IL: The Free Press.

Merton, R., & Kendall, P. (1946). The focused interview. *American Journal of Sociology, 51,* 541–557.

Meyer, C. (Ed.). (1983). *Social work in the eco-systems perspective.* New York: Columbia University Press.

Meyer, C. (1988). The ecosystems perspective. In R. A. Dorfman (Ed.), *Paradigms of clinical social work* (pp. 275–294). New York: Brunner/Mazel.

Middleman, R. (1978). Returning group process to group work. *Social Work with Groups, 1*(1), 15–26.

Middleman, R. (1980). The use of program: Review and update. *Social Work with Groups, 3*(3), 5–23.

Middleman, R. (1982). *The non-verbal method in working with groups: The use of activity in teaching, counseling, and therapy.* (Enlarged ed.). Hebron, CT: Practitioners Press.

Middleman, R., & Wood, G. (1990). Reviewing the past and present of group work and the challenge of the future. *Social Work with Groups, 13*(3), 3–20.

Milgram, D., & Rubin, J. (1992). Resisting resistance: Involuntary substance abuse group therapy. *Social Work with Groups, 15*(1), 95–110.

Miller, S., Nunnally, E., & Wackman, D. (1972). *The Minnesota couples communication program couples handbook.* Minneapolis: Minnesota Couples Communication Program.

Mills, T. (1967). *The sociology of small groups.* Englewood Cliffs, NJ: Prentice-Hall.

Milter, R. G., & Rohrbaugh, J. (1988). Judgment analysis and decision conferencing for administrative review: A case study of innovative policy making in government. In R. L. Cardy, S. M. Puffer, and J. M. Newman (Eds.), *Advances in information processing in organizations* (pp. 245–262). Greenwich, CT: JAI Press.

Mizrahi, T., & Rosenthal, B. (1998, March). *Complexities of effective coalition-building: A study of leaders' strategies, struggles, and solutions.* Paper presented at the Annual Program Meeting of the Council on Social Work Education. Orlando, FL.

Mondros, J., & Wilson, S. (1994). *Organizing for power and empowerment.* New York: Columbia University Press.

Montgomery, R. (Ed.). (1985). *Family seminars for caregiving: Helping families help.* Seattle: University of Washington Press.

Moore, C. (1994). *Group techniques for idea building.* Thousand Oaks, CA: Sage.

Moreno, J. (1934). *Who shall survive?* Washington, DC: Nervous and Mental Diseases.

Moreno, J. (1946). *Psychodrama* (Vol. 1). Boston: Beacon Press.

Morgan, D. (1997). *Focus groups as qualitative research* (2nd ed.). Thousand Oaks, CA: Sage.

Mullen, B., & Cooper, C. (1994). The relationship between cohesiveness and performance: An integration. *Psychological Bulletin, 115*(2), 210–227.

Mullen, E. (1969). The relationship between diagnosis and treatment in casework. *Social Casework, 50,* 218–226.

Mullender, A., & Ward, D. (1991). *Self-directed groupwork: Users take action for empowerment.* London: Whitney & Birch.

Munzer, J., & Greenwald, H. (1957). Interaction process analysis of a therapy group. *International Journal of Group Psychotherapy, 7,* 175–190.

Murphy, M. (1959). *The social group work method in social work education* (Project report of the Curriculum Study, Vol. XI). New York: Council of Social Work Education.

Murphy, M., DeBernardo, C., & Shoemaker, W. (1998). Impact of managed care on independent practice and professional ethics: A survey of independent practitioners. *Professional Psychology: Research and Practice, 29,* 43–51.

Myers, D., & Arenson, S. (1972). Enhancement of the dominant risk in group discussion. *Psychological Reports, 30,* 615–623.

Nadler, D. (1977). *Feedback and organizational development: Using data base methods.* Reading, MA: Addison-Wesley.

Nadler, D. (1979). The effects of feedback on task group behavior: A review of the experimental research. *Organizational Behavior and Human Performance, 23,* 309–338.

Napier, H. (1967). Individual versus group learning: Note on task variable. *Psychological Reports, 23,* 757–758.

Napier, R., & Gershenfeld, M. (1993). *Groups: Theory and experience* (5th ed.). Boston: Houghton Mifflin.

Newstetter, W. (1948). The social intergroup work process. In *Proceedings of the National Conference of Social Work* (pp. 205–217). New York: Columbia University Press.

Nixon, H. (1979). *The small group.* Englewood Cliffs, NJ: Prentice-Hall.

Northen, H. (1969). *Social work with groups.* New York: Columbia University Press.

Northen, H. (1995). *Clinical social work* (2nd ed.). New York: Columbia University Press.

Nosko, A., & Wallace, R. (1997). Female/male co-leadership in group. *Social Work with Groups, 20*(2), 3–16.

Nunnally, J. C. (1994). *Psychometric theory* (3rd ed.). New York: McGraw-Hill.

Nye, J., & Forsyth, D. (1991). The effects of prototype-based biases on leadership appraisals: A test of leadership categorization theory. *Small Group Research, 22,* 360–379.

Ollendick, T., & Hersen, M. (Eds.). (1984). *Child behavioral assessment.* Elmsford, NY: Pergamon Press.

Olmsted, M. (1959). *The small group.* New York: Random House.

Olsen, M. (1968). *The process of social organization.* New York: Holt, Rinehart & Winston.

Osborn, A. (1963). *Applied imagination: Principles and procedures of creative problem solving* (3rd ed.). New York: Charles Scribner's Sons.

Osgood, C., Suci, C., & Tannenbaum, P. (1957). *The measurement of meaning.* Urbana: University of Illinois Press.

Oxley, G., Wilson, S., Anderson, J., & Wong, G. (1979). Peer-led groups in graduate education. *Social Work with Groups, 1,* 67–75.

Papell, C. (1997). Thinking about thinking about group work: Thirty years later. *Social Work with Groups, 20*(4), 5–17.

Papell, C., & Rothman, B. (1962). Social group work models—possession and heritage. *Journal of Education for Social Work, 2,* 66–77.

Papell, C., & Rothman, B. (1980). Relating the mainstream model of social work with groups to group psychotherapy and the structured group approach. *Social Work with Groups, 3*(2), 5–23.

Parnes, S. (1967). *Creative behavior guidebook.* New York: Charles Scribner's Sons.

Parsons, R. (1991). Empowerment: Purpose and practice principle in social work. *Social Work with Groups, 14*(2), 7–21.

Parsons, T. (1951). *The social system.* New York: The Free Press.

Parsons, T., Bales, R., & Shils, E. (Eds.). (1953). *Working papers in the theory of action.* New York: The Free Press.

Patti, R. (1974). Organizational resistance and change: The view from below. *Social Service Review, 48*(3), 367–383.

Patton, M. (1990). *Qualitative evaluation and research methods* (2nd ed.). Newbury Park, CA: Sage.

Pearson, V. (1991). Western theory, eastern practice: Social group work in Hong Kong. *Social Work with Groups, 14*(2), 45–58.

Pence, R., & Paymar, M. (1993). *Education groups for men who batter: The Duluth model.* New York: Springer.

Pepitone, A., & Reichling, G. (1955). Group cohesiveness and the expression of hostility. *Human Relations, 8,* 327–337.

Perlman, H. (1970). The problem-solving method in social casework. In R. Roberts & R. Nee (Eds.), *Theories of social casework* (pp. 129–180). Chicago: University of Chicago Press.

Pernell, R. (1986). Empowerment and social group work. In M. Parnes (Ed.), *Innovations in social group work* (pp. 107–118). New York: Haworth Press.

Peters, A. (1997). Themes in group work with lesbian and gay adolescents. *Social Work with Groups, 20*(2), 51–69.

Pfeiffer, J., & Goodstein, L. (Eds.). (1984–1996). *The annual: Developing human resources.* San Diego, CA: University Associates.

Phillips, J. (1948). Report on discussion 66. *Adult Education Journal, 7,* 181–182.

Pincus, A., & Minahan, A. (1973). *Social work practice: Model and method.* Itasca, IL: F. E. Peacock.

Pinderhughes, E. B. (1979). Teaching empathy in cross-cultural social work. *Social Work, 2*(4), 312–316.

Pinderhughes, E. B. (1995). Empowering diverse populations: Family practice in the 21st century. *Families in Society, 76,* 131–140.

Pinkus, H. (1968). *Casework techniques related to selected characteristics of clients and workers.* Unpublished doctoral dissertation, Columbia University, New York.

Piper, W. (1992). *Adaptation to loss through short-term group psychotherapy.* New York: Guilford.

Piper, W. (1994). Client variables. In A. Fuhriman and G. M. Burlingame (Eds.), *Handbook of Group Psychotherapy* (pp. 83–113). New York: John Wiley & Sons.

Piper, W., Debbane, E., Bienvenu, J., & Garant, J. (1982). A study of group pretraining for group psychotherapy. *International Journal of Group Psychotherapy, 32,* 309–325.

Piper, W., & Joyce, A. (1996). A consideration of factors influencing the utilization of time-limited, short-term group therapy. *International Journal of Group Psychotherapy, 46*(3), 311–329.

Polansky, N. (Ed.). (1960). *Social work research.* Chicago: University of Chicago Press.

Pomeroy, E. C., Rubin, A., & Walker, R. J. (1995). Effectiveness of a psychoeducational and task-centered group intervention for family members of people with AIDS. *Social Work Research, 19*(3), 142–152.

Powell, T. (1987). *Self-help organizations and professional practice.* Silver Spring, MD: National Association of Social Workers Press.

Prapavessis, H., & Carron, A. (1997). Cohesion and work output. *Small Group Research, 28*(2), 294–301.

Prigmore, C. S. (1974). Use of the coalition in legislative action. *Social Work, 19*(1), 96–102.

Prince, G. (1970). *The practice of creativity.* New York: Harper & Row.

Proctor, E., & Davis, L. (1994). The challenge of racial difference: Skills for clinical practice. *Social Work, 39,* 314–323.

Rathus, J., & Sanderson, W. (1998). *Marital distress: Cognitive behavioral interventions for couples.* Northvale, NJ: Jason Aronson.

Rauch, J. (Ed.). (1993). *Assessment: A sourcebook for social work practice.* Milwaukee, WI: Families International.

Reagan-Cirinicione, P. (1994). Improving the accuracy of group judgment: A process intervention combining group facilitation, social judgment analysis, and information technology. *Organizational Behavior and Human Decision Processes, 58,* 246–270.

Reder, P. (1978). An assessment of the group therapy interaction chronogram. *International Journal of Group Psychotherapy, 28,* 185–194.

Redl, F. (1942). Group emotion and leadership. *Psychiatry, 5,* 573–596.

Redl, F. (1944). Diagnostic group work. *American Journal of Orthopsychiatry, 14*(1), 53–67.

Reid, K. (1981). *From character building to social treatment: The history of the use of groups in social work.* Westport, CT: Greenwood Press.

Reid, K. (1997). *Social work practice with groups: A clinical perspective* (2nd ed.). Pacific Grove, CA: Brooks/Cole.

Reid, W. J. (1992). *Task strategies: An empirical approach to clinical social work.* New York: Columbia University Press.

Reid, W. J. (1997). Research on task-centered practice. *Social Work Research, 21*(3), 132–137.

Reid, W. J., & Shapiro, B. (1969). Client reactions to advice. *Social Service Review, 43,* 165–173.

Rice, C. (1987). *Inpatient group psychotherapy: A psychodynamic perspective.* New York: Macmillan.

Richards, T. (1974). *Problem solving through creative analysis.* New York: John Wiley & Sons.

Richmond, M. (1917). *Social diagnosis*. New York: Russell Sage Foundation.

Rittenhouse, J. (1997). Feminist principles in survivor's groups: Out-of-contact. *Journal for Specialists in Group Work, 22*(2), 111–119.

Rittner, B., & Nakanishi, M. (1993). Challenging stereotypes and cultural biases through small group process. *Social Work with Groups, 16*(4), 5–23.

Rivas, R., & Toseland, R. (1981). The student group leadership evaluation project: A study of group leadership skills. *Social Work with Groups, 4*(3/4), 159–175.

Roback, H., Moore, R., Bloch, F., & Shelton, M. (1996). Confidentiality in group psychotherapy: Empirical findings and the law. *International Journal of Group Psychotherapy, 46*(1), 117–135.

Roback, H., Ochoa, E., Bloch, F., & Purdon, S. (1992). Guarding confidentiality in clinical groups: The therapist's dilemma. *International Journal of Group Psychotherapy, 42*(1), 81–103.

Robert, H. (1970). *Robert's rules of order*. Glenview, IL: Scott Foresman.

Roberts, R., & Northen, H. (Eds.). (1976). *Theories of social work with groups*. New York: Columbia University Press.

Robinson, J., & Shaver, P. (Eds.). (1973). *Measures of social psychological attitude* (2nd ed.). Ann Arbor: University of Michigan Press.

Robson, M. (1988). *Quality circles: A practical guide* (2nd ed.). Aldershat, Hants, England: Gower.

Roethlisberger, F. (1941). *Management and morale*. Cambridge, MA: Harvard University Press.

Roethlisberger, F., & Dickson, W. (1939). *Management and the worker*. Cambridge, MA: Harvard University Press.

Roethlisberger, F., & Dickson, W. (1975). A fair day's work. In P. V. Crosbie (Ed.), *Interaction in small groups* (pp. 85–94). New York: Macmillan.

Rohde, R., & Stockton, R. (1992, Winter). The effect of structured feedback on goal attainment, attraction to the group, and satisfaction with the group in small group counseling. *Journal of Group Psychotherapy, Psychodrama, and Sociometry, 44*(4), 172–179.

Rohrbaugh, J. (1979). Improving the quality of group judgment: Social judgment analysis and the delphi technique. *Organizational Behavior and Human Performance, 24,* 73–92.

Rohrbaugh, J. (1981). Improving the quality of group judgment: Social judgment analysis and the nominal group technique. *Organizational Behavior and Human Performance, 26,* 272–288.

Rohrbaugh, J. (1984). Making decisions about staffing standards: An analytical approach to human resource planning in health administration. In L. Nigro (Ed.), *Decision making in the public sector* (pp. 93–116). New York: Marcel Dekker.

Rokeach, M. (1968). *Beliefs, attitudes and values: A theory of organization and change*. San Francisco: Jossey-Bass.

Roller, B., & Nelson, V. (Eds.). (1991). The art of co-therapy: How therapists work together. London: Guilford.

Rooney, R. (1992). *Strategies for work with involuntary clients*. New York: Columbia University Press.

Rose, S. (1981). Assessment in groups. *Social Work Research and Abstracts, 17*(1), 29–37.

Rose, S. (1989). *Working with adults in groups: A multimethod approach*. San Francisco: Jossey-Bass.

Rose, S. (1991). The development and practice of group treatment. In M. Hersen, A. Kazdin, & A. Bellack (Eds.), *Handbook of Clinical Psychology* (pp. 627–642). New York: Pergamon Press.

Rose, S. (1998). *Group therapy with troubled youth*. Newbury Park, CA: Sage.

Rose, S., Cayner, J., & Edleson, J. (1977). Measuring interpersonal competence. *Social Work, 22*(2), 125–129.

Rose, S., & Edleson, J. (1987). *Working with children and adolescents in groups*. San Francisco: Jossey-Bass.

Rose, S., & Hanusa, D. (1980). *Parenting skill role play test*. Interpersonal skill training and research project, University of Wisconsin, Madison.

Rose, S., & LeCroy, C. (1991). Group treatment methods. In F. Kanfer & A. Goldstein (Eds.), *Helping people change* (4th ed., pp. 422–453). New York: Pergamon Press.

Rose, S., Tallant, S., Tolman, R., & Subramanian, K. (1987). A multimethod group approach: Program development research. *Social Work with Groups, 9*(3), 71–88.

Rosenthal, L. (1978). *Behavioral analysis of social skills in adolescent girls*. Unpublished doctoral dissertation, University of Wisconsin, Madison.

Rossi, P., Freeman, H., & Wright, S. (1979). *Evaluation: A systematic approach*. Newbury Park, CA: Sage.

Rothman, J. (1974). *Planning and organizing for social change: Action principles for social science research*. New York: Columbia University Press.

Rothman, J., Erlich, J., & Tropman, J. (Eds.). (1995). *Strategies of community intervention* (5th ed.). Itasca, IL: F. E. Peacock.

Rothman, J., & Tumblin, A. (1994). Pilot testing and early development of a model of case management intervention. In J. Rothman & E. J. Thomas (Eds.), *Intervention research: Design and development for human service* (pp. 215–233). New York: Haworth Press.

Rotter, G., & Portugal, S. (1969). Group and individual effects in problem solving. *Journal of Applied Psychology, 53,* 338–341.

Rounds, K., Galinsky, M., & Stevens, L. S. (1991, January). Linking people with AIDS in rural communities: The telephone group. *Social Work, 36,* 13–18.

Rubin, H., & Rubin, I. (1992). *Community organizing and development* (2nd ed.). New York: Macmillan.

Rutan, J. (1992). Psychodynamic group psychotherapy. *International Journal of Group Psychotherapy, 42*(1), 19–36.

Rutan, J. (1993). *Psychodynamic group psychotherapy* (2nd ed.). New York: Guilford.

Salazar, A. (1996). An analysis of the development and evolution of roles in the small group. *Small Group Research, 27*(4), 475–503.

Santhiveeran, J. (1998, October). *Virtual group meetings on the net: Implications for social work practice.* Paper presented at the meeting of the Association for the Advancement of Social Work with Groups, Miami, FL.

Sarri, R., & Galinsky, M. (1985). A conceptual framework for group development. In M. Sundel, P. Glasser, R. Sarri, & R. Vinter (Eds.), *Individual change through small groups* (2nd ed., pp. 70–86). New York: The Free Press.

Sarri, R., Galinsky, M., Glasser, P., Siegel, S., & Vinter, R. (1967). Diagnosis in group work. In R. D. Viner (Ed.), *Readings in group work practice* (pp. 39–71). Ann Arbor, MI: Campus Publishing.

Saunders, D. (1996). Feminist-cognitive-behavioral and process-psychodynamic treatments for men who batter: Interaction of abuser traits and treatment models. *Violence and Victims, 11,* 394–414.

Sax, G. (1996). *Principles of educational and psychological measurement* (4th ed.). Belmont, CA: Wadsworth.

Schachter, S. (1959). *The psychology of affiliation.* Stanford, CA: Stanford University Press.

Scheidel, T., & Crowell, L. (1979). *Discussing and deciding: A deskbook for group leaders and members.* New York: Macmillan.

Scheneul, J., Nastasi, B., Lecompte, M., & Borgatti, S. (1998). *Enhanced ethnographic methods: Audiovisual techniques, focused group interviews, and elicitation techniques.* Thousand Oaks, CA: Altamira Press.

Schiller, L. (1995). Stages of development in women's groups: A relational model. In R. Kurland and R. Salmon (Eds.), *Group work practice in a troubled society* (pp. 117–138). New York: Haworth Press.

Schiller, L. (1997). Rethinking stages of development in women's groups: Implications for practice. *Social Work with Groups, 20*(3), 3–19.

Schinke, S. P., & Rose, S. (1976). Interpersonal skill training in groups. *Journal of Counseling Psychology, 23,* 442–448.

Schlenoff, M., & Busa, S. (1981). Student and field instructor as group co-therapists. Equalizing an unequal relationship. *Journal of Education for Social Work, 17,* 29–35.

Schmidt, W. H., & Finnigan, J. P. (1993). *TQ Manager: A practical guide for managing in a total quality organization.* San Francisco: Jossey-Bass.

Schmitt, M., Farrell, M., & Heinemann, G. (1988). Conceptual and methodological problems in studying the effects of interdisciplinary geriatric teams. *The Gerontologist, 28*(6), 753–763.

Schopler, J. (1994). Interorganizational groups in human services: Environmental and Interpersonal Relationships. *Journal of Community Practice, 1*(3), 7–27.

Schopler, J., Abell, M., & Galinsky, M. (1998). Technology-based groups: A review and conceptual framework for practice. *Social Work, 43*(3), 254–267.

Schopler, J., & Galinsky, M. (1981). When groups go wrong. *Social Work, 26*(5), 424–429.

Schopler, J., & Galinsky, M. (1984). Meeting practice needs: Conceptualizing the open-ended group. *Social Work with Groups, 7*(2), 3–21.

Schopler, J., & Galinsky, M. (1990). Can open-ended groups move beyond beginnings? *Small Group Research, 21*(4), 435–449.

Schopler, J., Galinsky, M., & Abell, M. (1997). Creating community through telephone and computer groups: Theoretical and practice perspectives. *Social Work with Groups, 20*(4), 19–34.

Schriver, J. (1998). *Human behavior and the social environment* (2nd ed.). Boston: Allyn and Bacon.

Schuman, S., & Rohrbaugh, J. (1996, June). Meet me in cyberspace. *Government Technology, 9,* 32–34.

Schwartz, W. (1966). Discussion of three papers on the group method with clients, foster families, and adoptive families. *Child Welfare, 45*(10), 571–575.

Schwartz, W. (1971). On the use of groups in social work practice. In W. Schwartz & S. Zalba (Eds.),

The practice of group work (pp. 3–24). New York: Columbia University Press.

Schwartz, W. (1974). The social worker in the group. In R. W. Klenk & R. M. Ryan (Eds.), *The practice of social work* (pp. 208–228). New York: Wadsworth.

Schwartz, W. (1976). Between client and system: The mediating function. In R. Roberts & H. Northen (Eds.), *Theories of social work with groups* (pp. 171–197). New York: Columbia University Press.

Schwartz, W. (1981, April). *The group work tradition and social work practice.* Paper presented at Rutgers University, School of Social Work, New Brunswick.

Seaberg, J., & Gillespie, D. (1977). Goal attainment scaling: A critique. *Social Work Research and Abstracts, 13*(2), 4–9.

Seashore, S. (1954). *Group cohesiveness in the industrial work group.* Ann Arbor: University of Michigan Press.

Seely, H., & Sween, J. (1983, March). Critical components of successful U.S. quality circles. *Quality Circles Journal, 6,* 14–17.

Seligman, L. (1998). *Selecting effective treatments* (2nd ed.). San Francisco: Jossey-Bass.

Seligman, M. (1975). *Helplessness: On depression, development, and death.* San Francisco: W. H. Freeman.

Selltiz, C., Wrightsman, L., & Cook, S. (1976). *Research methods in social relations* (3rd ed.). New York: Holt, Rinehart & Winston.

Sexton, T., & Whiston, S. (1994). The status of the counseling relationship: An empirical review, theoretical implications, and research directions. *Counseling Psychologist, 22*(1), 6–77.

Shapiro, J., Peltz, L., & Bernadett-Shapiro, S. (1998). *Brief group treatment for therapists and counselors.* Florence, KY: Wadsworth.

Shaw, C. (1930). *The jack roller.* Chicago: University of Chicago Press.

Shaw, M. (1964). Communication networks. In L. Berkowitz (Ed.), *Advances in experimental social psychology* (Vol. 1, pp. 111–149). New York: Academic Press.

Shaw, M. (1976). *Group dynamics: The psychology of small group behavior.* New York: McGraw-Hill.

Shaw, M. (1980). *Role-playing.* La Jolla, CA: University Associates.

Sheldon, B. (1995). *Cognitive-behavioural therapy: Research, practice and philosophy.* London: Routledge.

Shepard, C. (1964). *Small groups: Some sociological perspectives.* San Francisco: Chandler.

Sherif, M. (1936). *The psychology of social norms.* New York: Harper & Row.

Sherif, M. (1956). Experiments in group conflict. *Scientific American, 195,* 54–58.

Sherif, M., & Sherif, C. (1953). *Groups in harmony and tension: An introduction of studies in group relations.* New York: Harper & Row.

Sherif, M., White, J., & Harvey, O. (1955). Status in experimentally produced groups. *American Journal of Sociology, 60,* 370–379.

Shils, E. (1950). Primary groups in the American army. In R. Merton & P. Lazarsfeld (Eds.), *Continuities in social research* (pp. 16–39). New York: The Free Press.

Shimanoff, S., & Jenkins, M. (1991). Leadership and gender: Challenging assumptions and recognizing resources. In R. Cathcart and L. Samovar (Eds.), *Small group communication: A reader* (6th ed., pp. 504–522). Dubuque, IA: William C. Brown.

Shipley, R., & Boudewyns, P. (1980). Flooding and implosive therapy: Are they harmful? *Behavior Therapy, 11*(4), 503–508.

Shulman, L. (1978). A study of practice skills. *Social Work, 23*(4), 274–280.

Shulman, L. (1999). *The skills of helping individuals, families and groups* (4th ed.). Itasca, IL: F. E. Peacock.

Shuster, H. D. (1990). *Teaming for quality improvement: A process for innovation and consensus.* Englewood Cliffs, NJ: Prentice-Hall.

Silbergeld, S., Koenig, G., Manderscheid, R., Meeker, B., & Hornung, C. (1975). Assessment of environment-therapy systems: The group atmosphere scale. *Journal of Consulting and Clinical Psychology, 43*(4), 460–469.

Silverman, M. (1966). Knowledge in social group work: A review of the literature. *Social Work, 11*(3), 56–62.

Siporin, M. (1975). *Introduction to social work practice.* New York: Macmillan.

Siporin, M. (1980). Ecological system theory in social work. *Journal of Sociology and Social Work, 7,* 507–532.

Slavson, S. R. (1939). *Character education in a democracy.* New York: Association Press.

Slavson, S. R. (1945). *Creative group education.* New York: Association Press.

Slavson, S. R. (1946). *Recreation and the total personality.* New York: Association Press.

Sluyter, G., & Mukherjee, A. (1993). *Total quality management for mental health and mental retardation.* Annandale, VA: National Association of Private Residential Resources.

Smith, A. (1935). Group play in a hospital environment. In *Proceedings of the National Conference of Social Work* (pp. 372–373). Chicago: University of Chicago Press.

Smith, H., & Doeing, C. (1985, Spring). Japanese management: A model for social work administration? *Administration in Social Work, 9*(1), 1–11.

Smith, K. K., & Berg, D. N. (1997). *Paradoxes of group life.* San Francisco: Jossey-Bass.

Smith, M. (1977). *Value clarification.* La Jolla, CA: University Associates.

Smith, M., Tobin, S., & Toseland, R. (1992). Therapeutic processes in professional and peer counseling of family caregivers of frail elderly. *Social Work, 37*(4), 345–351.

Smith, P. (1978). Group work as a process of social influence. In N. McCaughan (Ed.), *Group work: Learning and practice* (pp. 36–57). London: George Allen & Unwin.

Smucker, M., Dancu, C., & Foa, E. (1999). *Cognitive behavioral treatment for adult survivors of childhood trauma: Imagery rescripting and reprocessing.* Northvale, NJ: Jason Aronson.

Sonkin, D. (Ed.). (1995). What counseling approach should I use? In, *The counselor's guide to learning to live without violence* (pp. 31–45). Volcano, CA: Volcano Press.

Sosik, J., Avolio, B., & Kahai, S. (1998). Inspiring group creativity: Comparing anonymous and identified electronic brainstorming. *Small Group Research, 29*(1), 3–31.

Spielberger, C., Gorsuch, R., Lushene, R., Vagg, P., & Jacobs, G. (1983). *Manual for the stait-trait anxiety inventory.* Palo Alto, CA: Consulting Psychologists Press.

Spink, K., & Carron, A. (1994). Group cohesion effects in exercise classes. *Small Group Research, 25*(1), 26–42.

Starak, Y. (1981). Co-leadership: A new look at sharing group work. *Social Work with Groups, 4*(3/4), 145–157.

Stattler, W., & Miller, N. (1968). *Discussion and conference* (2nd ed.). Englewood Cliffs, NJ: Prentice-Hall.

Steckler, N., & Fondas, N. (1995). Building team leader effectiveness: A diagnostic tool. *Organizational Dynamics, 23*(3), 20–35.

Stein, L., Rothman, B., & Nakanishi, M. (1993). The telephone group: Accessing group service to the homebound. *Social Work with Groups, 16*(1/2), 203–215.

Steinberg, D. M. (1997). *The mutual-aid approach to working with groups: Helping people help each other.* Northvale, NJ: Jason Aronson.

Stern, R., & Drummond, L. (1991). *Practice of behavioural and cognitive psychotherapy.* New York: Cambridge University Press.

Stewart, D. W., & Shamdasani, P. N. (1990). *Focus groups: Theory and practice.* Newbury Park, CA: Sage.

Stockton, R., Rohde, R., & Haughey, J. (1992). The effects of structured group exercises on cohesion, engagement, avoidance, and conflict. *Small Group Research, 23*(2), 155–168.

Stogdill, R. (1974). *Handbook of leadership.* New York: The Free Press.

Stone, M., Lewis, C., & Beck, A. (1994). The structure of Yalom's Curative Factors Scale. *International Journal of Group Psychotherapy, 44*(2), 239–245.

Stoner, J. (1968). Risky and cautious shifts in group decisions: The influence of widely held values. *Journal of Experimental Social Psychology, 4,* 442–459.

Stouffer, S. (1949). *The American soldier, combat and its aftermath.* Princeton, NJ: Princeton University Press.

Strozier, A. (1997). Group work in social work education. What is being taught? *Social Work with Groups, 20*(1), 65–77.

Stuart, R. (1970). *Trick or treatment: Who and when psychotherapy facts.* Champaign, IL: Research Press.

Stuart, R. (1977). *Behavioral self-management: Strategies, techniques, and outcomes.* New York: Brunner/Mazel.

Stuart, R., & Davis, B. (1972). *Slim chance in a fat world.* Champaign, IL: Research Press.

Sue, D. W., & Sue, D. (1990). *Counseling the culturally different: Theory and practice* (2nd ed.). New York: John Wiley & Sons.

Sue, S., Zane, N., & Young, K. (1994). Psychotherapy with culturally diverse populations. In A. Bergin & S. Garfield (Eds.), *Handbook of psychotherapy and behavior change* (4th ed., pp. 783–812). New York: John Wiley & Sons.

Sundel, M., Glasser, P., Sarri, R., & Vinter, R. (1985). *Individual change through small groups* (2nd ed.). New York: The Free Press.

Sundel, M., Radin, N., & Churchill, S. (1985). Diagnosis in group work. In M. Sundel, P. Glasser, R. Sarri, & R. Vinter (Eds.), *Individual change through small groups* (2nd ed., pp. 117–139). New York: The Free Press.

Swenson, J., Griswold, W., & Kleiber, P. (1992, November). Focus groups method of inquiry/intervention. *Small Group Research, 23*(4), 459–474.

Tannenbaum, R., & Schmidt, W. (1972). How to choose a leadership pattern. In J. Lorsch & P. Lawrence (Eds.), *Managing groups and intergroup relations*. Homewood, CA: Dorsey Press.

Taylor, D., Berry, P., & Block, C. (1958). Does group participation when using brainstorming facilitate or inhibit creative thinking? *Administrative Science Quarterly, 3*, 23–47.

Taylor, N., & Burlingame, C. (in press). A survey of mental health care provider and managed care organization attitudes toward, familiarity with, and use of group psychotherapy. *International Journal of Group Psychotherapy.*

Taylor, R. (1903). Group management. *Transactions of the American Society of Mechanical Engineers, 24*, 1337–1480.

Teger, A., & Pruitt, D. (1967). Components of group risk-taking. *Journal of Experimental Psychology, 3*, 189–205.

Thelen, H. (1954). *Dynamics of groups at work.* Chicago: University of Chicago Press.

Thibaut, J., & Kelley, H. (1954). Experimental studies of group problem-solving process. In G. Kindzey (Ed.), *Handbook of social psychology* (Vol. 2, pp. 735–785). Reading, MA: Addison-Wesley.

Thibaut, J., & Kelley, H. (1959). *The social psychology of groups.* New York: John Wiley & Sons.

Thomas, E. (1978). Generating innovation in social work: The paradigm of developmental research. *Journal of Social Services Research, 2*(1), 95–115.

Thomas, E. (1990). Modes of practice in developmental research. In L. Videka-Sherman & W. Reid (Eds.), *Advances in clinical social work research* (pp. 202–217). Silver Spring, MD: National Association of Social Workers Press.

Thomas, E., & Rothman, J. (1994). An integrative perspective on intervention research. In J. Rothman & E. J. Thomas (Eds.), *Intervention research: Design and development for human service* (pp. 3–23). New York: Hawthorn Press.

Thoresen, C., & Mahoney, M. (1974). *Behavioral self-control.* New York: Holt, Rinehart & Winston.

Thorndike, R. (1938). On what type of task will a group do well? *Journal of Abnormal and Social Psychology, 33*, 409–413.

Thrasher, F. (1927). *The gang.* Chicago: University of Chicago Press.

Tolson, E., Reid, W., & Garvin, C. (1994). *Generalist practice: A task-centered approach.* New York: Columbia University Press.

Toseland, R. (1977). A problem-solving workshop for older persons. *Social Work, 22*(4), 325–327.

Toseland, R. (1981). Increasing access: Outreach methods in social work practice. *Social Casework, 62*(4), 227–234.

Toseland, R. (1990). Long-term effectiveness of peer-led and professionally led support groups for family caregivers. *Social Service Review, 64*(2), 308–327.

Toseland, R. (1993). Choosing a data collection method. In R. Grinnell (Ed.), *Social work research and evaluation* (4th ed., pp. 317–328). Itasca, IL: F. E. Peacock.

Toseland, R. (1995). *Group work with the elderly and family caregivers.* New York: Springer.

Toseland, R., & Coppola, M. (1985). A task-centered approach to group work with the elderly. In A. Fortune (Ed.), *Task-centered practice with families and groups* (pp. 101–114). New York: Springer.

Toseland, R., Decker, J., & Bliesner, J. (1979). A community program for socially isolated older persons. *Journal of Gerontological Social Work, 1*(3), 211–224.

Toseland, R., Diehl, M., Freeman, K., Manzanares, T., Naleppa, M., & McCallion, P. (1997). The impact of validation therapy on nursing home residents with dementia. *Journal of Applied Gerontology, 16*(1), 31–50.

Toseland, R., & Ephross, P. (1987). *Working effectively with administrative groups.* New York: Haworth.

Toseland, R., & Hacker, L. (1982). Self-help groups and professional involvement. *Social Work, 27*(4), 341–347.

Toseland, R., & Hacker, L. (1985). Social workers' use of groups as a resource for clients. *Social Work, 30*(3), 232–239.

Toseland, R., Ivanoff, A., & Rose, S. (1987). Treatment conferences: Task groups in action. *Social Work with Groups, 10*(2), 79–94.

Toseland, R., Kabat, D., & Kemp, K. (1983). An evaluation of a smoking cessation group program. *Social Work Research and Abstracts, 19*(1), 12–20.

Toseland, R., Krebs, A., & Vahsen, J. (1978). Changing group interaction patterns. *Social Service Research, 2*(2), 219–232.

Toseland, R., Labrecque, M., Goebel, S., & Whitney, M. (1992). An evaluation of a group program for spouses of frail, elderly veterans. *The Gerontologist, 32*(3), 382–390.

Toseland, R., Palmer-Ganeles, J., & Chapman, D. (1986). Teamwork in psychiatric settings. *Social Work, 31*(1), 46–52.

Toseland, R., & Reid, W. (1985). Using rapid assessment instruments in a family service agency. *Social Casework, 66*, 547–555.

Toseland, R., & Rivas, R. (1984). Structured methods for working with task groups. *Administration in Social Work, 8*(2), 49–58.

Toseland, R., Rivas, R., & Chapman, D. (1984). An evaluation of decision making in task groups. *Social Work, 29*(4), 339–346.

Toseland, R., & Rose, S. (1978). Evaluating social skills training for older adults in groups. *Social Work Research and Abstracts, 14*(1), 25–33.

Toseland, R., & Rossiter, C. (1989). Group interventions to support family caregivers: A review and analysis. *The Gerontologist, 29,* 438–448.

Toseland, R., Rossiter, C., & Labrecque, M. (1989). The effectiveness of peer-led and professionally led groups to support family caregivers. *The Gerontologist, 29*(4), 465–471.

Toseland, R., Rossiter, C., Peak, T., & Hill, P. (1990). Therapeutic processes in support groups for caregivers. *International Journal of Group Psychotherapy, 40*(3), 279–303.

Toseland, R., Rossiter, C., Peak, T., & Smith, G. (1990). Comparative effectiveness of individual and group interventions to support family caregivers. *Social Work, 35*(3), 209–219.

Toseland, R., Sherman, E., & Bliven, S. (1981). The comparative effectiveness of two group work approaches for the evaluation of mutual support groups among the elderly. *Social Work with Groups, 4*(1/2), 137–153.

Toseland, R., & Siporin, M. (1986). When to recommend group treatment: A review of the clinical and research literature. *International Journal of Group Psychotherapy, 36*(2), 171–201.

Toseland, R., & Spielberg, G. (1982). The development of helping skills in undergraduate social work education: Model and evaluation. *Journal of Education for Social Work, 18*(1), 66–73.

Tracy, E., & Biegel, D. (1994). Preparing social workers for social network interventions in governmental health practice. *Journal of Teaching in Social Work, 10*(2), 19–41.

Tracy, E., & Whittaker, J. (1990). The social network map: Assessing social support in clinical practice. *Families in Society, 71*(8), 461–470.

Trecker, H. (1956). *Group work in the psychiatric setting.* New York: William Morrow.

Trecker, H. (1972). *Social group work: Principles and practices.* New York: Association Press.

Trecker, H. (1980). Administration as a group process: Philosophy and concepts. In A. Alissi (Ed.), *Perspectives on social group work practice* (pp. 332–337). New York: The Free Press.

Triplett, N. (1988). The dynamogenic factors in pacemaking and competition. *American Journal of Psychology, 65*(1), 93–102.

Tropman, J. (1995). The role of the board in the planning process. In J. Tropman, J. Erlich, & J. Rothman (Eds.), *Tactics and techniques of community intervention* (3rd ed.) (pp. 157–170). Itasca, IL: F. E. Peacock.

Tropman, J. (1996). *Effective meetings: Improving group decision-making* (2nd ed.). Thousand Oaks, CA: Sage.

Tropp, E. (1968). The group in life and in social work. *Social Casework, 49,* 267–274.

Tropp, E. (1976). A developmental theory. In R. Roberts & H. Northen (Eds.), *Theories of social work with groups* (pp. 198–237). New York: Columbia University Press.

Trotzer, J. (1977). *The counselor and the group: Integrating theory, training and practice.* Pacific Grove, CA: Brooks/Cole.

Tuckman, B. (1963). Developmental sequence in small groups. *Psychological Bulletin, 63,* 384–399.

Tyson, T. (1998). *Working with groups* (2nd ed.). South Yarra, Australia: MacMillan Education.

Vaillant, G. (1995). *The natural history of alcoholism revisited.* Cambridge, MA: Harvard University Press.

Valacich, J. S., Dennis, A. R., & Connolly, T. (1994). Idea generation in computer-based groups: A new ending to an old story. *Organizational behavior and human decision processes, 57*(3), 448–467.

Van de Ven, A. (1974). *Group decision making and effectiveness: An experimental study.* Kent, OH: Kent State University Press.

Van de Ven, A., & Delbecq, A. (1971). Nominal versus interacting group processes for committee decision-making effectiveness. *Academy of Management Journal, 9,* 203–212.

VanGundy, A. B., Jr. (1988). *Techniques of structured problem solving* (2nd ed.). New York: Reinhold.

Vannicelli, M. (1992). *Removing the roadblocks: Group psychotherapy with substance abusers and family members.* New York: Guilford.

Vasquez, M., & Han, A. (1995). Group interventions in treatment with ethnic minorities. In J. Aponte & J. Wohl (Eds.), *Psychological inteventions and cultural diversity* (pp. 109–127). Boston: Allyn and Bacon.

Vinokur-Kaplan, D. (1995). Enhancing the effectiveness of interdisciplinary mental health teams. *Administration and Policy in Mental Health, 22,* 521–529.

Vinter, R. (Ed.). (1967). *Readings in group work practice.* Ann Arbor, MI: Campus Publishing.

Vinter, R. (1985a). The essential components of social group work practice. In M. Sundel, P. Glasser, R. Sarri, & R. Vinter (Eds.), *Individual change through small groups* (2nd ed., pp. 11–34). New York: The Free Press.

Vinter, R. (1985b). Program activities: An analysis of their effects on participant behavior. In M. Sundel, P. Glasser, R. Sarri, & R. Vinter (Eds.), *Individual change through small groups* (2nd ed., pp. 226–236). New York: The Free Press.

Vorrath, H. H., & Brendtro, L. K. (1985). *Positive peer culture* (2nd ed.). Chicago: Aldine.

Vroom, V. H., Grant, L., & Cotton, T. (1969). The consequence of social interaction in group problem solving. *Journal of Organizational Behavior and Human Performance, 4,* 79–95.

Vroom, V. H., & Yetton, P. (1973). *Leadership and decision making.* Pittsburgh, PA: University of Pittsburgh Press.

Wakefield, J. C. (1996). Does social work need the eco-systems perspective? Part I. Is the perspective clinically useful? *Social Service Review, 70*(1), 1–32.

Waldo, C. (1986). *A working guide for directors of not-for-profit organizations.* New York: Quorum Books.

Wall, V. D., Jr., Galanes, G. J., & Love, S. B. (1987). Small task-oriented groups, conflict, conflict management, satisfaction, and decision quality. *Small Group Behavior, 18,* 31–55.

Wall, V. D., Jr., & Nolan, L. L. (1987). Small group conflict: A look at equity, satisfaction and styles of conflict management. *Small Group Behavior, 18,* 188–211.

Wallach, M., & Wing, C. (1968). Is risk a value? *Journal of Personality and Social Psychology, 9,* 101–106.

Walls, R., Werner, T., Bacon, A., & Zane, T. (1977). *Behavior checklists in behavioral assessment: New directions in clinical psychology.* New York: Brunner/Mazel.

Walton, M. (1990). *Deming management at work.* New York: G. P. Putnam's Sons.

Wasserman, H., & Danforth, J. (1988). *The human bond: Support group and mutual aid.* New York: Springer.

Watson, S. R., & Buede, D. M. (1987). *Decision synthesis: The principles and practice of decision analysis.* New York: Cambridge University Press.

Watson, W., Johnson, L., & Merritt, D. (1998). Team orientation, self-orientation, and diversity in task groups: Their connection to team performance over time. *Group & Organization Management, 23*(2), 161–188.

Watzlawick, P., Weakland, J., & Fisch, R. (1974). *Change: Principles of problem formation and problem resolution.* New York: W. W. Norton.

Wayne, J., & Avery, N. (1979). Activities for group termination. *Social Work, 24*(1), 58–62.

Weaver, H. (1999). Indigenous people and the social work profession: Defining culturally competent services. *Social Work, 44*(3), 217–225.

Wech, B., Mossholder, K., Steel, R., & Bennett, N. (1998). Does work group cohesiveness affect individuals' performance and organizational commitment? A cross-level examination. *Small Group Research, 29*(4), 472–494.

Weinberg, N., Uken, J., Schmale, J., & Adamek, M. (1995). Therapeutic factors: Their presence in a computer-mediated support group. *Social Work with Groups, 18*(4), 57–69.

Weisner, S. (1983). Fighting back: A critical analysis of coalition building in the human services. *Social Service Review, 57*(2), 291–306.

Weissman, A. (1976). Industrial social services: Linkage technology. *Social Casework, 57*(1), 50–54.

Weissman, H. (Ed.). (1969). *Individual and group services in the mobilization for youth experiment.* New York: Association Press.

Wells, R. (1994). *Planned short-term treatment* (2nd ed.). New York: The Free Press.

Wheelan, S. (1994). *Group processes: A developmental perspective.* Boston: Allyn and Bacon.

Wheelan, S., & Hochberger, J. (1996). Validation studies of the group development questionnaire. *Small Group Research, 27*(1), 143–170.

Whitaker, D. (1975). Some conditions for effective work with groups. *British Journal of Social Work, 5,* 423–439.

White, B., & Madara, E. (1998). *The self-help sourcebook: Your guide to community and online support groups* (6th ed.). Nutley, NJ: Hoffman La Roche.

Whittaker, J. (1985). Program activities: Their selection and use in a therapeutic milieu. In M. Sundel, P. Glasser, R. Sarri, & R. Vinter (Eds.), *Individual change through small groups* (2nd ed., pp. 237–250). New York: The Free Press.

Whyte, W. (1943). *Street corner society.* Chicago: University of Chicago Press.

Widmeyer, W., & Williams, J. (1991). Predicting cohesion in a coacting sport. *Small Group Research, 22*(4), 548–570.

Wiener, L. S., Spencer, E. D., Davidson, R., & Fair, C. (1993). Telephone support groups: A new avenue toward psychosocial support for HIV-infected children and their families. *Social Work with Groups, 16*(3), 55–71.

Williams, O. (1992). Ethnically sensitive practice to enhance treatment participation of African American men who batter. *Families in Society, 73*(10), 588–594.

Williams, O. (1994). Group work with African-American men who batter: Toward more ethnically sensitive practice. *Journal of Comparative Family Studies, 25,* 91–103.

Wilson, G. (1976). From practice to theory: A personalized history. In R. W. Roberts & H. Northen (Eds.), *Theories of social work with groups* (pp. 1–44). New York: Columbia University Press.

Wilson, G., & Ryland, G. (1949). *Social group work practice.* Boston: Houghton Mifflin.

Wilson, G., & Ryland, G. (1980). The social group work method. In A. Alissi (Ed.), *Perspectives on social group work practice* (pp. 169–182). New York: The Free Press.

Wilson, S. (1980). *Recording: Working guidelines for social workers.* New York: The Free Press.

Winer, M. & Ray, K. (1996). *Collaboration handbook: Creating, sustaining, and enjoying the journey.* St. Paul, MN.: Amherst Wilder Foundation.

Winterfeldt, D., & Edwards, W. (1986). *Decision analysis and behavioral research.* New York: Cambridge University Press.

Wittman, H. (1991). Group member satisfaction: A conflict-related account. *Small Group Research, 22*(1), 24–58.

Wolf, T. (1990). *Managing a nonprofit organization.* New York: Prentice-Hall.

Woods, M., & Hollis, F. (1990). *Casework: A psychosocial therapy* (4th ed.). New York: McGraw-Hill.

Worchell, S. (1994). You can go home again: Returning group research to the group context with an eye on developmental issues. *Small Group Research, 25*(2), 205–223.

Wright, J., Thase, M., Beck, A., & Ludgate, J. (Eds.). (1993). *Cognitive therapy with inpatients: Developing a cognitive milieu.* New York: Guilford.

Wyss, D. (1973). *Psychoanalytic schools: From the beginning to the present.* New York: Jason Aronson.

Yalom, I. (1983). *Inpatient group psychotherapy.* New York: Basic Books.

Yalom, I. (1995). *The theory and practice of group psychotherapy* (4th ed.). New York: Basic Books.

Yost, E., Beutler, L., Corbishley, M., & Allender, J. (1985). *Group cognitive therapy: A treatment approach for depressed older adults.* Elmsford, NY: Pergamon Press.

Zajonc, R., Wolosin, R., & Wolosin, W. (1972). Group risk-taking under various group decision schema. *Journal of Experimental and Social Psychology, 8,* 16–30.

Ziller, R. (1957). Four techniques of group decision making under uncertainty. *Journal of Applied Psychology, 41,* 384–388.

name index